Principles of Economics

(8th *Edition*)

Principles of Economics

(8th *Edition*)

Dr. H. S. Agarwal
Professor of Economics (Retd.)
Agra College, AGRA

GLOBAL
professional
publishing

Original edition published by Ane Books

Global Professional Publishing Ltd
Random Acres
Slip Mill Lane
Hawkhurst
Cranbrook
Kent TN18 5AD
Email: publishing@gppbooks.com

ISBN 978-1-906403-64-5

Printed in the United Kingdom by 4edge

Preface to the Eighth Edition

In the present edition, almost every chapter has been revised and the text contains some significant alterations and additions. Besides, a number of new chapters added to the existing eight parts, three new parts have also been added. All diagrams have been redrawn and recast: *Part One* of the book now includes the new chapters on the Methodological Issues in Economics, Economic Models and The Role of Price Mechanism. New chapters in *Part Two* are Hicks Revision of Demand Theory and Recent Developments in Demand Theory. *Part Three* incorporates new chapters on the Traditional Approach of Production Function, Technical Progress and Production Function. *Part Four* includes new chapters on the Nature of Costs and Elasticity of Costs, Monopsony and Bilateral Monopoly, Limit Pricing Theories, Full-Cost Pricing Theory, Managerial and Behavioural Theories of the Firm and Theory of Games and Price Determination. *Part Five* incorporates some new chapters on Theories of Distribution, and Euler s Theorem. *Part Six* has been recasted. *Part Seven* on International Trade is a new part. It incorporates five chapters on Features of International Trade, The Theory of International Trade, The Heckscher-Ohlin Theorem of International Trade, Terms of Trade and Balance of Payment Mechanism. *Part Eight* on Income and Employment has been recasted. *Part Nine* includes a new chapter on Economic Planning. *Part Ten* on Public Finance is a new part. It includes seven chapters on Nature and Scope of Public Finance, Public Revenue, Public Expenditure, Public Debt, Deficit Financing, Fiscal Policy and Budget. *Part Eleven* on Economic System is also a new part. It contains four chapters on Capitalism, Socialism, Mixed Economy and Gandhian Economic Ideas. In the end of the book select bibliography has been added for furthur reading.

Besides the above alterations and additions, several new diagrams and illustrations have been added to improve the exposition of the complicated problems of Principles of Economics. Each chapter contains exercises and multiple choice questions to refurbish the memory of the students.

I am confident that this revised edition will not only help maintain its popularity but will enhance it still further.

The book is primarily meant for the undergraduate as well as postgraduate students of economics and will be equally useful for the students appearing for various competitive examinations and management courses.

Finally, I want to thank my wife Mrs. Shobha Agarwal and my son Pankaj Agarwal who rendered a lot of help in revising the book. The author also expresses his deep debt of gratitude to Ane Books Pvt. Ltd. for taking pains in bringing out the book in time. The author craves the indulgence of the reader for any errors of omission which he may come across in the course of his study of the book. The ultimate responsibility for the final product is that of the author.

Further suggestions from the teachers and the students for the improvement of the book shall be most welcome.

H.S. Agarwal

Contents

PART ONE

BASIC CONCEPTS

PART FOUR

PRODUCT PRICING

PART ONE
BASIC CONCEPTS

Chapter 1

The Nature and Scope of Economics

1. Introduction

There are different views regarding the nature and scope of economics. According to Prof. Pigou, "Economics is a positive science of what is and what tends to be; it is not a normative science of what ought to be." This view narrows the scope of economics too much. Sometimes, it is not possible to discuss "what is" without the knowledge of "what ought to be". On the other hand, Prof. Viner states that "economics is what the economists do". This widens the scope of economics too much. The economist performs many things which are entirely different from scientific discussion. Now to determine the scope of economics, we must understand the aim of economic studies. According to Prof. Marshall, the scope of economics includes the study of physical facts and human activities relating to production, consumption, exchange and distribution of wealth. Naturally, the study is concerned primarily with those activities which can be measured in terms of money. This part of economics can be called a positive science. It includes such rules of practical guidance in social and economic affairs as may be formulated by economists. Further, it includes a normative part, *i.e.* a discussion of how existing facts may be altered for the betterment of mankind. Hence, it is possible to state the scope of economics in more specific terms. Economics deals with problems relating to the consumption, production, exchange and distribution of wealth. Economists find out the ways by which the efficiency in production can be increased; they investigate the causes of low productivity, depression, unemployment and poverty. They also suggest the steps which can be taken for the removal of these evils from the economic system.

Thus, the nature and scope of economics are related to: What is economic's about? Is it a study of wealth or of human behaviour or of scarce resources? But it has been accepted by most economists that economics is the study of scarce resources which create the basic problem of an economy 'what, how and for whom'. This is the problem of all economic units which create economic activity. Like any other subject, the nature of economics is also concerned with economics as a science or an art or both.

2. The Subject Matter of Economics

The subject matter of economics is viewed by different economists in the following ways:

(*i*) Since the time of Adam Smith up till now economists have given different opinions regarding the subject matter of economics. With the change and development of social conditions, the subject matter of economics has also changed. If we look at the history of economic science, we may find that at first the main subject matter of economics was "Wealth." Adam Smith and other classical economists considered economics as a science of wealth.

(*ii*) The neo-classical economists added welfare in the subject matter of economics. Thus, in the time of Marshall it was considered as the science of both wealth and welfare.

(*iii*) According to Robbins and other modern economists, economics studies man and its behaviour. According to them, we are all aware of those matters which may be described as "economic" production and productivity, unemployment, the location of industry, the size of firms, monopolies, wages, profits, rent, interest, taxation, exports, imports, etc. Thus, the subject matter of economics is mainly concerned with the economic problem of the household, firms, and the administrative bodies.

(*iv*) But it is not possible to say exactly whether economics is related to wealth or human behaviour or scarce resources.

According to Boulding,[1] there are three types of human activity which may be described as economic: *(a)* Production, *(b)* Consumption, and *(c)* Exchange.

(*v*) But, if the subject matter of economics is viewed on micro basis, then it is clear that the entire micro economics is the analysis of the theories of price determination based on demand and supply of commodities.

(*vi*) A further part of the subject matter of economics is devoted to the

1. K.E. Boulding, *Economic Analysis*. Vol. I., *Microeconomics,* IVth Edition, pp. 3-4.

organisations which control and direct a large part of economic activity of a country, *e.g.*a limited company, a local institution, a public corporation or a government department.

(*vii*) Further, *Public Finance* is that part of the subject matter of economics which is concerned with the income and expenditure of Public Authorities (the Government and local authorities).

Thus, economics is a social science concerned with proper use and allocation of scarce resources for the achievement and maintenance of growth and stability. Now in the following section, we shall study the definitions of economics as given by various economists in detail to define the nature of economics.

3. Definition of Economics

One of the most controversial topics in economics is the definition of economics. The science of economics is sometimes called *political economy* or social economy, because it deals with the process by which people as a political group or society attempt to make economical use of the scarce resources of nature. The words *economics* and *economy* both come from the two Greek *terms—oikos* and *nemo*—-meaning "household management", as the management of the household activities is one of the most familiar fields for the practice of economy. Just as a family in the household must economize if it is to get the most out of its income, so society at large must utilize its resources wisely. Therefore, Aristotle described economics as a household management and stated how it was useful in acquiring, guarding and making proper use of wealth. In the 16th and 17th centuries, mercantilists, who were the leaders of economic thought since the time of Renaissance upto Adam Smith, understood that wealth was useful for state or the society and, therefore, economics was defined as the study of wealth. Like other social sciences, Economics developed out of the necessity to explain certain aspects of man's social and industrial environment. With the appearance of *Wealth of Nations* in 1776, 'Economics' saw the light of the day. In the early days it was called *Political Economy* and regarded as a branch of statecraft. Between 1760 and 1840, tremendous development of large scale production due to the Industrial Revolution changed the content of the subject.

At present, there are number of definitions of economics. A critical study of these definitions will make it clear that the growth of economics as a science has been most irregular and haphazard. For simplicity, the various definitions of Economics can be studied under the following four categories:

(*I*) 'Wealth' Definitions, (*II*) 'Welfare' Definitions, (*III*) 'Scarcity'

Definitions, and (*IV*) 'Growth' Definitions.

I. 'Wealth' Definitions

The classical school of economists defined economics as the science of wealth. Adam Smith, the father of modem economic theory, defined economics as ***"an enquiry into the nature and causes of wealth".*** J.B. Say, the follower of Adam Smith, regarded economics as "the practical science of the production and distribution of wealth". In other words, he looked upon economics as the study of laws that govern wealth. It was an art which enabled people to earn a revenue sufficient for themselves and the public services. According to the classical economists, self-interest was the only motive which actuated men in all their economic activities. Some of the followers of Adam Smith went further and gave rise to the idea that what economics was concerned with was not the ordinary man, but some sort of "economic man", who was extremely selfish, and who subordinated every other motive to that of earning money. Hence, the classical economists interpreted the term "wealth" in a very narrow sense to mean riches or abundance of money. The science of economics was made to suggest ways and means of increasing wealth of the state.

The "wealth" definition of economics came to be vigorously criticised, especially at the hands of **Carlyle**, **Ruskin**, and other literary writers (the **German Historical School**) of the 19th century. The English classical economists understood that self-interest was the only economic motive in the society where as, according to the Historical School, economics is concerned, not with the activities of an imaginary "economic man," but with those of ordinary men. Further, Adam Smith firmly believed in the harmony between individual and social interests; while the Historical School believed that individual interests were subordinate to social and national interests.

If the term "wealth" is rightly understood, the definition of wealth is more or less correct. As we shall see in the following discussion of the definition of economics, the word "wealth" is used in economics in a special sense. It does not mean riches or abundance of money as is understood in "wealth" definition. In a broad sense, it refers to those scarce goods and services which are used to satisfy the human wants. In other words, wealth is a means and the end is human welfare. Therefore, in economics we study those human activities which centre round wealth. Wants of man lead him to activity. Thus, economics is the study of these activities of man. As such, in economics, we study one of the most important aspects of human life, i.e. activities which lead to his welfare.

II. 'Welfare' Definitions

As the 'wealth' defintion has given rise to some misunderstandings, the emphasis has now been shifted from 'wealth' to 'welfare'. Marshall was the first economist who gave this idea. According to him, economics is still regarded as a study of wealth; but it is "on the other and more important side a part of the study of man."[2] He states that economics is no longer concerned with motives, but it is concerned with human activities. It does not study the activities of an economic man, but of ordinary man. Thus, Marshall defined economics as follows:

"Political economy or economics is a study of mankind in the ordinary business of life; it examines that part of individual and social action which is most closely connected with the attainment and with the use of the material requisites of well-being. Thus, on the one side, it is a study of wealth and on the other and more important side, a part of the study of man."[3]

The important features of Marshall's definition are explained in the following manner:

(*a*) *Human welfare.* Marshall used the term "economics" to examine the individual and social actions for the betterment of mainkind.

(*b*) *Ordinary business of life.* Marshall emphasized "economics is a study of mankind in the ordinary business of life". It is a study of human beings, not of animals or plants. Further, it deals with the economic aspect of the life of human beings and not political, social and religious. The term 'ordinary business of life' relates to how a person earns his income and how he spends it.

(*c*) *Wealth is a means.* In Marshall's definition, wealth is not considered as an end in itself but as a means to welfare, as a source for the betterment of human life. Further, it does not study the whole of human welfare but only a part of it, *i.e. economic* or *material welfare.*

After Marshall, **Pigou** also clearly defined economics as a study of economic welfare. His definition runs as follows:

"The range of our enquiry becomes restricted to that part of social welfare that can be brought directly or indirectly into relation with the measuring rod of money."[4]

This definition increases the scope of economics. It included all goods, material or non-material, which take a money price.

Edwin Cannan also defined economics in the following way:

"The aim of Political Economy is the explanation of the general causes on which the material welfare of human beings depends."

---

2. Marshall A., *Principles of Economics.* p. 1.
3. *Ibid.*
4. Pigou, A.C., *Economics of Welfare,* p. 1.

Criticisms of Welfare Definitions

The 'welfare' definition of Marshall and Pigou has in recent years been criticized on several grounds. The main critic of the 'material welfare' definitions is Prof. Lionel Robbins.[5]

(*a*) *Economics is only a social science.* Marshall assumes economics as a social science rather than as a human science. A social science studies the activities of those individuals who are the members of the society; while a human science studies all human beings, whether they live in an organised community or live outside the society. Although, Marshall used the word 'individual and social action' but by relating their activities to the measuring rod of money, he narrowed the subject matter of economics to the study of persons living in the society using some type of currency. Broadly speaking, the fundamental laws of economics apply to all human beings and, therefore, economics should be treated as a human science and not as a social science.

(*b*) *Classificatory.* Marshall's definition is assumed to be classificatory. He stated that economics dealt with only those activities which are not closely connected with the attainment and with the use of the material requisites of well-being. It means that there are two types of human activities economic and non-economic. Activities which are related to wealth, are economic activities and those which are not related to wealth, such as, political, social and religious are non-economic activities. Prof. Robbins objected to this type of distinction. He points out that in actual life, the distinction between the material and the non-material things is not so clear-cut as is assumed by Marshall. There are several things in our daily life which satisfy our basic needs, but they are not material in any sense of the term. According to Prof. Robbins, an economic problem will arise wherever scarce means are involved in the satisfaction of certain wants. Such a problem will arise even in the case of a person who lives outside the society and may not perform any economic activity in the sense of Mar shall. Therefore, economics should study the economic problem wherever and whenever it is found.

(*c*) *Material welfare.* According to Marshall, only those activities connected with the production and consumption of goods and services which aim at increasing material welfare can come under the scope of economics. In other words, Marshall's definition gave emphasis to economic welfare, while Prof. Robbins would have nothing to do with welfare at all. He points out that there are several activities which come under the purview of economics, but are hardly conducive to welfare. For example, activities relating to alcoholic drinks satisfy human wants and are studied in economics, but they are not conducive to human welfare. Prof. Robbins, therefore, states that "whatever economics

---

5. L. Robbins. *An Essay on the Nature and Significance of Economic Science.* 1932.

is concerned with, it is not concerned with the causes of material welfare as such".

(*d*) *Impossibility of quantitative measurement.* Further, the critics point out that welfare cannot be quantitatively measured. Even if money price is used as an instrument for the measurement of welfare, but it is only a rough and not a satisfactory measure of welfare. When two persons pay the same price for a commodity, it would not mean that both are getting an equal amount of utility or welfare. The welfare (utility) of a relatively poor person will be more than the other.

On the above grounds Prof. Robbins criticised the 'welfare' definition and developed a new definition of economics. His definition is also known as 'scarcity' definition. We shall discuss this definition in the following section.

III. 'Scarcity' Definitions

Until the beginning of 20th century, the 'welfare' definition of Marshall and Pigou was undoubtedly accepted by all the economists. But the publication of Prof. Robbins' book, *An Essay on the Nature and Significance of Economic Science* in 1932 created doubts in the minds of some economists regarding the welfare definition of Marshall, Pigou and others. In his book, Prof. Lionel Robbins defined economics in the following way:

"Economics is the science which studies human behaviour as a relationship between ends and scarce means which have alternative uses."

The main features of this definition may be analysed as below:

(*a*) *Human wants (ends) are unlimited.* In our daily life we reflect a number of wants. The fulfilment of one want gives rise to a number of new wants. Hence, wants are numerous and it is very difficult, rather impossible, to satisfy all the wants of a person. Therefore, a few urgent wants are made to be satisfied.

(*b*) *Means are scarce.* The means of a person by which his wants may be satisfied are limited. It leads to an economic problem as to which wants are to be satisfied by these limited means time and money at his disposal. No economic problem will arise if means are also unlimited.

(*c*) *Alternative uses of scarce means.* According to Robbins, for an economic problem the limited means should have alternative uses. If there are specific uses of these limited means, i.e. each may be put to only a single use and to none else, then there will be no economic problem as such. Therefore, means should have their alternative uses.

(*d*) *Problem of choice.* Further, the alternative uses of the limited means should possess varying degrees of importance, so that a fair selection among the different uses is possible. According to Milton Friedman, an economic problem exists whenever scarce means are used to satisfy alternative ends. If the means are not scarce, there is no problem at all; there is *Nirvana.* If the means are scarce but there is only a single end, the problem of how to use the means is a technological problem. No value judgements enter into its solution; only knowledge of physical and technical relatiooships.[6]

Hence modern economics is said to be based upon a theory of scarcity and choice.

The above economic problem developed the concept of *opportunity cost.* The true cost of using economic resources in any given project (or industry) is the loss of the alternative output which they might have produced. If we use a certain amount of land, labour and capital to build a factory, the economic cost (or opportunity cost) of the factory might be the houses which these resources could have produced. Hence, the *opportunity cost* represents the loss of the next most desired alternative. The purchase of a cinema ticket could be viewed in terms of the alternatives forgone—the opportunity cost might well have been a new fountain pen or a textbook of economics.

Again, the problem of choice which we find in Robbins' definition is universal. It is found everywhere and in all times. For, under the Robbins' definition, rich and poor, the businessman and the administrator of the nation, all are reduced to a common denominator. In other words, economics is not so much concerned with the theories of production and distribution of wealth, rather it is concerned with certain aspects of human behaviour. According to Eric Roll, "The laws which shall be derived from this definition shall be applicable to all the societies. The laws of choice, like the laws of gravitation, will the independent of the legal and political framework in which they work."[7] Similarly, Wickstead puts it, "Its laws are the laws of life and are applicable to fields that have no connection whatever with business or production of wealth." Hence the problem of choice has to be solved in dictatorships and democracies, in planned and unplanned economies, although different methods are applied in different economies.

Criticisms of 'Scarcity' Definitions

This definition is also not free from criticisms. According to the critics this definition of economics does not attach due importance to the social character of economics. An economist is not concerned with individual behaviour of individual ends unless and until the individual activities have consequences on other persons' behaviour or ends. For example, the problems of Robinson Crusoe are of no importance to the people of the modem society. The main criticisms of these definitions are the following:

(*a*) *Human welfare is ignored.* According to **Boulding,**[8] Robbins' definition makes the jurisdiction of economics too narrow. Economics is not only a

6. Milton Friedman, *Price Theory.* 1962, p. 6.
7. Eric Roll, *The Elements of Economic Theory,* p. 17.

study of "scarce means", but also of human welfare, as welfare is an end in itself.

(*b*) *Social character.* **Prof. Chaircross** suggests that to emphasise the social character of economics, the definition given by Robbins should be modified as follows: "Economics is a social science studying how people attempt to accommodate scarcity to their wants and how these attempts intertact through exchange."[9] It means that according to Chaircross the 'scarcity' definition converts economics into a pure science, a science that is concerned with the formulation of economic laws. It has nothing to do with the practicability of these economic generalisations. Most of the modem economists accept the Chaircross' modification of Robbins' definition.

(*c*) *Absence of practical aspect.* According to critics, the definitions of Robbins is based on theoretical analysis of human conduct. In this definition there is no place for morality and human welfare. There is complete absence of practical aspect in the Robbins' definition. This definition is purely theoretical.

(*d*) *No difference between ends and means.* Another criticism of Robbins' definition is that this definition does not distinguish between 'ends' and 'means'; because means are mere sources of enjoyment and the 'end' is nothing but satisfaction. Hence, enjoyment and satisfaction are one and the same thing.

(*e*) *Widened the scope of economics.* According to critics, Robbins has unnecessarily widened the scope of economic science. He did not agree with Marshall on the point of limiting the scope of economics merely to the human activities which can be measured with the aid of money. If this concept of Robbins is accepted, then in the absence of money, economics would become barren.

(*f*) *Non-economic aspect.* In Robbins' definition, a number of non-economic problems have been included under economic aspect. For example, when a person chooses to divide his time between work and leisure, it becomes a problem of economics. But in case the person spends his leisure for reading, writing and sleeping, economic problem does not arise.

Inspite of the criticism, the Robbins' definition presents the true picture of an economic problem. This is the reason why Prof. Robbins' definition is known as the best definition of economics.

Comparison between Robbins' Definition and Marshall's Definition

The definitions of economics as given by Marshall and Robbins have similarities as well as dissimilarities. The main points of similarity and difference can be discussed under the following headings.

---

8. Boulding, *Economic Analysis,* Chap. 1.
9. Chaircross, *Introduction to Economics.* Chap. 1.

Similarities. We find the following similarities in the two definitions:

(1) Both Marshall's and Robbins' definitions emphasise on the point that under economics we study man and his actions.

(2) Both the definitions have ignored the importance of wealth and have laid emphasis on the study of man and his activities.

(3) Robbins' and Marshall's definitions are similar in the sense that there is no fundamental difference between scarcity and welfare. What early economists called as 'wealth', Marshall called it as 'requisite of well being' and Robbins called it as 'scarce means'. Thus, 'wealth', 'requisite of well being' and 'scarce means' indicate one and the same thing in different terminology.

Dissimilarities. The main points of differences between the two definitions are the following:

(***a***) According to Marshall, economics is a social science under which we study the actions of those persons who live in the society. While according to Robbins, economics is a human science under which we study the conduct of all human beings whether they live in the society or not.

(***b***) According to Marshall, the scope of economics is limited, while according to Robbins, the scope of economics is sufficiently wide.

(***c***) Marshall's definition is based on materialistic conception and is, therefore, classificatory. Further, Marshall has distinguished between material and non-material economic activities. While, on the other hand, Robbins' definition is analytical. He analyses human behaviour and states that human behaviour is the subject matter of the science of economics.

(***d***) Marshall, in his definition, states that human behaviour is the ultimate 'end' of the science of economics. According to Robbins, the science of economics is 'neutral' between 'ends'. He states that there is no relationship between welfare and economics.

IV. 'Growth' Definitions

The 'growth' definition of economics has been given by a number of modern economists. This definition is very similar to that of Robbins' definition. It has modified the static view of 'scarcity' definition. According to **Prof. Boulding**, there are three types of human activity which may be described as "economic", viz., production, consumption and exchange. Study of these activities involves enquiry into certain "quantities", *e.g.* output of goods, the amount of accumulated stocks, prices, wages, interest and rent. These things are called "economic quantities". *Economics is a scientific study of economic quantities.* The collection of figures relating to economic quantities is the task of economic statistics and economic history and their interpretation is the task of economic analysis.'[10]

10. Boulding, *Economic Analysis,* Chap. 1.

Here, the views of **Prof. Samuelson** are also of great importance. According to him, "...logically there is nothing fundamental about the traditional boundaries of economic science. In fact, a system may be as broad and as narrow as we please depending upon the purpose at hand; and the data of one system may be the variables of a wider system depending upon expediency. The fruitfulness of any theory will hinge upon the degree to which factors relevant to the particular investigation at hand are brought into sharp focus."[11] Further, he puts economics as "the study of how men and society choose, with or without the use of money, to employ scarce productive resources which could have alternative uses, to produce various commodities overtime and distribute them for consumption now and in the future among various people and groups of society."

The most important implication of his 'growth' oriented definition is that it is not only dynamic in its scope but it is applicable even in a barter economy where money measurement is absent. The problem of choice may take place in a barter economy as well as in a money economy. The inclusion of time element makes the scope of economics dynamic. Human wants are not fixed or static. They change over time. Therefore, Samuelson's definition presents the choice problem in its dynamic setting. This definition also possesses universality in its applicability. Hence, it is an improvement over and above the 'scarcity' definition of Prof. Robbins.

4. The Central Problem of an Economy

The basis of all economic activities arises from the fact that there has never been in this world unlimited food, clothing, housing, and other material necessities of life which human beings require. Shortages of these items have always persisted in human society. Some of these may be attributed to the malfunctioning of the economy during periods of unemployment or underemployment, while some have been due to the scarcity of economic resources, such as, labour, capital and natural resources. Therefore, man is constantly confronted with the problem of choice. Our time and means are limited. We are continually considering how to allocate or 'economise' our resources and our time so as to get the most satisfaction from them. Doctor or lawyer, businessman or manufacturer, clerk or consumer—each is confronted with the need for making a choice. The choice between alternatives is the very foundation of the economic system.

11. Paul A. Samuelson, *Foundations of Economic Analysis,* p. 9.

Hence, any society, whether it is an advanced capitalist society, a communist state, a dictatorship, or a primitive tribe, must face the following basic economic problems:

(*i*) *What variety of goods should be produced and in what quantities.* This involves the allocation of scarce resources in relation to the composition of total output in the economy. Since the means and resources are scarce, the society has to decide about the goods to be produced.

(*ii*) *How these goods should be produced.* Here, the society has to decide who should produce the goods, the resources to be used and the methods of production to be adopted.

(*iii*) *How the goods produced should be distributed.* Here, some decision must be made on the manner in which the wealth is to be distributed among the citizens or the allocation of goods among the members of the society. How should the consumer goods and capital goods be distributed. The allocation of consumer goods among the households is made on the basis of exchange. Similarly, the distribution of income is determined by the quantity of resources contributed by a family in the form of services of labour, land, capital and enterprise towards production. The government may also influence the distribution of income through its policies of taxation and transfer payments.

(*iv*) *How efficiently the resources are being utilised.* Here the society has to see whether the resources are fully utilised or under utilised. In case the resources are not fully utilised, it has to find out the ways and means to utilise them fully. Thus it has to maintain full employment in the economy.

(*v*) *How to acquire an accelerated rate of growth.* Here the society has to see whether the resources of the economy are growing through time or are stagnant. If the economy is stagnant or growing slowly; its growth should be accelerated through a higher rate of capital formation.

All the above central problems of an economy are interrelated and interdependent. The first three problems relate to microeconomics and the last two problems relate to macroeconomics. *The solution to these problems lies in the price mechanism which we shall discuss later.* [12]

5. Society's Production Possibility Curve

The central problem of an economy as explained above can be represented graphically with the help of a production possibility curve (PPC). The PPC is an analytical tool which is used to illustrate and explain the problem of choice or economising process in a hypothetical economy or society. In every

12. For details see chapter on 'Price Mechanism' of this book.

economic society, the economising problem arises on account of the limited resources in relation to multiple (unlimited) ends. Prof. Samuelson[13] has used production possibility curve to clear the problem of scarcity and choice. Here the idea is that a full employment, full-production economy cannot have an unlimited output of goods and services in view of its limited resources. Thus to clear this idea, we make certain specific assumptions as under:

(*i*) We assume that the economy is operating at full employment level of output.

(*ii*) We assume that the available supply of factors of production is fixed, although it can be reallocated within limits among various uses.

(*iii*) We assume that during the course of time the state of technology remains constant.

(*iv*) Only two goods *X* (consumer goods) and *Y* (capital goods) are produced in different proportions in the economy.

(*v*) The same resources can be used to produce either or both of the two goods and can be shifted freely between them.

To simplify the problem, let us further assume that the economy is producing just two products—steel and wheat, or say, two types of goods—the capital goods and the consumer goods. Here steel is symbolic of capital goods and wheat is symbolic of consumer goods. Now, since the resources available in the economy are fixed; the maximum production of steel or wheat is also limited. It means that limited resources always mean limited output. Here more of steel can be produced only at the cost of less of wheat and vice versa. Thus the economy cannot increase the supply of both from its scarce resources. This is in fact the economic problems that the society has to face.

We may also clear this problem with the help of a simple imaginary example as shown in Table 1.1.

Table 1.1: *Production Possibilities of Steel and Wheat with Full Employment*

Products	*Production Alternatives*					
	A	*B*	*C*	*D*	*E*	*F*
Steel (units)	0	1	2	3	4	5
Wheat (units)	50	40	25	5	2	0

As is clear from the above table, at alternative *A* the economy may produce 50 units of wheat with zero steel from its (limited) available resources.

13. Paul A. Samuelson, *Economics,* 1961, pp. 19-24.

Similarly, at alternative *F* it can produce 5 units of steel with zero wheat. Both these alternatives are extreme and unrealistic as the society needs both steel and wheat. Thus as we move from *A* to *F*, the economy can produce steel and more of it only at lower levels of wheat. This is done by transfering resources away from the production of wheat (consumer goods) to the production of steel. If consumer goods are the current satisfaction (consumption) and capital goods are the future satisfaction (consumption) then we may say that in moving from *A* to *F*, the society is sacrificing current satisfaction (consumer goods) in the interest of future satisfaction (capital goods). Similarly in moving from *F* to *A*, the society is, in effect, choosing 'more now' (consumer goods) at the cost of 'much more later' (capital goods). It clearly means that the society can produce more of any goods only at the cost of the other product.

We may also represent the above illustration with the help of a production possibility curve or a transformation curve. In Fig 1.1, we represent steel along *Y* axis and wheat along *X* axis.

In Fig. 1.1 points *A, B, C, D, E* and *F* show the combinations of the two products that the society may produce from its limited resources. When we join these various points, we obtain a curve which is known as the Production Possibility Curve. This curve is also known as the Transformation Curve, because when we move from one point to another, say from *C* to *D*, we will be transforming wheat into steel by shifting resources from the production of wheat to the production of steel. Any point inside this curve, say point *R* indicates that resources are not being fully utilized. The society cannot go outside this curve (as point *K* in Fig 1.1) as its resources do not permit it to do so. This is the reason that the curve is also known as the frontier.

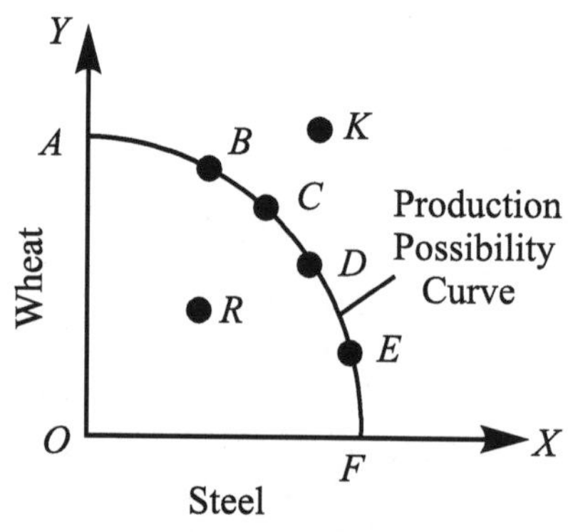

Fig.1.1

Uses or Applications of Production Possibility Curve

With the help of production possibility curve we can explain the basic problems of an economy such as the problem of unemployment, technological progress, economic growth and economic efficiency.

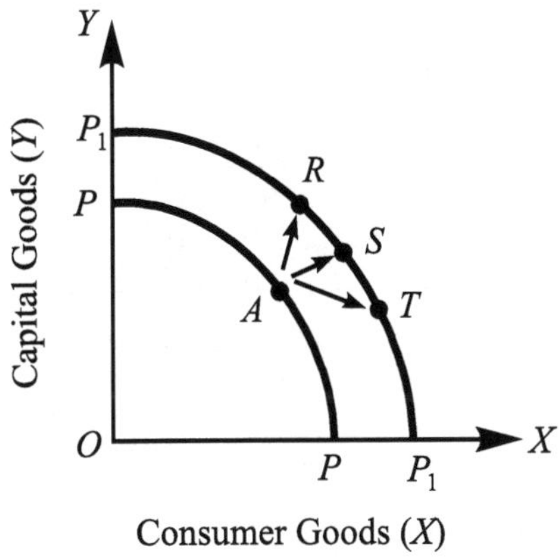

Fig. 1.2

(***a***) *Unemployment.* According to Keynes, there is always unemp-loyment in an economy. It is because of lack of effective demand or because of inequality between savings and investment in an economy. Thus if we relax the assumption of full employment of resources, we can find out the level of unemployment prevailing in the economy with the help of *PP* curve. It has been shown in Fig. 1.2. According to Lipsey, "The higher the proportion of resources unemployed, the closer will be the production possibility curve to the origin. In Fig. 1.2, the original production possibility curve of the economy is *PP* which depicts substantial unemployment in the economy. The economy can attain the level of full employment if it is able to go to any point on a higher production possibility curve P_1P_1. The economy can do so by employing its idle resources either producing more of capital goods, i.e. on point *R* on P_1P_1 curve, or more of consumer goods, i.e. point *T* on P_1P_1 curve or more of both the goods, i.e. at point *S* on P_1P_1 curve.

(***b***) *Technological Progress.* The economy is not able to get maximum returns of the available resources because of lack of technical progress. Technical progress enables an economy to get more output from the same quantities of factors of production. It is shown in Fig. 1.3. Initially, the economy is enjoying production possibility curve *PP* from its available resources. Now if the productive efficiency of the economy improves by technical progress, its *PP* curve will shift outward throughout to P_1P_1. The new P_1P_1 curve shows a higher level of both the consumer goods as well as the capital goods and the economy may enjoy say point *V* on P_1P_1curve.

Now suppose, the economy makes the technical progress in the production of only consumer goods, then it may shift to any point on PP_1 curve.

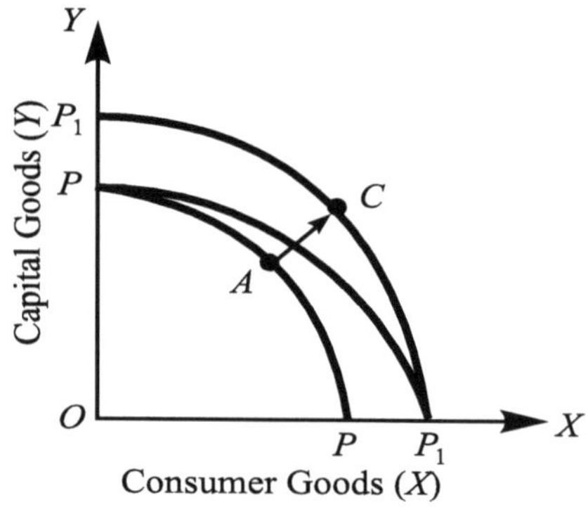

Fig.1.3

This curve may also enable the economy to produce more of both the goods although the technical progress has taken place only in the production of consumer goods.

(c) *Economic Growth.* Under this we may say that the quantities of factors of production like land, capital, labour and enterprise are fixed only in the short period. Development is a continuous and long-term process. Thus, these resources may change over time and shift the *PP* curve upwards as shown in Fig. 1.4. Now, if the economy is stagnant at point *R,* then economic growth will shift it to point *S* on production possibility curve *PP* and a further increase in factor quantities may shift the *PP* curve towards the right to P_1P_1 and the economy may go to any point on this higher production possibility curve, i.e. either point *R* or *S* or *T* as suits to the economy

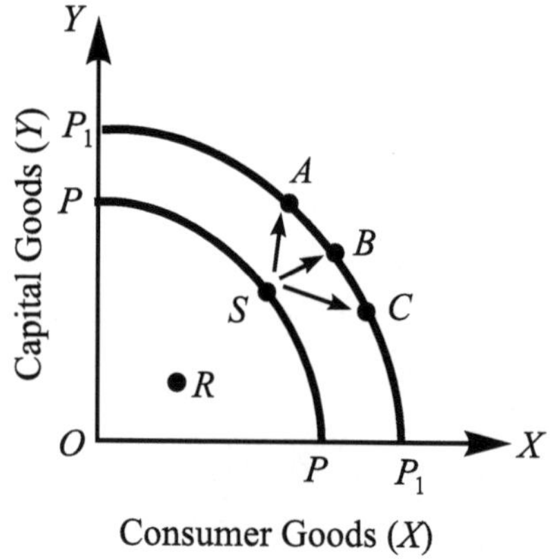

Fig. 1.4

(d) *Present goods vs Future goods.* Here we may say that if an economy allocates more of its resources in the present to produce capital goods than to consumer goods, it will have more of both kinds of goods in the future. It will thus acquire a higher rate of growth in the future. This is because of the fact that consumer goods satisfy the present wants while capital goods satisfy future wants. Figure 1.5 indicates the fact that the outward shift of the economy's future production possibility curve P_1P_1 from point R of the present curve PP is greater when more capital goods are produced in the future. Further, Fig. 1.6 shows lesser outward shift of the present curve $P\ P$ from point T to the future curve P_1P_1 when less capital goods are produced in the future.

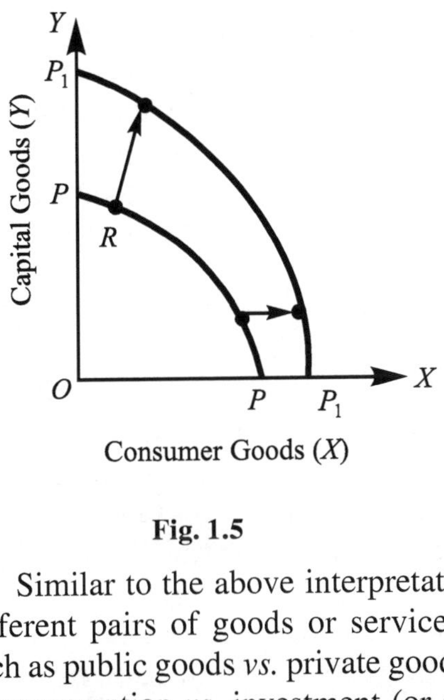

Fig. 1.5

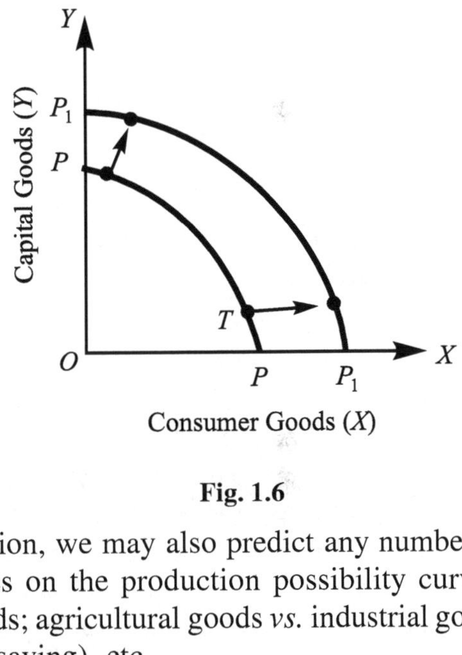

Fig. 1.6

Similar to the above interpretation, we may also predict any number of different pairs of goods or services on the production possibility curves, such as public goods *vs.* private goods; agricultural goods *vs.* industrial goods or consumption *vs.* investment (or saving), etc.

6. Circular Flow of Economic Activity

The above stated economic problem is solved by the three institutions (*i.e.* decision making agents) of an economy; namely, the households (or individuals), business firms and government. These decision making agents are actively engaged in three economic activities of consumption, production and exchange of goods and services in the society. They act and react in such a manner that all economic activities move in a circular flow and lead to full employment in the economy. First of all, we shall explain the nature of these agents and their role in decision making.

Households. The households perform two economic activities simultaneously. As agents of the factors of production, they supply productive inputs to the business firms and receive incomes in return in the form of rent, wages, interests and profits. At the same time, the households act as consumers as well and spend their incomes on consumer goods produced by the business firms.

Business Firms. The business firms are the producers and they take the decisions to manufacture goods and services. For this purpose, they procure different factors of production and make payments to them in the form of wages, rent, and interest, etc.

Government. In modern times, the government plays an important role in all types of economic systems, i.e. capitalist, socialist, and mixed economy.

All the above decision making agents take economic decisions to produce goods and to exchange them in order to consume them for satisfying the wants of the whole economy. Production, consumption and exchange are the three main activities of the economy. Consumption and production are to be performed simultaneously. They are interrelated and interdependent. Production leads to consumption and consumption necessitates production. These two activities are related to each other through the mechanism of exchange.

The Circular Flow in a Two-Sector Economy

Here we assume that there are only two sectors of the economy, i.e. the households and the business firms. Figure 1.7 presents a graphic analysis of the mode in which income flows between the households and the business firms. For simplicity, the economy has been divided into two markets, i.e. the product market and the factor market. The households (consumers) supply factors of production (such as land, labour, capital and enterprise) to business firms (producers), and receive money (income) for their services in different forms. Such receipts, in fact, constitute the total cost of production of goods and services produced in the economy. On the contrary, business firms sell consumer goods to households and receive money in return. In a simplified economy, the households are assumed to spend their entire income on the purchase of consumer goods and services. At the same time, the entire business receipts are paid out for the purchase of productive inputs from the households. Since there are no taxes, no savings and no foreign trade, the upper half of the circle would obviously be equal to the lower half. In other words, the flows of income between the factor and the product markets will not only be equal, but their size will also remain constant.

In Fig. 1.7, the upper half of the circle constitutes the market for consumer goods and shows the interaction between households, as buyers of such goods and the business firms, as sellers. By definition, prices of goods and services in this market form the connecting link between the flow of goods and the money payments.

In Fig. 1.7, the lower half of the circle shows the interaction between households and business firms in the factor market. In this case, the input prices constitute a link between the flow of inputs and money. In a simplified economy, the household receipts are equal to total cost of production. At the same time, cost of production is equal to the business receipts, which in turn are equal to total money spent on the purchase of goods and services.

Thus the two money flows are equal.

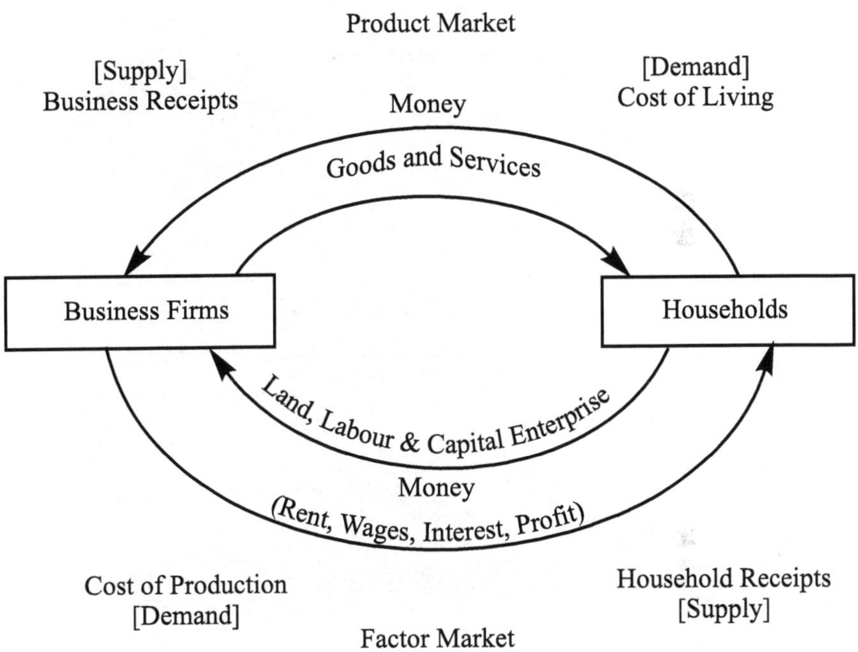

Fig. 1.7

The Circular Flow in a Three-Sector Economy

The above analysis of a simplified economy was based upon two-sector model. Now we add the government sector so as to make it a three-sector closed model of circular flow of economic activity. Now we will see that even if the goverment sector is added, the fundamental principles governing the circular flow of income would not show a significant difference. For the third sector, we add taxes and government purchases (or expenditure) in our presentation. Taxes are outflows from the circular flow and government purchases are inflows into the circular flow. The three-sector model of the circular flow of economic activity is shown in Fig. 1.8.

In Fig. 1.8 the government increases aggregate expenditure in the economy through purchases of services of the households, making transfer payments in the form of old age pensions, unemployment relief, sickness benefit, etc. and also through providing services like education, health, housing, water supply and other facilities. All such expenditures by the government are inflows into the circular flow. Contrarily taxes in the form of personal income taxes and commodity taxes paid by the households are outflows from the circular flow.

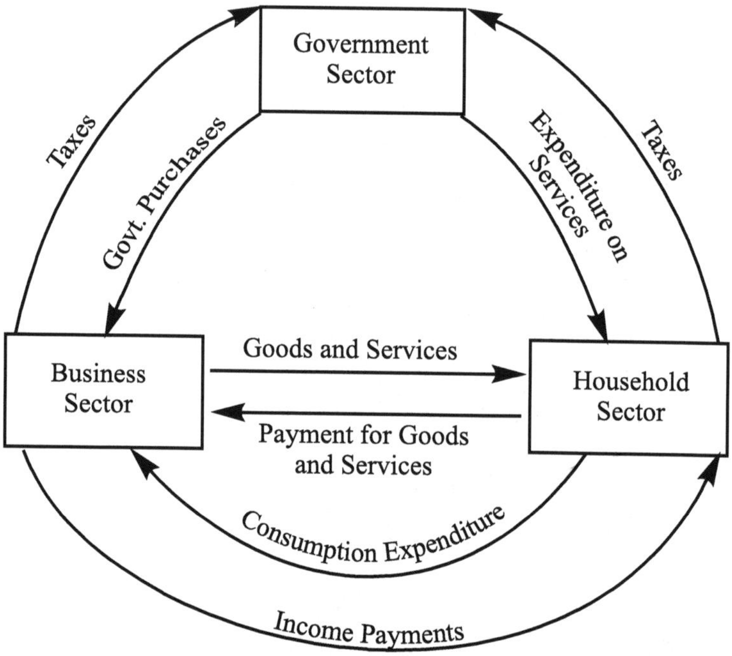

Fig. 1.8

Further, we may also see the circular flow between the business firms and the government. The government purchases all its requirements of goods from the business sector, gives subsidies and makes transfer payments to business firms in order to encourage their production. All these expenditures are inflows into the circular flow. Contrarily, all types of taxes paid by the business firms to the government are outflows from the circular flow.

Now we may discuss the combined effects between the three sectors together. As we know, taxes are a leakage from the circular flow. They tend to decrease consumption and saving of the household sector. Decreased consumption, in turn, reduces the sales and incomes of the firms. On the other hand, taxes on business firms tend to decrease their investment and production. The government fills this gap by making purchases from the business firms and buying services of the households exactly equal to the amount of taxes. Thus inflows equal outflows in the circular flow.

7. Economics as a Science

In order to understand the nature of economic laws, we have to indicate whether economics is a science or art? If it is a science, then is it a positive science or a normative science? In order to answer these questions, it is essential to know what science is and to what extent the characteristics of science are applicable to economics.

The systematized body of knowledge regarding a subject is commonly defined as "science". A science is not a mere collection of facts, but it indicates a relationship between cause and effect. In other words, it studies uniformities pervading a subject and tries to find out generalizations which we call laws. In this sense, physics is a science because it studies certain uniformities regarding the external universe. Also psychology is a science that studies the uniformities of the mental world. In the same sense, economics can also be regarded as a full-fledged science, because it studies the uniformities of human conduct in the ordinary business relations. It investigates the possibility of deducing generalizations as regards the behaviour of human beings and their economic motives. Hence, economics is a science, because it tries to discover the universal out of the chaotic facts. According to Prof. Marshall, "The economist seeks to discover the many in the one, the one in the many."

Some writers point out that the phenomena of science must be easily amenable to measurement. Here the claim of economics to be regarded as a science is based upon the fact that it deals with that part of man's actions which can be measured by the measuring rod of money. Like the chemist's balance, economics has an external measure for measuring human motives, and the measure is furnished by dollars or rupees, *etc*. Thus, of all social sciences, economics is the most exact; because none of the social sciences has got any external measure to make possible a definite quantitative measurement.

Here, one should remember that human motives cannot be accurately measured and that the moving forces of economic action can only be measured roughly and imperfectly. Therefore, economics which is the most perfect of all social sciences, is not exact as the physical science, because it deals with human motives which are very complex and variable. Although man is a rational being having the capacity of reasoning logically about the consequences of particular actions. In majority of cases human actions in response to a particular set of circumstances will follow a particular pattern. Marshall observed that, "Uniformity of reason implies some uniformity in human affairs." Therefore, it is possible to formulate economic laws. But, there are always exceptional individuals who may behave in an irrational manner. The economist assumes that such persons form only a small minority. But since they exist, we must accept that the laws of economics are true only in "general", *i.e.* they are statements which are true in the majority of cases and not universally. The physical sciences have developed a large body of laws possessing universal validity, and capable of quantitative measurement. But, economics cannot claim to have discovered such laws of universal validity, because of the nature of the subject matter of economics, *i.e.* the behavior of mankind.

Again, the existence of "free-will" in men prevents economics from being a science. Economists cannot claim precision for their laws. As men have free will, what guarantee is there that men will behave similarly under similar circumstances, so that there might be a homogeneous group of human actions for our study of economic science? But even admitting that men have free will, it is possible to build up an economic science on the following grounds:
(*i*) There are certain experiences which do not come within the purview of man's choice. Man cannot decide to feel pleased or sorry. These uncontrollable experiences help the economists to form general laws.
(*ii*) Some economic experiences of man are governed by laws of external nature beyond his control, *e.g.* the law of diminishing returns.
(*iii*) Free will does not mean that men act unreasonably. Even if they do so, we are in a position to foretell the course of their activities by means of the mathematical law of probability. But, on the whole, men behave reasonably. People usually buy a thing where it is cheap. A producer will sell more if the price of product increases. Because of this fact, we can predict the future course of human activities, and frame general laws.

Further, some writers say that "economics is not a science because economist disagree". According to Mrs. Barbara Wootton, "Whenever six economists are gathered, there are seven opinions."[14] This criticism is not true, because doctors frequently disagree but none contends that the study of medicine is not a science. Economists will not disagree so far as the facts are concerned; they may disagree on questions of policy. Moreover, the policy recommendations depend on the ethical ideas and political views. In a developing science, there are always differences of opinion.

It is, no doubt, true that economic prophecies are often found to be false by subsequent events. The reason for this must be sought, not in the unscientific nature of economic studies but in our ignorance of the causes at work. The laws of biology are not always borne out by subsequent events; but no one would, on that ground, deny that biology was not a science. The onset of a trade depression (economic forecast) can often be predicted a much longer time in advance than the coming of a cyclone (meteorological forecast). It means that sometimes economic forecasts are more reliable than meteorological

---

14. Barbara Wootton, *Lament for Economics* (1938), p. 14.

forecasts. Therefore, the task of the economist is the same as that of the natural scientist to apply the processess of sustained and unbiased argument to the data of observation and to determine the general laws of all events. Hence, the claim of economics to be regarded as a science cannot be denied on the ground that it lacks precision and prophetic power.

Now we can say that economic science is ordinarily regarded as a dry collection of abstract formulas having only a remote relation to the realities of human existence. The interests of all men are fundamentally compatible, that there is and can be no antagonism between the welfare of one and the welfare of all, that all mankind can live in peace and prosperity, provided that violence or threat of violence is reserved exclusively for the maintenance, by the State, of a free market in which goods and services are voluntarily exchanged without coercion from any quarter.

Nature of Economic Laws

There are various meanings of the term 'law'. It may mean a rule established in a community, permitting or prohibiting a course of action; it may mean a rule of procedure as the laws of games; it may mean an Act passed by the legislature; and it may mean a statement of causal relationship between two groups of phenomena. An economic law is a statement of tendencies, i.e. a statement that under certain conditions, we may assume a definite course of action from human beings in the aggregate. An economic law affirms that if certain causes exist, certain results are bound to ensue. All natural laws are laws in the same sense. Things fall on the ground as a result of the pull of the gravity, if nothing interferes to prevent them from falling. So also in economics, economic laws represent certain economic tendencies or principles expressing what is likely to happen, other things being equal. For example, the law of demand states that, *ceteris paribus,* demand for a commodity, will increase if its price falls and vice versa. According to Prof. Marshall, "A law of social science is a statement of social tendencies; that is, a statement that a certain course of action may be expected under certain conditions from members of a social group. Economic laws, or statements of economic tendencies, are those social laws which relate to branches of conduct in which the strength of the motives chiefly concerned can be measured by a money price."

Here it is important to note that economic laws deal with human behaviour. Human nature is not constant, and at times inconsistent; hence, economic laws can predict what men usually will do, but not with certainty what they actually will do. The laws of natural sciences are precise and exact. The law of gravitation is an exact statement and it is used for many mathematical calculations regarding the movement of the heavenly bodies. Therefore, the laws of economic science are not exact as those of the natural sciences.

Economic facts can be modified by human effort, but a law of physics cannot be modified by human effort. According to Seligman, "An economic law is a natural law so far as it states that given conditions will lead to given results. An economic law is not a natural law so far as it implies that human effort is important in modifying the conditions which lead to the results." Marshall has also pointed out that "the laws of economics are to be compared with the laws of tides rather than with the simple and exact law of gravitation." This means that economic laws as statement of tendencies, are only approximate. The laws of tides state how there is a rise and fall of tides twice a day under the influence of the sun and the moon, how there are strong tides at new and full moon, etc. Thus, these laws predict at what time the tide will probably be the highest on any day. Here the word 'probability' is used, because tides may not come at the expected hour owing to many unforeseen circumstances. Similarly, there are many unforeseen circumstances in human activities, as a result of which the expected course of action may not occur. It is why Prof. Seligman states that "economic laws are essentially hypothetical". It means that economic laws are conclusions drawn from certain assumptions or hypotheses. The economic relationship between cause and effect is subject to the condition that other things are equal. The proviso "other things being equal" is contained in all economic laws. But other things are not always equal and consequently in economics, definite conclusions cannot be predicted from definite facts. Economic laws are, therefore, described as hypothetical.

But in this sense, economic laws do not differ from other scientific laws. The laws of all other sciences are also hypothetical, i.e. they start from certain hypotheses and deduce certain consequences. As Prof. Marshall has pointed out, every scientific law will always contain conditions or the proviso "other things being equal". Then, what is the difference between the physical and economic law? The only difference is that the hypothetical element is specially prominent in economics. In physics, though there may be a complexity of forces at work, they can be definitely measured, and the results predicted. In economics, many of the forces cannot be measured; hence, no definite result can be predicted.

To conclude, economic laws, like scientific laws, would be correct if the assumptions are not inconsistent with one another and if the reasoning process is logical. If unpracticable or contradictory assumptions are made, the conclusions are not relevant or of value.

Economics as a Positive or a Normative Science

There are two types of science a positive science and a normative science. According to Keynes, "A positive science may be defined as a body of systematized knowledge concerning what is; a normative science or regulative science is a body of systematized knowledge relating to the object of what ought to be, and concerned with the ideal as distinguished from the actual. The object of a positive science is the establishment of uniformities; of a nonnative science the determination of ideals". These two conflicting views regarding the nature of economic science have been prevalent from the earliest days. Keynes also states that "The theory of economics does not furnish a body of settled conclusions immediately applicable to policy. It is a method rather than a doctrine, an apparatus of the mind, a technique of thinking which helps its processors to draw correct conclusions." According to this view, the object of economic science is to point out why certain effects follow from certain given causes. This means that the economist deals with facts and figures. He is to explore and explain, but not to point a moral or adorn a tale.

The positive character of economics has also been explained by Robbins in the following words: "It enables us to describe the distribution of resources which, given the valuations of individuals concerned, satisfies demand most fully. But it does not by itself provide any ethical sanctions. To show that, under certain conditions demand is satisfied more adequately than under any alternative set of conditions does not prove that the set of consideration is desirable. There is not a penumbra of approbation round the theory of equilibrium." Therefore, economics is not concerned with the rightness or wrongness of the existing social structure. For example, the economist cannot condemn the drink-trade, though as a social reformer he might oppose it; but as an economist, he is bound to consider the economics of the drink-trade. Further, economist cannot give any final judgement on any matter. For example, if in a society adopting a policy of living wage it is generally assumed that the gain by the absence of wage payments below the standard of living more than compensates for the unemployment and the losses it involves, such a policy cannot be condemned off-hand as undesirable. Policy is always based on a compromise between the economic, ethical and political aspects. The role of economist is to analyse the facts and to supply the results to the statesmen. Now, it is the task of the statesmen and the reformers to apply the results for increasing the welfare of the society.

Hence the old English Classical School was of the opinion that economics was purely a positive science which had no right to comment upon the rightness or wrongness of economic policy. The 20th century economist, Prof. Robbins gave similar views regarding the nature of economics. It is on this ground that Robbins and his followers are assumed to be as the Neo-classical School. The Historical School of Germany gave just the contrary view. These economists emphasise the normative functions of economics, According to Hawtrey, "Economics cannot be dissociated from ethics." This means that a strict neutrality on the ethical aspect of economic analysis cannot be maintained, for every step in economics carries an ethical import. Even Prof. Marshall states that "the ethical assumption which must always be present before the economist is that both the productive and monetary systems should be organized so as to open up to all the material means of a refined and noble life." According to Pigou, "Economic science is chiefly valuable neither as an intellectual gymnastics, nor even as a means of writing truth for its own sake, as a handmaid of ethics and the end of all economic activities is to promote human welfare. In other words, it is difficult to have an exclusively positive science even if we desire to do so. The economist cannot be as objective in his investigations as the physical or the chemist can. As Friedman puts it, economics is sometimes divided into two parts: positive economics and normative economics. The former deals with how the economic problem is solved; the latter deals with how the economic problem should be solved. For example, the effects of price or rent control on the distribution of income are problems of positive economics. On the other hand, the desirability of these effects on income distribution is a problem of normative economics. Therefore, economics is a positive science as well as a normative science.

8. Economics as an Art

The use of systematic knowledge is an 'art'. According to Prof. Keynes, "An art is a system of rules for the settlement of a given end." In this sense economics is an art. The economist presents the ways based on his theoretical knowledge and experience which help in reaching the optimum situation. For example, the law of equimarginal utility tells a consumer how to maximise his total utility or satisfaction.

More specifically, in order to make the decision, three kinds of information are required:

(*i*) a knowledge of the alternatives open to the decision-maker;

(*ii*) a knowledge of the consequences of choosing each of the alternatives, and

(*iii*) a criterion or rule that tells the decision-maker which of the sets of consequences is the most valuable to him. For example, a producer is trying to decide how much of a commodity to produce. His range of alternatives then consists of each of the possible quantities his industry is capable of producing. The consequences of choosing each alternative can be summarised by means of two numbers for each: the cost of producing that amount and the revenue which can be obtained from selling it. Now the objective of the producer is to make his profits as high as possible. This is his criterion; therefore, he searches the alternatives for the one which provides the greatest difference between Total Revenue *(TR)* and Total Cost *(TC)*. The economic law that marginal cost equals marginal revenue will provide this situation.[15]

Therefore, economics is both a science and an art simultaneously.

9. The Relation of Economics with other Subjects

The human behaviour is very complex. It is impossible to categorize it. Economics is a study of human activities which are affected by the circumstances and traditions of the society: legal, political, religious, moral, etc. These activities of human behaviour are so intermixed that it is impossible to separate them in water-tight compartments. In other words, human nature is indivisible. We study it in many social and human sciences, namely, history, psychology, sociology, politics, statistics, ethics, etc. In each social science we study some particular aspect of human behaviour. Thus, all social sciences are related and it is not possible to separate them. Economics is also a social science. Therefore, economics is closely related to all social sciences which deal with human behaviour.

Economics and Sociology. Sociology deals with the fundamental facts of all social life economic, political and historical, etc. and therefore, it is the general social science. Since economics is also one of the sciences, it is not possible to separate it from sociology. According to Comte, "Economics cannot claim to be a separate science, but must be included within sociology." It means that sociology is an all-comprehensive social science. It takes into consideration all the conclusions arrived at by different social sciences to make further conclusions. In other words, sociology is the fundamental social science of which other social sciences are differentiations. On the other hand, economics is a branch of sociology. It studies a particular aspect of human behaviour, not the whole of it.

Economics and Politics. Both Economics and Politics deal with human activities and are therefore, closely related. It is why the earlier writers used to regard Economics as a branch of Politics. The Greeks regarded Political Economy as the art of providing revenue for the state. Modern writers regarded economics as an art to be employed for farthering the purposes of the state.

---

15. Thus, a producer obtains maximum profit when

$$\frac{\partial R}{\partial q} = \frac{\partial C}{\partial q} \quad \text{where} \quad \frac{\partial R}{\partial q} = \text{Marginal Revenue}$$

and $$\frac{\partial C}{\partial q} = \text{Marginal Cost}$$

also $$\frac{\partial^2 R}{\partial q^2} > \frac{\partial^2 C}{\partial q^2} \text{(second order condition)}$$

Economics is the science of wealth in relation to man. Economic welfare of a country depends upon the system of government. Every modern government is closely connected with economic matters.

Further, the political organization of a country is often a reflex of its economic organization. Political movements are profoundly influenced by economic causes. State-socialism, Syndicalism, Fascism, and many other movements are not merely economic movements, but are political movements as well. Hence, the two are closely related.

Economics and Ethics. Economics and Ethics are also closely related. Ethics deals with principles of morality while economics deals with actually existing facts and the human welfare. But human behaviour is always influenced by moral considerations. Men's actions are usually guided by their ideas of what is proper. In other words, the normative aspect of economic science is economic ethics. The discussion of the relation of wealth to welfare shows the essentially ethical bent of the science. As we have already mentioned, economics is the handmaid of ethics and the end of all economic activities is to promote human welfare.

Further economic conclusions give certain data for the study of ethics and from these data ethics draws further conclusions. According to Seligman, "Economics, like ethics, is primarily a social science, the true economic action must in the long run be an ethical action."

Economics and History. History is a record of past events which also include economic events. The economist learns much by a study of past experiences. Historical facts can be used to formulate new economic theories. Their correctness may also be tested by the historical facts. Hence, the study of history is of a great help to the economist. Sir John Secley has summed up the mutual relationship between History and Economics in the following words: "Economics without History has no root. History without Economics has no fruit." History is a record of human behaviour and it is also a part of society. Thus, under both Economics and History, we study the human behaviour. It is, therefore, obvious that History and Economics are mutually related. A knowledge of history is important for correct appreciation of economics. Similarly, a knowledge of economics is essential for correct appreciation of history.

Economics is the foundation of History. According to Karl Marx, "History can be explained only through economic events. In order to have a correct knowledge about any system of Government, it is always necessary to have knowledge about the contemporary economic conditions and events of the country."

Economics and Statistics. Today, various methods of mathematical statistics are applied to the problems of economics. The economist, therefore, must have a fairly good grounding in the fundamentals of mathematical statistics. Since much of what is written in the field of economics and in other social sciences involves statistical analysis, any serious student of economics must know these fundamentals. Statistics, specially modern statistical theory, is of great importance to economists. Statistical methods of sampling are already useful for collecting the data which are the raw material of economic studies. Statistics has the additional advantage of giving an idea about the reality of the data. The use of probabilistic models is particularly suitable in the measurement of economic relationships that are difficult to measure exactly because of number of sources of error. Errors arise in economic data and relationships for a number of reasons. Firstly, there are errors of measurement. For example, a country's exports or imports are unlikely to be measured with complete accuracy as mistakes will be made on invoices, customs officials will often incorrectly record prices and quantities of goods moving into or out of customs houses and mistakes will be made in adding up individual items to get an export or import total. Secondly, errors are introduced when economic data are compiled on sampling basis. Thirdly, errors may arise because of random shocks such as war, natural disaster or variations in the weather. The economist makes use of various statistical methods to remove these errors as far as possible. Hence, the techniques of statistical inference enable the economist to make probabilistic statements concerning the parameters of theoretical models of economic processes.

Economics and Geography. Economics and Geography are also intimately related. Under Geography, we study man and the physical conditions around which he lives. Under Economics, we study the physical conditions which affect human behaviour. Thus it is clear that Economic and Geography are closely related.

Again, there are certain topics which are studied under both the subjects, e.g. climate, mineral resources, forests, animals, natural resources, etc.

Further, the economic conditions and development of a country is greatly influenced by its natural conditions. Therefore, Economics and Geography are closely related.

Economics and Psychology. As we know, Psychology is the science of mind. Under Psychology, we study the mental state of man and actions of his mind. The economic behaviour of man is purely the result of this mental behaviour. Since behaviour is conditioned by mind, economics is related to Psychology. The economic laws such as the Law of Diminishing Marginal Utility, the Law of Demand and the Law of Supply, etc. are based on Psychology. Hence, Psychology has always helped economic development. According to Robbins, "An economist should be a Psychologist also." The economic laws and facts can be tested through Psychology. Similarly, Economics also influences the Psychological laws.

Economics and Natural Sciences. Economics is related to natural sciences like Physics and Chemistry. Natural sciences deal with natural objects. Economics and Natural Sciences are to great extent comp-lementary to each other. The laws of economics are influenced by natural factors. Various discoveries made in the field of natural sciences affect economics. Economics creates a number of problems which the scientists have to tackle and solve. This has led to a number of researches in the field of natural sciences. Thus economics and technology go together. According to Prof. Stigler, "Whereas the economist is concerned only with the best allocation of scarce means among the competing ends, the technologist studies the best means to attain a specific end."

Exercises

1. Explain the nature and scope of economics.
2. "Economics is a study of man's actions in the ordinary business of life." Discuss.
3. Analyse different definitions of economics. Which of these definitions explain the correct nature of economics? Give reasons.
4. "Economics studies human behaviour as a relationship between unlimited ends and scarce resources having alternative uses." Do you agree with this statement? Why?
5. Define a Production Possibility Curve. Explain its uses in economic analysis.
6. Explain the circular flow of income in an economy.
7. Describe the role of households, firms and government in economic activity. Also describe their interrelationships.
8. "The science of economics has both positive and normative aspects." Explain.
9. Explain the nature of economics as a positive science and normative science. Is it a social science?
10. "The role of economist is to analyse and not to prescribe." Discuss the statement critically and examine its validity in the modern world with its emphasis on economic planning, growth, and welfare.
11. "The functions of an economist are to explore and explain and not to advocate and condemn." Discuss.
12. What are the types of problems to which economists attempt to find answers? Explain the value of economists' studies.
13. "Basic questions concerning right and wrong goals to be pursued cannot be settled by science as such. They belong to the realm of ethics and value judgements. The citizens must ultimately decide such issues. What the expert can do is to point out the feasible alternatives and the true costs that may be involved in the different decisions." (Samuelson). Discuss.
14. Explain the relationship of economics with other subjects.
15. "The object of economic analysis is not merely to discover the truth but also to assist in the solution of concrete problems." Comment.
16. Explain the central problem of an economy.

Multiple Choice Questions

17. (*i*) Who considered Political Economy as "an enquiry into the nature and causes of the wealth of nations" ?

(*a*) Adam Smith (*b*) J.S. Mill
(*c*) J.B. Say (*d*) F.A. Walker [*Ans.* (*a*)]

(*ii*) Which of the following embodies a more widely accepted definition of Economics?

(*a*) Science of wealth
(*b*) Science of material welfare
(*c*) A study of mankind in the ordinary business of life
(*d*) Science of choice-making [*Ans.* (*d*)]

(*iii*) Which of the following definitions of Economics includes the economic concept of 'scale of preferences'?

(*a*) Wealth Definition (*b*) Welfare Definition
(*c*) Scarcity Definition (*d*) Growth Oriented Definition [*Ans.* (*c*)]

(*iv*) To whom do you attribute the "Growth Oriented" definition of Economics?

(*a*) Milton Friedman (*b*) Lionel Robbins
(*c*) Paul A. Samuelson (*d*) J.M. Keynes [*Ans.* (*c*)]

(*v*) The fundamental problem faced by an economy is one of

(*a*) scarcity of resources and multiplicity of wants
(*b*) economic welfare of the society
(*c*) decision making by the government
(*d*) exchange and distribution [*Ans.* (*a*)]

(*vi*) Production possibilities curve (PP curve) does not s h o w

(*a*) How to produce
(*b*) What to produce
(*c*) For whom to produce
(*d*) Productive potential under conditions of disguised unemployment [*Ans.* (*d*)]

(*vii*) State whether economies is

(*a*) a positive science
(*b*) a normative science
(*c*) neither a positive nor a normative science
(*d*) a science or an art depending on who uses economics and for what purpose [*Ans.* (*d*)]

(*viii*) Who of the following emphasized the normative aspect of Economics as a science?

(*a*) Robbins (*b*) English Classical School
(*c*) Germen Historical School (*d*) None of the above [*Ans.* (*a*)]

(*ix*) The meaning of the word 'economic' is most closely associated with the word

(*a*) free (*b*) scarce
(*c*) unlimited (*d*) unrestricted [*Ans.* (*b*)]

Chapter 2

The Methodological Issues in Economics

1. Introduction

Every science follows certain methods for the formulation of its laws, principles and theorems. Since economics is a science, it also adopts certain methods for the discovery of its laws and theories. In fact, there are some scholars who recognize the claim of economics to be considered a science on the specific ground that it makes use of scientific methods in the forgoing of its theoretical tools and weapons. The generations being formulated by the economists are quite distinct from other sciences. All such issues are being discussed in the following section of this chapter.

2. The Nature of Economic Theory or Economic Laws

The aim of economics, like all other sciences, is to obtain generalisation or laws which would help us to understand the past and offer trustworthy guidance for the future. The task of a scientist is the discovery of laws. Every science uses terms such as hypothesis, theory and laws. We have a tentative hypothesis of facts. If the hypothesis can explain new facts and is not contradicted by new discoveries, it may be called as a theory. If a theory continues to stand test of time and experience, a law may be formulated.

What is a Theory?

According to Boulding, "Theories without facts may be barren, but facts without theories are meaningless." A theory, in fact, expresses a causal relationship between two sets of phenomena, one as cause and the other as effect. Marshall defined a scientific theory as "a general proposition or statement of tendencies, more or less certain, more or less definite." Every cause has a tendency to produce some definite result, if nothing happens to prevent it. Things fall on earth as a result of the pull of gravity, if nothing interferes to prevent them from falling.

Economic theories or economic laws represent certain economic tendencies or principles expressing what is likely to happen, other things being equal. For instance, the law of market demand states that *ceteris paribus,* consumers increase their purchases of the community when its price falls and vice versa. The phrase, "other things being equal" indicates the limitations within which many, if not all, economic laws operate. Human nature is changing and at times inconsistent; hence economics can predict what men usually will do, but not with certainty what they actually will do.

Steps of formulating an economic theory

The following steps are required to formulate an economic theory:

(*i*) *Selection of the Problem.* The first step is to clearly define the problem, because the following steps will depend upon the problem which is to be solved. The problem may be related to an individual unit (*i.e.* a consumer or a producer or a firm) which will be a problem of microeconomics, or it may be related to the entire society (*i.e.* the problem of unemployment, poverty or inflation, etc.) which will be a problem of macroeconomics.

(*ii*) *Collection of Data.* Once the problem is cleared, the second step is to collect the necessary data or facts pertaining to the problem to be explored. If the problem is related to micro units, then the data can be easily collected. But if the problem is related to macro units, then it may require many months or even years to collect the necessary data.

(*iii*) *Classification of Data.* After data collection, the next step is to arrange the data according to the aspects of the problem. For example, if the problem is to study the changes in the composition of population, then the census data may be collected and classified by sex, age groups, literacy, marital status, occupational distribution, etc.

(*iv*) *Formulation of Hypothesis.* After data classification, the researcher has to formulate the hypothesis. A hypothesis is a suggested answer to a problem by the help of which the cause and effect relationship is to be explained. The hypothesis is formed on the basis of the observed facts, experience or previous knowledge of the researcher. Here the researcher has to make certain underlying assumptions and conditions under which the hypothesis is to be tested. For example, the assumption may be that a consumer wants to maximise his satisfaction or total utility, *i.e.* on the basis of this assumption the theory of consumer behaviour can be developed.

(*v*) *Testing of Hypothesis.* After the formulation of hypothesis, the researcher has to test it. He has to see whether the formulated hypothesis explains the facts considered or not. The hypothesis should be tested by well established statistical techniques. Here the hypothesis should provide the answer to the problem which led to the enquiry. A successful tested hypothesis becomes a theory, otherwise it is to be rejected.

(*vi*) *Verification of Theory.* The tested hypothesis *i.e.* the theory may be verified by observation or by checking the consistency of the theory with related facts. When the theory is verified and proved true, possible solutions to the problem are formulated. Thus in the final stage, it becomes a law which tan be established in the economy.

3. Applications and uses of economic theories

(*i*) *To Provide tools of economic analysis.* Economic theories provide economic tools to the economists by which they analyse the economic problems of microeconomics and macroeconomics. They are applicable to all economic systems and all the countries of the world.

(*ii*) *Interpretation of economic phenomena.* With the help of economic theories, the economists may interpret and explain the economic phenomena of the real world. They can also suggest the possible solutions to the prevailing problems in various countries.

(*iii*) *Basis for predicting unobserved economic events.* Economic theories may explore the economic problems of the real world. For example, if we find that with the increase in the supply of sugar, the prices do not fall, given the demand for sugar, we can predict that there is likely to be shortage of sugar in the near future. The reason may be some natural calamity or expectation of some emergency in the economy.

(*iv*) *Formulation of economic policies.* The government has to seek the advice of the economists to formulate various public policies such as tax policy, export-import policy or policy of public expenditure. Here on the basis of various relevant economic theories, the economists are able to suggest the policy measures to the government related to various economic problems.

(*v*) *Judging the performance of the economy.* Economic theories help in judging the performance of various sectors of the economy.

4. Limitations of Economic Theories

(*i*) *Lack of reliable data.* All economic theories are based on available data related to the problem. If the data are not accurate or sufficient, then the thcorics will bccome unrealistic.

(*ii*) *Lack of correct predictions.* Economic theories are not able to make correct predictions regarding various issues, as they are based on human behaviour. The probability of accurate predictions in economics is much less than in physical sciences.

(*iii*) *Unrealistic assumptions.* The assumptions, on which the economic theories are based, are not realistic. For example, we assume that consumers and producers behave rationally. But we find that they never behave rationally. According to Boulding, "Economic analysis is not a perfect picture of economic life; it is a map of it. Just we do not expect a map to show every tree, every house, and every blade of grass in a landscape, so we should not expect economic analysis to take into account every detail and quirk of real economic behaviour."[1]

(*iv*) *Not applicable to economic policies.* Economic theories are not fully applicable to formulate economic policies, because the assumptions on which these theories are based become unrealistic in the context of the subject undertaken. They are different to actual economic situation. For example, most economic theories are based on the assumption of perfect competition and full employment. Now such situations are rarely in existence and therefore, the theories based on such assumptions can not be applied to form the economic policies for that particular area or field.

5. Methods of Economic Theories

Every science has its own methods of investigation. Broadly speaking, there are two methods of scientific studies available to the economists: (*i*) Deductive or abstract method, and (*ii*) Inductive or historical method. The deductive method involves reasoning from a few fundamental propositions, the truth of which is assumed. In other words, here first the principal factors in operation in any field of investigation are determined and then the consequences that will ensuer from the operation of these factors under given conditions, are deduced by a process of reasoning. Therefore, deductive method descends from the general to the particular. The inductive method, on the other hand, involves collection of facts, drawing conclusions from them and testing the conclusion by other facts founded on experience. Therefore, under inductive method, we go from the particular to the general. Here, the economic theorems (laws) are based on observed facts.

During the 19th century, there was a bitter controversy between the Classical School of Britain and the Historical School of Germany on the relative uses of deductive and inductive methods. The classical economists of the 19th century (J.S. Mill and others) used the deductive method, while the Historical School (notably Hildebrand and Frederick List) and Statistical School of modern times, uses the inductive method to formulate economic laws and theorems. It was first Schmollar and then Alfred Marshall who attempted to resolve the controversy between the deductive and inductive methods of economics. In the words of Alfred Marshall,"...induction and deduction are both needed for scientific thought as the left and right foot are both needed for walking."[2]

---

1. K.E. Boulding, *op. cit.,* p.11.
2. Alfred Marshall, *Principles of Economics,* p. 24.

Now we will explain the merits and demerits of the methods in the following section.

Deductive Method

This method is also known as the abstract, hypothetical or the "a Priori" method of economic analysis. The classical and neo-classical economists applied the deductive method in their investigations. They tried to deduce the whole of economic science from certain generalisations about human motives and habits. This method is called "hypothetical," because some of the assumptions or axioms may not correspond to the facts, but they are so near to the facts that they may be used as generalisations for drawing inferences. This method is also known as "abstract" method because the phenomenon is simplified after removing all the irrelevant facts. Therefore, under this method, economics provides certain analytical tools and principles which are assumed to be logically consistent and universally held and hence, no historical or empirical evidence is warranted to test them. For example, every consumer wants to achieve maximum satisfaction from his given limited income. Any evidence is hardly required to support it. It is a self-evident truth. Similarly, it is also self-evident truth that every firm tries to maximise its profits. For drawing further conclusions, we also assume that there is perfect competition in the market. In such a situation the price of a commodity is given for a firm. Therefore, to attain maximum profit, a firm will continue her production until the marginal cost equals the price of the product or marginal revenue. In other words, we conclude that for profit maximisation a firm should produce at a point where marginal cost equals marginal revenue.[3] In brief, deductive method may be described as the technique of an abstract or 'a priori' approach to the problems of economic science. From this, it is clear that under deductive process of study, we move from "general" to "particulars". When a general truth is found, which itself proves, then there cannot be any doubt about this truth. Once we are able to know the truth, it is taken to be fundamentally right and there does not arise any controversy about its truth and definiteness.

3. For profit maximisation, the first order necessary condition is that

$$\frac{\partial C}{\partial X} = \frac{\partial R}{\partial X}$$

and the second order sufficient condition is that

$$\frac{\partial^2 C}{\partial X^2} > \frac{\partial^2 R}{\partial^2 X}$$

where C = Total Cost, R = Total Revenue, X = Total Product.

However, according to Adam Smith, the founder of classical school, the deductive method is not an exclusive method. It is aided by inductive method in the formulation of economic laws and theorems. As Prof. Keynes pointed out, "Smith first raised political economy to the dignity of a deductive science, but he has also been regarded as the founder of the historical method (inductive method) in political economy."[4] Thus, Adam Smith used every method of economics that helped him in his investigations.

After Adam Smith, Malthus emphasized inductive reasoning in support of his population theory. But the later English School regarded Ricardo rather than Malthus for popularisation of the deductive method of reasoning. Later on, Senior, Mill and Walter developed the abstract method or deductive method of economics. According to Nassau William Senior, "The subject treated by the political economist is not happiness but wealth; his premises consist of a few general prepositions, the result of observation or consciousness and scarcely requiring proof or even formal statement which almost every man, as soon as he hears them, admits as familiar to his thoughts or at least as included in his previous knowledge and his inferences are nearly as general and, if he has reasoned correctly, as certain as his premises."[5] Thus, in the views of Prof. Senior, economics was a positive science where the conclusions were deduced 'a priori' from general considerations.

J.S. Mill and others also expressed similar views. According to them, the problem should be stated in the simplest form and then it should be gradually made complicated, because the actual world is very complex and complicated. If we deal with the complicated problems directly, then we will not be able to draw any final conclusion. For example, J.S. Mill stated that the subject of international trade is very complicated in itself. For this, Mill starts with very simple assumptions and then gradually introduces more and more complicated issues in his analysis till he derives a complete theory of international trade. Hence, the classical economists held the view that political economy was an abstract science where the conclusions were based upon few fundamental assumptions.

The deductive method, as used by modern economists can also be described as the method of *Intellectual Experiment.*[6] Here, Boulding argues that economic analysis includes price, wages and other various economic quantities. The real world of economic quantities and their relationships is very complicated: It is very difficult, rather impossible to understand the various economic effects of even a simple economic activity. In such situations,

---

4. Keynes, J.M., *The Scope and Method of Political Economy.*
5. Senior, N.W., *An Outline of the Science of Political Economy.*
6. K.E. Boulding, *Economic Analysis,* Chapter 1.

conditions and postulates which are simpler than reality are first assumed and the consequences are worked out. Gradually, more and more complex assumptions are introduced until reality is approached.[7]

This method is very similar to the method of pure mathematics. As Prof. Jevons argues, economics is essentially mathematical in character, taking the term mathematical to mean all enquiries that deal with quantitative relations. Economics is concerned with those phenomena whose quantitative aspect is of fundamental importance, and in those phenomena this method may be used gainfully.

Therefore, the deductive method may be classified into two types: (*i*) *non-mathematical deductive method,* and (*ii*) *mathematical deductive method.* The former was used by the classical and neo-classical economists while the latter was used by the modern economists. Edgeworth (1845-1926) was the only economist who applied mathematics to a considerable extent in the economic analysis in the 19th century. Later on, in France and Italy, the mathematical method occupied an important place in the development of economic analysis. In the words of Heinrich Yon Stackelberg, "Wherever quantitative analysis is necessary, there mathematics is employed...for the latter is only another name for quantitative analysis...All that mathematics can do is to produce precise thinking even about imprecise data." The modern writers are of the opinion that the mistake of the classical writers is their starting with insufficient data. According to Gide and Rist, "Even when the premises were correct, they were too ready to think and not careful enough to prove that their conclusions were always borne out by facts. No one can defend their incomplete analysis, their hasty generalisations or their ambiguous formulae."[8] The mistake of the classical school was not that they adopted the deductive method, but that they had too often mistaken the abstraction for the reality. The fault does not lie in the method, but in the doctrinal theory of some of the writers. Thus, Stiglar points out the profitability of mathematics in economics by saying that "mathematics can exhaust the implications of known quantitative relationships and it can often wring (squeeze) much information from only generally defined relationships. Mathematics is indeed the queen of sciences. Without mathematics one can give only an intuitive proof of complicated relationships; such as those expressed by Euler's theorem, Slutsky's equation, the theory of general equilibrium and certain theorems in the theory of games." Today, diagrammatical and mathematical methods occupy an important place in economic theory.

7. *Ibid.*, p. 11.
8. Gide and Rist, *A History of Economic Doctrines,* p. 396.

The chief advantage of such a method is that it leads to higher standards of precision in abstract economic reasoning. Chances of mistake are few. Another advantage of this mathematical deductive method is that it explains the relation of mutual dependence which may exist between different economic variables such as supply, demand and price. But the chief defect of this method is to attach too much importance to the method itself. It leads to intellectual toys and the real end disappears in the intellectual gymnastics of mathematical treatment. It is why Alfred Marshall opposed too frequent and avoidable use of mathematics. He stated, "The chief use of pure mathematics in economic questions seems to be in helping a person to write quickly, shortly and exactly, some of his thoughts for his own use; and to make sure that he has enough, and only enough, premises for his conclusion. But when a great many symbols have to be used, they become very laborious to anyone but the writer himself."[9]

Advantages of Deductive Method

The following are the main advantages of the deductive method of economics:

(*i*) *Simplicity.* Deductive method was not only used intensively by the classical economists, but it is also used in modern times. It is admitted that the use of deductive method is a very simple task. We start from a few assumptions and derive a number of conclusions. Therefore, it helps us to get results without any botheration of collecting facts and studying them.

(*ii*) *Limited use of experimentation.* The use of experimentation is very limited in economics and that increases the importance of this method of economics. As we know that experimentation can be made to a greater extent in the physical and chemical science, but the method of experimentation is not available in economic science and, therefore, the best alternative is to adopt the method of deductive reasoning. The deductive method does not assume the necessity of experimentation in economic analysis.

(*iii*) *Use of logic and mathematics.* As we have noted above, the deductive method is today known as mathematical method. It makes use of logic and mathematics which results in accurate conclusions or generalisations. Due to enough application of mathematical formulae, there remain very few chances of mistakes or inaccuracies in drawing inferences.

(*iv*) *Certainty and clarity.* Deductive method of analysis leads to exactness and certainty. This method is based on logic which is said to be an unfailing companion. If the reasoning is correctly used and assumptions are rightly taken, we always get correct conclusions. This method can easily correct the mistakes and results become quite clear.

---

9. A. Marshall, *op. cit.,* p. 9.

(*v*) *Effectiveness*. This method is very effective, if its assumptions are true. With the help of this method, we may forecast about the future. We can easily say that under certain given conditions how the individuals will react. For example, if the price of a commodity goes up, we can easily forecast that the demand for that, commodity will fall, while the supply of the same will rise.

(*vi*) *Universality*. The theories derived under the deductive method of reasoning are found to be universally true. They hold good in every country and in every period of history. For example, the law of diminishing utility states that if a number of units of a commodity are given to one person, he must feel after a certain stage that the utility of additional units will diminish.

(*vii*) *Impartiality*. The results deduced from this method are impartial. They are not affected by any favour or prejudice.

(*viii*) *Suitability*. This method is most suitable in the study of economic science. Since man is a rational being, he cannot be put to much experiment. It is with the help of reason alone that we can rightly interpret the human behaviour.

(*ix*) *Complementary*. According to Prof. Cairnes, "The method of deduction is incomparable when conducted under perfect checks, the most powerful instrument of discovery ever wielded by human intelligence." It is clear that where inductive method fails, it is the deductive method of analysis that comes to our rescue.

Limitations of deductive method

In spite of its advantages, the deductive method suffers from a number of limitations also. The main critics of the deductive methods are economists of the Historical School, which flourished mainly in Germany. They argued that theories must emerge if only adequate statistical or historical evidence is available to support them. According to their view, theories developed without facts are baseless. In the context of rapid changing circumstances no hypotheses may be assumed universally true. If the entire economic analysis is based on such axioms then the conclusions deduced from them will not be reliable. In brief, we find the following important limitations of the deductive method.

(*i*) *Lack of reliability*. Since classical theories are based on the aforementioned universally held axioms, they are true only when the axioms hold good. In other words, the condition of *ceteris paribus* is assumed throughout the process of reasoning. But most of these assumptions are not true in the changing world and therefore the conclusions drawn from them lack reliability.

(*ii*) *Lack of empirical evidence.* The followers of deductive method do not think it necessary to test their theories on the basis of facts or empirical evidence. Therefore in deductive process, there is danger of being too much abstract.

(*iii*) *Lack of personal experience.* This method ignores the importance of personal and historical experiences. It leads to conclusions having little or no connection with reality. If such results are applied in the formulation of government policies, then it will be followed by disastrous consequences.

Due to the above limitations of the deductive method, the economists belonging to the Historical School of Germany (notably Schmoller, Knies, Hildebrand, Roscher, etc.) developed a new method known as induction method of studying economic phenomena.

Inductive method

This method is also known as historical, empirical or 'a posteriori' method of economics analysis. The German School of economists advocated this method. They develop the economic science from economic history. They study particular instances from economic history and draw general conclusions from them. These conclusions are further verified by reference to subsequent economic facts. Thus, under this method *we go from particular to general.* The followers of this method believe that economic theory and economic laws have only a relative value. It is not possible to uniformally apply an economic law to all the countries and in all periods of history. The economists verify their conclusions from observation and analysis by subsequent economic facts. Observation and experiments are the chief instruments of this method. In this method, we make an attempt to connect the economic laws with reality and practical facts.

The rapid development in the science of statistics during recent years and the collection of data by governments and private individuals have enhanced the value of this method. From the data thus collected, valuable and scientific conclusions have been drawn. In this way the theorems and theories developed by this inductive method are more accurate and perfect than the abstract or deductive method.

According to Prof. Boulding, the inductive method may be classified into two types:[10] (*a*) Experimental Method, and (*b*) Statistical Method. Now we explain these forms in the following manner:

(*a*) *Experimental method.* prof. Boulding states that the experimental method has been very popular in chemistry, biology and other physical sciences; but it cannot be applied in economics except in narrow limited fields. This

10. K.E. Boulding, *op. cit.*, pp. 10-12.

method tests the validity of the generalisations (arrived at as a result of deductive reasoning) by resorting to the study of actual facts.

Since the economist lacks the laboratory facilities, he is unable to make necessary experiments. Moreover, economics is concerned with the behaviour of human beings where the experiments are not possible. As Prof. Albert L. Meyers states, "Human beings have wills of their own and resent being treated as guinea pigs for the purpose of social experimentation."[11] The economist, therefore, uses the statistical method.

(2) *Statistical Method.* This method consists in collecting figures regarding economic phenomena. The figures may be used to prove or disprove propositions derived theoretically or to correlate different phenomena and draw conclusions.

In economics, the statistical method is used as substitute for the controlled experimental method. Therefore, it fulfills the requirement. The statistical method is applied in the collection, classification and tabulation of facts and also applied to draw conclusions. Its results are based on sampling method and therefore covers the entire population (or region). For example, if we want to study the consumption pattern of one thousand labourers. Now we will apply the sampling technique where the family budgets of a sample of labourers (may be one hundred) will do the needful. The sampling method is a scientific procedure. Its results are reliable and we may also investigate the errors.

Advantages of Inductive Method

The inductive method of economics possesses the following main advantages;

(*i*) *Reliability of economic analysis.* The economic generalisations derived by this method are more reliable than the same under deductive method. Such generalisations are made on the basis of collected facts of the real world.

(*ii*) *Formulation of sound policy.* The conclusions arrived at by the process of induction may be tested on the basis of facts. They may be revised according to the changes in statistics. Such results are very well used in the formulation of government policies.

(*iii*) *Based on scientific procedure.* Under statistical method, we draw inferences on the basis of a representative sample. If we increase the size of the sample, then we may get more accurate results.

(*iv*) *Universality.* Since inductive reasoning is based on empirical facts, it may explain clearly the problem of any class, region or country. Such generalisations or theorems are based on very sure and realistic facts, and as such, their validity cannot be challenged.

---

11. Albert L. Meyers. *Elements of Modern Economics.* p. 2.

(*v*) *Complimentary.* The inductive method of reasoning is of positive advantages where the deductive method fails to interpret the results. Thus this method possesses the advantage of being complementary. We can easily testify the results drawn through deductive method by putting the results under experiments.

(*vi*) *Development of mental capacity.* With the help of this method, we can develop our mental capacity and increase our knowledge. It is possible because under this method, we clarify and verify the historical events by analysing the facts under which causes and effects are involved.

Limitations of Inductive Method

The inductive method is also not free from criticisms. It has been criticised on the following grounds:

(*i*) *Faulty statistics.* The statistical method or induction should be used with caution because statistics are in many cases faulty and co-relation is not causation. If two facts appear together, we cannot conclude that one causes the other; all that we can say is that there is a possibility that they may be so connected.

Moreover, the statistics related to human behaviour should not be assumed unbiased. Therefore, statistical results are accurate only on approximation.

(*ii*) *Limited scope.* Generally, we may not be able to collect data regarding all the economic units of the phenomena in all circumstances. It is very difficult to say whether the sample represents the entire population. This is the reason why theories based on induction lack the predictive power so profoundly embedded in the deductive method. Theories related to the pricing of products and productive services and macroeconomic theories of employment, interest and national income, are all deduced from certain widely accepted principles. Likewise, modern welfare propositions have also been deduced from the general, ethical principles of human behaviour.

(*iii*) *Imperfection.* The inductive method alone is unable to draw accurate economic generalisations unless it is supplemented by a process of deductive reasoning. Of course, it is true that we must establish and know the facts first of all. No science can develop without data or with incomplete data. The conclusions formed by general reasoning must also be verified by facts. To admit that is not to admit the uselessness of the deductive method. As Prof. Durbin states, "Facts do not speak for themselves. It is only by analysis, comparison, hypothesis and prophecy that they can be made to speak at all."[12] No science can develop without the aid of reason and hypothesis. Without the use of deductive reasoning, the historical or inductive method runs the

12. Durbin, "Methods of Research" in the *Economic Journal.* June 1938, p. 187.

risk of remaining purely descriptive. It can serve only to accumulate amass of unconnected and unserviceable facts.

(*iv*) *Costly method.* The inductive method is very costly. Collection off acts and data involve a number of experiments and require much investment. It is also necessary to provide sufficient training to the persons who are put for collection of data and conducting experiments.

(*v*) *Biased results.* The conclusions drawn with the help of this method are often not impartial. They are generally found prejudiced on account of individual likes and dislikes.

Complementarity of the Two Methods

As we have noted that neither the inductive method alone nor the deductive method alone can serve the purpose of economic analysis and investigation. Different methods are appropriate to different branches of economics. The mathematical method or the deductive method is very suitable for the theory of value while in trade cycles and monetary theory, inductive or statistical method is appropriate. Thus, both deduction and induction are useful in economic analysis. Hence, the two methods seem to be really complementary rather than rival methods. According to Pareto, "Discussion of method is a pure waste of time. The aim of the science is to discover economic uniformities, and it is always right to follow any path or to pursue any method that is likely to lead to that end." Marshall also observed, "Induction and deduction are both needed for scientific thought as the left and right foot are both needed for walking."[13] Adolf Wanger, a leading economist of the historical school also felt that "the true solution of the contest about method is not to be found in the selection of deduction or induction, but in the acceptance of deduction and induction. Each must be employed in the cases where it is specially adapted to the particular nature of the problem to be solved, and, as far as possible for it is not always possible there must be a combination of both, although in concrete cases one or the other will take precedence." It means that both the methods may be profitably employed by economists but in different propositions for different purposes.

Today, the modern economists find it more appropriate to blend the two approaches. According to Lipsey and Steiner, "Both induction and deduction are used in the scientific method which is applied in economic analysis."[14] Prof. Samuelson also remarks, "Properly understood, theory and observation, deduction and induction cannot be in conflict."[15]

---

13. Alfred Marshall, *op, cit.*, p. 24.
14. Lipsey and Steiner, *Economics.* p. 22.
15. Samuelson, P.A., *Economics,* 7th ed., 1967, p. 8.

Exercises

1. Describe the process of formulating an economic theory. What are the uses and limitations of economic theories?
2. "Induction and deduction are both needed for scientific thought as the left and right foot are both needed for walking" (Schmoller). Discuss and explain the uses and limitations of the two methods of economic analysis.
3. Explain the merits and demerits of inductive and deductive methods of economic analysis.
4. Discuss whether deduction or induction should be used as a method of study in economics.
5. Discuss the methods for the derivation of economic laws. Are these methods complementary?
6. Distinguish between deductive and inductive methods of reasoning and evaluate their usefulness in economic analysis.

Multiple Choice Questions

7. (*i*) Induction is the process of reasoning from
   (*a*) a part to the whole (*b*) particular to general
   (*c*) individual to universal (*d*) all of the above [*Ans.* (*d*)]

   (*ii*) Find out the correct statement
   (*a*) Deductive method descends from general to the particular
   (*b*) Inductive method descends from general to the particular
   (*c*) The classical economists emphasized inductive method
   (*d*) Deductive method depends on experimentation [*Ans.* (*a*)]

   (*iii*) What is true for inductive method ?
   (*a*) Static (*b*) Hypothetical
   (*c*) Empirieal (*d*) Ignores experimentation [*Ans.* (*c*)]

   (*iv*) What is true for deductive method ?
   (*a*) Supported by Historical School
   (*b*) Abstract
   (*c*) Realistic
   (*d*) Economic conditions assumed to be changing [*Ans.* (*b*)]

   (*v*) Which of the following statements has been drawn by inductive method?
   (*a*) A private firm will try to maximise its profits
   (*b*) All businessmen wish to buy at low price and sell at a high price
   (*c*) A consumer will buy from the cheapest market
   (*d*) The larger the stock of money with a person, the lower is the utility that he derives from it. [*Ans.* (*b*)]

   (*vi*) A theory is
   (*a*) an assumption (*b*) a hypothesis
   (*c*) a validated hypothesis (*d*) an if-then proposition [*Ans.* (*c*)]

   (*vii*) A theory expresses
   (*a*) the behaviour of people
   (*b*) a causal relationship between cause and effect
   (*c*) a positive relationship between dependent and independent variables
   (*d*) all of the above [*Ans.* (*b*)]

Chapter 3

Economic Models

1. Introduction

Model-building is another method of investigation. It is widely used by the present-day economists. A model states the relationship between a dependent variable and a number of independent variables. The economist has to study the relationships among economic variables in a world which is highly complex and complicated. Hundreds and thousands of economic forces are at work in the economy. Therefore, it creates a problem for the economist to isolate the effects of various economic variables in which he is interested from those many economic forces. Since so many things are excluded from the model, its conclusions must be accepted with particular caution. It is quite possible that one of the excluded variables may turn out to be crucially important. As such the conclusion may be misleading. Thus while framing a model one should incorporate all the important variables related to the problem. Economic models are generally setout in equation form with diagrams. A complete economic model will have as many equations as there are unknowns.

2. Meaning and Nature of Economic Models

Meaning of Economic Models

Economic theory is mainly concerned with relationships among economic variables. Demand function, consumption function, cost function, production function are some of the examples of the relations which are to be faced by all economists. In fact, the entire body of economic theory can be regarded as a collection of relations among variables. The universe of the study is very complex. Many factors affect one economic variable at one time. The main task of an investigator is to sort out the economic variables which are most closely linked with the phenomena we are going to analyse. The projected goal of a researcher is to reduce the economic analysis, as far as possible, to directly linked factors. It would be a happy state of affairs if important relationships could be reduced to simple mathematical formulas manipulated in mechanical ways. It is also very important to understand a theory well. Thus a concrete and well defined mathematical model is essential for testing the hypothesis and for economic policy formation. That is why the word 'model' occurs with increasing frequency in modern economic research.

In layman language, model is a simplification of reality. A model is an abstract representation of reality which clears what is relevant to a particular question at a particular time and neglects all other aspects. They are usually elaborated in terms of well-defined variables and functions. Prof. C.F. Christ wrote, "A model can be described by a list of endogenous variables, a list of exogenous variables and a list of specifications as to which variables are present in each equation."[1]

According to Prof. Edward J. Kane, "An economic model is a logical (usually mathematical) representation of whatever a priori or a theoretical knowledge economic analysis suggests is most relevant for treating a particular problem. Usually, a model takes the form of a system of equations embodying certain assumed interdependencies among more or less operationally defined variables."[2]

The information contained in a model is often referred to as a priori information or a priori restrictions or assumptions or the maintained hypothesis. A model establishes the main variables involved and connects them by means of mathematical statements. Thus a model simplifies the reality, points out the basic features of the problem and denotes a set of hypothesis.

Models are generally set out in the form of equations using mathematical symbols. Some models can be summed up in a single equation while others may consist of an impressive array of relations. The number of equations included in a model depends upon the objectives for which the model is constructed. Prof. C.F. Christ suggested some desirable properties that we would like our equations to have.

These properties are relevance, simplicity, theoretical plausibility, explanatory ability and forecasting ability.

Nature of Economic Models

Nowadays most of the sciences use models. But economic models are different from models of physical sciences. We study the human being made of flesh and bones. Thus to think of a rigid and exact model is a myth. Economic models study economic phenomena.

A statistical model denotes a set of hypothesis that permits statistical inference from the particular data under review. An economic model is usually

1. C.F. Christ, *Econometrics,* pp. 21-22.
2. Edward 1. Kane, *Economic Statistics and Econometrics,* p. 12.

adapted to yield a definite and precise formulation of the economic processes at work. The statistical model must specify the stochastic elements that are supposed to enter into the determination of the observations. Thus an economic model needs exact and precise knowledge while for statistical model the understanding of what is relevant to the particular observations at hand is far more important than a wide knowledge of economic theory.

Economic models are based upon abstract economic theory. Therefore their models are insufficient to permit an empirical application.

Economic models contain only established facts and theory, while new relation can be introduced into the initial statistical model. In the process of analysis, first, we construct a statistical model. It becomes economic model only after testing with data. Most of the economic models explain the phenomena as a whole. Statistical models on the other hand often include partial analysis all that can be achieved on available data. These are the models of special aspects of an economic phenomena. Economic models are concerned with the explanation of economic laws. While statistical models are designed to forecast about economic phenomena and to serve as aids to policy formation. These models are often called policy-models. Most of the economic models are prepared after the formulation of economic laws while construction of a statistical model is the starting point of any statistical investigation. Statistical models are classified according to the types of data involved, i.e. time series and cross section studies. Most of the time series-analysis are concerned with the national aggregates like national income, employment, consumption, etc. Usually cross-section studies are based upon surveys which yield direct information about economic conditions from microeconomic units like households, firms, etc.

Statistical methods used in economics are similar to those developed for other branches of study, but the nature of the data is quite different. The distinguishing feature of economic data is that they are non-experimental. A physical scientist concerned with some aspect of Boyle's Law can control the external conditions (temperature, *etc.*) within the four walls of a laboratory and can study that volume of gas at varying amounts of pressure. He can minimise the error of observations in a controlled atmosphere. In economic science we are not so fortunate with our raw materials. Here we cannot set up laboratory type situations, thus controlled experiments are not possible.

In economics, experiment is seldom possible. Nature does experiment with the economy by the cycle of day and night, winter and summer and good and bad harvest years. Here we deal with data pertaining to observations made about men. The numerous influences under which he lives and works, defy any attempt at controlled experiments. In the absence of controlled conditions, we simply record the consumer's behaviour, *e.g.* the purchases made by consumer at different price levels. Thus we get only associated set of prices and purchases which are made by different consumers under different conditions. The variations between observations are not subject to experimental control. Thus in physical sciences we have sound theoretical reasons for postulating a specific model, while in economics neither theoretical nor empirical reasons are available to justify the analysis. Economic behaviour is less predictable than physical sciences phenomena. All this results in unstable and unsupported laws. That is why economic laws are called mere statements of tendencies. No economic law can be so exact and stable as a physical science law.

3. Concepts in Model Building

When we have to work on an economic problem, we first frame a mathematical model which describes the events that we want to incorporate and the assumptions that are related to it. Thus a mathematical model contains three elements: (*i*) A dependent variable, i.e. the event to be explained; (*ii*) one or more independent variables, i.e. the factors by which the dependent variable is influenced; and (*iii*) the behavioural assumptions which explain the nature of causal relationships between explanatory and dependent variables.

An economic model consists of a set of behavioural relations and a set of equilibrium conditions. Thus we should specify the variables and the parameters that we want to include in the model. We may explain the various concepts used in model building as under:

1. **Variables.** A variable can be defined as something whose magnitude can change over a period of time. For example we may represent price by *P*, demand by *D* and supply by *S*.

Further a model may have dependent variable and a number of independent variables. A dependent variable is one whose magnitude will change as a result of a change in some other (independent) variable. An independent variable is one whose change is not influenced by the dependent variable. For example, when we define a demand functions as $D = f(P)$. It means that quantity demand is a function of price. Thus demand is a dependent variable and price is an independent variable.

Further, a model may have endogenous variables and exogenous variables. Endogenous variables are those whose values are determined within the model. On the other hand, exogenous variables are those values are determined outside the model. It must be remembered that a variable may be endogenous to one model and exogenous to another model.

Again, there may be flow variables and stock variables in the model. A flow variable is a quantity that can be measured in terms of specific time period while a stock variable is a quantity which can be measured in a point of time.

2. **Constants.** A constant is something whose magnitude does not change. Thus it is opposite to a variable. When a constant is joined to a variable, it is known as the coefficient of that variable.

3. **Parameters.** A parameter is a symbol which is constant for the purpose of any particular problem but may assume different values in different problems.

4. **Functional Relationships.** A functional relationship between two variables exists when a change in the value of one variable uniquely determines the change in the value of the other variables.

5. **Equations.** In economic models, three types of equations are used: (*i*) Definitional Equations, (*ii*) Behavioural Equations, and (*iii*) Equilibrium Equations.

(*i*) *Definitional Equations.* It specifies a relation between two alternative expressions having the same meaning. The sign (identically equal to) is used for such an equation.

(*ii*) *Behavioural Equation.* It specifies how a variable behaves in response to changes in other variables. A behavioural equation is always based on some definite assumptions on which the particular behaviour of the variable under study is based.

(*iii*) *Equilibrium Equation.* It explains the attainment of equilibrium. The equilibrium condition can be derived on the basis of behavioural equations.

4. Building a Micro Static Model

Let us construct a micro static model of an industry under perfect competition. The model can be framed by explaining a functional relationship among three variables: quantity demanded for the commodity (D), quantity supplied of the commodity (S) and the price of the commodity (P). Here D and S are the dependent variables while P is an independent variable.

Now the fundamental relationships can be established as under:

$$D = f(P) \qquad \text{...(1)}$$

$$S = f(P) \qquad \text{...(2)}$$

and

$$D = S \qquad \text{...(3)}$$

The important assumptions of the model are as under:

(*i*) Quantity demanded (D) is inversely related with price (P).

(*ii*) Quantity supplied (S) is positively related with price (P) but only after a certain minimum positive price.

(*iii*) D and S are stock variables.

(*iv*) The equilibrium condition is $D = S$

The Model

In this static market model, there are two behavioural equations and one equilibrium condition :

$$\left.\begin{aligned} D &= \alpha - \beta P \\ S &= \delta - \Upsilon P \end{aligned}\right\} \text{Behavioural Equations}$$

and $$D = S \text{ Equilibrium condition.}$$

where α, β, δ, and Υ are constants.

Suppose we have the following values for the above equations :

$$D = 400 - 100\,P \qquad ...(4)$$

$$S = -50 + 50\,P \qquad ...(5)$$

$$D = S \qquad ...(6)$$

Now substituting equation (4) and equation (5) into equation (6) we have

$$400 - 100\,P = -50 + 50\,P$$

or $$-100P - 50P = -50 - 400$$

or $$150P = 450$$

or $$P = 3$$

Putting the value of $P = 3$ in equation (4) and equation (5) we have

$$D = 400 - 100 \quad 3 = 100$$

$$S = -50 + 50 \quad 3 = 100$$

$\therefore$ $$D = S = 100$$

Thus the industry will be in equilibrium at price Rs. 3 when quantity demanded and supplied is equal to 100 units.

5. Limitations of Model Building

Economic models are statistical models. They give rise to statistical judgements and like all statistical judgements, they are subject to errors. These errors arise for the following reasons:

(*i*) *Misspecification.* The error may arise due to misspecification. Each variable is affected by so many economic variables at the time. If anyone of the relevant variable is left out and could not be included in our model, error of misspecification may arise.

Some variables may have been omitted because investigator did not suspect their presence. It may also happen that investigator has himself omitted them. In either case the error of misspecification arises. As our sphere of study is very complex, so many factors affect one factor at one time. In such a case it is impossible to include all the factors. Thus it is advisable to the investigator that he should emphasise the most closely linked variables and omit the others. In such a case misspecification error is bound to occur in our model.

(*ii*) *Non-availability of Data.* Error may also arise due to non-availability of data. Econometric study is largely based upon the assumptions that we have large samples of accurate data. But unfortunately we hardly find an example in which reliable and representative data are available. Our observations are based upon human beings made of flesh and bones. We do not expect them to behave exactly in the same manner in all circumstances. Since we cannot observe the economic phenomena in a controlled atmosphere, the behaviour of our samples is bound to change in changing circumstances. Thus in the absence of accurate data sampling error arises in the model.

(*iii*) *Wrong Assumptions.* Error may also arise due to wrong assumption about the relationship among the variables. It is possible that we may assume the relationship between variables as linear whereas it may be non-linear one. In such a case the forecast is bound to be incorrect. This type of error arises mainly due to misunderstanding of the investigator. Thus investigator must be well acquainted with the problem in his hand.

Exercises

1. What is an economic model? Explain the various concepts used in model building.
2. Discuss the meaning and nature of economic models.
3. Define an economic model and construct a microeconomic model.
4. What is an economic model? What are the uses and limitations of economic models?
5. Explain the following:
   (*a*) Variables
   (*b*) Constants
   (*c*) Parameters
   (*d*) Equations

Multiple Choice Questions

6. (*i*) A function refers to
   (*a*) the demand for a commodity
   (*b*) the supply of a commodity
   (*c*) the demand & supply of a commodity
   (*d*) The relationship between dependent variable and one or more independent variable [*Ans.* (*d*)]

   (*ii*) In an economic model
   $$D = f(P)$$
   an independent variable is
   (*a*) P (*b*) D
   (*c*) P&D (*d*) None of the above [*Ans.* (*a*)]

   (*iii*) Find out the correct statement
   (*a*) Prediction of economic models can not be refuted by empirical evidence
   (*b*) Model, transform verbal expressions into more scientific expressions
   (*c*) Models make no assumptions
   (*d*) Economic models are comprehensive and not partial [*Ans.* (*b*)]

Chapter 4

Microeconomics and Macroeconomics

1. Introduction

Microeconomics and macroeconomics are the two approaches to economic problems and economic analysis. These terms were first coined and used by Ragnar Frisch in 1933 and have now been adopted by the economists all the world over. *Microeconomics* studies the economic actions of a particular individual and a well-defined group of individuals, i.e. households, firms, industries, etc. and *macroeconomics* studies the broad aggregates, such as, total employment, the total consumption, and the aggregate national income. Microeconomics is also known as *partial analysis* and macroeconomics as *aggregate analysis*. It is because that microeconomics is the partial differentiation of the total (macro). This type of distinction is, in a sense, artificial, since aggregates are merely sums of individual figures. However, the distinction is justified by the basic differences in the objectives and methods of the two branches.

Before the distinction between microeconomics and macroeconomics came into vogue, the fundamental dichotomy was between price and income analysis. This dichotomy can be applied over into the micro and macro branches of economic theory. Normally, prices play a major role in the microeconomic analysis and its objective is to define price determination and the allocation of specific resources to particular uses. Macroeconomics, on the other hand, is the study of the economy as a whole, i.e. the determination of the levels of national income and aggregate resource employment. Here, one should not understand that income concepts are non-existent in microeconomics or that prices are ignored in macroeconomics. However, in the theories of microeconomics, the determination of incomes of individuals is encompassed within the general pricing process: people earn their incomes by selling factors of production, the prices of which are determined in the same manner as all other prices. On the other hand, prices are relevant in macroeconomic theories, but macrotheorists usually abstract from the problems of determining individual prices and their relations to one another and deal with aggregate price indices as determined by the level of aggregate spending. In simple words, microeconomics is related to particular individuals or particular business units, *i.e.* it includes the income of a particular individual, the output of a particular firm, etc. while macroeconomics is related to the economy as a whole, *i.e.* it includes the total income, total output and other aggregates relating to the whole economy.

Some economists prefer to begin their analysis of economic problems from the variables concerning individuals, individual firms and individual industries, *i.e.* microeconomics. Other economists prefer to begin their analysis from the broad aggregates or the national totals, *i.e.* macroeconomics. The greater part of Marshallian economics is concerned with microeconomics. The later works of Keynes *General Theory of Employment, Interest and Money* relate to macroeconomics. These two branches of economics are complementary and for a thorough discussion of economic problems, the micro and macro views of economic life are both necessary.

2. Microeconomics

Meaning of Microeconomics

According to Boulding, "Microeconomics is the study of particular firms, particular households, individual prices, wages, incomes, individual industries, particular commodities." From this definition, it is clear that under microeconomics we study particular economic organism; for instance, individual prices, wages or incomes; economic behaviour of individual consumers and producers, *etc.*

According to Prof. Lerner, "Microeconomics consists of looking at the economy through a microscope, as it were, to see how the millions of cells in the body economic the individuals or households as consumers, and the individuals or firms as producers play their part in the working of the whole economic organism." For example, in microeconomic analysis, we study the demand of individual consumer for a good and from there go on to derive the group demand for the good. The study of microeconomics clears the economic status of the individual units. It helps us in determining the remuneration of individual units.

Types of Microeconomics

Microeconomics has been divided into following three types:

(*i*) *Simple Micro-statics.* It studies different microeconomic variables and their relationships at a given point of time under the conditions of equilibrium. It, therefore, assumes that the values of microeconomic variables will remain unchanged[1] and for this reason a simple micro-static model does not involve time period.

---

1. In a static model, the equilibrium value of a dependent variable will remain unchanged so long as the magnitude of dependent variable (S) remain unchanged.

For example, the equilibrium price of a commodity in the market is established at a point where the demand is equal to the supply. Now, as long as the demand function *DD* and supply function *SS,* as shown in Fig. 4.1, remain unchanged, the price of the commodity will stick to *OP.* Micro-statics discusses the question of how an equilibrium price is arrived at in a market where demand and supply functions are known and remain unchanged.

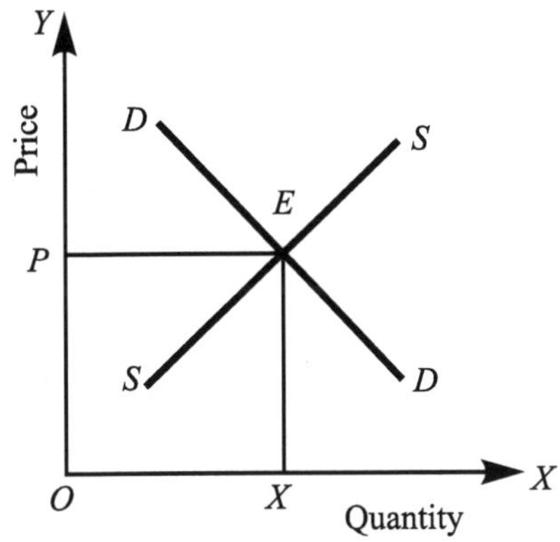

Fig. 4.1

(*ii*) *Comparative Micro-statics.* It compares the equilibrium positions at different points of time. In micro-statics, we assume that there is no change in the demand and supply functions. But due to a change in the independent variable, the demand function or the supply function or both will shift and the market will reach a new state of equilibrium giving a new price. This new equilibrium position will also be studied under micro-statics. But in comparative micro-statics, we compare the two equilibrium positions and will throw no light on the process by which the new equilibrium has been arrived at.

It has been shown in Fig. 4.2. The old equilibrium point is *E.* Due to

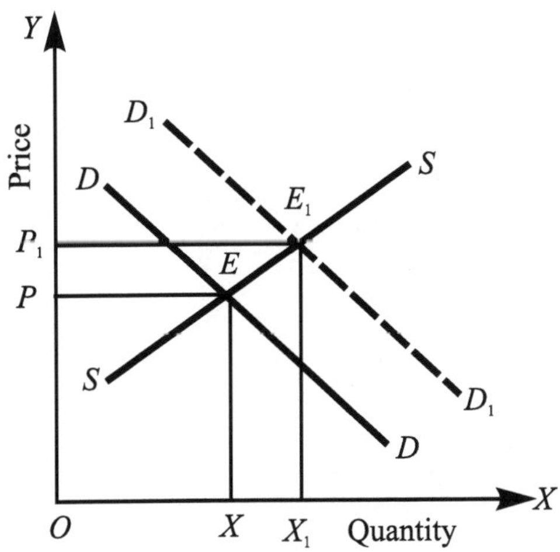

Fig. 4.2

a change in some independent variable, the demand function shifts upward from *DD to* D_1D_1. It results in a new equilibrium position at E_1, where the price is OP_1 and quantity demanded and supplied is OX_1. These two equilibrium positions are compared by the comparative micro-statics.

(*iii*) *Microdynamics* (*The Cobweb Model*). It explains lagged relationship between the microeconomic variables. Microdynamics throws full light on the happenings in the market during the period of transition from one static equilibrium to another. It is a study of disequilibrium. More specifically, it studies the process through which the new equilibrium in the market is established. The Cobweb Model is used to explain the dynamics of demand, supply and price over long periods of time. As prices move up and down in cycles, quantities produced also seem to move up and down in a counter cycle manner.

For example, in Fig. 4.3 the initial price of a commodity is fixed at *OP* where the quantity demanded and supplied is *OX*. Now, due to a change in some independent variable, the demand curve *DD* shifts upward to D_1D_1. As a result, a disequilibrium will occur in the market. This will be followed by a series of disequilibria before the final equilibrium is arrived at and a new equilibrium price takes place. As soon as demand increases, supply cannot be increased at the same moment. Therefore, the immediate effect of the upward shift in the demand curve is that the suppliers enjoy a higher price *XA*. It is due to the fact that the supply is perfectly inelastic at a given point of time. This sharp increase in price in the market period will attract the suppliers to increase their supply in the short run. This leads to increase in the supply at the level OX_1. It will result in a decrease in price by *BC*. But at this price the demand decreases to OX_2. This level of output again leads to an increase in price to the level OP_3.

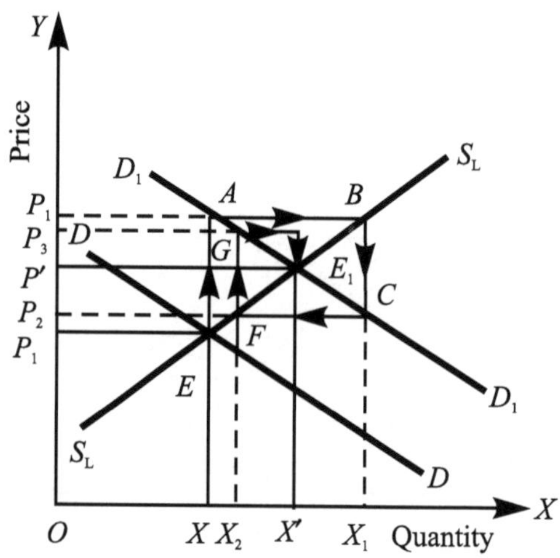

Fig. 4.3

This process will continue until the new equilibrium is established at point E_1 where the price is OP' and quantity supplied and demand is OX'. This entire process is studied under microdynamics.

Uses of Microeconomics

According to Prof. Bilas, the main uses of microeconomics are the following:

(*i*) *Price Determination and Allocation of Resources.* Microeconomics is useful in the determination of price and for the allocation of resources between alternative uses. We shall see that demand-supply model is used in price-theory. The model states that price is determined by the forces of demand and supply, and at equilibrium price, the quantity demanded equals quantity supplied. If price increases then the quantity demanded will be less than quantity supplied.

Further, microeconomics studies the behaviour of an individual consumer, family, firm and industry. Suppose we want to study steel industry. For this, we will study the cost situations of various steel producing units. Their element of competition will also be studied. The demand and supply for their products will be studied. The price of steel will be determined by the aggregate demand and aggregate supply of steel. This price will be given to all steel producing units in the industry. The firms in the industry will determine individually their level of outputs of steel. In microeconomics, we will also study the factor-employment by these various firms in the industry.

(*ii*) *Determination of Economic Policy.* Microeconomics, to some extent, states the relevance of economic policies of the government. The effect of direct and indirect tax on consumption and production of a commodity can easily be found by the analysis of microeconomics. Not only this, but the rationale of price policy and wage policy of the government can also be determined by the analysis of the allocation of resources by a firm under microeconomics. Microeconomics will also state whether the rationing is justified or not in the interest of citizens of a country.

(*iii*) *Optimum Utilisation of Factors of Production.* We may also find the situation of optimum utilisation of resources for a consumer and a producer by the help of microeconomics. Microeconomics provides the law of substitution by which a consumer will maximise his satisfaction when the ratio of marginal utilities equals the ratio of various commodities. Similarly, a producer will maximise his profit when the ratio of marginal product of factors of production equals the ratio of their prices. This situation will be the situation of maximum welfare on micro level.

Mathematically, a consumer maximises satisfaction when,

$$\frac{MU_1}{P_1} = \frac{MU_1}{P_1} \quad \frac{MU_2}{P_2} = ... = \frac{MUn}{Pn}$$

where *MU* is marginal utility and *P* is price. The subscripts 1, 2...*n* indicate the respective commodities.

Also a producer maximises profit or minimises costs when,

$$\frac{MU_1}{P_1} = \frac{MP_2}{P_2} = ... = \frac{MPn}{Pn}$$

where *MP* is marginal product and *P* is price. Subscripts 1, 2, ...*n* indicate the respective factors of production.

(*iv*) *Linear Programming.* Microeconomics provides the technique of linear programming by which a producer takes a number of important decisions. He can know which factor is available in abundance and whose supply is scarce in quantity. This knowledge helps a farmer or an entrepreneur to mix the factors of production in an optimum manner and can increase his income. Linear programming also investigates the best possible production process among the alternative production processes to attain maximum income.

Hence, we can say that microeconomics provides such important tools which are helpful in determining the optimum mix of commodities and optimum distribution of income among the factors of production. Therefore, microeconomics is an important branch of economic analysis.

Limitations of Microeconomics

As we have seen that microeconomics is very useful in economic analysis, yet it has its own limitations. The important limitations are the following:

(*i*) It does not throw light on the collective activity of the national economy. Today the policies which affect the entire economy such as tax-policy and expenditure policy of the government, monetary policy, fiscal policy, etc. are assumed to be of greater importance. These policies do not come within the purview of microeconomics, but are studied under macroeconomics.

(*ii*) Microeconomics assumes other things remaining the same and has based its results on the assumption of full employment in the society. These assumptions do not hold in real life. Lord Keynes criticised this assumption and stated that "To assume full employment is to assume our difficulties away." It is why the reliability of microeconomic results becomes doubtful.

In spite of these two limitations, microeconomics possesses its own importance. It is widely used in the problems of macroeconomic analysis.

3. Macroeconomics

Meaning of Macroeconomics

According to Boulding, "Macroeconomics deals not with individual quantities, as such, but with aggregates of these quantities; not with individual incomes, but with national income; not with individual prices, but with price level; not with individual outputs, but with national output."

He further states that "Macroeconomics is that part of the subject which deals with the great aggregates and averages of the system rather than a particular item in it, and attempts to define these aggregates in a useful manner and to examine their relationship."

According to Prof. Ackley, "Macroeconomics also uses aggregates smaller than for the whole economy, but only in a context which makes them sub-divisions of an economywide total. Macroeconomics also uses aggregates, but not in a context which relates them to an economywide total."

From the above definitions, it is evident that macroeconomics concerns itself with those aggregates which relate to the whole economy. Macroeconomics also discusses the sub-aggregates of the large aggregates relating to the whole economy, but these sub-aggregates, unlike the aggregates of microeconomics which examine aggregates relating to a particular product, a particular industry or a particular market, cut across various products and industry.

Types of Macroeconomics

Macroeconomics has been divided into following three types:

(*i*) *Simple macrostatics.* It studies relationships between macroeconomic variables in a stationary situation. It is concerned with equilibrium points and not the process through which it is attained. Hence, macrostatics deals with the final equilibrium of the economy at a particular point of time. For example, the position of final equilibrium can be shown by the following Keynesian equation:

$$Y = C + I$$

where Y = Total Income, C = Total Consumption, I = Total Investment

The above equation explains the relationship between three macroeconomic variables Y, C and I. The equality between Y and $C + I$ indicates the equilibrium position. It does not involve the study of time analysis. The above macrostatic model can also be shown diagrammatically. In Fig. 4.4, a 45° line indicates that at all points on this line the equality between Y and $C + I$ exists. The consumption schedule is shown by C and the combined consumption and investment schedule is shown by $C + I$. The equilibrium point will be attained at E where the equilibrium national income is OY. This equilibrium position E will be studied under macroeconomics.

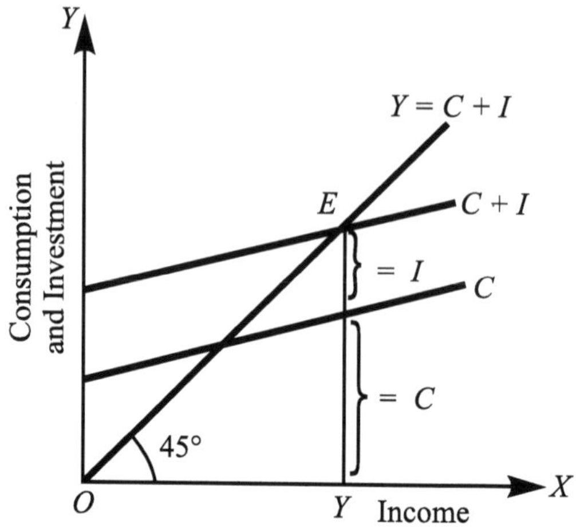

Fig. 4.4

(*ii*) *Comparative macrostatics.* It involves a comparative study of different macrostatic equilibrium positions which are attained by the economy. But it does not study the process of adjustment by which the economy shifts from one equilibrium position to another equilibrium position.

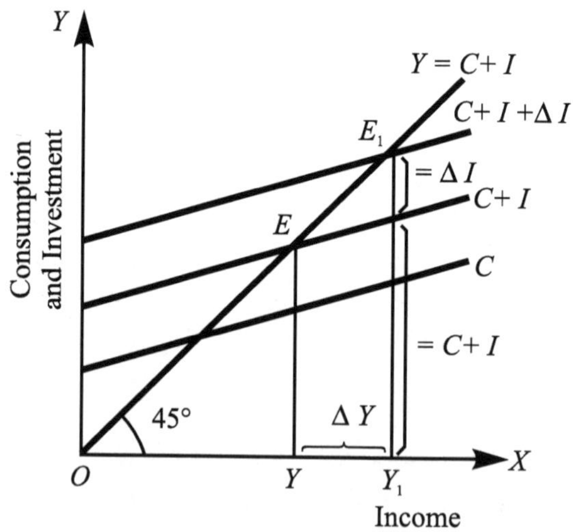

Fig. 4.5

For example, if there is an increase in investment (Δ*I*), then the initial level of income (*OY*) will be disturbed. In Fig. 4.5, the equilibrium is attained at point E_1, where the new level of equilibrium income is OY_1. Comparative macrostatics studies these two equilibrium positions *E* and E_1. and does not talk about the process through which the equilibrium takes place. It states that when aggregate investment increases by ΔI, the aggregate increase in income will be ΔY.

(*iii*) *Macrodynamics.* This concept has recently been developed by some eminent economists like D.H. Robertson, J.R. Hicks, M. Kalecki, J. Timbergen, R.F. Harrod, E.D.Domar and P.A. Samuelson. It studies the process through which a new equilibrium is established after a change in independent macroeconomic variables. According to Prof. Kurihara, "Macroeconomics enables to separate the process of trial and error into a series of continuously changing reactions and indicates the cause and effect. It analyses the discrete or continuous changes of aggregates, the sequence of cause and effect events arising from some initial change and the time paths (roots) of macroeconomic variables."[2] In other words, it studies fluctuations of income at various points of time, and, therefore, involves period analysis.

For example, initially the economy is in equilibrium at point *E* in Fig. 4.6. At point *E* the equilibrium income is *OY*. Now there is an increase in investment (ΔI) which leads to an increase in the aggregate expenditure. The community's expenditure increases the level of aggregate income in the next period to a level of OY_1. At this increased new level of income people will spend more on consumption goods (*C*) and therefore the next period's total expenditure ($C + I$) increases to Y_1C. Further, this increase in expenditure raises the level of aggregate income and consequently the consumption expenditure. This process continues until the final (long-run) equilibrium point *E*′ is attained where the new level of equilibrium national income is *OY*′. Hence, the entire process is studied under the macrodynamics.

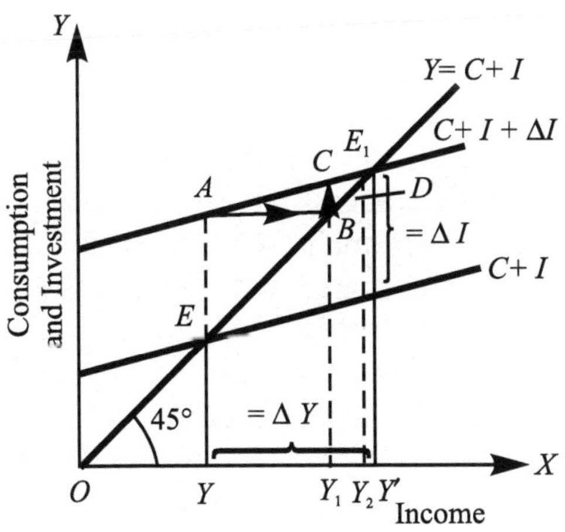

Fig. 4.6

2. Kenneth K. Kurihara, *Introduction to Keynesian Dynamics.*

Uses of Macroeconomics

The old economists emphasised particularly the problems of microeconomics. They were not interested in the concepts of total national income, total national employment and total investment. But, during the last 40-45 years macroeconomics has gained much popularity. The 1930s worldwide depression compelled the world economists to think over the macroeconomic policies. Since the publication of Keynes' famous book, *General Theory of Employment, Interest and Money* in 1936, macroeconomics has been growing fast. In this context, the following points are important:

(*i*) *Determination of Economic Policies of the Government.* The study of macroeconomics becomes indispensable for formulation and successful execution of economic policies of the government. The main objective of the government is to attain maximum social benefit. It is not concerned with the benefit of an individual, but it is concerned with the collective benefits (welfare) of the individuals. Therefore, it is concerned with the regulation of aggregates of the economic system, the general price-level, the general level of production, consumption and investment, the general volume of trade, etc. This means that accurate and reliable data of the aggregative variables are the first prerequisite for the formulation of sound public policies. For example, in a country like India population is rapidly increasing and, therefore, necessary macro decisions must be taken for creating the situation of more employment in the economy. Further, a lack of effective demand creates unemployment in more developed countries. For this, necessary monetary and fiscal policies are adopted.

In this way, macroeconomics contributes a lot in the determination of government economic policies which affect the level of national income, price and employment. Future targets of saving and investment may also be determined with the help of macro quantities.

(*ii*) *Economic Planning.* The developed and developing countries of the world are making use of economic planning for their economic development. Economic planning is concerned with aggregative variables and therefore, it comes under macroeconomic analysis. The rates of saving and investment are determined and efforts are made to increase them. The annual rate of economic growth is also determined and efforts are made to achieve it. In this way, a number of aggregative variables are used in economic planning.

(*iii*) *Development of Microeconomic Theories.* The study of macroeconomics is useful even for the purpose of building and developing microeconomic theories. The determination of wage in an industry will be influenced by the general wage rate of the economy. Similarly, the price of a commodity will also be influenced by the prevailing general price level in the economy. In the situations of inflation, generally the prices will increase, while in the years of depression the prices will go down. Thus, no microeconomic law can be formulated without a pre-study of macroeconomics.

(*iv*) *International Comparisons.* Macroeconomics provides necessary information for international comparisons. For example, a comparative study of average national income, consumption and saving between different countries requires macroeconomic information.

(*v*) *The Necessity of Separate Knowledge of the Aggregates.* The aggregates are not merely sums of individual units. They possess their own peculiarities. According to Prof. Boulding,[3] it is not possible to discover the behaviour pattern of the aggregates simply by generalising from the behaviour of the individual units. As he points out that the forest is an aggregation of trees, but it does not possess the characteristics and behaviour-patterns of individual trees. The forest has its own characteristic and behaviour pattern which is to be distinguished. As we know that an individual tree grows and decays, while a forest goes on for ever with exactly the same internal composition in regard to the behaviour of the trees that constitute it. The reason is very clear: as individual trees grow, mature and decay, new trees spring up to take their places and the forest goes on for ever.

Similarly, an economy is not merely a sum of independent economic units. As old industries are destroyed and new industries are created, the economy moves on for ever. Thus, the knowledge of total economy possesses its own importance.

Macroeconomic reasoning can take account of many relationships which are not applicable to individual parts. For example, for any individual or group of individuals, income and expenditure on currently produced output obviously can and usually will be different magnitudes; but for a whole society, income and expenditure (properly defined) can always be shown to be equal. Any individual can save without investing or invest without having previously saved, but carefully defined saving and investment must be identical for the whole economy. One country's imports may well exceed its exports, but for all countries combined, total imports and exports must obviously be equal. Similarly, one firm (or industry) can increase its output and employment by binding workers away from other firms; when there is full employment, industry as a whole cannot increase total labour input so as output (because full employment exists). Hence the study of macroeconomics is useful in both theory and practice.

Limitations of Macroeconomics

In spite of the growing popularity macroeconomics is not free from its limitations. The important limitations are as follows:

(*i*) It is a complicated task to find out total national income by the help of the estimates of prices of different goods and services. Wholesale price index numbers are made to find out general price level. These index numbers involve the problems of weighing, averaging and a number of other difficulties.

3. Boulding, K.E., *A Reconstruction of Economics,* p. 173

(*ii*) The aggregates which are homogeneous in nature can lead to accurate results. But sometimes we may have to take into our account aggregates which are non-homogeneous in character. Results based on these heterogeneous aggregates are not accurate and we should always avoid such problems.

(*iii*) Due to imperfect knowledge of statistical techniques, some persons may predict the aggregates in a false way. For example, the agricultural prices decrease by 50 per cent while industrial prices increase by 50 per cent, the general price level remains the same, because the two types of price changes neutralise each other. In such a situation one may advise the government to make no change in its policy, because general price level remains the same. But actually the government needs to implement a policy which helps the farmers who get a loss due to fall in their product prices. Thus, sometimes the aggregate results may be misleading. It requires special ability to predict the results in such a situation.

(*iv*) An aggregate change may not influence all the sectors of the economy in the same manner. For instance, a general rise in prices does not mean that the prices of all the commodities have increased and have increased in the same proportion. It is quite possible that the prices of a few commodities may rather decrease. Further, due to this aggregate change, some sectors may be affected more adversely than others. On the other hand, some individuals may be benefited more than the others.

4. Interdependence of Micro- and Macroeconomics

Microeconomics deals with the division of total output among industries, products, and firms and the allocation of resources among competing uses, *i.e.* it deals with the behaviour of individual units. On the other hand, macroeconomics deals with economic affairs in "the large", *i.e.* with the aggregates of individual decision-making units. Therefore, the two branches seem to be independent of each other. As we know that the size of an individual unit is assumed to be so small that it has no bearing on the aggregate demand, supply or prices. Similarly, an increase in macroeconomic units, such as, the GNP of a country or the level of employment will make no effect on an individual unit.

In spite of these differences, the two branches are not assumed to be mutually exclusive. Actually, the line between microeconomic and macroeconomic theory cannot be precisely drawn. A truly "general" theory of the economy would clearly embrace both; it would explain individual behaviour, individual outputs, incomes, and prices; and the sums or averages of the individual results would constitute the aggregates with which macroeconomics is concerned. Such a general theory exists, but its very generality leaves it with little substantive content. Rather, to reach meaningful results, we find that we must approach macroeconomic problems with macroeconomic variables and microeconomic problems with microeconomic variables. Prof. Samuelson has rightly expressed this relationship in the following words: "There is really no opposition between micro and macroeconomics. Both are absolutely vital. And you are only half educated if you understand the one while being ignorant of the other."

Exercises

1. Distinguish between microeconomics and macroeconomics. Explain the uses and limitations of macroeconomic analysis.
2. Explain and distinguish between macro and microeconomic analysis. Can we use both these methods of economic analysis together?
3. Distinguish between microeconomics and macroeconomics. "To have proper appreciation of the working of economic forces it will be necessary to supplement the study of one by the study of the other." Do you agree with this statement?
4. What is the difference between static, comparative static and dynamic microeconomic analysis? Discuss their principal characteristics and the areas of their use.
5. Define macroeconomics. What are the various types of macroeconomics? Discuss their usefulness in economic analysis.

Multiple Choice Questions

6. (*i*) Microeconomic theory studies how a free enterprise economy determines
   (*a*) the price of goods (*b*) the price of services
   (*c*) the price of economic resource (*d*) all of the above [*Ans.* (*d*)]

   (*ii*) Microeconomics deals primarily with
   (*a*) comparative statics, partial equilibrium and positive economic
   (*b*) comparative statics, general equilibrium and positive economics
   (*c*) comparative dynamics and normative economics
   (*d*) all of the above [*Ans.* (*a*)]

   (*iii*) Macroeconomics is the study of
   (*a*) individual economic units (*b*) economy as a whole
   (*c*) price theory (*d*) all of the above [*Ans.* (*b*)]

   (*iv*) Microeconomics is primarily concerned with comparative statics rather than dynamics.
   (*a*) True (*b*) False
   (*c*) Uncertain [*Ans.* (*a*)]

   (*v*) Who was the first economist to have coined the terms microeconomics and macroeconomics?
   (*a*) J.M. Keyncs (*b*) Ragner Nuruse
   (*c*) Ragner Frisch (*d*) M. Dobb [*Ans.* (*c*)]

   (*vi*) State which of the following refers to the macroeconomic approach from a national angle?
   (*a*) Per capita income of the country
   (*b*) Capital-output ratio in steel industry
   (*c*) Unemployment among the educated people
   (*d*) Inflation in the economy [*Ans.* (*b*)]

   (*vii*) Microeconomics uses
   (*a*) Slicing Method (*b*) Lumping Method
   (*c*) Monetary Analysis (*d*) Income Analysis [*Ans.* (*a*)]

Chapter 5

Economic Statics and Economic Dynamics

1. Introduction

The distinction between statics and dynamics is of vital importance for the proper understanding of modern economic theory. These words are also used in physical sciences, but in economics the meaning of the two terms is different from the meaning given to them in physical sciences. According to the dictionary meaning the word 'static' means 'causing to rest or stand' and the word 'dynamic' means 'causing to move'. These dictionary meanings clearly indicate the basic distinction between the two terms. The analysis of both these types is designed for different purposes. According to Stonier and Hague, "Static analysis mainly discusses the question of how, for example, an equilibrium price is arrived at in a market where the demand and supply curves are known and remain unchanged. Static analysis, therefore, shows us how consumers, firms, industries and whole economies can remain in stable, or static equilibrium at certain levels of prices, output, income and employment."[1] On the other hand, economic dynamics refers to a state where the rates of output, income and employment are changing. Most economists do not agree about what actual economic statics and dynamics mean. Yet, many of them have explained the distinctive features of the two methods.

It was first Auguste Comte (1798-1857), a French sociologist who introduced the two concepts of Statics and Dynamics in the domain of social science. But these two terms were first employed in economics by John Stuart Mill who was influenced by Comte. Today, these terms have been developed and popularised by modern economists.

The most important thesis on economic statics and dynamics has been developed by J.R. Hicks. According to him, "We call economic statics those

1. Stonier and Hague, *A Textbook of Economic Theory,* 1964, p, 499.

parts of economic theory where we do not trouble about dating: economic dynamics are those parts where every quantity must be dated. For example, in economic statics we think of an entrepreneur employing such quantities of factors and producing by their aid such quantities of products but we do not ask when the factors are employed and when the products come to be ready. In economic dynamics, we do ask such questions; and we pay special attention to the way changes in these dates affect the relations between factors and prices."[2] Thus, economic dynamics are those parts of economic theory where the question of dates comes in and is not only important but also inevitable. Statics studies stationary situations in which there are no changes and, therefore, they do not require any comparison with past or future.

In a stationary state, the factor analysis of the present may be employed to predict the future. In the views of Prof. Hicks, it is only a change in the system which causes the analysis to be dynamic. He states that changes will cause things to be different at different dates and, therefore, they make the analysis dynamic.

Many economists have criticised Hicks' definition. They expressed the view that the dynamic theory of Hicks includes many problems where methods of static analysis are called for. Prof. Hicks has not appreciated that dynamics is not something which should be applied to have a comparative study of the two phenomena. Such a study could be called comparative statics. Hicks only emphasises that dynamic economics or economic dynamics includes an element of change which is, according to subsequent economists, not valid.

Harrod, in this context, states, "Hicks appears to be analysing the effects of once-over change in fundamental conditions. There is no recognition that a different technique may be required for analysing the effects of continuing changes." Harrod thus wants to base the definition of dynamic economics on continuing changes as against those which take place once for all. Harrod further states, "One change over is the same thing as a once-over change in taste." In a dynamic system, the determinant will not be the existence of a certain expectation or once-over change in that expectation. This may itself be determined by a rate of change in some other fundamental condition. The effects of a once-over change in expectation are likely to continue to be handled by the method of economic statics.[3]

According to Ragnar Frisch the most important basis of dynamics is the analysis of the *process of change and not the non-stationarity* of the system analysed. He argues, "By static analysis is meant a method of dealing with economic phenomena that tries to establish relations between the elements of

2. J.R. Hicks, *Value and Capital,* p. 115.
3. Harrod, R.F., *Towards a Dynamic Economics,* 1949.

the economic system, prices and quantities of commodities all of which have the same point of time." "Dynamic economic analysis is one in which we consider the magnitudes of certain variables on different points of time and introduce certain equations which embrace at the same time several of those magnitudes at different instants."[4] Thus, dynamic study analyses the influences of relative factors in relation to a change in some particular economic variable.

Further, William Baumol, an American economist, believes that economic dynamics is prediction, *i.e.* it enables us to answer many questions about the present and the future on the basis of the historical facts of the past. Baumol also believes that the purpose of economic dynamics is not only forecasting market trends, but also relating these trends to different events, past and present. As he puts it, "Economic dynamics is a study of economic phenomena in relation to preceding and succeeding events."

The main difference between the definitions of William Baumol and Ragnar Frisch lies in the fact that while Prof. Baumol believes that the basis of economic dynamics is the predictability, Prof. Frisch considers it to be the analysis of a process. There are a number of other economists who define economic dynamics as the study of the processes through which the final position of equilibrium is reached via a series of adjustments over time. Prof. Hicks and Prof. Harrod, on their part, confine themselves to the definition of the contents of economic dynamics. According to Prof. Hicks, the concept of economic dynamics is economic statics involving time, and not dynamic as such.

2. Economic Statics

In economic statics, we study the laws of equilibrium. Here we assume certain factors to be constant and then study their results. Prof. Marshall observed, "The forces to be dealt with are, however, so numerous that it is best to take a few at a time and to work out a number of partial solutions as auxiliaries to our main study. Thus, we begin by isolating the primary relations of supply, demand and price in regard to a particular commodity. We reduce to inaction all other forces by the phrase, *other things being equal.* We do not suppose that they are inert, but for the time being, we ignore their activity. This scientific device is a great deal older than science; it is the method by which consciously or unconsciously sensible men deal from time immemorial with every difficult problem of ordinary life. In the second stage, more forces are released from the hypothetical slumber than had been imposed on them. Gradually, the area

4. R. Frisch, "Propagation Problems and Impulse Problems in Dynamic Economics," *Economic Essays* in *Honour of Gustav Cassel.*
5. Alfred Marshall, *op. cit.,* Preface, pp. 14-15.

of dynamical problem becomes larger; the area covered by provisional statical assumptions becomes smaller."[5]

The basic idea in economic statics is clearly a notion of equilibrium and hence of forces in equilibrium. As compared with mechanics, the notion of forces is much more or less troublesome in economics. However, a majority of economists use the terms like equilibrium and tendency in the sense of statical modes and mathematical limits. While in a physical set-up of mechanical equilibrium, the forces unavoidably act through things having mass weights or springs and hence act upon these mass as well as upon each other. If friction (disagreement) could be eliminated from such a system, it would never actually come from any other position to a stationary equilibrium and would perpetually oscillate or move around the same circuit which could be represented by an equation. It is rather crude in economics to attribute any continuing divergence of conditions from those of theoretical equilibrium to a friction as sometimes economists do, since the theory of a frictionless system calls not for equilibrium but for perpetual oscillation. It seems that the analogy in the minds of economists for discussing the tendency toward equilibrium is that of movement against a viscious friction, with inertia absent or negligible.

The method of economic statics is generally associated with the concept of a stationary state which is only a methodological fiction (or imaginary method); more specifically, a simplifying device or a tool of analysis. As Prof. Walter Eucken puts it, "The static state has never been realised historically. Large changes in data have been constantly occurring, occasionally only small changes but never no changes at all."[6] In the basic economic law of uniform prices in a market, the assumption of perfect competition is common. Only the time dimension seems to carry over directly and be available for use in the field of economics. We cannot reduce the economic process of quantitative terms unless we can give workable meaning to space and to mass. We constantly speak of frictions in economic changes and even of degrees of position or identity, yet, it is not always possible to use the notion (idea) of social forces and processes in a definite sense which might be represented by perfect coordinates. It may be added that the problems in economic statics are those problems connected with equilibrium conditions which do not involve any variations in the time element. An equilibrium for a specified model is characterised by a lack of tendency to change. For this reason the analysis of equilibrium is known as statics.

As already stated, statics analysis discusses the question of how, for example, an equilibrium price is arrived at in a market where demand and supply functions are known and remain unchanged. In economic statics the

6. Walter Eucken, *The Foundation of Economics,* 1950, p. 204.

equilibrium value of a dependent variable will remain unchanged so long as the independent variable remains constant. For this reason, such a static model involves no dating of economic variables. The theory of product pricing is a good example of economic statics. Here we presume that the price of the commodity will be determined by the forces of supply and demand existing at a particular time. Let us assume the following:

$$Dt = \alpha - \beta Pt \text{ (Demand Function)} \quad ...(1)$$

$$St = a + bPt \text{ (Supply Function)} \quad ...(2)$$

where Dt = quantity demanded,

St = quantity supplied,

Pt = price of the commodity,

β = slope of demand function,

b = slope of supply function

a and α are constants and t is time period.

In equilibrium,

$$Dt = St$$

or $$\alpha - \beta\, Pt = a + b\, Pt$$

or $$bPt + \beta Pt = \alpha - a \quad ...(3)$$

or $$Pt(b + \beta) = \alpha - a$$

$$Pt = \frac{\alpha - a}{b + \beta} \quad ...(4)$$

which is the equilibrium price.

Similarly, if saving and investment functions are known, we may find the equilibrium national income where savings are equal to investment. The equilibrium level of income will remain unchanged, so long as the saving and investment functions remain unchanged.

Scope of Static Economics

The classical economists in the past have made an extensive use of the methods of economic statics. Today, the various assumptions associated with the static analysis have narrowed down the scope of static economics in the study of real world problems. The important assumptions of economic statics are perfect knowledge, absence of uncertainty, given consumer tastes, given population, perfect fact or mobility, etc. Some of these assumptions are quite unrealistic and for this reason the static analysis is rendered incapable of any application in the real world. But in spite of this fact, Prof. Harrod remarks, "I am sure that statics will remain an important part of the whole." The method of economic statics is the only device to make the treatment of complex problems easier and clearer.

Even today economic statics covers the following problems of the economic statics:

(*i*) The problem of free trade will be studied under the method of economic statics.

(*ii*) Monopoly price-determination may also be regarded as the part of economic statics; because it is based on the assumption that the behaviour pattern of the buyers and sellers remains the same with the passage of time. Here, it is the marginal cost and not the average cost of production which governs price of the product.

(*iii*) Since the law of diminishing marginal utility assumes no time interval in the consumption of a commodity, it comes within the purview of economic statics.

(*iv*) The economic behaviour of a man or the law of equi-marginal utility is also studied under static economics, because it is based on a timeless consideration.

(*v*) The comparative costs theory of international trade is studied under economic statics so far as it assumes perfect mobility between factors of production within the country and absence of change, etc.

(*vi*) The marginal analysis comes under economic statics.

(*vii*) Economic statics can study those problems arising out of the once-over changes. When the once-over changes take place in any of the assumptions of economic statics, the relevant static equations may define the position of the new static equilibrium.

Under relatively more stable conditions, that is, conditions undergoing slower processes of change, the static analysis serves as theoretical analysis as a framework or setting of given conditions with reference to shorter period adjustments. These short-run adjustments have the character of tending to establish equilibrium with reference to their respective given conditions at any given time. According to Prof. Hicks, economic statics includes the theories of traditional economics which are studied without reference to time element. According to Prof. Tinbergen, static economics can be used to study the long-run tendencies of certain cases, i.e. the determination of the final results.

Advantages of Economic Statics

The main advantages of economic statics are given below:

(*i*) We can understand the working of the complex economic system with the help of this method.

(*ii*) We can understand the nature of the functioning of the economic system only when we study economic statics, i.e. the position of static equilibrium.

(*iii*) The study of dynamic economics requires a pre-study of static economics. In order to understand the various implications of dynamic analysis, we must know the contents of economic statics, as the study of the laws of rest is necessary to understand the laws of motion.

(*iv*) Economic statics is a simple method because it assumes several things remaining the same while studying an economic law.

Limitations of Economic Statics

The limitations of this method are mostly based upon its unrealistic assumptions.

The main weaknesses of this device are given below:

(*i*) Static analysis is largely unrealistic and unsuitable for many purposes. The problems which involve dating are not studied by this method.

(*ii*) It assumes no change in both the dependent variable and the independent variable under consideration and, therefore, ignores a comparative study of the economic phenomena.

(*iii*) If we make a change in any of the variables (independent variables), it affects our final conclusions.

(*iv*) In the real world where rapid changes take place, the economic statics cannot provide accurate results. Its results are misleading.

3. Comparative Statics

In a static analysis, we are concerned with the stationary state or the non-evolutionary process. In other words, in a static economic model, the values of both the dependent variables as well as the independent variables are assumed to be constant and they explain the economic phenomena at a given point of time. More specifically, the process of the adjustment of such variables towards equilibrium does not cause any shift in any of the independent variables, and consequently the equilibrium position remains unchanged. But in a comparative static analysis, there may be a change in the independent variable, and here, we analyse its impact on the dependent variable. In other words, a shift will take place due to a change in independent variable and it will lead to a new equilibrium position. A method which compares these two equilibrium positions is referred to as the method of comparative statics.

It must be borne in mind that comparative statics oblivates the path which has been followed while moving from one static equilibrium to another. In this method, we, however, study the evolutionary process in a series of equilibria, and often compare the new position of equilibrium to the old one. In the words of Prof. Lipsey, "Comparative statics involves a comparison of the new equilibrium position (E_1) with the original equilibrium position (E)....We wish to form an hypothesis about the effect of some change in data for example, the introduction of a tax or a change in the conditions of demand. We start from a position of equilibrium and then introduce the change to be studied. The new equilibrium position is determined and it is compared with the original one. The differences in the two positions of equilibrium must be due to changes in the data that were introduced. This analysis, which is based on a comparison of two positions of equilibrium, is called comparative static equilibrium analysis."[7]

Therefore, the method of comparative statics deals only with the final equilibrium positions. Suppose, in our previous static model of demand and supply, the demand function (1) shifts upward due to an increase in the value of α caused by a change in some independent variable, say, income and with the values of α, b and β remaining unchanged in equation (4), price will increase. In other words, in period $(t+1)$, due to an increase (upward shift) in the demand function, the price level $(Pt + 1)$ will be higher than Pt. Mathematically,

$$Pt = \frac{\alpha - a}{b + \beta} \qquad \ldots(5)$$

also

$$P_{t+1} = \frac{\alpha^1 - a}{b + \beta} \qquad \ldots(6)$$

If

$$\alpha^1 > \alpha \qquad \ldots(7)$$

then

$$P_{t+1} < Pt \qquad \ldots(8)$$

Comparative statics, therefore, compares the two equilibrium prices. Comparative statics also occupies an important place in economic analysis, particularly in the theories of monopolies and competition. But it is unable to study the path which the market follows when it shifts from one position of equilibrium to another. This would call for economic dynamics which explains how one situation emerges out of the preceding situation.

4. Economic Dynamics

Various economists have defined economic dynamics in different ways. According to Prof. J.R. Hicks, dynamic economics includes only those parts of economic theory where every quantity must be dated.[8] According to Prof. R.F. Harrod, economic dynamics is the study of an economy in which the rates of output are changing.[9] Harrod has observed, "Dynamics will specially be concerned with the effects of continuing changes and with the rates of change in the values that have to be determined." In the words of Prof. William J. Baumol, "Economic dynamics is the study of economic phenomena

7. Richard G. Lipsey, *An Introduction to Positive Economics* (1964), p. 118.
8. J.R. Hicks, *op. cit.*, p. 115.
9. R.F. Harrod, *op. cit.*, p. 5.

in relation to preceding and succeeding events." According to Prof. Lipsey, "Dynamic analysis may be defined as the study of the behaviour of systems, single markets or whole economics, in disequilibrium conditions." According to Hicks, "Economic dynamics refers to those parts of economic theory where the problem of dating is conspicuously important." Similarly, Prof. Ragnar Frisch has defined dynamic economics as "one whose behaviour over a time is determined by functional equations at which variables at different points of time are involved in an essential way." Thus, the main concern of all these definitions of economic dynamics is with the dates. This implies that unlike the static analysis economic dynamics explains lagged relationship between the dependent and the independent variables.

There are economists who define dynamic economics in relation to equilibrium. According to these economists dynamic economics studies the process through which the final position of equilibrium is reached through a series of adjustments over a series of time. Baumol states that dynamic economics has the power of forecasting future.

Economic growth and fluctuations are studied with the help of dynamic analysis. During 1930s and 1940s many theories regarding dynamic analysis have been developed. Frisch, Kelecki and Samuelson developed mathematical analysis in relation to economic fluctuations. They are helpful to understand the causes of economic fluctuations. On the other hand, Harrod in England and Domar in America developed the theories of economic growth. In the field of national income analysis, economists like Robertson, Haberler, Hansen, Machlup and others have emphasised the use of dynamic processes. The Swedish economists (notably, Gunnar Myrdal, Bertil Ohlin, Lindall and Lundberg) have made use of dynamic models to discuss national income analysis. Today, the theories of interest and profit are also studied under dynamic analysis.

In simple words, complex problems in economics, especially when they involve movements towards a constantly changing equilibrium, may be analysed by economic dynamics. Several examples of this type from both microeconomics and macroeconomics can be given. If we assume that consumption expenditure (C) in period t is determined by the income (Y) received in the preceding time period, i.e. $t - 1$, then such type of relationship will be studied under economic dynamics. Mathematically,

$$Ct = f(Y_{t-1})$$

or

$$Ct = f(Yt)...$$

Similarly, we may also define such a relationship from microeconomics. Here it may be assumed that the supply of a commodity in period t may be a function of its price prevailing in previous period, i.e. $t - 1$. Mathematically,

$$St = f(P_{t-1})$$

or $$S_{t+1} = f(Pt)$$

or $$S_{t+2} = f(P_{t+1})$$

or $$S_{t-1} = f(P_{t-2})$$

or $$S_{t-2} = f(P_{t-3})$$

Thus, economic dynamics defines lagged relationships between the dependent and the independent variables. *Cobwebs theorem* is the simplest model of these dynamics of demand, supply and price. The essential features of the model are:

$$Dt = f(Pt) \qquad ...(9)$$

and $$St = f(P_{t-1}) \qquad ...(10)$$

Hence, supply of lagged one period behind price. Agricultural commodities provide good examples of lagged supply functions. Suppose, this year's price of wheat (Pt) is high. Now farmers make their plans for next year (t+1); each of them assuming that next year's price will be high too. But in the following year the price actually falls because in the time period, t+1, the supply of wheat is greater than the demand. Here, the main assumption of the theorem is that nothing is stored and entire production is in the market. It clears that quantity demanded in any period depends upon the price in that period, but quantity supplied depends upon the price in the previous year. In other words, equations (8) and (9) hold in the real world. Taking the linear versions of unlagged demand and lagged supply functions as

$$Dt = \alpha - \beta\, Pt$$

where $$\alpha > 0, \beta > 0 \qquad ...(11)$$

and $$St = a + b\, P_{t-1}$$

where $$\alpha > 0, b > 0 \qquad ...(12)$$

In equilibrium

$$Dt = St$$

or $$\alpha - \beta Pt = a + b\, P_{t-1}$$

or $$\beta Pt + b\, P_{t-1} = \alpha - a$$

For simplicity we shift the subscripts of time period ahead by one period (*i.e.* change $t - 1$ to t and t to $t + 1$), we get

$$\beta Pt + 1 + b\, Pt = \alpha - a$$

or $$P_{t+1} = \frac{\alpha - a}{\beta} - \frac{b}{\beta} Pt \qquad ...(13)$$

Now we get the time path for price and quantity variations we put

10. If required please see the detail in Alpha C. Chiang, *Fundamental Methods of Mathematical Economics,* 1967, Chapter 16.

$t = 0, 1, 2, \ldots$ in equation (13) and finally get the resulting equation of time path[10] as

$$Pt = \left(P_0 - \frac{\alpha - a}{\beta + b}\right)\left(-\frac{b}{\beta}\right)t + \frac{\alpha - a}{\beta - b} \qquad \ldots(14)$$

On the basis of above formula, Prof. Chiang presents three basic points:

(*i*) The amount $\frac{\alpha - a}{\beta - b}$ of the equation (14) can be taken as the equilibrium price of the model, i.e.

$$\overline{P} = \frac{\alpha - a}{\beta - b}$$

Substituting it in (14), the equation can be rewritten as,

$$Pt = (P_0 - \overline{P})\left(-\frac{b}{\beta}\right)t + \overline{P} \qquad \ldots(15)$$

(*ii*) In equation (15), $(P_0 - \overline{P})$ shows the difference between the initial price and equilibrium price and its sign will determine whether the time path will commence above or below the equilibrium.

(*iii*) The difference between β and b will determine the Cobweb phenomenon (or disequilibrium phenomenon). Here, β represents the slope of the supply function.

Hence, the analysis of the path travelled between the new and the initial equilibrium position is economic dynamics. Hicks also agrees that the presence of expectations is sufficient to characterise an economy as dynamic. He says, "Once the missing element of the anticipations is added, equilibrium analysis can be used, not only in the remote stationary conditions to which many economists have found themselves driven back, but even in the real world in disequilibrium."[11]

Advantages of Economic Dynamics

As we have already discussed, the importance of economic dynamics has always been realised. Even in the development of classical theories, economic dynamics was assumed to be equally important with economic statics. Later on, more emphasis has been given to economic dynamics. The main advantages of economic dynamics are the following:

(*i*) As we know, economic statics can study only the final result of a change from one equilibrium position to another equilibrium position. It cannot

11. J.R. Hicks, *op. cit.*, p. 115.

study the process of the change or the problems of transitional period. For this, economic dynamics is used.

(*ii*) The complex economic phenomena, such as, cyclical fluctuations and secular growth are reasonably studied under dynamic economics.

(*iii*) Moreover, it is used to correct the unrealistic nature of economic statics. As we know, economic statics is based on unrealistic assumptions, such as, perfect knowledge, absence of uncertainty, given consumer tastes, given population, perfect factor mobility, etc. It further assumes a stationary state to exist. All this leads to unrealistic conclusions. Economic dynamics is free from these unrealistic assumptions and, therefore, is much nearer to reality than economic statistics.

(*iv*) This method is highly flexible. It can develop a number of models to explore all the possibilities concerning a particular problem. Most of the modern theories of trade cycles are based on the dynamic models of Ragnar Frisch and Paul A. Samuelson.

Limitations of Economic Dynamics

The method of economic dynamics possesses the following weaknesses:

(*i*) Although economic dynamics is more realistic than economic statics, yet it is essentially very complex and only a highly trained mathematician and economist could make full use of it.

(*ii*) The method of economic dynamics is not yet fully developed and therefore, possesses a limited scope in present-day economic analysis.

From the above, one can conclude that both economic statics and economic dynamics, are complementary to each other. Economic analysis can neither do without dynamics nor can it do without statics. Some of the problems of economic analysis can only be solved by the help of economic dynamics while many others can be better tackled by the simple static economics. A few problems are there which can be solved with the collective application of both the methods. Thus, economic statics and economic dynamics are both needed for the study of economic analysis.

Exercises

1. What are the differences between economic statics and economic dynamics? Discuss their principal characteristics and the areas of their use.
2. "I call economic statics those parts of economic theory where we do not trouble about dating; economic dynamics are those parts where every quantity must be dated" (J.R. Hicks). How far do you agree with the above statement?
3. Distinguish between economic statics and economic dynamics. Explain the importance and shortcomings of statics as a methodological device.
4. Write a lucid note on the concept of economic dynamics.
5. What do you understand by economic dynamics? Discuss in brief the main methods by

which economists have sought to cope with dynamic problems.

6. Describe the Cobweb Model with the help of micro and macro variables.

Multiple Choice Questions

7. (*i*) In micro-static model, supply and demand relationship determines price at a
   (*a*) point of time (*b*) period of time
   (*c*) constant range of time (*d*) none of the above [*Ans.* (*a*)]

   (*ii*) Micro-dyamics analysis is
   (*a*) the demand supply model at a point of time
   (*b*) the cobweb model
   (*c*) the income-consumption model
   (*d*) all of the above [*Ans.* (*b*)]

   (*iii*) Among the following economists, who has not adopted the method of dynamic analysis?
   (*a*) Karbacki (*b*) Tinbergen
   (*c*) Frisch (*d*) J.M. Keynes [*Ans.* (*d*)]

   (*iv*) Which of the following does not relate to dynamic analysis?
   (*a*) $D_t = f(P_{t+1})$ (*b*) $C_t = f(Y_{t-1})$
   (*c*) Principle of Acceleration (*d*) Doctrine of comparative costs [*Ans.* (*d*)]

   (*v*) Which of the following relates to comparative statics ?
   (*a*) The law of diminishing marginal utility
   (*b*) The law of monopoly value
   (*c*) The Quantity Theory of Money
   (*d*) The theory of rent [*Ans.* (*c*)]

   (*vi*) Which of the following statements is correct ?
   (*a*) The static model is much difficult and complex to work out than dynamic method
   (*b*) Dynamic analysis excludes the time element
   (*c*) Static method makes the assumption of cetcris paribus
   (*d*) Dynamic method relates to macroeconomics only [*Ans.* (*c*)]

Chapter 6

The Concept of Economic Equilibrium

1. Introduction

The concept of economic equilibrium forms the core of economic theory. The modern economics is known as equilibrium economics.[1] The term "equilibrium" means a position from which there is no tendency to move. Economists sometimes regard the concept of an unchanging or frictionless world useful, even though it is a pure abstraction. They call it a stationary state or the static state, i.e. a state of balance or a state of rest. This concept helps in theorising about ultimate tendencies of prices, although we must always keep this in mind that any such perfect balance does not exist in the real world. There may be a tendency to it, but it is a tendency very much interfered with by counteracting influences. The disturbing factors are sometimes more obvious than the balancing tendencies.

The economy of a nation is said to be in a state of equilibrium when the effective demand for every commodity and every factor of production is exactly equal to its respective supply. From the point of view of an individual producer, equilibrium position will be attained when he enjoys maximum profit. Similarly, for a consumer equilibrium will be reached at a point when he gets maximum satisfaction from his given income spent on different goods and services. Once, an individual is in equilibrium, he sticks to it because any reallocation of his limited income (resources) will decrease his total utility or satisfaction (profits). Also, an industry will be in equilibrium when there is no tendency for the size of the industry to change, i.e. when no firms want to leave it and no new firms wish to enter into it. If these conditions did not exist, the adjustment would be incomplete and in a competitive system with freedom for price to move, reactions would result tending to correct the situation.

We know that so long as production is not correctly adjusted to demand, price discrepancies arise so as to correct the situation (of disequilibrium).

1. George J. Stigler, *The Theory of Price,* p. 26.

When through-out the economic system production is in perfect equilibrium with the demand, there is no further tendency for prices to change unless some new developments, such as, change in consumers' tastes, or a new invention or different production technique were introduced into the situation.[2] Any change of this type will lead to readjustment in the prevailing price structure until new equilibrium takes place in the economy.

In a dynamic economy, the effects on the distribution of resources are so frequent and disturbing elements are so strong that perfect equilibrium is never attained and the system is always in maladjustment. We face frequent changes in prices in response to the changed situations of demand and supply, but there will always be a tendency which will lead to a more balanced adjustment.

It is, however, possible to find general equilibrium prices and the forces which determine the prices of all goods together by mathematical methods, such as, input-output analysis, linear programming and identification, *etc*. The procedure comprises setting up of a set of simultaneous algebraic equations in which the choices of ultimate consumers, the existing quantities of factor-inputs and the technical requirements of industries for these factor inputs are clearly specified, while the prices of finished products and the factors of production are left unspecified. Econometricians have constructed such equations and demonstrated that an inter-dependent system of prices for all commodities can be determined theoretically by such mathematical methods. These equilibrium prices summarize the important determinants of economic activity.

2. Classification of Equilibrium

Equilibriums can be classified in several important respects. The main kinds of an economic equilibrium are the following:

(*i*) Stable, Unstable and Neutral Equilibrium

According to Prof. A.C. Pigou, "A system is in *stable equilibrium* if, when any small disturbance takes place, forces come into play to re-establish the initial position; it is in *neutral equilibrium* if, when such a disturbance takes place, no re-establishing, but also no further disturbing forces, are evoked, so that the system remains at rest in the position to which it has moved; it is in *unstable equilibrium* if the small disturbances call out further disturbing forces which act in a cumulative manner to drive the system away from its initial position. A ship with a heavy keel is in stable equilibrium; an egg lying on its side in neutral equilibrium; an egg poised on one of its ends in unstable equilibrium."[3]

2. *Ibid.* A stationary economy or a state of equilibrium may be defined as one in which there are no changes in the three fundamental set of data Tastes, Resources and Technology.
3. A.C. Pigou, *Economics of Welfare*, 1932, pp. 794-95.

Similarly, Prof. Scheneider has also explained clearly the distinction between a stable and an unstable economic equilibrium. According to him, "A position of equilibrium corresponding to a given set of data may be said to be stable if a disturbance of the position leads to a revision of economic plans, and therewith to a change in the disposition of the individual economic units which leads the system back again in the course of time to the initial equilibrium position. On the other hand, if the reason of the individual's economic plans, and of the resulting dispositions, does not lead back to the initial equilibrium position, there we may say that the equilibrium is unstable."[4]

Further, in the words of Prof. Schumpeter, "A *stable equilibrium value* is an equilibrium value that, if changed by a small amount, calls into action forces that will tend to reproduce the old value; *a neutral equilibrium value* is an equilibrium value that does not know any such forces; and an *unstable equilibrium value* is an equilibrium value, change in which calls forth forces which tend to move the system farther and farther away from the equilibrium value. The ball that rests at the bottom of a bowl illustrates the first case; a ball that rests on a billiard table, the second case; and a ball that is perched on the top of an inverted bowl, the third case."[5]

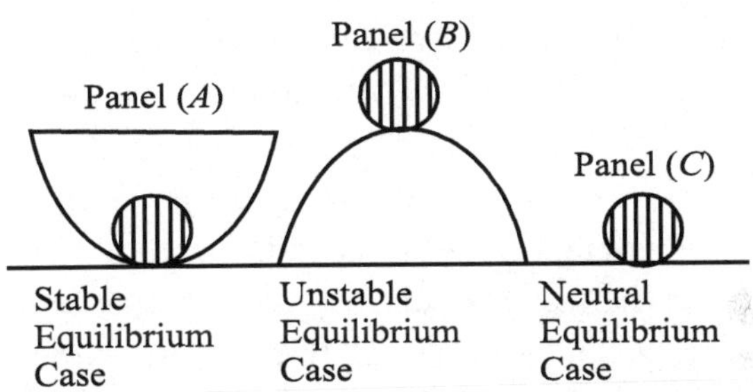

Fig. 6.1

We may now illustrate these three cases with the help of Fig. 6.1. In Fig. 6.1, panel (*A*) shows the case of stable equilibrium where the ball rests at the bottom of the bowl. If its position is disturbed, the ball will again come to its original position. In Fig. 6.1, panel (*B*) shows the case of an unstable equilibrium where the ball is balanced at the top of the invested bowl. If its position is even slightly disturbed, the ball will roll down and will never return to its original position. In Fig. 6.1, panel (*C*) shows the case of neutral equilibrium where the ball rests on a billiard table (or on the flat ground). If its position is disturbed, the ball will move away from its original position and will again rest at some new place. In other words, in the case of neutral equilibrium, if the position is disturbed, it will find a new equilibrium position.

4. Eric Scheneider, *Pricing and Equilibrium,* pp. 234-35.
5. Schumpeter, *History of Economic Analysis,* p. 178.

Similarly, we may also illustrate the three cases of equilibrium with the help of a demand and supply model of economic analysis. Under the conditions of perfect competition, the equilibrium price has a tendency to maintain itself so long as the underlying demand and supply conditions remain unaltered.

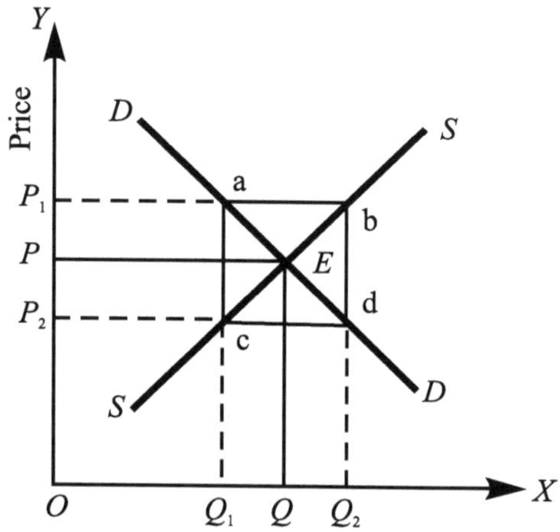

Fig. 6.2

In Fig. 6.2, market demand curve *DD* is negatively sloped while market supply curve *SS* is positively sloped. At *p* point *E,* the demand is equal to the supply and therefore, *OP* is the stable equilibrium price. Any other price will be unstable; because if the equilibrium price *OP* is disturbed, then the forces of demand and supply will again lead price to its original position. For instance, if price rises to OP_1' then at this price, quantity demanded is OQ_1, while quantity supplied is OQ_2. In other words, the quantity supplied (OQ_2) is more than the quantity demanded (OQ_1). This will lead to a reduction in price to the level of *OP* where the quantity demanded is equal to the quantity supplied. In the same way, if price falls to OP_2, then the quantity demanded is OQ_2 while the quantity supplied is OQ_1. In this situation quantity demanded is more than quantity supplied. Therefore, it will lead to an increase in the price to the level of *OP,* where again the quantity demanded is equal to the quantity supplied. It illustrates the case of a stable equilibrium.

Now, we explain *unstable economic equilibrium.* Here also we take the case of demand and supply model. But in this case, we assume that the demand curve is positively sloped while the supply curve is negatively sloped. This will happen only in the case of a 'Giffen good' where the negative income effect is so strong that it swamps the positive sub-stitution effect of a price change. In normal situations, we do not find such cases. In Fig. 6.3, an increase in price from *OP* to OP_1 leads to excess demand *(AB),* because demand increases from *OQ* to OQ_1 while supply decreases from *OQ* to OQ_2. As a result of this, the price again increases. Similarly, a decrease in price from *OP to* OP_2 will lead to excess supply, because demand decreases from OQ to OQ_3 while supply increases from OQ to OQ_4. As a result of this, price again falls. In both the situations, price never returns to its original position but moves away and away from the original position. This is the case of an unstable equilibrium.

Now we shall discuss the neutral economic equilibrium. As we know, under this equilibrium, if the initial equilibrium position is disturbed,

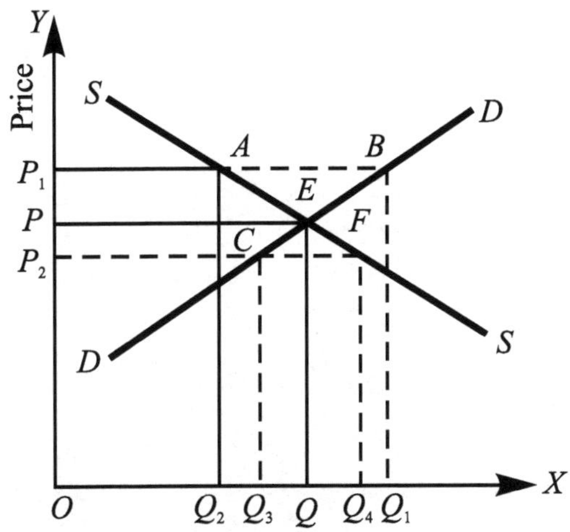

Fig. 6.3

then the disturbing forces will lead to a new equilibrium position. The neutral equilibrium is classified into two types (*a*) Static Neutral Equilibrium, and (*b*) Dynamic Neutral Equilibrium.

Static Neutral equilibrium has been shown in Fig. 6.4 and Dynamic Neutral Equilibrium has been shown in Fig. 6.5.

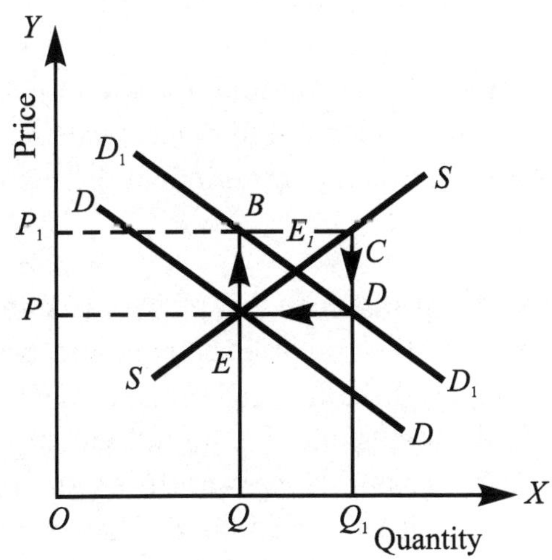

Fig. 6.4

In Fig. 6.4, the initial equilibrium point is E, whereas at OP price the demand and supply are equal to OQ. If price increases to OP_1, then the new equilibrium point will be E, where the quantity demanded and supplied remains the same, i.e. at OQ. Thus between the price range PP_1 (or EE_1) the market is in neutral equilibrium.

In Fig. 6.5, an increase in demand will lead to an increase in price

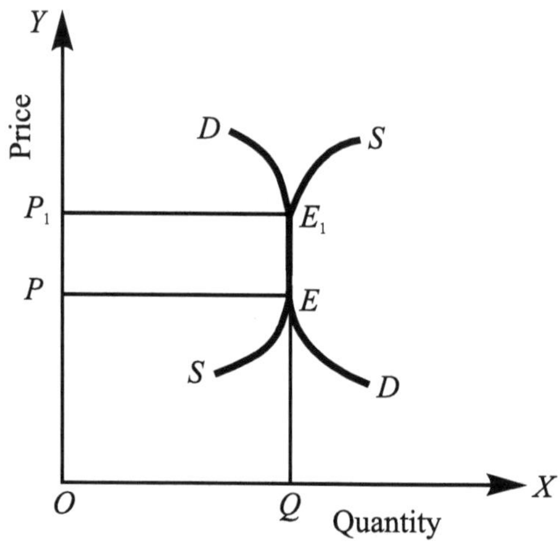

Fig. 6.5

from OP to OP_1. At this increased price, the producers will have the initiative to produce OQ_1 amount of the commodity. But at this level of output the demand price OP is less than the supply price OP_1, and, therefore, the producers will curtail their supply to the extent of OQ. But again, at this level demand is more than supply. Thus, it will further lead to an increase in price to the extent of OP_1. In this way, price and quantities will fluctuate along the equilibrium point E.

Now, it is important to note that among the three types of equilibrium, it is only the stable equilibrium which is used to analyse the complex economic phenomena by the economists. The unstable and the neutral equilibrium are only of theoretical importance.

Stability Conditions of Equilibrium—Walras *vs.* Marshall

As we have noted above, equilibrium price and quantity are determined by the equality of demand and supply. Equilibrium is characterized by the acquiescence of buyers and sellers in the status quo, i.e. no individual in the market has an incentive to modify his behaviour. However, the existence of an equilibrium point does not guarantee that it will be attained. There is no guarantee that the initital price will happen to be the equilibrium price. Moreover, changes in consumer preference will generally shift the demand curve, and innovations will shift the supply curve. Both these forces will tend to disturb an established equilibrium position. The disturbance (change) may lead to a new equilibrium situation, but there is again no reason to assume that it will be attained. More specifically, an equilibrium is stable, if a disturbance results in a return to initial equilibrium and it is unstable if the disturbance does not lead to the original equilibrium position.[6]

Now, the question is as to what are the stability conditions of equilibrium? In this context, we shall discuss two types of views: The Walrasian View and the Marshallian View, under both the *static stability* and the *dynamic stability* conditions.

Static stability conditions. We have already mentioned that a disturbance usually creates an adjustment process in the market. For instance, if the actual price is less than the equilibrium price, the adjustment may consist of some buyers raising their bids (offers) for the commodity. Static analysis abstracts from the time path of the adjustment process and considers only the nature of the change, i.e. whether it is toward, or away from, equilibrium. In Fig. 6.6, the excess demand[7] is positive at the price OP_1, and negative at the price OP_2.

Stability conditions are derived from the assumptions about the market behaviour of buyers and sellers.

The Walrasian stability condition. It is based on the assumption that buyers tend to raise their bids (offers) if excess demand is positive and sellers tend to lower their prices if excess demand is negative. If this assumption holds good, a market is stable if a price raise diminishes excess demand.[8] In other words, Walras assumes that it is price that adjusts itself to quantity changes. The excess demand price is defined as the difference between the price that buyers are willing to pay and the price that sellers are charging for a given quantity. In Fig 6.6, there is a positive excess demand price at OQ_1, quantity, (i.e. the demand price Q_1A is more than the supply price Q_1B or $Q_1A > Q_1B$, and a negative excess demand price at OQ_2 quantity, i.e. the demand price Q_2F is less than the supply price Q_2C_2 or $Q_2F < Q_2C$.) Now, according to the Walrasian stability condition, when excess demand is positive, then the buyers will increase the price and if it is negative then the sellers will reduce the price, as a result of which the equilibrium position E in Fig. 6.6 is attained.

6. P.A. Samuelson, *Foundations of Economic Analysis*, 1948, pp. 260-62. He states that it is not a rigorous definition of stability and is only one of several alternative definitions.
7. Mathematically, the excess demand at price P can be defined as,

   $E(P) = D(P) - S(P)$

   It is positive, or $E(P) > 0$ if $D(P) > S(P)$

   It is negative, or $E(P) < 0$ if $D(P) < S(P)$
8. It means that the first derivative of excess demand with respect to price must be negative

   or $\dfrac{dE(P)}{dP} = E'(P) = D'(P) - S'(P) < 0$

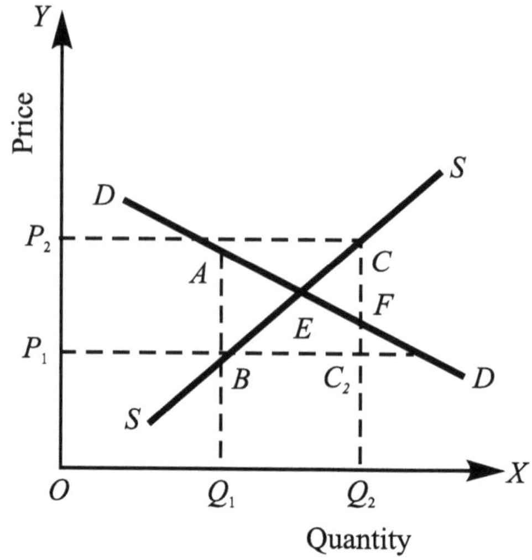

Fig. 6.6

The Marshallian stability condition, on the other hand, is based on the assumption that producers will tend to raise their output when the excess demand price is positive and lower it when it is negative. In other words, Marshall's analysis is based upon the assumption that quantity adjusts to price changes. If excess demand price is positive, the producer realises that consumers are offering a higher price than he is charging and concludes that he can profitably increase the quantity supplied. Also, if excess demand price is negative, the producer curtails the quantity supplied. As we may notice in Fig. 6.6, when excess-demand price is positive (*i.e.,* $Q_1A > Q_1B$), then it means that consumers are ready to pay more price which the producers want, therefore, producers will increase the supply. When supply increases, it will lead to a decrease in price and that again leads to increased demand; as a result of which equilibrium will be attained at point *E*. Analogous reasoning holds for the converse case.

In this way, both the Walrasian and the Marshallian stability conditions are satisfied if the demand curve is negatively sloped and the supply curve is positively sloped, as shown in Fig. 6.6. The ordinary supply-demand situation is, therefore, stable according to both the Walrasian and Marshallian definitions.

However, if the supply curve is negatively sloped, an equilibrium cannot be stable according to both the definitions.[9] Also, in such a case both the conditions Walrasian and Marshallian stability conditions cannot be

9. The supply curves which may have negative slope are the supply curves for primary inputs, such as, labour and product supply curves in the presence of external economies or diseconomies. Unstable equilibria may occur only in these cases.

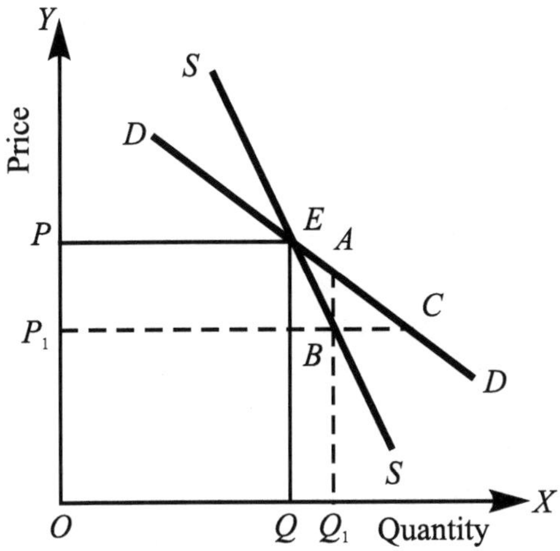

Fig.6.7

fulfilled simultaneously. Both the conditions are applied in opposite directions. If an equilibrium is stable in the Walrasian sense, then the equilibrium will be unstable in the Marshallian sense. The converse is also true. First of all, we will study these stability conditions with the help of straight line demand and supply curves.

The equilibrium is stable in the Walrasian sense if the supply curve is steeper than the demand curve and unstable in the opposite case. Equilibrium is stable in the Marshallian sense if the supply curve is less steep than the demand curve and unstable in the opposite case. These concepts are illustrated in Figs 6.7 and 6.8 respectively.

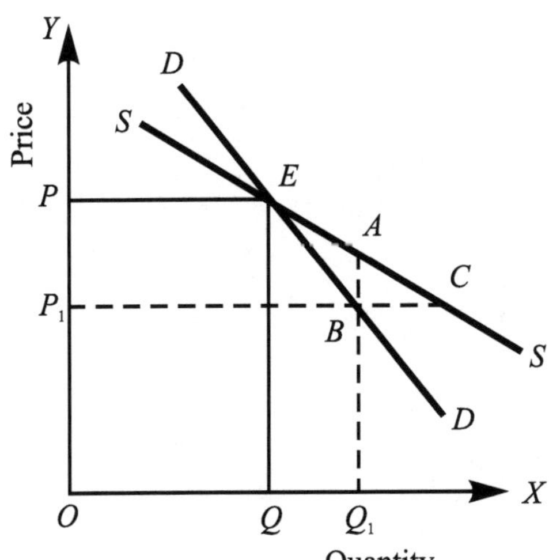

Fig. 6.8

Fig. 6.7 illustrates the Walrasian stable and Marshallian unstable equilibrium. In Walrasian sense, at price OP_1, the excess demand BC is positive (because demand is more than supply or $P_1C > P_1B$), therefore competition among consumers will tend to raise the price to the extent of OP and excess demand diminishes. Hence the equilibrium is stable at point E in Fig. 6.7. But, in Marshallian sense, at price OP_1, the quantity supplied is OQ_1; the corresponding excess demand price AB is positive (because $Q_1A > Q_1B$). The consumers are ready to pay more price than the actual price. Therefore, the quantity produced will tend to increase, but the excess demand price increases too. Thus, the actual price and quantity move farther away from the equilibrium point E.

Now, Fig. 6.8 illustrates the stable equilibrium in Marshallian sense and unstable equilibrium in Walrasian sense. In Marshallian sense, at price OP_1, the excess demand price AB is negative (because $Q_1B < Q_1A$, i.e. demand price is less than supply price.) It inspires the producers to reduce their supply from OQ_1 to OQ. Price increases and demand decreases, as a result of which the original equilibrium point E is attained. But in Walrasian sense, at price OP_1, the excess demand BC is negative because $P_1B < P_1C$. It will inspire the sellers to make a further reduction in their price. Thus both price and quantity move farther away from the equilibrium point E. Hence, the equilibrium is unstable. Theoretically, a negatively sloped supply curve may intersect the demand curve at several points. Such a case is illustrated in Fig. 6.9. Each intersection defines an equilibrium position. In Walrasian sense, the successive equilibrium points A, B, C are alternatively stable and unstable.[10] The supply curve is steeper than the demand curve at point A, and therefore, the equilibrium is

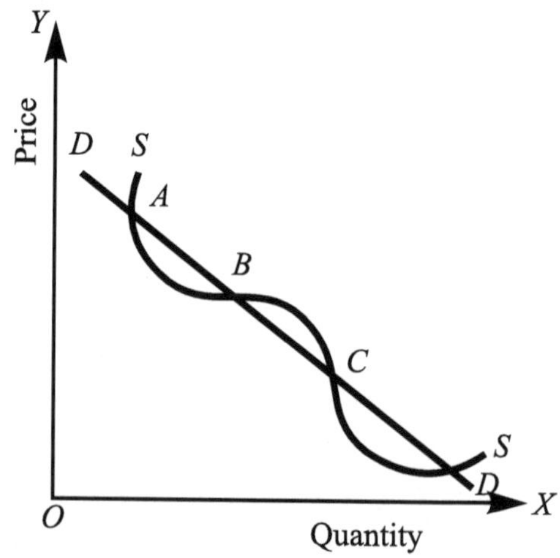

Fig. 6.9

10. The arrangement here is based on the Walrasian behaviour assumption. Analogous arrangement can be given in terms of the Marshallian assumption. In that case the above successive equilibrium points A, B, C of Fig. 6.9 will represent alternatively unstable and stable equilibrium positions.

stable at this point. Similarly, at point *B* the supply curve becomes less steep than the demand curve and, therefore, the equilibrium is unstable at point *B*. By a similar reasoning, point *C* again represents a stable equilibrium. It is also known as a case of 'multi-equilibrium'.

Thus, the views of Prof. Marshall and Prof. Walras regarding the stability conditions of equilibrium are just opposite to each other. The reason may be that Prof. Marshall and Prof. Walras have developed their ideas about the stability conditions assuming different time periods. Marshall defines his stability conditions in the context of equilibrium in which the adjustment is made by quantity changes. Walras, on the other hand, defines his stability conditions assuming a short-time period in which adjustment is made by changes in price. Therefore, one cannot say a *priori* whether the Walrasian or Marshallian condition is more plausible in reality. In any concrete situation stability of equilibrium can be assessed only after empirical information has been collected, concerning the behaviour patterns of the buyers and sellers in the market.

Dynamic stability conditions. As we have explained, the static stability conditions are stated in terms of change of excess demand with respect to price or the rate of change of excess demand price with respect to quantity. This type of analysis (static) makes no effort to investigate time path of the adjustment process. We cannot expect instantaneous (immediate) adjustments in the present model of demand and supply. If the initial price is not equal to the equilibrium price, it changes and new equilibrium takes place. If the new price is still different from the equilibrium price, it is again forced to change. This process continues until equilibrium is reached.[11] This is known as the dynamic nature of the model.

Equilibrium is stable in the dynamic sense if the price converges to (or approaches) the equilibrium price over time. It is an unstable equilibrium if the price change is always away from equilibrium. Dynamic stability may also be defined in terms of the convergence of the quantity supplied to the equilibrium quantity. The former definition corresponds to the Walrasian and the latter to the Marshallian definition of dynamic stability conditions. Both static and dynamic stability depend upon the slopes of the demand and supply curves. But the static and dynamic approaches to stability are fundamentally different. Static stability need not imply dynamic stability, but dynamic stability implies static stability. The reason is that dynamic analysis is a more inclusive tool for investigating the properties of equilibrium. Static analysis concerns itself only with the direction of the adjustment and neglects the magnitude of the adjustment from period to period.

---

11. The prices which are recorded from period to period are potential, rather than realized prices until equilibrium is reached.

After the development of dynamic economics, the stable and unstable equilibrium situations are explained with the help of Cobweb theorem.[12]

(ii) Short-run and Long-run Equilibrium

An economic equilibrium may also be classified as short-run and long-run equilibrium. Such type of classification was made by Prof. Marshall who for the first time introduced the element of time in the theory of value. In the short-run, individual firms seek to maximize profits or minimize losses. The scale of plant is fixed for each firm. Available techniques of production and input-prices determine the individual firm's costs.[13] Losses are increased by some firms and profits are made by others. No firm operates unless the price of its product exceeds average variable costs. The supply is adjusted to the changes in demand with the existing means of production because the time is too short to vary the means of production or the scale of plant. Such an equilibrium is termed as *short-run equilibrium.*

In the long-run those resources (or costs) that were fixed in the short-run become variable. These are the costs that constitute the plants of individual firms. As they become variable, it becomes possible for individual firms to change scale of plant, for firms to exit from those industries in which losses occur, and for firms to enter those industries which make profits provided entry or exit of a firm is easy, as it is under conditions of pure and monopolistic competition. Therefore, in the long-run the time available to adjust the supply to change in demand is quite adequate. The supply can be adjusted to the changes in demand by varying the means of production (or scale of plant) and the resulting equilibrium is called *long-run equilibrium.*

In other words, long-run equilibrium will be reached when all resources are so allocated that their respective marginal revenue products *(MRP)* are equalized in all alternative uses. No shortage or surpluses occur for any resource; that is, the marginal revenue product of each is equal to its price, *i.e.* $MRP = P$. When the equilibrium allocation of resources is achieved, each firm will be using resources in the least-cost combination. Finns will adjust their scales of plant in such a way that their long-run marginal cost equals marginal revenue $(LMC = MR)$, and will use least-cost resource combinations for the outputs which they produce.[14]

The difference between the two types of equilibrium short-run and long-run equilibrium can be illustrated with the help of an example of perfect competition. Here, short-run equilibrium requires that each firm must produce

12. Hendersen and Quandt, *Microeconimic Theory—A Mathematical Approach,* pp. 11 3-23.
13. In our discussion on the short-run equilibrium, we distinguish between "fixed" costs and "variable" costs. The maximum loss that a firm may accept will not exceed its fixed costs.
14. It holds only in the case of perfect competition when entry is free.

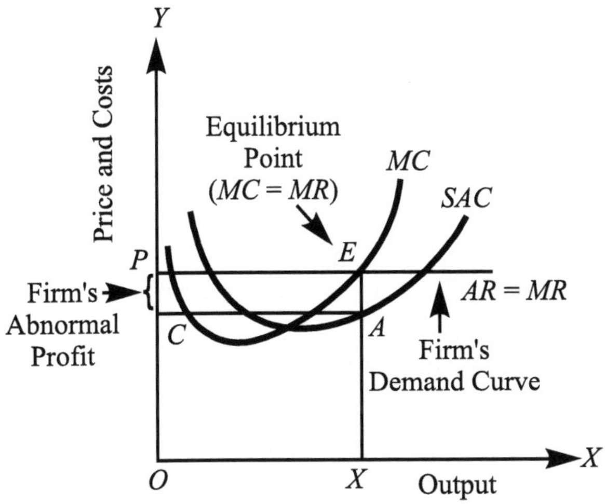

Fig.6.10

that level of output for which its marginal cost equals marginal revenue *(MC = MR)*. On the other hand, long-run equilibrium requires that each firm must produce that level of output for which its *MC = MR = AR = AC.*

Fig. 6.10 shows the short-run equilibrium, while Fig. 6.11 shows the long run equilibrium of a perfectly competitive firm. In Fig. 6.10, the equilibrium point *E* indicates that the firm is producing *OX* level of output where its *MC = MR*. It is a profit-maximising output and the firm has no incentive to deviate from this. The firm's total abnormal profits are shown by the area of rectangle *(PEAC)*.

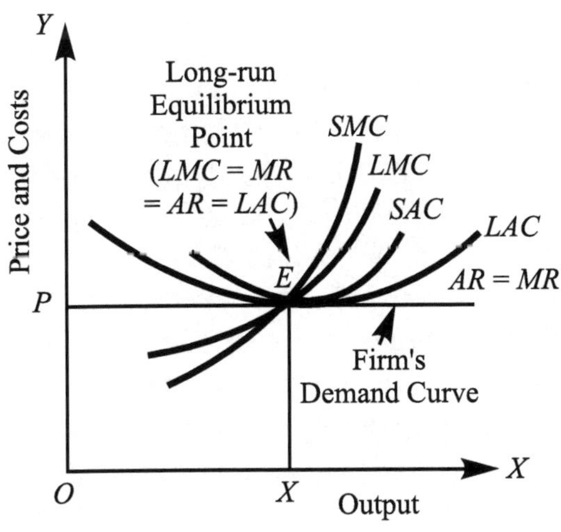

Fig. 6.11

Fig. 6.11 shows the case of long-run equilibrium. Here, the equilibrium point *E* indicates that the firm will produce *OX* level of output where its $MC = MR = AR = AC$. The important point to notice here is that the abnormal profits of the firm disappear due to the entry of new firms in the market. Also for the firm, there is no incentive to increase or decrease the scale of plant or the output. This also means that long-run equilibrium of the firm also requires the short-run equilibrium to exist at the same time. But the converse may not be true; that is short-run equilibrium of the firm (or the industry) can exist even though there is long-run disequilibrium of the firm (or the industry).

(*iii*) Unique and Multiple Equilibrium

Acoording to Prof. Stigler, "Equilibrium may be unique or multiple. A position of unique equilibrium arises if there is a single set of prices and quantities which fulfill the conditions of equilibrium. Multiple positions of equilibrium exist when several different sets of prices and quantities will meet the equilibrium conditions. The study of multiple equilibrium positions is essentially formal; no important empirical cases have yet been advanced to illustrate it....In general, a unique position of equilibrium will be treated as the typical case."

In this sense, Fig 6.6 represents the situation of a single or unique equilibrium which is very common to the real world, while Fig 6.9 represents the situation of multiple equilibrium which is very rare in the real world.

(*iv*) Static and Dynamic Equilibrium

As we have already explained, static equilibrium represents a stationary state. According to Prof. Mehta, "Static equilibrium which maintains itself outside the period of time under consideration." It is such a gainful situation which every consumer, firm, industry or factor-input wants to achieve and when it comes, nobody would like to leave it. A consumer is in static equilibrium if he gets maximum satisfaction from his limited income to be spent on various goods and services. Deviation from this position will necessarily reduce his total satisfaction. Similarly, a firm is in static equilibrium if she gets maximum profit and will have no initiative to increase her output. In the same way, an industry will be in static equilibrium if no firm has the incentive to enter into it and no firm wants to exit from it. In other words, an industry is in equilibrium if all the firms (which constitute it) are earning only normal profits.

An economic system, on the other hand, may be said to be in a dynamic equilibrium if its total stock changes at a constant rate, and if the rates of production and consumption of all items of the stock increase at the same time. According to Prof. Mehta after a certain time period when the equilibrium position is disturbed, then it is said to be dynamic equilibrium. Today, the concept of dynamic equilibrium is explained with the help of Cobweb theorem.

In real world, the concept of dynamic equilibrium is of little importance in interpreting economic change; but the concept of static equilibrium is realistic and is generally used to interpret the economic change.

(*v*) Partial and General Equilibrium

According to Prof. Stigler, "Equilibrium may be partial or general. A partial equilibrium is one which is based on only a restricted range of data; a standard example is the price of a single product, the prices of all other products being held fixed during the analysis. General equilibrium is ostensibly based on all of the data relevant to the problem which is being studied: the corresponding example would be the prices and outputs of all industries. The method of partial equilibrium analysis is associated with Marshall and the Cambridge School; that of general equilibrium with Walras and the Lausanne School." In simple words, an equilibrium pertaining to a single variable a single price or a consumer or a firm or an industry may be called partial or particular equilibrium. More specifically, it studies the movements of particular individuals, firms or industries towards equilibrium on the basis of given economic data. General equilibrium, on the other hand, deals with the economy as a whole.

The economic analysis of Prof. Marshall is related to the study of partial equilibrium. While analysing the behaviour of an individual consumer or a firm or a sector of the economy, it is generally assumed that the changes in these individual units make no effect on the rest of the economy. In other words, micro-economic analysis of economic units is based on the assumption of "ceteris paribus". Thus, all micro-economic studies are concerned with partial or particular equilibria. Generally, partial equilibrium analysis is related to two types of problems:

(1) Problems which are related to a particular aspect of the economic behaviour of an individual consumer, firm or an industry. For example, if the workers of a particular industry go on strike, the effects of such strike are likely to remain confined to that particular industry only.

(2) Problems which are concerned with the *first order* effects of an economic disturbance of any kind. For example, suppose a rearmament programme increases the demand for steel suddenly and substantially. Partial equilibrium analysis will provide answers to the first-order effects on the steel industry what happens to its prices, its output, its profits, its demand for resources, resource prices and resource employment levels. However, the first-order effects by no means end the repercussions from the initial disturbance. In other words, it will continue even after the steel industry has attained a new equilibrium position.

Partial or particular equilibrium analysis will be helpful in reviewing the operation of a free enterprise economy. In a free enterprise economy, individual consumers seek to maximise satisfaction. In terms of utility analysis, each consumer will spend his limited income among different goods and services in such a way that the marginal utility of the dollar spent on them must be the same.

A firm will be in equilibrium, if it does not want to make any change in its production. In the short run, its marginal cost equals marginal revenue *(MC = MR)* and in the long run it performs the conditions of complete equilibrium, i.e. *MC* + *MR* = *LAC*. Thus, the firm earns only the normal profit and does not want to leave the industry. In the analysis of a firm, the production technique, and prices of goods and factor inputs are given.

Similarly, an industry will be in equilibrium, if all the firms in the industry enjoy normal profit and the number of firms is fixed.

There are two main limitations of the partial equilibrium analysis:

(*a*) It does not deal with the economy as a whole. It is limited to a particular phenomenon of the economy.

(*b*) It assumes other things remaining the same; therefore, it cannot be used as a policy guide.

Due to these limitations, the study of general equilibrium is required. The general equilibrium analysis considers all the sectors of an economy simultaneously. It attempts to deal explicitly with inter-relationships between different sectors of the economy. The concept of general equilibrium implies that all economic units all consumers, firms, industries and factor inputs are in equilibrium. If some units were in equilibrium and others were not, those in disequilibrium will move toward equilibrium. In other words, general equilibrium for the entire economy could exist only if all economic units were to achieve simultaneous partial equilibrium adjustments, as all economic units are assumed to be inter-dependent.

According to Prof. Leftwich, a line of demarcation between particular equilibrium analysis and general equilibrium analysis is hard to draw. Instead of establishing a dichotomy, it will be preferable to think in terms of moving along a continuum from particular to general equilibrium, or from first-order effects of a disturbance to second-order effect and further of higher-order effects. For instance, in price and output determination under perfect competition, we are concerned first with the (partial) equilibrium of the individual firm. Next, we extend the analysis to an entire industry. Then we observe, how a purely competitive free enterprise economy operates according to consumer tastes and preferences. This shows progressive movement from the application of particular analysis to the application of general equilibrium analysis.

According to Prof. Stigler, the main advantages of general equilibrium analysis are the following:

(*a*) It provides a demonstration that equilibrium in any particular sector of the economy is not incompatible with equilibrium in other sectors.

(***b***) It provides an outline of the general structure and the working of the economy as a whole.

(***c***) It is of great assistance in discovering which data are relevent to any specific problem.

When the impact of an economic disturbance is of sufficient magnitude to have repercussions throughout most of the economy, general equilibrium analysis provides the more relevant answers regarding its ultimate effects.

There are two principal variants of general equilibrium analysis.

(***a***) *Walras Model* which discusses general equilibrium in mathematical terms. Here the interdependence of economic units is shown through a system of simultaneous equations relating many economic variables to each other. There are as many variables to be determined as there are equations relating them.

(***b***) *Leontief's Input-Output Analysis.* It is an empirical descendant of the abstract Walrasian approach. It divides the economy into a number of sectors or industries, including households and the government as the sectors of final demand. Here, the inter-dependence of each industry on the others is established, statistical data provide an informative and useful picture of the inter-industry flows of goods, services and resources.

The Walrasian Model of General Equilibrium

The general equilibrium situation of Prof. Walras is static in which all prices are in equilibrium and demand and supply of the products are equal on equilibrium prices. Walras developed a system of equations to explain the state of general equilibrium. He distinguished between product-markets and factor-markets. In the product-markets, the goods are supplied by the business firms or industries and the same are demanded by the consumers. In the factor-markets, the households (or consumers) supply factor-inputs, such as, land, labour, capital, etc. to the industries and in return receive incomes from the industries. Therefore, consumers are buyers in the product-markets and sellers in the factor-markets. Similarly, the industries are sellers in the product markets and buyers in the factor-markets.

Assumptions of the Model

The Walrasian model is based on the following assumptions:

(***a***) The income and tastes of the consumers are given and constant.

(***b***) There is perfect competition in both the markets the product market and the factor market.

(***c***) Factors of production are perfectly mobile.

(***d***) Constant returns prevail in the economy.

(***e***) All the units of a product or service are homogeneous.

(***f***) Production technology is unchanged.

(***g***) Factors of production are fully employed.

Under these assumptions the economy is in equilibrium of the demand and the supply of each product or service are equal. The unknown variables in the Walrasian Model are the prices and quantities of the factors of production used in the production of each product. Walras called them technical coefficients. If there are *n* commodities and *m* factor-inputs, then there would be *n* commodity-prices and *m* factor-prices. It will create *n* *m* technical coefficients. The whole system of Walrasian equations can be explained in the following manner: An economy consists of X_1, X_2,…*Xn* quantities of n-commodities; P_1, P_2,… *Pn* are the prices of *n*-commodities; R_1,R_2. . . *Rn* are the quantities of *n-factor* inputs; w_1, w_2…wn are the prices *n-factor* inputs; and *aij* are the fixed technical coefficients of the ith factor input in producing *j*th products, (*i* = 1, 2,... *n,* and *j* = 1, 2,…*n)*

All the prices are measured in terms of one commodity, X_1which is known as the numeraire. For example, the price of X_2 is that quantity of X_1which is exchanged for an unit of X_2. In this way, the Walrasian system is the system of commodity-exchange where the numeraire is used to measure a single unit and p_1=1.There is no intermediate commodity and the commodities are directly produced by the given factor-input quantities. The economy is in equilibrium position when the demand for each commodity is equal to its supply. Walrasian model keeps supply equations equal to demand equations. Thus, there are two sets for each equation; one is for individual consumers and producers which is represented by small letters (x_1, x_2,…and r_1 r_2…r_n) and the other set is for the economy as a whole which is represented by capital letters (X_1, X_2 …… X_n and R_1, R_2…R_n).

Walras assumes that each consumer has its own demand for those productive services which he supplies and he tries to maximise his satisfaction from his given constraints the fixed income and the fixed prices of the commodities. Thus, the budget equation of a consumer can be written as

$$x_1 p_1 + x_2 p_2 + \ldots + x_n p_n = r_1 w_1 + r_2 w_2 + \ldots . r_n w_n \qquad \ldots(1)$$

In this way there will be *n* equations of consumers which will determine *n* quantities of various commodities. In all *n* variables are expected. Now, we may write the demand of individual consumers for the various commodities in the following manner.

$$\left.\begin{array}{l} X_1 = f_1(p_1, p_2, \ldots . p_n \,;\, w_1, w_2, \ldots .. w_n), \\ X_2 = f_2(p_1, p_2, \ldots . p_n \,;\, w_1, w_2, \ldots .. w_n), \\ \vdots \\ X_n = f_n(p_1, p_2, \ldots . p_n \,;\, w_1, w_2, \ldots .. w_n), \end{array}\right\} \qquad \ldots(2)$$

By adding the demand functions of the individual consumers under (2) we may construct the market demand equations of the commodities. If *xij* indicates the demand of *i*th (*i*= 1, 2,..,*n*) product for the *j*th (*j*= 1, 2…*k*) consumer, then the market demand equations for the products X_1 X_2, … Xn are developed in the following manner.

$$
\begin{aligned}
X_1 &= x_{11} + x_{12} \ldots x_{1k} \\
X_2 &= x_{21} + x_{22} + \ldots x_{2k} \\
M & \\
X_n &= xnl + xn2 + \ldots x_{nk}
\end{aligned}
\qquad \ldots(3)
$$

Thus, like the, individual demand functions, the market demand equations depend upon the prices of various commodities and factor-inputs. We may write these market demand functions in the following manner:

$$
\left.
\begin{aligned}
X_1 &= F_1(p_1, p_2, \ldots. p_n \,;\, w_1, w_2, \ldots.. w_m) \\
X_2 &= F_2(p_1, p_2, \ldots. p_n \,;\, w_1, w_2, \ldots.. w_m) \\
\\
X_n &= F_n\ (p_1, p_2, \ldots. p_n \,;\, w_1, w_2, \ldots.. w_m)
\end{aligned}
\right\}
\qquad \ldots(4)
$$

On supply side, for equilibrium, the price of each commodity must be equal to its unit-cost. For example, the per unit production of the first commodity requires all units of first factor-input, a_{12} units of the second factor-input and so on. In this way we will have *n* equations ;

$$
\begin{aligned}
a_{11}w_1 + a_{12}w_3 + \ldots + a_{1m}w_m &= p_1 \\
a_{21}w_1 + a_{22}w_2 + \ldots + a_2 m w_m &= p_2 \\
an_1 w_1 + an_2 w_2 + \ldots anm wm &= p_n
\end{aligned}
\qquad \ldots(5)
$$

An equilibrium in the product market will be maintained if the quantity offered by the factor inputs is equal to the quantity of their productive services. The total quantity of factor-inputs will depend upon the market price of the finished goods and their (factors) own prices own prices as shown by (5). Thus, we will have a set of *m* equations as

$$
\begin{aligned}
R_1 &= F_1(\,p_1, p_2, \ldots pn; w_1, w_2, \ldots w_m \\
R_2 &= F_2(\,p_1, p_2, \ldots pn; w_1, w_2, \ldots w_m \\
Rm &= Fm(\,p_1, p_2, \ldots p_3; w_1, w_2, \ldots w_m
\end{aligned}
\qquad \ldots(6)
$$

The economy will be in equilibrium when the market supply equals market demand, *i.e.* equations (4) and (6) are assumed to be equal.

Thus, Walrasian Model states that any individual who demands a commodity, is, by definition, prepared to supply, in exchange, an amount of money (or other commodities) of equal value. Similarly, anyone who supplies some product would demand, in exchange, its value equivalent in money (or other commodities).

In terms of aggregate demand and supply, we have

$$\sum_{i=j}^{n} PiSi = \sum_{i=j}^{n} PiDi \qquad \text{...(7)}$$

Where S represents the supply[1] of the commodity and D represents the demand for the commodity. But Walras'Model explains that one of the general equilibrium equations is redundant (excessive). But the model indicates that by subtraction it can be shown that the money value of the quantity supplied and that of quantity for X_1 must also necessarily be equal. Because we have

$$\sum_{i=j}^{n} PiSi = \sum_{i=j}^{n} PiDi$$

and also

$$\sum_{i=2}^{n} PiSi = \sum_{i=2}^{n} PiDi$$

then, by definition,

$$P_1S_1 = P_1D_1$$

or

$$S_1 = D_1$$

Hence, the quantity supplied must be necessarily equal to the quantity demanded.

Criticisms of the Walrasian Model

The main criticisms of is model are the following:

(1) It is based on a number of unrealistic assumptions. Its assumptions are far from the reality. Perfect competition, which is the basis of this model, is only an imaginary concept.

(2) This model is static in nature. It assumes *ceteris paribus.* But in real world, the tastes and preferences of the consumers are changing. Constant returns to scale are not found in the long run. Further, the cost situations are different for different producers.

(3) The model assumes a set of simultaneous equations which makes it complicated. A non-mathematical student of economics is unable to understand it.

Exercises

1. Discuss the significance and the concept of equilibrium in economic theory.
2. What do you understand by the term 'equilibrium'? What are the various types of equilibrium?
3. Distinguish between the conditions for stable and unstable equilibrium.
4. Define stable, unstable and neutral economic equilibrium. Prove with suitable diagrams that equilibrium is actually achieved in the real world from time to time.

5. Write a lucid note on the Walrasian Model of General Equilibrium.
6. Distinguish between partial and general equilibrium. What are the advantages and limitations of general equilibrium analysis?
7. Write short notes on the following:
   (*i*) Short-run and Long-run Equilibrium.
   (*ii*) Unique and Multiple Equilibrium.
   (*iii*) Static and Dynamic Economic Equilibrium.
8. Distinguish between static and dynamic equilibrium. Explain your answer with the help of diagrams and equations.
9. Define equilibrium and show with the help of the Cobweb theorem that under given conditions equilibrium can actually be achieved in practice.

Multiple Choice Questions

10. (*i*) Which of the following is most closely associated with general equilibrium analysis?
    (*a*) everything depends on everything else
    (*b*) cateris paribus
    (*c*) the equilibrium price of a good or service depends on the balancing of the forces of demand and supply for that good or service
    (*d*) none of the above [*Ans.* (*a*)]

    (*ii*) The market equilibrium of a commodity is determined by
    (*a*) the market demand for the commodity
    (*b*) the market supply of the commodity
    (*c*) the balancing of the forces of demand and supply of the commodity
    (*d*) any of the above [*Ans.* (*c*)]

    (*iii*) The long-run equilibrium of a firm under perfect competition requires that each firm much produce that level of output at which its
    (*a*) $MC = MR = AR = AC$ (*b*) $MC = MR$
    (*c*) $AR = AC$ (*d*) $P = MR$ [*Ans.* (*a*)]

    (*iv*) Of the following economists, who is considered as master of partial equilibrium analysis ?
    (*a*) J.S. Mill (*b*) Alfred Marshall
    (*c*) A.C. Pigon (*d*) J.M. Keynes [*Ans.* (*b*)]

    (*v*) What is applicable to total analysis?
    (*a*) Assumption of Ceteris paribus (*b*) Incomplete and unrealistic
    (*c*) Mathematical Treatment (*d*) Independent Economic variables
    [*Ans.* (*c*)]

    (*vi*) Which of the following situations illustrates unstable equilibrium?
    (*a*) A ball that rests at the bottom of a bowl
    (*b*) A ball that rests on a billiard table
    (*c*) A ball that perched on the top of an inverted bowl
    (*d*) None of the above [*Ans.* (*c*)]

Chapter 7

The Role of Price Mechanism

1. Introduction

In every economy, some fundamental problems arise and the economy has to face them. Since these problems are common for all economies whether they are rich or poor, capitalist or socialist, they are known as the central problems of an economy. This must be remembered that the root of all these problems is the 'law of scarcity'. Had the resoures been unlimited like sunshine and air, there would have been no problem whatsoever. In different economies these problems are attempted to be solved differently.

These problems are:

(*i*) *What to produce?* That is what commodity is to be produced and in what quantity?

(*ii*) *How to produce?* That is what methods and techniques of production are to be used?

(*iii*) *For whom to produce?* That is what are the people for whom the economy has to produce? This also means how the national income or national output is distributed?

Besides the above problems, every economy has to face two more problems. But they can be included in the above three central problems. However, they can be put up as below:

(*iv*) *What should be the rate of growth of an economy?* That is what measures should be adopted by an economy to acquire an accelerated rate of growth? This problem is more important in an underdeveloped economy.

(*v*) *How to secure smooth working of an economy?* That is what measures should be adopted by an economy for its smooth growth? This problem is more relevant to a develped economy.

All the above problems are solved by the price mechanism. In fact, mechanism is a system of economic organisation in which each individual in his capacity as a consumer, producer and factor-owner is engaged in economic activity with a large measure of freedom. In every society there are legal and social institutions which govern it. The individual economic actions must confirm the system prevailing in an economy. Now we shall see how does the price mechanism play its role in solving the above central problems in various types of economies.

2. Role of Price Mechanism in a Free Enterprise Economy

Under a free enterprise economy, the price mechanism works through the demand and supply of goods and services in a competitive market. These in turn are determined by their prices. Prices determine the level of production of different goods and services. They also organise production and distribute it among the people of the society. We shall discuss all these problems in the following manner:

(*i*) *What and how much to produce?* In a free enterprise or capitalist state the choices are made by the people through the *price mechanism.* In such a system everything has a price. All the goods produced have a market price as do the factors (land, labour and capital) which produce them. Everyone receives money for what he sells (e.g. the worker sells his services) and uses this money to buy the goods he desires. If more of any particular product is desired there will be an increased demand for that commodity. This increase in demand will tend to raise its price and cause more of it to be produced. If more of any particular commodity is being produced than people desire, then the excess supply will cause its price to fall and producers will supply less of that commodity. We can say, therefore, that the manner in which people spend their income decides *what goods shall be produced and in what quantities.* It is the money votes of the people, votes which they place in the market, which decide the pattern of production. Buying a commodity is equivalent to voting for its production.

According to Friedman, "The votes of the members of a free enterprise exchange economy are manifested through prices which, in turn, reveal the standards of the society. Given these standards, there must be some machinery to translate these values or choices into productive activity. Productions must be organised both among and within industries. This is accomplished by the price system through the interaction of two sets of prices: price of products and price of resources. Prices of products in relation to the costs of producing them determine the distribution of resources among industries; the relative prices of factors, in turn, determine the coordination of factors within industries."[1]

The problem can also be explained with the help of Fig. 7.1. Here we

1. Milton Friedman, *Price Theory: A Provisional Text,* 1970, p. 9.

assume that the economy produces consumer goods (*X*) and capital goods (*Y*). In deciding the level of output of the economy it has to choose that combination of goods *X* and *Y* which is possible within the available resources of the economy. The PP_1 curve is the production possibility curve of the economy. Thus it can not choose point *R* which lies below the production possibility curve as it indicates the economic inefficiency of the system in the form of unemployment of resources. It is also not possible for the economy to choose any point outside the production possibility curve, say, point *T* which is not allowed by its available resources. It will, therefore, choose any point

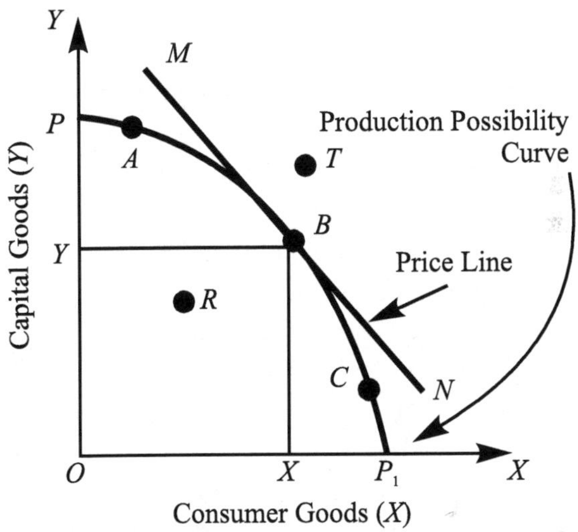

Fig. 7.1

among *A, B,* or *C* which lies on the production possibility curve. Since the total factor-endowment (or total cost) is fixed, the slope of production possibility curve will depict the change in the relative costs only, or the ratio of marginal cost of consumer goods (*X*) and capital goods (*Y*). Thus, its slope may be defined as:

$$\frac{\partial C}{\partial X} \bigg/ \frac{\partial C}{\partial Y}$$

where C = Total costs, X = Consumer goods, Y = Capital goods.

The straight line *MN* shows the relative prices or $\frac{P_X}{P_Y}$. The optimum allocation of resources (in a free economy) will be done at that level where

$$\frac{\partial C}{\partial X} \frac{\partial C}{\partial Y} = \frac{P_x}{P_y}.$$

Thus, in the present situation *OX* quantity of consumer goods and *OY* quantity of capital goods will be produced. If the relative prices change, the optimum level of factor used and the corresponding composition of output will also change.

(*ii*) *How to produce?* The problem 'how to produce' means the problem of choosing the technique or method of production. There are various alternative methods of production and the economy has to choose those techniques of production which would maximise production but minimise costs. This is possible only when the production resources are utilised in the best possible manner. The utilisation of resources in turn depends, upon the various factors and conditions which govern the productivity and efficiency of factors of production.

First of all, the choice is between the labour-intensive technique or capital-intensive technique. Labour-intensive technique of production means the use of more labour and less capital. In underdeveloped economies where labour is plenty and capital is relatively scarce, labour-intensive technique of production will be better. On the other hand, capital-intensive technique refers to the use of more capital and less labour. In economies where labour is relatively scarce, capital-intensive methods of production are more suitable.

Secondly, there is the question of specialisation or division of labour. To produce more goods at less cost of production specialisation is essential. Under specialisation right man is placed at the right place. Specialisation brings about —(*a*) the use of modern and uptodate capital, (*b*) the use of each capital asset up to its full capacity, (*c*) inventions and innovation, and (*d*) economical use of raw material.

Thirdly, comes the question of organisation. Production is the result of the joint efforts of the factors of production. Better organisation will, therefore, increase the magnitude of output and lower the cost of production. The factors of production should be so employed as to equalise their marginal utilities. This means that the allocation of the various factors should be according to the principle of substitution.

Lastly, the economy has to decide regarding the localisation of the various firms. Since the factors of production are not equally distributed over all parts of the economy, different places are to be chosen for different firms. In the matter of localisation, the economy should take the following factors into consideration: (*a*) Natural advantages to the firms, viz. facilities to raw material, power, transport, suitable climate, etc.; (*b*) economic advantages of the firms, viz. nearness to the market, availability of cheap labour, capital, etc. (*c*) other advantages, viz. political patronage, regional reputation, etc. Through localisation of industries or firms both internal and external economies are obtained. These economies reduce the cost of production. Here again, the problem is solved differently in different economies. In a capitalist economy the problem is solved by price mechanism.

As we know wages, rent, interest and profits are the prices paid by the entrepreneur (producer) for the services of the factors of production which make up the cost of production. Every producer aims at using the most efficient production process. An economically efficient production process is one which produces goods with the minimum costs. The choice of a production process will depend upon the relative prices of the factor services and the quantity of goods to be produced.

All this will be decided by competition between different producers. The more efficient producers will be able to supply a commodity at a lower price than less inefficient producers. Price competition will decide the methods of production which the society uses. Those producers who are best able to meet the demands of the consumers will succeed and make profits; the inefficient will make losses and go out of business. The large farm will tend to replace the small farm if this leads to lower production costs. Electricity will be generated from oil rather than coal if this means cheaper electricity. Motor cars will be manufactured by large-scale mass production methods if consumers demand cheap standardised models rather than expensive specially designed cars.

(iii) For whom to produce? The problem 'for whom to produce' is relative to the problem of 'what to produce'. We cannot decide the problem of what to produce unless we first know the people for whom the economy has to produce. We must make sure whether we have to produce for rich or poor; young or old; men or women; civil people or military people and soon. This is clearly the problem of the distribution of national income. People with different incomes will demand different goods and services. The producers will take into account the demand for these goods and services and produce accordingly. The solution of the problem depends upon the type of the economy. In a capitalist economy or free capitalist enterprise system, price plays a vital role and settles the problem of allocation of productive resources. In such an economy capitalists produce those goods which are used by rich people since they have more purchasing power. They pay huge prices for these goods and producers earn huge profits. Thus goods like motor cars, refrigerators, air conditioners, etc. will be produced more. The result is that poor people do not get even their bare necessities.

According to Friedman, every society must provide some means of dividing the total wealth among individuals of the society. In a free enterprise exchange economy this task is accomplished by the price system. Individuals in such a society separately own the resources used in production. They get claim on the product by selling their services in the market for a price. The total claim of any individual is determined by the quantity of resources he owns and the prices at which he is able to sell all the services of these resources. Factor prices or the return per unit of time per unit of resource in conjunction with the distribution of ownership of resources thus determine the distribution of total wealth or product among the individuals in the society.[2]

In other words, the share of the national wealth which any individual enjoys depends on the level of his income. Incomes are paid in the form of money, but money is merely a claim to goods and services. The higher a person's income, the greater is his purchasing power and the share of the nation's wealth available to him. The manner in which the wealth of a society is distributed depends, therefore, on the way in which personal incomes are determined.

Now, income is derived in two ways, either in return for some kind of labour, or from the ownership of property. The income which people receive as a reward for labour is known as wages. Income derived from the ownership of property takes the form of rent, dividends and interest, and is paid to the owners of land and capital. The levels of these incomes are governed by conditions of supply and demand in the markets for the factors of production (land, labour and capital). Rent, wages and interest are prices, and whether these prices are high or low depends upon their supply and the society's demand for the products which they help to make.

Hence, under a free enterprise or capitalist economy, the goods which are produced, the methods of production used, and the incomes of the factors of production, are all determined by the price mechanism operating in free markets. It is a system of profits and losses.

Limitations of Price Mechanism in a Free Market Economy

(*i*) *Production is guided by the demand of the elite and not by the need of the poor.* It is pointed out that even if the system worked perfectly in the manner described above, many persons would not consider it perfect. Commodities would obviously tend to go to those with most money. The system produces those goods which people demand, but demand implies the ability to pay. Hence, in this system, we may find the rich enjoying luxuries while the poor lack necessities. Only those goods would be produced which appear to offer the prospect of profit. It is, therefore, doubtful whether the system would provide such things as public parks, a universal system of education, or a national health service, etc.

(*ii*) *Non-existence of perfect competition.* In actual life, competition is not perfect, but it is found to be imperfect. There is not a single country in the world today which adheres to the principles of *laissez faire*. Most of

2. *Ibid.*, pp. 9-10.

capitalist economies have converted themselves into mixed economies-whatever objectives they may have before them.

(*iii*) *Price mechanism leads to unemployment and stagnation.* Economists, businessmen and government officials in rich countries increasingly recognize that their country must maintain a sufficiently high rate of development if deep depression is to be avoided and the possibility of stagnation averted. Unless the rate of development is sufficiently high, a rich country may suffer from general over-production and face a long-run problem of unemployment.

(*iv*) *Nationalisation of social services.* Measures aimed at nationalisation of social services also tend to modify the price system in favour of mixed economy.

3. Role of Price Mechanism in a Mixed Economy

The system we have described above is commonly known as a system of *private enterprise.* This particular type of organization allows private individuals to own the means of production. Private persons are allowed to buy and own land, buildings, machines, *etc.* to hire labour, and to produce and sell goods and services. But the competitive condition required of a free market which never existed in actual fact. Furthermore, the doctrines of the *laissez faire* philosophers were neither completely accepted by all nor left unchallenged. The alternative to this is a system of *public enterprise.* In this case the means of production are owned and controlled by public authorties (*i.e.* the state or local councils). In our own country and in most western countries there are mixed systems where both private and public enterprises operate side by side.

Our economic structure is based on the system of private enterprise. Property can be privately owned and people are economically free, subject to the obedience to the laws, to use their time and means as they like. The state protects the right of the individual to control his property and his goods. Economic freedom means that the individual is free to do as he likes with his own property and with his own time and energy. Economic freedom and private enterprise do not preclude the possibility of State enterprise or "public" enterprise. Our economic system is one of comparative freedom: the freedom of the individual, whether acting alone or in conjunction with others, is restricted by the standards set up by society to ensure the welfare of the community as a whole.

The economy of the US is still primarily a free enterprise economy, but it is more accurately described as a "mixed economy", a "dual economy" or as "mixed capitalism"; all these phrases indicating that both private enterprise and government play important roles. The extent of intervention by the government in the economy is indicated by the following: regulation of banks, the establishment of a strong Federal Reserve System; anti-trust regulation; a broad social security programme; the equalisation of bargaining power between capital and labour; controls on farm production; subsidies to many different types of businesses; protection of consumer interests from false and misleading advertising and business practices; the regulation of public utilities engaged in inter-state commerce; the regulation of monetary system, the redistribution of income, production of some products, specially during World War II; and governmental assumption of the responsibility to use the means at its disposal to help maintain full employment.

Similarly in Great Britain, a considerable part of the economy used to be under the direct control of public authorities. The coal industry, the electricity and gas industries, the railways, a part of road haulage, and most civil aviation, were some of the industries which are controlled by the state. Many local authorities in UK operated local omnibus services, built houses, built and controlled schools, and provided public baths and public parks, etc. In addition to this form of public enterprise which provided goods, and services directly, the state controlled, and still does, the operations of private enterprise. The Factory Acts govern the conditions under which people are allowed to work in factories. The Companies Acts lay down the methods by which companies are allowed to conduct their financial affairs. The Monopolies and Restrictive Practices Acts supervise and control the procedures of businessmen in fixing their prices and the manner which they supply their goods to the public. The Distribution of Industry Acts are designed to influence the decisions of businessmen in the location of their factories. The various Public Health Acts and Weights and Measures Acts also affect the manner in which business is carried on in Great Britain as do European Union regulations.

Many countries have adopted economic planning as a national policy. Not only the socialist and communist, but even some of the capitalist countries have introduced and adopted the concept of planned economy. Great Britain has made tentative move towards national planning, although it has not set up any central planning body to direct the operations of the British economy in detail. But it did inaugurate the broad programme of planning designed to achieve full employment, agricultural development, restoration of foreign trade, housing, construction and increased social security through measures of control.

In present time, some economists feel that it could be possible to adopt the idea of central planning in a capitalist economy. They hold the opinion that planning could be worked out without too much encroachment on the rights of the private sector. They have worked out a system of planning that allows the price system to function as much as it now does but to achieve a better balance between demand and supply than is possible in an unplanned system, through an intelligent manipulation of the monetary system.

Let us now study as to how the central economic problems are attempted to be solved in a mixed capitalist enterprise system. We take these problems one by one.

(*i*) *What to produce and in what quantity?* In a capitalist economy profit motive or price mechanism decides as to what commodity and in what quantity is to be produced. Generally, the producers are induced to produce those commodities which can be sold for higher prices and which promise them high profits. In a mixed capitalist economy also price mechanism solves this problem. But in such an economy, the government keeps on interfering for general welfare of the people. In these economies, the government undertakes the production and distribution of essential goods and services. The private enterprise is also allowed to exist for all other non-essential goods and services. But this sector also functions under the supervision and control of the government. The government adjusts demand and supply of goods. To remove the scarcity of certain goods, the government gives to the producers of these goods incentives like bounties, tax rebates, etc. and to discourage the production of certain goods, the government provides disincentives like imposing of higher taxes on those commodities.

(*ii*) *How to produce?* The problem 'how to produce' means the problem of choosing the method or technique of product on. In a free market economy or capitalist economy this problem is solved automatically. In order to maximise his profits, each producer tries to reduce his cost of production. He would choose that method or technique of production which is the cheapest and which minimises the cost of production. The factors of production are available in the market at different prices. The producers also come to the market to purchase them. In order to maximise their profits, the producers would purchase more of those factors whose price is low and less of those whose price is relatively high. In this way the problem of the choice of method of production is solved by the price mechanism. Thus, under free market economy or capitalist economy, price mechanism allocates the productive resources. But in a mixed capitalist economy, the allocation of productive resources between different uses is done partly through the government direction and partly through price mechanism. In the public sector, all decisions as to 'how to produce' are taken by the government whereas in the private sector price mechanism decides the allocation of the resources among different lines of production. This decision is done on the basis of profit motive. But even in private sector the working of price mechanism is regulated by the government rules and regulations.

(*iii*) *For whom to produce?* In a mixed capitalist economy need of the poor people are kept in mind by the government. The government undertakes the production and distribution of certain essential goods and services for the best interests of the society. Through price control and rationing the government ensures the supply of goods to both the rich and the poor classes of the society. The government imposes high direct taxes and reduces the purchasing power of the rich. Also the government levies high duties on the production of luxury goods and reduces their production. On the other hand, the government provides many social securities to the poor people.

4. Role of Price Mechanism in a Socialist Economy

The price mechanism is regarded as a distinguishing feature of a free market economy. It has little relevance in a socialist economy. Economic planning under socialism plays the same role as is played by the price mechanism in a capitalist economy. Here the Planning Commission is required to solve the basic central problems of what to produce, how to produce and for whom to produce. It makes an estimate of the entire economic, human and natural resources at its command. The commission has to decide upon the various commodities which the economy should produce with the available resources. It takes the social welfare aspect and the development related goals of the nation while choosing the technique of production to be used. The price mechanism in a capitalist economy operates in such a way that production takes place only to meet the demands of all these people who have considerable amount of disposable income. Production of those commodities is neglected which belong to the poor man's basket in a socialist economy. But in a socialist economy income inequalities are dramatically reduced so that everyone has an adequate amount of disposable income. While determining the pattern and size of output the Planning Commission has to see to it that its decisions in this regard are such that they ensure the availability of commodities for all in the market. Every economic plan of the nation which determines the economy's pace and pattern of development should necessarily incorporate the elements

(*i*) the way in which national income is to be distributed between consumption and accumulation, and

(*ii*) the manner in which investment is to be allocated among the different sectors of the economy.

The major characteristics of economic planning are as follows:

(*i*) Economic planning is conscious and delibrate process which aims at attaining certain specific objectives and target within specified time limit.

(*ii*) It implies within the national economy of a single and undivided authority invested with the power of taking all the decisions on the basis of the comprehensive survey of existing and potential resources in the country.

(*iii*) Planning is comprehensive in nature, it covers in an integrated manner all the important sectors of the national economy.

(*iv*) Economic planning is characterised by the use of limited resources on the basis of pre-determined priorities with a view to attain maximum welfare of the commodity.

(*v*) Economic planning covers not only planning of production of goods and services but also covers patterns of distribution of income and wealth as conceived by the planning authority.

The central planning authority is vested with the responsibility of preparing blue print for the allocation of resources among the different sectors of the economy and among the different uses within the different sectors. Different functions of the central planning authority are

(*a*) to fix prices of goods,

(*b*) to fix prices of factor services,

(*c*) to determine the rate of capital accumulation, and

(*d*) to decide the resource allocation.

It would be seen that the central planning decision regarding what, how and for whom to produce can not be disputed. Thus in a socialistic economy the freely functioning price mechanism and consumer choices no longer decide what goods and services are to be produced. Those decisions invariably have to be taken by the central planning authority.

Exercises

1. Describe how resources are allocated in a free market economy.
2. Explain how resources are allocated in a socialist economy.
3. What do you understand by price mechanism? Discuss its role in an economy.
4. Explain the role of price mechanism in a mixed capitalist economy.
5. Describe how the price system solves the fundamental problems of an economy through the forces of demand and supply.
6. Explain in brief the central economic problems of an economy.

Multiple Choice Questions

7. (*i*) The optimum allocation of resources in a free economy will be done at that level where

(*a*) $\frac{\partial C}{\partial X} \frac{\partial C}{\partial Y} = \frac{P_X}{P_Y}$ (*c*) $TC = TR$

(b) $P_X = P_Y = AR = MR$

(d) None of the above [Ans.(a)]

(ii) In which type of system the role of price mechanism is assumed to be significant?

(a) Free Enterprise Economy

(c) Planned Economy

(b) Controlled Economy

(d) All of the above [Ans.(a)]

(iii) The central problem of an economy consists of

(a) What and how much to produce?

(c) For whom to produce?

(b) How to produce?

(d) All of the above [Ans. (d)]

(iv) In a free enterprise economy the problem of what, how and for whom are solved by

(a) A planned committee

(b) The price mechanism

(c) The elected representatives of the people

(d) None of the above [Ans.(b)]

PART TWO
DEMAND THEORY

Chapter 8

The Utility Analysis

1. Introduction

In economics the study of consumer behaviour occupies an important place. The problem of a consumer consists of things: *(a)* the object, *(b)* the constraints, and *(c)* the decision variable. The object of a consumer is to maximise his total utility (satisfaction). He always tries to perform those economic activities which add to his total satisfaction. The constraints are the limited means. A consumer is unable to satisfy all of his wants from his given income. Thus, his decision variable is the quantity purchased of various commodities. He is to follow a law which enables him to attain maximum satisfaction.

Two approaches have been developed to deal with the problem of a consumer: (*i*) The Cardinal Utility Approach, and (*ii*) The Ordinal Utility Approach developed by Alfred Marshall. The indifference curve approach is the more recent approach or the modern approach developed mainly by Prof. Hicks. At the present time the former can be thought of as a special case of the latter. The cardinal utility approach will be discussed in this chapter and the indifference curve approach will be deferred to the next chapter. The modern economists have also developed two other approaches the revealed preference approach and the cardinal utility approach involving risky choices or the modern utility approach which will be discussed in the following chapters.

The concept of utility, which we will define shortly, was employed by the classical economists of the late 18th and 19th centuries. The 20th century version of the concept is the neoclassical. The utility approach was developed in the 1870s with the simultaneous publication of major works by three economists working independently. These were William Stanley Jevons (1835-1882) of England, Karl Menger (1880-1921) of Austria, and Leon Walras (1840-1921) of France. Later on, in 1890, Alfred Marshall made a pioneering effort by bringing the concept of price in line with marginal utility.

2. The Meaning of Utility

With given constraints, *i.e.* given prices of goods and services and given income, a consumer makes his purchases according to his tastes or desires or preferences or wants. A consumer may desire a unit of good *X* more than that of a unit of good *Y*, because commodity *X* gives him more utility. Utility means the power to satisfy a want. Any commodity or service which can satisfy a human want is said to have utility. According to Wicksteed, "Utility as an economic concept, means only desireness. "It signifies only the fact that a thing is wanted, that it is expected to satisfy a given want. It does not mean usefulness, as is generally assumed. The consumption of a particular commodity may be harmful, illogical or immoral; nevertheless, if it satisfies some want of somebody, it is deemed to possess utility from the economic standpoint. Therefore, we can very well say that utility is subjective, not objective. Utility resides in the mind of the consumer. The consumer knows it by introspection.

The term utility is commonly used as equivalent to satisfaction. But in economics, it has a different meaning. The amount of satisfaction actually obtained from the consumption of a thing is a psychological entity which is incapable of measurement, because it varies according to time, place, and the mental makeup of the individual concerned. The intensity of a person's desire for a commodity depends upon his habits, tastes and various other circumstances. At different times, the intensity of desire may be different. A consumer thinks of utility when he is buying a commodity but he secures satisfaction only after its consumption. To avoid confusion between utility and satisfaction some economists (like Wicksteed) use the term "significance" in place of utility. Wicksteed states that a thing has economic significance if it is scarce in relation to human wants, whatever may be the satisfaction it gives. Some economists use the term "intensity of desire" which seems better. Hence, utility is the measure, not of usefulness, nor of satisfaction, but of the intensity of desire. In fact, the entire theory of consumer behaviour is based on the assumption that utility and satisfaction are synonymous or that the expected satisfaction from a commodity is equal to the realised satisfaction.

3. Cardinal and Ordinal Utility

The terms cardinal and ordinal are borrowed from the vocabulary of mathematics. The numbers 1, 2, 3, 4, 5, *etc.* are cardinal numbers. The number 2, for example, is twice the size of number 1. In contrast, the numbers 1st, 2nd, 3rd, 4th, 5th, *etc.* are ordinal numbers. Such ordinal numbers are ordered or ranked, and there is no way of knowing, just from the ranking, what is the size relation of the numbers. The second one might be or might not be twice or thrice as big as the first one. The ordinal numbers 1st, 2nd, 3rd, 4th and 5th could be 50, 100, 150, 200 and 250 or they could be 50, 51, 52, 53 and 70. All we can know of the ordinal numbers is that the second number is greater than the first, the fourth is greater than the fifth, etc.

The concept of cardinal utility assumes that the measurement of utility of different commodities is possible. For example, the consumption of an apple may give 40 units of utility whereas the consumption of an orange may give only 20 units of utility. From this, it is clear that the utility of an apple is just twice the utility of an orange. On the other hand, the concept of ordinal utility permits us to say that the consumer prefers an apple to an orange, or prefers a cup of coffee to a glass of milk. It means that ordinal utility analysis is unable to compare the quantities of the two commodities. The neoclassical (Marshallian) utility approach assumes that utility can be measured. The units of measurement are arbitrary; they are called "utils". Thus, under some given conditions, the utility of an apple is 40 utils and that of an orange is 20 utils. This is just another way of saying that one apple has twice as much utility as one orange. Contrarily, the concept of ordinal utility (indifference curve approach) maintains that quantities of utility are inherently immeasurable theoretically and conceptually, as well as practically. These economists argue that the theory of consumer behaviour can be explained without the idea of measurable utility.

4. Measurement of Utility

There are two views on the question whether utility can be measured. Pareto, Hicks and other economists are of the opinion that utility cannot be measured in quantitative terms. According to them, utility is a subjective concept. The mental attitude on which utility depends differs from person to person. For the same consumer it differs from time to time. Even at a particular moment of time it is impossible to calculate the utility of a commodity in physical terms. All that a consumer can say is whether he prefers a cup of tea to a glass of milk. As such, it is not possible to measure directly the utility of a commodity.

But the 19th century economists (W. Stanley Jevons, Leon Walras, Alfred Marshall, etc.) are of the opinion that it is possible to measure utility indirectly by finding out how much a consumer is prepared to sacrifice in order to get one unit of a certain commodity. According to Prof. Marshall, "If we find a man in doubt whether to spend a few pence on a cigar, or a cup of tea, or on riding home instead of walking home, then we follow ordinary usage, and say that he expects from them equal utilities."[1]

1. Marshall, *op. cil.*, p. 15. We have substituted the word "utilities" in place of "pleasures".

Marshall argued that utility is correlative to want or desire. He conceded to the fact that wants cannot be measured directly. However, he developed an indirect measure for it in "the price which a person is willing to pay for the fulfillment or satisfaction of his desire or want". In other words, Marshall provided a cardinal measurement of utility. Higher the price paid by a consumer for a commodity higher shall be its utility and vice versa. Price can, thus, be a measure of the utility of a commodity. In this way, a consumer is assumed to be capable of assigning to every commodity a number representing the amount of utility associated with it. The utility numbers could be manipulated in the same fashion as weights. For example, we assume that the utility of Q_1 is 10 units and the utility of Q_2 is 40 units. The consumer would like Q_2 four times as strongly as Q_1. Therefore, difference between utility numbers could be compared.

5. Total Utility and Marginal Utility

Total utility is the sum of the utilities obtained from each unit consumed. The more of the commodity a consumer consumes per unit of time, the greater will be the total utility or satisfaction from it up to a certain point, At some rate of consumption total utility from the commodity will reach a maximum. The consumer will not be capable of enjoying any greater satisfaction from it even though more of it were thrust upon him. This is called his *saturation point* for that commodity.[2] For example, if a consumer consumes *n* units of commodity *X*, then the total utilities derived from these *n* units will be referred to as the total of *n* units, symbolically,

$$TUn = \sum_{i=1}^{n} Xi$$

where TUn = Total Utility of n units, Xi = Utility of i_{th} unit

Σ = is the notation of the sum total, n = Total number of units consumed.

Marginal utility, on the other hand, is defined as the change in total utility resulting from a one unit change in consumption of the commodity per unit of time. In other words, marginal utility is the additional utility which a person derives from a small addition to his stock of the commodity in question. Thus, the marginal utility of *n* units of commodity *X* is the difference between the total utility of *n* units and the total utility of *n*–1 units of the commodity, symbolically,

$$MUn = Tun{-}TUn{-}1$$

2. After attaining the saturation point, if the consumer is forced to consume more of the same commodity, it will cause his total utility to decrease. The study of the segment of the total utility curve beyond the saturation point is of no importance for our purposes.

where MUn = Marginal utility of n units
TUn = Total utility of n units
$TUn-1$ = Total utility of $n-1$ units

The marginal utility of any quantity can also be stated as the slope of the total utility curve for the same quantity. Mathematically,

$$MU = \frac{d(TU)}{dX} = \text{Slope of total utility curve.}$$

Since marginal utility defined as an increase in the total utility due to the consumption of an additional unit of a commodity, total utility will increase till the marginal utility remains positive or $\frac{d(TU)}{dX} > 0$. When marginal utility becomes negative, or $\frac{d(TU)}{dX} < 0$, total utility will decrease. When marginal utility is equal to zero, or $\frac{d(TU)}{dX} = 0$, total utility becomes maximum. Table 8.1 and Fig. 8.1 show the relations between total utility and marginal utility. Table 8.1 indicates that the total utility is nothing but the sum of the marginal utilities.

Table 8.1: Total Utility and Marginal Utility

Units of Commodity X	*Total Utility (TU)*	*Marginal Utility (MU)*
0	0	—
1	40	40
2	75	35
3	95	20
4	105	10
5	105	0
6	95	–10
7	75	–20

In Fig. 8.1, the upper part shows thc total utility curve and the lower part of the figure displays only the increases in total utility, *i.e.* the marginal utilities of different units of the commodity. The slope of total utility curve at a point is the gain of utility at that point and is equal to the height of the marginal utility curve at the corresponding quantity of the commodity. When the total utility curve reaches the maximum at point *E,* its slope becomes zero as shown by the horizontal line *AB* that is tangent at the maximum point *E*. Marginal utility is zero when total utility is a maximum. Further, when total utility is declining, its increases are negative, which is something as stating that marginal utility is negative.

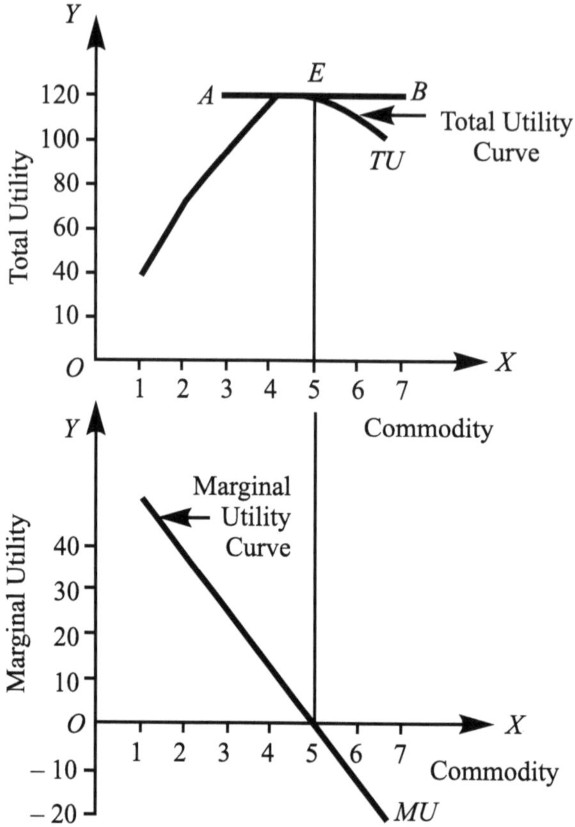

Fig. 8.1

The economic meaning of zero marginal utility is that the consumer has all that he desires of the commodity. Also, he would not care if he loses a unit of the commodity *(MU = O)*. In our diagram the 5th unit that is marginal unit whose marginal utility is zero and therefore, the consumer will buy 4 units of the commodity. In Fig. 8.1, we have assumed that the units are divisible and therefore, the *TU* curve and the *MU* curve are presented in smooth lines. The important relations are summarized in Table 8.2.

Table 8.2

Total Utility	*Marginal Utility*
1. Increasing at an increasing rate	increasing
2. Increasing at a constant rate	constant
3. Increasing at a decreasing rate	decreasing
4. Becomes constant	zero
5. Decreasing	negative

Importance of the Concept of Marginal Utility

The concept of marginal utility is of extreme importance in economic theory, particularly in price theory. With the help of this, price of a commodity is determined in the market. Consumers do not pay more price than its marginal utility that they derive from the use of that commodity. As we know that an individual demands a particular commodity because of the satisfaction or utility he receives from consuming it. When he consumes more units of the same, the marginal utility diminishes. Thus the individual will not be ready to pay a price higher than the marginal utility of the commodity. This fact explains why certain prices are higher than other prices. Commodities which provide higher marginal utility can be sold at higher price.

The concept of marginal utility is helpful in explaining the *diamond-water paradox* — is more useful than diamond but diamond is more costly than water. The price of a commodity is related to its marginal utility. Water being available in plenty commands no price. This is because relative importance of water brings down its marginal utility to zero. While, on the other hand, diamonds being scarce have a very high marginal utility and have a high price.

6. Law of Diminishing Marginal Utility

The law of diminishing utility is a generalisation deduced from observations of human nature. As we get more and more of a commodity, the want for that commodity diminishes. The want of a thirsty man for water is very strong, but after he takes one glass of water, his intensity of desire for another glass of water becomes less. This tendency towards diminishing utilities from successive doses of the same commodity is operative in all types of commodities and services. The rate of diminishing utility may be slow for some commodities, or rapid for others, but the tendency is still operative and a point will come when further additions of the commodity would yield no utility at all. This generalisation is known as the law of diminishing marginal utility. This law has been stated by Boulding as follows:

"As a consumer increases the consumption of anyone commodity, keeping constant the consumption of all other commodities, the marginal utility of the variable commodity must eventually decline."[3]

According to Marshall, the law of satiable wants or of diminishing (marginal) utility can be defined in the following words :

".... the additional benefit (marginal utility) which a person derives from a given increase of his stock of a thing, diminishes with every increase in the stock he already has."[4]

3. Boulding, K.E., *Economic Analysis,* 1950, p. 616
4. Marshall, *Principles of Economics,* p. 79.

Translating the law of diminishing marginal utility in terms of price, Marshall argued that the price a person is willing to pay rather than go without a thing, would also diminish with every increase in its stock. For example, we may assume that a person will be just willing to pay $20 for one pair of shoes. Then $20 measures the marginal utility of one pair of shoes to him. The second pair of shoes will give him less satisfaction than the first and hence, he is ready to pay less price for it, say $15. Now $15 measures the marginal utility of the second pair of shoes. Similarly, for the successive pairs of shoes he will offer lower and lower prices, until a point will come when he will refuse to purchase any more pairs of shoes.

Prof. William J. Baumol expressed the law in another way. According to him, when we have only a little of a particular commodity, we put it to the most urgent use. As we get more and more of it, we begin to putting it to less urgent uses. It happens so because we give priority to more highly valued uses. If we have only one piece of cake we give it to our child; if we have two we give the second to our wife, a third we keep for ourselves and a fourth we give to our mother-in-law (assuming that mother-in-law lives with family).[5]

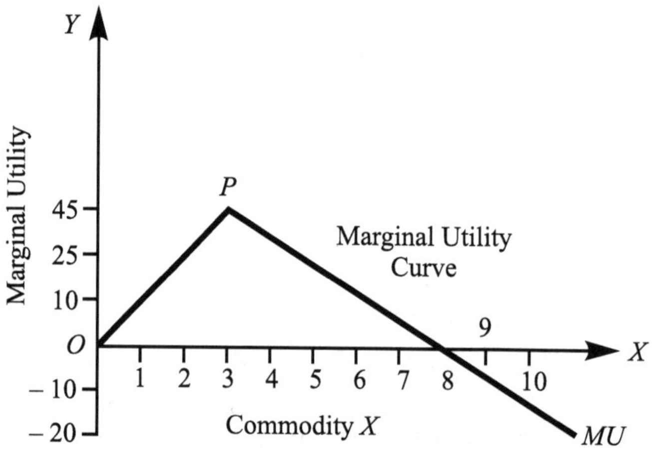

Fig. 8.2

Thus, the marginal utility of a commodity diminishes as its quantity increases. But it is possible that, in the first stage of consumption, intensity of our desire may increase. In such a situation marginal utility will increase and as a result, total utility will increase at an increasing rate. But a situation will certainly appear when the law of diminishing marginal utility will become operative.

5. William J. Baumol, *Economic Theory and Operations Analysis,* 3rd Edition, p. 205.

Fig. 8.2 explains that the consumer gets higher marginal utility from the second unit of the commodity than the first one. The third unit still yields more utility, but thereafter from the fourth unit of the commodity the marginal utility starts declining.

Also, the marginal utility of the eighth unit is zero and no rational consumer would like to consume the commodity after this level, even if the commodity is available tree of cost. As we observe that the 9th and the 10th units of the commodity yield negative marginal utilites, i.e. the total utility will decline from the successive consumption of the commodity. As a practical matter no consumer will reach the saturation point (where total utility is maximum and marginal utility is equal to zero) for any good that commands a price, except by accident. Thus, the negative slope of the marginal utility curve explains the law of diminishing marginal utility. This law is applicable only under certain assumptions.

Assumptions of the Law

The main assumptions of the law of diminishing marginal utility are the following:

(*i*) *The units of the commodity must be relevantly defined.* The law of diminishing marginal utility holds only if the units of a commodity are relevantly defined. For example, the law holds for pairs of shoes but not for a single shoe. An unit must be complete for its consumption or use.

(*ii*) *The tastes are given and unchanged.* The law holds for individual commodities wanted by individual consumers with given tastes. If the taste of a consumer changes, so that he likes a commodity more, then the marginal utility of the commodity in question increases.

(*iii*) *The units of the commodity are homogeneous.* All the units of a commodity must be the same in all respects, i.e. in size and quality, etc. If the units are no homogeneous then the law will not hold.

(*iv*) *There in no time-lag between the consumption of the two units of a commodity.* The law holds only when the process of consumption is continuous without any time-interval. For example, if a consumer drinks three glasses of water at a time. Then the marginal utility of each will decline. But if he drinks the second glass and third glass of water at an interval of two hours, then the marginal utility of these glasses of water will rather increase; thus the law fails.

(*v*) *The income and prices of the commodity and its substitutes are given.* If the price decreases or income increases, then the consumer will buy more of the commodity. Also, if the price of substitutes falls, the consumer will buy more quantity of the commodity in question and the law fails.

Hence, for the law of diminishing marginal utility to hold, the above conditions must exist.

Exceptions to the Law of Diminishing Marginal Utility

In fact, there is no real exception to the law of diminishing marginal utility. But some exceptions arise when we misinterpret the law. The following are the important exceptions to the law.

(*i*) There are certain groups of commodities, the marginal utility of which does not diminish with every increase in the stock of them. In the collection of curios and antiques, stamps, old paintings, coins, etc. the law of diminishing marginal utility does not hold. A person may desire the additional units of the curios articles, or stamps with increasing intensity. But according to Prof. Viner,[6] this is no exception to the law; if we take a complete set as the proper unit of observation. For instance, if there are known to be in existence two pearls of the same type, these two should be taken as one unit. The addition of pearls of the same type to this unit will yield diminishing utility. In other words, a person will not pay higher prices in acquiring the same type of stamps or coins. Therefore, it is not a real exception to the law of diminishing marginal utility.

(*ii*) It is said that the law of diminishing marginal utility does not hold in the consumption of liquor. The additional doses of liquor will yield increasing marginal utility to a drinker. But this argument is not correct because a drinker is not a rational consumer and we do not study his irrational behaviour in economics.

(*iii*) It is said that the law fails when there is a large number of consumers to consume a commodity. The marginal utility of one set of telephone, for example, rises with increasing use of telephones.[7] Similar is the case with fashion or style commodities. But the law still remains true with regard to those commodities that at any given period of time, given the extent of the use of the commodity, the marginal utility of additional units diminishes. For instance, we may imagine a situation when all the families of a city possess telephone facility; then it is certain that an additional set of telephone will yield lessened satisfaction to the same family.

(*iv*) It is also said that the law does not apply to money. A person gets increasing marginal utilities from additional amounts of money. This is particularly true in the case of a miser. But in the long run, the law will also apply to the miser. Moreover, the miser is not assumed to be a rational man and therefore, his activities are not studied in economics.

The above exceptions are not real and hence the law of diminishing marginal utility is the universal law applicable in all cases of consumption. According to Taussig, "The tendency shows itself so widely and with so few exceptions that there is no serious inaccuracy in speaking of it as universal. The law of

---

6. Viner, "The Utility Concept in Economic Theory", *Journal of Political Economy,* 1925.
7. Chapman, *Outlines of Political Economy,* p. 32.

diminishing marginal utility is of paramount importance, because it is the basis of the law of demand, and provides adequate reason for the negative slope of the demand curve.

Criticisms of the Law of Diminishing Marginal Utility

Like the other laws of economics, the law of diminishing marginal utility is subject to the following limitations:

(*i*) The law of diminishing marginal utility holds only if "other things remain the same", i.e. the habits, tastes, temperament and income of the consumer do not change. If any of the thing change, the law may not be true. In real life, these things are changing.

(*ii*) The law may not operate in the initial stages of consumption, i.e. for very small increments of the commodity. If thirsty person is offered water in teaspoons, the utility he gets from the second teaspoon of water will be greater than that from the first one.

(*iii*) This law assumes no time-gap in the consumption of various units of a commodity. In practical life it is not necessary that all the units of a commodity are consumed at a time.

(*iv*) This law assumes utility measurable in terms of money. Marshall took this assumption for analytical purposes, but modern economists criticise this assumption. According to them, utility is a subjective concept and its quantitative measurement is not possible.

In spite of these limitations, the law of diminishing marginal utility assumes a great theoretical and practical importance.

Importance of the Law of Diminishing Marginal Utility

The law of diminishing marginal utility possesses the following points of importance:

(*i*) *Basis of the law of demand.* The law of diminishing marginal utility is one of the fundamental laws of economics. The basic law of demand is based on this law. The law of demand states that more amounts of a commodity will be purchased at a relatively lower price. The reason for this is that as more and more units of a commodity are purchased and consumed, its marginal utility to the consumers becomes less and less. And the consumer will be ready to pay the price of a commodity just equal to its marginal utility (or $MU_i = P_i$).Therefore, the additional units of a commodity will be purchased only at a lower price. The law of demand, thus, has been directly based on the law of diminishing marginal utility.

(*ii*) *Basis of the progressive tax-policy.* The government can formulate a progressive tax-policy on the basis of the law of diminishing marginal utility. Adam Smith emphasized the canon of "ability to pay tax" which was later presented in terms of marginal utility of money by Prof. Pigou.They argued that the marginal utility of money or wealth is more for the poor than for the rich. This is the reason why the rich have to pay tax at a progressive rate and the poor at a lower rate.

(*iii*) *Basis of the policy of redistribution of wealth.* The government's public expenditure policy is also based on the law of diminishing marginal utility. The government's tax-cum-expenditure policy helps in transferring the purchasing power from richer to the poorer classes. It leads to an equi-distribution of wealth in the society.

(*iv*) *Determination of optimum level of consumption.* This law helps in the determination of the optimum level of consumption. It is attained at a point where the marginal utility of the commodity equals its price. We shall discuss this concept in the following section of this chapter.

7. The Law of Equi-marginal Utility

To solve the problems of a consumer which we have discussed in the beginning of the chapter, Marshall gave his famous Principle of Equi-Marginal Utility. The law of equi-marginal utility is also known as the law of substitution, or the law of economy in expenditure, or the law of maximum satisfaction or the principle of income allocation, etc. Marshall defined this law in the following manner:

"If a person has a thing which he can put to several uses, he will distribute it among these uses in such a way that it has the same marginal utility in all. For, if it had a greater marginal utility in one use than another he would gain by taking away some of it from the second use and applying it to the first."[8]

Thus, a consumer attains maximum total utility from his available resources (income) only when the marginal utilities of all the goods consumed are equal. Symbolically,

$$MU_1 = MU_2 = MU_3 = \ldots MUn \qquad \ldots(1)$$

where MUi indicates the marginal utility of the ith commodity and $i = 1, 2, \ldots n$.

Marshall stated that in a barter economy, equalization of marginal utilities is not possible, because there i no common measurement of value. In a money economy, price becomes a common denominator of value. Hence, the law of equi-marignal utility is useful only in money economy. If the prices of all the commodities are equal, the consumer attains maximum total utility... when $MU_1 = MU_2 = MU_3 = \ldots = MUn$. If prices (Pi) of various goods are different, then the consumer will attain maximum total utility only when the following condition holds:

8. *Alfred Marshall, op. cit.*, p. 98.

$$\frac{MU_1}{P_1} = \frac{MU_2}{P_2} = \frac{MU_3}{P_3} ..... = \frac{MUn}{Pn} \qquad ...(2)$$

Assumptions of the Law

The law of equi-marginal utility is based on the following assumptions:

(*i*) Utility is measurable in terms of money.

(*ii*) The income of the consumer is limited and remains constant.

(*iii*) There is perfect competition in the market. It means that the consumer is unable to change the price of those commodities which he consumes. The consumer has to accept the market prices in the determination of his budget.

(*iv*) The marginal utility of money remains constant.

(*v*) The utility schedule of a commodity is independent of the utility schedules of the other commodities.

(*vi*) The law of diminishing marginal utility holds.

On the basis of above assumptions, the law of equi-marginal utility can be explained clearly with the help of an example. Suppose that the consumer purchases two commodities commodity *X* and commodity *Y* the prices of which are P_x and P_y respectively. As long as P_x and P_y are fixed or constant, a dollar's worth of *X* or a dollar's worth of *Y* represents a certain quantity (utility) of *X* or of *Y*. Suppose, that the consumer's marginal utility schedules for *X* and *Y* are those of Table 8.3.[9]

Now the question is as to how should the consumer allocate his income between *X* and *Y*? Here we suppose that the consumer has an income of $10. The consumer will spend his first dollar on commodity *X*, because it gives him 50 units of utility which is the highest in his utility schedule of Table 8.3. Now the consumer also spends his second dollar on commodity *X* which will increase his total utility by 45 units; whereas, if instead he spends it on *Y*, it would increase total utility by 38 units only. Hence, the second dollar will be spent on *X*. Similarly, the third dollar will also be spent on *X*. But the 4th

9. Here we assume that the marginal utility schedule of each commodity is independent of the level of consumption of the other commodity. It enables us to allocate our income among the two commodities in such a way that leads to maximum satisfaction. If *X* and *Y* were substitutes, the more of *X* consumed, the lower the marginal utility of *Y* would be at various consumption levels of *Y*. If they were complementary, the more of *X* consumed, the higher the marginal utility of *Y* would be at various consumption levels of *Y*.

Table *8.3*

Money Units Spent	*Marginal Utility for Commodity X (MUx)*	*Marginal Utility for Commodity Y (MUy)*
1st Dollar	50 (1)	38 (4)
2nd "	45 (2)	36 (5)
3rd "	40 (3)	32 (7)
4th "	35 (6)	25 (10)
5th "	30 (8)	18
6th "	25 (9)	15
7th "	20	10
8th "	15	5
9th "	10	2
10th "	5	1

dollar will not be spent on *X*, because it will increase his total utility only by 35 units; whereas if it is spent on *Y*, it will increase total utility by 38 units. Thus, the 4th dollar will be spent on *Y*. The 5th dollar will again be spent on *Y*. The 6th on *X*, the 7th on Y and 8th on *X;* and the 9th and 10th, one each on *X* and *Y*. The order in which he spends his $10 on *X* and *Y* commodities is shown in brackets in Table 8.3. In this way, when the consumer spends all his income, he should be enjoying six dollars' worth of commodity *X* and four dollars' worth of commodity *Y*. The marginal utilities of the last dollar spent on *X* and of the last dollar spent on *Y* are equal to 25 units.
In other words,

$$\frac{MU_X}{P_X} = \frac{MU_Y}{P_Y} = 25$$

It satisfies the consumer's objective of getting maximum total utility. In our example, the total utility of $10 spent on *X* and *Y* is equal to the total utility derived from the consumption of commodity *X* plus the total utility derived from the consumption of commodity *Y*, i.e.

$$\begin{aligned} TU_{x+y} &= TU_x + TU_y \\ &= [50 + 45 + 40 + 35 + 30 + 25] + [38 + 36 + 32 + 25] \\ &= 225 + 131 \\ &= 356 \text{ units} \end{aligned}$$

If the consumer disturbs this allocation of income, then he would not be able to secure the maximum total utility from his consumption. For instance, if he transfers his 10th dollar from *Y* to *X*. Now giving up a dollar's worth of *Y* will decrease his total utility by 25 units. The additional dollar's worth of *X* will increase his total utility by 20 units. So that, the transfer results in a net loss of 5 units of utility to his total satisfaction. If the transfer were made from X to Y, the net loss would be equal to 7 units of utility. Hence, no other allocation of consumer's income will yield as much satisfaction as the one set by the law of equi-marginal utility.

The above explanation can also be made with the help of a diagram. In Fig. 8.3, the marginal utility curves for X and Y commodities are MU_x and MU_y respectively. The equilibrium point is E where the marginal utility of X is equal to the marginal utility of Y. At this equilibrium point the consumer will attain maximum satisfaction by spending OM income on commodity X and MO' income on commodity Y. Any other allocation of his limited income OO' on these two commodities will not yield him maximum satisfaction.

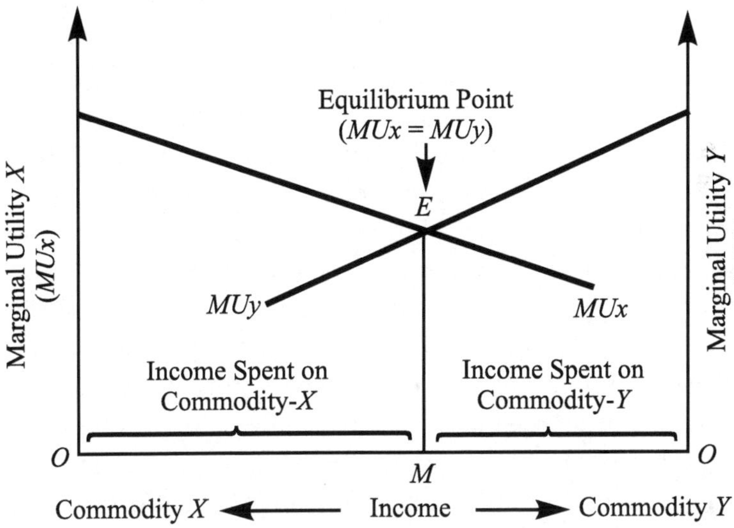

Fig. 8.3

The principle of equi-marginal utility can be extended to as many goods as confront the consumer and is not limited to the two commodities. The first necessary condition for maximising total utility will be

$$\frac{MU_X}{P_X} = \frac{MU_Y}{P_Y} = \frac{MU_Z}{P_Z} \qquad ...(3)$$

If there are only two commodities under the consumption, then the proportionality condition (3) becomes

$$\frac{MU_X}{P_X} = \frac{MU_Y}{P_Y}$$

or

$$\frac{MU_X}{MU_Y} = \frac{P_X}{P_Y} \qquad ...(4)$$

where $\frac{MU_X}{MU_Y}$ = the ratio of the marginal utilities of the two commodities X and Y

$\frac{P_X}{P_Y}$ = the ratio of the prices of the two commodities X and Y.

Thus, in equilibrium, the ratio of their marginal utilities must be equal to the ratio of their prices.

The above necessary condition does not take into account the income restraint under which the consumer operates. Thus, the second sufficient condition of consumer equilibrium can be written as

$$I = XP_X + YP_Y + ZP_Z + \ldots + NP_N \quad \ldots(5)$$

where I represents consumer's income, P_X , P_Y, P_Z .... P_N are the prices of various commodities and X, Y, Z, ...N are the respective quantities bought.

The original law of equi-marginal utility as developed by Prof. Marshall does not assume the second condition of equilibrium to hold, while the modern interpretation of the law of equi-marginal utility is based on this assumption that under the income constraint a consumer will attain maximum satisfaction only if the equality between the ratio of marginal utilities and the ratio of prices exist. Nevertheless, there is no basic difference between the Marshallian concept and modern interpretation of the law of equi-marginal utility. If the prices of all the goods are assumed to be the same, will get similar conclusion from them. Prof. Boulding has represented this law in terms of "weighted marginal utility". In his opinion the weighted marginal utility of a commodity indicates the ratio of its marginal utility to its price. It means that the consumer attains maximum satisfaction only when the weighted marginal utilities of all the goods included in the budget of a consumer are equal. In the words of Prof. Boulding, "The best division of expenditures is that at which the weighted marginal utilities in all lines of expenditure are equal."[10]

Applications or Importance of the Law of Equi-Marginal Utility

The law of equi-marginal utility is of great practical importance in economics. According to Prof. Marshall, the law of equi-marginal utility or returns is a universal law applicable to every branch of economic activity. Some of its important applications are described below.

(*i*) *Determination of an optimum budget.* As we have already discussed, a consumer has unlimited wants and limited means to fulfil them. All the wants are not fulfilled with his limited means. Now, the question before the

10. K.E. Boulding, *Economic Analysis,* Vol. I, *Microeconomics.* Fourth Edition, pp. 527-28.

consumer is as to which commodities should be included in his budget and how much of them should be purchased. The law of equi-marginal utility provides him the answer. According to this law, he distributes his limited income among various commodities in such a way that the last dollar spent on each of them gives equal utility. By doing so, he gets maximum satisfaction, *i.e.* optimises his budget.

(*ii*) *Determination of saving and consumption.* Every consumer has *to* decide how much of his income should be put for saving (i.e. for future consumption) and how much for consumption. In other words, the economists call it the rate of time preference. According to Prof. Marshall, a rational consumer will distribute his resources between his present needs and future needs in such a way that the marginal utility of the last dollar put in saving equals the marginal utility of the last dollar put in consumption. Thus, the law of equi-marginal utility helps the consumer in solving the problem of the allocation of income between consumption and saving.

(*iii*) *Determination of least cost combination of resources.* According to Marshall, the principle of substitution is also used in the field of production.[11] Like a consumer, an entrepreneur also uses his limited factor inputs in the production process in such a way that the marginal product of each factor input becomes equal. He constantly substitutes one factor of production for another, until the marginal returns from all the factors are equal. The modern economists state that the least cost combination off actors of production will be attained at a point when the ratio of their marginal products is equal to the ratio of their prices. Thus, if there are only two factors of production, say labour *(L)* and capital (*K*), then

$$\frac{MP_L}{P_L} = \frac{MP_K}{P_K}$$

or
$$\frac{MP_L}{MP_K} = \frac{P_L}{P_K}$$

where MP_L = Marginal product of labour, MP_K = Marginal product of capital, P_L = Price of labour, P_K = Price of capital

(*iv*) *Expenditure of time.* Prof. Boulding relates the Marshall's law of equi-marginal utility to the expenditure of limited time (24 hours). He states that a person should spend his limited time among alternative uses, in such a way that the marginal utility gained from those uses must be equal, *i.e.* he gets maximum satisfaction. Thus the optimum utilization of time is possible through this law.

11.Marshall, *op. cil.,* pp. 295-99.

(*v*) *Determination of exchange.*[12] The important part of economic activity deals with exchange among individuals. Exchange will take place only when both the parties gain from it. It is the prospect of gain that causes voluntary exchange to occur. This point can be illustrated with the help of utility analysis. Suppose, there are two consumers, *A* and *B*. Each holds the stocks of two commodities, *X* and *Y*. Now suppose, initially (before exchange) for *A*, I unit of *X* equals 2 units of Y and for *B*, I unit of *X* equals two-third units of *Y*. Now exchange will take place, and *A* will exchange *Y* for *X* and *B* will exchange *X* for *Y*. Exchange will continue till *A* gets more than one-half units of *X* for 1 unit of Y and *B* gets more than two-third units of *Y* for 1 unit of *X*. In equilibrium (*i.e.* at a point where exchange stops),

$$\frac{MU_K}{MU_Y} \text{ for } A = \frac{MU_X}{MU_Y} \text{ for } B$$

In such a situation, both the consumers will attain maximum total satisfaction.

Limitations of the Law of Equi-Marginal Utility

The criticisms of this law are based on the unrealistic assumptions that the law assumes in the beginning. The points of criticisms are the following:

(*i*) *The measurement of utility is not possible.* The law assumes that the utility of a commodity is measurable in terms of money. As Prof. Marshall states that the price a consumer is willing to pay for a commodity is its utility for him. But modern economists argue that when two persons are paying equal price for a given commodity, it would not mean that both are getting the same level of utility. Thus, utility is a subjective concept which cannot be measured in quantitative terms.

(*ii*) *Utilities are inter-dependent.* Marshall's law of equi-marginal utility is based on the assumption that commodities are independent, and, therefore, their marginal utilities are also independent. But in real life, we see that commodities are either substitutes or they are complementary. Their utilities are, therefore, inter-dependent.

(*iii*) *The marginal utility of money is not constant.* The law assumes that the marginal utility of money remains constant. But it is not true. The marginal utility of money increases with every decrease in its available stock. Further, the marginal utility of money for a rich person is less than that for a poor person.

(*iv*) *Indivisibility of goods*[13] According to Prof. Boulding, this law is applicable only if commodities (or money, time, etc.) are divisible because the weighted marginal utilities of various commodities in terms of money (MU_x/P_x)

12. Leftwich, *The Price System and Resource Allocation,* Fourth Edition, pp. 66-68.
13. Boulding, *op. cit.,* pp. 530-31.

will be made equal only if the commodities. are purchased in small pieces. But there are certain commodities which are not divisible, such as, a house, a car, a cooler, etc. In such cases, the law of equi-marginal utility will not be applicable.

(v) *Indefinite budget period.*[14] According to Prof Boulding, another difficulty of the law is the indefinite budget period. Normally, one year is assumed to be a budget period. But there are certain commodities under the consumption of a person whose durability (or life) is more than one year. For such commodities, it is difficult to calculate the marginal utility. Thus, the law is not applicable in these situations.

In conclusion, we can say that due to the above criticisms, the Marshall's law of equi-marginal utility is not widely used in practical life. Prof. Hicks and his followers developed a new approach-indifference curve approach-to solve the problem of a consumer. This new approach will be discussed in the next chapter.

Exercises

1. Explain fully the law of diminishing marginal utility. What is the practical importance of this law? Do you think that the law is universally applicable?
2. Define utility. Explain the relationship between total utility and marginal utility with the help of a diagram.
3. State and explain the law of equi-marginal utility. What are its assumptions and limitations? .
4. How does a consumer maximise his total utility function under the utility analysis?
5. Explain the 'law of proportionality' in consumption. Discuss its limitations.
6. Explain the importance of the law of equi-marginal utility. What are its limitations?
7. "The application of the Principle of Substitution extends over almost every field of economic enquiry." (Marshall). Explain this statement.
8. Define utility. Distinguish between marginal utility from total utility. Prove that the total utility of a commodity is maximum only when its marginal utility is zero. Illustrate your answer with the help of a diagram.
9. Explain the law of ideal allocation of income by the consumer.

Multiple Choice Questions

10\. (*i*) Utility is always related to
(*a*) Usefulness (*c*) Profit
(*b*) Want satisfying power (*d*) Maximum returns [*Ans.* (*b*)]

(*ii*) The Cardinal Utility Approach was developed by
(*a*) Marshall (*c*) Fisher
(*b*) Hicks (*d*) Samuelson [*Ans.* (*a*)]

(*iii*) Total Utility is maximum when Marginal Utility is
(*a*) Positive (*c*) Zero
(*b*) Negative (*d*) Maximum [*Ans.* (*c*)]

(*iv*) Marginal Utility (*MU*) is equal to Average Utility (*AU*) when
(*a*) *MU* is maximum (*c*) *AU* is minimum
(*b*) *AU* is maximum (*d*) *MU* is minimum [*Ans.* (*b*)]

14. *Ibid.*

Chapter 9

The Theory of Indifference Curve

1. Introduction

The Marshallian utility analysis suffers from a number of weaknesses. The most important weakness of this old approach was related to its cardinal measurement of utility. To overcome this difficulty the modern economists have developed an alternative approach based on indifference curve analysis. This new indifference curve approach does not deny the existence of utility but makes use of it in a different way. It states that utility is measurable only in principle, but its magnitude cannot be assigned real numbers. In other words, this concept is based on the assumption that utility cannot be measured in absolute terms.

The technique of indifference curve was originally invented by the nineteeth century English economist, F.Y. Edgeworth[1] who employed it to show the possibilities of exchange between two persons; he did not employ indifference curves to explain consumer's demand. About a decade later, Fisher also independently discovered the technique of indifference curves. Prof. Fisher tried to build a theory of consumer's equilibrium based on indifference curves but could not go beyond discussing the question of substitutes and complementary goods. An important point to note is that both Edgeworth and Fisher, the inventors of indifference curves, continued to believe in the cardinal measurement of utility. In 1906, the Italian economist, Vilfredo Pareto[2] modified the 'Edgeworth Technique'. Pareto held that the notion of measurability was not necessary to derive the theorem of demand. He proved that the theorems of demand, which were originally derived from the concept of utility, could be derived from ordinal utility hypothesis represented by indifference curves. Pareto thus rejected the measurability of utility but adopted the principle of complementary goods which, according to him, depended upon the measurability of utility. His whole thinking was, therefore, full of inconsistency.

1. Francis Y. Edgeworth, *Mathematical Physics,* 1881.
2. Vilfredo Pareto, *Manual d' economic politique,* 1908.

Johnson was the next economist who extended the theory of ordinal utility analysis. He stated that variations in quantity demanded as a result of changes in prices and incomes were quite independent of the measurability of utility. He called indifference curves as constant utility curves or simple utility curves. In his own words, "There are no lines in the figure which measure the utility itself. The several utility curves are arranged in a scale of increasing value as we pass to the right and above; and thus the 'distance' (measured arbitrarily) from one curve to another 'indicates' (without measuring) the increase in utility. But this means of measurement does not affect any economic problem. Neither does economist need to know the marginal (rate of) utility of commodity. What is needed is a representation of the ratio of one marginal utility to another. In fact, this ratio is precisely represented by the slope of any point of the utility curve (indifference curve)."

Pareto and Johnson were followed by the Russian economist, E.E. Slutsky, who in an article, published in 1915, further refined the technique of indifference curves. Slutsky consolidated the ideas of ordinal utility hypothesis and demand analysis based upon indifference curves. His utility function was an object of scale of preferences. He did accept the inter-relation of economic utility and psychological utility, but deduced empirical tests of only psychological hypothesis. If the marginal utilities of goods are independent, we can test the hypothesis by the equation it implies. Slutsky assumed that the increment of utility obtained by moving from one combination to another is independent of the path of movement and offers an empirical test of its validity.

The real elaboration of the indifference curves was made by Hicks and Allen. In 1934, J.R. Hicks and R.G.D. Allen wrote an article, 'A Reconstruction of the Theory of Value' in *Economica* (Feb., May 1934) presenting the indifference curve analysis. A detailed treatment of the new approach is to be found in Hicks' famous work entitled, *Value and Capital* published in 1939. The new analysis or the indifference curve analysis is also known as substitution analysis. Here, the diminishing marginal rate of substitution (*MRS*) is the basic concept.

The great merit of indifference curve analysis is that it leads to ordinal measurement of utility. The consumer needs not assign specific amount to the utility he derives from the consumption of a good or a combination of goods. He is simply capable of comparing the different utilities or satisfactions in the sense whether one level of satisfaction is equal to or lower than or higher than another. He cannot determine how much one level of satisfaction is higher or lower than the other. For the purpose of explaining the consumer's behaviour, it is quite sufficient to assume that the consumer is able to rank his preference consistently. Thus, the ordinal measurement of utility has a greater element of realism than the cardinal measurement of utility. It is why the indifference curve analysis is now regarded as superior to the old utility analysis.

Again, indifference curve analysis explains the consumer's behaviour without assuming constant marginal utility of money. Marshall had assumed that the marginal utility of money remains constant where there is a change in the price of a good. In real life, the marginal utility of money does not remain constant. Thus, the old theory leads to contradiction while the indifference curve technique validly derives the demand theorem.

Again, the indifference curve analysis makes greater note of the fact of the price change on the demand of goods by distinguishing between income effect and substitution effect. The new approach divides the price effect into two parts — the substitution effect and the income effect. The distinction between these two effects enables us to gain better understanding of the effect of a price change on the demand for a commodity. Normally, the amount demanded of a commodity rises as a result of the fall in its price, due to two reasons: (*i*) real income rises as a result of, the fall in price, representing income effect; and (*ii*) the goods whose price falls become relatively cheaper than others; therefore, the consumer substitutes it for others, representing substitution effect. In the new approach, income effect is distinguished from the substitution effect by the method of 'compensating variation'.

In this way, it is widely believed that in difference curve analysis is a definite improvement upon the utility analysis.

2. Assumptions of Indifference Curve Analysis

The indifference curve analysis is based on the following important assumptions :

(*i*) *Complete knowledge about the market.* The consumer possesses full knowledge about all matters pertaining to his consumption decisions. For example, he knows the complete range of goods and services available in the market. He also knows the technical capacity of each commodity to satisfy his want. He possesses the information regarding the prices of various goods and services.

(*ii*) *Entire income is spent on consumption.* The budget constraints of a consumer are the given prices of different goods and services and the constant income of the consumer. If Y is defined as the consumer's money income, then the constraints can be written in the following manner:

$$Y = \sum_{i=1}^{n} piqi$$

where pi and qi refer to the price and quantity of the ith commodity respectively. Under the budget constraint, we have assumed that the consumer spends his entire income to attain his objective of maximising satisfaction.

(*iii*) *Scale of preference can be expressed.* Every consumer has a scale of ordered preferences which enables him to compare any two combinations of two or more goods and to decide whether or not a given combination of any two goods, say Q_1 and Q_2, is preferred, not preferred or equivalent to any other combination of Q_1 and Q_2. Naturally, he can indicate when between two particular combinations of goods he is *indifferent,* i.e. likes them equally. It must be noted that indifference in this context does not mean indecision. It only implies that the consumer assigns the same rank order to both the combinations of goods.

The taste of the consumer can therefore be described with the ideas of preference and indifference. If he can choose between two goods or combinations of goods, he always prefers one to the other or else he is indifferent. Here we observe that the only assumption is that the consumer prefers or is indifferent. Why he prefers can be left out of it ? And so can by how much the consumer prefers. This last is the assumption omitted in the indifference curve analysis and is not needed.[3]

(*iv*) *Preference towards a combination of goods.* The indifference curve analysis assumes that the consumer is not interested in anyone commodity at a particular time as asserted by the utility analysis, but he is interested in a combination of goods and services. He is able to compare the total satisfaction derived by one particular combination of goods with that given by other.

(*v*) *Rational behaviour.* The indifference curve analysis also assumes that the consumer acts in a rational manner.

(*vi*) *Falling marginal rate of substitution.* The marginal rate of substitution of one commodity for another is always falling.

3. Meaning of Indifference Curves

A consumer possesses a definite scale of preferences for goods and services. Each scale of preference consists of a number of alternative combinations of two or more goods, which give the consumer the same amount of satisfaction, so that if he chooses any out of many alternative combinations, he is neither better nor worse off. He is, therefore, found indifferent towards these various

3. Consumers often experience difficulty in making choices. Suppose that the consumer prefers *A* to *B* and *B* to C, but it is harder to make the choice of *A* over *B* than of *B* over *C*. It then can be hypothesised that the difference of (cardinal) utility between *A* and *B* is less than between *B* and C. Consumers are also sometimes inconsistent. Suppose a consumer chooses *A* over *B* by 70 per cent of the time, and *B* over C, 90 per cent of the time. Here again it can be argued that the difference of (cardinal) utility between *A* and *B* is less than between *B* and C.
Thus, to make the choices (or selection) consistent, we assume that if

$A > B$

and $B \sim C$ (in place of $B > C$)

then $A > C$

when the symbol $\sim$ shows indifference between the two situations.

combinations. Such combinations of commodities as between which an individual is indifferent are called *indifference combinations.*

On the basis of above description one can think of combinations of numerous commodities which yield an equal level of satisfaction to the consumer. For convenience we assume that there are only two commodities under consumption. The points of indifference, at a particular level of satisfaction, when joined together produce a curve which is known as the indifference curve. In other words, *an indifference curve* is *a locus or path indicating different combinations of commodities X* and *Y which yield an equal level of satisfaction.* An indifference curve is also known as an isoutility or satisfaction curve.

For the purpose of drawing an indifference curve, we require an indifference schedule. An indifference schedule may be defined as a schedule of various combinations of the two commodities that will equally be acceptable to the consumer. According to Prof. Watson, "An indifference schedule is a list of combinations of two commodities, the list being so arranged that a consumer is indifferent to the combinations, preferring none of any others."[4]

An imaginary indifference schedule is given in Table 9.1.

Table *9.1:* Indifference Schedule

Combinations	*Quantity of X*		*Quantity of Y*		*Total Satisfaction*
I	1 *X*	+	20 *Y*	=	Z
II	2 *X*	+	12 *Y*	=	Z
III	3 *X*	+	7 *Y*	=	Z
IV	4 *X*	+	4 *Y*	=	Z
V	5 *X*	+	3 *Y*	=	Z

In Table 9.1, five different combinations of *X* and *Y* commodities are given. By definition all these combinations give the consumer the same level of total satisfaction Z. Thus, the consumer is indifferent as to whether he gets the first combination of 1 unit of *X* + 20 units of *Y*, or the second combination of 2 units of *X* + 12 units of *Y*, or the last fifth combination of 5 units of *X* + 3 units of *Y*. We find from the indifference schedule that, while the quantity of *X* is increasing, that of *Y* is diminishing. This is true because the consumer has to remain at the same level of total satisfaction. When the consumer is at the second combination, he is less eager to keep commodity *Y* than when he is lower down on the fifth combination. That is why, he is willing to surrender 8 units of *Y* for 1 unit of *X* in the former position and only

4. D.S. Watson, *Price Theory and Its Uses,* p. 77.

1 unit of *Y* for 1 unit of *X* in the latter position. But in all cases he derives the same total satisfaction. We have discussed only one indifference schedules but there may be a number of indifference schedules of the two commodities. The various indifference scheflu les may represent different levels of total satisfaction yielded by a consumer.

Now, if the indifference schedule is plotted on a graph and the various points of combinations are joined by a curve, then the resulting curve is the indifference curve [see Fig. 9.1(A)]. Several other indifference curves can be drawn on the same principle. They will represent different levels of total satisfaction. But all points on any indifference curve, must represent the same level of satisfaction. Also, the higher the indifference curve, the more will be the level of satisfaction. It is because of the fact that as the consumer shifts to the right from one indifference curve to another, he gets more of one or both the commodities. For example, in Fig. 9.1 (B) at point *C* on indifference curve IC_2, he gets the same units of *Y* as at point *f* on indifference curve IC_1 but more units of commodity *X*. Thus, point C is preferred to *point f*.

From the above description, it is clear that an indifference curve shows nothing about the absolute amount of satisfaction or utility derived by the consumer. It merely shows the various combinations which will give equal satisfaction to the consumer. In fact indifference curve is a curve showing equal satisfaction in different combinations of goods. Every point given on indifference curve represents a different combination. It is, therefore, a matter of indifference for the consumer whether he chooses one combination or the other. The consumer is found as indifferent between all such combinations, which represent the same level of satisfaction.

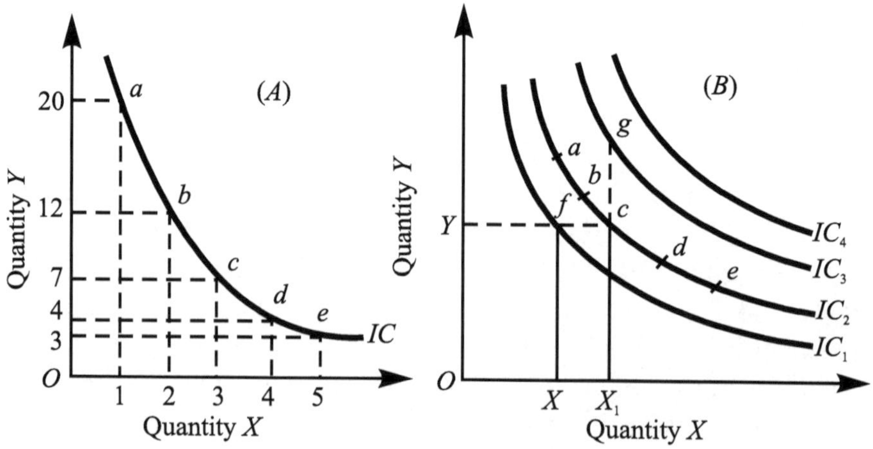

Fig. 9.1

A family of indifference curves is known as *indifference map.* In Fig. 9.1 (B) we represent an indifference map of four indifference curves IC_1, IC_2, IC_3, and IC_4. The indifference curve, labelled higher number, is preferred to one labelled lower number. In the words of Stonier and Hague, "An indifference curve is, thus like a counter line on a map which shows all places at the same height above sea level. Instead of representing height, each indifference curve represents a level of satisfaction. It is, however, quite impossible to measure levels of satisfaction in the way that one can measure heights above sea level. There are obviously no units of measurement. One can say whether one indifference curve represents a higher or lower level of satisfaction than another, but one cannot say by how much satisfaction is higher or lower."[5]

Thus, it must be noted that though by definition, every combination of *X* and *Y* on indifference curve IC_2 is preferred to every other combination of *X* and *Y* on indifference curve IC_1, there may be infinite number of indifference curves in between, and by definition, all of them will also be preferred to IC_1.[6]

4. Marginal Rate of Substitution (MRS)

According to Leftwich, "The marginal rate of substitution of *X* for *Y* (MRS_{XY}) is defined as the amount of *Y* the consumer is just willing to give up to get an additional unit of *X* (and still remain on the same in difference curve)."[7]

Table 9.2 explains the concept of diminishing marginal rate of substitution. To get a second unit of *X*, the consumer is ready to give up 8 units of *Y*. For a third unit of *X*, he can give up the consumption of only 5 units of *Y*; for a fourth unit of *X*, he is ready to sacrifice only 3 units of *Y* and for a fifth unit of *X*, he will sacrifice only one unit of *Y*. It means that, as the consumer gets

Table 9.2

Combinations	*Quantity of X (in units)*		*Quantity of Y (in units)*	*Marginal Rate of Substitution* (MRS_{XY})
I	1 *X*	+	20 *Y*	—
II	2 *X*	+	12 *Y*	1 *X* = 8 *Y*
III	3 *X*	+	7 *Y*	1 *X* = 5 *Y*
IV	4 *X*	+	4 *Y*	1 *X* = 3 *Y*
V	5 *X*	+	3 *Y*	1 *X* = 1 *Y*

5. Stonier and Hague, *A Textbook of Economic Theory*, p. 45.
6. In general, an indifference curve can be represented on the basis of (ordinal) utility function as

$$U = f(x.\ y)$$

where *U* is a constant. An indifference map is generated by assigning different values to *U*.
7. Richard H. Leftwich, *The Price System and Resource Allocation*, 4th edition, p. 72.

more and more units of X; he is willing to surrender fewer and fewer units of Y for each additional unit of X. This because of the fact that the importance of good X in terms of Y goes on falling with each addition to his total of the former (good X). This feature of the consumer's behaviour is known as the *principle of diminishing marginal rate of substitution.*

As mentioned above, a consumer gets the same level of satisfaction along a given indifference curve. It means that an increase in the quantity of commodity X is always accompanied by a similar decrease in the quantity of commodity Y and thus the marginal rate of substitution must be negative. Symbolically,

$$MRS_{XY} = -\frac{\Delta Y}{\Delta X} \qquad \text{... (1)}$$

Where ΔX represents change in X and ΔY represents change in Y.

Equation (1) represents the slope of indifference curve at a particular point. Since each addition in X leads Y to diminish less and less, the numerical value of the slope of indifference curve also goes on falling. This situation has been shown in Fig. 9.2.

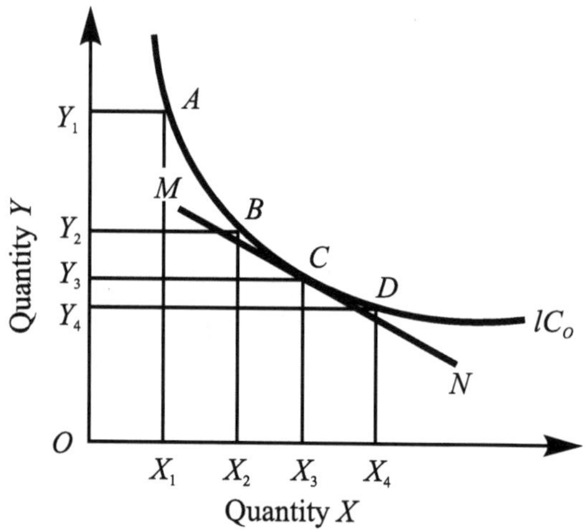

Fig. 9.2

In Fig. 9.2, the total satisfaction remains constant between combination point A, B , C, and D on indifference curve IC_0. However, the composition of commodity X and commodity Y changes while the consumer moves from point A to B, B to C and C to D. According to Prof. Hicks, the gain in utility got by consuming more of X is equal to the change in the quantity of X (ΔX or dX) multiplied by the marginal utility of X. Again, he states that this gain in utility must be equal to the loss in utility resulting from a negative change in the quantity of Y (ΔY or dY) multiplied by the marginal utility of Y. Thus, we may write

$$U = f(X, Y)$$

and $$dU = f_1\, dX + f_2\, dY = O \quad ...(2)$$

where dU represents the change in total utility, U (satisfaction), f_1 and f_2 are the marginal utilities of X and Y respectively.

Also, from (2) we get

$$f_1\, dX = f_2\, dY$$

or $$\frac{f_1}{f_2} = -\frac{dY}{dX}$$

or $$\frac{f_1}{f_2} = -\frac{dY}{dX} = MRS_{XY} \quad ...(3)$$

where by equation (1), $-dY/dX$ is the marginal rate of substitution. For a marginal increment of X in Fig. 9.2, $-dY/dX$ can be interpreted as the slope of the indifference curve IC_0 by the tangent MN at point C. Thus, MRS_{XY} is nothing but the slope of an indifference curve. It is also clear from equation (3) that MRS_{XY} measures the ratio of the marginal utility of Y to the marginal utility of X. This implies that MRS and marginal utility are similar concepts. According to Prof. Hicks, although utility is not measurable, we may still give a precise meaning to the ratio of the marginal utilities, when the quantities of both the commodities are given. In his opinion, this quantity is represented by the slope of an indifference curve; and the slope of indifference curve represents the ratio of the marginal ulitity.[8]

5. Properties or Characteristics of Indifference Curves

There are five basic properties or characteristics of indifference curves:

(*i*) Indifference curves have a negative slope,

(*ii*) Indifference curves are convex to the origin,

(*iii*) Indifference curves never intersect,

(*iv*) Indifference curves need not be parallel to each other, and

(*v*) A higher indifference curve is always preferred to a lower one.

Now we shall discuss in detail the above properties of indifference curves in the following manner:

(*i*) *Indifference curves have* a *negative slope.* It means that each indifference curve slopes downward from left to the right as shown in Fig. 9.3 (*a*). The negative slope implies that if the consumer is to attain the same level of satisfaction, then for an increase in the stock of one commodity he is required to forgo certain units of the other commodity. As stated above, in utility terms

$$f_1 dX = f_2(-dY)$$

8. J.R. Hicks, *Value and Capital,* pp. 19-20.

or $$\frac{f_1}{f_2} = \frac{dY}{dX}$$

which is nothing but the negative slope of indifference curve.

To put it differently, if an indifference curve does not have a negative slope, then the three possible situations may be that: (*i*) it is horizontal to *X* axis, or (*ii*) it is vertical to *X* axis, or (*iii*) it may have a positive slope. These three inconceivable situations are shown in Fig. 9.3 (*b*), 9.3 (*c*) and 9.3 (*d*) respectively. If we are able to disprove these three possibilities, then the only true situation of indifference curve is its downward sloping represented in Fig. 9.3 (*a*).

Suppose, an indifference curve is a horizontal line as shown in Fig. 9.3 (*b*). As the consumer moves from point *A* to *B* an increase in the quantity of *X* is unaccompanied by any change in the quantity of *Y*, and thus the consumer gets more satisfaction at point *B* than at point *A* on the same indifference curve. But, by definition, this would not be the true situation of indifference curve.

Now suppose an indifference curve is a vertical line as shown in Fig. 9.3 (*c*). Here also, as the consumer moves from point *A* to *B*, the amount of *X* remaining the same while the amount of *Y* decreases and therefore, the consumer gets more satisfaction at point *A* than at point *B*. In this situation too, total satisfaction (utility) changes with every movement along the curve and hence, by definition, this will not be the true shape of an indifference curve.

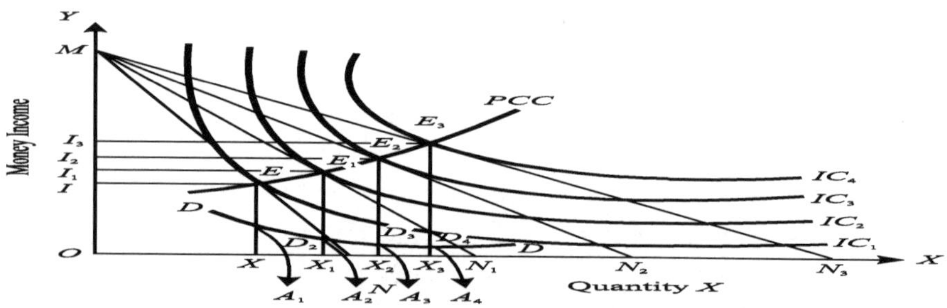

Fig. 9.3

Finally we assume that an indifference curve is a positively sloping curve as shown in Fig. 9.3 (d). Here, as the consumer moves from point *A* to *B*, the quantity of both the commodities decreases and thus the consumer gets more satisfaction at point *A* than at point *B*. Hence, by definition, we also reject this case.

Now, we are also to say that in neither of the three cases (horizontal, vertical and upward sloping curves), the consumer remains *indifferent* between two points and in such cases he is not substituting one commodity for another. But in a true case he must substitute one commodity for another, because his total satisfaction remains the same. Only on a curve that slopes downwards to the right, this requirement is fulfilled. Therefore, indifference curve must slope downward from left to the right.

(*ii*) *Indifference curves are convex to the origin.* This is an important property of an indifference curve which can be derived from the *law of diminishing marginal rate of substitution.* Convexity implies that the consumer is prepared to sacrifice decreasing quantities of *Y* for each given increment in the quantity of *X*. In other words, the greater the number of units of *X* that are acquired, the smaller will be the number of units of *Y* that will be substituted to maintain the given level of satisfaction.

If marginal rate of substitution is constant, the indifference curve would be a straight line and if it is increasing, then the indifference curve would be a concave. In real world, the *MRS* is neither constant nor increasing, but it is diminishing as we move from left to right. Since the principle of diminishing marginal rate of substitution holds in real life, we may explain it with the help of a convex indifference curve as in Fig. 9.4.

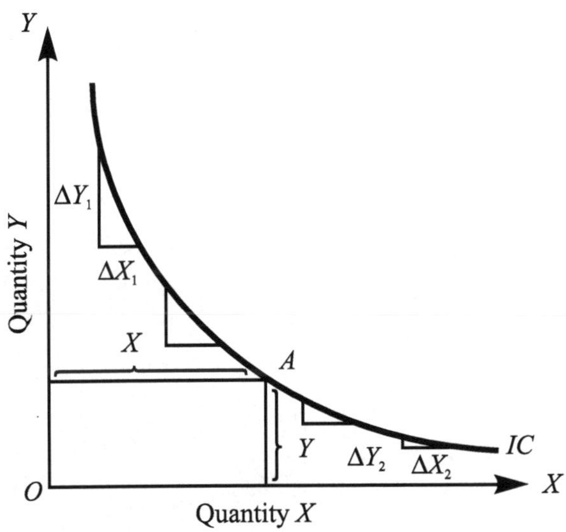

Fig. 9.4

At the top of the curve, the consumer gives up ΔY_1 of *Y* for ΔX_1 of *X* as he slides down the curve. Here the consumer has lots of *Y* and not much of *X;* hence, he is willing to forgo ΔY_1 units of *Y* to get ΔX_1 units of *X*. Thus, the length ΔY_1 is greater than the length ΔX_1 at the top of the curve. But as the consumer moves down to the right of the curve, the relative quantities of *X* and *Y* change. In Fig. 9.4, the distance ΔX is uniform for each time. The lengths of the lines ΔY become shorter and shorter as the consumer moves to the right of the curve *IC*. This signifies that when the consumer has lots of *X* and not much of Y, he will be ready to sacrifice a little of Y to get the same number of units of X. As we see in Fig. 9.4, how short is the length of ΔY_2 at the bottom of the curve IC. Thus, it proves the principle of diminishing marginal rate of substitution $\left(\frac{\Delta Y}{\Delta X}\right)$, and an indifference curve is always convex to the origin. But the degree of convexity of an indifference curve depends upon the ease or difficulty of substitution between the two goods.

(*iii*) *Indifference curves never intersect.* We know that each indifference curve represents a particular level of satisfaction and, therefore, it must be different from other indifference curves. To prove the property that two indifference curves never cut each other, let us assume a situation where the two cut each other as shown in Fig. 9.5. In Fig. 9.5 indifference curve IC_1 cuts indifference curve IC_2 at point A. Now we take a point B on IC_1 which gives lower satisfaction than a point C on IC_2. But by definition of indifference curve we may write the following equality:

On IC_1, $A = B$
On IC_2, $A = C$
then $B = C$ ...(4)

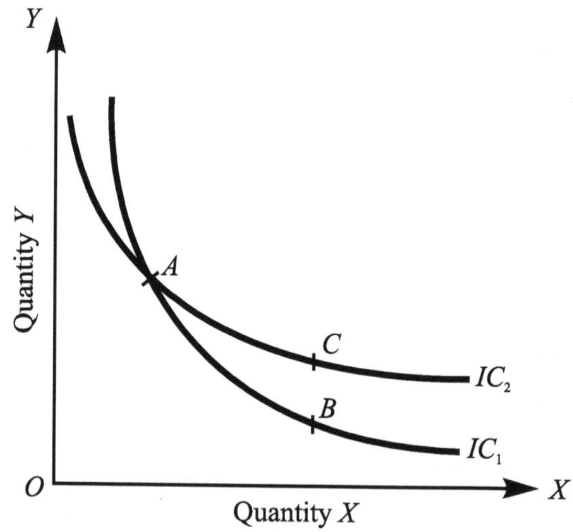

Fig. 9.5

Now, mathematically the equality (4) should hold, but as stated above, point B lies on IC_1 while point C lies on IC_2 and, therefore, the two levels of satisfaction are unequal. The equality (4) is clearly impossible and, therefore, indifference curves can never intersect each other.

(*iv*) *Indifference curves need not be parallel to each other.* As we have noted, indifference curves have a negative slope and the marginal rate of substitution between the two commodities need not be the same in all indifference curves. It depends upon consumer's preference which may change according to his economic position. Thus, it follows that indifference curves may be parallel or may not be parallel as the situation may be. Fig. 9.6 indicates that some indifference curves are parallel while some others are not parallel.

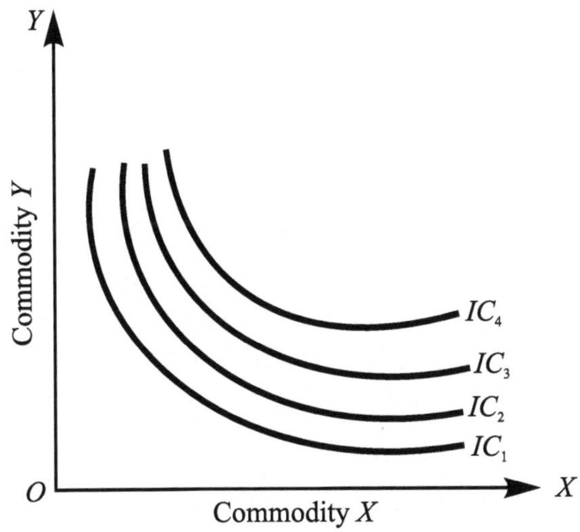

Fig. 9.6

(*v*) *A higher indifference curve is always preferred to a lower one.* We have already explained that on higher indifference curves the consumer gets more of one or both the commodities. If marginal utilities of these commodities are positive, then the consumer will certainly get more satisfaction on higher indifference curves. Naturally, a, higher indifference curve will always be preferred to a lower one. Mathematically we may write

$$Y = F(U)$$

where $U = f(X, Y)$ and Z is a constant.

Now, total utility (U) along an indifference curve is constant, but Z is an increasing function of U. It means that higher the indifference curve, more will be the level of satisfaction. It also implics that if more units of both the commodities X and Y (or at least one of them) are offered to the consumer, total utility function, U, will go on increasing and as a result, Z will increase.

6. The Budget Constraint Line or the Price Line

Before we discuss consumer's equilibrium, it is better to understand his budget line. Because, unless we have this information we cannot know how much of the two commodities the consumer will buy. The indifference map helps him only to put various sets of combinations in a certain imaginary order of preference. But, by itself, it does not tell him as to which particular combination to buy. In reality, the consumer is constrained by his money-income and the respective prices of the two commodities in question. If there is no such constraint, the consumer would maximise his total satisfaction by consuming X and Y to that level where the ratio of their marginal utilities becomes zero, *i.e.*

$$\frac{\partial U / \partial U}{\partial X / \partial Y} = 0$$

or

$$\frac{MU_X}{MU_Y} = 0$$

In other words, a consumer would like to go to the highest indifference curve. But this would not be the case in the real world and he has to confine his decision under his given constraints. His budget constraints are referred to as his "opportunity factors" which consist of three factors: (*i*) given money income (I); (*ii*) price of commodity X (P_X); and (*iii*) price of commodity Y (P_Y). If he spends his entire income on X and Y, then the budget equation becomes:

$$I = XP_X + YP_Y \qquad ...(5)$$

where I, P_X, and P_Y are exogenous variables and X and Y are endogenous variables.[9]

If the consumer spends his entire income on commodity X, then his budget equation becomes:

$$I = X.\ P_X$$

or

$$X = \frac{I}{P_X} \qquad ...(6)$$

Similarly, if he spends his entire income on commodity Y, then his budget equation becomes:

$$I = Y.P_Y$$

or

$$Y = \frac{I}{P_Y} \qquad ...(7)$$

Equations (6) and (7) are the two extremes within which a consumer is able to fix quantities of X and Y to be purchased. There may be a number of combinations of X and Y which can be purchased by the given budget constraint. These combinations are shown by the help of a budget line in Fig. 9.7.

---

9. Exogenous variables are those variables which are determined from outside and assumed to be constant in the model. Here income of the consumer price of X and Y are given from outside and thus are exogenous variables. Endogenous variables, on the other hand, are the variables which are determined within the model. Here the quantities of X and Y are to be determined and thus the variables X and Y are endogenous.

From equation (5) we may derive the equation of a budget line in the following manner :

$$I = X.P_X + Y.P_Y$$

or
$$Y = \frac{I}{P_Y} - \left(\frac{P_X}{P_Y}\right)X$$

or
$$Y = a - bX \quad ...(8)$$

where
$$\frac{I}{P_Y} = \text{constant or intercept}$$

$$b = \frac{P_X}{P_Y} = \text{slope of the budget line}$$

Equation (8) is the equation of a straight line. Here the ordinate intercept *a* shows the quantity of commodity *Y* when commodity *X* is not purchased at all. In Fig. 9.7, *MN* is the price line which is also known as *the consumption possibility curve* or *total outlay curve.*

Let the consumer's money income be \$100 and the price of *X* be \$10 per unit and the price of *Y* be Rs. 5. Then the equation of the budget line will become

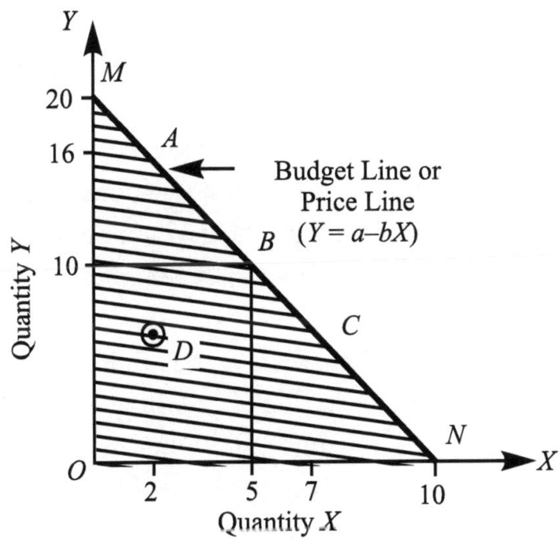

Fig. 9.7

$$Y = 20 - 2X$$

Here, the consumer could buy 10 units of *X* if he spent his entire *X* income on *X*, and he could buy 20 units of *Y* if he spent his entire income on *Y*. A straight line between 10 *X* and 20 *Y* shows every possibility of spending the income on the two commodities at their given prices. If we look at Fig. 9.7, we find that the consumer can buy 20 *Y* and zero *of X* or 16 *Y* and 2*X*, or

10Y and 5X, or 6Y and 7X, etc. These possible combinations are shown by the points M, A, B, C and N on the price line MN.

Further, the consumer can also buy any quantity inside the shaded area under the price line MN, such as, combination R; but if he does this, he is not spending all of his income. To attain the objective of maximum satisfaction we assume that the consumer spends his entire income on his consumption. Also, the consumer is unable to purchase a combination of X and Y which lies outside the area of the price line such as point S in Fig. 9.7. The reason is that his constraints do not allow him to go beyond the price line MN. Thus, the problem of the consumer is to select a point (combination) on the price line which gives him maximum satisfaction. This will be discussed under the equilibrium of the consumer in the following section.

7. Equilibrium of the Consumer

How much of X and Y does the consumer purchase? In order to answer this question, we have to bring together the two earlier diagrams of the consumer's indifference map and the price line. This has been illustrated in Fig. 9.8. The price line MN indicates the various combinations of the two commodities X and Y which the consumer can purchase with the given income and given prices of the two commodities. In Fig. 9.8, the family of indifference curves IC_1, IC_2, IC_3 and IC_4 indicates the liking or preference of the consumer. In the absence of the budget line, the consumer would like to remain on the highest indifference curve IC_4, but with the given money income, the highest attainable level of satisfaction for the consumer is IC_2. Indifference curves IC_3 and IC_4 are beyond the approach of the consumer, as their attainment requires larger money income than what he has in his pocket.

Also, even on the indifference curve IC_2, only one particular combination point E is conceivable to the consumer and other points such as C or D are beyond the consumer's approach, as they lie outside the price line MN.

Thus, point E represents a unique combination of X and Y and it gives maximum satisfaction to the consumer. In other words, point E is the equilibrium point of the consumer where the equilibrium quantities of X and Y are OX_0 and OY_0 respectively. Here, we may notice that the point A and B on IC_1 are fairly attainable by the consumer, since they lie on the price line. But none of them represents the equilibrium point, because in this case the consumer has to remain on a lower indifference curve.

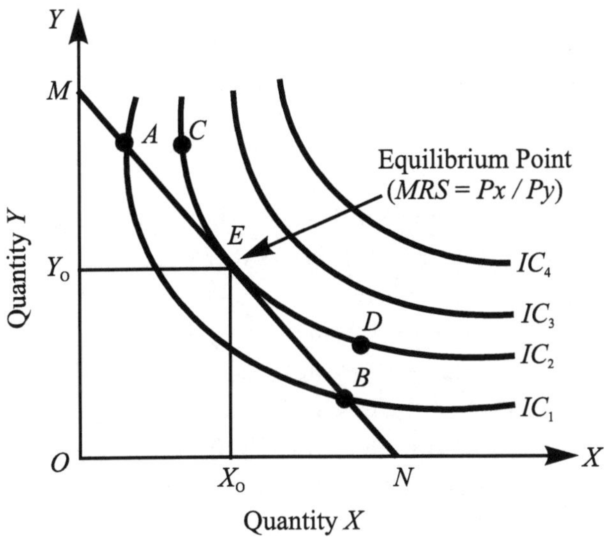

Fig. 9.8

On the basis of above analysis, we may conclude that a consumer maximises his total satisfaction at a point where the indifference curve touches is tangent to the price line. Mathematically,

$$MRS = \frac{P_X}{P_Y} \qquad \text{... (9)}$$

where MRS represents the slope[10] of the indifference curve $\left(\frac{PY}{PX}\right)$ and $\frac{P_X}{P_Y}$ is the slope of the price line.

Here, we may observe that the Marshallian utility approach to consumer behaviour also predicted the same conclusion as equation (9). In utility terms, we may write :

$$\frac{MU_X}{MU_Y} = \frac{dU}{dX} \Big/ \frac{dU}{dY} = \frac{P_X}{P_Y}$$

or

$$\frac{P_X}{P_Y} = \frac{PY}{PX} = MRS_{XY} \qquad \text{...(10)}$$

10. The absolute value of the slope is taken here. That is the minus sign, for the slope of indifference curve is ignored. To do so is usual.

Thus, Marshallian and Hicksian conclusions are similar at the optimisation level. However, their approaches are still different, because Marshall's approach is based on the cardinal measurement of utility while Hicks' approach is based on the ordinal measurement of utility.

8. Abnormal Indifference Curves and Corner Solution

In certain abnormal cases, the point where the indifference curve is tangent to the price line does not give maximum satisfaction to the consumer. These abnormal situations are the following:

(*i*) When indifference curves are straight lines,

(*ii*) When indifference curves are concave to the origin,

(*iii*) When indifference curves are convex to the origin, but their slope is either greater or lower than the slope of the price line.

In the first case, the condition of tangency is not fulfilled because the price line and the indifference curve are merged into each other. In such a situation the equilibrium is indeterminate. This case has been illustrated in Fig. 9.9 (a). When the slope of indifference curve IC_0 is everywhere more or less steep than the slope of the price line *MN*, equilibrium will be attained at the corner point where the two curves meet each other. These situations have been shown in Fig. 9.9 (b) and 9.9 (c). The corner solutions are made at points *M* and *N* respectively. Under these situations, however, the consumer buys either *X* or *Y* and certainly not both.

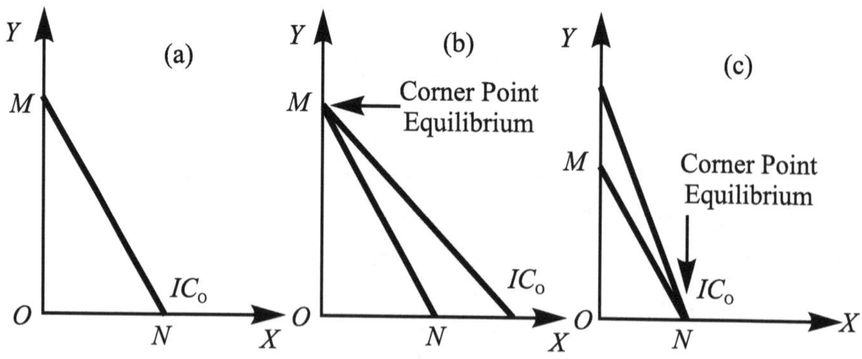

Fig. 9.9

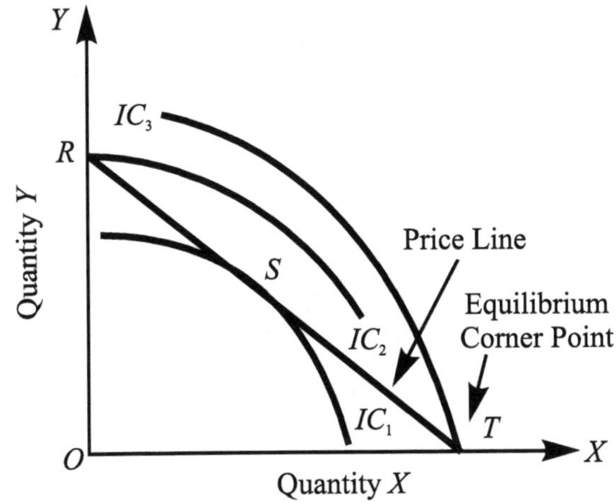

Fig. 9.10

In the second case (Fig. 9.10), when the indifference curves are concave, rather than convex, the MRS_{XY} increases as the consumer moves along the indifference curves. The condition of tangency (or the first order marginality condition) is satisfied at point $S\left(MRS_{XY} = \frac{P_X}{P_Y}\right)$, but this point of tangency does not satisfy the objective of the consumer to attain maximum satisfaction. At point S, he remains on a lower indifference curve IC_1. In this situation, the consumer can increase his satisfaction by moving to point T which lies on a higher indifference curve IC_3. At point T, the consumer will specialise in the consumption of X alone. It is also possible that the consumer may specialise in the consumption of Y alone. It will depend upon the nature of the slope of indifference curves.

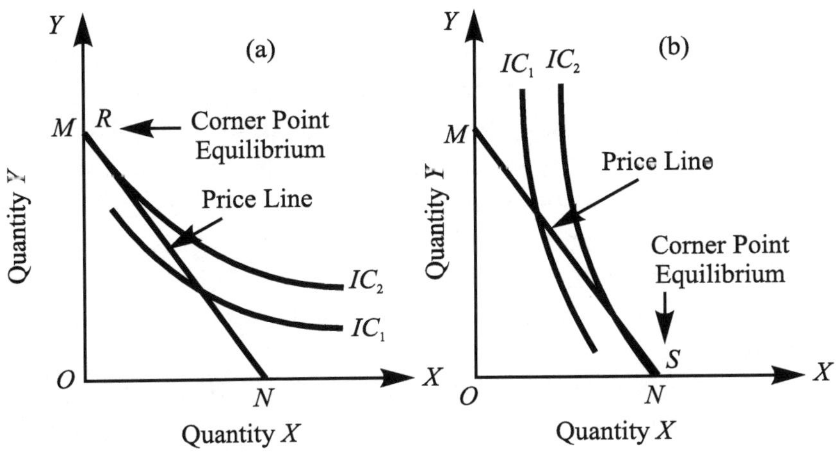

Fig. 9.11

In the third case, Fig. 9.11 (a) and (b), when the indifference a curves are convex to the origin, but it does not fulfil the condition of tangency ($MRS_{XY} = P_X/P_Y$); the consumer consumes only one commodity in the optimum situation. If the slope of indifference curve is less steep than the price line, *i.e.*

$$MRS_{XY} < \frac{P_X}{P_Y}$$

the consumer's equilibrium will be attained at the corner point *R* in Fig. 9.11 (*a*). Here the consumer spends his entire income on commodity *Y* and consumes *OM* units of *Y* only. If, on the other hand, the slope of indifference curve is more steep than the price line, *i.e.*

$$MRS_{XY} > \frac{P_X}{P_Y}$$

the consumer's equilibrium will be attained at the corner points in Fig. 9.11 (*b*). Here the consumer spends his entire income on commodity *X* and consumes *ON* units of *X* only.

These above are the cases of corner equilibria which do not hold in real life. Normally, consumers buy commodities in groups. They do not purchase a single commodity. Thus, these situations are particular situations where the ordinal utility function of the consumer is transformed as a function of only one commodity.

9. The Income Consumption Curve and the Income Effect

As we know that the Marshallian Utility approach is based on the assumption that the marginal utility of money is constant. It means that changes in consumer's money income do not affect the *MRS* between money and any particular commodity. It also implies that the demand for a commodity is independent of consumer's money income. But according to Prof. Hicks, the demand for a commodity is influenced by changes in consumer's income, although the magnitude of the effect depends on the nature of the commodity under consumption and the consumer's preference. It is in this context that the indifference curves analysis helps us to understand as how much the consumer's demand for a commodity changes in response to a given change in the income of the consumer or the price of a commodity. In other words, with the help of indifference analysis we are able to derive consumer's Engel curve (income-quantity) for a commodity or his demand curve (price-quantity relationship) for it.

In this section we shall consider, how the consumer's demand for a commodity will respond to changes in his income, with prices and his tastes remaining constant.

In general, the higher the income of a consumer, the more of a commodity he will buy. If the equation of his constraint is given as:

$$Y = \frac{1}{Py} - \frac{P_X}{P_Y}X$$

where $1/P_Y$ is the ordinate intercept and Px/Py is the slope of the budget line. If the money income (I) increases while the price ratio or the slope Px/Py remains the same, the ordinate intercept will increase and the new price line will be parallel to the old price. Thus, an increase in the consumer's income will cause his price line or outlay curve to shift upwards to the right. This new price line is tangent to a higher indifference curve. It means an increase in income puts the consumer on to a higher level of satisfaction. Similarly, a decrease in income will cause his price line to shift down-wards to the left and the consumer comes down to a lower indifference curve.

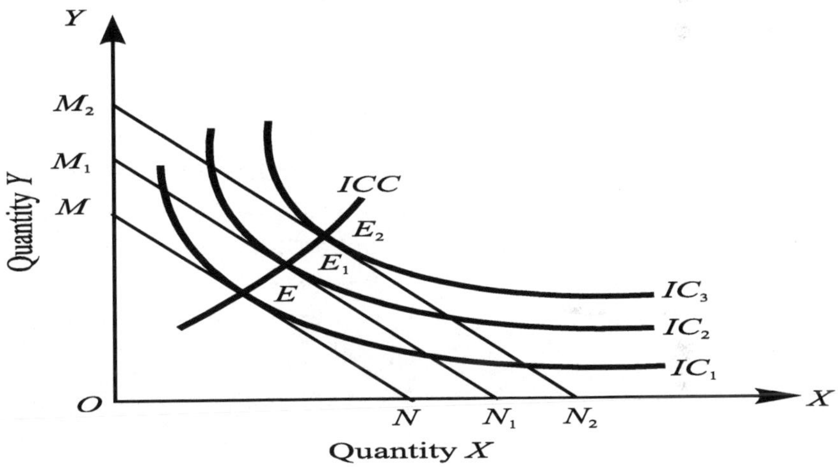

Fig. 9.12

This is shown in Fig. 9.12. The initial equilibrium position is at point E where the indifference curve IC_1 is tangent to the price line MN. If income increases, then the budget line shifts from MN to M_1N_1 and further from M_1N_1 to M_2N_2. The corresponding equilibrium position will also shift from point E to E_2 and further from E_1 to E_2. According to Prof. Hicks, the income consumption curve (*ICC*) is derived by joining these tangency points. The *ICC* shows the way in which consumption varies when income changes but prices of the two commodities remain unchanged. In other words, the *ICC* indicates the income effect of a given change on consumer's money income.

In general (for normal goods), income consumption curves (*ICC*) slope upwards to the right, showing that as the consumer's income increases, his purchases of the two commodities also increase. But this need not be so in all cases.

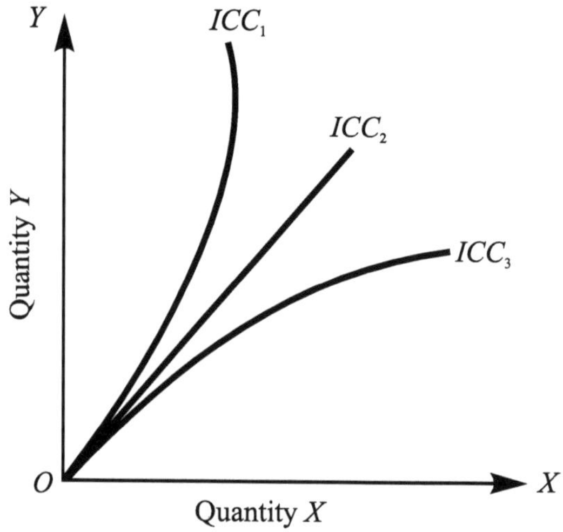

Fig. 9.13

For instance, in Fig. 9.13, we have three income consumption curves ICC_1, ICC_2 and ICC_3 which show that both the commodities X and Y are normal goods. Because as the consumer's income increases, he buys more of both. In Fig. 9.13, ICC_2 shows a more or less proportionate increase in expenditure on both the goods; ICC_1 shows the expenditure on commodity X is increasing but less than proportionately; and ICC_3 shows that the expenditure on commodity X is increasing more than proportionately.

In other words, on ICC_1

$$\frac{\partial X}{\partial I} < \frac{\partial Y}{\partial I} \text{ also } \frac{\partial X}{\partial I} > 0, \frac{\partial Y}{\partial I} > 0$$

On ICC_2 we have

$$\frac{\partial X}{\partial I} < \frac{\partial Y}{\partial I} \text{ also } \frac{\partial X}{\partial I} > 0, \frac{\partial Y}{\partial I} > 0$$

On ICC_3, we have

$$\frac{\partial X}{\partial I} < \frac{\partial Y}{\partial I} \text{ also } \frac{\partial X}{\partial I} > 0, \frac{\partial Y}{\partial I} > 0$$

Let us now discuss another case of income consumption curve where the consumer's expenditure on a particular good, instead of increasing, may actually decrease. This happens only when one of the goods is inferior.[11] The consumer consumes this inferior good in large quantities only when he is poor or his income is low. When his income increases he shifts his consumption of inferior good to a superior one. This phenomenon is known as Giffen's Paradox. These cases of inferior goods are shown in Fig. 9.14 (*a*) and 9.14 (*b*).

11. In the case of an inferior good, the quantity demanded decreases with increase in income, i.e., income effect is negative, or $\partial X/\partial I < 0$ when x is an inferior good.

$$\frac{\partial X}{\partial I} < 0 \text{ but } \frac{\partial Y}{\partial I} > 0$$

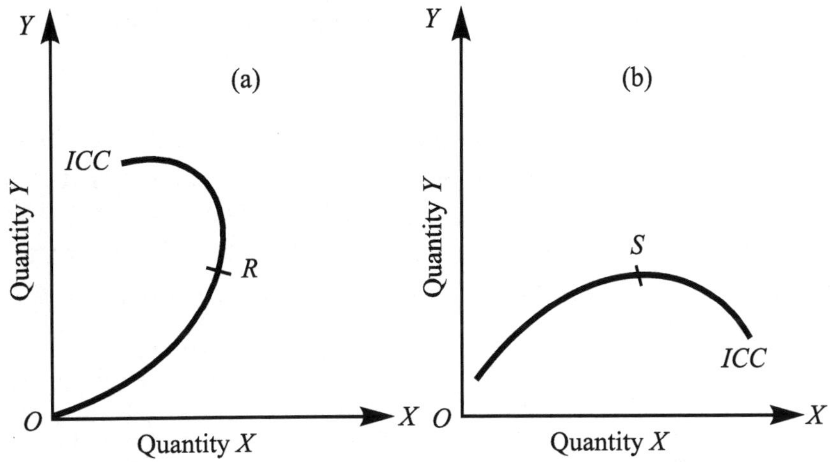

Fig. 9.14

Figure 9.14 (*a*) shows that after *R*, despite an increase in income, the consumer buys smaller quantity of *X*. In this situation, the *ICC* bends backward and *X* is termed as an inferior goods, while *Y* still remains to be a superior good, *i.e.*

Similarly, Fig. 9.14 (*b*) shows that after point *S*, despite an increase in income, the consumer buys smaller quantity of *Y*. In this case, the *ICC* slopes downward to the left after point *S* and it explains the inferior nature of good *Y*. Here, we have

$$\frac{\partial X}{\partial I} < 0 \text{ but } \frac{\partial Y}{\partial I} > 0$$

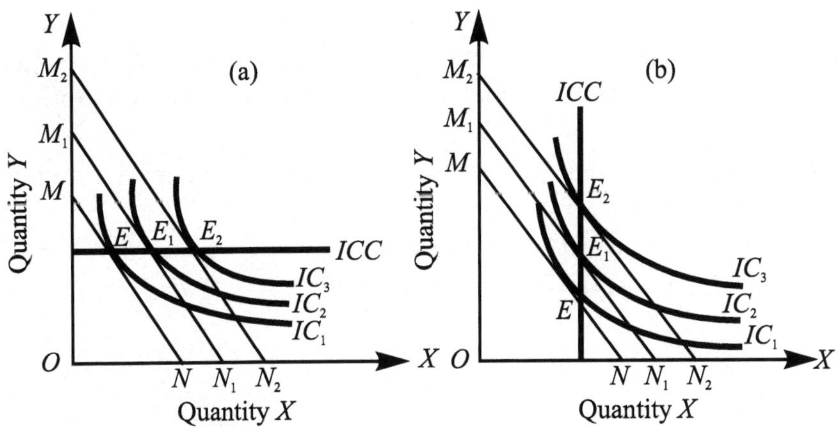

Fig. 9.15

Further, an income consumption curve may be horizontal. In this case, commodity *X* is a superior good because its consumption increases as income increases and commodity *Y* is a neutral good[12] because its consumption neither increases nor decreases with an increase in the money income of the consumer. This situation has been illustrated in Fig. 9.15 (*a*). Similarly, when *Y* is a superior good and *X* is a neutral good, the income consumption curve would be a vertical line. This situation has been illustrated in Fig. 9 .15 (*b*). Here, the consumption of *Y* increases as the money income of the consumer increases while the consumption of *X* remains unchanged at *OX*.

Now, on the basis of above discussion, we may sum up the relationship between the income consumption curves and the kind of goods to which they relate in Table 9.3.

Table 9.3

Shape of the Income Consumption Curve (ICC)	*Kind of Goods*	
	X	*Y*
Negative slope (ICC_1)	Superior	Inferior
Horizontal slope (ICC_2)	Superior	Neutral
Positive slope (ICC_3)	Superior	Superior
Vertical slope (ICC_4)	Neutral	Superior
Backward slope (ICC_5)	Inferior	Superior

The five types of *ICC* curves stated in Table 9.3 have been shown in Fig. 9.16. Their respective slopes indicate the nature of the commodities.

ICC_1 slopes negatively. Here after point *E*, the commodity *Y* becomes inferior while commodity *X* is still a superior good.

ICC_2 becomes horizontal after point *E* and thus *X* is a superior commodity while *Y* is a neutral good or necessary commodity; because after further increase in income after point *E*, the consumer does not increase its quantity.

ICC_3 is positively sloped which indicates that the two commodities *X* and *Y* are normal goods.

ICC_4 becomes vertical after point *E* and thus *Y* is a superior commodity and *X* becomes a neutral good or a necessary good.

ICC_5 bends backward after point *E* and thus commodity *X* becomes inferior while *Y* still serves as a superior good.

12. Leftwich, *The Price System and Resource Allocation,* Fourth Edition, pp. 66-68.

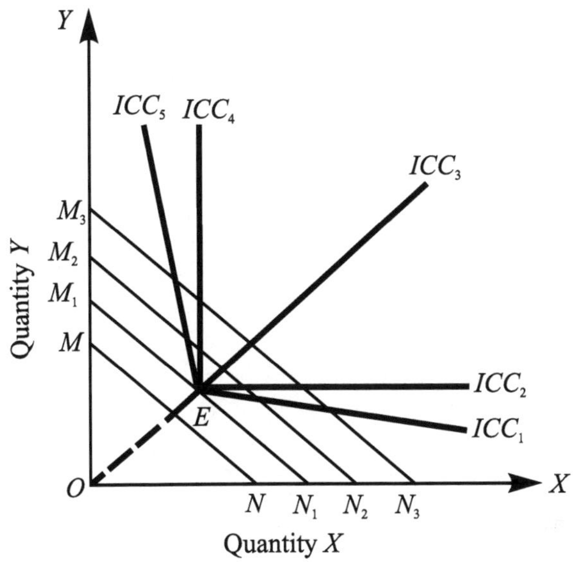

Fig. 9.16

The above conclusions can also be expressed in terms of Engel Curves. Prof. A. Engel developed the laws of family expenditure on the basis of Engel Curves. This curve represents those quantities of a commodity which a consumer would purchase at different levels of money income assuming the prices and the preferences remaining unchanged.

10. The Substitution Effect

According to Stonier and Hague, "A substitution effect occurs when the relative prices of goods change in such a way that the consumer in question is no better or worse off than he was before, but has to re-arrange his purchase in accordance with new relative prices."[13]

Here, it is assumed that when the price of *X* decreases, the price of *Y* would simultaneously increase. It is also assumed that the consumer's money incomes change in such a way as to compensate for the change in his real income consequent upon a fall in the price of *X* so that the consumer remains on the same indifference curve. The substitution effect is shown in Fig. 9.17.

13. Stonier and Hague, *op. cit.*, p. 57.

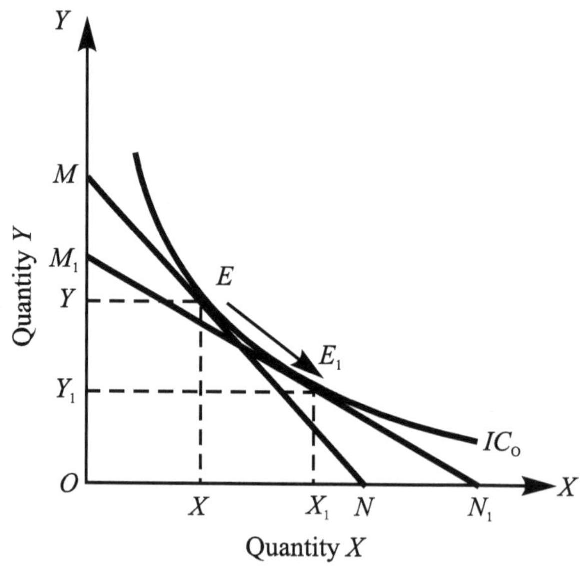

Fig. 9.17

In Fig. 9.17, the consumer is in equilibrium at point E on IC_0 buying OX units of X and OY units of Y. Suppose the relative prices of the two goods have changed, *i.e.* the price of X falls while the price of Y rises. The relative change in the prices takes place in such a manner that the new price line M_1N_1. touches the same indifference curve IC_0 at point E_1. It means that the rise in the price of Y is compensated by an increase in the income of the consumer in terms of a fall in the price of X. Thus the consumer remains on the same indifference curve. He only readjusts his purchases of the two goods at the new equilibrium point E_1. The new combination of the two goods is $OX_1 + OY_1$. It is clear that in the new situation the consumer has more of X *which* is cheaper and less of Y *which* is dearer. The movement from equilibrium point E to E_1 indicating the increase of XX_1. quantity of X purchased by the consumer is called the substitution effect of the relative price change.

In the words of Prof. Hicks, it has been a *compensating variation* in the consumer's income in terms of quantity of X to the extent of NN_1, so that the rise in the price of Y is cancelled out. As a result, the consumer remains on the same indifference curve IC_0 and the movement along this indifference curve from E to E_1 is due to the substitution effect.

Now we will explain the *substitution effect when the price of only one commodity changes*. Let us assume that the price of commodity X falls while the price of commodity Y remains the same. Now the consumer will substitute X for Y. The substitution occurs even if we assume that the increase in real income (as a result of the fall in the price of X) is not available. Now, the increase in the purchase of commodity X and to a given fall in the price of X after deducting the part which is brought about by the increase in real income is called the substitution effect of a given fall in the price of commodity X alone. Fig. 9.18 illustrates this substitution effect.

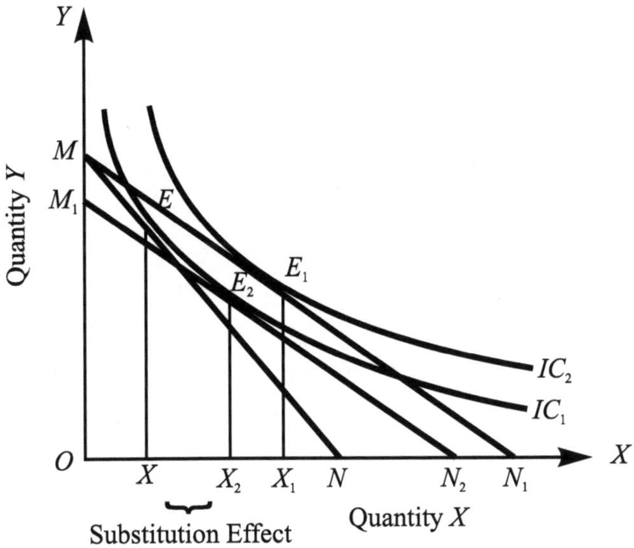

Fig. 9.18

In Fig. 9.18, the original price line is MN and the consumer is in equilibrium at point E where indifference curve IC_1 touches the price line MN. At original equilibrium point E, the consumer consumes OX quantity of commodity X. Now the price of X falls and a new price line MN_1 takes place. The increase in the real income of the consumer in terms of commodity X is the distance NN_1.The new equilibrium position of the consumer is at point E_1 on the higher indifference curve IC_2. In the new situation, the consumer buys OX_1 quantity of X. We know that the movement from point E_1 on IC_1 to point E on IC_2 is partly due to the income effect and partly due to the substitution effect of a given fall in the price of X. To get the substitution effect we need to eliminate the income effect. For this, we draw a line M_1N_2 parallel to the price line MN_1 in such a way that it is tangent to the old indifference curve IC_1 at point E_2. Thus the movement from E_1 to E_2 (i.e. from OX to OX_2 or the distance X_1 X_2) is the income effect and the movement from E to E_2 (i.e. from OX to OX_2 or the distance X_1 X_2) is the substitution. In other words, if we reduce the money income of the consumer by MM_1 amount (= N_2N_1 amount in terms of commodity X), his real income will remain constant (as in the initial stage) because with his reduced money income he can now get the same level of satisfaction (since both the points E and E_2 lie on the same indifference curve IC_1). Thus, the fall in the price of X results in a net increase of XX_1 in the quantity of X. Of this XX_2 is the substitution effect and X_2X_1 is the income effect. It also shows that the price effect represents the combined operation on income and substitution effects.

11. The Price Consumption Curve and the Price Effect

As already explained, a change in the price of a commodity not only induces the consumer to buy more or less because the relative price (P_X/P_T) has altered, but it also affects the demand for a commodity via "income effect" of a change in price. In other words the real income of the consumer is inversely related to the change in price. However, this aspect of consumer demand will be discussed later on. Here we shall discuss the "direct effect" of a change in price assuming that the consumer's income remains constant and the prices of all other commodities remain unchanged. The curve which shows the price effect is known as price-consumption curve (*PCC*). With the help of indifference curve analysis we derive the price consumption curve, and the demand curve for a commodity can directly be derived from the price consumption curve.

Our initial equation of the budget line or price line is

$$Y = \frac{I}{P_Y} - \frac{P_X}{P_Y} X$$

Now, if the price commodity X (P_X) falls, then the intercept (I/P_Y) of the line remains unchanged while the slope (P_X/P_Y) decreases. This has been illustrated in Fig. 9.19 (a) where the original price line is *MN* and the new price line becomes MN_1. The consumer shifts from his initial equilibrium point E to the new equilibrium point E to the equilibrium point E_1. If we join these two points of equilibrium then the resulting curve is known as price consumption curve is (*PCC*). The shift from E to E_1 is termed as price effect.

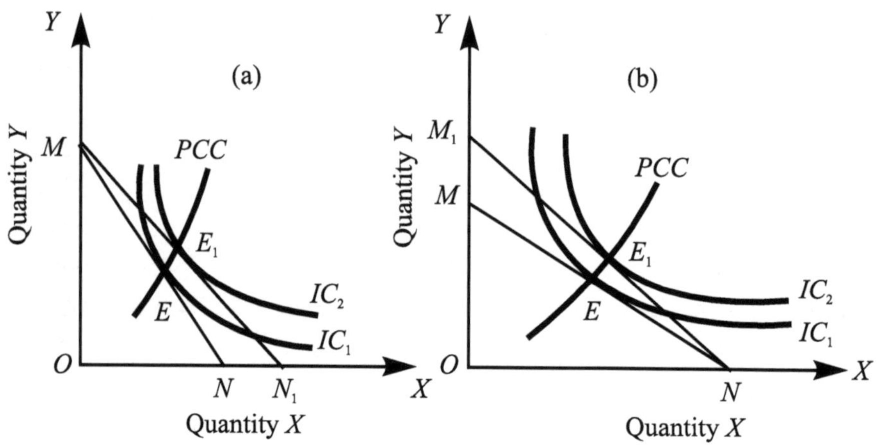

Fig. 9.19

Similarly, if the price of commodity Y (i.e. P_Y) falls, then the ordinate intercept of the price line (P_X/P_Y) will increase and the slope of price line (P_X/P_Y) will also increase. As a result of this, the price line MN shifts to M_1N in Fig. 9.19 (b). In this situation also, the consumer moves from a lower indifference curve IC_1 to a higher indifference curve IC_2. The locus of the equilibrium points E and E_1 is called the price consumption curve and the shift from E to E_1 is called price effect.

Like income consumption curve, the price consumption curve (*PCC*) may have a negative, positive, zero or infinite slope indicating the nature of the commodities, i.e. whether the commodities are superior, inferior or neutral. In the rare case of a "Giffen Good" it may even be backward bending.

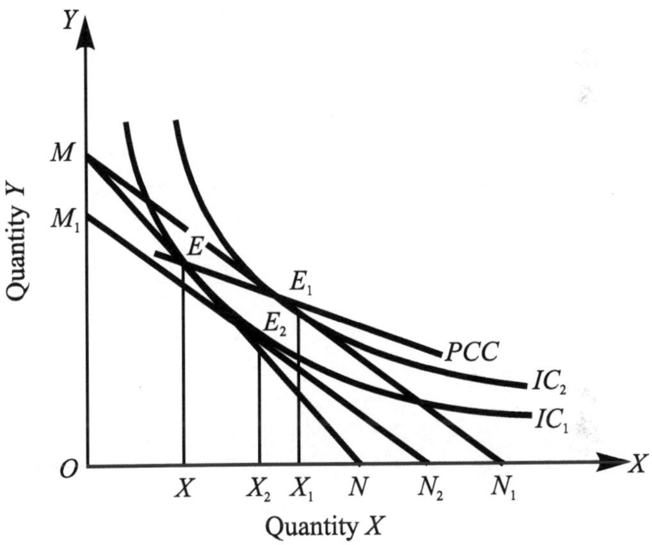

Fig. 9.20

Let us first take the most general type of price consumption curve the curve which slopes downwards to the right as shown in Fig. 9.20. In this case, commodity X is a superior or normal good, because unless the income effect of a price change (i.e. fall in price) is positive, the *PCC* cannot have a negative slope. In other words, the income effect here is positive. The original price line is MN where the consumer gets maximum satisfaction, a point E on IC_1. Due to a fall in the price of X, the price line shifts to MN_1, and the new point of equilibrium is E_1. Originally, the consumer was consuming OX units of X_1, but in the new situation his consumption increases to OX_1. The net increase in the consumption of X is equal to XX_1. This is the price effect which is due to the combined operation of the income effect and the substitution effect. If we want to know the income effect,[14] then we need to separate the substitution effect from the income effect. The technique is simple. We draw a line M_1N_2 parallel to the price line MN_1 in such a way that the line M_1N_2 is tangent to IC_1 at point E_2. Now the movement from E *to* E_2 along IC_1 represents the substitution effect. On commodity X, it is equal to XX_2. If we subtract this from the net increase in the quantity of X (or price effect = XX_1), we get income effect which is equal *to*X_1X_2. Since this income effect is positive, or

$$\frac{\partial X}{\partial I} = X_1X_2 > 0$$

we conclude that commodity X in this case (Fig. 9.20) is a superior good or a normal good.

The second type of price consumption curve which is horizontal is X-axis whose slope is zero as shown in Fig. 9.21. Here the original equilibrium position is at point E on IC_1. If the price of X falls, then consumer attains a new equilibrium point E_1 on IC_2. The net increase in the quantity demanded of X is XX_1. Of this, the distance XX_2 is due to the substitution effect and the remaining part X_2X_1 is due to income effect since, here also, income effect is positive, i.e.

$$\frac{\partial X}{\partial I} = X_2X_1 > 0$$

The commodity X is a superior or normal commodity.

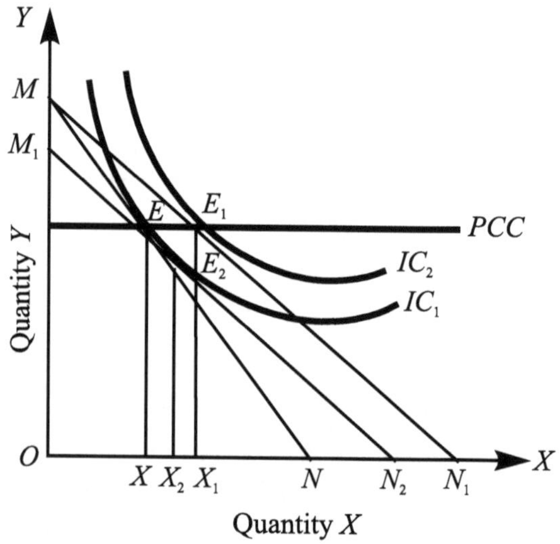

Fig. 9.21

14. Because to find out whether the good is superior, inferior or neutral, we need to know the income effect. As is known, good X is inferior if the income effect, $\frac{\partial X}{\partial I} < 0$. Similarly, for a superior or normal good, and for a neutral good, $\frac{\partial X}{\partial I} > 0$ and for a neutral good $\frac{\partial X}{\partial I} = 0$.

The third type of *PCC* is a vertical line with an infinite slope as shown in Fig. 9.22. Here, if the price of *X* falls, there will be no increase in the quantity demanded. For instance, in Fig. 9.22, the original equilibrium point is *E* where the consumer buys *OX* quantity of *X*. Now due to a fall in the price of *X*, the price line shifts from *MN* to MN_1 and the new equilibrium point would be E_1. At this new equilibrium position the consumer again buys *OX* quantity of *X*. Thus, there is no change in the quantity of *X*, or price effect is zero, *i.e.*

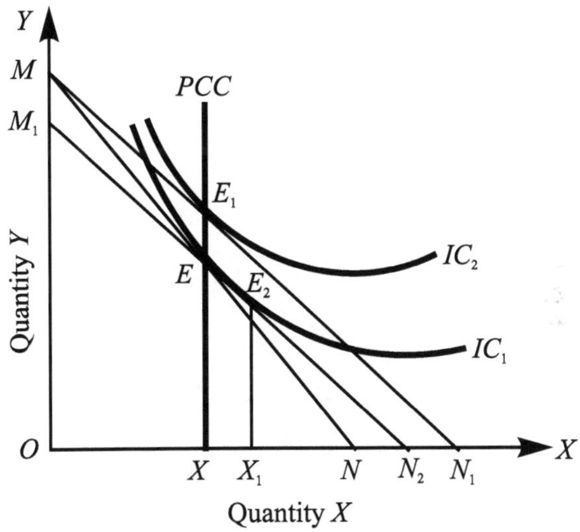

Fig. 9.22

$$\frac{\partial X}{\partial P_X} = 0 \text{ because } \partial X = 0$$

This can happen when the negative income effect just cancels the positive substitution effect which in Fig. 9.22 is represented by XX_1. In other words,

$$\frac{\partial X}{\partial P_X} = XX_1 < 0$$

The negative income effect shows that the commodity *X* is an inferior or *subnormal commodity.*

The fourth type of price consumption curve is a backward bending curve as shown in Fig. 9.23. Here, as a result of a fall in the price of commodity *X*, the quantity demanded of *X*, instead of increasing, decreases. For instance, in Fig. 9.23, the original price line is *MN* where the equilibrium point is *E*. At point *E* the consumer buys *OX* of *X*. Now, if price of *X* falls, it will lead to a new price line MN_1. The new equilibrium point is E_1 where the consumer buys only *OX* quantity of *X*. Thus, the consumption of *H* decreases from *OX* to OX_1. This happens only when the negative income effect is stronger than the positive substitution effect. In Fig. 9.23, the negative income effect is equal to X_1X_2 (= $X_1X + XX_2$) while the positive substitution effect is XX_2. Obviously,

$$X_1X_2 > XX_2$$

Thus, the commodity X is definitely an inferior commodity. Here, it is a special type of inferior good which in economics is known as the "Giffen Good".

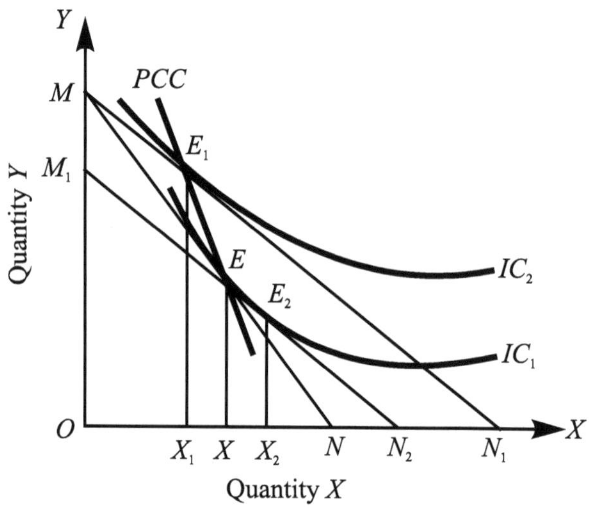

Fig. 9.23

We have discussed above the four important types of price consumption curves. But there may be a number of other shapes of *PCC*. Thus negatively sloping and horizontal *PCC* show the upper limit while the backward bending and vertical *PCC* show the lower limit. Between these two limits, there is a large range of positively sloping *PCC* where it is difficult to say straightaway whether the goods are superior, inferior or neutral. All that can be said is that the steeper the positive slope of the *PCC*, the greater is the likelihood for X to be an inferior commodity and vice versa. Here we can illustrate the three cases of positively sloping *PCC* with the help of Fig. 9.24 (*a*), (*b*) and (*c*) respectively.

In Fig. 9.24 (*a*), the net increase in the quantity demanded of X, as a result of a fall in its price, is equal to XX_1. Of this the substitution effect is equal to XX_2 and income effect is equal to X_2X_1.

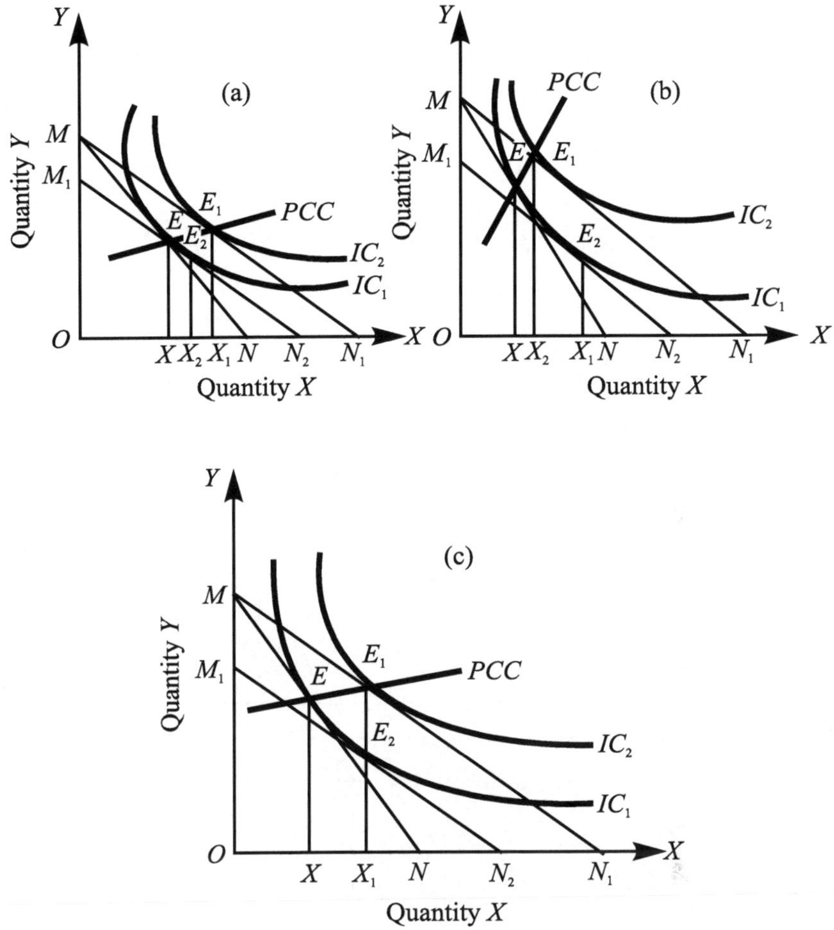

Fig. 9.24

Since income effect is positive, i.e.

$$\frac{dX}{dI} = X_2X_1 > 0$$

the commodity X is a superior or normal commodity.

In Fig. 9.24 (b), the net increase in the quantity demanded of X, as a result of a fall in its price, is XX_1. This has been calculated by subtracting the negative income effect X_2X_1 from the positive substitution effects XX_2. Thus the negative income effect neutralises a part of the positive substitution effect. But anyhow, since the income effect is negative, i.e.

$$\frac{dX}{dI} = X_2X_1 < 0$$

the commodity X is, an inferior or sub-normal commodity.

Also, in Fig. 9.24 (c), as the consequent upon the fall in price of X, the net increase in the quantity demanded of X is XX_1. Here the income effect is zero and, therefore, the entire increase in X is due to the positive substitution effect. Since the commodity X is a neutral commodity.

$$\frac{dX}{dI} = 0$$

Now we may sum up the above cases of price consumption curves in Table 9.4.

Table 9.4.

Shape of the Price Consumption Curve (PCC)	*Nature of the Commodity*
Negatively sloping (PCC_1)	Superior
Horizontal sloping (PCC_2)	Superior
Positively sloping (PCC_3) and PCC_4)	Uncertain (may be superior, inferior or neutral)
Vertical sloping (PCC_5)	Inferior
Backward sloping (PCC_6)	Inferior

The various types of PCC curves stated in Table 9.4 are shown in Fig. 9.25. Their respective slopes indicate the nature of commodity X.

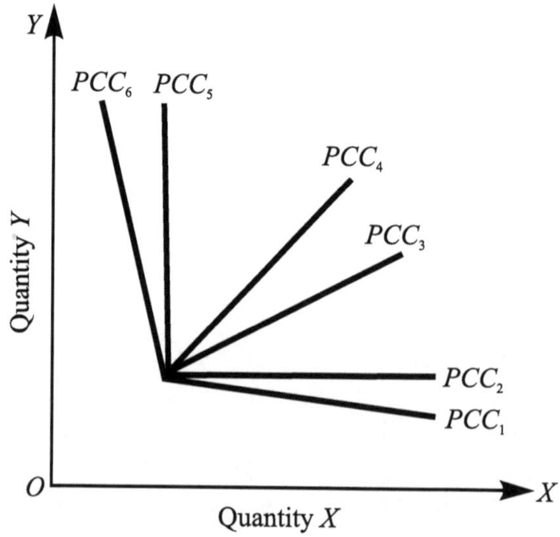

Fig. 9.25

12. Separation of Price Effect into Income and Substitution Effects—Slutsky *vs* Hicks

As we have noted above that a fall in the price of commodity *X* leads to an increase in its quantity demanded. The total increase in the quantity demanded of *X* is, however, the result of the combined action of the substitution and income effect of a given price change. Thus,

Price Effect = Substitution Effect + Income Effect

Here, we are interested to know that of the total price effect (*i.e.* total increase in the quantity demanded of *X*) how much is contributed by the substitution effect and how much is contributed by the income effect.

As we know, when the price of commodity *X* falls (the money income of the consumer remaining the same), the real income of the consumer increases. In other words, with the same money income, the consumer can now purchase larger quantities of both the goods *X* and *Y*. Now in order to find out how much of this (total) increase in the quantity demanded of *X* is due to the fall in the price *alone* (or due to substitution effect), it is necessary to keep the real income of the consumer constant. This can be done by reducing the money income of the consumer (through income tax, etc.) to the extent that his real income remains constant.

Two approaches have been developed so far to define the level of constant real income or the income effect.

(*i*) Slutsky's Approach.

(*ii*) Hicks's Approach.

The first approach has been developed by the well-known Russian economist Prof. Fugen Slutsky. Slutsky states that to keep the real income of the consumer constant, we should reduce his money income to the extent that he should be just able to purchase the original combination of the two commodities (if he desires). This can be done by drawing a line parallel to the new price line which passes through the original combination of the two commodities *X* and *Y*. This approach, however, has been criticised on the ground that here the *apparent real income* remains constant and not the real income of the consumer. Because, this approach enables the consumer to enjoy a higher indifference curve (as he may move to a new point on the drawn price line which lies on a higher indifference curve).

The second approach has been developed by the well-known British economist, J.R. Hicks. According to this approach, in order to keep the real income of the consumer constant, we should reduce his money income to the extent that he is just able to enjoy the original indifference curve. This can also be done by drawing a parallel line to the new price line which at some point touches the original indifference curve.

The difference between the two approaches is clear that the former approach empahsises the attainment of the original combination of the two goods while the latter approach emphasises the attainment of the original level of total satisfaction. Fig. 9.26 illustrates the difference between the Slutsky and Hicks's approaches to income effect.

In Fig. 9.26, *MN* is the original price line which is tangent to IC_1 at the point *E*. The original equilibrium point *E* indicates that the consumer buys *OX* quantity of commodity *X*. Now suppose the price of *X* falls and, therefore, the price line shifts rightward to the new position of MN_1. The new equilibrium point is E_1 where the indifference curve IC_3 touches the price line MN_1. At this new equilibrium point E_1 the consumer buys OX_1 quantity of *X*. Thus the net increase in the quantity demanded of *X* (as a result of the fall in the price of *X*) is equal to XX_1. This increase of XX_1 is due to the combined contribution of the income and substitution effects. Now we are interested to find out that how much of this total increase in quantity demanded of *X* ($=XX_1$) is due to the substitution effect alone. In order to separate the two effects (substitution effect and income effect), We shall apply the techniques separately.

Let us first adopt the Slutsky approach. For this we draw a line M_1N_2 parallel to the new price line MN_1 in such a way that it passes through the original equilibrium (combination) point *E*. It means that we have reduced the money income of the cconsumer to the extent of the distance MM_1

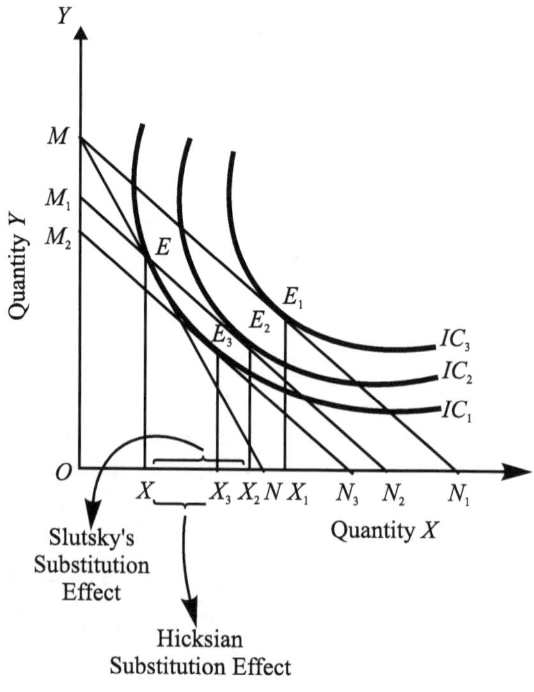

Fig. 9.26

(in terms of commodity *Y*) on axis *Y* or N_2N_1 (in terms of commodity *X*) on axis *X*. In Slutsky's opinion the line M_1N_2 keeps the consumer's real income constant. Now on the price line M_1N_2, the consumer can buy the original combination of X and Y at the point E, if he so likes. But as a rational consumer, he would not buy the old combination of the two commodities at point E and moves on to the point E_2 which lies on a higher indifference curve IC_2. At this point E_2, the quantity demanded of X increases from OX to OX_2 which is the direct effect (substitution effect) of the price change. In other words under Slutsky's approach, the substitution effect is equal to XX_2. If we subtract this substitution effect (XX_2) from the total effect (XX_1), we get the income effect (X_2X_1). Thus,

Income effect (X_2X_1) = Total price effect (XX_1) – Substitution effect (XX_2).

This is the Slutsky approach of separating the price effect into the substitution effect and the income effect.

Now we employ Hicks's approach. According to his approach, to keep the real income constant the money income of the consumer should be reduced to the extent that he is forced to go back to the original indifference curve. For this we draw a line M_2N_3 parallel to the new price line MN_1 in such a way that it touches the original indifference curve IC_1 at point E_3. At point E_3, the consumer's real income remains the same in the sense that he gets the same level of total satisfaction as the original point E, because both the points E and E_2 lie on the same indifference curve IC_1. But at point E, the consumer buys only OX quantity of X while at point E_3, he buys OX_3 quantity of X. Thus the substitution effect is equal to XX_3. From the total increase in the quantity demanded of X due to the fall in its price, i.e. XX_1, if we deduct the substitution effect, XX_3; then the remaining portion X_3X_1 is the income effect, or

Income effect (X_2X_1) = Total price effect (XX_1) – Substitution effect (XX_3).

This is Hicks's approach of separating the price effect into the substitution effect and the income effect.

It is now possible for us to sum up the relationship between the total price effect, the substitution effect and the income effect of the two approaches in Table 9.5.

Table 9.5

	Method	*Fall in the Price of X*	*Total Price Effect*		*Substitution Effect or Direct Price Effect*		*Income Effect*
1.	Slutsky's	$-\Delta P_x$	XX_1	=	XX_2	+	X_2X_1
2.	Hicks's	$-\Delta P_x$	XX_1	=	XX_3	+	X_3X_1

Table 9.5 shows that the fall in the price of X and the total price effect on the

quantity demanded of X are the same in the two approaches. But the substitution effect of direct effect is more under the Slutsky's approach than it is under the Hicks's approach because in Fig. 9.26 we observe that

$$XX_2 > XX_3$$

It means that income effect is less under the Slutsky's approach than under the Hicksian approach, or

$$X_2X_1 < X_3X_1$$

Now as regards to the comparative importance of the two methods, Hicks's method seems to be more scientific than Slutsky's method. Because under Hicks's method, the substitution effect is such that the consumer remains on the same indifference curve due to a fall in the price of X. His real income remains the same because he becomes neither better off nor worse off as a result of the substitution effect. While under the Slutsky's approach, the consumer would enjoy a higher indifference curve which gives greater total satisfaction as a result of the substitution effect. Here, one is not able to say that the consumer's real income is constant. Thus, Hicksian approach is more reliable in the interpretation of the substitution effect and the income effect than the Slutsky's approach.

The above analysis clearly indicates the fact that the substitution effect is always positive. Because a cheaper commodity (due to a fall in the price) is always substituted for a dearer commodity.

In mathematical terms, the substitution effect will always have a negative sign, because

$$\left(\frac{\partial X}{\partial P_X}\right)_{u=c} < 0$$

where $\left(\frac{\partial X}{\partial P_X}\right)_{u=c}$ indicates the direct price effect when the consumer remains on the same indifference curve or total utility remains constant. Here, ∂P_X if is negative (i.e. the fall in the price of X), then ∂X will be positive (i.e. the quantity demanded of X increases), and thus the product $\frac{\partial X}{\partial P_X}$ will be negative.

But we are not sure about the nature of the income effect. In the case of a normal or superior good, the sign of the income effect will be positive, i.e.

$$\left(\frac{\partial X}{\partial I}\right)_{p=c} > 0$$

It means that given the prices of the commodities, an increase in the consumer's money income (∂I) will lead to increase in the quantity demanded of X (∂X). If on the other hand, the given commodity X is an inferior or a sub-normal commodity, then the income effect will be negative, or

$$\left(\frac{\partial X}{\partial I}\right)_{p=c} < 0$$

It means that given the prices of the commodities, an increase in the money income of the consumer ($+\,\partial I$), will lead to decrease in the quantity demanded of X ($-\partial X$).

Thus the product $\frac{\partial X}{\partial I}$ will be negative.

If the commodity is a neutral commodity, the income effect will be zero, i.e.

$$\left(\frac{\partial X}{\partial I}\right)_{p=c} = 0$$

It means that given the prices of the commodities, an increase in the money income of the consumer ($+\partial I$), will lead to a zero change in the quantity demanded of X (or $\partial X = 0$). Thus the product $\frac{\partial X}{\partial I}$ will be zero.

Prof. Slutsky has presented the relationship between the price effect, the substitution effect (direct price effect) and the income effect in an equation which is called the *Slutsky Equation.* The equation can be written in the following manner:

$$\underbrace{\frac{\partial X}{\partial P_X}}_{\text{Total Price Effect}} = \underbrace{\left(\frac{\partial X}{\partial P_X}\right)_{u\,=\,\text{constant}}}_{\text{Substitution Effect}} + \underbrace{X\left(\frac{\partial X}{\partial I}\right)}_{\text{Income Effect}} \frac{P_X}{P_Y} = \text{constant}$$

13. Derivation of the Demand Curve from the Price Consumption Curve

As demonstrated above, the price consumption curve shows the relationship between the change in the price of a commodity and the corresponding changes in the quantity demanded of the commodity by the consumer. The conventional demand curve also indicates the similar relationship that how much quantity of a commodity would be demanded by the consumer at different prices assuming *ceteris paribus.* It may, therefore, be hypothesised that the consumer's demand curve for a commodity must be related in some way to his *PCC* curve.

As a matter off act, the *PCC* as well as the demand curve yield the same information about the demand-price relationship. But in spite of this similarity, there are also some differences between these two curves The *PCC* and the demand curve of the consumer. The important are the following:

(1) The *PCC* is drawn with the two commodities represented on the two axes one say *X* on the *X* axis and the other say *Y* on the *Y* axis. On the other hand, the demand curve is drawn with only one commodity, say *X* represented on the *X* axis and its price represented on the *Y* axis.

(2) In the case of *PCC,* the prices of the commodities are not mentioned directly but slope of the price line indicates the ratio of the prices of the two commodities *X* and *Y.* While in the case of the conventional demand curve price of the commodity is directly mentioned on the vertical axis.

(3) The *PCC* clearly brings out separately the income effect and the substitution effect of a change (rise or fall) in the price of a commodity; while the conventional demand curve is unable to separate the two effects.

(4) The *PCC* also indicates the size of the consumer's money income while the conventional demand curve does not provide this information.

The above differences indicate the comparative importance of the two curves the *PCC* and the demand curve. But if we are given the indifference map of the consumer and the money income of the consumer along with the price of all other goods (labelled as *Y* in our example), we can easily derive the demand curve of an individual consumer from his price-consumption curve. Generally, two different methods are employed to derive the demand curve from the price consumption curve. We shall discuss them separately in the following manner.

Method I

Under this method we shall derive the demand schedule of a consumer from his *PCC.* In Fig. 9.27, the consumer's money income has been represented on *Y* axis and the quantity of commodity *X* has been represented on *X* axis.

Suppose the line of attainable combinations or the price line is initially *MN.* Now if the price of *X* falls, then the price line *MN* will shift upwards to the right. In Fig. 9.27, we have drawn the different price lines *MN,* MN_1, MN_2, MN_3 and MN_4 showing different prices of commodity *X,* namely *PX,* PX_1, PX_2, PX_3 and PX_4. The consumer's initial equilibrium position is at point *E* where he buys *OX* quantity of *X.* Here the price per unit of *X* is calculated by dividing the total money income of the consumer (*OM*) to the quantity of *X* that can be purchased with the entire money income. So that, the initial price of *X* (i.e. say PX_0) would be equal to the ratio

$$\frac{OM}{ON} = PX_0$$

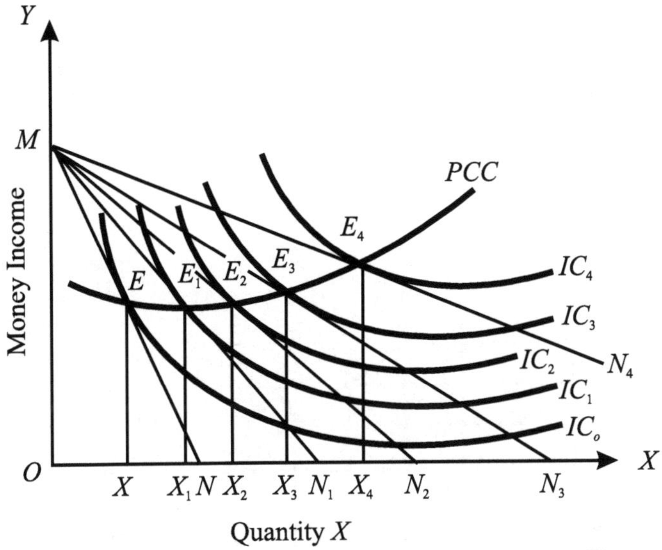

Fig. 9.27

At this initial price (OM/ON), the consumer buys OX quantity of X. Similarly, on the price line MN_1, the equilibrium position is at point E_1 where the consumer buys OX_1 quantity of X at the price OM/ON_1. Likewise, we may easily calculate the various price of commodity X and the respective quantities of X purchased by the consumer. This information has been summarised in Table 9.6.

Table 9.6

Price of the commodity X (*PX*)	*Quantity Demanded of X* (*X*)
(1)	(2)
$PX_0 = \frac{OM}{ON}$	OX
$PX_1 = \frac{OM}{ON_1}$	OX_1
$PX_2 = \frac{OM}{ON_2}$	OX_2
$PX_3 = \frac{OM}{ON_3}$	OX_3
$PX_4 = \frac{OM}{ON_4}$	OX_4

Table 9.6 shows the demand schedule of the consumer. We can now easily construct the conventional demand curve on the basis of the price-quantity information mentioned in Table 9.6. Figure 9.28. indicates the

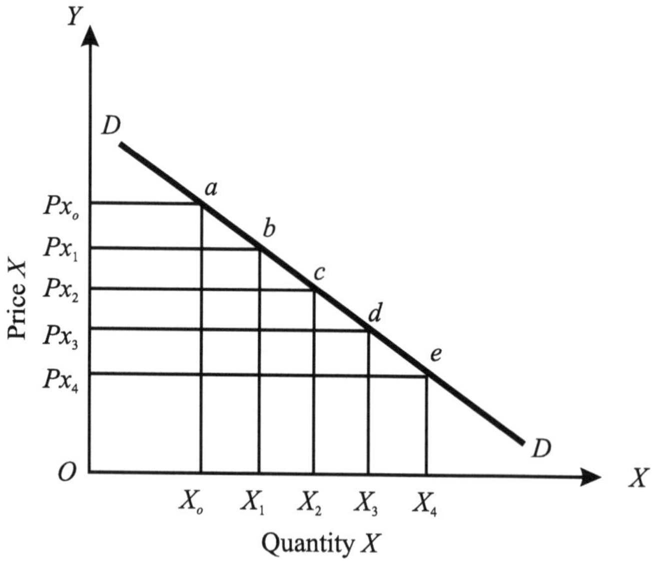

Fig. 9.28

resulting demand curve. Since the denominator of the column 1 of Table 9.6 is increasing, we write,

$$PX_0 > PX_1 > PX_2 > PX_3 > PX_4$$

As the price decreases, the quantity demanded of X increases, i.e.

$$OX < OX_1 < OX_2 < OX_3 < OX_4$$

In other words, we can say that the law of demand holds. By plotting these various points of the demand schedule we obtain the demand curve DD as in Fig. 9.28.

Method II

Under this method the demand curve is drawn in the same diagram in which price consumption curve is constructed as shown in Fig. 9.29. In Fig. 9.29, horizontal axis measures the quantity of X while the money income is measured on the vertical axis. In this case the trade-off is between the purchase of X and the money which would be used for buying other goods (including Y). The slope of the price line is now simply the price of X (because slope, here, is defined as the ratio of total money income to the maximum attainable quantity of X or alternatively, the income spent on X divided by the actual quantity purchased which is nothing but the price of X).

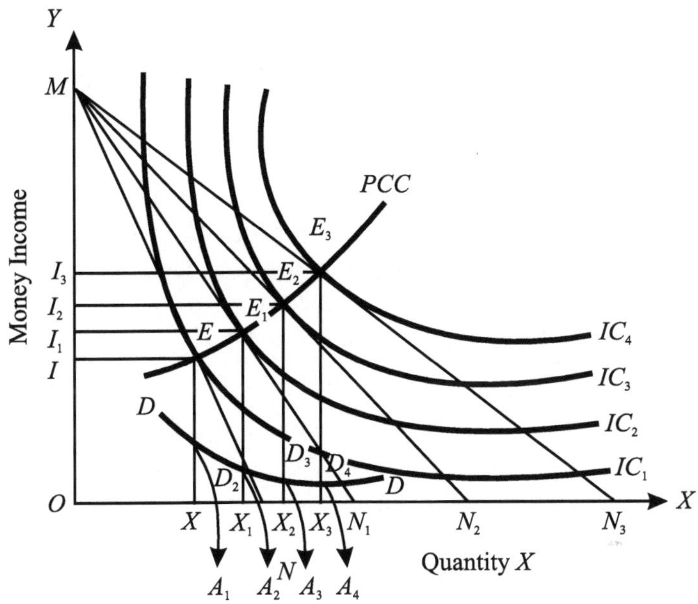

Fig. 9.29

In Fig. 9.29, the initial equilibrium point is *E* where consumer buys *OX* units of *X*. At this point he spends *MI* units of money on *X* and saves *OI* units of money for other goods. As the price *X* falls, the budget line rotates from *MN* to MN_1, then to MN_2, and finally to MN_3 as shown in Fig. 9.29. The equilibrium quantity of *X* bought increases each time the price of *X* falls. First it increases from *OX* to OX_1, then to OX_2 and finally to OX_3. Money income spent on *X* however, decreases from *MI* to MI_1, then to MI_2, and finally to MI_3. Thus a fall in the price of *X* induces the consumers to increase his demand for *X*. This is known as the law of demand.

The *PCC* curve has been usually drawn by joining the various equilibrium points *E*, E_1, E_2, and E_3. Here the price consumption curve tells us the total expenditure that is incurred on *X* at different prices. We, therefore, call the *PCC* as the "Total Outlay Curve" in relation to commodity *X*.

But this curve gives us no information about the price per unit of *X* when different quantities are purchased by the consumer. This information (i.e. the various prices of *X*) can be obtained by dividing the total expenditure incurred on *X* by the number of units of *X* bought by the consumer. If we obtain this information, i.e. the price per unit of *X* when different quantities of it are purchased by the consumer, then it becomes very easy to draw the demand curve of the individual consumer.

The demand curve DD in Fig. 9.29 has been derived by establishing price quantity relationship at different levels of price. Thus, at different levels of price, one unit of X has been marked off from the equilibrium quantities. For instance, to the right of EX along the X axis, one unit of X (it may be a kilogram, a litre, or a metre as the case may be) is represented by the distance XA_1. We, when draw the line D_1A_1 parallel to the price line MN. Since D_1A_1 is parallel to the price line MN. It represents the same price (slope of the line) per unit of X as MN. Since XA_1 represents one unit of X, therefore, D_1X represents the price per unit of X (because price = $D_1X/XA_1 = D_1X$ since $XA_1 = 1$) when OX is purchased by the consumer. Thus D_1 is first point on the consumer's demand curve DD. Here price D_1X should be considered equivalent to OM/ON. Similarly, we mark off one unit of X to the right of point X_1 on the X axis at an equal distance of X_1A_2 (=XA_1) and draw a line D_2A_2 parallel to the price line MN_1). Now since the slope of price MN_1 indicates the price of X when OX_1 units of X are purchased by the consumer, the slope of the line D_2A_2, i.e. $\dfrac{D_2X_1}{X_1A_2}$ also indicates the price per unit of X. Here $X_1A_2 = 1$, therefore the price of X would be equal to D_2X_1. Thus, at price D_2X_1 the consumer purchases OX_1 quantity of X. In this way point D_2 is another point on the consumer's demand curve DD. In a similar manner, we can find out point D_3 and D_4 showing the consumer's demand for commodity X when the price unit is D_3X_2 and D_4X_3 respectively. If we join together the points D_1, D_2, D_3 and D_4, we may obtain the consumer's conventional demand curve DD.

14. Comparative Demand Curves

The conventional demand curve derived above shows that the price and quantity are inversely related. It makes no attempt to explain the change in quantity demanded as a result of the substitution effect distinctly from the one resulting from the income effect of a change (fall or rise) in price. The above analysis is therefore, based on the Marshallian approach. Prof. Hicks and Prof. Slutsky criticised this approach. They hold the opinion that a change in price would lead to an opposite change in the consumer's real income. As already explained the increase in quantity demanded of X due to fall in its price is divided into two parts one is attributed to the income effect and other remaining part is attributed to the substitution effect (or the direct price effect). Here, both Hicks and Slutsky state that response of quantity demanded to a change (fall) in price should be analysed exclusively on the basis of the substitution effect (or direct price effect), i.e. by ignoring the income effect. In other words, under the derivation of the demand curve the Marshallian approach emphasises the total price effect, i.e. the total change in quantity demanded in the event of a price change while Hicksian and the Slutskian approaches assume the consumer's real income constant and then analyses the effect of a price change on quantity demanded, i.e. exclusively on the basis of substitution effect. To put it differently, Marshallian approach considers the effect of an absolute change in the price of a commodity on quantity demanded in the derivation of the demand curve, while the other two approaches Hicks and Slutsky consider the effect of relative price change, i.e. *PX/PY* on the quantity demanded of the commodity.

Again, in spite of this fact that both Hicksian and Slutsky approaches give emphasis to the substitution effect in the derivation of the demand curve, the two are not altogether identical. As we have already noticed, assuming the consumer's real income constant, Prof. Hicks intends the consumer to remain on the same indifference curve and allows him to select a new combination of *X* and *Y* along the original indifference curve; while Slutsky intends the consumer to enjoy the original equilibrium point. It means, to purchase the original combination of *X* and *Y*, Slutsky provides much compensation (negative or positive as the case may be) to the consumer.

Now assuming the real income of the consumer constant, we may derive the demand functions of the two approaches (Hicks and Slutsky) from Fig. 9.30. In Fig. 9.30, the money income has been shown on the *Y* axis and the

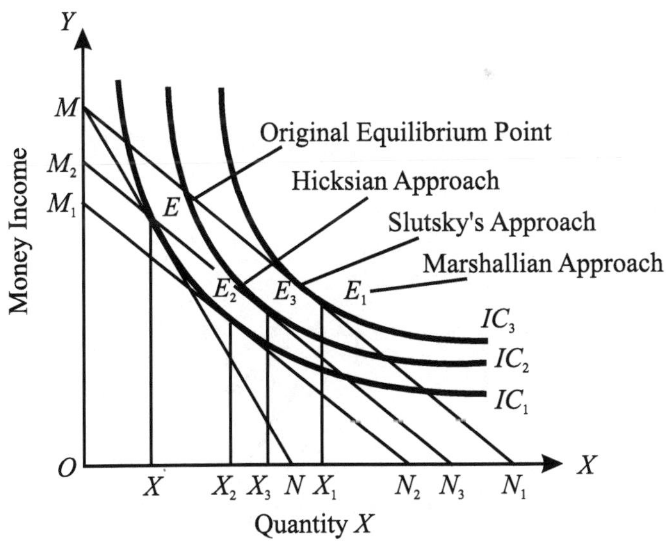

Fig. 9.30

quantity of commodity *X* on the *X* axis. The price of commodity *X* is known by the slope of the respective price lines *MN*, MN_1 and MN_2. For example, at the original equilibrium point *E*, the consumer buys *OX* quantity of *X* at the price *OM/ON*. But when the price of *X* falls to OM/ON_1, then the conventional total quantity demanded of *X* would be OX_1, while according to Hicks and Slutsky it would be OX_2 and OX_3 respectively. This information of the three different demand functions Marshall, Hicks and Slutsky has been shown in Table 9.7.

Table 9.7

Price of X	*Total Quantity of X purchased*	*Quantity of X purchased according to Hicks*	*Quantity of X purchased according to Slutsky*
$PX_0 = \frac{OM}{ON}$	OX	OX	OX
$PX_1 = \frac{OM}{ON_1}$	OX_1	OX_2	OX_3

The information of Table 9.7 can be represented graphically by the three different demand curves Marshall, Hicks and Slutsky as shown in Fig. 9.31. The demand curves in Fig. 9.31 have been drawn under the assumption that a change in the price leads to an opposite change in the quantity demanded. In other words, Fig. 9.31 depicts the demand for a normal good in relation to

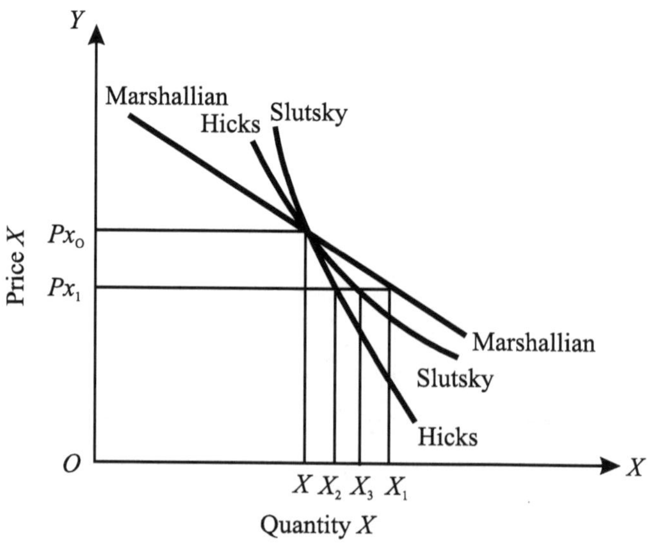

Fig. 9.31

price. At the original price OPX_0, the quantity demanded was *OX*. When the price falls from OPX_0 to OPX_1, under the Marshallian approach (i.e. total price effect) the consumer increases the quantity of X to OX_1; but under Slutsky's approach the consumer increases the quantity of X to OX_2, while under Hicksian approach the increase in quantity of X is only equal to OX_2. In other words, the elasticity of demand will be lower if examined under Slutskian approach and still lower if viewed from Hicksian approach. Symbolically,

$$Ed \text{ (Marshall)} > Ed \text{ (Slutsky)} > Ed \text{ (Hicks)}$$

In spite of the above differences, the common characteristic to all the three demand curves of Fig. 9.31 is their negative slope. It means that for a normal good, the price and quantity demanded are inversely related in all the three cases of demand curves.

15. Derivation of the Income Demand or Engel Curve

With the help of indifference curve analysis, we may derive the income demand curve or the Engel curve from the income consumption curve (*ICC*). The Engel curve represents the relationship between the income of the consumer and the quantity of X demanded by the consumer. It has been shown in Figs. 9.32 and 9.33.

In Fig. 9.32 the income consumption curve slopes positively which indicates that as the money income of the consumer increases, he will buy more of the two goods X and Y. For instance as income increases, the price

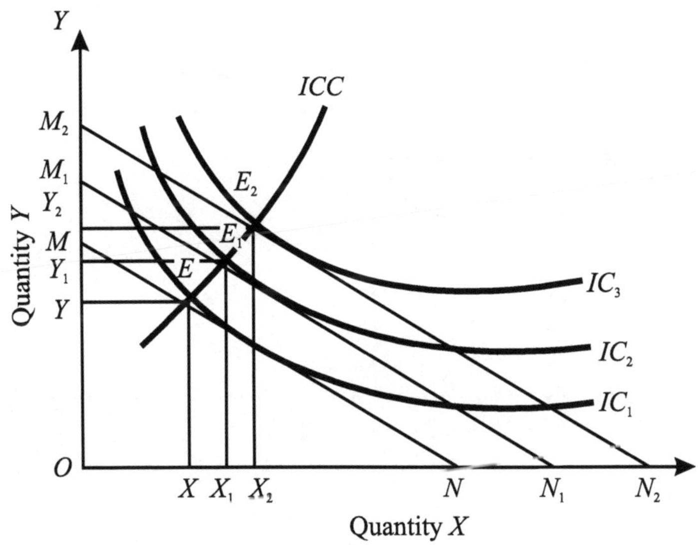

Fig. 9.32

line shifts to the right from MN to M_1N_1 and then to M_2N_2 respectively. These lines are parallel to each other, because the slope of the price line or price ratio P_X/P_Y remains constant. If X and Y are normal goods, the increase in income increases the quantity of X taken from OX to OX_1, then to OX_2 and the amount of Y taken from OY *to* OY_1 then to OY_2.

Engel curves or income demand curves for X and Y can be plotted from the data provided from Fig. 9.32. Here we draw an Engel curve *DD* in Fig. 9.33. Money income of the consumer is measured on the vertical axis while quantities of X are measured on the, horizontal axis. Now from Fig. 9.32 we can read that with money income OM the consumer buys OX quantity of X. This is plotted as point A on Fig. 9.33. From Fig. 9.32 we again note that when income increases from OM to OM_1, the consumer will buy OX_1 of X. We plot this as point B on Fig. 9.33. Similarly, from Fig. 9.32 we find that when income rises to OM_2, the consumer buys OX_2 units of X. We plot this as point C on Fig. 9.33. Now if we join these points then the resulting curve is the income demand curve *DD*. This demand curve slopes upwards rather downwards which, shows a positive relationship between the money income of the consumer and the demand for X. The slope of the demand curve will show the respective elasticity of demand for the commodity. In the case of a

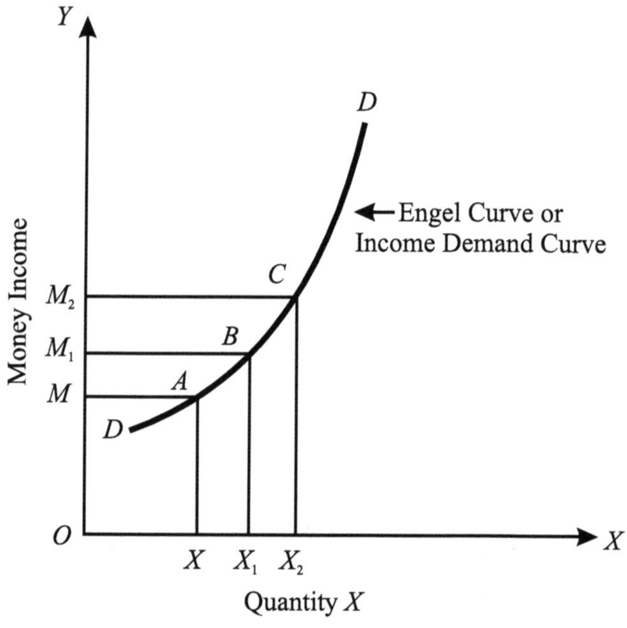

Fig. 9.33

superior commodity as assumed in our above example, the *ICC* as well as the Engel curve will be positively sloped and the income elasticity of demand will be positive. In the case of an inferior good, the *ICC* will be backward bending, showing a negative relationship between income and consumption changes and, therefore, the income demand curve or the Engel curve will also have a negative slope showing that as income increases, the quantity demanded of *X* decreases. In this case, the income elasticity of demand will be negative.

16. Elasticity of Demand and the Price Consumption Curve (PCC)

From the price consumption curve (*PCC*) we not only derive the demand curve for a commodity, but the slope of the *PCC* also indicates whether the elasticity of demand for the commodity *X* is unitary, greater than one, or less than one.

In Fig. 9.34 (a), the slope of price consumption curve is zero because it is horizontal to *X* axis. It indicates that the elasticity of demand is unitary, because it states that total expenditure incurred on *X* remains unchanged. In other words, a percentage fall in the price of *X* is equal to the percentage increase in the quantity demanded of *X* and thus leaving the total expenditure incurred on the commodity unchanged. Symbolically,

$$Ed = \frac{\text{Percentage change in the quantity demanded of } X}{\text{Percentage change in the price of } X}$$

$$= -\frac{\Delta X / X}{\Delta P_X / P_X} = 1$$

because $\Delta X/X = \Delta P_X/P_X$

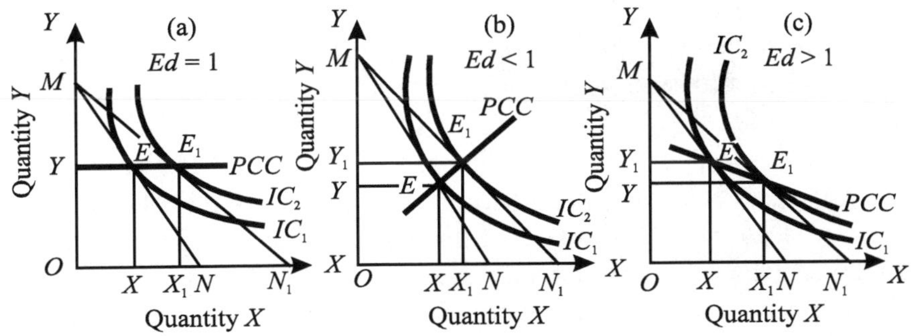

Fig. 9.34

In Fig. 9.34 (b), the *PCC* slopes upward which indicates that the elasticity of demand for *X* is inelastic. Because when price of *X* falls, the quantity demanded of *X* increases from *OX* to OX_1, but the total expenditure (in terms of *Y*) incurred on *X* falls from *MY* to MY_1. In other words, the percentage increase in the quantity demanded of *X* is less than the percentage fall in its price. Thus the elasticity of demand for *X* is less than one. Symbolically,

$$Ed = \frac{\Delta X / X}{\Delta P_X / P_X} < 1$$

because $\Delta X/X < \Delta P_X/P_X$

In Fig. 9.34 (*c*), the *PCC* slopes downwards to the right indicating that the elasticity of demand for *X* is elastic. Because when price of *X* falls, the quantity demanded of *X* increases from *OX* to OX_1, while at the same time the amount of money income (in terms of *Y*) spent on it also increases from *MY* to MY_1. It means that the percentage in quantity demanded of *X* is greater than the percentage fall in its price. Thus, the price elasticity of demand for *X* is greater than one. Symbolically,

$$Ed = \frac{\Delta X / X}{\Delta P_X / P_X} > 1$$

because $\Delta X/X > \Delta P_X/P_X$

17. Applications of Indifference Curve Analysis

As we have already explained, indifference curve analysis is useful in the derivation of the demand curve of an individual consumer for particular products. However, indifference curve analysis can also be fairly used in the fields of consumption, production, exchange and distribution. It may also be used to explain the impact of various government policies related to rationing, taxation, international trade, etc. Here we shall narrate some of the Important uses of indifference curve analysis in the following section:

(*i*) *Optimisation in a Barter Economy* (*or the Determination of the Rate of Exchange*). A situation where prices are not expressed in monetary units, is generally called a barter economy. The first application of indifference curve analysis relates to the determination of the rate of exchange between two commodities bartered by two individuals. In 1881, Prof. Edgeworth[15] made the first attempt to show the limit within which exchange could take place between the two individuals. Assuming the scale of preferences of the individual's and the supplies of the commodities given, he laid down the limits of exchange with the help of his famous box diagram and pointed out that it is not possible to ascertain the precise rate at which the two commodities will exchange. The most that can be done is to indicate the limits within which the exchange ratio must lie, its actual position within these limits is determined by the relative abilities of the two individuals to bluff, to coerce, to harangue, and the like. This has been illustrated in Fig. 9.35.

15. Edgeworth, E.N., *Mathematical Physics*. 1881, p. 20.

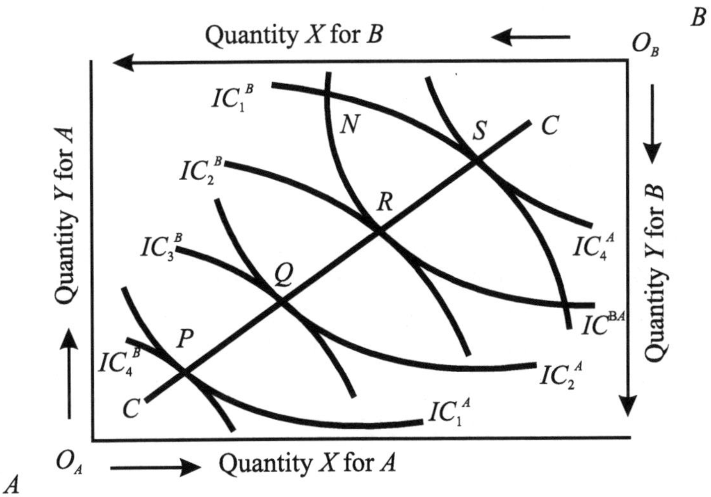

Fig. 9.35

Let us assume that the two individuals are *A* and *B;* and the two commodities are *X* and *Y.* In Fig. 9.35, *A*'s family of indifference curves (showing the scale of preference) is IC_1^A, IC^A_2, IC^A_3, and IC_4^A and starts with the origin O_A. Likewise, *B*'s family of indifference curves (showing his scale of preferences) is IC_1^B, IC_2^B, IC_3^B, and IC_4^B and starts with the origin a O_B. The two persons *A* and *B* get maximum satisfaction in exchange where their indifference curves touch each other. In other words, the slope of indifference curves of *A* and *B* must be equal. Since the slope of indifference curve represents the marginal rate to substitution of *X* for *Y* (*MRSxy*), we may write the condition:

$$MRSxy \text{ for } A = MRSxy \text{ for } B$$

It is clear from Fig. 9.35 that the above marginality condition is satisfied at the points *P, Q, R* and *S*. These points are the equilibrium points of exchange. The locus or path of these points is *CC* which is generally known as the *Contract Curve.*

To prove that the touching points *P, Q, R,* and *S* are the relevant points for exchange, we assume a new point of exchange *N* where the indifference curves of *A* and *B* cut each other. Now we will see that the total welfare can be increased by moving point *N* to *S* or *R*. In other words, at point *N* only one of the individuals will give his acceptance for exchange and the other will not; thus exchange will not be possible. On the other hand, at point *S* or *R* both will agree for exchange and thus exchange between them will take place. We summaries the positions of *A* and *B* at the point *N, R* and *S* in the following manner.

	A	B
At point N	IC_3	IC_1
At point R	IC_3	IC_1
At point S	IC_4	IC_1

Now if we compare point N and R, then we find that A gets the same level of satisfaction on both the points as he remains on IC_3, but B gets more satisfaction on point R (because he enjoys IC_2), then point N (lies on IC_1). It means that B will give his acceptance on point R and A will have no objection for this point and thus exchange will take place only on point R and not on N.

Similarly, if we compare points N and S, then we find that at point S both agree for exchange because A shifts to a higher indifference curve IC_4 (from a lower indifference IC_3 at point N) while B does not lose anything (because at both the points he remains on IC_1). Thus, point N will not be the relevant point of exchange while point S will be the relevant point of exchange. Now, it is proved the every point on the contract curve represents a position of final contract between the two individuals.

(ii) Determination of Tax Policy. A second application of indifference curve analysis lies in the determination of a tax policy. With the help of indifference curves we can show that income-tax (direct tax) is better than an equivalent sales-tax or an excise tax (indirect-tax). This can be proved by means of Fig . 9.36. In this figure X axis represents the commodity taxed and Y axis the consumer's money income. The consumer's (or tax payer's) money income is equal to OM. We now draw the price line MN, whose slope is equal to Px/Py. Since Py is equal to unity (the price of \$1 is 1), the slope of the price line MN equals Px. If there is no tax on the consumer, then the individual will buy MX quantity of commodity X at a total expenditure of XE dollars and will initially enjoy point E on IC_3.

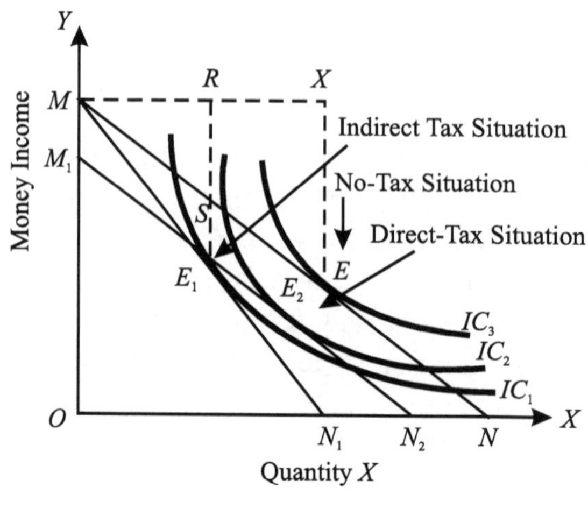

Fig. 9.36

If a tax is imposed on commodity *X*, then the price of *X* will rise. The new price line will become MN_1, where the equilibrium point is E_1. At E_1, the consumer buys *MR* quantity of *X* at a total cost of RE_1 of which SE_1 will be taxes.[16] In this situation of indirect tax, the consumer enjoys indifference curve IC_1. If an equal amount of tax is levied on the income of the consumer, his income is reduced to OM_1 (where $MM_1=SE_1$), but the slope of the price line M_IN_2 retains its former slope since the price of *X* is unaffected. The consumer's equilibrium point will be E_2 which lies on IC_2. It proves that the consumer will be on a higher indifference curve if a certain amount of money is taken from him by a personal income tax than if it is raised by means of a commodity tax.

(*iii*) *Explaining the Effects of Subsidies.* Subsidy is generally provided by the government to help consumers (low income groups) in such a way that

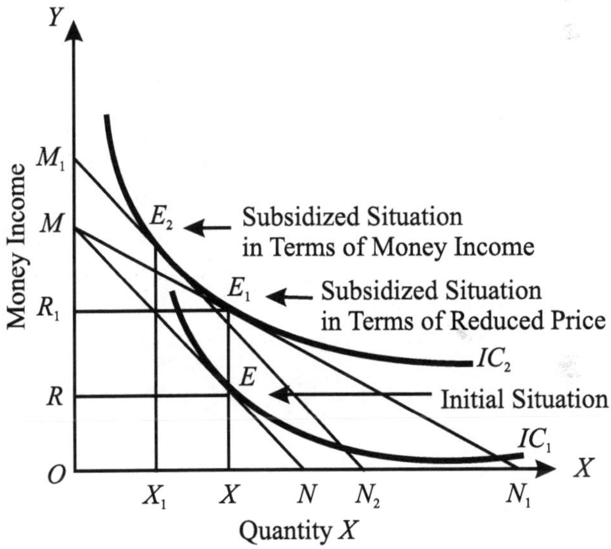

Fig. 9.37

they are able to purchase goods at a price lower than the market price. Here the question is: whether the benefit to the consumer(s) is more than the cost of the subsidy to the government. This has been illustrated in Fig. 9.3 7. Suppose, consumer's money income is *OM* and in the absence of any subsidy his price line is *MN*. The consumer was originally optimising the use of his money income at point *E* where he was placed on the indifference curve IC_1. Now if government provides him commodity *X* at (fair) lower prices, then

16. Here we assume that the rise in price of *X* will be just equal to the amount of the tax.

his price line shifts to MN_1. At this new price line, the consumer's equilibrium position is at point E_1 on IC_2 where he buys OX quantity of X at a total expenditure of MR_1. Originally, the consumer was required to pay a total expenditure of MR to purchase same quantity OX of commodity X. This means that the government provides RR_1 amount of money in terms of subsidy. But the consumer does not get this amount in cash (*i.e.* in money units). If it could be given in terms of money income, then the amount would be equal to MM_1. Now as far as the individual consumer is concerned, he is equally benefited from both types of transfer payments (*i.e.* either in cash or in terms of price reduction); because he remains on the same indifference curve IC_2 (where $E_1 = E_2$). But the cost of the subsidy to the government is more when it is given in terms of price reduction than in terms of money (because $RR_1 > MM_1$). Thus, the subsidy should be given in cash terms than in terms of air prices. Moreover, the consumer purchases lesser amount of X at point E_2 than at point E_1. The government also wants to curtail the consumption and thus cash-subsidy is recommended in place of the other type of subsidy.

(*iv*) *Explaining the Effects of Rationing.* Indifference curves are also used to explain the effects of rationing. There are different methods of rationing. For example, the first method is that each consumer is entitled to a fixed quantity of the commodity. The second method is that the consumer is entitled to get ration according to his taste and preference. Now with the help of indifference curves we can show that the second method of rationing is better than the first method.

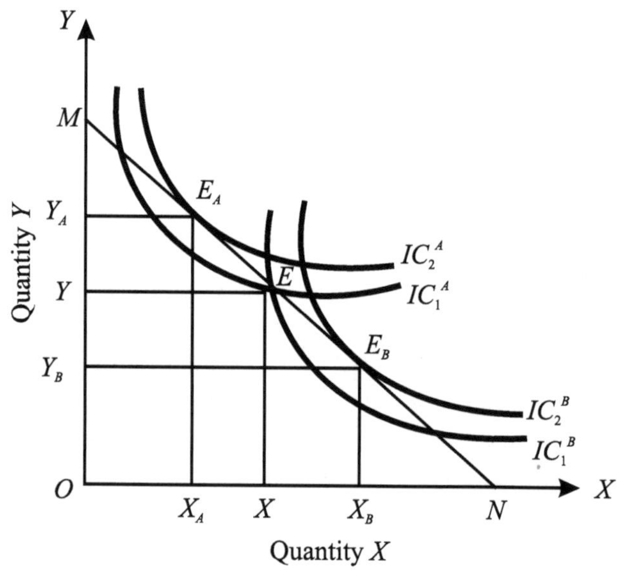

Fig. 9.38

We assume that the two consumers, A and B have the same amount of money income at their disposal. Also, there are two commodities X and Y where the rationing is imposed. The prices of the two commodities are also given. In Fig. 9.38, MN is the price line. The indifference curves (which show their respective tastes) of A and B are given as IC_1^A, IC_2^A, IC_1^B and IC_2^B respectively to the first method of rationing both A and B get fixed quantities of X and Y, i.e. OX of X and OY of Y. The forced equilibrium point for both is E where A enjoys IC_1^A and B enjoys IC_1^B. Now, if the second method of rationing is introduced, then both the consumers will buy X and Y according to their tastes.In such a situation A will enjoy equilibrium point E_A which also lies on a higher indifference curve IC_2^A and B will enjoy equilibrium point E_B which also lies on a higher indifference curve IC_2^B. A's combination of the two commodities X and Y will be $OX_A + OY_B$ and B's combination of the two commodities X and Y will be $OX_B + OY_B$. Thus under the second scheme both the consumers get higher level of satisfaction. Here we may notice that total quantities of X and Y sold in the market remain the same, because when B buys XX_B more of X, then he has to sacrifice the purchase of Y to the level of YY_B. Similarly when A buys YY_A more of Y, then he reduces the purchase of X to the level of XX_A. Thus the controlled quantity of commodities X and Y remaining the same, the distribution according to consumer preferences will lead to higher satisfaction.

(v) *Derivation of the Supply Curve of Labour.* Here we consider the attitude of a consumer toward his income. A consumer sells his services (labour) to business firms. The indifference curve analysis can be used to indicate the supply of labour available at different wage rates. The supply curve of labour can easily be derived from the *Wage Offer Curve,* provided the indifference map of labour and the entire range of wage-rates are known to us. In general, a consumer would like to earn higher incomes and for this he has to work more. In other words, more work means the sacrifice of some leisure.[17]Since leisure is also necessary for life, a consumer has to make balance between work and leisure. In other words, the gain in utility from more income has to be balanced against the loss of utility from less leisure. Obviously, there is a direct substitution of income for leisure, and vice versa. The utility function of the consumer can be written as,

$$U = f(L, I) \qquad \ldots(1)$$

where L indicates leisure and stands for the money income of the consumer. Again the money income of the consumer is a positive function of work (N). Symbolically,

17. Here leisure means the time not spent in remunerative work, i.e., in earning money income.

$$I = f(N)$$

or $$I = w.\,N \qquad ...(2)$$

where w is a coefficient or represents wage rate.

also $$w = \frac{1}{N} \qquad ...(3)$$

Now a number of indifference curves may be drawn by assigning different values to the utility function (1). In Fig. 9.39 we have drawn four indifference

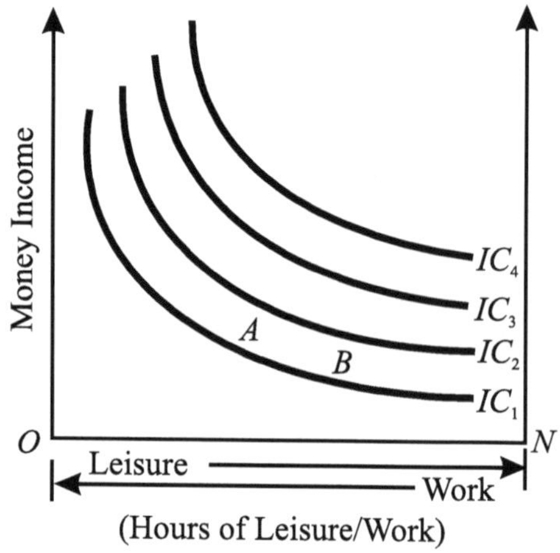

Fig. 9.39

curves IC_1, IC_2, IC_3 and IC_4 showing various combinations of income and leisure. The vertical axis shows money income in dollars and the horizontal axis shows leisure/work. When we read the horizontal axis from left to right, it shows hours of leisure per week and when we read it from right to left, it shows hours of work per week. Moreover, by definition, along an indifference curve, the total utility obtained from work (or income) and leisure remains constant. For instance, on indifference curve IC_1, if the consumer shifts from combination point *A* to combination point *B*, then he sacrifices income but gains enough leisure to compensate, so that he is indifferent between these two combinations. Mathematically, the slope of such indifference curve can be written as

$$-\frac{\partial I}{\partial L} = \frac{\partial U}{\partial L} \bigg/ \frac{\partial U}{\partial I} \qquad ... (4)$$

The slope (or shape) of indifference curve, here, represents the attitudes toward income and leisure.

Now the different hourly payments or wage rates (w) can be represented by the slope of wage lines. In Fig. 9.40, we have drawn four wage lines showing different wage rates.

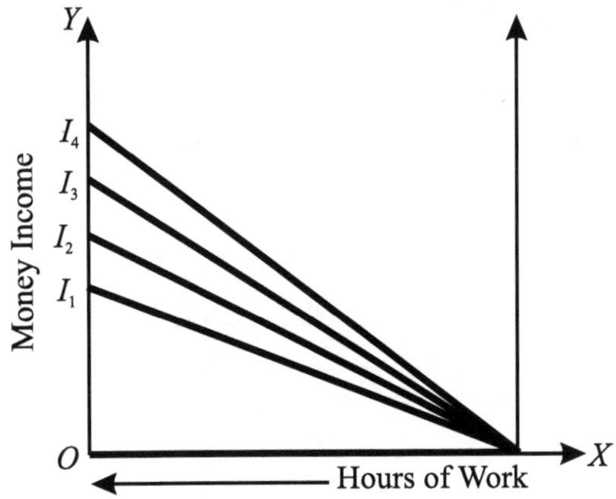

Fig. 9.40

Now for optimisation, the rational consumer wants to be on the highest reachable indifference curve. Thus, he will select that point where the indifference curve is tangent to the respective wage line. In Fig. 9.41, the wage lines are tangential to the indifference curves IC_1, IC_2, IC_3, IC_4 at points E_1, E_2, E_3, E_4 respectively. Joining these various points of equilibrium, we obtain the wage offer curve. Its meaning is that the wage rate rises, the individual first works more hours and then works fewer hours. The wage-offer curve may take any shape depending upon shapes of the indifference curves. Thus the wage offer curve indicates that at difference wage levels

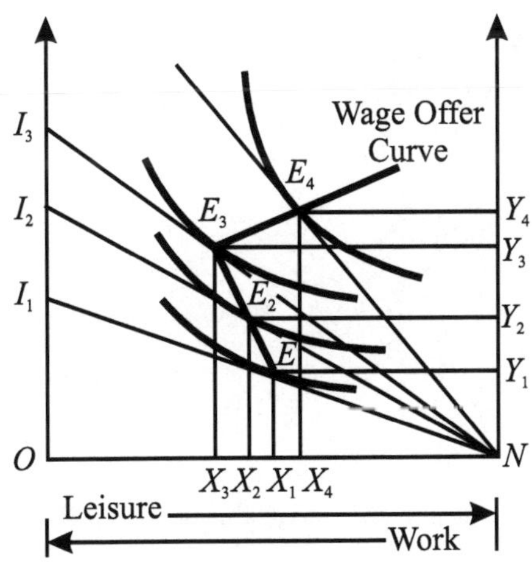

Fig. 9.41

how many hours of work the consumer is ready to offer. This information can be rearranged and presented in an ordinary price-quantity diagram. This is shown in Fig. 9.42. Here the curve *SS* is a supply curve of labour showing the relation between wage rates (price) and the number of hours (quantity) worked at each.[18] The backward bending supply curve in Fig. 9.42 is the supply curve for an individual labour (consumer). But the same curve can also be made to stand for a group of labourers in a labour market, when the supply curves of different labourers are added.

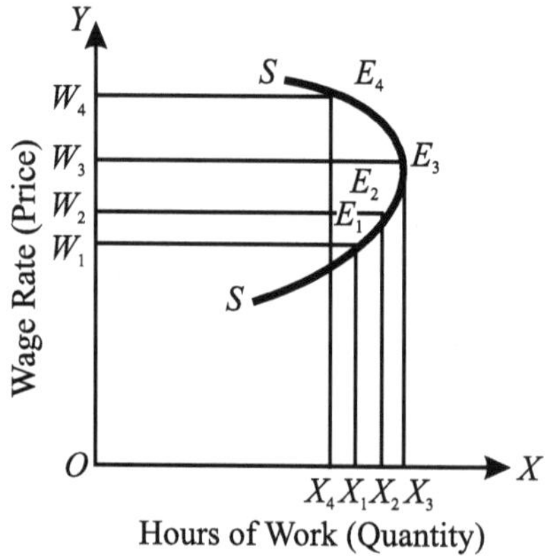

Fig. 9.42

(*vi*) *Explaining the Theory of Index Numbers.* Index number indicates the changes in the level, and thus enables us to compare the standards of living in two different periods or situations. Here we assume that the consumer's preference between the two goods remains the same, i.e. the same indifference curves apply for both the periods.

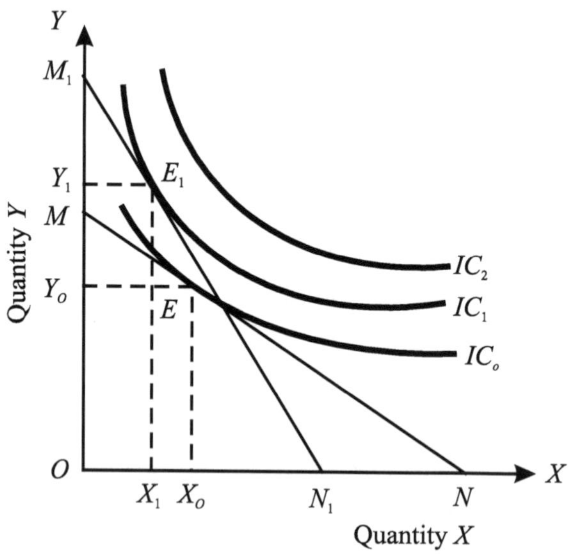

Fig. 9.43

18. The wage offer curve in Fig. 9.41 and the supply curve of labour in Fig. 9.42 face in opposite directions. The reason is obvious that Fig. 9.41 measures work from right to left, whereas Fig. 9.42 measures work from left to right.

In Fig. 9.43, we have drawn three indifference curves IC_0, IC_1 and IC_2 which represent the consumer's satisfaction from goods X and Y in both the periods. MN represents the price line in the initial period O, and M_1N_1 represents the price line in the current period I. Initially or in the base period the consumer was enjoying point E on IC_0 where he was buying OX_0 units of X and OY_0 units of Y in current year when price of X increases and that of Y decreases, the consumer's new equilibrium point becomes E_I on IC_1. At point E_1, he buys OX_1 of X and Oy_1 of Y. Since E_1 lies on a higher indifference curve than the equilibrium point E attained in the base year, the consumer is better off.

The above analysis can be put in the form of real income index numbers in the following manner:

$$I_0 = \frac{P_{X0}\,X_0 + P_{Y0}\,Y_0}{P_{X0}\,X_0 + P_{Y0}\,Y_0} \times 100 = 100$$

and
$$I_1 = \frac{P_{X1}\,X_1 + P_{Y1}\,Y_1}{P_{X0}\,X_0 + P_{Y0}\,Y_0} \times 100$$

where I_0 and I_1 are the index numbers in the base year 0, and the current year 1. P_{X0} represents the price of X in the base year, P_{X1} represents the price of X in current year, P_{Y0} is the price of Y in the base year and P_{Y1} is the price of Y in the current year. Similarly X_0, Y_0 represent the quantities of X and Y in the base year and X_1, Y_1 represent the quantities of X and Y in the current year.

If $I_1 > I_0$, it means the consumer is better off because his current year's real income is greater as compared to the base year's real income.

In general, the index number would be obtained by the following formula:

$$I_{01} = \frac{\sum_{i=1}^{n} P_{1i} X_{1i}}{\sum_{i=1}^{n} P_{0i} X_{0i}}$$

where X_{1i} denotes the current year quantities of various products ($i = 1,\ldots n$) and P_{1i} denotes their respective current year prices. Similarly X_{0i} denotes the base year quantities of various products ($i = 1,\ldots n$) and P_{0i} denotes the irrespective base prices.

Prof. Laspeyre (like Prof. Slutsky) stressed on the base year quantities whereas Prof. Paasche emphasised the current year quantities for both numerator and the denominator. Thus, the Laspeyre Index number can be stated as:

$$I_{01} = \frac{\sum_{i=1}^{n} P_{1i} X_{0i}}{\sum_{i=1}^{n} P_{0i} X_{0i}}$$

and the Paasche Index number can be stated as :

$$I_{01} = \frac{\sum_{i=1}^{n} P_{1i} X_{1i}}{\sum_{i=1}^{n} P_{0i} X_{1i}}$$

(*vii*) *Explaining Changes in Tastes and Preferences.* As we have explained earlier, the slope of an indifference curve explains the relative preferences (or tastes) of the two commodities. If his tastes and preferences remain the same, then the slopes of different indifference curves will also remain identical. In other words, the indifference curves will be parallel to each other in the event of a rise in the *X* money income of the consumer, i.e. he will purchase larger quantities of both the commodities. This case has been illustrated in Fig. 9.44. Initially, the consumer's equilibrium position is at point *E* where his indifference curve IC_1 is tangent to the original price line *MN*. If his money income increases, then the price line shifts from *MN* to M_1N_1 and the new equilibrium position becomes E_1, At point E_1 IC_2 is tangent to the price line

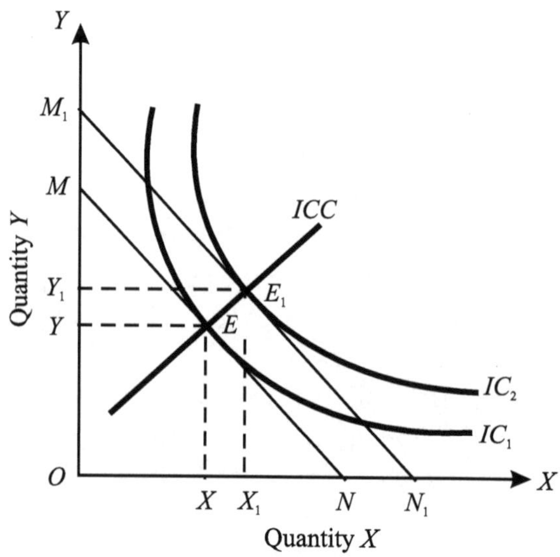

Fig. 9.44

M_1N_1 and it is also parallel to the old indifference curve IC_1. It indicates that the consumption of both the commodities increases.

Now, let us assume that an increase in income leads to change in his tastes. In such a case the slope of the indifference curves will not be the same. In other words, they would not be parallel to each other. The changing slope will indicate whether he prefers more of X to Y or more of Y to X. In Fig, 9.45, it is clear that if the consumer assigns higher preference to X than before, he will move from point E on IC_1 to point E_1 on IC_2. The slope of IC_2 is higher

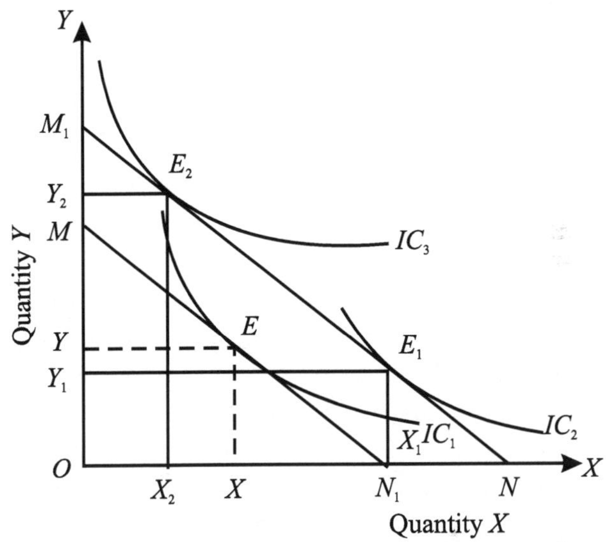

Fig. 9.45

than the slope of IC_1 which implies that along indifference curve IC_2 the relative marginal utility of $X \left(\frac{MU_X}{MU_Y} = MRS \right)$ is higher than the corresponding marginal utilities along IC_1, symbolically,

$$MRS_{XY} \text{ of } IC_2 > MRS_{XY} \text{ of } IC_1$$

or
$$\frac{MU_X}{MU_Y} \text{ of } IC_2 > \frac{MU_X}{MU_Y} \text{ of } IC_1$$

It means X is preferred to Y, and thus commodity Y may be termed as an inferior commodity. The quantity of Y decreases from the initial level of OY to OX_1 despite a rise in cosumer's money income.

Hence, a change in taste leads to an increase in the quantity of (X from OX to OX_1) at the cost of Y (because the consumer moves from E to E_1).

On the other hand, if as a result of an increase in consumer's income he assigns higher preference to Y than before, he will move from IC_1 to IC_3. The consumer's new equilibrium position is E_2 where he buys OY_2 of Y and OX_2 of X. Thus, the consumption of Y increases to the extent of YY_2 while that of X decreases to the extent of XX_2. It is so because the slope of IC_3 or the ratio of marginal utilities all along IC_3 is lower than the corresponding slope or the ratio of marginal utilities, all along IC_1. Symbolically,

$$MRS_{XY} \text{ of } IC_3 > MRS_{XY} \text{ of } IC_1$$

or $$\frac{MU_X}{MU_Y} \text{ of } IC_3 > \frac{MU_X}{MU_Y} \text{ of } IC_1$$

Therefore, commodity Y is more preferable to commodity X, i.e. its utility has increased as a result of an increase in the consumer's money income.

(*viii*) *Measurement of the Consumer's Surplus.* Prof. Hicks makes use of indifference curve analysis in the measurement of the consumer's surplus attained by an individual consumer from certain commodity. In Fig. 9.46, the consumer's imaginary indifference curve is IC_I which states that the consumer is ready to pay MI_1 money for OX units of X rather than going without it. Also, the consumer is indifferent to point M or R, as both the points lie on the same indifference curve IC_1. In this case, the consumer actually needs to sacrifice MI amount of money (or EQ) at the equilibrium level of quantity OX. Thus, he is able to save II_1 (or ER) amount of money which is the measure of his consumer's surplus. Hence, indifference curve analysis is also of much help in the measurement of consumer's surplus which is of paramount importance in various welfare policy determinations.

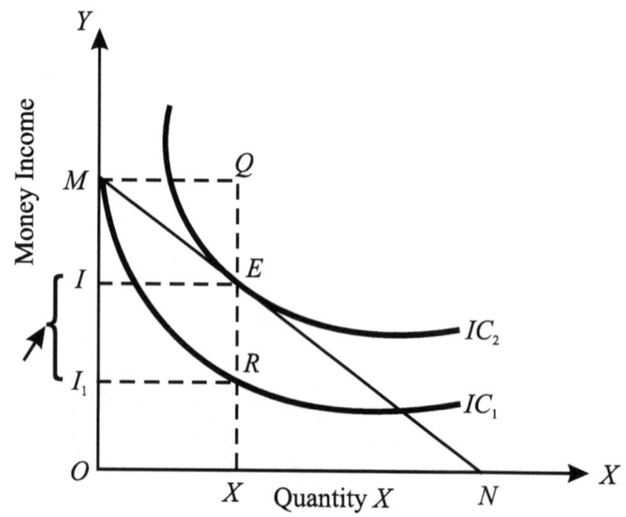

Fig. 9.46

These above are the important applications of indifference curves. Besides, it is fairly used in the determination of various government policies.

17. Comparative Study of Utility Analysis and Indifference Curve Analysis

If we compare the two approaches, we find that the indifference curve analysis is an improvement over the old conventional demand analysis which is based on utility concept. In this connection the following points may be noted:

(*i*) *The indifference curve analysis is not based on the cardinal measurement of utility, while the utility analysis is based on the cardinal measurement of utility.* Under indifference curve analysis we take into account merely the preference of the consumer which is found on the basis of comparison between different levels of satisfaction. We do not bother about the measurement of psychological satisfaction, but depend upon choices of the consumers.

(*ii*) *The utility analysis assumes the price of other goods to be constant while the indifference curve analysis don't have such assumptions. The* utility analysis does not consider the price of the other commodities and assumes that the prices of other commodities are constant. But in real life the prices of other commodities do not remain the same. Changes in the prices of other goods influence the commodity under consideration. The indifference curve analysis takes into account the changes in the prices and quantity of other commodities.

(*iii*) *The utility approach is a single commodity approach while the indifference curve analysis is a two commodity model.* Under utility analysis, Dr. Marshall confines himself to a single commodity model and fails to analyse correctly the multi commodity models. It is also unable to explain the relationships of substitution and complementary. The indifference curve analysis, on the other hand, successfully deals with all such cases.

(*iv*) *Utility analysis assumes that the marginal utility of money is always constant and therefore, it ignores the income effect of price change.* Thus it fails to distinguish between the two components of price effect. In other words, the utility analysis fails to explain the income effect and the substitution effect of a change in the price of commodity. It indicates that demand rises with a fall in price, but it does not indicate how much of it has gone up due to change in income and how much due to substitution effect.

The indifference curve analysis does not assume the marginal utility of money to be constant; and therefore, it enables us to distinguish between the income effect and substitution effect of a price change.

(*v*) *Indifference curve analysis develops the theory of demand.* The indifference curve approach developes the general theory of demand through the ordinal utility theory which enables us to enunciate the general theorem of demand in the following manner:

(*a*) The demand for a good varies inversely with price when the income elasticity of demand for that good is zero or positive.

(*b*) The demand for good varies inversely with price when the income effect of a change in price is smaller than the substitution effect.

(*c*) The demand for a good varies directly with price, when the income elasticity of demand for that good is negative and the income effect of a change in price is larger than the substitution effect.

When either the first or the second condition is fulfilled, the law of demand based on utility analysis holds good; but when the third condition applies we get the Giffen case of positively sloping demand curve. This is the reason that Giffen case is an exception of Marshallian law of demand. The problem of inferior goods was a paradox to Marshall. Hicks' explanation (or indifference curve analysis) of a Giffen case is that the negative income effect is so powerful that it outweighs the positive substitution effect and hence when the price of a Giffen good falls, its demand also falls, instead of rising.

These above points clearly shows that indifference curve analysis is an improvement over the utility analysis in explaining the consumer's demand.

18. A Critical Appraisal of the Indifference Curve Analysis

Since the outcome of Prof. J.R. Hicks' book *Value and Capital* in 1939,[19] the indifference curve analysis has been widely accepted by the modern economists, and it has been greatly elaborated in various directions. As we know, today indifference curves are used in the explanation of many economic phenomena. The modern economists (Hicks, Allen and others) claim that the indifference curve analysis is superior to marginal utility analysis, in that it avoids the allegedly untenable assumption (implicit in utility approach) that consumers can measure the amounts of utility in the various goods that they buy. The indifference curve analysis assumes only "that the consumer is able to decide whether two combinations of goods are equivalent or whether he prefers one to the other; but it is not assumed that he can tell by how much he prefers one combination to the other."[20]

An indifference curve represents the consumer as being able to tell exactly how many units of commodity *Y* will compensate him for loss of one unit of commodity *X* (or vice versa); and he is supposed to be able to do this for any two goods or more goods, or for any good as against all the others put together. This would appear to necessitate his measuring the amounts of utility in every economic good. Otherwise, how can he know much more of

19. Although, Prof. Hicks did not originate the indifference theory, yet it was his exposition and elaboration of the indifference curve that gave its present position in economics.
20. George J. Stigler, *The Theory of Price,* p. 76.

one exactly balances little less of one (or all) of others? There is just as much measurement implied in the one theory as the other. And both the terminology and the mechanics of the indifference curve analysis are more awkward than the marginal utility explanation.

Another advantage of indifference curve analysis over the cardinal utility analysis is that the former explains the income and substitution effects of a given change in the price of commodity and thus it enables us to derive the *real income constant demand curve* which proves a more general and more inclusive theorem of demand than the Marshallian law of demand.

Beyond this, the indifference curve analysis is open to the same criticisms that we raised against the old utility analysis. It is why some economists argue that it (indifference analysis) is merely the utility analysis put in a new garb. According to Prof. Robertson, the new (indifference curve) analysis is only the old wine put into a new bottle. Instead of the concept of utility, it introduces the term 'preference'. Instead of the cardinal numbers (1, 2, 3,…etc.), it makes use of the ordinal numbers (first, second, third, etc.) to indicate the consumer's preferences. The concept of marginal utility has been replaced by the concept of marginal rate of substitution. Similarly, the assumption of diminishing marginal utility has been replaced by the new principle of diminishing marginal rate of substitution.

Like the old utility approach, the new indifference curve approach assumes that consumers are entirely rational in spending their money, and they proceed to plan their expenditure by a complicated process of mathematical calculation. Thus neither of the approaches is correct. As a complete and realistic explanation of how consumer purchases are actually determined, both the approaches the cardinal utility approach and the ordinal indifference curve approach are faulty.

Exercises

1. What are the weaknesses of the Marshallian utility approach? Show how does the indifference curve technique overcome these weaknesses in the law of demand?
2. What are the characteristics of indifference curves? How would you explain a consumer's equilibrium with the help of these curves?
3. Show the effect of a change in income and a change in the price on consumer's demand with the help of indifference curves.
4. What do you understand by indifference curves? Explain fully the uses of indifference curve.
5. State and explain the concept of diminishing marginal rate of substitution (MRS). Whether this law is superior to that of the law of diminishing marginal utility?
6. Explain that the point of tangency between indifference curve and the price line alone is the point of consumer's equilibrium.
7. (*a*) Differentiate between "income effect" and "substitution effect" caused by the change in the price of a commodity.

(*b*) Under what conditions may the fall in the price of the commodity lead to a reduction in the demand for it?

8. Supposing that utility can be measured. Show that utility analysis and indifference curve analysis give the same conditions of equilibrium of the consumer. Use diagram and/ or formula to prove your answer.
9. What is Giffen Paradox? Explain it with the help of indifference curves.
10. What do you mean by a price consumption curve? Is it possible to derive the price-quantity demand curve from the consumption curve?
11. Write short notes on the following:
    (*i*) The Diminishing Marginal Rate of Substitution
    (*ii*) The Budget Line or the Price Line
    (*iii*) Indifference Curves Map
    (*iv*) Abnormal Indifference Curves and Comer Solution
    (*v*) Comparative Demand Curves
    (*vi*) Engel Curves or Income Demand Curves
    (*vii*) Elasticity of Demand and Price Consumption Curve.
12. Explain with the help of a diagram the concept of indifference curves. How far is it an improvement over the utility concept?

Multiple Choice Questions

13. (*i*) An indifference curve indicates, other things remaining the same,
    (*a*) combinations of goods *X* and *Y* which yield equal level of satisfaction.
    (*b*) combinations of goods *X* and *Y* which a consumer would prefer to any others.
    (*c*) a consumer's preference for any two goods.
    (*d*) the amount of commodities *X* and *Y* that a consumer will buy at given prices.
    [*Ans.* (*b*)]

    (*ii*) An indifference curve
    (*a*) slopes upward from right to left.
    (*b*) slopes upward from original point.
    (*c*) slopes downward from left to right.
    (*d*) is parallel to the *Y* axis. [*Ans.* (*c*)]

    (*iii*) An indifference curve is always
    (*a*) concave to the origin. (*b*) convex to the origin.
    (*c*) a vertical straight line. (*d*) a horizontal straight line. [*Ans.* (*b*)]

    (*iv*) Indifference curve is convex to origin since
    (*a*) MRS_{XY} decreases
    (*b*) MRS_{XY} increases
    (*c*) MRS_{XY} remains the same
    (*d*) Marginal utility of commodity *Y* is decreasing as one increases the consumption of commodity [*Ans.* (*a*)]

    (*v*) Which of the following figures can not be an indifference map?

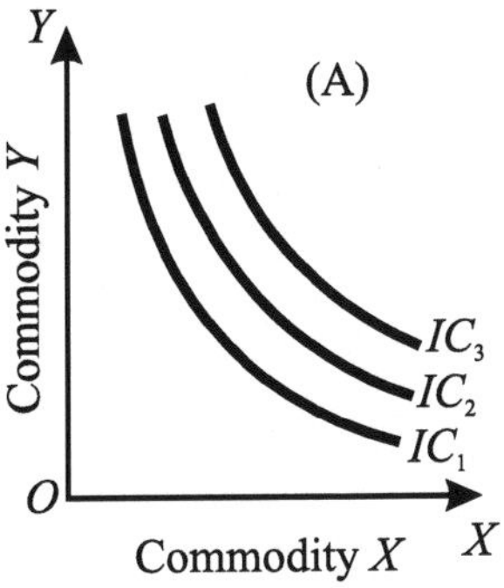

Fig. A

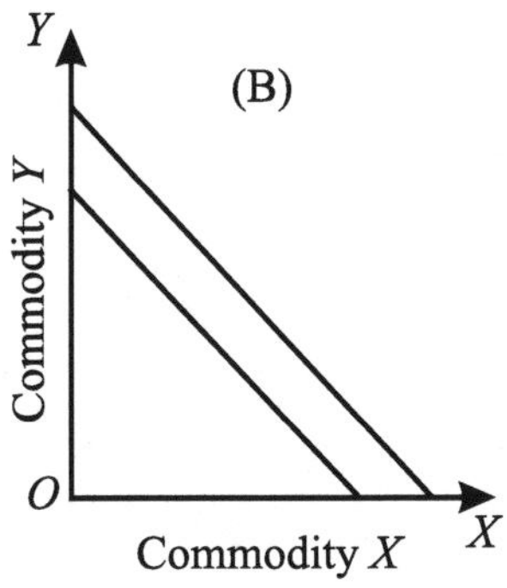

Fig. B

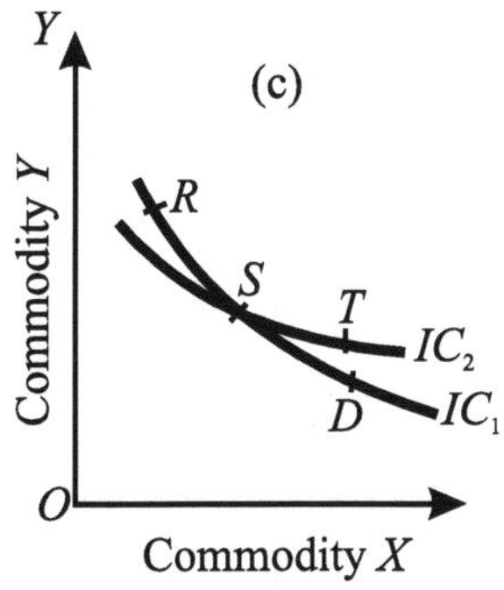

Fig. C

(*a*) *B* and C (*c*) *A* and *B*
(*b*) *C* and *A* (*d*) *A*,*B and C* [*Ans.* (*a*)]

(*vi*) The slope of an indifference curve shows
(*a*) the price ratio (*c*) factor substitution
(*b*) the diminishing *MRS* (*d*) level of indifference [*Ans.* (*b*)]

(*vii*) The statement *A* = *B* = 100 utilities implies
(*a*) an ordinal measure of utility only
(*b*) a cardinal measure of utility only
(*c*) an ordinal and a cardinal measurement of utility
(*d*) none of the above [*Ans.* (*c*)]

(*viii*) At equilibrium, the slope of an indifference curve is
(*a*) equal to the slope of budget line
(*b*) greater than the slope of budget line
(*c*) less than the slope of budget line
(*d*) any one of the above [*Ans.* (*a*)]

Chapter 10

The Concept of Consumer's Surplus

1. Introduction

The idea of consumer's surplus is of enormous importance in economics both from theoretical as well as practical point of view. It was first developed by a French engineer-economist, Arsene Jules Dupuit in 1844. Later on, Alfred Marshall improved a popularised concept of consumer's surplus in 1879 in his *Pure Theory of Domestic Values.* He termed the concept as "Consumer's Rent". But in his later work, *Principles of Economics,* he called it "Consumer's Surplus.

2. Meaning of Consumer's Surplus

When we buy a commodity for consumption, we gain some utility by consuming it; at the same time we lose some utility in terms of the price that we need to pay for it. In the beginning, utility gained is usually higher than the utility lost; and we go on buying a commodity so long as the utility gained continues to exceed the utility lost. The law of diminishing marginal utility tells us that the utility derived from each successive unit of a commodity, however, goes on diminishing. Moreover, the price of the commodity, remains constant. Thus, a point will come when the utility gained equals the utility lost, and at that point we stop our purchases. It will not be worthwhile to increase the purchases beyond this point since the utility gained is smaller than the utility lost in terms of price. It means that we normally make the purchases only when our utility is greater than the price we pay for the commodity. In other words, we buy the commodity only if we expect a surplus of utility or satisfaction from it. This surplus of utility or satisfaction acquired by the consumer is known as the Consumer's Surplus.

Thus, consumer's surplus can be defined as the difference between the satisfaction which the consumer derives from the commodity and that which he forgoes in order to procure that commodity. To put it differently, the satisfaction that consumer obtains from the consumption of a commodity may be measured by the price he would pay for it rather than go without it; while the satisfaction he loses in procuring a commodity is measured by the price he actually pays for it. As such, consumer's surplus is defined as the excess of what a consumer would pay over what he actually pays. According to Dr. Marshall, "The excess of the price which he would be willing to pay rather than go without the thing, over that which he actually does pay, is the economic measure of this surplus satisfaction. It may be called *consumer's surplus.*"[1]

3. Measurement of Consumer's Surplus

Two different approaches have been developed to measure the consumer's surplus. The first is the Marshallian approach based on the utility analysis and the second is the Hicksian approach based on the difference curve analysis. We explain the two approaches in the following section.

4. Marshallian Approach to Consumer's Surplus

Marshall derives the economic measurement of consumer's surplus from the demand curve (marginal utility curve). In Fig. 10.1, *DD* is the demand curve which shows the set of prices that the consumer is willing to pay

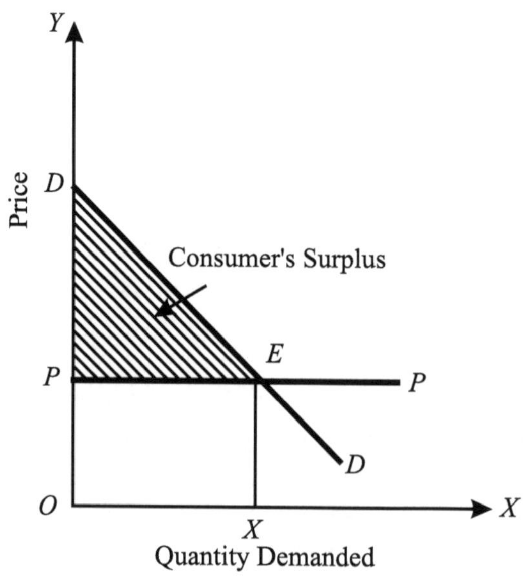

Fig. 10.1

1. A. Marshall, *op. cit.*, p. 103.

for successive units of a commodity. The demand curve *DD* is based on the marginal utility. Since the price of the commodity is fixed by the market, it is constant for all units for our consumer. In Fig. 10.1, *PP* is the price line which is horizontal to *X*-axis. At this given price, the consumer buys *OX* quantity of the commodity. Thus, the area *ODEX* indicates the total amount of money the consumer is willing to pay for *OX* quantity of the commodity. The area *OPEX* indicates the total amount of money that he actually pays for *OX* quantity of the commodity purchased. Thus, the shaded area *PDE* represents the consumer's surplus.

To make it more clear, let us take a numerical example. Suppose, a consumer goes in the market with 120 paise in his pocket with a view to purchasing some oranges. He thinks that the utility of the first orange will be equal to 100, of the second 80, of the third 60, of the fourth 40, of the fifth 20 and of the sixth zero. Now the price per orange in the market is 20 paise. Let us also assume that one unit of utility is equal to one paisa. Now the consumer will purchase the first four oranges without any hitch because the utility of each of them exceeds 20 which he will have to pay per unit (price). He will also buy the fifth orange because he will derive 20 paise worth of utility from it, which is just equal to its price. Now, he will stop his purchases at this point. The consumer's surplus derived by him from the purchase of oranges is shown in Table 10.1.

Table 10.1 states that the total utility derived from 5 units of oranges is qual to 300 paise and the price paid for these five oranges is equal to 100 paise. Thus, the total consumer surplus is 300-100 = 200

Table 10.1

(in Paise)

Units of Oranges	*Marginal Utility (Imaginary Price)*	*Actual Price*	*Consumer's Surplus*
1st	100	20	80
2nd	80	20	60
3rd	60	20	40
4th	40	20	20
5th	20	20	0
Total	300	100	200

The consumer's surplus can also be expressed by a mathematical formula as given below:

$$C.S. = TU - (P \quad N)$$
$$= \Sigma MU - P \times N$$

where TU is the total utility, MU the marginal utility, P is the price of the commodity and N indicates the units of oranges purchased and consumed. Also Σ (sigma) indicates the sum total. If we supplement the necessary information in our above formula from Table 10.1, then we get

$$
\begin{aligned}
C.S. &= 300 - 20 \quad 5 \\
&= 300 - 100 \\
&= 200 \text{ paise.}
\end{aligned}
$$

It is obvious that the consumer's surplus derived from some commodities is much greater than that from the other. There are many comforts and luxuries of which the prices are very much below those which many people would pay rather than go entirely without them; and which, therefore, afford very great consumer's surplus. Good examples of such types of commodities are matches, tea, salt, newspaper, and a postage stamp, etc.[2]

The above concept of individual consumer's surplus can very well be extended to the society as a whole. According to Marshall, if we assume that interpersonal differences in income, tastes, fashion, etc. are cancelled out, we can measure the total surplus satisfaction enjoyed by the society as a whole. This can be calculated by the simple process of adding together the consumer's surpluses enjoyed by all the consumers individually.

Assumptions of Marshallian Approach

The Marshallian concept of consumer's surplus is based on the following important assumptions:

(*i*) *Marshall assumes that there is a fixed relationship between utility and satisfaction.* As we know that utility implies expected satisfaction while satisfaction means actual or realised satisfaction. Utility is measured at the time of purchasing a commodity whereas satisfaction is derived when it is consumed. Thus, utility is different from satisfaction. A commodity may possess more utility, but when consumed the realised satisfaction may not be to that extent. But Marshall assumes that there is a definite relationship between expected satisfaction (utility) and realised satisfaction.

(*ii*) *Marshall assumes that the marginal utility of money is constant throughout the process of exchange.* This assumption is very important because no comparison can be made in the absence of this assumption, and it becomes difficult to calculate consumer's surplus.

(*iii*) *It assumes all the assumptions of the demand analysis.* The idea of consumer surplus is based on the demand curve or the marginal utility curve

---

2. According to Marshall, this benefit may be called the benefit he derives from his opportunities or from his environment; or to recur to a word that was in common use a few generations ago, from his conjecture (the sum total of the technical, economic, social and legal conditions).

(according to Dr. Marshall, the two curves are the same). Thus, the assumptions underlying the demand curve become the assumptions of Marshallian approach to consumer's surplus. It includes *ceteris paribus* conditions.

(*iv*) *It assumes that the utility of a commodity depends upon the quantity of that commodity alone.* In other words, each commodity is an independent commodity. It means, the commodity in question has no substitutes. In the case of substitutes, all substitutes should be grouped as one commodity.

(*v*) *Other things remaining the same.* It assumes that differences in incomes, fashions, and tastes, etc. between consumers are to be cancelled out.

The Marshallian approach to consumer's surplus holds only if the above assumptions are accepted.

Criticism of Marshallian Approach to Consumer's Surplus

The Marshallian Approach to the measurement of consumer's surplus has been criticised by Ulisse Gobbi, Cannan, Nicholson, Taussig, Hicks, Samuelson and others. According to Prof. Hicks, Marshall's concept of consumer's surplus has been based on certain assumptions which are not tenable in actual life. Thus the concept has been criticised on the basis of its unrealistic assumptions. The important criticisms of Marshall's concept of consumer's surplus are given below:

(*i*) *Utility cannot be measured numerically.* Marshall's approach is based on the assumption that utility is measurable. But utility cannot be measured numerically; it can only be realised. Due to this limitation, Prof. Hicks has explained the concept with the help of indifference curve technique.

(*ii*) *Marginal utility of money does not remain the same.* Marshall's approach also assumes that the marginal utility of money is constant throughout the process of exchange. But this is not true; because when the consumer buys some quantity of a commodity, his stock of money is correspondingly reduced with the result that the marginal utility of money increases. The law of diminishing marginal utility also states that the greater the stock of money, the smaller is the marginal utility and vice versa. Thus, Marshall's assumption of constant marginal utility of money does not hold in real life.

(*iii*) *Utility is interrelated.* Another assumption of the approach is that the utility of each good depends on the quantity of that good alone. In other words, it assumes that utility of any commodity is independent. The critics have challenged this assumption. The utility of a commodity also depends upon its related goods.

(*iv*) *Substitutes are available.* Further, a commodity may possess a number of substitutes and it is neither possible nor feasible to assume the various substitutes of a commodity as one commodity.

(*v*) *Assumptions are unrealistic.* Again Marshall's concept of consumer's surplus is based on the demand curve. Critics point out that it is not possible to know the whole demand schedule of the commodity in question. It is difficult to know that how much price the consumer is willing to pay for each unit of the commodity because complete list of demand prices is not available. Thus, we cannot calculate the accurate estimate of consumer's surplus. Moreover, the assumption of *ceteris paribus* does not hold in real life.

(vi) *Utility and satisfaction are different.* Marshall assumes that there is a definite relationship between utility and satisfaction. But the facts of experience do not follow the relationship. The satisfaction may not always be proportional to utility. It is possible that in the cases of utility we may obtain some consumer's surplus, but in the case of (realised) satisfaction, we have to incur losses. Thus, Marshall's assumption that satisfaction is directly proportional to utility is not valid in real life.

(vii) *Other things do not remain the same.* Again, the critics do not accept Marshall's assumption that the differences in incomes, fashions and tastes, etc. are cancelled out in order to measure the consumer's surplus of the society as a whole. This is only an arbitrary assumption. There are large number of purchases in the market with different incomes, fashions and tastes, etc. Different people act differently to a particular economic situation. All this will lead to a number of difficulties in the measurement of consumer's surplus of the society as a whole.

These above are the important limitations of Marshall's measurement of the consumer's surplus.

5. Hicksian Approach to Consumer's Surplus

Prof. Hicks derives the measurement of consumer's surplus from the indifference curve analysis. It has been shown in Fig. 10.2. In Fig. 10.2, consumer's money income has been measured along *Y*-axis while the *X*-axis measures the quantity of commodity *X*. Let us assume that the consumer has *OM* of income. If he spends his entire income on *X*, he would get *ON* quantity of *X*. Thus, *MN* is the price line which touches the indifference curve IC_2 at point *E*. At point *E*, he gets *OX* quntity of *X* and *OY* amount of

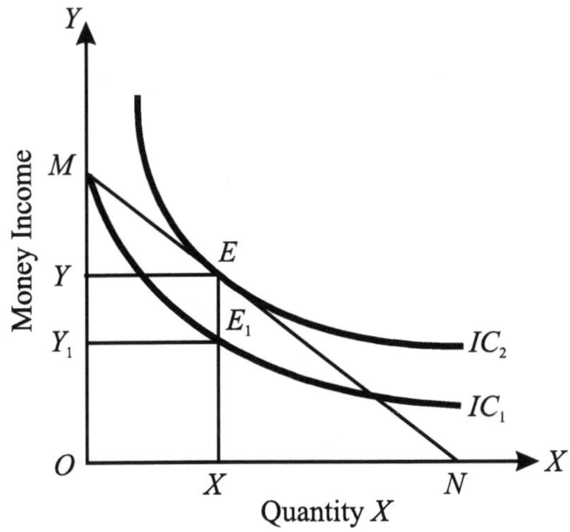

Fig. 10.2

money income. In other words, in equilibrium he spends *YM* money for *OX* quantity of *X*. Now, let us assume that the consumer does not know the price of *X*. In the absence of the price line, the imaginary indifference curve IC_1 indicates that for *ON* quantity of *X*, consumer is willing to spend MY_1 amount of money income and would like to remain at point E_1 on IC_1. But actually he has to spend *MY* money income for the same quantity. Thus the difference (MY_1 – *MY*) YY_1 is consumer's surplus. In other words, consumer's surplus is the difference between the imaginary price and the actual price.

Further, we can also have the effect of a price change or income change upon consumer's surplus through the indifference curve technique. This has been explained in the following section.

Change in Price and Consumer's Surplus

Here we assume that the price of *X* falls but the money income of the consumer remains unchanged. Due to a fall in the price of *X*, the price line *MN* shifts MN_1 in Fig. 10.3. Originally, the consumer was in equilibrium at point *E* where he got *OX* quantity of *X* and OY amount of money income. In other words, he was purchasing *OX* quantity of *X* with *MY* of money income. His consumer's surplus at point *E* was shown by YY_1 (= EE_1). In the new situation when the price of *X* decreases, it enables the consumer to enjoy equilibrium point E_2 with a combination of *OX* quantity of *X* and OY_2 amount of money income. In other words, he needs to spend MY_2 money for the same *OX* quantity of *X*. It implies that at point E_2 this consumer's surplus has increased to Y_2Y_1.

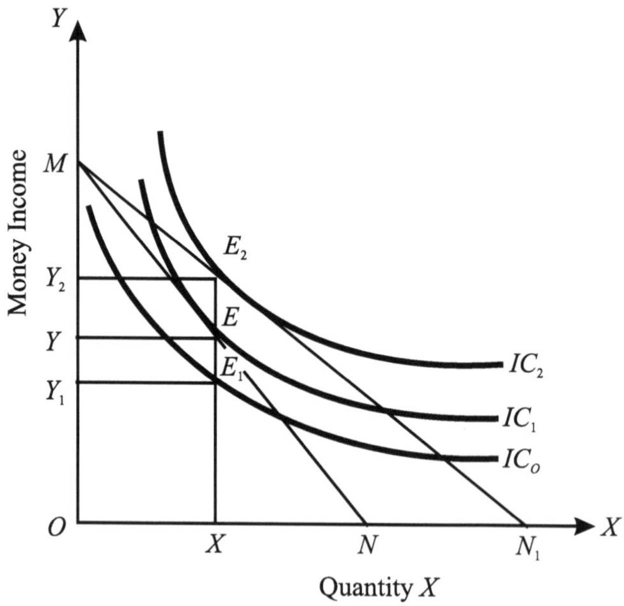

Fig. 10.3

Similarly, the students can also show the effect of a rise in price of *X* on consumer's surplus assuming that money income remains the same.

Change in Income and Consumer's Surplus

This case has been illustrated in Fig. 10.4. Here we assume that the money income of the consumer changes while the price of the commodity remains the same. Let us assume that the money income of the consumer increases. Due to an increase in money income the line shifts from *MN* to M_1N_1. Originally, the consumer's price line was *MN* which touches the indifference curve IC_1 at point *E*. His original consumer's surplus was YY_1 (= EE_1), because the consumer was willing to pay MY_1, amount of money for *OX* quantity of *X*. If consumer's income increases from *OM* to OM_1 his new price line becomes M_1N_1 (assuming that the price of *X* remains constant). In this new position of increased income the consumer's preference schedule has changed. The original imaginary indifference curve was IC_0 but in the new position the imaginary indifference curve would be IC_2. It indicates that the consumer is now ready to pay M_1Y_2 amount of money for the same *OX* quantity of *X*. But he is able to get the same quantity of commodity *X* by actually paying only M_1Y_3 amount of money (here we may note that M_1Y_3 = M Y_2 because the price of *X* and the quantity purchased remain the same). Thus, the new consumer's surplus is Y_3 Y_2 (= E_2E_3) which may be equal to or more or less than the original consumer's surplus. The amount of consumer's surplus depends upon the slope of imaginary indifference curves IC_0 and IC_2. If the slope of IC_0 and IC_2 is the same, then in both the situations (the initial situation and the increased income situation) the consumer's surplus will be the same.

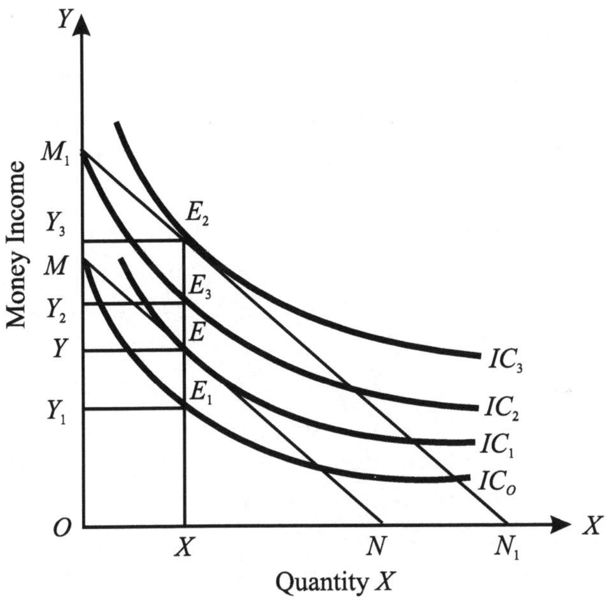

Fig. 10.4

6. Hicks' Reformulation of the Concept of Consumer's Surplus[3]

In the above analysis Prof. Hicks has defined consumer's surplus as the difference between the imaginary price and the actual price of the commodity. This is very similar to that of Marshallian measurement of the consumer's surplus. But later on, Prof. Hicks defined the concept of consumer's surplus in a slightly different way. He defined consumer's surplus as "that sum of money which must either be paid to or taken away from the consumer consequent upon a change in his economic position in such a manner as to leave his total satisfaction unaffected." To put it differently', the consumer remains on the same difference curve despite the change in his economic position. The changes in his economic position may take place via the changes in the quantity of the commodity or the price of the commodity. We discuss them under the following headings.

3. J.R. Hicks, The Consumer s Surpluses , *Review of Economic Studies,* 1943-44, Vol. II.

Changes in the Quantity of the Commodity

As we know, commodity's surplus using from the opportunity to purchase a commodity. It the opportunity to purchase is lost or is taken away, pay, by the government, the consumer surplus will also disappear. Suppose the government stops the open purchase of sugar by the consumers and subjects it to the permit system. Only that person is allowed to purchase sugar who purchase a permit issued by the government. Let us suppose that a person has a monthly income of $1000 and also purchase a permit to purchase sugar. Let in further suppose that the person is prepared to give up his sugar permit if he is paid a sum of B 20 lieu of it. Then B 20, according to Hicks, con........ the quantity-equivalent variation in income. It is a measure of consumer's surplus, because the consumer considers an income of $1000 plus the permit to purchase sugar as equivalents to an income of $1020. when the consumer receives B.20 in lieu of having forgave his right to purchase sugar, his total satisfaction remains the same. In other words, the sum of B.20 received by him compensates that person for the loss of satisfaction that he has suffered consequent upon forgoing the permit for sugar. Now let in suppose that the income of that person is $1000; but he has no sugar permit in his possession. When another person having a sugar permit approaches him and desires to sell that permit to him, the person is prepared to buy it for, let us say, a sum of B.16. Then B.16, according to Hicks, is quantity compensating variation in income because that person commodes an income of $1000 as qua........... to an income of $984 plus the opportunity to by sugar. When that person pays B 16 is lieu of having received the permit, his total satisfaction remains the same. In other words, the loss of satisfaction suffered by him on parting with B 16 has been compensated by the acquisition of the right to buy sugar.

We shall now illustrate quantity-equivalent variation in income and quantity-con........ variation income with the help of indifference curves.

In Fig. 10.5, we measure sugar along the horizontal axis OX an money income along the vertical axis OY. The consumer has a money income of OM. The income price line MN represents the price of sugar. The consumer is in equi.......... of point E on IC_2 buying OS of sugar paying YM of money. Now, suppose the consumer loses his sugar permit and con........also the right to purchase sugar.[4] The question is now is how much additional amount of money-income the consumer needs to be given to compensates him for the loss of the right to purchase sugar so that he remains on the same

4. Here, we should remember the assumption that only that person is able to purchase sugar who possesses the sugar permit. Sugar is completely controlled by the government.

indifference curve IC_2. as the diagram shows, if the consumer is given MM_3 additional money income, he will be fully compensated for the loss of the right to purchase sugar, so that he will remain on the some indifference curve IC_2. if he is given MM_3 of additional income, he will more from E to M_3 on the Y-axis and yet he will remain on the some indifference curve. At point M_3 he will combine zero unit of sugar with OM_3 of money. Thus the consumer needs to be given MM_3 sum of additional money-income to compensate him for the loss of the right to by sugar. MM_3, therefore, con.......

Quantity-equivalent variation in income.

Now let us suppose that in the ini.........situation, there is no sugar permit available to the consumer. Then later on a sugar permits made available to the consumer. He can now buy sugar with this permit and this enables him to enjoy consumer's surplus from sugar. The problem now is how much money income should be taken away from the consumers to neutralize his consumer's surplus so that he is neither better of nor worse of than before. As shown in Fig. 10.5, the consumer finds himself initially at the point M on IC_0 comparing zero unit of sugar with OM of money. This is the portion when sugar is not available to him. Then a sugar permit is issued to him and he is enabled to buy sugar at a price indicated by the price line MN. This helps the consumer in reaching equilibrium. At point E on indifference were IC_2 with OS of sugar and OY of money. Having reached at point E, the consumer is obviously on the higher indifference curve IC_2 showing that he is now better off than before. But the question is that the consumer is not to be allowed to become bitter off than before. His total satisfaction is to remain the same. This can be ensured only if the consumer is parched back to original indifference curve IC_0. As shown in Fig. 10.5, the consumer can be pursed back to IC_0 only if MM, amount of income is taken away from him. MM, therefore, cons....... Quantity-com. Variation in income

Hicks *vs.* Marshall's Measure

If we examine Hicks' quantity-equivalent variation and quantity-compensating variation and Marshall's consumer's surplus[5], then we find that Hicks' surplus in both the 4 types of measurements is higher than that of Marshall's suplus, when the money income of the consumer and the price of the commodity are given. Marshall measures the consumer's surplus as the difference between the price which he would be prepared to pay and the price which he actually

5. Prof Hicks defines consumer s surplus in terms of quantity-equivalent variation and quantity-compensating variation while Marshall used the term consumer s surplus for Hicks quantity variations.

pays to buy the equilibrium quantity of the commodity. In Fig. 10.5, the former price of the quantity OS is TE_1 while the latter price of the same quantity OS is TE. Thus, Marshall's consumer's surplus is EE_1. If the consumer had the freedom to buy any quantity of the commodity, he would

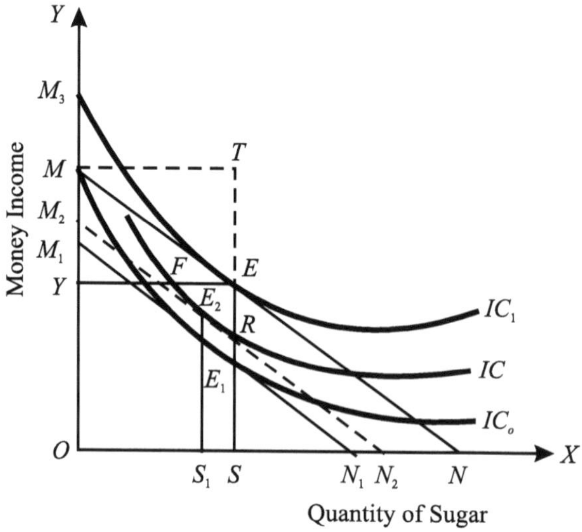

Fig. 10.5

have wished to buy OS_1 quantity of the commodity where he enjoys a higher indifference curve IC. This is because points F and E_1 both lie on IC_0 and if the consumer shifts from E_1 to F he is able to increase his income as consequent of the shift in the price line from M_1N_1 to M_2N_2. Now keeping himself on the price line M_2N_2 the consumer can get a higher satisfaction if he moves from F to E_2 on the same price line M_2N_2. Since point F lies on IC_0 while point E_2 lies on IC_1 which is higher than IC_0, the consumer is able to get a higher level of satisfaction at point E_2. At point E_2, he buys OS_1 (which is $< OS$) quantity of the commodity. If, however, the indifference curves are parallel, then there will be no difference between the two approaches. The assumption of parallel indifference curves is equivalent to the assumption of constant marginal utility of money. In other words, in the case of parallel indifference curves, there will be no income effect and the Hicksian consumer's surplus will be equal to that of Marshallian consumer's surplus.

Changes in the Price of the Commodity

Like the quantity changes, the price changes are also of two types:

(*i*) Price-equivalent variation.

(*ii*) Price-compensating variation.

Under the price-equivalent variation, when the price of the commodity increases, the income of the consumer is to be increased, so that he remains on the same indifference curve. While under the price-compensating variation, when the price of the commodity decreases, the income of the consumer is to be reduced, so that he remains on the same indifference curve.

This has been illustrated in Fig. 10.6. Suppose, consumer's money income is *OM* and the initial price line is *MN*. Originally, the consumer's equilibrium point is *E* where the price line *MN* touches the indifference curve IC_2. At point *E*, the consumer buys *OX* quantity of the commodity with *RE* amount of money income. Now if the price of commodity *X* increases, then the price line shifts leftwards to MN_1 which touches the lower indifference curve IC_1 at point E_1. Now the question is that how much income he should be given, so that he may again reach his initial indifference curve. Figure 10.6 shows that the increase in the price of commodity *X* will be compensated by providing MM_1 amount of additional income to the consumer. This will enable the consumer to attain E_2 initial indifference curve IC_2. Therefore, according to Hicks, MN_1 amount of money income is the *price-equivalent variation in income.*

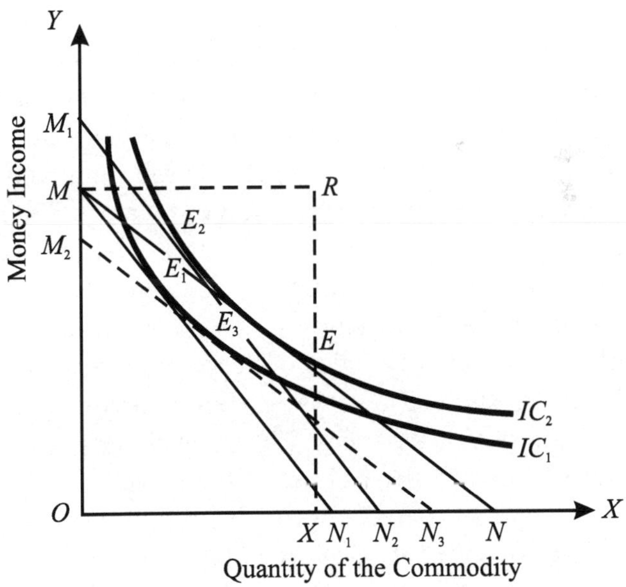

Fig. 10.6

Now, let us assume that the original price line is MN_1 which is tangent to indifference curve IC_1 at point E_1. If the price of *X* falls, the original price line MN_1 shifts to the new price line *MN* which touches a higher indifference curve IC_2 at point *E*. Now the question is that how much money income of the consumer should be reduced, so that in the new situation he is made neither worse nor better off. Fig. 10.6 indicates that the consumer's money income should be reduced by MM_2 to push the consumer back to his original indifference curve IC_2. Here, the consumer's equilibrium point is E_3 which lies on the same indifference curve as the point E_1. Thus, according to Prof. Hicks, MM_2 amount of money incomes is the *price compensating variation in income.*

7. Importance of Consumer's Surplus

The concept of consumer surplus is of great importance in theoretical as well as in practical fields. It is an important instrument of government policies. It occupies and important place in welfare economics. It is also fairly used in taxation and price determination. Some of the important uses of the concept of consumer's surplus are given below:

(i) *It helps us to make a comparative study of the satisfaction derived by different classes.* People receive their incomes in the shape of money. But their real income should be calculated in terms of satisfaction which they derive by spending their monetary income. Therefore, in comparing the income of a person (class) with that of another, we should look at the real income or satisfaction derived from money income. An idea of real income or satisfaction from money income can be had with the help of consumer's surplus. Thus, if we desire to calculate the real income of the same class of persons in two countries, we should calculate the consumer's surplus enjoyed by them. For instance, the average money income of the labour class is \$200 per month in India and the same class can earn \$300 in Australia. Now, it is possible that \$200 in India may afford more consumer's surplus than \$300 in Australia. In such a case the labour class will enjoy greater satisfaction in India than in Australia. Similarly, we can get an idea of the economic position of the same class of people in the same country at different times by calculating the consumer's surplus enjoyed by them. Thus consumer's surplus is used to make a comparative study of the welfare of the people.

(*ii*) *The concept of consumer's surplus is used in the determination of a fair tax-policy.* The government of every country has to collect revenue by imposing taxes. But it makes every endeavor to impose only such taxes which might yield substantial revenue to cause as little harm to the people as possible. Marshall has proved on the basis of consumer's surplus that the government should impose taxes on an increasing cost industry and it should provide economic subsidies to decreasing cost industry.

(*a*) *Tax on an increasing cost industry and consumer's surplus.* We know that a tax brings additional revenue to the government (it can be assumed as the benefit aspect of the tax) and on other hand, it leads to a rise in the price of that commodity with a corresponding reduction in the consumer's surplus of the people (it can be assumed as the loss aspect of the tax). Now, a tax can be considered a good tax only if the benefit (in terms of government revenue) is greater than the loss (in terms of consumer's surplus). According to Marshall, a tax on an increasing cost industry is a good tax. This can be illustrated with the help of a diagram. In Fig. 10.7, *DD* and *SS* are the respective demand and supply curves of the increasing cost industry. These curves cut each other at

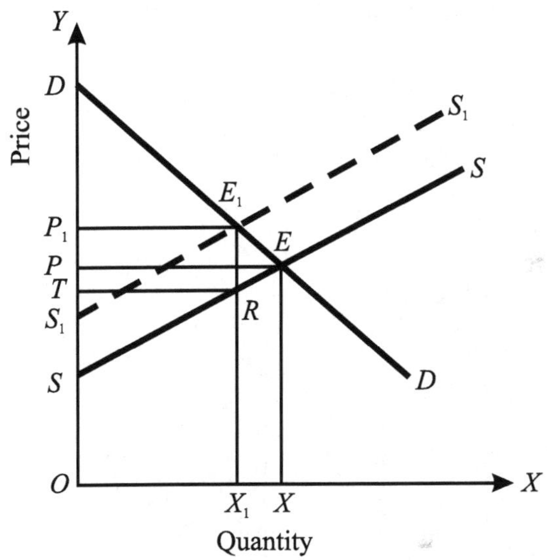

Fig. 10.7

point *E* where *OX* quantity of *X* is bought at *OP* price and the consumer's surplus is equal to the area *DEP.*

Now if tax is levied on commodity *X,* then the supply curve shifts upwards to S_1S_1 which cuts the demand curve *DD* at point E_1. Now the consumer's surplus is reduced to the area DE_1P_1 because price has increased from *OP* to OP_1. Thus, the loss to "consumer's surplus is equal to the area P_1E_1EP. But per unit tax on OX_1 quantity is RE_1 ($=TP_1$). Thus, the government collects revenue to the amount of P_1E_1TR which is clearly greater than the loss of consumer's surplus (P_1E_1EP). Thus, such type of tax on an increasing cost industry is justified. .

(*b*) *Economic subsidy to a decreasing cost industry and consumer's surplus.* As we know that economic subsidy (bounty) leads to a decrease in the price of the commodity and consequently the consumer's surplus increases with an increasing economic burden of the government. If the amount of consumer's surplus is greater than the economic subsidy, then the economic subsidy is justified. This can be illustrated by the following figure. In Fig.10.8, *SS* curve indicates the decreasing cost conditions of the industry. If economic bounty is given to the industry, it shifts to S_1S_1. The initial price of the industry was equal to *OP* but now it becomes OP_1.

The total increase in consumer's surplus is equal to the area P_1E_1EP. The per unit economic subsidy on *OX* quantity is E_1R (= TP_1). Thus the total economic subsidy amounts to be the area TRE_1P_1 which is less than the total increase in consumer's surplus P_1E_1EP. Thus, an imposition of tax on a decreasing cost industry is not justified but in place an economic bounty is well justified. It leads to enough increase in consumer's surplus.

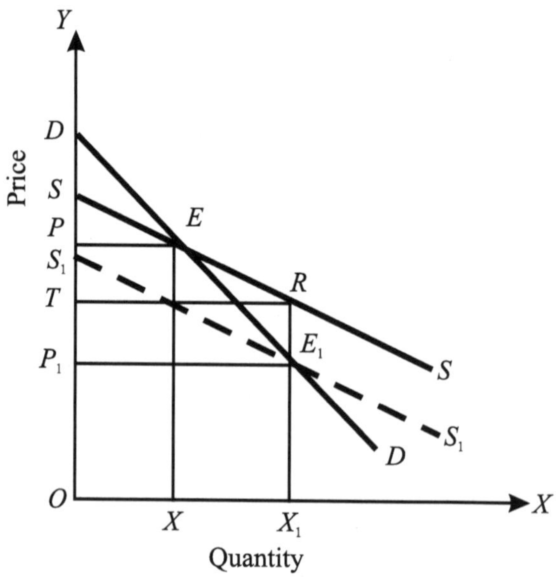

Fig. 10.8

(*iii*) *The concept of consumer's surplus has practical importance to the monopolist in the determination of the price for his product.* If he possesses the knowledge about the consumer's surplus, he can get maximum profit by adopting the policy of price discrimination. He can sell his product at a higher price in that market where the consumer's surplus of the people is found to be very high and at lower price where consumer's surplus is found to be low.

(*iv*) *The concept of consumer's surplus states that the burden of indirect taxes is more than of direct taxes (income-tax).* When a tax is levied on a commodity, the consumer has to curtail his consumption. It leads to a greater loss of consumer's surplus. If the same amount of tax is collected through income-tax, then the consumer can minimise his loss of consumer's surplus by reducing a little (marginal) consumption of various commodities under his consumption. Thus, normally, direct tax leads to a minimum loss of consumer's surplus because the consumer can readjust his expenditure on various commodities.

(*v*) *We can measure the gains from international trade with the help of consumer's surplus.* According to Heckscher-Ohlin theory of international trade, we should import those commodities whose costs of production are higher in our country and should export those commodities which are cheaply produced in the home country. By doing thus, we may be able to increase the consumer's surplus of the society which is the net gain from international trade.

(*vi*) *The concept of consumer's surplus enables us to realise the difference between 'value in-use' and 'value-in exchange'.* In our real life, we realise almost daily that some commodities are very useful and also cheap in market, e.g. match box, postcard, salt, newspaper, etc. For these items, we are ready to pay much more than what we actually pay, if the alternative is to go without them.

(*vii*) *The doctrine of consumer's surplus enables us to compare the advantage of environment and opportunities.* We may compare the conditions of one period with those of the other period or of one country with those of another country with the help of consumer surplus. Thus, we can make a comparative study of the economic conditions of people at different times and of different countries. The consumer's surplus is the index of welfare. The larger the consumer's surplus, the better off the people.

Thus, the concept of consumer's surplus is of great importance. Prof. Samuelson has also accepted the idea of consumer's surplus. According to him, "The privilege of being able to buy a vast array of goods at low prices cannot be overestimated."[6] It helps the government to take proper public decisions.

Exercises

1. What do you understand by consumer's surplus? How far can it be measured?
2. Explain graphically the concept of consumer's surplus. What difficulties are encountered in its measurement? Show the theoretical and practical importance of this concept.
3. Discuss the importance of consumer's surplus in the theory of monopoly and taxation.
4. Critically examine the concept of consumer's surplus. How far has Professor Hicks succeeded in improving this concept?
5. How do indifference curves help us in understanding the concept of consumer's surplus?
6. Explain Marshallian doctrine of consumer's surplus. What is the contribution of Hicks towards the doctrine of consumer's surplus?
7. Show how the concept of consumer's surplus is based on the distinction between total utility and marginal utility.
8. "If we put Marshall's question and ask how much more the consumer would be prepared

to pay rather than go without the thing, we get the compensating surplus." (J.R. Hicks). Illucidate.

9. Explain Hicks' reformulation of consumer's surplus in terms of quantity variation and price variation.

Multiple Choice Questions

10. (*i*) Consumer surplus is described as
    (*a*) extra quantity bought
    (*b*) low price available
    (*c*) difference between imaginary price and actual price
    (*d*) none of the above [*Ans.* (*c*)]

    (*ii*) Consumer's surplus is higher in the case of
    (*a*) buyer's surplus
    (*b*) differential surplus
    (*c*) indifference surplus
    (*d*) extra personal gain [*Ans.* (*a*)]

    (*iii*) Consumer's surplus is highest in the case of
    (*a*) necessaries
    (*b*) comforts
    (*c*) luxuries
    (*d*) conventional necessaries [*Ans.* (*a*)]

    (*iv*) In which of the following fields the concept of consumer's surplus is useful?
    (*a*) monetary policy
    (*b*) tax policy
    (*c*) investment policy
    (*d*) fixing remuneration of factors of production [*Ans.* (*b*)]

Chapter 11

The Revealed Preference Theory of Demand

1. Introduction

The theory of revealed preference has been developed by Prof. Paul A. Samuelson of America[1]. This theory is different to that of Marshall's utility approach and Hicksian indifference curve approach. As we have noticed that the Marshallian utility approach to consumer behaviour is based on the assumption that utility is measurable and the Hicksian indifference curve approach to consumer behaviour is based on the assumption that the consumer is able to tell his preference among the various alternative combinations of the two commodities. These assumptions are unrealistic assumption. The Samuelson's revealed preference theory of demand is free from such unrealistic assumptions and it seeks to enunciate the demand from observed market behaviour of the consumer. Thus, it is third root of 'the logical theory of demand' and has been called by Hicks as the Direct Consistency Test under strong ordering. The theory is based on the fact that 'choice reveals preference.' In other words, the theorem of revealed preference draws its conclusions about the preferences of the consumer from the reactions of the consumer to price changes that take place in the market.

2. Assumptions of Revealed Preference Theory

Now, before we explain the theory let us understand the assumption on which the theory is based. The important assumptions of the theory are given below:

(*i*) The tastes and preferences of the consumer are given and they remain unchanged during the period of analysis.

(*ii*) The consumer prefers more goods to less in any situation.

---

1. P.A. Samuelson, *Foundations of Economic Analysis,* 1947, Ch. V-VI and "Consumption Theorems in terms of over compensation rather than indifference comparisons," *Economica,* February 1953.

(*iii*) The consumer chooses only one combination of the two commodities on agiven income-price line (or budget line).

(*iv*) The consumer's choice is based on strong ordering.

(*v*) The consumer's choices are consistent. Here, consistency or transitivity implies that once combination *A* is preferred to *B*, the latter must never be revealed preferred to *A*.

(*vi*) Revealed preference will alter only if the price is sufficiently lowered.

(*vii*) The theory is based on the assumption of transitivity. Transitivity, however, refers to three term consistency. If *A* is preferred to *B*, and *B* is to *C*, then the consumer must prefer *A* to *C*. This assumption is necessary for the revealed preference theory, if the consumer is to make a consistent choice from given alternative situations.

(*viii*) Income elasticity of demand is positive, i.e. more good is demanded when income rises, and less when income falls.

3. Choice Reveals Preference

Prof. Samuelson's theory of demand is based on the revealed preference axiom or hypothesis which states that choice reveals preference. In this context, a consumer buys a combination of two goods, either because he likes it in relation to the other combinations or it may be cheaper as compared to others. The idea of the revealed preference theory of demand has been explained in Fig. 11.1. Given the income of the consumer and the prices of the two commodities, *MN* is the income-price line in Fig.11.1. Triangle *OMN* is the area of consumer's selection. The consumer can select any of the combinations *A, B, C*, and *D* with the help of his given constraints under the price line *MN*. Now the consumer will decide to buy some particular combination of the two commodities *X* and *Y* because he likes it more than the others or because it happens to be cheaper. If the consumer chooses to buy combination *A*, then *A* is *revealed preferred* to *B*, and combinations *C* and *D* are *revealed inferior* to *A*. To put it differently, combinations *A* and *B* both lie on the same price line *MN* and, therefore, are equally costly and equally good. If both are equally costly and also equally good, and even then the consumer buys combination *A*, the conclusion is obvious that the consumer buys *A* because he likes *A* better. It means that by purchasing combination *A*, the consumer has revealed his preference for it. On the other hand, combinations C and *D* are revealed inferior because they are lying to the left of the price-income line *MN*. Also, in Fig. 11.1, combination *E* lies outside the price-income line which indicates that it is more expensive and the consumer is unable to buy it with his given constraints. Thus, combination *A* is revealed preferred to all other combinations where the consumer buys *OX* quantity of *X* and *OY* quantity of *Y*. Therefore, this choice becomes preference and strong ordering *preference hypothesis* is the basis of Prof. Samuelson's revealed preference theory.

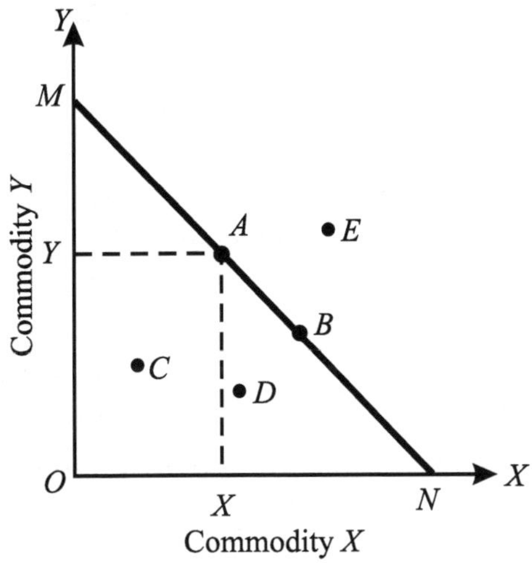

Fig. 11.1

The strong ordering preference hypothesis implies that there is a definite ordering of the various combinations of the two commodities in the consumer's scale of preferences. The selection (choice) of a particular combination by the consumer reveals his definite preference for it over all other combinations that are possible. Under the indifference curve approach, the consumer was assumed to be indifferent to the various alternative combinations on an indifference curve, but under the revealed preference approach, the consumer reveals a definite preference for one particular combination of the two commodities. In Fig. 11.1 the consumer chooses combination *A* out of various alternative combinations available to him and there is no possibility of *A* being indifferent to any other combination (say *B*) on the same price line under strong ordering hypothesis. But according to Prof. Hicks, strong ordering implies that the chosen combination is preferred to all other combinations below the price-income line but may be indifferent to the combinations on the same price-income. In Prof. Hicks' own words, "The difference between the consequences of strong and weak ordering, so interpreted amounts to be more than this, that under strong ordering the chosen position is shown to be preferred to all other positions in and on the triangle, while under weak ordering it is preferred to all positions within the triangle but may be indifferent to other positions on the same boundary as itself."[2]

2. J.R. Hicks, *Revision of Demand Theory* (1956), p. 43.

The assumption of the revealed preference theory also states that the consumer has to choose one and only one particular combination of the available combinations. It implies that he cannot be indifferent between any two combinations on the price-income line. Thus, according to Prof. Samuelson, strong ordering implies a definite preference and there is no question of indifference relationship between the various alternative combinations. To this extent, the revealed preference theory is an improvement over the previous two theories of demand the Marshallian utility analysis and the Hicksian indifference curve analysis.

Prof. Samuelson's revealed preference approach can also be explained in terms of index numbers. Let us assume that in a given situation, X_1 and X_2 represent the two combinations of various goods and P_0 represents the prevailing price level. If the total cost of combination X_1 at price P_0 is considered to be not greater than the total cost of combination X_2 at price P_0' we may write the consumer's preference function in the following manner:

$$X_1P_0 \leq X_2P_0 \qquad ...(1)$$

The condition (1) implies that the expenditure incurred on combination X_2 would also have adequate to buy combination X_1. In other words, combination X_1 is within the buying range of the consumer when he chooses X_2. X_2 combination is, thus, revealed preferred to X_l Consistency or transitivity implies that once X_2 is "revealed" preferred to X_1 the latter must never be revealed preferred to X_2.

Here, it should be clearly noted that the condition (1) or the revealed preference will change if the price is lowered sufficiently. In other words, in a changed situation, X_1 can be revealed to be preferred to X_2 if

$$X_2P_1 \leq X_1P_1 \qquad ...(2)$$

where P_1 is the price level of the changed situation.

The theory of revealed preference is based on the axiom that the condition (2) can never hold if the condition (1) does hold. Also, if (2) holds, then (1) cannot hold. In other words, let us assume that X_1, X_2...X_k are the various combinations of the commodities. Now, if X_2 is revealed to be preferred to X_1, which is revealed to be preferred to X_3..., which is revealed to be preferred to X_k; then X_k must never be preferred to X_2. This axiom ensures the strong ordering or the transitivity of revealed preferences.

4. Revealed Preference Theory and the Demand Theorem or the Law of Demand

The conventional law of demand states that there is an inverse relationship between the price of a commodity and its demand. Other things being equal, the quantity demanded will increase if the price of the commodity decreases

and it will decrease if the price increases. Prof. Samuelson has derived the law of demand from his revealed preference theory assuming that the income elasticity of demand is positive. He recalls the demand theorem as the *fundamental theorem of consumer behaviour* and defines it in the following words: "Any good (simple or composite) that is known always to increase in demand when money-income alone rises must definitely shrink in demand when its price rises." It means that the demand for a good always increases with an increase in income, and obviously, it would always decrease when the price of the good increases. The "fundamental theorem" (demand theorem), therefore, states that positive income elasticity implicitly depicts the consumer will increase his purchases of the lower priced good and consequently the demand curve will slope negatively.

We may also illustrate the demand theorem on the basis of revealed preference hypothesis in two stages (*i*) by assuming a rise in price, and (*ii*) by assuming fall in price.

In Fig. 11.2 *MN* is the original price-line (budget line). The area *OMN* represents the area of consumer's choice. Suppose, the consumer chooses combination point *E* where he buys *OX* quantity of commodity and *OY* quantity of commodity *Y*. Thus, initially point *E* reveals his preference. Or, point *E* is revealed to be preferred to all other combinations on and under the triangle *OMN*. Now suppose that the price of commodity *X* increases the price of commodity *Y* remains the same, i.e. the new price line (or budget line) becomes MN_1. Here, we have proved that in the new situation the consumer will buy less of *X*, *i.e.* he will purchase less than *OX* quantity of *X*, because the price of *X* has increased. The new price line MN_1 indicates that point *E* will not be possible for the consumer to buy, because it lies beyond the budget line MN_1.

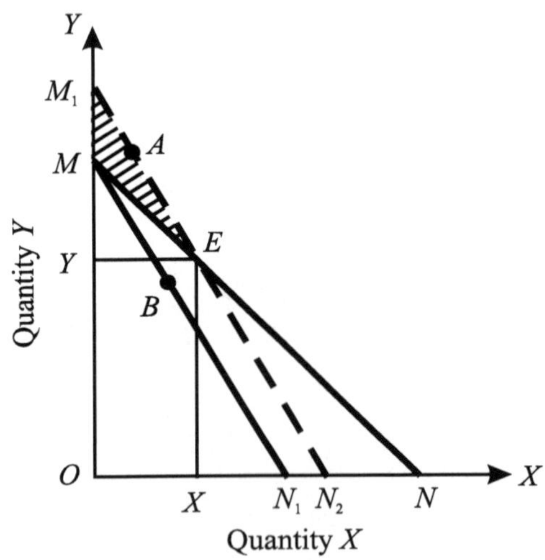

Fig. 11.2

Now let us assume that the consumer is given sufficient extra income which enables him to buy the original combination point *E*. Due to a sufficient increase in income the price line shifts to M_1N_2 which is parallel to the price line MN_1. The price line M_1N_2 passes through point *E*. Thus the area of consumer's choice becomes OM_1N_2. Now under the new price line M_1N_2, the consumer can choose point *A* or any other point on segment M_1E of the new budget line M_1N_2. This is because of the fact that segment M_1E will provide higher quantities of both the commodities to the consumer than the segment *ME* of the old initial price line *MN*. Moreover, the choice of the consumer for the remaining part (EN_2) was also available under the initial situation of the price line *MN*. But the choice on M_1E was not available to the consumer before when the price line was *MN*. Under the consistency assumption, the consumer will not select any point on the EN_2 segment of the budget line M_1N_2 except of course point *E* itself because segment EN_2 lies below segment *EN*. Therefore, there are two alternatives open to the consumer; either to buy the old combination point *E* (i.e. *OX* of *X* and *OY* of *Y*) or to choose any combination on segment *M.E*, i.e. above point *E* which will mean less quantity of *X* (*i.e.* less than *OX*) and more quantity of *Y* (*i.e.* less than *OY* of *Y*).

Hence, even after the consumer is given sufficient income to compensate the loss of a price increase (in commodity *X*), the consumer demands either the same quantity of *X* or a smaller quantity of *X* at higher price. If somehow the extra income is not given to the consumer, then he will definitely buy a smaller quantity of *X* at a higher price. Thus the inverse relationship between price and demand is proved.

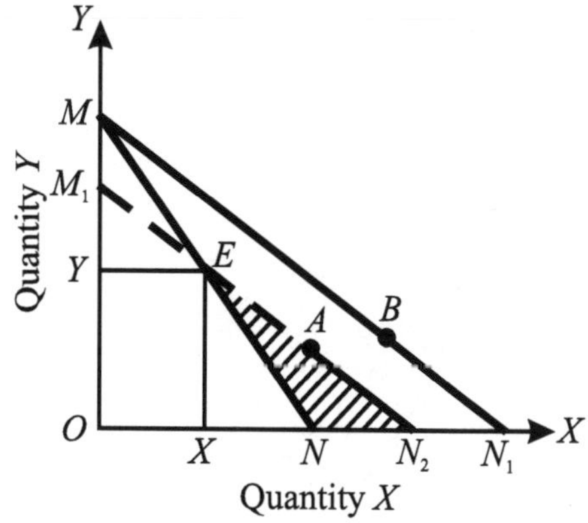

Fig. 11.3

Further, we can also explain the demand theorem by assuming a fall in the price of *X*. In Fig.11.3 *MN* is the original budget line. At this price line, the consumer chooses point *E* which is revealed to be preferred to all other available combinations. Here the consumer buys *OX* of *X* and *OY* of *Y*. Now

suppose the price of X falls assuming the price of Y to be the same the new price line becomes MN_1, and the area of consumer's choice is OMN_1. Now if some income is taken away from the consumer via taxation (income-tax), *i.e.* he comes down to a lower price line M_1N_2. Now he can choose either point A or some other point on the segment EN_2. He will not chooses any point on the remaining segment M_1E of the budget line M_1N_2 because it (the segment M_1E) lies to the left of (below) the segment ME of the original price line MN. Thus, the consumer can choose either point E ($OX + OY$) or some other combination beyond E to the right (or segment EN_2 which is above the segment EN of the original price line MN), which would mean more of X and less of Y. If the consumer's money income remains the same, *i.e.* remains on the price line M_1N_2, he will always demand a higher quantity of X (provided that the income elasticity of demand for X is positive which has already been assumed by Prof. Samuelson between price and demand is proved.

5. Price, Income and Substitution Effects Under Revealed Preference Approach

The income and substitution effects of a price change can be explained with the help of a diagram. In Fig. 11.4 MN is the original price line. Suppose, the consumer chooses point E, so that it indicates the quantities of the two commodities X and Y which are revealed to be preferred to any other point on MN. Now suppose that the price of commodity X falls while the price of commodity Y is assumed to be constant; the price line becomes MN_1. At this new price line MN_1, the consumer chooses point E_1. The movement from point E to E_1 is due to the price effect and the price effect comprises the substitution effect and income effect. In order to separate these effects, we assume that the consumer's money income is reduced to the extent that he comes down to his original point E; or the price-income line passes M_1N_2 through point E. Now the consumer will choose any point to the right of E on segment EN_2. Let us assume that this is point E_2. At this point E_2, the consumer buys more of $X(OX_2 > OX)$ which is due to substitution effect. If thc incomc of the consumer is not reduced, so that he remains on the price-income line M_1N_2, he will move from E_2 to E_1 purchasing more of X ($=X_2X_1$ units) purely due to income effect. Thus, as indicated in Fig. 11.4 XX_1 is the price effect which is divided into two parts, the substitution effect (XX_2) and the income effect (X_2X_1). It is to be noted that the Samuelson's explanation of the substitution effect is different from that of indifference curve analysis. In the case of indifference curve analysis, the consumer moves from one combination to another on the same indifference curve and his real income remains constant.

But in the revealed preference theory, indifference curves are not assumed and the substitution effect is a movement along the price income line arising from changing relative prices.

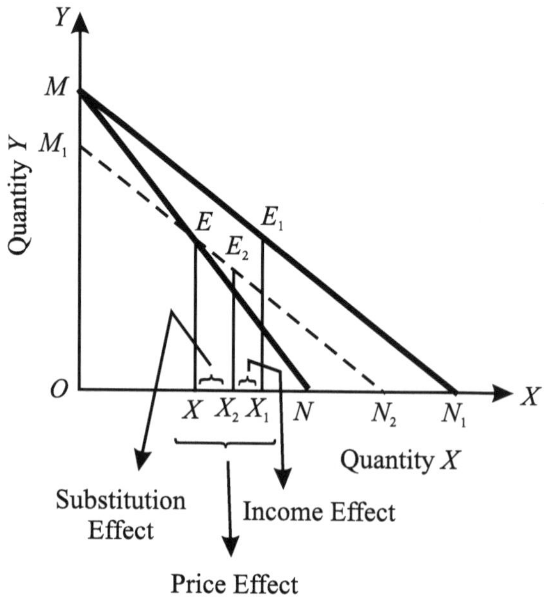

Fig. 11.4

6. Derivation of Demand Curve from Revealed Preference

We may also derive the demand curve from the revealed preference hypothesis. This can be explained with the help of Fig. 11.5. In panel (*A*) of Fig. 11.5 money is measured along the vertical axis while commodity *X* is measured along the horizontal axis. *MN* is the original price-income line on which the consumer shows his preference at point *E* and buys *OX* of commodity *X*. Suppose that the price of commodity *X* falls. As a result of this, the price-income line shifts to MN_1. On this line the consumer may reveal his preference, say at point *B*, where he buys a larger quantity OX_1 of commodity *X* which has resulted in his increased demand from *OX* to OX_1.

Now if we withdraw the increased real income (as a result of a fall in price) equal to MM_1 then M_1N_2 will become his new price-income line which is drawn parallel to MN_1 and passes through point *E*. The new triangle OM_1N_2 becomes his area of choice. Since the consumer was showing his original preference at point *E* on the original price-income line *MN*, therefore all points above *E* on the segment EM_1 of the line M_1N_2 are inconsistent with his choice. This is because of the fact that he will not have less quantity of commodity *X* when price falls. He will therefore reject all combinations above point *E* and either choose combination *E* or any other combination in the shaded triangle NEN_2. If the MM_1 amount of money taken from the consumer is returned to him, he will again be at point *B* on the price-income line MN_1 where he buys larger quantity OX_1 of *X* than before. The shift from point *E* to point *B* develops the relevant demand curve in panel (*B*) of Fig. 11.5.

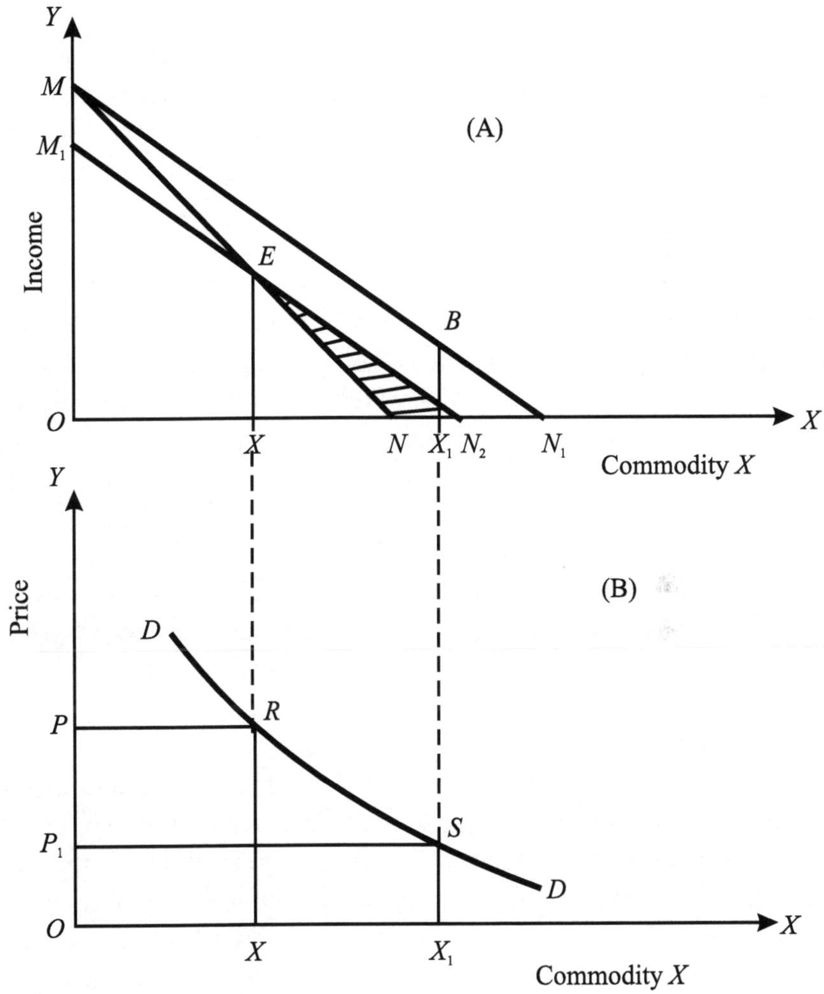

Fig. 11.5

As we have shown income on the vertical axis in panel (*A*), the price of commodity can be calculated by dividing the total money income by the number of units of *X* purchased. Thus the initial price of *X* would be *OM*/*ON*

(=*OP* in panel *B*) where the quantity demanded is *OX*. When the price of *X* falls to OM/ON_1 (= OP_1 in panel *B*) then the quantity demanded or purchased would be OX_1. Now in panel (*B*) we may plot this information and join the points *R* and *S* to get the relevant demand curve *DD*.

7. Superiority of Revealed Preference Theory

The above discussed revealed preference approach is superior to the Hicksian ordinal utility approach (indifference curve approach) on the basis of following points:

(*i*) *Consumer behavioural aspect.* The revealed preference approach does not involve any psychological introspective information about the behaviour of the consumer. Instead it shows a behaviouristic analysis based on observed consumer behaviour in the market. Thus the revealed approach is more realistic than the earlier utility approach developed by Marshall and Hicks.

(*ii*) *Assumption of continuity.* The revealed preference approach rejects the continuity assumption of the utility and indifference curve approach. An indifference curve is a continuous curve where the consumer may choose any combination of two goods. Samuelson believes that there is discontinuity because the consumer can have only one combination. Once it is selected, the consumer does not talk about the others. Following this argument, later on Hicks in his *Revision of Demand Theory* does not talk about this assumption and replaced it by the assumption of strong and weak ordering.

(*iii*) *Assumption of rationality.* Hicks, theory of indifference curve is based on the assumption that the consumer always behaves rationally to maximise his satisfaction from given income and given prices of goods and services. Samuelson's demand theory (revealed preference theory) is superior because it does not talk about rationality or the law of diminishing marginal utility in his analysis.

(*iv*) *Explanation of substitution effect.* Samuelson's demand theorem is more realistic as an explanation of consumer behaviour towards the substitution effect than the Hicksian approach. Samuelson permits the consumer to shift to a higher price-income situation (i.e. price line) in case of a fall in price shift while Hicks puts the consumer on the same indifference curve. This improvement was later also admitted by Hicks when he dropped the compensating variation principle in his revision of demand theory.

8. Defects of the Revealed Preference Theory

The Samuelson's theory of revealed preference suffers from a number of limitations. The following are the important defects of the theory :

(*i*) *Strong ordering hypothesis is not correct.* According to Prof. Armstrong, the revealed preference theory ignores the possibility of indifference in the behaviour of the consumer. The strong ordering hypothesis of Prof. Samuelson completely rejects the indifference points on the same price-income line. He states that only and only one point is revealed to be preferred over the other points available to the consumer. But the critics say that if the preference of the consumer is to be made from a number of combinations available to the consumer, then the possibility of indifference in the behaviour of the consumer cannot be overlooked.

(*ii*) *Behavioural factors have been ignored.* The theory is based upon the behaviour of the consumer to changes in (market) price-level. But actually the behaviour of consumers is also affected by other factors which the theory has completely ruled out.

(*iii*) *Conditional approach.* The Samuelson's revealed preference theory of demand is conditional and not general. It is based on the fundamental postulate that the income elasticity of demand for the commodity is positive. But if the income elasticity of demand (or income effect) is negative, the theory fails. To put it differently, if income elasticity of demand is negative, the theory is unable to determine accurately the change in demand in response to a change in price.

(*iv*) *Giffen's paradox has not been explained.* The theory does not explain Giffen's paradox, because Giffen's paradox is related to the negative income elasticity of demand which the theory does not assume. In the case of a Giffen good, the negative income effect is very strong which overcomes the positive substitution effect. Thus the exclusion of the Giffen's paradox is a great drawback of the new approach. This is the reason why Prof. Hicks' indifference curve theory of demand is more comprehensive than Prof. Samuelson's fundamental theorem of consumption.

(*v*) *Welfare purpose has been ignored.* The revealed preference analysis does not serve that welfare "purpose" of the demand theory. It only serves the economic purpose of the demand theory. Sometimes, it is possible that a consumer has chosen a wrong point, but the revealed preference theory does not permit him to correct the mistake. Thus, it is only an academic exercise and is not based upon the rational behaviour of a consumer in the market.

The above points of criticism indicate that the revealed preference theory of demand is not an improvement over the Hicks-Allen indifference curve analysis. Nevertheless, it can be assumed as an alternative of the old approaches to the consumer behaviour.

Exercises

1. Explain the revealed preference theory of consumer behaviour.
2. Write a critical note on the theory of revealed preference.
3. Explain that how Prof. Samuelson has derived the conventional (Marshallian) law of demand from his revealed preference theorem.
4. Illustrate the Fundamental Theorem of Consumption as developed by Prof. Samuelson.
5. "Choice reveals preference." Explain this statement.
6. Bring out the improvements introduced in demand analysis by the theory of revealed preference.
7. Assess the impact of revealed preference on the theory of demand.
8. Derive the demand curve from the theory of revealed preference.
9. Explain the superiority of revealed preference over the utility and indifference curve approach to consumer behaviour. What are the defects of the theory of revealed preference?

Multiple Choice Questions

10. (*i*) Who has developed the revealed preference theory of demand?
    (*a*) Marshall (*c*) Samuelson
    (*b*) Hicks (*d*) Baumol [*Ans.* (*c*)]

    (*ii*) Samuelson's revealed preference theory of demand is based on the assumption:
    (*a*) consumer's behaviour is rational
    (*b*) income elasticity of demand is positive
    (*c*) income elasticity demand is negative
    (*d*) all of the above. [*Ans.* (*b*)]

    (*iii*) Revealed preference approach is superior to the Hicksian ordinary utility approach to consumer behaviour because
    (*a*) it does not involve any psychological introspective information about the behaviour of the consumer
    (*b*) it admits the assumption of continuity
    (*c*) it is based on the assumption that the consumer always behaves rationally to maximise his satisfaction
    (*d*) none of the above [*Ans.* (*a*)]

Chapter 12

The Modern Utility Analysis of Choices Involving Risk or Uncertainty

1. Introduction

We have already discussed in previous chapters that the neo-classical economists constructed a cardinal utility theory as a part of their analysis of consumer demand. The cardinal utility measure was designed to give information about the psychological state of the consumer or the businessman the magnitude of his desires and the psychic gains and loss incurred by the alternative actions which are available to him. We have also seen that under ordinal analysis (indifference curve approach), a large class of decision processes can be explained with the aid of information about the individual's preference, with no attempt to assign magnitudes to them. The consumer is certain about his income, tastes and the goods he purchases and maximises his satisfaction by choosing that combination which gives him the highest total utility. But in reality, many goods and services involve risk or uncertainty,[1] such as investment in shares or stocks, insurance and gambling.

Thus it is, however, found useful to go beyond an ordinal utility measure whenever question of risk arises. Our analysis of consumer behaviour (Marshallian utility approach, Hicksian indifference curve approach and Samuelson's revealed preference approach) had so far assumed that there is certainty about incomes. But, in reality, consumers have to make choices under a state of uncertainty. Individual face uncertainties or risks about future income, returns of investment and future demand for certain product, etc. Thus, outcomes of the alternative choices available to the decision-maker are

1. Here we should know the difference between risk and uncertainty. A risky situation has more than one possible outcome and the risk-taker is aware of all possible outcomes and he knows the probability of each one occurring. On the other hand, an uncertain situation is one where the precise nature of these outcomes is not known and therefore probability to the outcomes can not be determined.

sometimes known only in probabilistic form. The neo-classical (Marshallian) and the ordinal utility approaches to consumer behaviour fails to hold in such a situation of uncertainties. It was Neumann and Morgenstern who in their theory of Games and Economic Behaviour studied the behaviour of an individual in risky situations and developed a new theory (known as *N-M Theory*) in 1944. This theory is termed as "Modern Utility Theory" of consumer behaviour. The *N-M* theory lays down a rational course of action for an individual who is confronted with a highly uncertain situation.

This modern utility theory is also sometimes known as Bernoullian utility theory after Danial Bernoulli, the 18th century Swiss mathematician who got interested in the problem known as "St. Petersburg Paradox" and provided hypothesis for resolving this paradox. St. Petersburg paradox refers to "why people are unwilling to make bets at better than 50-50 odds when their mathematical expectations of winning money in a particular kind of gamble are greater the more money the bet."[2]

The modern utility theory was later refined by Friedman and Savage and by Markowitz. We shall explain these different views on choices involving risk or uncertainty in the following section of this chapter.

2. The Bernoulli Hypothesis or the St. Petersburg Paradox

The neo-classical utility analysis (cardinal as well as ordinal) studies only consumer behaviour in regard to the choices among quite certain and risk less alternatives. In their theory, a consumer faces no uncertainties regarding the availabilities of goods and services, their prices and the size of his income and so forth. With full knowledge and information about these things, the consumer makes his choice and maximises utility from his given money income. Thus according to these neo-classical theories, the consumer is a rational being who does not indulge in gambling or even in fair bet with 50-50 odds. The reason for such a rational behaviour was explained by Danial Bernoulli, the 18th century Swiss mathematician. When he was at St. Petersburg in 1732, he found that Russians were unwilling to make bets even at better than 50-50 odds knowing fully that their mathematical expectation of winning money in a particular kind of gamble were greater the more money they bet. This contradiction is known as St. Petersburg Paradox. To make it more clear, Bernoulli took the help of a game. It requires the tossing of a coin until it falls heads up. If head occurs on the first toss, the player gets £ 2 and the game stops. If it occurs in the second throw, £ 2^2 = £ 4 is paid and the game stops. If head appears for the first time after n tosses, then £ 2^n is paid to the player. How much would a rational individual be willing to take part in this

2. S.D. Watson, *Price Theory and Its Uses,* 2nd edition, 1970, p. 122.

game? In other words, what is the expected money value of the pay-off to such a game? The expected monetary value of the game is infinite. The probability that head will occur on the first toss of the coin is 1/2. The probability of obtaining head for the first time on the *n*th toss is $\left(\frac{1}{2}\right)^n$. Since there is no finite number of throws within which guarantee can be given that a head will occur, the expected pay-off of the game or the expected monetary value of the game would be

$$E\ (M) = \left(\frac{1}{2}\right)2 + \left(\frac{1}{2}\right)^2 2^2 + \left(\frac{1}{2}\right)^3 2^3 + ... + \left(\frac{1}{2}\right)^n 2^n$$

$$= \sum_{n=1}^{\infty}\left(\frac{1}{2}\right)^n 2^n = 1 + 1 + 1 + ... + 1...$$

$$= \infty \text{ (infinity)}$$

As the *E*(*M*), *i.e.* the expected monetary value of the game is infinity, a person whose objective is to maximise expected monetary value would willing to pay everything he has to play the game. Bernoulli resolved the St. Petersburg Paradox by saying that a rational individual will take decisions under risky and uncertain situations on the basis of expected utility rather than expected monetary value. He further contended that marginal utility of money to the individual declines as he has more of it. Since the individual behaves on the basis of expected utility from the extra money he wins in a game and the marginal utility of money to him declines as he has extra money, a rational individual will not 'play the game', that is, will not make a bet. It is in this way that Bernoulli resolved St. Petersburg Paradox.

Bernoulli's St. Petersburg Paradox can also be explained with the help of a diagram. In Fig. 12.1, we measure money (thousands of dollars) along the *X*-axis and marginal utility of money along the *Y*-axis. Suppose a person has 10,000 dollars with him and can make a bet at even odds, (*i.e.* 50-50 odds) of winning or losing 1,000 dollars. If he wins the bet, money with him will rise to \$11,000 (*i.e.* \$10,000 + \$1,000). If as a result of an increase in money with him, his expected marginal utility of money declines, then the expected marginal utility of extra one thousand rupees to him which is shown by the rectangle *TUVW* is less than the extra marginal utility of the previous one thousand dollars (i.e. 10th thousand which he has to put to bet) which is shown by the rectangle *RSTU*. In other words, the gain in utility in the case of his winning the bet is less than the loss of utility in the case of his actually losing the bet, though in terms of the monetary value the gain and loss is the identical (*i.e.* \$1,000). Thus under the assumption of

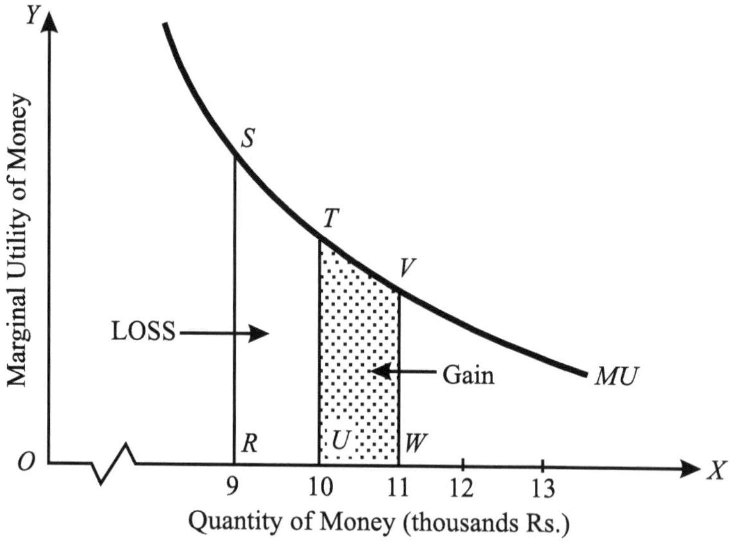

Fig. 12.1

diminishing marginal utility of money, the expected gain in utility is less than the expected loss of utility from $1,000 involved in the bet, a rational consumer will therefore not make a bet with 50-50 odds.

However, game theorists Von Neumann and Morgenstern who studied individual's behaviour in situations of risk and uncertainty as in betting or gambling found it necessary and useful to go beyond an ordinal utility measure. They emphasised that in risky and uncertain situations, the outcomes of the alternative choices are known only in probability form, for instance, if an individual chooses alternative *A,* and has one chance in four of ending up with $10,000 and three chances in four of ending up with $100. In such situations involving probabilities (*i.e.* risky and uncertain situations), Von Neumann and Morgenstern felt it necessary to go beyond ordinal ranking of various alternatives and to construct cardinal utility measure (popularly known as *N-M* Index) for ranking of various risky and uncertain alternatives.

3. The Neumann-Morgenstern Method of Measuring Utility

J. Von Neumann and O. Morgenstern in their book *Theory of Games and Economic Behaviour* developed the method of cardinal measurement of expected utility from risky choices which are faced in gambling, lottery tickets, etc. On the basis of such a cardinal utility index called *N-M* Index, rational decisions are made by the individuals in case of risky situations.

Now, before we construct the *N-M* utility index, it is better to understand the basic assumptions on which the theory is based. The important *assumptions* of the *N-M* theory are the following:

(*i*) It assumes that the outcomes of a consumer's decisions are unknown, but the consumer is capable of assigning some probabilities to different alternative choices.

(*ii*) It assumes that the values of the outcomes are different and assignment of different probabilities to them is required to construct a utility index.

(*iii*) A utility index can be used to predict the consumer's choice in risky situations, provided the following axioms are observed.

(*a*) *Transitivity* (*complete ordering*). This axiom states that for the two alternatives *A* and *B*, the consumer must choose anyone of the three conditions: the consumer chooses (prefers) *A* to *B*, or *B to A*, or he is indifferent between them. However, if *A* is preferred to *B* and *B* is preferred to *C*, *A* is preferred to *C*, i.e.

$$A > B > C$$

This above is the condition of transitivity.

(*b*) *Continuity of preferences.* This axiom states that if $A > B > C$, then there exists some probability P ($1 > P > 0$), such that the consumer is indifferent between outcome *B* with certainty and outcome *A* and *C* with probabilities *P* and ($1-P$) respectively.

(*c*) *Indifference.* Assume that the consumer is indifferent between *A* and *B* and that *C* is any outcome whatsoever. If one lottery ticket offers outcomes *A* and *C* with probabilities *P* and ($1-P$) respectively and the other ticket offers outcomes *B* and *C* with the same probabilities *P* and ($1-P$), then the consumer is indifferent between the two lottery tickets.

(*d*) *Desire for high probability as success.* Assuming the two lottery tickets with indentical prizes, the consumer will prefer that one which possesses the higher probability of winning.

The N-M Utility Index

Now in the context of above assumptions, we may construct the *N-M* utility index. A utility index explains numerically the preference of an individual (consumer). It shows the expected utility of different outcomes. According to Professors Von Neumann and Morgenstern, the utility function can be measured by the following method, "consider three events *C*, *A*, *B* for which the order of the individual's preferences is the one stated. Let *X* be a real number between *O* and 1 such that *A* is exactly equally desirable with the combined event consisting of a chance of probability ($1-\alpha$) for *B* and the remaining change of probability α for *C*. Then we suggest the use of A as a numerical estimate for the ratio of the preference of *A* over *B* to that of Cover *B*. " We may put this method in the form of a mathematical formula:

$$A = B(1-\alpha) + \alpha C \qquad ...(1)$$

where α indicates the probability of happening the event. If *P* is put in place of α, we may write the equation (1) as under:

$$A = B(1 - P) + PC \qquad ...(2)$$

If the preferences (choices) are given, we may construct a cardinal utility index with the help of the above formula. Suppose, the three situations are *C*, *A* and *B* respectively. Now if situation *A* is certain and the probability of *C* is *P* and that of *B* is $(1 - P)$. Also, their respective utilities are $U(A)$, $U(B)$ and $U(C)$, then we may define the formula of utility index as below:

$$U(A) = PU(C) + (1 - P)\,U(B) \qquad ...(3)$$

because it is hoped that the consumer will try to maximise his utility, therefore the utility of the certain situation *A* is equal to some value of *P* which is the expected utility of situations *C* and *B*. Now for the construction of a utility schedule on the basis of the above, *N-M utility* index, we need to assign utility numbers to any two of the situations. These utility numbers (values) are purely arbitrary, but we should note that more utility value is to be assigned to a relatively preferred situation.

Suppose we assign 20 units of utility to *C* and 1 unit of utility to *B* and the value of *P* (probability) is $\frac{2}{5}$ then

$$U(A) = \frac{2}{5}(20) + \left(1 - \frac{2}{5}\right)(1)$$

$$= 8 + \frac{3}{5} = 8.6 \text{ units}$$

Similarly, with the same probability value, we may calculate different numerical value for $U(A)$ by assigning different utility numbers to *B* and *C*. The *N-M* utility index of Table 12.1 has been constructed by taking $P = \frac{2}{5}$.

Table 12. 1 : The N-M Utility Index

Situation	*U(A)*	*U(B)*	*U(C)*
1	8.6	1	20
2	15	5	30
3	22	10	40
4	29	15	50
5	36	20	60

The utility index of Table 12.1 states that the consumer's order of preference will be *C*, *A*, *B* respectively. Thus the consumer attempts to maximise his expected utility even in the face of uncertainty.

The *N-M* utility index has been criticised on the ground that it is based on expected utility values and thus it provides no justification to a change in the marginal utility of money. According to Henderson and Quandt, "The utilities in the Von Neumann-Morgenstern are cardinal in a restricted sense. They are derived from the consumer's risk behaviour and are valid for predicting his choices as long as he maximises his expected utility. They are derived by presenting him with mutually exclusive choices; therefore, it is meaningless to attempt to infer from the utility of event *A* and the utility of event *B*, the utility of the joint event *A* and *B*."

Some of the limitations of *N-M* theory have been removed by the Friedman-Savage Hypothesis. This has been discussed in the following section.

4. Friedman-Savage Hypothesis

Milton Friedman and L.J. Savage developed a better interpretation of consumer's behaviour in situations involving risk. According to them, the marginal utility of money decreases if the money income of the consumer is below to a certain level; it (the marginal utility of money) increases if the money income varies between this level and a level above this level; it again decreases if the money income increases further. This has been shown in Fig. 12.2. The income utility curve *U* (Y) indicates the

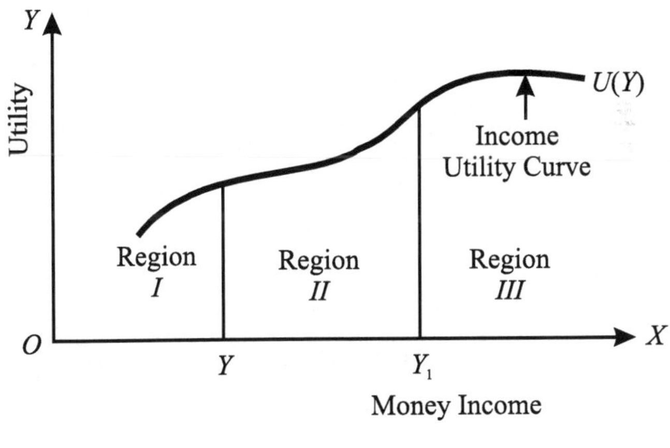

Fig. 12.2

three situations. In the beginning it is concave to the horizontal axis, then it becomes convex and then it becomes convex to the *X*-axis. If the income is below *OY*, the consumer prefers insurance. Thus the region *I* is of insurance where the consumer prefers a *certain* loss in income due to a little probability of heavy losses. If the income of consumer is between *OY* and OY_1., he comes under the middle income group *II*. In that situation he prefers gambling. Because the convex part of *U*(*Y*) curve indicates the increasing marginal utility of money. Thus, the people of this income group are anxious to bear risk for the improvement in their economic situation. The people under the lower income group *I* may also be attracted a little towards gambling, provided their income is very near to *OY*. Now the people whose income is above *OY*, come under region *III*. The marginal utility of money for them decreases. They would be ready to play gambling or will not prepare for risk until the situation of risk becomes favourable for them. This region explains St. Petersberg's paradox.

Thus, the Friedman-Savage theory is based on the assumption that the utility depends upon the levels of money income. Suppose the consumer's incomes from various alternatives bearing no risks are Y_1, Y_2, and Y_3, etc. and their respective utilities are given by $U(Y_1)$, $U(Y_2)$, and $U(Y_3)$, etc. Now the consumer will choose art alternative which yields him an income that gives him maximum total utility (or satisfaction). But if the alternatives involve risks, then the choice becomes difficult.

Now in such a situation of risk, the consumer will assign different probabilities for different income levels. This will help to find out consumer's preference. Suppose *A*, *B* and *C* are three alternatives involving risks. Each of them contains a set of alternative incomes associated with their respective probabilities. The consumer may prefer *A* to *B*, *B* to *C*, or may be indifferent between *A* and *B*. Now, the choice of the consumer will depend upon the utility attached to various probability distributions of income. Suppose we are given the relevant information for the outcome *A* as under. Outcome *A* yields incomes Y_1 (\$230), Y_2 (\$550) and Y_3 (\$640) with the respective probabilities P_I (= 0.1), P_2 (= 0.5) and P_3 (0.3). We are also given the respective utilities of incomes as $U(Y_1)$ = 200 utils, $U(Y_2)$ = 400 utils and $U(Y_3)$ = 600 utils. Now we may calculate the utility of the income *A* by the following formula :

$$
\begin{aligned}
U(A) &= P_1U(Y_1) + P_2U(Y_2) + P_3U(Y_3) \\
&= 0.1(200) + 0.6(400) + 0.3(600) \\
&= 20 + 240 + 180 = 440
\end{aligned}
$$

Similarly, the expected utilities of the other outcomes *B* and *C* can be calculated. The consumer's behaviour in ranking the outcomes *A*, *B* and *C* will depend upon their expected utilities. He will choose that outcome which gives him maximum satisfaction.

5. The Markowitz Hypothesis

Both the Bernoullian hypothesis and the Friedman-Savage hypothesis assume that marginal utility of money depends on the absolute level of income. When

N-M utility index is prepared for an individual for various levels of income, his choice pertaining to risky situations can be ascertained. Prof. Markowitz has criticised the Friedman-Savage hypothesis for its assertion that 'very poor' and 'very rich' will be unwilling to take risk and therefore would not like to perform gambling, etc. and it is only the middle income group that will go into it. According to Prof. Markowitz, marginal utility of money income relates only to changes in the level of money income rather than to the absolute money income with this assumption, he states that why most people prefer insurance and also play gambling. He takes the deviations from the present income of the individual as determining the attitude of people towards risks. The Markowitz hypothesis states that with small increases in income from the present level, the marginal utility of money income increases but huge increases in income from the present level, the marginal utility of money will rather diminish. Similarly, with small decreases in income from the present level, the marginal utility of money income, while huge decreases in income from the present level will yield diminishing marginal utility of money.

Markowitz hypothesis can also be explained with the help of a diagram as in Fig. 12.3. Here *MU* curve shows the marginal utility of money at different levels of money income. In Fig. 12.3, the curve has three inflexion points, *R*, *S*, and *T* and four segments *ST, TB, SR,* and *RA* as against two inflexion points and three segments in *MU* curve of Friedman-Savage hypothesis. M_0

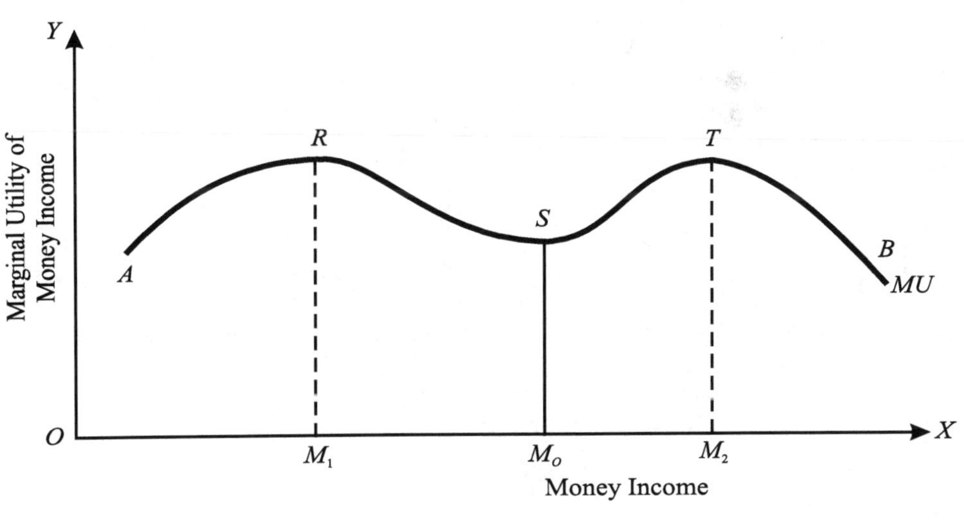

Fig. 12.3

in Fig. 12.3 is the present level of income. As the individual's income increases from M_0 to M_2, the marginal utility of money increases along *ST* segment. However, increases in income beyond M_2 will yield diminishing marginal utility of money. On the other hand, small decreases in money income from M_0 to M_1, will yield increasing marginal utility of money income but huge decreases in money income, so that to the left of M_1 will lead to diminishing marginal utility of money.

Thus, it is clear that as per Markowitz hypothesis, small increases in money income will yield rising marginal utility of money, but large increases in money income will bring about diminishing marginal utility of money, hence an individual will be willing to accept small fair bets but will be reluctant to take risks involving big amounts of money.

Exercises

1. Discuss critically the modern utility analysis of choice involving risks.
2. Write a short note on Neumann-Morgenstern utility index.
3. What do you mean by Friedman-Savage Hypothesis? Illustrate your answer with the help of a diagram.
4. "The ordinal utility system breaks down as soon as we introduce uncertainty of expectation with regard to the consequences of choice." Comment on the method suggested by Von Neumann and Morgenstern to solve this problem.
5. Write a lucid note on Bernoulli Hypothesis.
6. Explain the modern utility analysis of risky choices along with its various refinements.
7. Write a note on Markowitz Hypothesis.

Multiple Choice Questions

8. (*i*) 'St. Petersburg Paradox' has been developed by
   (*a*) Bernoulli
   (*b*) Morgenstern
   (*c*) Savage
   (*d*) Markowitz [*Ans.* (*a*)]

   (*ii*) *N-M* utility index is based on the assumption:
   (*a*) the choices of an individual are transitive
   (*b*) probability lies between *O* and 1.
   (*c*) uncertainty or risk does not possess utility or disutility of its own
   (*d*) all of the above [*Ans.* (*d*)]

   (*iii*) Which statement is correct about Markowitz Hypothesis :
   (*a*) small increases in money income yield rising marginal utility of money
   (*b*) large increases in money income bring about diminishing marginal utility of money
   (*c*) the individual will be willing to accept small fare bets but will be reluctant to take risks involving large amount of money
   (*d*) all of the above [*Ans.* (*d*)]

Chapter 13

Hicks' Revision of Demand Theory (Demand Theory of Logical Ordering)

1. Introduction

Prof. Hicks wrote a book *A Revision of Demand Theory* in 1956 in which he revised his demand theory which he explained in his earlier book *Value and Capital.* Hicks realised that his earlier explanation to the theory of demand was weak and too elliptic. Among the chief reasons which prompted him to undertake the revision of his earlier theory are the development of Samuelson's revealed preference approach, the rise in the application of econometrics and the emergence of mathematical theories of strong and weak orderings. Hicks was mainly influenced by the revealed preference hypothesis and the logic of strong ordering used by Samuelson and his followers to derive the theory of demand. Thus in his revision of demand theory, he gives emphasis on econometric approach to the theory of demand. He states that the demand theory which is useful for econometric purposes is definitely superior to the one which does not serve such purposes. According to him, "There can be no doubt that econometrics is now a major form of economic research, a theory which can be used by econometricians is to that extent a better theory that one which can not." But still Hicks is of the opinion that only ordinal measurement of utility is possible. He therefore, continues to make use of the concept of ordinal utility in his revision of demand theory as well. It is to be noticed that Hicks has not taken the help of indifference curve in any of the theories which he developed at a later stage. He has pointed out various disadvantages of the indifference curve technique. He says that geometrical method of indifference curve is fully effective and useful for representing only quite simple cases, especially those in which the choice concerns quantities of two goods only. When the problem is extended to more than two goods, then we can not escape mathematics to solve it. Further, he points out that geometrical method is based upon the assumption of continuity, a property which the geometrical field does have but which the economic in general does not." He, therefore, gives up the assumption of continuity in his revision of demand theory. Now we shall explain below how Hicks develops his new method of preference hypothesis and bases his demand theory on it.

2. Preference Hypothesis and Logic of Ordering

In the formulation of his revised demand theory, Hicks assumes preference hypothesis on the part of an ideal consumer. He explains the preference hypothesis as follows: "The ideal consumer (who is not affected by anything else except the price of the commodity) chooses that alternative, out of the various alternatives open to him, which he prefers most, or ranks most highly. In one set of market conditions he makes one choice, in others other choices, but the choices he makes always express the same ordering, and must, therefore, be consistent with one another. This is the hypothesis made about the behaviour of the ideal consumer."

It is clear that the consumer in a given market situations chooses the most preferred combination of goods and in different market situations, he will choose different combinations, but his choices in different market situations will be consistent with each other. Hicks further states that "the demand theory which is based upon the preference hypothesis turns out to be nothing else but an economic application of the logical theory of ordering." Hence before deriving his revised demand theory from preference hypothesis, he explains the "logic of order". In this context he draws out difference between strong ordering and weak ordering. Finally, he develops his demand theory on weak ordering type of preference hypothesis.

Strong and Weak Ordering Distinguished

The distinction between strong ordering and weak ordering may be explained as follows:

Strong Ordering. A set of items is strongly ordered, if each item has a place of its own in the order and each item could then be assigned a number and to each number there would be one item and only one item which would correspond.

Weak Ordering. A set of items is weakly ordered if the items are clustered into groups but none of the items within a group can be put ahead of the others. Thus, a weak ordering implies a division into groups in which sequence of groups is strongly ordered, but in which there is no ordering within the groups.

The indifference curve analysis is based on weak ordering because all the points on the same indifference curve are not ordered, though all are equally desirable (or occupy same place in the order) but the consumer is indifferent to others. On the other hand, revealed preference approach implies strong ordering because it assumes that the choice of a combination reveals consumer's preference. Choice can reveal preference for a combination only if all the alternative combinations are strongly ordered. It simply means that under weak ordering, the consumer chooses a point and rejects others open to him, then the rejected points need not be inferior to the point actually selected by him but may be indifferent to it.

The above analysis of strong ordering and weak ordering as applied to the theory of demand can be explained with the help of diagrams. First we explain the strong ordering in Fig. 13.1. Here Hicks assumes that there are two commodities *X* and *M*. Commodity *X* is an individual good and commodity *M* (money) is a composite good representing all goods and services other

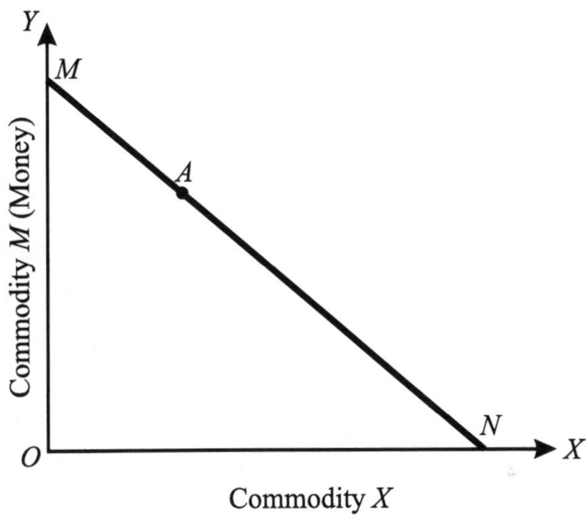

Fig. 13.1

than *X*. Commodity *M* (money) is measured along the vertical axis while commodity *X* is measured along the horizontal axis. Given the income of the consumer and the price of *X*- and *M*, the price income situation of the ideal consumer (who acts according to preference hypothesis) is shown by the line *MN*. Now the consumer may opt any combination in or on the triangle *MON*. The point *A* on the line *MN* represents the actual choice of the consumer. Now the question is how his act of choice of *A* from among the available alternatives in and on the triangle *MON* is to be interpreted. If the available alternatives are strongly ordered, then the choice of *A* by the consumer will show that he prefers *A* over all other available alternatives. In Samuelson's language he 'reveals his preference' for *A* over all other possible alternatives which are rejected. Thus, under strong ordering, the consumer shows definite preference for the selected alternative, there is no question of any indifferent positions to the selected one. But such type of strong ordering has been criticised by Hicks on the following grounds:

(*i*) In Samuelson's version of the preference hypothesis in its strong ordering form, it can not be assumed that all the geometrical points, which lie within or on the triangle *MON* represent effective alternatives. A two dimensional continuum point can not be strongly ordered.

(*ii*) Hicks states that if commodities are assumed to be available only in discrete units, so that the diagram is to be conceived as being drawn on squared paper and the only effective alternatives are the points at the corners of the squares and, therefore the selected point must also lie at the corner of a square, then the strong ordering hypothesis is acceptable. Since in real world such a situation never arise because of the use of money. Thus, in making a choice between commodity *X* available in discrete units and the finely divisible commodity *M* (money), strong ordering has to be given up. It is on the basis of this reasoning of Hicks that he rejects Samuelson's strong ordering hypothesis.

Weak Ordering in the Hicks' Demand Theory

Hicks makes use of weak ordering hypothesis in his demand theory. In the words of Prof. Hicks, "If the consumer's scale of preference is weakly ordered, then his choice of a particular position *A* does not show (or reveal) that *A* is preferred to any rejected position which is preferred to *A*. It is perfectly possible that some rejected position may be indifferent to *A*; the choice of A instead of that rejected position is then a matter of choice."

If preference hypothesis in its weak ordering form is adopted, then it provides very little information about the consumer's behaviour that the basic propositions of demand theory can not be derived from it. Thus Prof. Hicks introduces an additional hypothesis along with the weak ordering hypothesis, so that basic proposition of the demand theory can easily be derived. As we have already noted in the earlier section that under additional hypothesis, "the consumer will always prefer a large amount of money to a smaller amount of money, provided that the amount of good *X* at his disposal is unchanged." Here it should be remembered that it is not necessary to adopt this additional hypothesis if strong ordering form of preference hypothesis is applied. But this additional hypothesis is very reasonable and is always implicit in economic analysis. Now when this additional hypothesis along with weak ordering preference hypothesis is adopted, we may get the positive solution, as shown in Fig. 13.2. Here let us assume that from all available combinations in and on the triangle *MON*, the consumer chooses *A*.

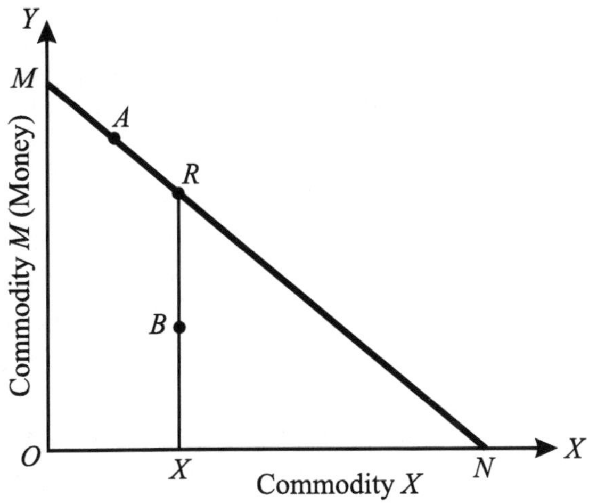

Fig. 13.2

Under weak ordering hypothesis alone, the choice of *A* rather than *B* means that either *A* is preferred to *B*, or *A* and *B* are positions of indifference. But this proposition of weak ordering does not hold if another position *R* is taken on the line *MN* through the vertical line *XB*. Under the additional hypothesis, *R* is preferred to *B* because the consumer prefers more of money (i.e. commodity *M*) at point *R* to less of money (i.e. commodity *M*) at point *B*, given the same quantity of *OX* of commodity *X*. If *A* and *B* are points of indifference, it follows from the transitive condition that point *R* is preferred to point *A*. But according to the weak ordering hypothesis, no other position is preferred to point *A* within and on the triangle *MON* which means that *R* has already been rejected in favour of *A*. Therefore points *A* and *R* may be of indifference. It follows that if *A* and *R* are points of indifference, then the alternative that *A* and *B* points are indifferent must be ruled out. Therefore the logic of weak ordering states that the point *A* on the line *MN* is preferred to *B* which lies within the triangle *MON*. But what can not be explained is that point *A* is preferred to point *C* or any other point on the line *MN*. Thus drawing the difference between the implications of strong and weak ordering, Prof. Hicks states, "The difference between the consequence of strong and weak ordering so interpreted amounts to no more than this: that under strong ordering the chosen position is shown to be preferred to all other positions within and on the triangle, while under weak ordering, it is preferred to all positions within the triangle, but may be indifferent to other positions on the same boundary as itself."

3. The Direct Consistency Test

Following Samuelson, Prof. Hicks also assumes consistency of choice behaviour on the part of the ideal consumer who reveals an unchanged scale of preferences. Prof. Hicks calls this consistency test as the direct consistency test. Here the direct consistency is the economic expression of the two-term consistency condition on the theory of logic of order. Besides the consistency of consumer's choices, Hicks proves the hypothesis on the basis of inconsistency also. It can be explained with the help of a diagram. In Fig. 13.3, commodity *X* is measured along the horizontal axis and the composite commodity *M* (money) is measured on the vertical axis. Given the income of the consumer and the price of *X*, the choices open to the consumer are shown by the area of the triangle *MON*. The point *A* on the line *MN* represents the actual choice of the consumer. The preference hypothesis in its strong ordering form (Samuelson's version) represents *A* to be preferred to all other combinations within the triangle *MON*. While in its weak ordering form, it implies that point *A* is preferred to all combinations within the triangle and is either preferred or indifferent to other points on the line *MN*.

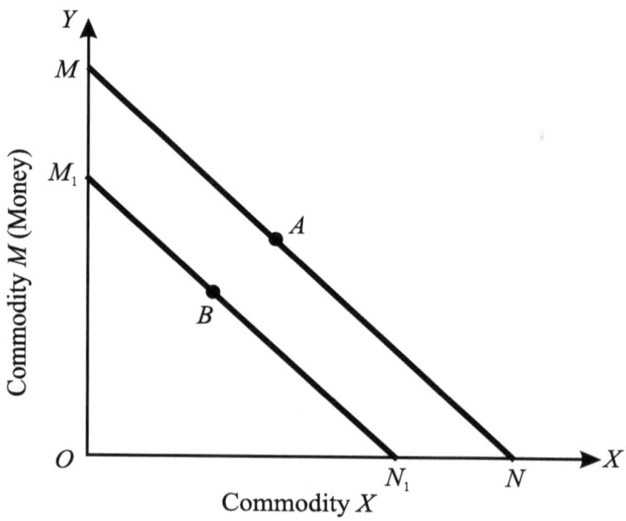

Fig. 13.3

Now let us take another market situation represented by the price-income line M_1N_1 where the price of *X* is different and the income of the consumer mayor may not be different. The various alternative combinations open to the consumer in the new situation are represented by the triangle M_1ON_1. Point *B* on the line M_1N_1 represents the actual choice of the consumer in the new situation. Similar kind of preference, as in situation *A*, will follow in situation *B* under strong and weak form of preference hypothesis.

Since the consumer acts according to the unchanged scale of preference in both situations, the preferences by him in the two situations must be consistent with each other. The behaviour of the consumer will be inconsistent if he reveals his preference for combination *A* over combination *B* in situation *A*, when both the combinations *A* and *B* are available in both the situations. But in the case of weak ordering, the possibility of indifference has also to be considered. Thus, the various cases of consistency or inconsistency that may arise under strong ordering and weak ordering may be analysed in the following manner:

(*i*) *First Case.* The first situation may be when one of the two price-income lines lies wholly outside the other. In Fig. 13.4 we assume that the line *MN* lies above M_1N_1 throughout its length. In situation *A*, point *B* lies within the triangle *MON* and therefore the consumer prefers point *A* to *B* both under strong and weak ordering. In the *B* situation, point *A* is not available (as it lies outside the triangle M_1ON_1). Therefore the consumer's choice of *A* in the *A* situation is quite consistent with his choice *B* in the *B* situation. But there is no inconsistency in these two situations. This in fact is the Samuelson's version of revealed preference hypothesis.

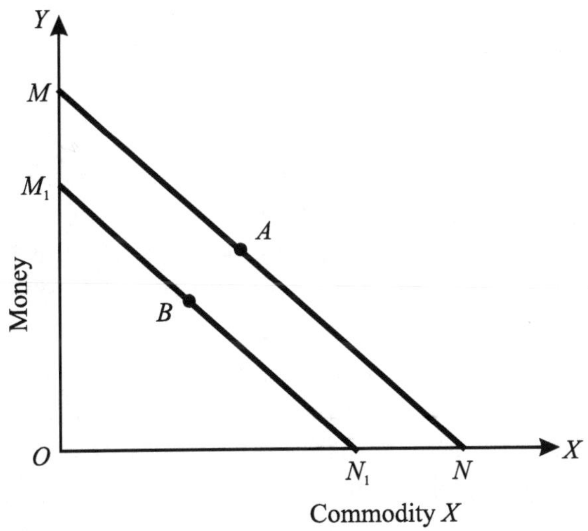

Fig. 13.4

(*ii*) *Second Case.* The second situation may be when one of two price-income line does not lie wholly outside the other, that is the two lines intersect each other at the same point. This case has been shown in Fig. 13.5 when line *MN* lies outside the line M_1N_1 on the left of the cross point *R* (so that it represents a higher income) and lies inside the price-income line M_1N_1 on the right of the cross point *R* (so that it represents a lower income). When two

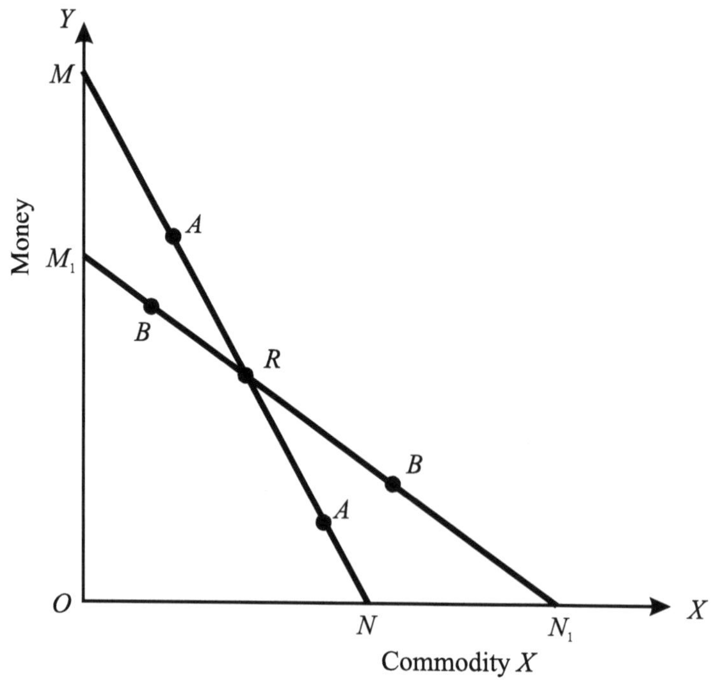

Fig. 13.5

price-income lines intersect each other then the following possibilities are created :

(*a*) The first possibility is one when the choices available to the consumer in the two situations *A* and *B* lie to the left of the cross point *R* (or above point *R*). In the *A* situation, *B* lies within the triangle *MON*. Thus the consumer prefers *A* to *B* and is indifferent to *B* (weak ordering). In the *B* situation, *A* is not available to him, because it lies outside the triangle M_1ON_1. Thus his choice of *B* in situation *B* is consistent with his preference for *A* in situation *A*.

(*b*) The second possibility is that when both the selected positions *A* and *B* respectively in the two situations lie to the right of the cross point *R* (or below *R*). In this case, point *B* is preferred to point *A* because *A* lies within the triangle M_1ON_1 and the consumer is also in different to *A*. Here point *B* is not possible to the consumer in situation *A*. Thus, his choice of *A* in the situation *A* is consistent with his preference for *B* in situation *B*. Thus, in this case also the consumer's choice behaviour is quite consistent.

(*c*) The third possibility is that when *A* lies outside to the left of the cross point *R*, and *B* outside to the right of it (in the area $MARBM_1$). In this case, in *A* situation *A* is chosen because *B* lies outside his approach and in *B* situation only *B* is chosen because *A* lies outside his approach. The question of preference of one over the other does not arise in this case. Thus, the choices are consistent in both the situations under both strong and weak ordering whatever is adopted by the consumer.

(*d*) The fourth possibility is that when the two selected points *A* and *B* lie inside the cross point *R*, i.e. *B* to the left of *R* and *A* to the right of *R* (as shown by the area M_1BRAN in Fig. 13.5). In this case there is inconsistency in the behaviour of the consumer. In situation *A*, point *A* is preferred to *B* because *B* lies within the triangle *MON*. Similarly in situation *B*, point *B* is preferred to *A* because *A* lies within the triangle M_1ON_1. In either of the situations, the consumer is indifferent to the other choice. But he can not prefer *A* to B and *B* to *A* simultaneously. Therefore, we find inconsistency in the consumer's behaviour under both strong and weak orderings.

(*iii*) *Third Case.* Here we may show a group of special cases when the two price-income lines intersect each other but one of the two choice positions lies at the cross point while the other choice position may lie either outside or inside the cross point. These cases can be explained with the help of a diagram as in Fig. 13.6.

(*a*) The first case is one where point *A* lies on the cross and *B* outside the cross to the left of *A*. In the *A* situation, point *A* is preferred to *B* because *B* lies within the triangle *MON* and the consumer is indifferent to point *B*. But in *B* situation on the line M_1N_1 point *A* is also there. Under strong ordering *B* reveals a preference over *A* in the *B* situation, though *A* reveals a preference over *B* in the *A* situation. Thus, there is inconsistency because both cannot be chosen to each other. Under weak ordering in *B* situation, either *B* is preferred to *A* or *B* is indifferent to *A*. Thus, there is again inconsistency in the consumer behaviour.

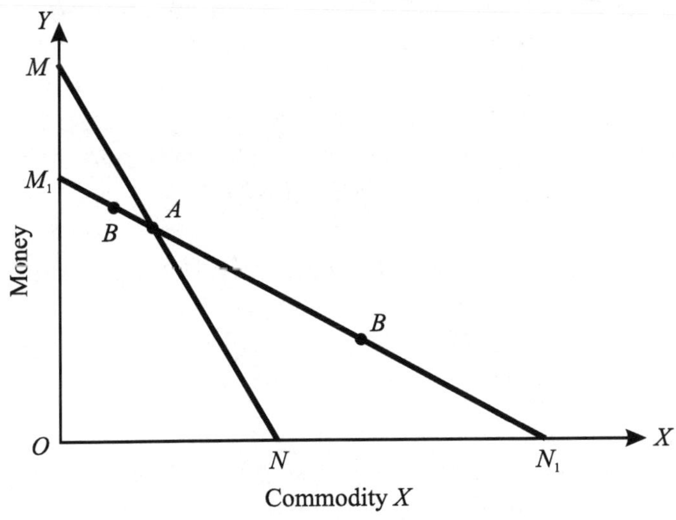

Fig. 13.6

(*b*) The second case is that when *A* lies on the cross and *B* outside the cross to its right as in Fig. 13.6. In this case *B* lies outside the reach of the consumer in situation *A*. Therefore, there is no inconsistency in choice *A* in the *A* situation. In the *B* situation *B* is preferred to *A*. Under weak ordering, it implies that either *B* is preferred to *A* or *B* is indifferent to *A*. So, there is no inconsistency because *B* is not available in the *A* situation.

(*iv*) *Fourth Case.* Here both *A* and *B* lie at the cross (can not be presented in Fig.), the consumer can not have any preference for one situation over the other and hence there can be no inconsistency in his choice.

It is clear from the above analysis that we reach the same conclusion in all cases from the direct consistency test whether we are applying strong ordering or weak ordering hypotheses. On either hypothesis, there is inconsistency in the following two cases:

(*a*) When both points *A* and *B* lie within the cross.

(*b*) When one point lies at the cross and the other within the cross.

Though the weak and the strong forms of preference hypothesis give the same result in regard to the consistency tests, but it should be remembered that the arguments by which they achieve the result are different.

4. Demand Theory of Weak Ordering

Prof. Hicks develops his revised demand theory on the basis of weak ordering (along with additional hypothesis) and the direct consistency test. He first builds the theory of demand for a single commodity, i.e. for the behaviour of the consumer confronted with a market in which the price of only one commodity changes while the prices of other goods are held constant. He derives the law of demand by dividing the effects of a price change into substitution effect and income effect. The main task is to separate out the substitution effect. The substitution effect can be separated from income effect by the following two methods: (*i*) The Method of Compensating Variation, and (*ii*) The Method of Cost Difference.

Derivation of Law of Demand by the Method of Compensating Variation

In Fig. 13.7, we measure money along the vertical axis and commodity *X* along the horizontal axis.[1] Given a certain price of the commodity *X* and income of the consumer, the price income line is drawn as *MN*. Now

1. Here the reader should note that following Hicks we have not shown the horizontal axis in Fig. 13.7. It is only because of the assumption that the consumer is spending an extremely large proportion of his income on the commodity in question. Thus the horizontal axis will be somewhere at the bottom of the page. It is only the top portion of the diagram that counts and hence shown in Fig. 13.7.

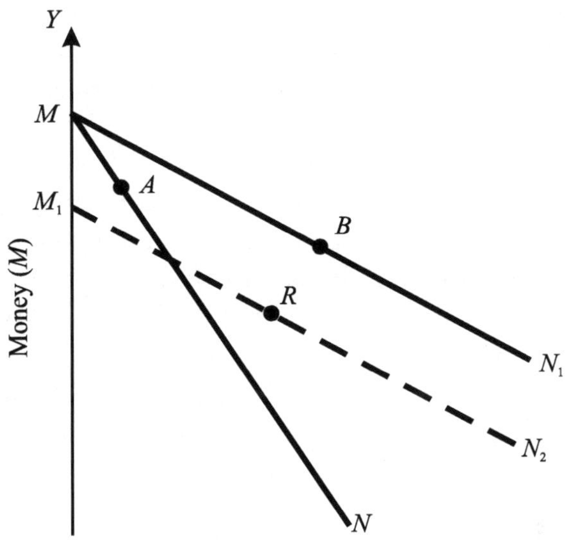

Fig. 13.7

assume that on this initial line *MN,* the consumer selects the combination *A*. Now suppose that the price of commodity *X* falls and money income (*i.e.* prices of other composite items) remaining unchanged; the price-income line becomes MN_1 Now the consumer has to select a new combination on line MN_1. It follows from the consistency test that so long as some quantity of *X* is consumed, any position (point) on line MN_1 must be preferred to point *A*. In other words, whether the selected new position *B* on MN_1 lies to the left of *A* or to the right of *A* or exactly above *A,* it will be preferred to *A;* this is because of the fact that *A* lies within the triangle MON_1. Now the question is where the position *B* on MN_1, will lie; that is whether it will lie to the right of *A,* or to the left of *A* or exactly above *A*. The position *B* lying to the right of *A* means that the quantity demanded for commodity *X* rises as a result of all in its price; and the position *B* lying to the left of *A* implies that the quantity demanded for commodity *X* falls with the fall in its price, and further the position *B* lying exactly vertical above *A* would mean that the consumer does not change the consumption of *X* even if its price falls.

Thus, now the question is whether the quantity of *X* consumed rises, falls or remains the same with a fall in the price of *X*. The answer to this question, as a whole, can not be deduced from the consistency test. As stated above, it is perfectly consistent for there to be a rise, or a fall or no change in quantity of *X* as a result of a fall in the price of *X*. However, if the fall in the price of *X* is associated with a reduction in income, then it can be shown from the consistency test that the quantity demanded for *X* must rise or remain the same, it can not fall. When the income of the consumer is reduced by an appropriate amount along with a fall in the price of *X*, the remaining effect of the change in price (fall in price) on the quantity demanded for *X* will be due to substitution effect. It is clear now that it can be shown from the consistency test that due to substitution effect to the fall in the price of *X*, the consumption of *X* must rise or remain the same, it can not diminish. The rest of the total effect of change in price is the income effect. In which direction (*i.e.* negative or positive) the income effect of the fall in price of *X* works, can not be shown with the help of consistency test. In fact it will depend upon the nature of the commodity which is based on the observation of the consumer.

It follows from the above fact that in order to indicate the substitution effect on the demand for a commodity we make a suitable reduction in income along with the fall in price of commodity *X*. The movement from point *A* on line *MN* to point *B* on line *MN* as a result of the change (fall) in price represent the price effect. In order to find out the substitution effect from the price effect, we have to reduce the gain in real income accruing to the consumer due to a fall in the price of *X*. In other words, income of the consumer is reduced by so much amount that the intermediate position *R* is arrived at the new lower price but with lower income where the consumer is indifferent[2] to the initial position *A*.

According to the indifference curve hypothesis, the movement of the consumer from point *A* to *R* is the substitution effect which is positive. Now it is easy to show from the consistency theory that in what direction the substitution effect works. Since the consumer is indifferent between the positions *A* and *R*, the opportunity line M_1N_2 must intersect the line *MN*. This is because of the line M_1N_2 were to lie wholly outside *MN*, then *R* would be shown to be preferred to *A*; and if line M_1N_2 were to lie wholly inside *MN*, then *A* would be shown to be preferred to *R*. Similarly if *A* and *R* are to be indifferent, *A* and *R* can not lie both to the left or both to the right of cross point (not shown in the diagram) of the lines on which they lie. Again, if the two positions *A* and *R* lie within the cross, or one at the cross and other within the cross, inconsistency of choice will come into the picture. Thus, the only alternatives left are: (*i*) both positions *A* and *R* lie outside the cross; (*ii*) from positions *A* and *R*, one lies at the cross and the other outside the cross; and (*iii*) both positions *A* and *R* lie at the cross. These three are the only possible cases if *A* and *R* are to be indifferent and if the consumer's choice is to be consistent. In any of these cases, it should be noted that either

2. According to J.R. Hicks, "On this interpretation the substitution effect measures the effect of the change in relative prices, with real income constant, the income effect measures the effect of the changes in real income."

the consumption of X increases or remains the same. This is one part of the price effect (*i.e.* fall in the price of X)[3]. Thus, here we conclude that when the price of X falls, the consumer moves from position A to B and the consumption of X tends to rise. The movement from A to B is the price effect which is composed of the movement from A to R via the substitution effect and from R to B through the income effect. Thus, the theorem is proved that the demand curve is downward sloping.

Derivation of Law of Demand by the Method of Cost Difference

Although the above method of compensating variation is perfectly valid for the derivation of law of demand, yet the alternative method of cost difference is more convenient for this purpose. This method was evolved by Prof. Samuelson and has been used by Hicks to derive the law of demand. According to this method, when the price of commodity X falls, the real income of the consumer is reduced in such a way that he is just able to buy the original combination A as shown in Fig. 13.8. Hicks says that income is accordingly reduced by the difference between the cost of his previous (A) consumption of X at the old price and at the new price. It can be illustrated in Fig. 13.8.

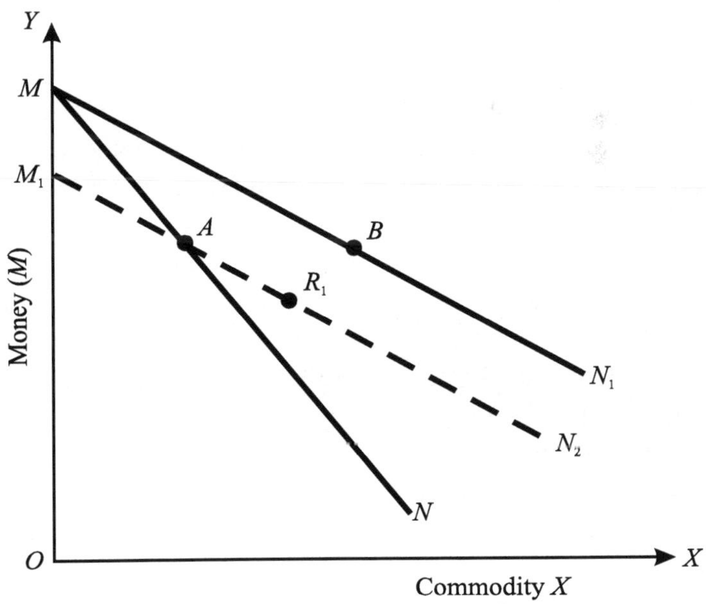

Fig. 13.8

3. The other part (i.e. when price rises) can also be explained in a similar way. Here we need not to repeat it.

Let us assume that *MN* is the original price-income line and *A* is the initially selected combination. When the price of *X* falls, the consumer goes to point *B* on new price line MN_1. The shift from *A* to *B* is known as price effect, which is to be divided into substitution effect and income effect by the cost difference method. Under the cost difference method, the fall in price of *X* is accompanied by the reduction in income of the consumer by such an amount which will put the consumer just able to buy the original combination *A*. Hence, the cost difference in Fig. 13.8 is MM_1 and the income of the consumer is reduced by M_1N_2 in such a way that the line M_1N_2 passes through the old (initial) combination *A*. On the line M_1N_2, the consumer will be at position R_1. Thus the movement from *A* to R_1 is the substitution effect. For a consistent choice the possibilities open to the consumer are: (*i*) that the situation *R*, lies to the right of *A;* and (*ii*) that *A* and R_1 coincide (when under changed situation M_1N_2, the consumer chooses point *A* instead of R_1).

Since in case (*i*) the consumption of *X* will tend to rise from position *A* to *R* and in case (*ii*) it (i.e. the consumption of *X*) will tend to be constant as a result of the situation effect. As in the compensating variation method, if the reduced income of the consumer is returned to him, he will again move to point *B* on MN_1 line. Since point *B* lies above and to the right to R_1 the income effect from R_1 to *B* is positive; the consumer consumes more of *X* as a result of the income effect. Here *X* is a superior or normal good. Thus, the law of demand holds.

Inferior Goods, Giffen Goods and Law of Demand

The Case of Inferior Good. If *X* is an inferior good with negative income elasticity of demand; a fall in the price of *X* will reduce the demand for *X*. The positive substitution effect being greater than the negative income effect in case of most inferior goods, even here the consumer will tend to increase the consumption of commodity *X* when its price falls. This is shown in Fig. 13.9.

In Fig. 13.9, we assume that the commodity *X* is an inferior good and initially the consumer is at point *A* on line *MN*. Now with fall in the price of *X* the opportunity line (income-price line) shifts from position *MN* to MN_1. Accordingly, the consumer moves from point *A* to point *B*. This movement is known as price effect. This is divided into substitution effect and income effect. The substitution effect is the movement from *A* to R_1 and the income effect is the movement from R_1 to *B*. As a result of substitution effect (*A* to R_1), the consumer will consume more of *X;* but he will consume less of *X* when he moves from R_1 to *B* as a result of negative income effect. It is clear that the positive substitution effect being greater than the negative income effect, thus the consumer consumes more of *X*. This is clearly indicated in the lower part of Fig. 13.9 where at the initial price *OP*, the consumer consumes

OX quantity of *X* and when price falls to OP_1, he consumes a greater quantity OX_1. The demand curve *DD* passes through the points *A* and *B*. Thus even in the case of an inferior good, the demand curve may slope negatively. This inverse price-demand relationship will hold in most cases of the inferior goods (provided it is not a Giffen good).

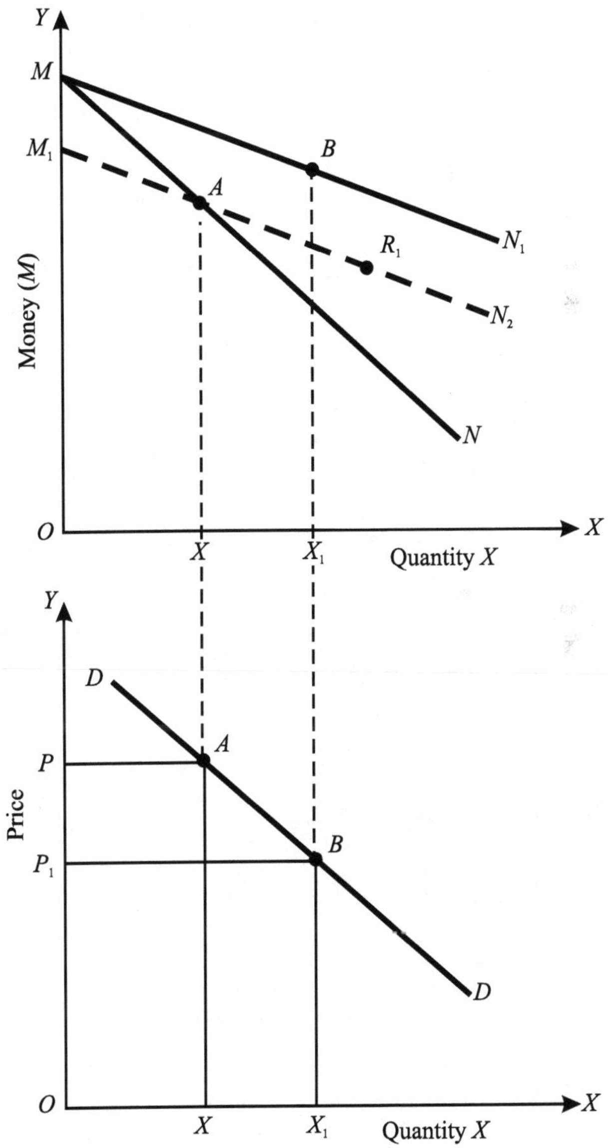

Fig. 13.9

The Case of Giffen Good. The inferior goods, for which there is positive relationship between price and quantity demanded, are known as Giffen goods. Thus, the Giffen goods are exceptions to the law of demand. They can occur only when the following three conditions are fulfilled:

(*i*) the commodity must be an inferior good with a negative income elasticity of significant size,

(*ii*) the substitution effect must be small,

(*iii*) the proportion of income spent upon the inferior good must be large.

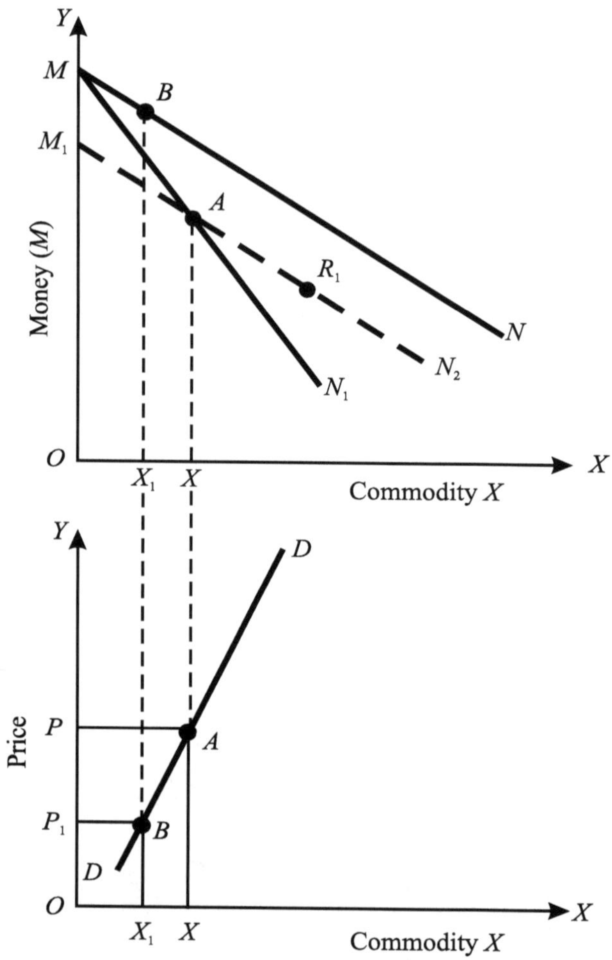

Fig. 13.10

The case of a Giffen good is shown in Fig. 13.10. Here initially the consumer is at point *A* on the line *MN*. With the fall in the price of *X*, he moves from *A* to point *B* on line MN_1. Since commodity *X* is a Giffen good, the consumer will consume less than before. This is shown by point *B* which lies to the left of *A*. Thus, going from *A* to *B* is price effect. Now it is to be divided into two parts, i.e. the substitution effect and the income effect. The substitution effect is the movement from *A* to R_1 while the negative income effect is the movement between point R_1 and *B*. Since negative income effect is larger than the positive substitution effect, *B* lies even to the left of *A* showing on overall fall in the consumption of *X* as a result of a fall in the price of inferior good *X*. This is shown in the lower part of Fig. 13.10. Here the consumer consumes *OX* quantity of *X* at *OP* price. When the price of *X* falls to OP_1, he consumes less quantity, *i.e. OX,* (it is clear that $OX_1 < OX$). The relevant demand curve *DD* passes through these points *A* and *B*. It is a positively sloping demand curve with a positive relationship between the price and the quantity demanded for commodity *X*. According to Hicks, "It is very unlikely that the three conditions for the Giffen case to occur will be satisfied in the case of any ordinary commodity. Thus, although exceptions to the law of demand are theoretically possible, the chance of their occurrence is in practice negligible."

5. Superiority of Hicksian Logical Ordering Theory of Demand

Hicks' Revision of Demand Theory is superior to the cardinal and indifference curve approaches in following respects:

(*i*) *Different from Samuelson's Approach.* Hicks does not follow Samuelson's behaviouristic approach to study consumer's behaviour but instead uses the technique of logical ordering on the part of the consumer to establish the theorems of demand. The cardinal theory fails to analyse the effect of price change into substitution effect and income effect.

(*ii*) *Sound Methodology.* Fritz Machlup points out that "The methodological position underlying Hicks approach is eminently sound. He is free from positivist behaviouristic restrictions on the study of consumer's behaviour, and he also avoids contentions about the supposely empirical assumptions regarding rational action. Instead, he starts from a fundamental postulate, the preference hypothesis."[4]

(*iii*) *Avoids Unrealistic Assumptions.* Hicks's revised theory of demand is free from unrealistic assumptions of cardinal and ordinal approaches, namely continuity and maximising behaviour on the part of the consumer. He has not used indifference curves in his analysis and therefore avoids the assumption of continuity. Further, instead of assuming that consumer always tries to

4. Fritz Machlup, "Professor Hicks' Revision of Demand Theory", *American Economic Review,* March 1957.

maximise his satisfaction, he now, like Samuelson, relies on consistency in the behaviour of the consumer which is a more realistic assumption.

(*iv*) *Applicability to More than Two Goods.* The previous theory of indifference curves could be applied only in the context of two goods, but now the revised theory of demand can be applied even to more than two goods. It is done by deducing from preference hypothesis and logic of order.

(*v*) *Distinction between Weak Ordering and Strong Ordering* is *Possible.* For the first time Hicks makes the distinction between weak ordering and strong ordering forms of preference hypothesis. He has based his revised theory of demand on weak ordering which recognises the possibility of indifference in consumer's scale of preferences.

(*vi*) *Distinction between Inferior Goods and Giffen Goods has been Drawn.* Hicks has clearly explained the distinction between normal goods, inferior goods, and Giffen goods through his new logical weak ordering theory. This he has done by classifying the income effect and the substitution effect from the price effect. Samuelson's revealed preference theory has not been able to distinguish between inferior goods and Giffen goods.

Exercises

1. Explain with the help of diagrams, the Hicks' revision of demand theory.
2. How does J.R. Hicks derive the law of demand directly from the assumption of weak ordering without using indifference curves? Supplement your answer with suitable diagrams.
3. "Demand theory which is based upon the preference hypothesis, turns out to be nothing else but an economic application of the logic of ordering itself. " J.R. Hicks. Comment on the statement.
4. Explain clearly "the direct consistency test" as developed by J.R. Hicks. Derive his demand theorem on this basis.
5. Distinguish between weak ordering and strong ordering. Which one would you select for deriving a demand curve and why?
6. Explain the case of an inferior good and a Giffen good with the help of cost difference method as developed by J.R. Hicks.
7. Explain in brief the superiority of Hicksian logical ordering theory of demand over the cordinal and ordinal approaches.

Multiple Choice Questions

8. (*i*) Which of the following assumptions has been undertaken by Hicks in formulating his revised demand theory:

   (*a*) preference hypothesis (*b*) rationality of the consumer
   (*c*) assumption of continuity (*d*) all of the above [*Ans.* (*a*)]

   (*ii*) Who has developed the demand theory of logical ordering?

   (*a*) Marshall (*c*) Samuelson
   (*b*) Hicks (*d*) Allen [*Ans.* (*b*)]

   (*iii*) Which of the following concepts has been explained by J.R. Hicks?

   (*a*) Indifference Curve Analysis (*b*) Weak Ordering Hypothesis
   (*c*) Direct Consistency Test (*d*) All of the above [*Ans.* (*d*)]

Chapter 14

Law of Demand and Elasticity of Demand

1. Introduction

In economics, the words 'demand' and 'supply' have their own importance. The whole study of economic science is based upon the scientific study of 'demand and supply' and their relationship. The proverb, "teach a parrot to say 'supply' and 'demand' in reply to every question, and he will be a good economist" shows the importance of these two terms in economic science. As a matter of fact the entire theory of value is explained by demand and supply. But in the present chapter we shall only deal with demand theory.

By demand we mean the amount of some commodity which an individual wishes to purchase in a given market in a given period of time at a given price. In our economy the consumer is nominally free to spend his income as he wishes. The sale of a few consumption goods is restricted by the state, and in time of war or other great emergency other goods may be restricted; but these exceptions do not seriously weaken the general rule that the consumer has liberty of choice in his expenditure.

However, consumers' freedom of choice is limited by certain circumstances that are inherent in economic life. One limit is made by the productive power of the community. In poor societies, where the output of goods is not more than sufficient to provide the barest necessities, the range of choice open to the consumers is very narrow. Only in the rich societies with huge natural resources, much capital equipment, and modern technology, we may find a great enough variety of goods to make the range of choice very wide. Even in such societies, some consumers may find their choices painfully restricted by the smallness of their personal incomes. Further, consumer choices are also swayed, more or less, by the persuasive power of advertising. Some economists understood it as an important factor in the determination of (American) consumers' demand.

Besides, there are various other social influences that shape the choices of the consumer. A person is not an independent cause, exerting his will in complete freedom in every situation. He is rather a very complicated man, governed by basic biological urges, personal temperament and tastes, acquired habits, family surroundings, social institutions, contemporary activities, and many other influences all inextricably intermingled. In choosing how he will spend his limited income, there is often opportunity for him to exercise his individuality, but to a great extent he will be controlled by habits, customs, *etc.*

Now the question arises that how a consumer will divide his limited income among the range of goods that are available to him? As we know, if he is a rational consumer or an "economic man", he will spend wisely, seeking always the greatest amount of benefit for his money or income. Different goods would have for him different utilities,[1] taking into consideration all the factors that influence his desire. We can think of him as making a comparison of these desires, and arranging the various goods he might buy in a scale of preferences, beginning with those which he considers of most importance, and ending with those of least.

Again, the utility of a good diminishes gradually as more and more of it is consumed.[2] Therefore, the total utility or total satisfaction derived from the limited income will be the maximum when the utilities of the last dollar spent for each are equal. Some economists have represented this above analysis as an explanation of the behaviour of consumer demand. The modern theory of demand rests on the structure built by Alfred Marshall (1842-1924). Through his *Principles of Economics,*[3] he moulded the thinking of his following generations of British and American economists.

2. Meaning of Demand

In economics the term 'demand' is used in a particular sense. According to Stonier and Hague, "Demand in economics means demand backed up by enough money to pay for the good demanded."[4] In the absence of purchasing power, demand is not effective. For instance, many people would probably like to have a big modernised house, a brand new car, a summer cottage, etc. But they have no effective demand for these things. In order for them to have a demand for these things, they must be *able* and *willing* to buy them. Hence the use of the term "effective demand" has a particular meaning in economics.

1. As we have already defined utility as "the power to satisfy a want." But utility must not be construed as the objective properties of a good. It is really a subjective thing the desire for its possession excited by a good in the mind of the person who contemplates it.
2. The law of diminishing utility explains this situation.
3. Alfred Marshall, *Principles of Economics,* London, Macmillan, 1st ed., 1890 and 8th ed., 1920.
4. Stonier and Hague, *A Textbook of Economic Theory,* 3rd ed., p. 15.

Demand then shows us the quantities of goods that people are willing to purchase at different prices. As Benham rightly points out, "The demand for anything, at a given price, is the amount of it which will be bought per unit of time at that price. Demand means always demand at a price, the term has no significance unless a price is stated or implied."

The demand has the following four characteristics:

(*i*) *Price.* The demand is always at a price. If we say that there is a demand for one thousand motor-cars in the market, this type of statement is meaningless. The person must state the price at which he is prepared to purchase the said quantity of the commodity.

(*ii*) *Time.* Demand must mean demand per unit of time, per month, per week or per day.

(*iii*) *Market.* Demand is always held in the market. Market is a set of points of contact between buyers and sellers. It need not be a definite geographical area.

(*iv*) *Amount.* Demand is always a specific amount of money (price) which a person is willing to purchase. It is not an approximation, but is to be expressed in numbers.

A demand schedule, as we shall note shortly, shows us how much of some product people will buy at different price. On the other side of the picture, supply tells us the quantities of goods that producers are willing to sell at different prices.

3. The Law of Demand

Generally speaking, the amount of a commodity people (consumers) are willing and able to buy varies with the price. The lower the price, the more people tend to buy of a commodity, and the higher price the less people tend to buy. In fact, the 'law of demand' states that the quantity of a product demanded varies inversely with the price. Putting it more concisely, we can say, the lower the price, the greater the effective demand; or, the higher the price, the less the effective demand. It follows from this law that sellers cannot get as high a price for a large quantity as for a lesser quantity. The greater the quantity of a good they are trying to sell, the lower the price must be.

We should note, however, that this law is a generalisation to which there are *some exceptions.* Mainly, there are two situations in which this law will not hold true, but they are exceptional. If the price of a thing is declining, and it is expected to fall still further, buyers may hold off until they think it has reached the bottom, so as to get it at the lowest possible price. This is particularly true of dealers and speculators; but it also holds for consumers in certain situations. But when the bottom has been reached, consumers will buy more than they would at a higher price, so that the general principle inherent in the law is valid, even for this case. The other exception runs directly counter to the principle. There are a few commodities (like diamonds) that are bought largely for the prestige that they confer upon the possessor. To display a diamond necklace or a big diamond in a ring confers a distinction upon the wearer as a person of great wealth. If diamonds were to become so inexpensive that even the poor could have plenty of them, they would no longer carry any prestige, and the demand for them might fall off. Notwithstanding the existence of a great many such goods, for most commodities the law of demand is a valid generalisation.

Alfred Marshall defines the law of demand as follows: "The greater the amount to be sold, the smaller must be the price at which it is offered in order that it may find purchasers; or, in other words, the amount demanded increases with a fall in price, and diminishes with a rise in price. Marshall understood it as the general law of demand. It will be proper to make it clear that like the other laws of economics, the law of demand holds only when other things remain the same. This assumption is known as the assumption of *ceteris paribus.* We shall explain this condition of the law under demand function.

4. The Demand Function

In a given market in a given period of time, the demand function for a commodity can be defined as the relationship between the various amounts of the commodity demanded and the determinants of those amounts. Generally, the determinants of the demand for a commodity are the following:

(*i*) The price of the commodity,

(*ii*) The incomes of the consumers,

(*iii*) Tastes of the consumers, and

(*iv*) The price of other commodities.

In general, therefore, the demand function for a commodity can be written as

$$Dx = f\,(Px\ P,\ Y,\ T) \qquad \text{...(1)}$$

where Dx = Quantity of commodity X demanded per unit of time,

Px = Price of the commodity X,

P = Average price of other commodities,

Y = Income of the consumer,

T = Taste of the consumer.

The accurate or exact form of such a demand function depends on how consumers respond to changes in the value of each of the determinants. If prices of other commodities, income and taste are all assumed to be a constant, the demand function (1) reduces to the simple form,

$$Dx = (Px) \qquad \text{...(2)}$$

The demand function (2) states that the demand for a commodity (X) is a function exclusively of its own price (Px).

But when the other determinants are not held constant or when structural changes occur in the economy over a time period, then a dynamic demand function may be used to allow for all changes. Econometrics is the subject that combines economic and statistical theory for the purpose of measuring actual economic relations. Mathematical models are developed on the basis of economic theory. Statistical methods and techniques are used to estimate the values of the parameters of these mathematical models from the empirical statistics collected for the purpose.

Demand functions are generally homogeneous, of degree zero in prices and income, *i.e.* if all prices and income change in the same proportion, the quantity demanded remains unchanged.[5]
where

5. To prove this statement or property of the demand function, we assume that the total utility function and the budget constraints of a consumer are given as

$$U = f(q_1, q_2)$$

and $$Y = P_1q_1 + P_2q_2$$

where q_1 and q_2 are the amounts of the two commodities Q_1 and Q_2 consumed by the consumer and $p\text{-}_1$ and p_2 are the respective prices. Y represents the total income of the consumer.

If all prices and income change in the same proportion, say by k times, then equation of budget constraint becomes,

$$kY = (kp_1)\, q_1 + (kp_2)\, q_2$$

We now write the Lagrangean function as

$$V = f(q_1, q_2) + \lambda[kY - kp_1q_1 - kp_2q_2]$$

For maximisation of the utility function, we have

$$\frac{\partial V}{\partial q_1} = f_1 - \lambda kp_1 = 0 \qquad ...(i)$$

$$\frac{\partial V}{\partial q_2} = f_2 - \lambda kp_2 = 0 \qquad ...(ii)$$

$$\frac{\partial V}{\partial q} = kY - kP_1q_1 - kp_2q_2 = 0 \qquad (iii)$$

From (i) and (ii) we get

$$\frac{f_1}{f_2} = \frac{p_1}{p_2}$$

It, Therefore, proves that a proportionate (equal) change in income and prices would not affect the optimum combinations of the two commodities under consideration. The second order condition also remains unaffected.

Table 14.1: A's Demand Schedule for Oranges

Price per kg. (in Dollars)	*Quantity Purchased (in kgs.)*
16	1
15	2
14	3
13	4
12	5
11	6

If income, price of other commodities, tastes and other independent variables are held constant, the demand function takes the simple form $Dx = f\ (Dx)$. This form of the demand function can vary considerably as long as the demand curve is monotonic (*i.e.* it always moves in the direction) with quantity varying inversely with price.

Demand Schedule and Demand Curve

Demand Schedule. According to Prof. Alfred Marshall, a demand schedule is a list of prices and quantities. In other words, a demand schedule states the relation between the two variables of price and quantity. In Table 14.1 we have a hypothetical illustration of *A's* demand schedule for oranges. In this table we see that at a price of \$16 per kg., the consumer *A* buys 1 kg. of oranges; if instead the price were \$15, the quantity demanded would be 2 kg. and so on.

A demand schedule does not say what the price is. It only says that amounts would be bought at different possible prices. The lower the price, the larger is the quantity that is bought. Similarly, the higher the price, the smaller the quantity. Therefore, Table 14.1 is a "demand schedule", which, in turn, is defined as a list of the quantities of any economic goods that will be purchased in a given market at a given time.

Demand Curve. The material in Table 14.1 can be made into a demand curve, as shown in Fig. 14.1. The vertical axis represents price and the horizontal axis quantity.[6] We proceed by plotting first purchases at \$16. To do this we read up the vertical axis until we come to \$16 point; then we go across to the right until we come to \$11 on the quantity scale and place a dot there. We do the same thing for the other prices. We then connect these

---

6. Some mathematical economists reverse the axes on the ground that quantity is the dependent variable, which belongs on the Y-axis. To put price on the Y-axis and quantity on the X-axis is a convention established by Prof. Alfted Marshall.

points by drawing a smooth curve through all of them. This is our "demand curve". This demand curve shows the relationship between the two variables of price and quantity in particular the manner in which quantity is demanded upon price. The demand curve is always so called, even when it happens to be a straight line.

According to Friedman, "A demand curve of a particular group for a particular commodity can be defined as a locus of points, each of which shows the maximum quantity of the commodity that will be purchased by the group per unit time at a particular price. It represents an attempt to relate a rate of flow to a price at an instant of time. For many problems, it is useful to conceive of a demand curve as boundary line separating two spaces, the space to the

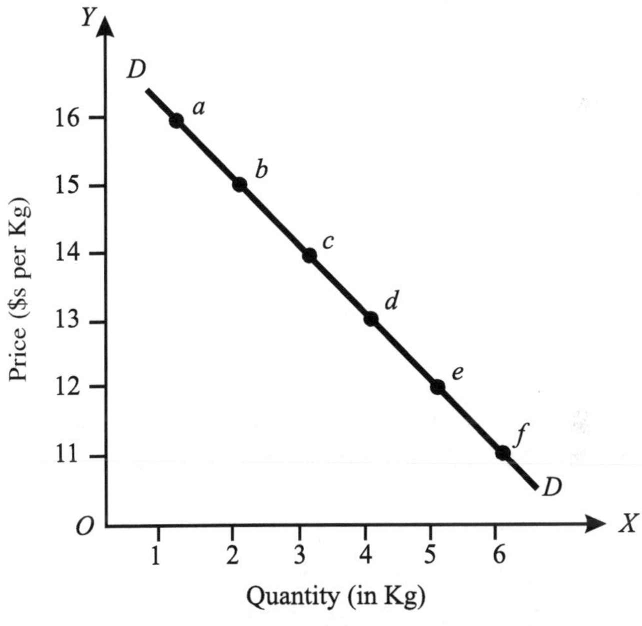

Fig. 14.1

left of the demand curve representing points that are attainable under the given conditions of demand, in the sense that demanders would be willing to buy the indicated quantity at the indicated price, and the space to the right of the demand curve representing points that are unattainable in the sense that demanders would not be willing to buy the indicated quantity at the indicated price."[7]

7. Milton Friedman, *Price Theory—A Provisional Test* (First Indian ed., 1920), pp. 13-14.

Fig. 14.1 shows the demand curve for one person, and it is downward sloping. With other persons or families it may be different, although it will tend to be a decreasingly downward-sloping curve. It is possible that a higher income person would purchase more oranges at each given price. In such a case the curve would be farther to the right; or, lower income person might buy less at each price, in which case the curve would be to the left.

Market Demand Curve

Figure 14.1 illustrates the demand curve of an individual consumer, which, in terms of the total number of consumers, constitutes only a small part of the total demand for this particular product. This individual consumer's demand has little influence on the price and quantity of oranges sold, but the total demand for this or any other product does influence the market price and the quantity sold. The market demand curve (or schedule) is the sum of the demand curves (or schedules) of all consumers. As noted above, such schedules are made up of the reactions to prices of many consumers, each of whom decides how much of a given commodity it is worth while to buy. At high prices he buys less, and at low prices he buys more. Also, at certain prices some consumers will purchase very little, some a lot as price increases or decreases; some consumers will vary their purchases very little, some will vary their purchases significantly. Thus, the demand curves for all consumers show different slopes, different positions and different shapes. By adding up the potential purchases of all the consumers at each possible price, we get the demand schedule (curve) for the market.

To give a very simple illustration, suppose there are only three possible buyers oranges in a given market. We can picture their possible purchases in Table 14.2.

Table 14.2: Market Demand Schedule

Price per kg. (in $s.)	*Effective Demand of Oranges (in kg.)*			*Total Effective Demand of the Market (in kg.)*
	Consumer A	*Consumer B*	*Consumer C*	
16	1	–	–	1
15	2	1	–	3
14	3	2	1	6
13	4	3	2	9
12	5	4	3	12
11	6	5	4	15

The schedule of demand for the market will then be shown in the last column, which is obtained by adding the demands of *A*, *B* and *C* horizontally across the table for each price. By plotting this schedule on a graph, we would get the required curve. In Fig. 14.2, the individual demand curves are added to arrive at the market demand curve.

Fig. 14.2 indicates that the demand curve for the market may not be a linear demand curve while the individual consumers may have linear demand curves.

Mathematically, we can say that

$$Dx = Dx_1 + Dx_2 + Dx_3 +$$

or

$$Dx = \sum_{i=1}^{n} Dx_i \qquad \ldots(3)$$

where Dx = Market demand for commodity X

Dx_i = i^{th} consumer's demand for commodity X

n = Total number of consumers.

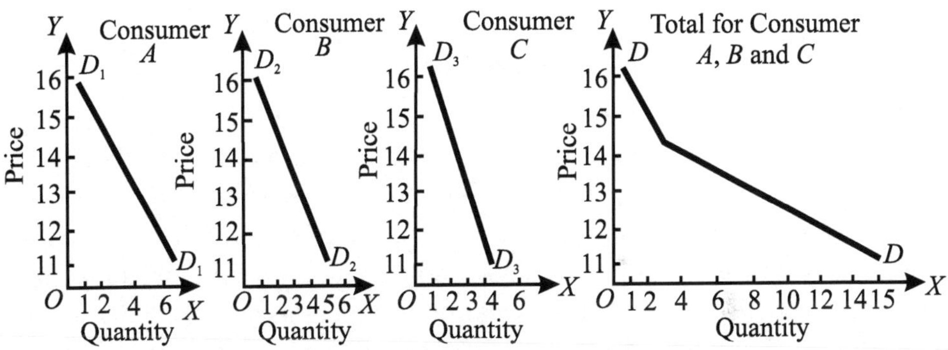

Fig. 14.2

5. Types of Demand

We normally study three types of demand: (*i*) Price Demand, (*ii*) Income Demand, and (*iii*) Cross Demand.

As we have already discussed, price demand shows us the quantitics of goods that people are willing to purchase at different prices, assuming *ceteris paribus*. It is the price demand that the economists frequently make use of. Figure 14.3 illustrates the case price-demand curve which has a negative slope indicating an inverse relationship between the price and the quantity demanded. Figure 14.3 shows that at price *OP*, the quantity demanded is *OX;* when price increases to OP_1, the quantity demanded reduces to OX_1; also when price falls to OP_2, quantity demanded increases to OX_2.

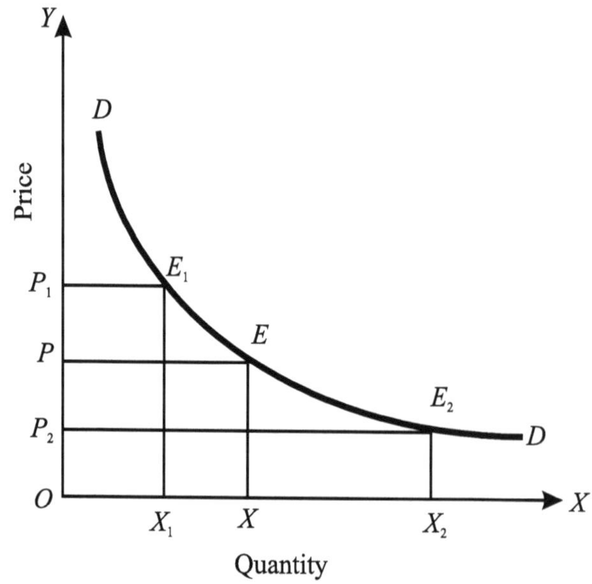

Fig. 14.3

Similarly, income demand shows us the quantities of goods that people are willing to purchase at different income levels, assuming other things remaining the same. For superior goods or normal goods, the income demand curve will have a positive slope, and for inferior goods, or Giffen goods, the income demand curve will be of a backward-bending type. Figure 14.4 shows the income demand curve for a superior or normal commodity. At *OY* level of income, the consumers buy *OX* quantity of commodity *X*. If income increases to OY_1,then people will demand OX_1 quantity of the commodity and for higher levels of income, more of commodity *X* will be demanded.

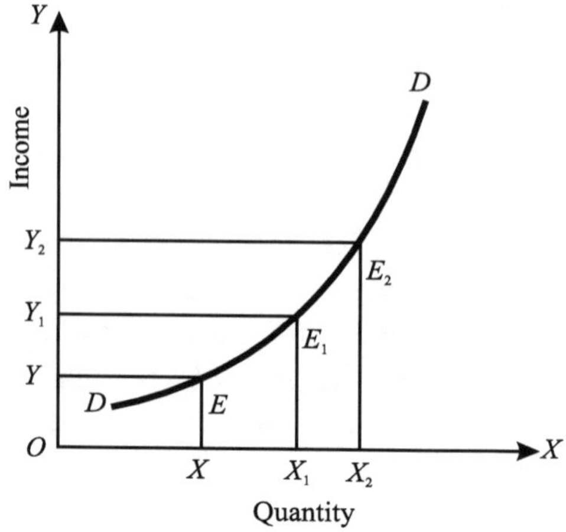

Fig. 14.4

Figure 14.5 indicates the case of an inferior good or a "Giffen good."[8] Here with every rise in income of a consumer above *OY* level of income will lead to a fall in quantity. At *OY* level of income, the consumer purchases *OX* quantity of commodity *X*. If his income increases to OY_1, then he demands only OX_1 of the commodity.

Now cross demand shows us the quantities of commodity *X* that people are willing to purchase at different prices of other commodities, say commodity *Y* (some related commodity), assuming *ceteris paribus*. Here, we may draw two types of demand curves-demand for substitutes and demand for complementary goods.

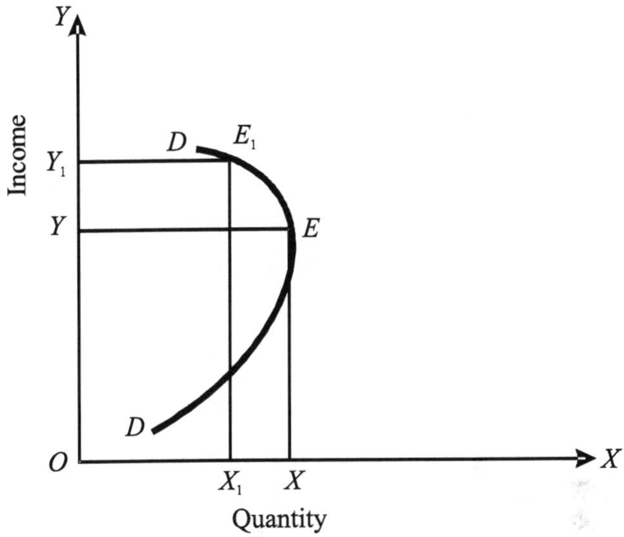

FIG. 14.5

There are some commodities whose demand decreases as a result of an increase in the price (prices) of other commodity (or commodities), or their demand expands due to a decrease in the price (or prices) of other commodity (or commodities). Such commodities are known as complementary commodities. The demand curve of these complementary goods has been drawn in Fig. 14.6. This demand curve is very similar to the normal or general demand curve.

---

8. Although Giffen good is an inferior good, but every inferior good cannot be a Giffen good. Because in the case of an inferior income effect is negative, but in the case of a Giffen good the negative income effect is strong enough to more than swamp the positive substitution effect of a given price change.

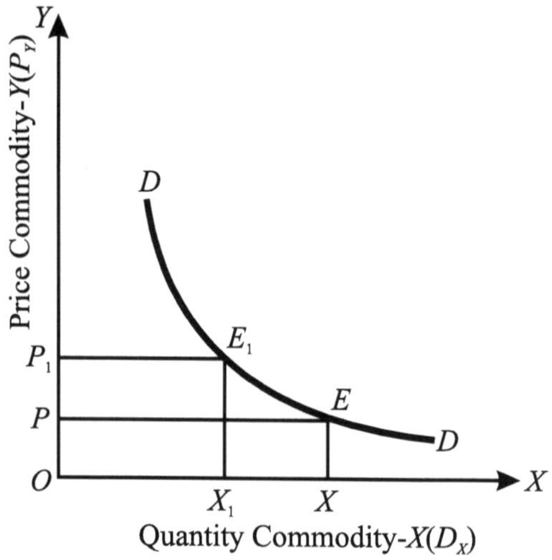

Fig. 14.6

In Fig.14.6, *X* and *Y* are complementary goods. If price of *Y* increases from *OP* to OP_1, then the demand for *X* decreases from *OX* to OX_1.

Figure 14.7 shows the demand curve of substitute goods. It has a positive slope, because a decrease (or increase) in the price of *Y* will lead to a decrease (or increase) in the demand for *X*.

The demand for complementary goods is also known as *joint demand.* For example, there is a joint demand for tennis rackets and tennis balls, automobiles and automobile tyres. More generally, the demand for any product is always a joint demand for the resources used to produce it. Also, the demand for any commodity or service may be a *composite demand,* compounded out of the demand for a number of different uses, e.g. demand for leather is a composite demand of the demand for leather for shoes, for pocket books, etc. Of these various types of demand, the one frequently used is the price-demand.

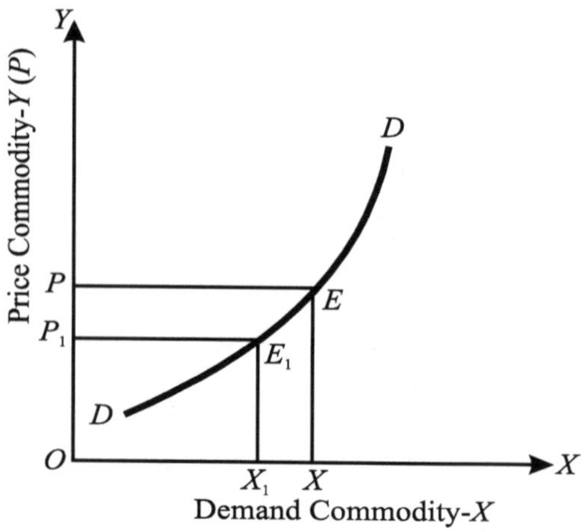

Fig. 14.7

6. The Determinants of the Demand Curve[9]

As we have already discussed under the demand function that the following fundamental factors will determine the demand for a commodity:

(*i*) *Price of the Commodity.* The first and the most important obvious determinant is the price of the commodity which is being demanded. As the law of demand states, in general, larger quantities of a commodity will be purchased at lower prices. We also observe that a 10 per cent reduction of price will lead to very different percentage increases of purchases of various goods; the elasticities of demand for various commodities are most diverse.

(*ii*) *Urgency of Consumer Needs.* The other thing that affects elasticity of demand is the urgency of consumers' need for the commodity in question. In the case of luxuries, demand is usually pretty elastic. These are items which we can do without; consequently, when they become more expensive, we curtail our purchases of them. Conversely, when they become cheaper, we buy them more freely. The demand for necessities, on the other hand, is usually more or less inelastic. For instance, if the price of bread were doubled, purchases would not decrease very greatly. Consumers would feel that they must have their usual quantity of bread, even at the high price. Rather than be deprived of it. They would go without other things that they considered less essential. Demand is also inelastic in the case of commodities which are very low in price, but for a different reason. Such things as matches, salt, or spool cotton, which cost but a few paise, represent so small a percentage of our total expenditures that we buy all we desire of them without much thought of economy. Lower the price, and very few more will be bought. for everyone has already all that he needs. Raise the price to even double what it was, still the amount is so small that consumers will not greatly curtail their purchases. However, if the price were raised ten or a hundred fold, this would no longer be true, and a considerable reduction in consumption (demand) might be made.

(*iii*) *The Degree of Substitution.* The degree to which substitutes for a given commodity are available also has much to do with elasticity of demand. Commodities for which there are good substitutes will have high demand elasticities; commodities for which there are only poor substitutes will have low elasticities.

(*iv*) *Income of the Consumer.* Another determinant of the quantity demanded by a consumer is his income. *Ceteris paribus,* there will be some correlation between income and demand elasticities, however, changes in income will be accompanied by changes in the purchases of various goods and services. The income elasticity of demand will assume different values for different goods. Necessities are not much responsive to changes in income while goods are very responsive to changes in income. Generally speaking,

9. George J. Stiglar, *The Theory of Price,* pp. 86-88.

the influence of income change upon the demand for commodities will depend upon the value of the marginal propensity to save of the consumers. The lower the marginal propensity to save, the more will be the income elasticity of demand and vice versa.

(*v*) *Price of Related Goods.* One of the important determinants of demand is the prices of the related goods. In the case of substitute goods, if the price of commodity *Y* falls, then it will lead to a reduction in the demand for commodity *X*. Similarly, if the goods are complementary, then a rise in the price of *X* will lead to a reduction in the demand for *Y*, because *X* and *Y* both are jointly demanded.

(*vi*) Size *of Population.* The demand for a good will also depend upon size of the population in the economy. An increase in population will lead to an increase in the demand for a good and vice versa.

The future expectations about the price of the commodity and the various policies of the government are also some of the determinants of the demand for a commodity. We, generally, assume these determinants of demand to be constants while drawing a demand curve. Any change in any of these other determinants will lead to a shift in the demand curve.

7. Change in Demand and Change in Quantity Demanded

According to Friedman, in the demand analysis, it is necessary to make a clear distinction between "demand" in the *schedule sense* and "demand" in the *sense of quantity demanded.* Here we must be very careful about our use of the words, because the concept of changing demand in everyday speech is clouded with some confusion, which must be clarified. In this conext the following statements are important: (*i*) "The price went up and therefore demand went down", and (*ii*) "Demand went up and therefore price went up." Each statement separately looks sensible, yet the two are clearly contradictory if the word "demand" is supposed to have the same meaning in both. Of course, it does not. In the first statement the word demand means quantity demanded, while in the second statement the word demand means demand schedule.

Sometimes, we find that the demand does not change only because of a change in price. Demand can, and does, increase or decrease without any change in price. In such case, when the price remains the same but the demand either increases or decreases, the entire demand curve is shifted either to the right or to the left. It shifts to the right in the case of an increase in demand and to the left in the case of a decrease in demand. This is called change in demand. We refer to these changes as *shifts in the demand curves.* In other words, there has some force at work which has altered the demand situation such that there will be a shift in it. These forces which influence the demand curve are many.

An increase in consumer income may result in a willingness on the part of consumers to buy a larger quantity of a product at each price. In this case our demand curve will shift to the right (from *DD* to D_1D_1 for example) as shown in Fig. 14.8. If, on the other hand, consumers decide to purchase less of a product at each price, then the demand curve will shift to the left from *DD* to D_2 D_2 (for example), as shown in Fig. 14.8. A change in income may bring a change in consumer preference, but other factors, such as technology, may also change preferences and tastes. Therefore, it should be noticed again that, when we say *demand increases,* we mean that there is an increase in the amount that consumers will purchase at each particular price, and vice versa. Such a change (increase or decrease in demand) is described as a shift in the demand curve. This is different from a movement along a demand curve.

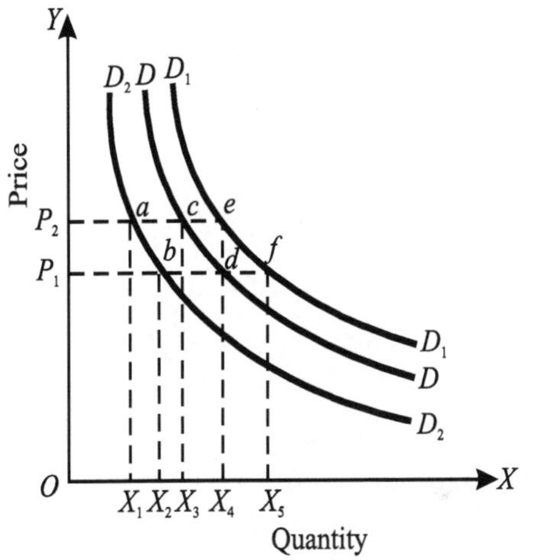

Fig. 14.8

When we talk about extension (or expansion) of demand and contraction of demand, then we refer to the movement along the same demand curve. Extension of demand means an *increase in the quantity demanded* while contraction of demand means a *decrease in the quantity demanded.* Hence, an increase (or decrease) in demand should not be confused with an increase (or decrease) in the quantity demanded because of a fall (rise) in price. A change in the quantity demanded as a result of the change in the price of a given commodity alone (other factors such as income, technology, etc. remaining unchanged) does not require the drawing of a new demand curve as shown in Fig. 14.9.

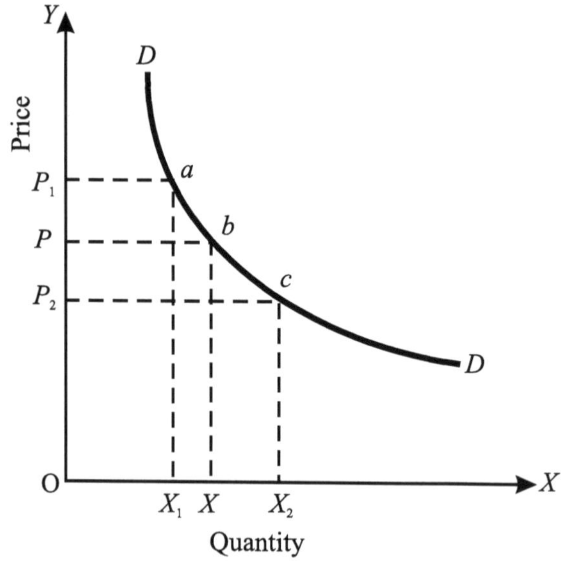

Fig. 14.9

Figure 14.9 indicates that when price increases from *OP* to OP_1, quantity demanded reduces from *OX* to OX_1. Also, if price falls to OP_2, quantity demanded would increase to OX_2. On a particular demand curve, the movement from one point to another represents the law of demand, because it indicates the effect of a price change on the quantity demanded assuming *ceteris paribus.*

8. Reasons for the Negative Slope of the Demand Curve

There, are the following reasons for the negative slope of the demand curve or for the operation of the law of demand:

(*i*) *The Law of Diminishing Marginal Utility.* According to the law of diminishing marginal utility, as a consumer consumes more of a given commodity, the marginal utility of the additional units will diminish. Further, the price of a commodity that the consumer is ready to pay will not be greater than the marginal utility of it. Therefore, a consumer will buy more units of a commodity only if its price goes down. Hence, the law of demand holds.

(*ii*) *Substitution Effect.* The law of demand states that when the price of a commodity goes down, its demand will rise. The reason is that substitutes of the commodity are available in the market. If the price of a commodity goes down, other things being the same (*i.e.* the prices of its substitutes remain unchanged), the consumer would like to substitute this commodity in place of other substitute goods. To what extent the substitution takes place will depend upon the degree of substitutability. This part of a rise in the demand for a good due to a fall in its price is known as substitution effect.

(*iii*) *Income Effect.* When the price of a commodity goes down, the real income of the consumer will increase. In other words, if the consumer buys the same basket of goods, he can easily save a part of his money income. This amount can be spent on any commodity, depending upon the desire of the consumer. Since the consumer, buys more of a commodity as its price declines, this means he is spending more on it. This part of increase in consumption is known as the income effect.

The above are some of these important reasons for the negative slope of the demand curve. But we may also find certain exceptions of it which we have already explained.

9. Elasticity of Demand

Under the demand function we have seen that the demand for a commodity is a function of its own price, the prices of related goods, and the income and taste of the consumer. A change in any of these independent variables will lead to a change in the demand for the said commodity or the dependent variable. If we assume the other factors such as the prices of related goods, the income and the taste of the consumer, etc. as constant, then we can relate the quantity demanded directly to the price of the commodity under consideration. When price changes, the quantity demanded usually changes, but what will be the extent of the change in quantity in relation to the change in price? Will a small change in price bring about a large change, a small change, or no change in the quantity demanded?

We have already noted that the demand curves of different consumers have different slopes and shapes. Similarly, different commodities have demand curves which differ in slope and shape, some being rather steep and some tending to be flat. The steepness of the demand curve is caused by increases (or decreases) in quantity demanded as price decreases (or increases) and by the entry (or withdrawal) of additional buyers into the market as price increases (or decreases). The difference in consumer response in quantity demanded to price changed is expressed with the concept of *elasticity of demand.*

The elasticity of demand refers to a particular behaviour of a demand curve. It tells us something about how the quantity demanded responds to changes in price. The degree to which quantity demanded responds to a change in price is known as the elasticity of demand. If a small change in price causes a relatively large change in the quantity demanded, we say that demand is elastic. If the change in the quantity demanded is relatively small, then demand is said to be inelastic. It is important to note that we are concerned with *proportionate* change in price and quantity, and not with *absolute* changes.

Elasticity will, therefore, be different at each and every price, and it can only be meaningful when related to small changes in price. Elasticity of demand is the relationship between proportionate change in price and the resulting proportionate change in quantity demanded.

The concept of elasticity of demand was mainly developed by Marshall. According to him, "The elasticity (or responsiveness) of demand in a market is great or small, according to the amount demanded increases much or little for a given fall in price, and diminishes much or little for a given rise in price."

In the words of Albert L. Meyers, "The elasticity of demand is a measure of relative change in the amount purchased in response to relative change in price on a given demand curve."

Modern economists, however, define the elasticity concept in a mathematical way. For instance, Prof. R.G. Lipsey states that "Elasticity of demand may be defined as the ratio of the percentage change in the quantity demanded to percentage change in price." Mrs. Joan Robinson defines it more clearly. According to her, "The elasticity of demand at any price or at any output, is the proportional change of amount purchased in response to a small change in price, divided by the proportional change of price."

These above definitions analysed only the responsiveness of demand to a given change in price, and thus obliviated the effect of a variation in the prices of other commodities or in the income of the consumer. In their views, demand is a function of price alone, and therefore, they discussed only price elasticity of demand. In the modern analysis of consumer behaviour, however, the following elasticities of demand are considered important, albeit their relative significance may be different in different situations (*i*) Price Elasticity of Demand, (*ii*) Cross Elasticity of Demand, (*iii*) Income Elasticity of Demand, (*iv*) Demand Elasticity of Substitution.

Price elasticity is, of course, the most important among the above elasticities of demand. That is why the concept of price elasticity of demand is popular among the economists. Now we shall discuss these various concepts under the following analysis.

I. Price Elasticity of Demand

Alfred Marshall was the first economist to give a clear formulation of price elasticity as the ratio of a relative change in quantity to a relative change in price. Let *Ed* stand for price elasticity of demand. Then mathematically, the formula for calculating the price elasticity of demand can be written as :

$$Ed = \frac{\text{Percentage change in quantity demanded}}{\text{Percentage change in price}}$$

$$= \frac{\frac{\Delta X}{X} \times 100}{\frac{\Delta P}{P} \times 100}$$

$$= \frac{\Delta X}{X} \Big/ \frac{\Delta P}{P}$$

$$= \frac{\Delta X}{X} \times \frac{P}{\Delta P}$$

or $$Ed = \frac{\Delta X}{\Delta X} \cdot \frac{P}{X}$$

Also $$Ed = \frac{dX}{dP} \cdot \frac{P}{X}$$

Here, X is quantity, P is price, and Δ (delta) is the symbol meaning "a change in". Thus, $\Delta X/X$ is a relative change in quantity, and $\Delta P/P$ is a relative change in price. Generally, a negative sign is put before the term $dX/dP.\ P/X$, which simply indicates that quantity demanded and price are inversely related. *Ed* is also called the coefficient of elasticity of demand. It is a pure number, that is, it stands by itself being independent to units of measurement. When numerical estimates are possible, the coefficients of elasticity of different commodities can be directly compared. The value of the coefficient *Ed* will lie between O and ∞. If *Ed* equals 1, demand has unit elasticity. If *Ed* is less than 1, but more than zero, demand is inelastic. If the coefficient is zero, demand is said to be perfectly inelastic. If the coefficient is greater than 1, but less than ∞, demand is elastic. If it is ∞, demand is said to be perfectly elastic. Thus, the value of the coefficient *Ed* will tell us the nature of the demand curve. Conveniently, we put the following five categories of the demand curve.

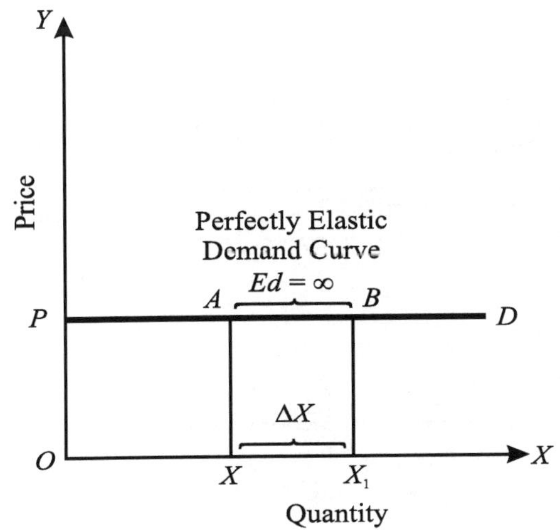

Fig. 14.10

(*a*) *Perfectly Elastic Demand.* It refers to that situation where a small rise in price will cause the quantity demanded to be zero. In such a situation price of a commodity remains constant. In a perfect competitive firm, the demand curve is perfectly elastic. The numerical value of the coefficient *Ed* will be infinite, or

$$Ed = \frac{dX}{dP} \cdot \frac{P}{X} = \infty \qquad \text{because } dP = 0$$

It should, however, be noted that cases of perfectly elastic demand are very rare in actual life and, therefore, only of theoretical importance. Figure 14.10 indicates this situation where the price *OP* is fixed and at this fixed price any quantity of the commodity can be sold. In short, perfectly elastic demand for a commodity refers to those cases in which the quantity demanded is independent of price.

(*b*) *Elastic Demand.* It refers to that situation where the proportionate change in quantity demanded is much greater than the proportionate change in price. In such a case the numerical value of the coefficient *Ed* will take the limit $1 < Ed < \infty$ or normally,

$$Ed = \frac{dX}{dP} \cdot \frac{P}{X} > 1$$

which implies that the relative change in quantity demanded is much greater than the relative change in price, or $\frac{dX}{X} > \frac{dP}{P}$. For example, a 10

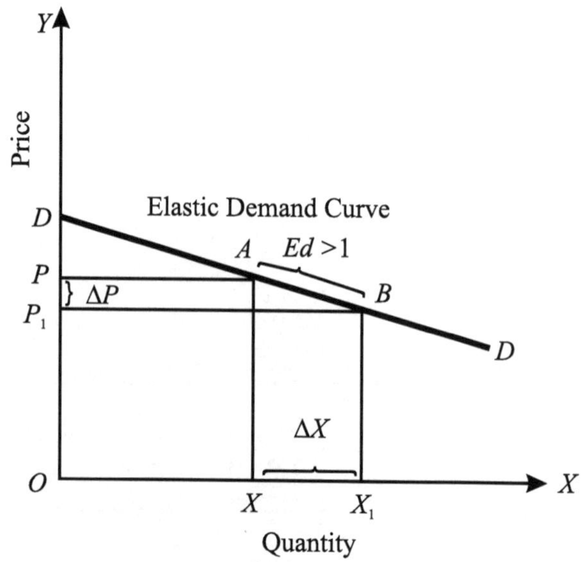

Fig. 14.11

per cent change in price will lead to a 20 per cent change in quantity demanded, then

$$Ed = \frac{20 \text{ per cent}}{10 \text{ per cent}} = 2$$

This case has been shown in Fig. 14.11.

(*c*) *Unit Elasticity of Demand.* It refers to that situation where the proportionate change in quantity demanded is equal to the proportionate change in price. In such a case the numerical value of the coefficient *Ed* will be equal to unity, i.e.

$$Ed = \frac{dX}{dP} \cdot \frac{P}{X} = 1$$

because $$\frac{dX}{X} = \frac{dP}{P}$$

This case has been shown in Fig. 14.12.

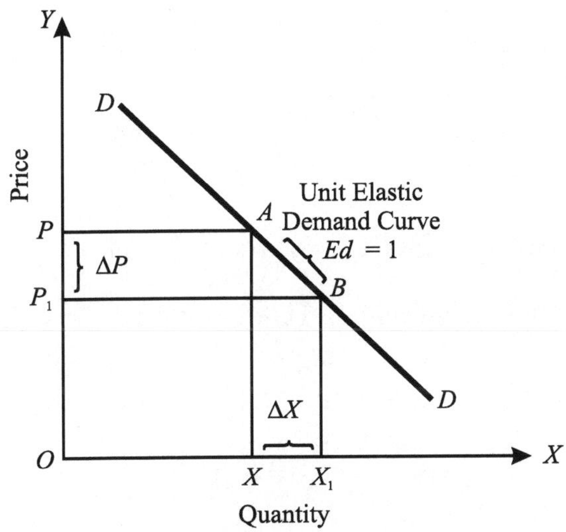

Fig. 14.12

(*d*) *Inelastic Demand.* It refers to that situation where the proportionate change in quantity demanded is less than the proportionate change in price. In such a case the numerical value of the coefficient *Ed* will take the limit, $0 < Ed < 1$, or normally,

$$Ed = \frac{dX}{dP} \cdot \frac{P}{X} < 1 \quad \text{because} \quad \frac{dX}{X} < \frac{dP}{P}$$

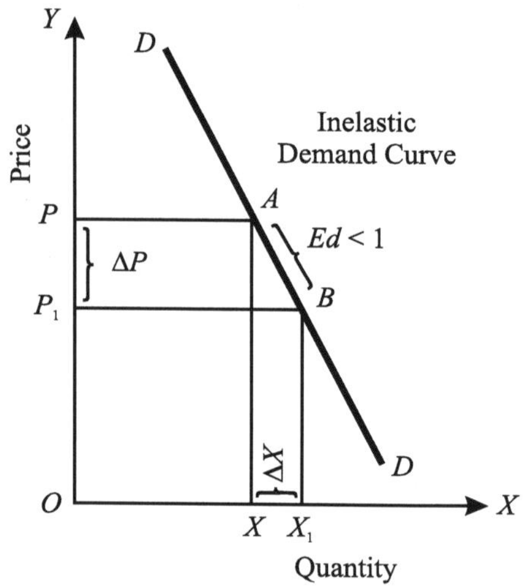

Fig. 14.13

For example, a 10 per cent change in price will lead to a 5 per cent change in quantity demanded, then

$$Ed = \frac{5 \text{ per cent}}{10 \text{ per cent}} = \frac{1}{2} \text{ which is} < 1$$

This case is shown in Fig. 14.13, where the ratio $\frac{\Delta X}{\Delta P}$ or $\frac{dX}{dP} < 1$.

(e) Perfectly Inelastic Demand. It refers to that situation where quantity demanded is perfectly independent of price changes. In such a case the demand is non-responsive and the value of the coefficient *Ed* will be equal to zero, i.e.

$$Ed = \frac{dX}{dP} \cdot \frac{P}{X} = 0$$

because $dX = 0$

This situation has been shown in Fig. 14.14 where the demand *OX* is fixed. If price increases or decreases, it will be unable to make any change in quantity demanded. This case is rarely found in real life.

It should, however, be noted that the first and the last categories of price elasticity of demand are unrealistic situations. We cannot visualise any situation in which the quantity demanded is independent of price, or where

$$Ed = \infty \text{ and } Ed = 0$$

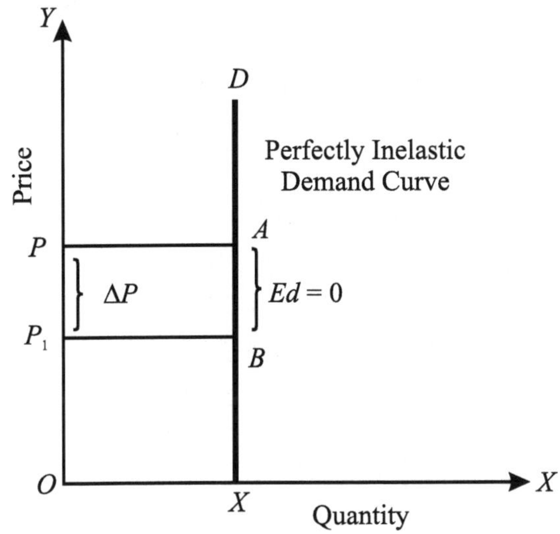

Fig. 14.14

changes in price do induce changes in the quantity demanded, although the magnitude of such change may be different for different commodities. Hence, in reality the demand for a commodity may be elastic, unitary elastic or inelastic. More specifically,

$$|ED| \begin{matrix} > \\ = \\ < \end{matrix} 1$$

Further, it should be remembered that a demand curve does not have the same elasticity throughout its entire length. Therefore, the above classification of the price elasticity of demand applies to the different segments of a demand curve. A demand curve will change its elasticity at different points. But there are three cases of perfectly elastic, perfectly inelastic and unit elastic demand curves, where it possesses only one elasticity throughout its entire length. These are exceptions to the general rule.

Measurement of the Price Elasticity of Demand

The price elasticity of demand can be measured in several alternative ways. We shall discuss the following three methods of measurement (1) Total Outlay or Expenditure Method, (2) Point Method, and (3) Arc Method.

(a) *Total Outlay or Expenditure Method.* This method was devised by Alfred Marshall. Marshall said that the price elasticity of demand can be measured on the basis of change in total outlay (or expenditure) following a change in the price of a commodity. In the words of Marshall, "If the elasticity of demand be equal to unity, any fall (or rise) in price will cause a proportionate rise (or fall) in the amount brought (quantity demanded) and, therefore, it will make no change in the total outlay which purchasers make for the commodity." Therefore, in this method, we consider the change in price and the consequent change in the outlay on the purchase of the commodity. If we multiply the quantity purchased by its price, then we get total outlay incurred on it, i.e.

Total Expenditure = Quantity Demanded Price

If with a price increase, total spending increases also, then demand is *inelastic.* If, with a price reduction, total spending declines, the demand is also *inelastic.* If, with a price increase, total spending declines, the demand is *elastic.* If, with a price reduction, total spending increases, demand is elastic. In other words, if total spending changes in the same direction as the change in price, demand is inelastic; if total spending changes in the opposite direction of a change, then demand is elastic. If total spending remains the same as price goes up or down, we have unitary elasticity. Examine the demand schedule of Table 14.3.

Table 14.3: Elastic Demand, Unitary Elasticity and Inelastic Demand

Price ($s.)	*Quantity Demanded*	*Total Revenue ($s.)*	*Demand Elasticity*
10	100	1,000	Elastic Demand
9	120	1,080	(*Ed* > I)
8	140	1,120	Unitary Elasticity
7	160	1,120	(*Ed* = 1)
6	180	1,080	Inelastic Demand
5	200	1,000	(*Ed* < 1)
4	240	960	

From Table 14.3 we draw the following conclusions:

(*i*) If demand is elastic, a given fall in price causes a relativey larger increase in the quantity demanded. From this it follows that a drop (rise) in price causes consumers to make a larger (lesser) money expenditure on a commodity whose demand is elastic.

Table 14.4: Changes in Price, Outlay and Elasticities of Demand

Nature of the Change in Price	*Change in Total Expenditure (Outlay)*	*Value of the Coefficient (Ed)*	*Nature of the Elasticity of Demand*
I. Effect of a fall in price	(*a*) Decrease	$Ed < 1$	Inelastic
	(*b*) Increase	$Ed > 1$	Elastic
	(*c*) Constant (No change)	$Ed = 1$	Unitary Elastic
II. Effect of a rise in price	(*a*) Decrease	$Ed > 1$	Elastic
	(*b*) Increase	$Ed < 1$	Inelastic
	(*c*) Constant (No change)	$Ed = 1$	Unitary Elastic

(*ii*) If demand has unit elasticity, a fall (or rise) in price causes no change in expenditures.

(*iii*) If demand is inelastic, a fall (or rise) in price causes consumers to spend less (more) money on the commodity.

The relations between elasticity and expenditure are stated in more general form in Table 14.4.

These relationships may be illustrated graphically. In Fig. 14.15 the area OP_1AX_1 (total revenue) exceeds the area *OPBX* and illustrates a situation where demand in this price range (*OP* to OP_1) is inelastic.

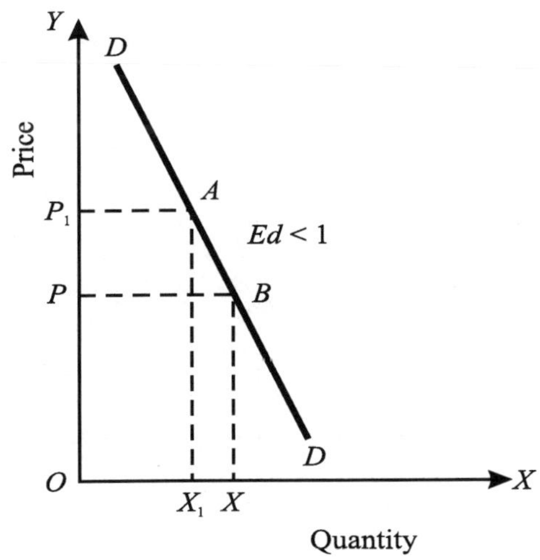

Fig. 14.15

Figure 14.16 shows a situation where demand is elastic in the price range OP OP_1, because here total revenue is greater at lower price (i.e. the area OP_1 BX_1 > $OPAX$).

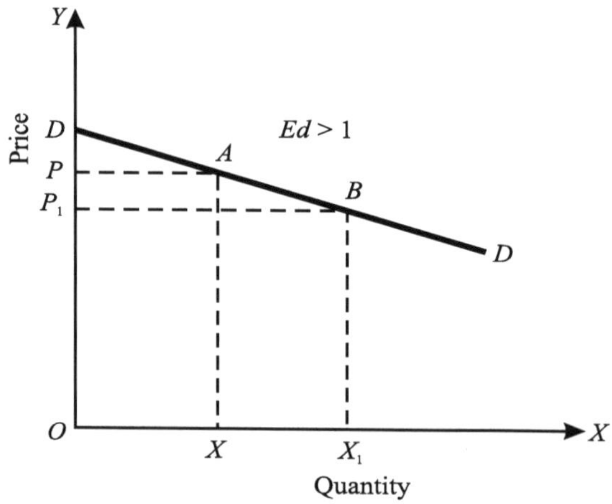

Fig. 14.16

Fig. 14.17 illustrates the interesting case where the elasticity of demand is unity and the total revenue will be the same at all prices (i.e. $OPAX= OP_1BX_1$.

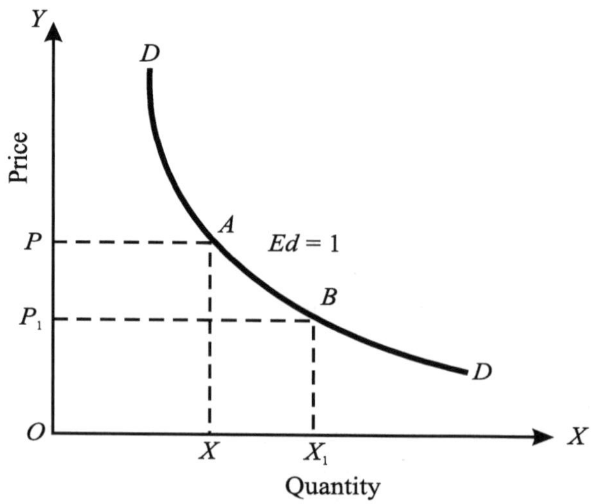

Fig. 14.17

The relationship between the total outlay and price elasticity of demand can also be shown by the help of Fig. 14.18. In Fig. 14.18 we take three different price ranges: from OP to OP_1, from OP_1 to OP_2, and below OP_2. If price falls from OP to OP_1, total outlay increases and the total outlay curve slopes downward to the right. Also, if price increases from OP_1 to OP, the total outlay decreases as shown by the segment AB of the curve sloping upward to the left. Thus, over the price range OP to OP_1, elasticity of demand is greater than one or the demand is elastic.

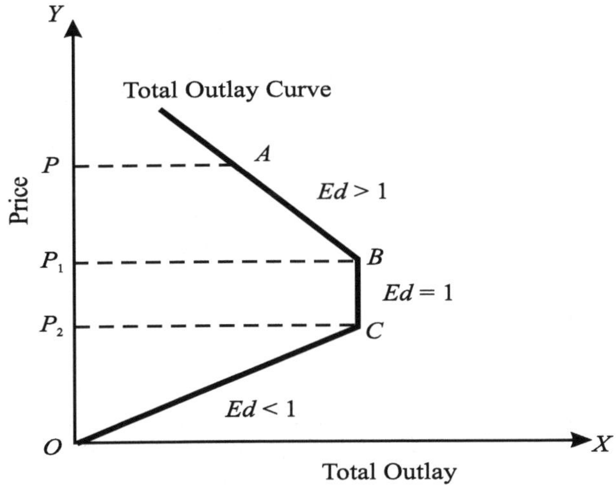

Fig. 14.18

If price falls from OP_1 to OP_2 or it rises from OP_2 to OP_1, total outlay remains the same. Therefore, the elasticity of demand over the price range $OP_1 - OP_2$ will be unitary elastic ($Ed = 1$). Over the price range OP_2, total outlay decreases as price falls; thus the elasticity of demand is inelastic ($Ed < 1$).

The main limitation of the total outlay method is that it simply classifies the price demand into elastic, inelastic and unitary elastic. This method is unable to measure the elasticity in numerical terms, i.e. it does not explain the situation of perfectly elasticity elastic demand ($Ed = \infty$) and the situation of perfectly inelastic demand ($Ed = \infty$).

(*b*) *Point Method or Point Elasticity of Demand.* The point method of measuring price elasticity of demand has also been developed by Prof. Alfred Marshall. Under total outlay method, the terms "elastic" and "inelastic" have been applied to the whole demand for a commodity. This is correct only for some purposes, but not for others, because the demand for a commodity can be elastic in one price range and inelastic in another. The degree of elasticity

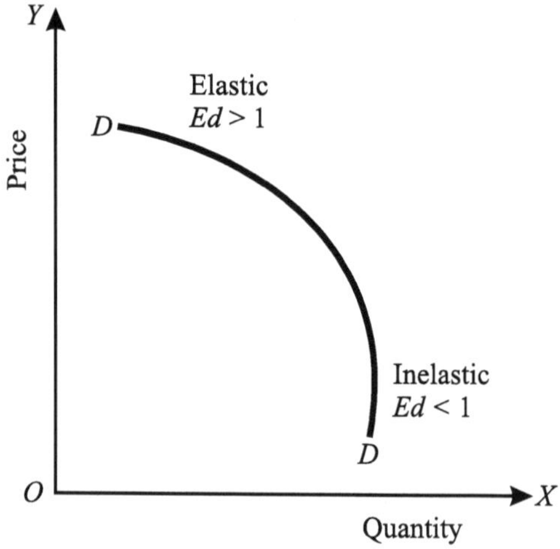

Fig. 14.19

or inelasticity as indicated by the size of the coefficient (*Ed*)—can also vary from one price range to another. Figures 14.19 and 14.20 show two demand curves. We may notice that the demand curve in Fig. 14.19 is elastic at high prices and inelastic at low prices. The demand curve in Fig. 14.20 is just the opposite. Both kinds of demand curves are possible. Hence, by itself, "price range" is not a precise expression. The coefficient of elasticity could vary within some given range, as well as from one price range to another. Thus, precision requires that the elasticity of demand must be measured at a point on a demand curve.

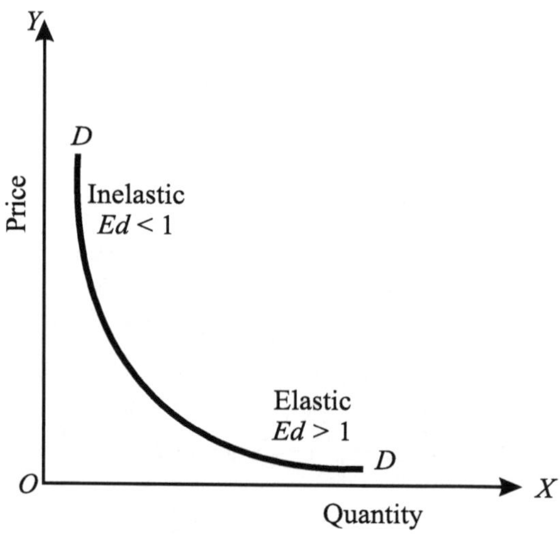

Fig.14.20

Point elasticity of demand is the corresponding concept for each particular point on the demand curve. But, at any such point, there is no change in price or $\Delta P = O$ and also there is no change in quantity, or $\Delta X = O$. We, therefore, define point elasticity in much the same way as the derivative concept used in the beginning, that is, we take the point elasticity to be the limit of the arc elasticity where the arc (a segment of the demand curve) is made smaller and smaller to arrive at the definition:

$$\text{Point elasticity of demand} = \frac{dX}{dP} \cdot \frac{P}{X}$$

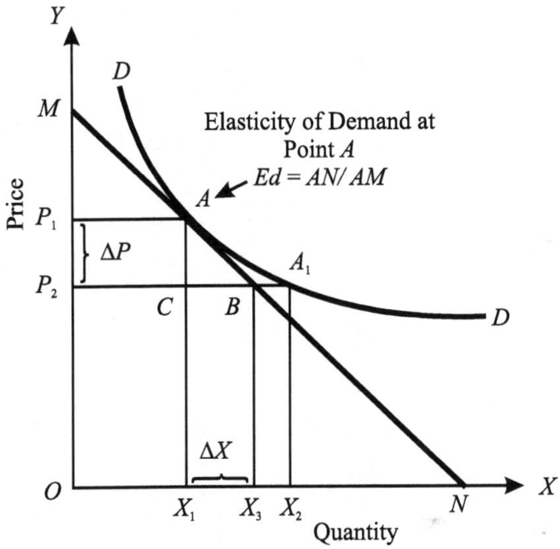

Fig. 14.21

Figure 14.21 shows how to find the elasticity at a point A on the demand curve DD. If price changes from OP_1 to OP_2, then the quantity demanded will increase from OX_1 to OX_2. Now the consumer is at point A_1 of the same demand curve. Since we want to measure elasticity of demand at a particular point A on the demand curve DD, we therefore draw a straight line MN which is tangent to the demand curve at point A. The slope of the line MN is the same throughout. We here assume that point A_1 is very near to point B (as the limiting case) and, therefore, $OX_2 \equiv OX_3$. At point A and B the slope is the same. Now we supplement the information in our above formula of *Ed,* i.e.

$$Ed = \frac{dX}{dP} \cdot \frac{P}{X} \qquad ...(5)$$

where dX = change in quantity, dP = change in price, P = original price, X = original quantity

In Fig. 14.21, $dX = X_1X_3$ and $dP = P_1P_2$.

Similarly, $X = OX_1$ and $P = OP_1$.

Substituting these values in (4) we obtain

$$Ed = \frac{X_1X_3}{P_1P_2} \cdot \frac{OP_1}{OX_1} \qquad ...(6)$$

But

$$\frac{X_1X_3}{P_1P_2} = \frac{CB}{AC}$$

$\therefore$

$$Ed = \frac{CB}{AC} \cdot \frac{OP_1}{OX_1}$$

Furthermore, by the theorem of similar triangles $\Delta ABC = \Delta AX_1N$; thus

$$\frac{CB}{AC} = \frac{X_1N}{AX_1} = \frac{X_1N}{OP_1} \qquad ...(7)$$

$\therefore$

$$Ed = \frac{X_1N}{OP_1} \cdot \frac{OP_1}{OX_1}$$

$$= \frac{X_1N}{OX_1} \qquad ...(8)$$

But $\frac{X_1N}{OX_1} = \frac{AN}{AM}$, hence the coefficient of price elasticity at point A is approximately,

$$Ed = \frac{AN}{AM} \qquad ...(9)$$

Hence, elasticity of demand at point A is equal to AN.

If $AN = AM$ then $Ed = 1$

If $AN > AM$ then $Ed > 1$

If $AN < AM$ then $Ed < 1$

If $AN = 0$, then $Ed = 0$

If $AM = 0$, then $Ed = \infty$

This proves the theorem that elasticity of demand at various points on the same demand curve is different. Equation (8) states that along a linear demand curve as shown in Fig. 14.22, the elasticity coefficient will increase if point A (where $Ed = 1$) approaches M and exactly at point

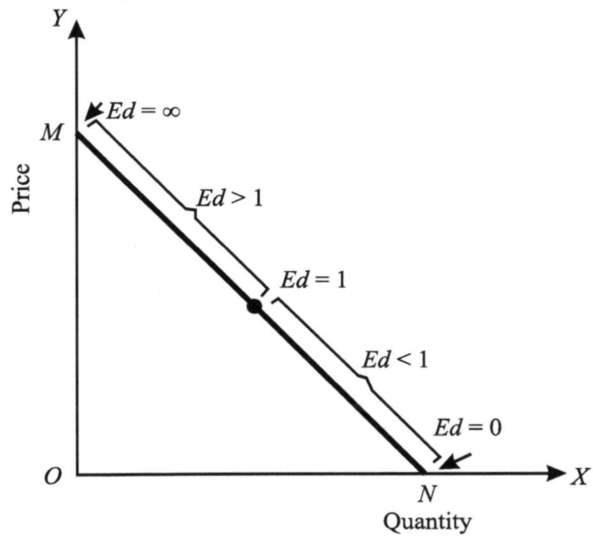

Fig. 14.22

M, $Ed = \infty$. Similarly, the elasticity coefficient *Ed* will decrease if point *A* leads to *N* and exactly at point *N*, $Ed = 0$.

(c) *Arc Method or Arc Elasticity of Demand.* The important limitation of the point method is that it is used only when a demand curve is known, either by assumption or through a statistical calculation based on many observations of prices and quantities. In real life, only scanty data are available, the data being a few price-quantity observations of purchases of a commodity. In other words, the change in price may not be infinitesimal, i.e. it may be finite. We do not possess such information about minute changes in price and quantity. We may possess demand schedules in which there are wide gaps in price as well as the quantity demanded. In such a situation, the elasticity of demand cannot be measured at a point on the demand curve. Instead, the problem is now related to the measurement of elasticity over a certain range of values of price and quantity, or over a certain arc of the demand curve. Thus, there is another method of price elasticity known as arc elasticity of demand. An arc is a portion or a segment of a demand curve.

The question now is the appropriate formula for arc elasticity. Differential calculus cannot help us measure the arc elasticity of demand, as the demand curve *DD* in Fig. 14.23 has different slopes at points *A* and *B*.

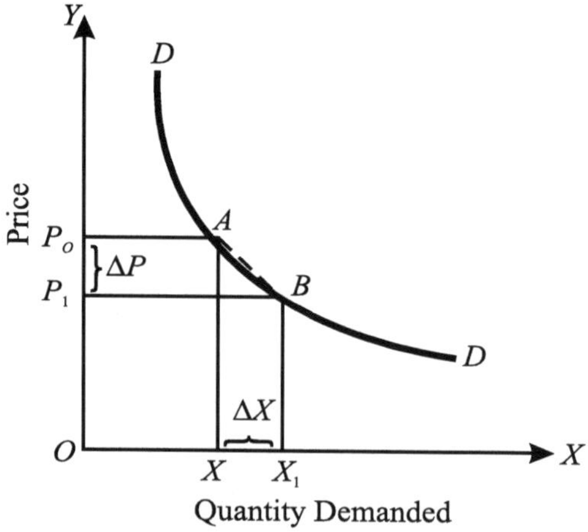

Fig. 14.23

Arc elasticity is a measure of the average responsiveness to price change exhibited by a demand curve over some finite stretch of the curve as *AB* in Fig. 14.23. In Fig. 14.23, we may very well find the absolute change in price ($\Delta P = P_1 - P_0$) and the absolute change in quantity demanded ($\Delta X = X_1$ X_0). But what are the exact values of *X* and *P* ? Since a number of values may occur between X_0X_1 and between P_0P_1, no unique value of these variables (*X* and *P*) is called for by the definition. It is customary for this purpose to use the average of the two end values of *X*, that is, $X = (X_1 + X_0)/2$, and to do the same for $P = (P_1 + P_0)/2$. Hence the arc elasticity of demand is defined by the expressions:

$$Ed = \frac{\Delta X}{\Delta P} \cdot \frac{P}{X}$$

$$= \frac{X_1 - X_0}{P_1 - P_0} \cdot \frac{(P_1 + P_0)/2}{(X_1 + X_0)/2}$$

$$= \frac{X_1 - X_0}{P_1 - P_0} \cdot \frac{P_1 + P_0}{X_1 + X_0}$$

$$= \frac{X_1 - X_0}{P_1 + P_0} \cdot \frac{P_1 + P_0}{X_1 - X_0} \qquad \text{...(10)}$$

where X_0 = Old level of quantity
X_1 = New level of quantity
P_0 = Old price
P_1 = New price

It is, however, to be remembered that the concept of arc elasticity of demand is not as precise as that of point elasticity of demand. But, on the other hand, arc elasticity is a real concept which is applicable in real life.

Elasticity and Slope of the Demand Curve

Elasticity of demand must not be confused with the slope of the demand curve. As we have seen, elasticity will be different at every price. The slope of the demand curve may remain constant and yet its elasticity may be different at different points on the same demand curve. In Fig. 14.22, we have a straight line demand curve whose slope is uniform but the elasticity changes throughout the length of the curve. In the middle of the curve at point *A*, elasticity is equal to unity; below the mid-point *A*, it is less than unity; and above the mid-point *A*, it is greater than unity. Hence, the slope and the elasticity are not one and the same thing. The exceptions to this general rule, that elasticity will be different at every price, are:

(1) Where the demand curve is a rectangular hyperbola (slope keeps changing), elasticity is unity at every price.

(2) Where the demand curve is perpendicular to the quantity axis; elasticity of demand is zero.

(3) Where the demand curve is perpendicular to the price axis; elasticity of demand is infinite.

In conclusion, we may say that no demand curve (except the rectangular hyperbola demand curve, or the vertical or the horizonal straight-line demand

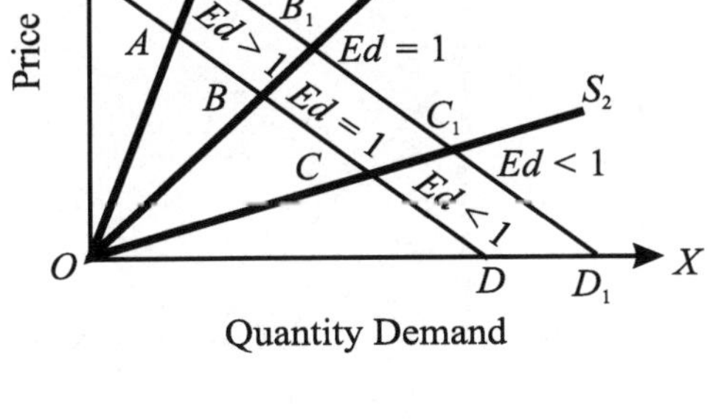

Fig. 14.24

curve) will have a single elasticity throughout its length. It will have different elasticity on different points of it.

Further, we can also compare elasticity on different points of two demand curves. In Fig. 14.24, we draw two straight-line demand curves *DD* and D_1D_1 parallel to each other. If we draw a line through the origin point *O*, it cuts the two demand curves at points of equal elasticities. As shown in Fig. 14.24, the straight lines *OS*, OS_1, OS_2 cut the demand curves *DD* and D_1D_1 at points of equal elasticity. The elasticity of demand on the demand curve *DD* at points *A*, *B*, *C* is the same as that of the demand curve D_1D_1 at points A_1, B_1, and C_1. The elasticity at points *B* and B_1 is equal to unity, while the elasticity at point *A* and A_1 is more than one and at points *C* and C_1, it is less than one. In brief,

At points *A* and A_1 $Ed > 1$

At points *B* and B_1 $Ed = 1$

At points C and C_1 $Ed < 1$.

Now if we draw a line perpendicular to *X*-axis, it will cut the lower demand curve at a point of lower elasticity and the higher demand curve at a point of higher elasticity (see Fig. 14.25). In Fig. 14.25, we have two demand curves– *DD* the lower demand curve and D_1D_1 the higher demand curve. *MN* is the vertical line which cuts the two demand curves *DD* and D_1D_1 at the points *A* and A_1 respectively. Elasticity at point *A* is lower than the elasticity at point A_1,

Similarly, if we draw a line perpendicular to the *Y*-axis or horizontal to the *X*-axis, it will cut the lower demand curve at a point of higher

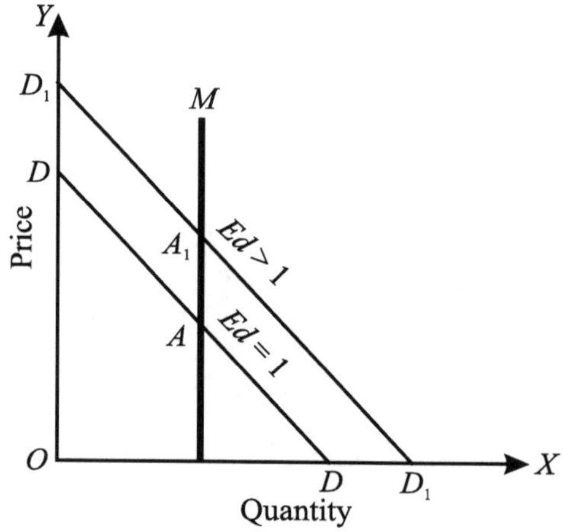

Fig. 14.25

elasticity and the higher demand curve at a point of lower elasticity. In Fig. 14.26, *MN* is a horizontal line to *X*-axis. It cuts the demand curve *DD* at point

A and demand curve D_1D_1 at point A_1 respectively. Now the elasticity at point A is higher than the elasticity at point A_1.

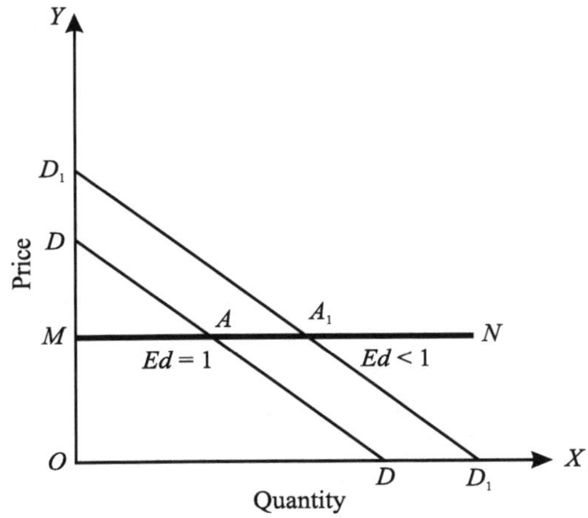

Fig. 14.26

The Determinants of Price Elasticity of Demand

A question normally arises that as to what makes the demand for one commodity elastic and the demand for another inelastic? The determinants of price elasticity of demand for a commodity can be studied under the following headings:

(*i*) *The number and closeness of* its *substitutes.* The available substitutes for a commodity are the most important determinants of the price elasticity of demand. If a product has many close substitutes in the relevant price range, its demand is almost certain to be highly elastic. If the producer of such a commodity were to raise his price, consumers buy less of the commodity and buy more of its substitutes. If the producer reduces the price, the consumers desert the substitutes and buy the commodity in (relatively) much larger quantities. The more close substitutes the commodity has, the more elastic will be the demand for it. The demand for cigarettes will be inelastic because there are no close substitutes, but the demand for a particular brand of cigarettes will be elastic because there are a number of very effective substitutes in the relevant price range.

(*ii*) *The importance of the commodity* in *buyers' budgets.* The proportion of consumer's income which is spent on the commodity will be an important determinant of the price elasticity of demand. Where this proportion is very small, demand will tend to be inelastic. Matches account for a very small part of our total spending and a relatively large increase in their price would not have any great effect on the quantity demanded. Also, the demands for soap, salt, ink, and for many other similar commodities are highly inelastic, because the typical household spends only a few paise a week on each of them. The percentages of family budgets devoted to such commodities are exceedingly small. We, however, notice that the demands for such commodities are inelastic and not perfectly inelastic.

(iii) Degree of necessity. It is sometimes held that the demand for necessities is inelastic and the demand for luxuries elastic. The demand for necessities, such as, bread, potatoes, water, and clothing is certainly inelastic, but is this not another aspect of the availability of substitutes? There are no close substitutes for these articles in the relevant price ranges. The demand for luxuries will be elastic, it is argued, because if their prices rise, we can manage without them. But the demands for motor cars, petrol, cigarettes and alcoholic drinks have proved to be extremely inelastic. There are hardly 'necessities' in the strict sense of the word. The use of word as 'luxury' and 'necessity' raises many problems. In an economy where incomes are steadily rising, the luxuries of one generation become necessities for the next.

(iv) Habit of the consumers. It is also an important factor determining the elasticity of demand. Some commodities are habit-forming tobacco and alcohol are good examples and the demand for such goods will tend to be inelastic.

(v) The *number of uses of the commodity.* Here we may say that the more uses a commodity can be put to, the more elastic its demand. If a commodity has only a few uses, its demand is likely to be inelastic. The various uses of a commodity can be put in the order of their importance. If the price of a commodity is very high, consumers will put the few units they buy only to the most important use of the commodity. At successively lower prices, more of the commodity is purchased, to be devoted to the less important uses.

(vi) Time and *Elasticity.* The demand for a commodity always exists in some period of time which can be a day, a week, a month, a season, a year or a period of several years. Elasticity of demands varies with the span (length) of time periods. In general, demand is more elastic (or less inelastic), the longer the period of time. The longer the period of time, the greater is the case of substitution for both consumers and producers. If for instance, the price of fuel oil should increase but not the prices of other fuels, it is likely that the consumption of fuel oil in the month after the price increase would diminish very little. The demand for fuel oil in anyone month's period, then, is probably highly inelastic. But the demand over a year is certain to be less inelastic,

because a year is long enough for people to change their plans about the kinds of furnaces to install. Over a period of, say, five years or more, the demand for fuel oil is probably highly elastic, because such a period is long enough to permit full substitution. Thus, time is also an important determinant of price elasticity of demand.

Any judgement of the elasticity of demand for a commodity must take all these above determinants into account. They can reinforce one another, or work in opposite directions.

II. Cross Elasticity of Demand

In real problems of demand analysis, commodities stand in more or less definite clusters of substitutes and complements. Under the demand function we have seen that demand for a commodity is not only a function of its own price but also a function of the prices of related goods. Hence, the idea of elasticity of demand can also be applied in a situation where two commodities are related to each other. The concept of cross elasticity of demand is useful in handling inter-commodity relations. Once more, we assume that two commodities *X* and *Y* are related, ie. a change in the price of one will certainly affect the demand for the other. The expression of cross elasticity of demand is

$$Ed^* = \frac{\text{relative (percentage) change in the quantity demanded of commodity } X}{\text{relative (percentage) change in the price of commodity } Y}$$

$$= \frac{\Delta X}{X} \Big/ \frac{\Delta Py}{Py}$$

$$= \frac{dX}{X} \Big/ \frac{dPy}{Py}$$

$$= \frac{dX}{dPy} \cdot \frac{Py}{X} \qquad \text{...(11)}$$

where X = quantity demanded for commodity X, Py = price of commodity Y.

The cross elasticity of demand for commodity *X* may be positive or negative, depending upon the nature of relationship between *X* and *Y* commodities.

The coefficient (*Ed*) is positive if *X* and *Y* are substitutes because the price change and the quantity change are in the same direction. If the price of *Y* goes up, so does the quantity demanded of *X*, and vice versa. But if commodities *X* and *Y* are complements, the coefficient (*Ed*) is negative because changes in the price of one commodity cause opposite changes in the quantity demanded of the other.[10]

Let us assume the two commodities are Coca Cola and Pepsi. If the price of Coca Cola increases, people in large number will drink Pepsi. The cross elasticity in such a case would therefore be positive, because the change in the demand for Pepsi and the change in the price of Coca Cola move in the same direction. The closer two commodities are substitutes for each other, the greater is the size of the cross-elasticity coefficient. Close substitutes have high cross-elasticity of demand. Two commodities are poor substitutes for each other, if the cross elasticities are low.

If the two goods are complementary products, such as sugar and tea, the cross elasticity will be negative. Because, an increase in the price of sugar would reduce its demand, and simultaneously, the demand for the tea will also fall. Thus, the two variables, the change in the price of sugar and the change in the demand for tea move in opposite directions. Therefore, the cross elasticity of demand for complementary goods will be negative.

Sometimes, it is possible that the two goods *X* and *Y* are neither substitutes nor complements, *i.e.* they are unrelated or independent goods. In such a situation the cross elasticity of demand for the independent goods will be zero.

The above three situations of cross elasticity of demand can be illustrated diagrammatically in panels (*a*), (*b*) and (*c*) of Fig. 14.27. Panel (*a*) of Fig. 14.27 explains that an increase (decrease) in the price of *Y* will lead to an increase (decrease) in the quantity of *X*. Thus the two goods will be labelled as substitutes and the cross elasticity of demand will be positive ($Ed^* < 0$). Panel (*b*) of Fig. 14.27 explains that an increase (decrease) in the price of *Y* will lead to a decrease (increase) in the quantity of *X*. Thus, the two goods will be labelled as complements and the cross elasticity of demand will be negative ($Ed^* < 0$). Panel (*c*) of Fig. 14.27 explains that an increase or decrease in the price of *Y* will make no effect on the quantity of *X* and, therefore, the cross elasticity of demand will be zero ($Ed^* = 0$).

10. Such definition that substitutes have positive cross elasticity of demand and complements have negative cross elasticity of demand are valid for commodities bought in markets, i.e., for the mass behaviour of consumers. For an individual consumer however, mathematical reasoning can show that such definitions might not be correct. It is a question of the income effect.

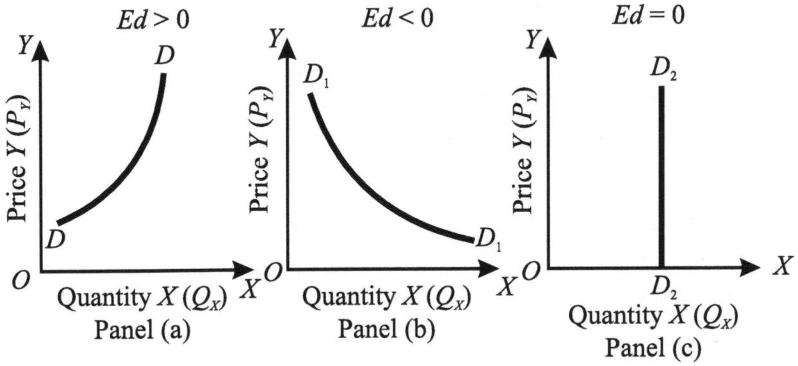

Fig. 14.27

We can, however, say that for the perfectly substitutable products, the cross elasticity of demand is highly positive and generally tends to be infinity. And, for the perfectly complementary goods, the cross elasticity of demand may assume any value below zero. In brief,

for substitutes, $0 < Ed^* < \infty$

for complements, $-\infty < Ed^* < 0$ ... (12)

III. Income Elasticity of Demand

Under the demand function, we have seen that consumer's income is one of the determinants of his purchases of a commodity. The income elasticity of demand is defined as the responsiveness of demand, *ceteris paribus* to the change in consumer's money income. In other words, it may be defined as the ratio of the proportionate (percentage) change in the quantity demanded to the proportionate (percentage) change in income. Symbolically,

$$Ey = \frac{\text{Proportionate change in the quantity demanded of } X}{\text{Proportionate change in money income}}$$

$$= \frac{\Delta X}{X} \Big/ \frac{\Delta Y}{Y}$$

$$= \frac{\partial X}{\partial Y} \cdot \frac{Y}{X} \quad \text{...(13)}$$

where X = commodity, and Y = income.

Normally, income elasticity of demand for a commodity is positive, except in the case of inferior goods where the income effect is negative. In the case of an inferior good, the demand varies inversely with income, and, as a result, the income elasticity of demand is negative. The five possible income demand curves are shown in panels (*a*), (*b*), (*c*), (*d*) and (*e*) of Fig. 14.28. The geometrical properties of an income-demand curve are the same as those of a supply curve. Panel (*a*) of Fig. 14.28 explains a *high income elasticity of demand.* Here the value of the coefficient *Ey* is greater than unity. In this case increases in income are accompanied by relatively larger increase in quantity demanded.

The *unitary demand* curve is drawn in panel (*b*) of Fig. 14.28. Here the value of the coefficient (*Ey*) is equal to unity. It explains that the proportionate change in quantity is equal to the proportionate change in money income.

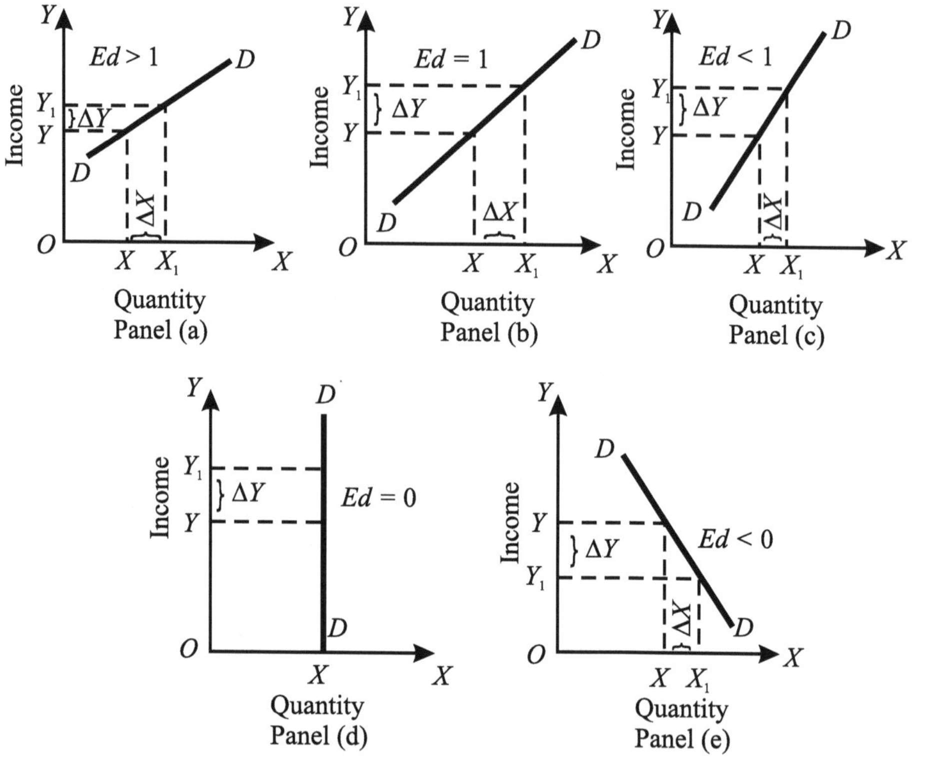

Fig. 14.28

The case of *low income elasticity* of demand is shown in panel (*c*) of Fig. 14.28. Here the relative change in quantity demanded is less than the relative change in money income. The value of the income elasticity coefficient (*Ey*) is less than unity.

The case of *zero income elasticity of demand* is shown in panel (*d*) of Fig. 14.28. It shows that quantity bought is constant regardless of changes in income. The value of the coefficient (*Ey*) is equal to zero.

The case of *negative income elasticity of demand* is shown in panel (*e*) of Fig. 14.28. It explains that less is bought at higher incomes and that more is bought at lower incomes. The value of the coefficient (*Ey*) is less than zero or negative.

Here, we may notice the important difference between the price elasticity and income elasticity of demand. If the coefficient is greater than one, income elasticity is "high"; if the coefficient is less than one, income elasticity is "low". In contrast, demand is "elastic" if the coefficient of price elasticity is greater than one, and "inelastic" if it is less than one.

Goods differ widely in their income elasticities. Ornaments, jewellery, automobiles, precious stones, etc. are the examples of goods whose income elasticities tend to be high. In contrast, soap, salt, matches, newspapers, etc. are the examples of low income elasticities of demand. The proportion of income spent on a good is a major determinant of its income elasticity of demand. An exception to this definition is probably housing. Housing takes a considerable part of consumer's income; it seems to have an income elasticity equal to unity. But goods that people regard as expensive, as luxuries, generally have high income elasticities. Therefore, the best way to define luxuries is that goods whose income elasticity of demand is high are luxuries. Similarly, necessities can be defined as goods whose income elasticities are low. It is quite possible that for one time a commodity may be necessary one, but for another time it becomes a comfort or luxury.

In modern times, economists have developed another concept, *the concept of income sensitivity* of consumption expenditure, which is very similar to the concept of income elasticity. Income elasticity is concerned with changes in physical units purchased, whereas income sensitivity deals with changes in dollar expenditures. The income sensitivity of a commodity in a period of time is measured by calculating the percentage change in dollar expenditures associated with a one per cent change in disposable income in the same period. Income sensitivity, therefore, also has a coefficient. But these coefficients of income sensitivity are only approximations and rough estimates, because there is still no method developed to disentangle the effects of changes in income from the effects of changes in prices and tastes.[11]

---

11. See Donald S. Watson, *op. cit.*, p. 109. The American Department of Commerce has found that the following commodities and services have high income sensitivities (coefficients equal to 1.5 or more) : telephone service, automobiles, air transportation, television repairs and foreign travel. Commodities and services with low income sensitivities (coefficients less than 0.5) are exemplified by shoes, clothing, local bus transportation and dental care.

Income Elasticity of Demand and the Propensity to Consume

We may define income elasticity of demand in terms of the average and marginal propensities to consume. The marginal propensity to consume (*MPC*) may be defined as the ratio of change in consumption expenditure to the change in income, i.e.

$$MPC = \frac{\Delta C}{\Delta Y}$$

where ΔC = Change in consumption, ΔY = Change in income

The average propensity to consume (*APC*) may be defined as the ratio of aggregate consumption to aggregate income, i.e.

$$APC = \frac{C}{Y}$$

where C = Total Consumption, Y = Total Income

Now, income elasticity of demand can be defined as the ratio of the proportionate (percentage) change in consumption expenditure to the proportionate (percentage) change in income. Symbolically,

$$Ey = \frac{\text{Proportionate change in consumption expenditure}}{\text{Proportionate change in income}}$$

$$= \frac{\Delta C}{C} \Big/ \frac{\Delta Y}{Y}$$

$$= \frac{\Delta C}{\Delta Y} \cdot \frac{Y}{C} \qquad \text{...(14)}$$

where C = Original Consumption, Y = Original Income, ΔC = Change in Consumption Expenditure, ΔY = Change in Income.

Since, $\frac{\Delta C}{\Delta Y} = MPC$ and $\frac{C}{Y} = APC$,

We may write,

$$Ey = \frac{MPC}{APC} \qquad \text{... (15)}$$

Equation (15) states that income elasticity of demand is the ratio of marginal propensity to consume to average propensity to consume.

Income Elasticity of Demand and Engel Curves

According to Christian Lorenz Ernst Engel, a nineteenth century economist, the quantity demand is directly related to the consumer's money income.

Prof. Engel's analysis of family revealed that the responsiveness of demand to a change in income is different for different goods. He showed these relationships between the income and the quantity demanded by the help of Engel curves.

According to Ferguson, "An Engel curve is a function relating equilibrium quantity purchased of a commodity to the level of money income." We know that a change in demand as a result of a change in money income will depend on the nature of the commodity in question. Figure 14.29 presents three out of a number of Engel curves, each indicating a different type of demand response to a given change in income.

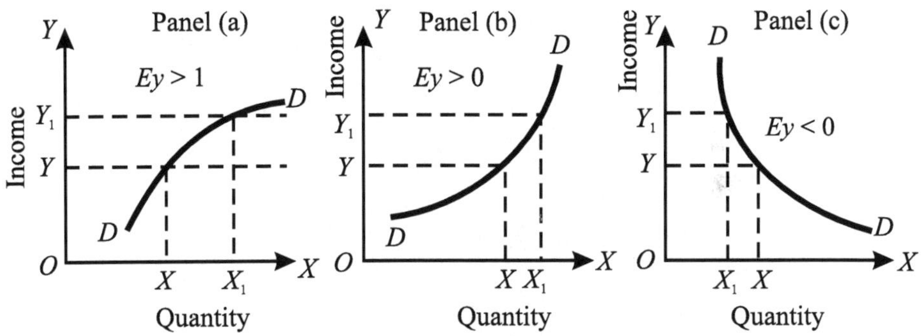

Fig. 14.29

It is very clear from Fig. 14.29, that an equal increase in consumer's money income from OY to OY_1, the demand for commodity X increases relatively more in the case of a superior good (see panel (*a*) of Fig . 14.29) as compared to the normal good (see panel (*b*) of Fig. 14.29). Further, in the case of an inferior good, an increase in income from OY to OY_1 will reduce the quantity of X purchased from OX to OX_1
(see panel (*c*) of Fig. 14.29).

We can, therefore, write

for the superior goods, $Ey > 1$
for the normal goods, $Ey > 0$
for the inferior goods, $E < 0$

Now, given the indifference curve map and different levels of income, the Engel curve can be easily derived from the slope of the Income Consumption Curve (*ICC*).

IV. Demand Elasticity of Substitution

The concept of elasticity of substitution is of great importance in modern economic analysis. It is the corresponding concept of substitution effect. Elasticity of substitution may be defined as the degree to which one commodity can be substituted for another as a consequence of a given change in their price ratio.

In other words, elasticity of substitution is the proportionate change in the ratios of two goods to the proportionate change in the price-ratio. Symbolically,

$$Es = \frac{\text{Proportionate change in the commodity quantity ratio}}{\text{Proportionate change in the commodity price ratio}}$$

$$= \frac{\Delta\left(\frac{X}{Y}\right) \Big/ \frac{X}{Y}}{\Delta\left(\frac{Px}{Py} \Big/ \frac{Px}{Py}\right)}$$

$$= \frac{\Delta\left(\frac{X}{Y}\right)}{\Delta\left(\frac{Px}{Py}\right.} \times \frac{\frac{Px}{Py}}{\left.\frac{X}{Y}\right)}$$

$$= \frac{\partial\left(\frac{X}{Y}\right)}{\partial\left(\frac{Px}{Py}\right)} \times \frac{\frac{Px}{Py}}{\frac{X}{Y}} \qquad \text{...(16)}$$

where $\frac{X}{Y}$ = quantity ratio of goods X and Y, $\frac{Px}{Py}$ = ratio of prices of X and Y.

Now, we may draw the following three conclusions:

(a) If two goods are perfect substitutes for each other, elasticity of substitution will be infinite, or $Es = \infty$.

In this case the rate of substitution between them will be constant or uniform. A fall in the price of commodity X, assuming the price of commodity Y to be a constant will induce a consumer to substitute commodity X completely for commodity Y. But in real life we do not find such cases of infinite elasticity of substitution. In case the two commodities are perfect substitutes, they should be considered as one commodity.

(b) If two commodities are close substitutes for each other, elasticity of substitution will be greater than one, or $Es > 1$.

(3) If there is no possibility of any substitution between them, so that, they are used in fixed proportions, elasticity of substitution will be equal to zero, or $Es = 0$.

In between these two extreme values of the coefficient, $0 \leq Es \leq \infty$, we may have high or low elasticity of substitution depending upon whether the rate of substitution is falling rapidly or slowly. We may also represent these cases diagrammatically with the help of indifference curves. The elasticity of substitution coefficient in terms of indifference curve analysis can be written as,

$$Es = \frac{\text{Proportionate change in the ratio of } X \text{ and } Y}{\text{Proportionate change in the marginal rate of substitution } (MRS) \text{ of } X \text{ in terms of } Y}$$

In other words, elasticity of substitution measures that rate at which the marginal rate of substitution (*MRS*) of *X* for *Y* diminishes when the consumer buys relatively more of *X* and less of *Y*. Thus the slope of indifference curves ($\Delta X/\Delta Y$) explains the relative importance of *X* and *Y* in the measurement of preferences. The more flat the indifference curve, the lesser will be the *MRS* of *X* for *Y*. It means that for an additional unit of *X*, the consumer is ready to sacrifice less and less amount of *Y*. Various combinations of two commodities on an indifference curve are the best substitutes for one another. The substitution elasticities are expressed in terms of substitution effect in panel (*a*) and (*b*) of Fig. 14.30. In panel (*a*) of Fig. 14.30 the original equilibrium point is set where the indifference curve *IC* touches the price line *MN* at point *E*. At point *E*, the consumer consumes *OX* of *X* commodity and *OY* of *Y* commodity. In a new situation of price change, the relevant price line is M_1N_1 and the new equilibrium point is E_1 where the original indifference curve touches the price line M_1N_1. At point E_1 the consumer consumes OX_1 of *X* commodity and OY_1 of *Y* commodity. Therefore, the movement from *E* to E_1 represents the substitution effect. For XX_1 quantity of *X*, the consumer sacrifices YY_1 quantity of *Y*. The slope $\Delta Y/\Delta X$ is less than one; the difference curve is flat; and, therefore, elasticity of substitution is highly elastic.

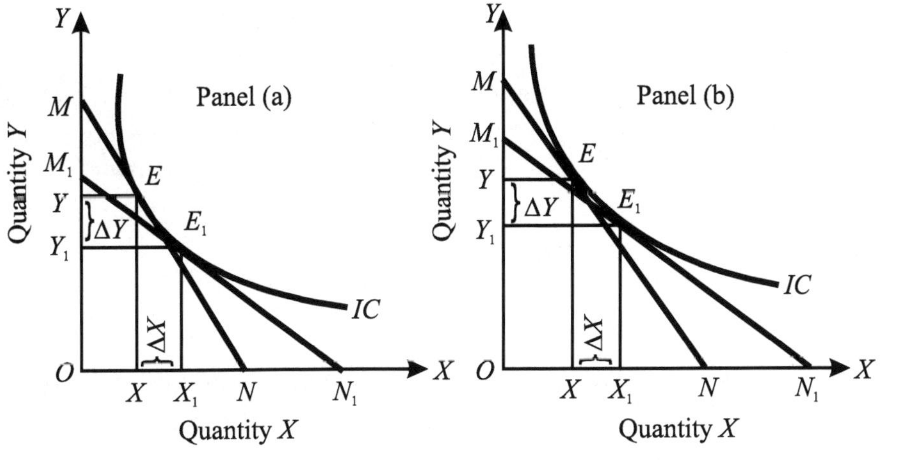

Fig. 14.30

In contrast, the steeper the indifference curve, the higher will be the marginal rate of substitution (*MRS*). It means that to consume an additional unit of *X*, more units of *Y* are to be sacrificed. In this situation, the elasticity of substitution of *X* for *Y* will be *less elastic*. In panel (*b*) of Fig. 14.30, for attaining an additional quantity XX_1 of commodity *X*, the consumer has to sacrifice YY_1 quantity of *Y* commodity (and $YY_1 > XX_1$). The movement from equilibrium point *E* to E_1 on the same indifference curve *IC* represents the substitution effect. The ratio $\Delta Y/\Delta X$ is relatively higher which means that the slope of indifference curve is more steep in panel (*b*) of Fig.14.30.

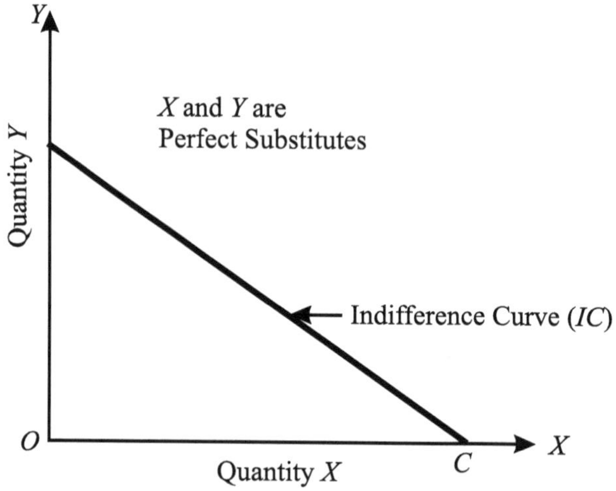

Fig. 14.31

When the two commodities are perfect substitutes, the indifference curve is a straight line, as shown in Fig. 14.31. *X* and *Y* will be deemed as perfect substitutes. Here, the slope of indifference curve is the same throughout, and the marginal rate of substitution between the two commodities remains constant. If the *IC* is a 45° line to *Y*-axis, the two goods are exchanged in fixed ratio (i.e. 1 : 1). If the two goods *X* and *Y* are identical, the marginal rate of substitution between them is infinite. Since indifference curve will never be a straight line, and therefore, phenomena of perfect substitutes are out of the scope of substitution effect.

10. Mathematical Relationship between Elasticities

We have discussed the three main types of demand elasticities, namely, price elasticity of demand, income elasticity of demand and the elasticity of substitution. Now, we can explain the relationship between these three types of elasticities by the help of a formula given below:

$$Ed = \lambda Ey + (1 - \lambda)Es \qquad ...(17)$$

where Ed = Price Elasticity of Demand, Ey = Income Elasticity of Demand, Es = Elasticity of Substitution, λ = Constant

As we know, price effect is divided into two parts: the income effect and the substitution effect; the price elasticity of demand depends upon the income elasticity of demand, on the one hand, and the elasticity of substitution on the other. If price of a commodity falls, the quantity demanded will increase. But the increase in quantity demanded will depend upon two things.

(1) The proportion of the money spent on the commodity and the nature of the income effect. Due to a fall in price, the real income of a consumer increase. Now, whether this increase in real income is spent on the commodity whose price has fallen, or whether it is spent on the other commodity under consumption. It may also be possible that the consumer buys more of both the goods or he may purchase lesser quantity of the cheaper commodity if it is an inferior commodity. If the proportion of income spent on a commodity (whose price has fallen) is A, then the total income effect is equal to (λ Ey).

(2) The remaining proportion of income spent on the other commodity is $(1 - \lambda)$. Therefore, the second influence on the quantity demand of a commodity (whose price has fallen) is the substitution effect which is equal to $(1 - \lambda)$ Es.

The first effect, i.e. the income effect can be positive, zero or negative depending upon the nature of the commodity (whose price has fallen). The second effect, i.e. the substitution effect will always be positive; because the natural tendency of a consumer is to buy more of the cheaper commodity. The total price effect on the quantity demanded of a commodity will be the sum of these two effects. We may illustrate these relationships with the help of some numerical examples.

Suppose, $Ey = 3$ (Elastic)

$Es = 2$ (Elastic)

and $\lambda = \frac{1}{3}$

then,

$$Ed = \frac{1}{3} \; 3 + (1 - \frac{1}{3}) \quad 2$$

$$= 1 + \frac{4}{3} = 2.3$$

Therefore, price elasticity of demand is highly elastic or $Ed > 1$.

If both the income elasticity of demand (Ey) and the elasticity of substitution (Es) are equal to unity, i.e. $Ey = 1$ and $Es = 1$, then the price elasticity of demand will also be equal to unity ($Ed = 1$), irrespective of the

proportion of income spent on the commodity. For instance, if $\lambda = \frac{1}{3}$ and $Ey = 1$ and $Es = 1$,
then

$$Ed = \frac{1}{3}\ 1 + (1 - \frac{1}{3})\ 1$$

$$= \frac{1}{3} + \frac{2}{3} = 1$$

In this way, we can find out the price elasticity of demand by the formula (15), if we know the income elasticity of demand, the demand elasticity of substitution and the proportion of income spent on the commodity.

11. Average Revenue, Marginal Revenue and Elasticity of Demand

As we have explained above that when demand is unitary elastic, total revenue[12] (or receipts) remains constant even after the effective demand has changed in response to a change in price. If demand is highly elastic, total revenue varies inversely with prices. If demand is inelastic, total revenue varies directly with price. Now, we explain the relationship between average revenue (*i.e.* price), marginal revenue and the elasticity of demand.

Marginal revenue (*MR*) can be defined as the slope of the total revenue (*TR*) function. In other words, *MR* is defined as the change in *TR* for a unit change in output (*X*). To calculate *MR,* we take the first derivative of *TR*. Thus,

$$TR = P \cdot X \qquad \text{...(18)}$$

where P = price of the product, X = output or quantity demanded

$$\therefore \qquad MR = \frac{d(TR)}{dX} = P + X\frac{dP}{dX}$$

or

$$MR = P\left(1 + \frac{X}{P} \cdot \frac{dP}{dX}\right)$$

$$= P\left(1 + \frac{1}{Ed}\right) \qquad \text{...(19)}$$

---

12. It should, however, be made clear that total expenditure on a product incurred by consumers is identical with total revenue obtained by the producers from different output levels at different prices, or *TE* = *TR*.

where $Ed = \frac{dX}{dP} \cdot \frac{P}{X}$, and $P = AR$

or
$$MR = P\left(1 - \frac{1}{|Ed|}\right) \quad ...(20)$$

If we ignore the sign of the coefficient *Ed*.

or
$$Ed = \frac{P}{P - MR} \quad ...(21)$$

The important results based on the above relation under (20) are:

(*a*) If $Ed = 1$, then $MR = 0$

(*b*) If $Ed > 1$, then $MR > 0$

(*c*) If $Ed < 1$, *then* $MR < 0$

Diagrammatical Representation

If we are given a linear demand function (or AR-function), we can show that the marginal revenue curve will also be linear and its slope will be twice as much as compared to the slope of the demand curve. First, we may examine

Table 14.5: Demand, Average Revenue, Marginal Revenue and Elasticity of Demand

Quantity of Commodity X (in units)	*Price or Average Revenue (AR)*	*Total Revenue (TR)*	*Marginal Revenue (MR)*	*Elasticity of Demand* $Ed = \frac{P}{P - MR}$
0	22	0	–	–
1	20	20	20	∞
2	18	36	16	9
3	16	48	12	4
4	14	56	8	2.3
5	12	60	4	1.5
6	10	60	0	1
7	8	56	–4	0.67
8	6	48	–8	0.43
9	4	36	–12	0.25
10	2	20	–16	0.11

the relationship between the three types of revenues (*TR, AR,* and *MR*) and the elasticity of demand (*Ed*) with the help of hypothetical data given in Table 14.5.

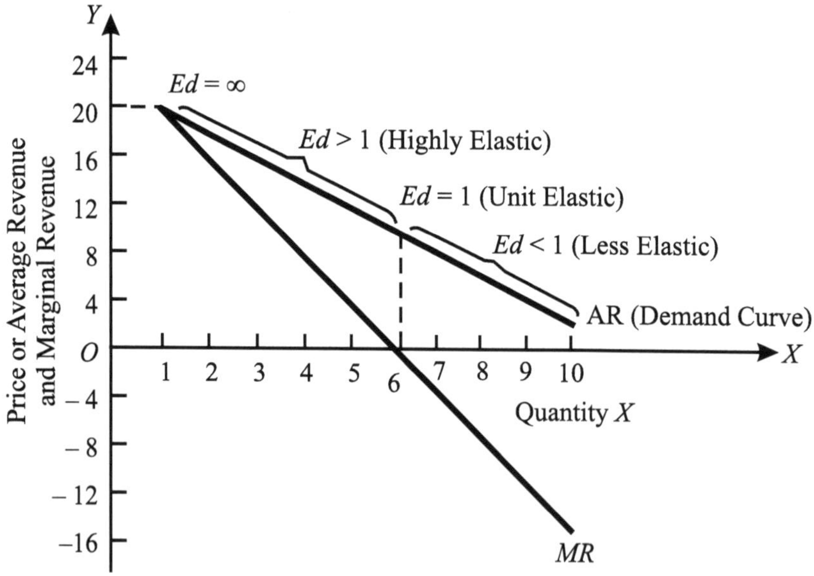

Fig. 14.32

It is evident from the Table 14.5 that when average revenue equals marginal revenue, the elasticity of demand will be infinite. As average revenue falls, the marginal revenue also falls, but the fall in the marginal revenue is more than that of the average revenue. If we draw the average and the marginal revenue curves, both will start from the same point, but throughout its length, marginal revenue curve would remain below the average revenue curve, as shown in Fig. 14.32.

In Fig. 14.32, we have drawn the *AR*-curve and the *MR*-curve on the basis of the hypothetical data provided in Table 14.5. It is clear that the elasticity of demand is unity where $MR = 0$. The elasticity of demand is highly elastic ($Ed > 1$) so long as $MR > 0$. The elasticity of demand becomes inelastic in the range of negative marginal revenue.

A more general case of the relationship between *AR, MR* and *Ed* is shown in Fig. 14.33. Suppose, we take point *E* on the demand curve or the *AR*-curve. At the point *E, OX* amount of commodity *X* is sold at price *OP.* The total revenue according to the Average Revenue Curve is *OXEP,* and according to the marginal revenue curve, it is area *OXED.* Since total revenue in both the cases is the same, therefore

Total Revenue, $OXEP = OXED$

where $OXEP = OXBAP + AEB$, and $OXED = OXBAP + DPA$

Therefore, we write

$$OXBAP + AEB = OXBAP + DPA$$

or

$$AEB = DPA$$

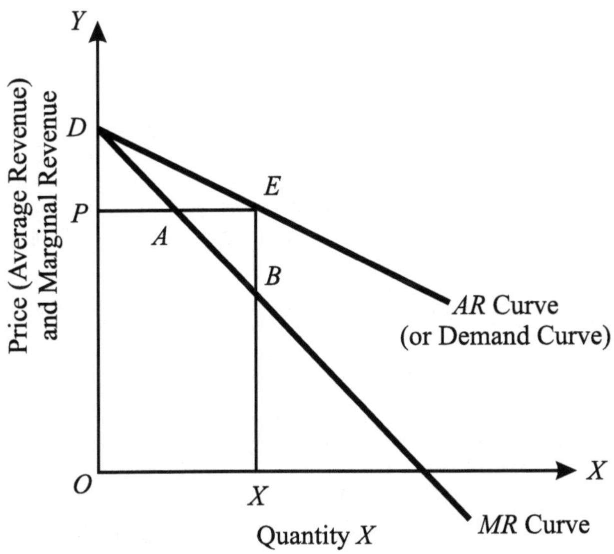

Fig. 14.33

Now the triangles *AEB* and *DPA* are equi-angular triangles. Hence they are equal in all respects. It means that,

$$DP = EB$$

and

$$PA = AE$$

Thus, marginal revenue curve falls twice as rapidly as the average revenue curve.

Further, according to the point elasticity of demand, the elasticity at point *E* on the demand curve is equal to $\frac{OP}{PD}$ or we may write,

$$Ed = \frac{OP}{PD} = \frac{EX}{EB} = \frac{EX}{EX - XB}$$

$$= \frac{\text{Average Revenue}}{\text{Average Revenue} - \text{Marginal Revenue}} \quad ...(22)$$

If we denote Average Revenue by *A*, and Marginal Revenue by *M*, then we may write (22) as below:

$$Ed = \frac{A}{A - M} \quad ...(23)$$

From (23), the elasticity of demand can be found if Average Revenue and Marginal are given.

Similarly, marginal revenue can be calculated, if Average Revenue and Elasticity of Demand are given, i.e.

$$M = A\left(1 - \frac{1}{Ed}\right)$$

or

$$M = A\left(1 - \frac{E_d - 1}{Ed}\right) \qquad ...(24)$$

Also, Average Revenue can be found, if elasticity of demand and marginal revenue are given, *i.e.*

12. Significance of the Concept of the Elasticity of Demand

The theory of elasticity of demand plays an important role in the solution of economic problems and the determination of various economic policies. Many of the applications of the concept of price elasticity of demand have to do with pricing decision of business firms or government agencies that directly or indirectly regulate price. All too often decisions on prices fail to take elasticity into account, or give it insufficient attention. Changes in costs usually dominate on prices; costs can be calculated, and higher costs usually seem to be valid justification for higher prices. Even if demand and its elasticity cannot always be calculated, they should not be ignored.

(*i*) **Determination of price under monopoly.** A monopolist has to consider the elasticity of demand for his product when he determines its price or changes the existing price. If the elasticity of demand for his product is highly elastic, he will maximise his profits by fixing a lower price; because at a lower price he is able to increase his sales. If the elasticity of demand for his product is less elastic or highly inelastic, he is in a position to fix a high price for the commodity. If he fails to study the elasticity of demand for his product, he would not be able to optimise his profits in the market.

(*ii*) **Determination of price under discriminating monopoly.** The policy of price discrimination can be successfully implemented only on the basis of different elasticities of demand in different markets of the same product. A monopolist will fix a higher price in a less elastic market and a lower price in a more elastic market. By doing so, he will be able to attain maximum total revenue.

(*iii*) **Determination of prices of product mix.** Some commodities are jointly produced such as wheat and grass, cotton and cotton seeds, etc. It is difficult to find out their separate costs of production. In such a situation, their prices are determined only on the basis of their elasticities of demand.

The prices of relatively inelastic goods are higher and prices of relatively more elastic goods are lower.

(*iv*) **Determination of the prices of public utilities.** The concept of elasticity of demand is also of much importance in the determination of the prices of public utility services. Economic welfare of the society to a very large extent depends upon the cheap availability of the essential products like water, electricity, cooking gas, transportation, etc.

Public utilities possess a public interest and hence it is desirable that those industries for whose products the demand is inelastic must be declared public utilities and they should be controlled by the government. The government will distribute these products at fair prices and therefore, will remove the fear of restricted output and high prices.

(*v*) **Determination of various government policies.** The concept of elasticity of demand is helpful in the formulation and determination of various government policies:

(*a*) *Policy of granting protection.* The government provides protection or subsidy to those industries whose demand for their products is elastic. As a result, they are unable to face foreign competition until the prices of their products are reduced through subsidy.

(*b*) *Explaining the paradox of poverty in the midst of plenty.* The concept of elasticity of demand also explains the paradox of poverty in the midst of plenty. A bumper crop of foodgrains, the demand for which is inelastic, might spell economic disaster instead of bringing prosperity among the producers (farmers) because a rich harvest will bring less and not more money to them. Therefore, a protective policy must be framed in favour of the farmers.

(*c*) *Tax-policy.* The Finance Minister considers the elasticity of demand for a product while imposing a tax on it. It will help the government to make a correct probable estimate of the tax-revenue. Moreover, taxes impose burden upon the final tax-payers (consumers) and this burden should be equally distributed between the different groups of tax-payers. In other words, the equity canon of taxation must be justified. The problem of incidence of taxation depends upon the elasticities of demand and supply of the goods taxed. A proper tax policy will be determined only when the authority has a perfect knowledge about the elasticities of demand and supply.

(d) **Determination of international trade policies.** The concept of elasticity of demand plays a significant role in solving the problems of international trade, such as, the problem of terms of trade, gains from trade, balance of payments, etc.

(*a*) *Determination of the terms of trade.* The terms of trade are determined by the mutual elasticities of demand of the two countries for each other's goods. The "terms of trade" implies the rate at which one unit of a domestic product will exchange for some units of a foreign commodity. A country's gains from trade will therefore, depend upon the elasticity of "demand" and the terms of trade. If we export goods whose demand is inelastic and import goods whose demand is elastic, we shall gain from international trade. Because, in such a situation, we may get higher price of our exports and would be ready to pay a lower price for the imports.

(*b*) *Determination of tariff policy.* We know that export-import duties will increase the internal prices of the commodities. The elasticity of demand for the protected goods depends upon the increase in the domestic prices. If the elasticity of demand for protected goods is elastic, an increase in their prices will lead to fall in their quantity demanded. If, on the other hand, demand is elastic, the burden of increase in price will be borne by the people as a result of the policy of export-import tariffs.

(*c*) *Determination of the policy of devaluation.* The policy of devaluation will be successful only when the country possesses the perfect knowledge of the elasticities of its exports and imports. Due to devaluation a country's exports become cheaper and imports dearer. But an increase in exports will take place, only when the elasticity of demand for our exports is elastic. Similarly, our imports will be reduced only when the import elasticity is elastic. In other words, devaluation will be helpful in correcting the disequilibrium of the balance of payment, only the sum of the elasticity of our exports and imports is greater than one.

Exercises

1. What do you mean by elasticity of demand? Explain its theoretical and practical importance.
2. Distinguish between point elasticity and arc elasticity of demand.
3. What are the kinds of price elasticity of demand? How would you measure the price elasticity of demand?
4. Explain the relationship between average revenue (or price), marginal revenue and the elasticity of demand.
5. What is cross elasticity of demand? How will you express the nature of the commodities with the help of this elasticity?
6. Explain the concepts of income, elasticity of demand and substitution elasticity of demand.
7. What are the determinants of elasticity of demand? Why elasticity of demand is always negative?
8. What do you understand by elasticity of supply? What are its determinants?
9. "Elasticity of demand, therefore, depends equally on the shape of the price consumption curve, which depends, in turn, on the nature of income effect and of the substitution effect." Thus, elasticity of demand depends upon two other elasticities. Discuss.
10. Prove that elasticity of demand is different at different points on the same demand curve.

11. Write a short note on demand function and supply function. How will you draw the demand curve from the demand function?
12. Distinguisn between' increase in demand' and 'expansion of demand'. Bring out those conditions under which demand increases with the increase in prices.
13. State the law of demand. Why do demand curves slope downwards to the right?
14. Define the term elasticity of demand. What is the relation between elasticity of demand and the slope of the demand curve?
15. "'Flatness' and 'steepness' are not the perfect tests for elasticity." Explain.
16. Explain the concept of elasticity of demand and distinguish between elastic and inelastic demand with the help of diagrams. What are the factors which explain variations in elasticity?
17. Define elasticity of demand. How are income arid cross elasticities of demand for a commodity determined?

Multiple Choice Questions

18. (*i*) An individual's demand for goods is
(*a*) the amount he will buy at any given price
(*b*) the total amount he is able to buy
(*c*) his ability to buy a given quantity
(*d*) the satisfaction he obtains from a given quantity [*Ans.* (*a*)]

(*ii*) In the typical demand schedule, quantity demanded
(*a*) varies directly with price
(*b*) varies proportionately with price
(*c*) varies inversely with price
(*d*) is independent of price [*Ans.* (*c*)]

(*iii*) A fall in the price of a commodity leads to
(*a*) a shift in demand
(*b*) a fall in demand
(*c*) a rise in the consumer's real income
(*d*) a fall in the consumer's real income [*Ans.* (*c*)]

(*iv*) In the case of a Giffen good, like bajra, a fall in its price tends to
(*a*) increase the demand
(*b*) reduce the demand
(*c*) change demand in an abnormal way
(*d*) make the demand remain constant [*Ans.* (*b*)]

(*v*) If ten goods are complements, this means that a rise in the price of one commodity will induce
(*a*) an upward shift in demand for the other commodity
(*b*) a rise in the price of the other commodity
(*c*) a downward shift in the demand for the other commodity
(*d*) no shift in demand for the other commodity [*Ans.* (*c*)]

(*vi*) When the price of a substitute of commodity *X* falls, the demand for *X*
(*a*) rises (*c*) remains unchanged
(*b*) falls (*d*) any of the above [*Ans.* (*b*)]

(*vii*) Consider a demand curve which takes the form of a straight line cutting both axis. Elasticity at the mid-point of the line would be
(*a*) 0 (*c*) 1.5

(*b*) 1.0 (*d*) 2.0 [*Ans.* (*b*)]

(*viii*) If the quantity demanded remains unchanged as its price changes, the coefficient of price elasticity of demand is

(*a*) greater than 1 (*c*) smaller than 1

(*b*) equal to 1 (*d*) zero [*Ans.* (*d*)]

(*ix*) Cross elasticity of demand between two perfect substitutes will be

(*a*) very high (*c*) zero

(*b*) very low (*d*) infinity [*Ans.* (*d*)]

(*x*) If the income elasticity of demand is greater than 1, the commodity is

(*a*) a necessity (*c*) an inferior good

(*b*) a luxury (*d*) an on-related good [*Ans.* (*b*)]

Chapter 15

The Concept of Consumer's Sovereignty

1. Introduction

In a laissez-faire economy or capitalism, consumption occupies a very important place in the science of economics. It is, in fact, the beginning and the end of all economic activity. Human beings undertake economic activities merely because they have wants which call for satisfaction. It is existence of wants and need of their satisfaction which lead to economic efforts. Human wants constitute the mainspring which sets all the economic forces to work. Consumption is, as such, the starting point in Economics. Again, all economic activities are undertaken with one ultimate purpose, namely, the satisfaction of wants. The production, exchange and distribution of wealth, have only this final aim. It is consumption which gives the initial push to production. Production, thus, is directed and stimulated by consumption.

It is said that "under capitalism, the *consumer* is *the king.* "He is completely free to spend his income in the manner he thinks best. It is the desires of the consumers which govern the volume and direction of all productive activity in a capitalistic economy. Therefore, he ultimately determines what commodity should be produced and what should not be produced. Every producer endeavours to meet the requirements of consumers because his aim is to sell the maximum amount of goods produced by him and this he cannot do unless the consumer has a desire for it. If the consumers are satisfied, business prospers and production expands. But if the consumers happen to dislike a commodity or think that its price is too high, its production will sooner or later come to an end. Thus, under capitalism, a consumer is a sovereign and his sway extends over the entire realm of economic activity.

2. Meaning of Consumer's Sovereignty

Every manufacturer, before he initiates his production, has to study the nature of consumer's behaviour. Manufacturers try to find out better and more profitable methods to satisfy the consumers. Thus, consumers direct and guide production.

Further, it is the intensity of consumers' desires which determines prices in the market. Consumption, thus, exerts its influences on exchange also. Without consumption there would have been no exchange. Distribution, i.e. the flow of income of landlords, labourers, capitalists and organisers, is also influenced by the consumption (standard of living) of each of these classes. Standard of living determines their efficiency and on efficiency depends their shares in the national income.

"Standard of living" refers to the necessaries, comforts and luxuries which a person is accustomed to enjoy. In other words, standard of living of the people means the quantity and quality of the consumption. The concept, which is used to show the ways of life of different social classes and the general level of prosperity, is usually measured in terms of amount of income which each class of people has to spend. The standard of living of a group of people governs the commodities which individuals of that group desire and the choices they make. Standard of living gives us the readymade choices of food, dress, house, entertainments, etc. of the consumer. It is thus the model of consumer's living.

In short, free expression about the tastes and preferences of the consumers is known as *consumer's sovereignty.* It can be found only in capitalism where the price mechanism reflects the preferences of the consumers. National welfare and prosperity very much depend on the nature of the consumption of the consumers. Other things remaining the same, the more voluminous the consumption, the greater is the prosperity. But the composition of the commodities consumed is a very important matter. If the commodities are wisely selected and are useful, progress of the individuals and the country is certain. But in the absence of wise expenditure, no amount of richness can bring real happiness and progress.

3. Limitations of Consumer's Sovereignty

The sovereignty of the consumer under capitalism is, however, subject to the following limitations:

(*i*) *Limited Income.* Today the incomes of most of the people are very low while only a few consumers get sufficient income. Consequently, a large number of consumers are unable to express freely their tastes and preferences. They spend only on necessities. In actual practice, therefore, production of those goods cannot be affected which a consumer may desire to have because he has not the necessary money left for their purchase. Thus, poverty or limited income of the consumer reduces the sovereignty of the consumer.

(*ii*) *State Interference.* Sometimes it is possible that the consumer has to confine his tastes and preferences only to those goods and services which are produced in the country. This limits the consumer's sovereignty. It so happens because the government of the country does not adopt a free policy of imports.

(*iii*) *Limited Availability of Technical Knowledge.* The consumer may not desire a commodity which cannot be produced with the aid of present-day technology. For example, if the consumer desires a 'flying carpet' or the 'Aladdin's lamp', then in such cases his desire will not be fulfilled, because the available technology cannot produce such things. Thus, to this extent he has to limit his sovereignty.

(*iv*) *Situation of Inflation.* If the prices of commodities are constantly increasing, then the consumer has to make necessary changes in his budget, which reduces the importance of his liking and preferences.

(*v*) *Monopoly Power.* Under perfect competition, the consumer enjoys greater freedom of consumption, but under monopoly, there is very little freedom of consumption. He has to purchase the type of commodity produced by the monopolist and requires to pay the price fixed by the monopoly firm. This, therefore reduces consumer's sovereignty.

(*vi*) *Social Traditions and Customs.* Social traditions and customs affect the preferences of the consumer and he has to curtail sovereignty in the light of such traditions of the society.

(*vii*) *Rationing.* In the situation of rationing, the consumers can consume only those commodities which are provided by the ration. He has to restrict his consumption of goods and services accordingly. Thus, in rationing, the consumer's sovereignty is seriously reduced.

(*viii*) *Advertising.* Today advertising has become a major factor in the determination of consumer's choice. In advanced countries like U.S.A., U.K. and Japan, advertising plays an important role. The manufacturers spend a good amount of money on advertising. The consumers are subject of advertisement in their selection of choices. To this extent the sovereignty of the consumer is to be reduced.

4. Desirability of Consumer's Sovereignty

We find conflicting views regarding the desirability of consumer's sovereignty. One group of economists is of the opinion that in matters of consumption the consumer should be allowed full freedom to take his own decisions. There must be no government interference on consumption. According to them the consumers are the best judges of their own interests. But the other group of economists (socialist) opposed the idea of granting perfect freedom of choice to the consumers. They gave the following arguments against the consumer's sovereignty:

(*i*) According to the critics, there are vast economic inequalities in a capitalistic economy. The richer sections may enjoy the freedom of choice of consumption, but the (overwhelming majority of) poor sections will be deprived of their preferences. Thus, all people will not be enjoying consumer's sovereignty in a capitalistic economy.

(*ii*) Critics point out that consumer's sovereignty will lead to uneconomic utilisation of resources of the country. According to them, the consumers' choices are often irrational.

(*iii*) According to the socialists, full freedom of consumption to the consumers will not be a wise step even in their own interests. Suppose consumers are habitual of drinking. This is harmful for their health. Now the state should come forward to restrict the consumption of alcoholic liquors and save the consumers from its harmful effects. Thus, complete freedom of consumption is not desirable.

From the above discussion, it is clear that there must be some restriction on consumer's sovereignty.

Exercises

1. Write a brief note on consumer's sovereignty.
2. Is the consumer's sovereignty desirable? Give reasons for your answer.
3. "Under capitalism, the consumer is the king." Benham. Explain this statement.
4. What do you understand by consumer's sovereignty? Do you agree with the view that in modern times "the consumers are bulked together and treated *en masse,* not like a king, but a herd of sheep".
5. What is meant by consumer's sovereignty? How far is it real and what are its functions?
6. "In a free economy, there are few restrictions upon the consumer's freedom of choice." Discuss this statement.

Multiple Choice Questions

7. (*i*) Consumer's sovereignty is primarily found under
   (*a*) capitalism (*c*) mixed economy
   (*b*) socialism (*d*) all of the above [*Ans.* (*a*)]

   (*ii*) Under consumer's sovereignty, we find that
   (*a*) consumer is the king
   (*b*) consumption is the starting point in economics
   (*c*) all economic activities are undergone with one ultimate purpose, namely, the satisfaction of wants
   (*d*) all of the above [*Ans.* (*d*)]

Chapter 16

Recent Developments in Demand Theory

1. Introduction

The neo-classical and modern approaches to consumer behaviour based on cardinal and ordinal utility analysis have been the main concern of theoretical economic analysis. In recent years, economists have questioned their practical applicability and have developed some economic models to explain the consumer behaviour in a more realistic manner. These newly developed approaches have been explained in the following section of this chapter.

2. The Pragmatic Approach

The law of demand is a fundamental law of economics. On the basis of this law, the modern economists have formulated multivariate demand functions. Here the demand for a commodity is a function of a number of independent variables rather than the price of that particular commodity. Some of these independent variables are the prices of related goods, income of the consumers, tastes of the consumers, etc. In fact, these multivariable demand functions are primarily concerned with the market demand of the consumers and not that of an individual consumer. Further, some demand functions are related with various groups of commodities rather than a single particular commodity, for example, demand for foodgrains, demand for durable items, inferior items or for services, etc. To develop such demand functions, economists are making use of econometric methods and tools. This is the pragmatic approach to the previous theories of demand. Here we may explain a few such demand functions in the following manner.

(*i*) The Constant Elasticity of Demand Function

The constant elasticity of demand function is extensively used in various statistical studies conducted by a number of economists in recent years. Here we establish a relationship between demand and its such determinants as price of the commodity, prices of related goods income of the consumer, etc. Further, it is assumed that the price of related goods and the incomes of the consumer are constant. Hence the price-quantity relationship in the demand function is isolated. So far as the shape of the demand curve is concerned, it would be fitted on the basis of the statistical data given to us.

The usual type of constant elasticity demand function can be mathematically written as

$$qx = q_x = Ap_x^{\alpha} \cdot p_y^{\beta} \cdot I^{\gamma} \cdot u \qquad ...(1)$$

where qx = quantity demanded for commodity X; A = constant; P_x = price of X, α = price elasticity of demand; p_y = price of related goods; β = cross elasticity of demand; I = income of the consumer; γ = income elasticity of demand; e = base of natural logarithms, ft = a trend factor for tastes.

The above stated function under equation (1) is known as the constant elasticity of demand function because the coefficient of elasticity of demand, i.e., α, β, and γ are assumed to be constant.

Proof. In order to prove the above stated function, we take the logarithms of quantity and price of X, assuming other determining variables as constant.

For demand function of constant price elasticity, we have

$$\alpha = \frac{\Delta qx / qx}{\Delta px / px} \text{ is a constant}$$

Now using the property that arithmetic changes in the logarithms represent proportionate changes in the variable, we can write

$$\Delta \log qx = \alpha \, \Delta \log px$$

where

$$\Delta \log qx = \frac{\Delta qx}{qx}$$

$$\Delta \log px = \frac{\Delta px}{px}$$

and

$$\alpha = \frac{\Delta qx / qx}{\Delta px / px} \text{ where } b \text{ assumed to be constant}$$

Now, generalising, the constant-elasticity of demand function of px, py, and I, we may write it in the logarithmic form as

$$\log qx = \log A + \alpha \log px + \beta \log py + \gamma \log I + ft \log e \qquad ...(2)$$

Converting equation (2) to its natural units, we get

$$qx = A \cdot P_x^{\alpha} \cdot p_y^{\beta} \cdot I^{\gamma} e^{ft} \qquad ...(3)$$

Hence proved.

Graphical Representation. In order to represent the above function graphically, we may take some hypothetical set of data and show it with the help of a cluster diagram as in Fig.16.1. The fitted demand curve is *DD* which depicts constant price elasticity of demand.

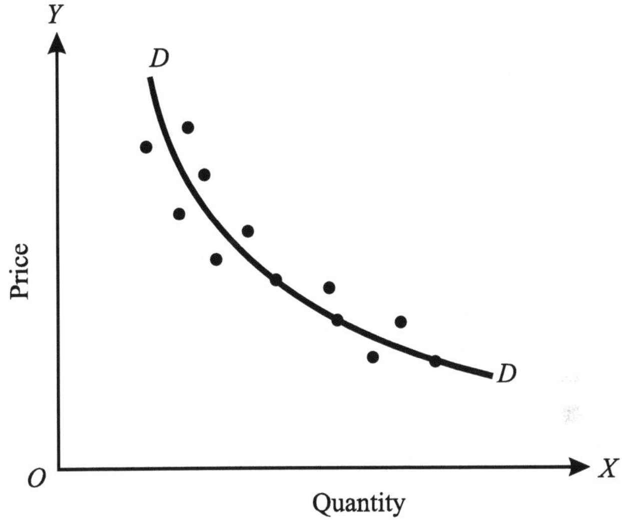

Fig. 16.1

When we express the demand function of equation (3) as a homogeneous function of degree zero, then it is to be done by introducing relative prices and real income in the demand function, as shown below:

$$qx = \left(\frac{px}{p}\right)^{\alpha} \cdot \left(\frac{py}{p}\right)^{\beta} \cdot \left(\frac{I}{p}\right)^{\gamma} \qquad ...(4)$$

where p is a general price index.

(*ii*). The Dynamic Demand Function

The dynamic demand function is also called as the distributed lag models of demand. Here we use the lagged values of the quantity demand and of income as independent variable which affect the quantity demanded in any particular period. They are based on the stock-adjustment principle which states that current demand decisions are influenced by past behaviour of the consumers. It means that here quantity demanded in current period depends on past levels of income and demand. Thus, a distributed-lag model of demand and income may be written as

$$q_t = f(p_t, p_{t-1}, \ldots, q_{t-1}, q_{t-2} \ldots, I_t, I_{t-1}, \ldots) \qquad ...(5)$$

where q_t = demand for the commodity in current period *t;* p_t = price of the commodity in period *t;* p_{t-1} price of the commodity in period *t*–1 (*i.e.* the previous period); q_{t-1} = demand for the commodity in period $t-1$; q_{t-2} = demand for the commodity in period $t-2$; I_t = Income of the consumer in period t (*i.e.* current period); I_{t-1} = Income of the consumer in period $t-1$ (*i.e.* the past income).

Thus, the dynamic demand function shows that the current demand decisions are influenced by past level of price, demand and income along with the current price and current income. Here, in particular we may discuss the demand functions of the durable items as well as non-durable items,

(*i*) *Demand Function for Durable Items.* The above dynamic demand function is based on *Nerlove's stock adjustment principle.* When it is applied to durable item, it may take the following form:

$$q_t = \beta\, q_{t-1} + \gamma\, I_t \qquad \text{...(6)}$$

where q_t = quantity demanded in current period t; I_t = income in current period t; q_{t-1} = quantity demanded in past period *t-1;*

β and γ are constant parameters.

This function may be derived as below:

Let
$$q^*_t = cI_t \qquad \text{...(7)}$$

where q^*_t = desired level of durable items; I_t = current income level; c is a constant parameter.

Since the consumer is not able to buy the desired level of durable items from his current limited income. Thus, the consumer buys only a part of his desired quantity of durable items in each period of the actual change from the quantity purchased in the previous period is $q_t - q_{t-1}$; then this is only a fraction k of the desired change. Thus

$$q_t - q_{t-1} = k\,(q_t^* - q_{t-1}) \qquad \text{...(8)}$$

where $(q_t - q_{t-1})$ is the actual change, $(q_t^* - q_{t-1})$ is the desired change and k is the coefficient of stock adjustment, and $0 < k < 1$.

Now substituting equation (7) into (8) we have

$$q_t - q_{t-1} = k\,(cI_t - q_{t-1})$$

or
$$q_t = k\,(cI_t) - q_{t-1}) + q_{t-1}$$

or
$$q_t = (kc)\, I_t + (1-k)\, q_{t-1}$$

Now assuming $(kc) = \gamma$ and $(1 - k) = \beta$

we arrive at original equation (6) as below:

$$q_t = \gamma\, I_t + \beta\, q_{t-1} \qquad \text{... (9)}$$

Hence proved.

(*ii*) *Demand Function for Non-durable Items.* We have seen that the Norlove stock adjustment principle is applied to explain the dynamic demand function for durable items; it has been extended to non-durable items by H.S. Houthakker and L.D. Taylor through their *habit formation principle.* Here the current demand for non-durable items (q_t) depends on, among other things, the previous demand for items based on habit (that is q_{t-1}). Now the demand function may assume the form as below:

$$q_t = A + \alpha_1 p_t + \alpha_2 \Delta p_t + \alpha_3 I_t + \alpha_4 \Delta I_t + \alpha_5 q_{t-1} \qquad ...(10)$$

where A = constant; p_t = price in period t (current period); Δp_t = change in price; I_t = income in period t (current period) ; ΔI_t = change in income; α_1, α_2, α_3, α_4, and α_5 are parametric coefficient.

In fact, for non-durable items, the demand function may be derived from durable item demand function, which depends upon the current period price, stocks of durable items, stocks of non-durable items and on current period income.

(*iii*). The Empirical Demand Function

As we know that the general demand function for a commodity can be stated as

$$q_x = f(p_x, p_y, I, T, ...) \qquad ... (11)$$

where q_x is the quantity demanded for commodity X; P_x is the price of X; P_y is the price of related goods (i.e. substitutes or complements), I is the income of the consumer and T represents taste of the consumer and so on. But such a demand function has no relevance for empirical purpose. It simply points out that the quantity demanded for a commodity is a function of a number of variables without mentioning any particular functional form for the relationship between the dependent variable q_x and the independent variables, p_x, p_y, I, T, and so on.

Thus, when we want to estimate an empirical demand function, it is essential to specify what measurable impact the prices of related items may have on the demand for the commodity under consideration. If tastes remain constant over a period of time, it may be deleted from the function. But when taste is to change over time, then we have to introduce a time variable. If the taste changes due to some economic or political reasons for some period, then we have to introduce a dummy variable. In such situations one more term is to be introduced in the function and that is the error term which incorporates the effect of any other factor which could not be included in the function either for one reason or the other.

Further, if the size of the coefficient, linking the various independent variables with the dependent variable, are to be estimated, a particular functional form needs to be selected. The two common forms are (*a*) "Linear Demand Function; and (*b*) Exponential Demand Function.

(*a*) *Linear Demand Function.* The linear demand function can be written as:

$$q_x = A + \alpha_1 P_x + \alpha_2 P_y + \alpha_3 I + \alpha_4 T + \alpha_5 D + u \qquad ...(12)$$

where A = constant; P_x = price of X; P_y = price of related goods Y; I = Income of the consumer; T = Taste; D = Dummy variable; u = Error Term; α_1, α_2, α_3, α_4 and α_5 are coefficients.

Now if required data are available for each of the variables, then we may apply the technique of multiple regression to estimate the intercept (A) and value of the coefficient (α_1, α_2, α_3, α_4 and α_5) showing the impact of each independent variable on the dependent variable. Once they are estimated, it becomes a simple task to find out the quantity demanded for any set of value for each of the independent variables. This is worked out by inserting these values into the equation (12).

(*b*) *Exponential Demand Function.* The exponential demand function is an alernative to the linear demand function. It can be written as

$$q_x = A . p_x^{\alpha} . p_y^{\beta} . I^{\gamma} . u \qquad ...(13)$$

where α, β and γ are the elasticities of demand with respect to price of the commodity X, price of the related goods Y and the income of the consumer (I) respectively.

The above demand function (13) can also be written in a linear form by taking the help of logarithms as below:

$$\log qx = \log A + \alpha \log px + \beta \log py + \gamma \log I + \log u \qquad ...(14)$$

The above equation can be estimated by the method of multiple regression assigning direct estimates of the different elasticities of demand.

Limitations of Demand Functions

Under the pragmatic approach to demand theory we come across a number of satistical problems in estimating the various demand functions. Some of the problems may be mentioned as below:

(*a*) *Problems of Index Numbers.* The problem of aggregation of individual values and individual items is to be faced. It leads to the use of index numbers, but there are many limitations associated with the construction of index numbers such as the problems related to collection of data, choice of commodities, choice prices, choice of average and the problem of assigning weights.

(*b*) *Problems of Multicolinearity.* When there is simultaneous change in all the independent variables then the problems in assuming the impact of each independent variable are to be faced. It is the problem of multi co linearity.

(*c*) *Problems of Lack of Data.* The method of multiple regression provides only the best fit to the data. But the best fit may not be very correct because of incomplete information regarding the independent variables. Thus, the demand function may explain only a very small part of the variation in quantity demanded.

(*d*) *Unrealistic Assumptions about the Error Term.* The estimated value of the individual coefficient in the demand function are only good estimates, if the assumptions regarding the error term are valid. If not, then necessary corrections are to be made before we go to any conclusion.

(*e*) *Problem of Identification.* The problem of identification arises in estimating the demand curve. The demand curve drawn on the basis of a set of observation relating to the price of a commodity and its demand is 'the best fit'. When the supply curve shifts, the points traced out by the supply curve might identify the demand curve also. Hence to solve the problem of identification, one has to deal with simultaneous equations rather than only one single equation for the demand function.

3. The Linear Expenditure System (Les)

Prof. R. Stone[1] developed the model of linear expenditure system (*LES*). It was based on utility function from which demand functions are derived. Thus, the approach of this system (*LES*) is similar to the indifference curve approach. Nevertheless, we may point out two major differences between the two approaches: (*i*) the indifference curves are concerned with individual commodities while the *LES* approach is concerned with groups of commodities; (*ii*) under indifference curves approach, commodities are substitutable, while under *LES,* substitution between the items is avoided.

Assumptions of LES Model

The main assumptions of the *LES* model are the following:

1. There are five groups of consumer goods, namely *A, B,* C, *D* and *E.*
2. Each group of consumer goods includes all substitutes and complements.
3. Substitution between groups are not possible while substitution may take place within each group of items.
4. Consumer's income remains constant.
5. The consumer buys certain minimum quantity of each group, irrespective of their prices.
6. The consumer always acts rationally, i.e. he always tries to maximise his total utility function from his given constraints.
7. Utilities are additive.

1. R. Stone, "Linear Expenditure System and Demand Analysis", *Economic Journal,* 1954.

Frame work of the LES Model

In the context of above mentioned assumptions, Prof. Stone has formulated an additive utility function of groups of items in logarithms as below:

$$U = \sum_{i=1}^{n} \alpha_i \log (q_i - R_i) \qquad ...(15)$$

By assumption,

$$U = U_A + U_B + U_C + U_D = U_E$$

or $$U = (q_1 - R_1)^{\alpha_1}, (q_2 - R_2)^{\alpha_2} ... (q_n - R_n)^{\alpha_n}$$

or $$U = \alpha_1 \log (q_1 - R_1) + \alpha_2 \log (q_2 - R_2) + ... + \alpha_n \log (q_n - R_n) \qquad ...(16)$$

Here $0 < \alpha_i < 1; C \geq 0; (q_i - C_i) > 0$

Since the consumer maximises his total utility function, subject to the budget constraint, so that mathematically we may write the problem in the form of a model as below:

Maximise $$U = \alpha_1 \log (q_1 - R_1) + ... + \alpha_n \log (q_n - R_n)$$

Subject to $$I = \sum_{i=1}^{n} p_i q_i \qquad ...(17)$$

Now maximisation of the constraint utility function gives the following demand function:

$$q_i = R_i + \frac{\alpha_i}{p_i}(I - \Sigma p_i R_i) \qquad ...(18)$$

where q_i = quantity demanded of *i*th group of items; R_i = minimum quantity of *i*th group of items; α_i = marginal budget share, i.e. how much expenditure on *i*th group rises as total income changes by one unit; p_i = price index of *i*th group of items; I = consumer's total money income; $\Sigma p_i R_i$ = subsistence level of income of the consumer which is necessarily be spent for his survival. $(I - \Sigma p_i R_i)$ = supernumerary income of the consumer which is left over and above the subsistence level of income for the consumer.

The demand function formulated under equation (18) can also be written as:

$$p_i q_i = p_i R_i + \alpha (I - \Sigma p_i R_i) \qquad ...(19)$$

Equation (19) explains the consumer's expenditure on *i*th group of items; i.e. $p_i q_i$ = Subsistence expenditure $(p_i R_i)$ + Supernumerary expenditure $[\alpha_i (I - \Sigma p_i R_i)$.

4. The Indirect Utility Function (Linear Programming Technique)

The indirect utility function explains the problem of utility maximisation in terms of linear programming technique. Here we may write the problem as below:

$$\left.\begin{array}{ll}\text{Maximise} & u(q) \\ \text{Subject to} & \sum_{i=1}^{n} p_i q_i \le I\end{array}\right\} \quad \ldots(20)$$

where q_j = quantity of ith commodity; u = utility derived from the quantity consumed (q); p_i = price of ith commodity; I = income of the consumer.

Let us assume that $\lambda_i = \frac{p_i}{I}$ where λ_i are normalised prices, then the utility-maximisation problem can be written as:

$$\left.\begin{array}{ll}\text{Maximise} & u(q) \\ \text{Subject to} & \sum_{i=1}^{n} \lambda_i q_i \le I\end{array}\right\} \quad \ldots(21)$$

Here the utility-maximisation problem (21) has two sets of n variables:

(*i*) consumption quantities $q_1, q_2, \ldots q_n$ and

(*ii*) normalised prices $\lambda_1, \lambda_2, \ldots \lambda_n$

The optimal consumption quantity is stated by the system of demand function as under

$$q_i = f_i(\lambda) \text{ where } i = 1, 2, \ldots n \quad \ldots(22)$$

The maximum utility level is obtained by substituting the optimal consumption quantity of equation (22) into the utility function of equation (20). This optimal consumption quantity, in turn, depends on the income level and the vector of prices as shown in the system of demand function in equation (22). This results the indirect utility function as:

$$V(\lambda) = u\,[f_1(\lambda), f_2(\lambda), \ldots, f_n(\lambda)] \quad \ldots(23)$$

where V is the indirect utility function because it depends indirectly on the income level and the price vector (λ) or a set of normalised price, λ.

Properties of the Indirect Utility Function

The following are the important properties of the indirect utility function:

1. If u is continuous; then V is also continuous at all positive sets of λ.
2. V does not rise because if price is increased or income is lowered, it can not increase maximal utility.

3. V does not necessarily fall when there is the ith normalised price, even if u is increasing in the ith consumption quantity.

4. If there is corner solution, i.e. $q_i = 0$, rising p makes no effect on consumer's utility. For example, if the price of Maruti car is raised, it does not affect the utility level of most consumers.

The Dual of Indirect Utility Function

The dual of utility-maximisation problem is the utility minimisation problem which may be stated as below:

$$\left.\begin{array}{ll} \text{Maximise:} & V(\lambda) \\ \text{Subject to:} & \sum_{i=1} \lambda_i q_i \leq 1 \end{array}\right\} \qquad \text{...(24)}$$

To minimise the utility level, the consumption quantity q is assumed to be fixed and a normalised price vector λ is selected. The solution of this minimisation problem is represented by the following set of n equations:

$$\lambda_i = \phi_i(q) \qquad i = 1, 2, \ldots n \qquad \text{...(25)}$$

Assuming $i = 1,2$, (i.e. there are only two commodities under consideration) then the budget equality of the minimisation problem is

$$\lambda_1 q_1 + \lambda_2 q_2 = 1$$

solving it for λ_2 we get

$$\lambda_2 = \frac{1 - \lambda_1 q_1}{q_2}$$

$$= \left(\frac{1}{q_2}\right) - \lambda_1 \left(\frac{q_1}{q_2}\right)$$

Here $\left(\frac{1}{q_2}\right)$ is the budget constraint for commodity. Similarly, the budget constraint for commodity 1 is $\left(\frac{1}{q_1}\right)$.

5. The Consumer Expenditure Function

The consumer expenditure function states that how the consumer minimises his expenditure, given the prices of goods and the utility level. The derivation of the consumer expenditure function is based on the linear programming technique. The problem can be stated as:

$$\left.\begin{array}{ll}\text{Maximise:} & \sum_{i=1}^{n} p_i q_i \\ \text{Subject to:} & u(q) \geq u\end{array}\right\} \qquad \ldots(26)$$

where $p_i\ q_i$ is the total expenditure which is to the condition that the utility level be not less than u. The solution to the problem (26) depends on the values of prices (p) and utility level (u) which may be stated as:

$$q_i = \psi_i(P, u) \quad \text{where } I = 1, 2, \ldots n \qquad \ldots(27)$$

Substituting this function into the objective function (26) results a function which shows the minimum level of expenditure that may attain the utility level u, given prices p as below:

$$\sum_{i=1}^{n} p_i \cdot \psi_i(p,u) \qquad \ldots (28)$$

This equation (28) is the final consumer expenditure function.

Exercises

1. Explain the pragamtic approach to the theory of demand.
2. State and derive the constant elasticity of demanded function and the dynamic demand function.
3. Discuss the empirical demand function. What are the limitations of such a demand function?
4. Explain Prof. R. Stone's Linear Expenditure System.
5. Explain the indirect utility function. Also illustrate its dual.
6. Explain briefly the consumer expenditure function.
7. What are the important developments in the theory of demand? Explain them briefly.

Multiple Choice Questions

8. (*i*) Which of the following is related to the dynamic demand function
   (*a*) distributed lag models of demand
   (*b*) lagged value of quantity demanded and of income of the consumer
   (*c*) stock adjustment principle
   (*d*) all of the above [*Ans.* (*d*)]

   (*ii*) Which is the linear demand function
   (*a*) $q_x = A + a_1 p_x + a_2 p_y + a_3 I + a_4 T + u$
   (*b*) $q_x = Ap_x^{\alpha} \cdot p_y^{\beta} \cdot I^{\gamma} \cdot u$
   (*c*) Both of the above (*a*) and (*b*)
   (*d*) None of the above [*Ans.* (*a*)]

PART THREE
THEORY OF PRODUCTION

Chapter 17

Traditional Approach of Production Function

1. Introduction

A producer in microeconomic theory is that economic entity which combines various factors of production for the purpose of transforming them into outputs. Since it is assumed that the producer is also the supplier of a product to the consumers, it seems logical to term him as the firm. Thus, a firm combines factors of production in order to produce one or more products and then offers this product (or products) for sale to consumers. There are two important theories in this process (*i*) the theory of production; and (*ii*) the theory of costs. The theory of production analyses the physical relationship between inputs and outputs, while theory of costs presents the relationship between the levels of output and the levels of costs (the outlay incurred on different inputs used in producing a given output), production functions, which embody the technical and technological conditions of production, are in a sense more basic than cost functions. If factor prices are given, then cost functions can be derived from production functions. Production functions have been very well explored and widely discussed. Recently, a new kind of production function has been introduced into the discussion under the name of 'linear programming'. Hence, this is a field of paramount importance in economics. According to D.R. Klein, "in classifying the different relationships implied by the theory of the firm according to their degree of autonomy, we rate the production function in a very high position. By the autonomy of a relation, we mean the extent to which that relation will remain valid under differing circumstances. Particularly, if we are estimating statistical relations from a sample, we mean by an autonomous relation, one that will be valid in the fresh samples that may be collected under environmental conditions different from those at hand in the sample being used for estimation."[1]

1. Lawrence R. Klein, *An Introduction to Econometrics,* p. 84.

This chapter deals with production theory in the traditional manner while the modern approach in terms of the isoquant-isocost analysis is explained in the next chapter.

2. The Production Function

A production function is a precise way to represent a technology involved in the process of production. An entrepreneur transforms his inputs into outputs, subject to technical rules specified by his production function. The production function tells us how much output we can hope if we have so much of labour and so much of capital and so much of land, etc.

A production function is a mathematical expression to the relationship between the quantities of inputs employed and the quantity of output produced.

The concept is perfectly general. Any specific production function may be given by (*i*) a single point, (*ii*) a single continuous or discontinuous function, and (*iii*) a system of equations.

Though we are mainly concerned with the second category which is most general also; we shall give brief attention to the first and third categories also. Briefly, we can say that the basic relationship between physical inputs and physical outputs is referred to as a production function. A production function is a technical or engineering relation between input[2] and output. Since money prices do not appear in it, it merely depicts the physical relationship between the output and the inputs.

Mathematically, such a basic relationship between the inputs and the output may be expressed as:

$$X = f(L, K, N, \ldots)$$

where X = output of a commodity per unit of time; L = labour; K = capital; N = land and other natural resources.

The above equation shows that the quantity of output produced (X) depends upon the quantities of different factors (L, K, N,...) available to the firm. The above function shows that there exists some relationship between output X and the quantities of inputs L, K, N, etc but it does not tell us the specific form which this relationship is assumed to have. This unspecified relationship is denoted by the letter f. If the form of the function f is given, that is, if the right hand of the equation is given in a specific mathematical form, we can then fully find out by the use of mathematical methods the nature of the relationship.

---

2. An input is any good or service which contributes to the production of an output. It may be true that an input of one production may be output of another production. Besides these produced inputs, we may also have unproduced inputs.

In the simplest case, where there are assumed to be only two inputs, labour (L) and capital (K) and one output (X), the production function becomes,

$$X = f(L, K)$$

And the maximum production that a firm can produce from various combinations of L and K can be presented by a two-way table as in Table 17.1.

In Table 17.1 along the left side we have taken various labour units, going from 1 unit to 10 units of labour. Similarly, along the top right hand side, amount of capital has been taken, going from 1 unit to 10 units of capital. If we are interested in knowing exactly what output there will be when 5 units of capital and 2 units of labour are available, then our answer will be

Table 17.1: The Physical Production Schedule

Units of *Labour* (*L*) ↓ / *Capital* (*K*) →	*1K*	*2K*	*3K*	*4K*	*5K*	*6K*	*7K*	*8K*	*9K*	*10K*
1L	12	14	16	16	14	13	12	11	10	9
2L	20	24	26	28	30	32	33	32	31	30
3L	24	32	36	38	40	42	44	46	48	50
4L	24	40	44	48	50	52	54	56	58	60
5L	22	44	52	56	60	62	64	66	68	70
6L	20	48	60	64	70	72	74	76	78	80
7L	18	48	64	72	78	82	84	86	88	90
8L	16	48	68	80	44	88	92	96	98	100
9L	14	46	72	82	90	96	100	104	108	112
10L	12	44	76	84	96	104	108	112	118	120

that given this amount of input the producer will be able to produce 30 units of X. Similar answers will be given to other combinations of labour and capital units. Thus for any combination of labour and capital, the production function tells us how much product we shall have (using, of course, the best methods as decided by the technical engineer).

Table 17.1 shows not only the output levels obtained from different combinations of L and K but also states the relative changes in inputs and the output. If we move vertically, then we assume capital (K) to be constant and try to analyse the responsiveness of output (X) to various levels of labour (L) units. On the other hand, if we move horizontally, then we assume labour (L) to be constant and try to analyse the responsiveness of output (X) to various levels of capital (K) units. If both are variable, we move diagonally and try to find out their responsiveness on output levels.

Two things must be noted in respect of production function:

(1) Production function, like the demand function, must be specified with reference to a particular period of time. Thus, production function expresses a flow of inputs resulting in a flow of output in a specific period of time.

(2) Production function of a firm is determined by the state of technology. When the technology advances, the production function changes with the result that the new production can yield greater flow of output from the given quantities of inputs, or smaller quantities of inputs can be used for producing a given quantity of output.

Short-Run Production Function and Long-Run Production Function

In economic theory, we are interesed in two types of input-output relations or production functions:

(1) *Short-Run Production Function.* Here we study the production when the quantities of some inputs are held constant and the quantity of some other input (or quantities of few inputs) are varied. This kind of input-output relation forms the subject matter of the law of variable proportions.

When one input is increased while other inputs are kept constant, the resulting output, as we have shown in Table 17.1 increases first at an increasing rate, then at a constant rate and then at a decreasing rate. These three different situations lead to the formation of three different laws of returns. When the percentage increase in output is more than the percentage increase in a single input, the situation is of law of increasing returns. When the percentage increase in output is equal to percentage increase in input" then it will be a situation of law of constant returns. When percentage increase in output is less than the percentage increase in input, then the situation is of law of diminishing returns. The first two laws hold only temporarily, and therefore, the law of diminishing returns will take place in the economy.

(2) *Long-Run Production Function.* Here we study the input-output relation by varying all inputs. This forms the subject matter of the laws of returns to scale.

As we have three types of laws of returns, similarly, we also have three types of laws of returns to scale. But in the case of returns to scale, we examine the relationship between all inputs and the resulting output. In other words, all inputs vary in the same proportion under the case of returns to scale. *In the case of returns to scale, the production is homogeneous.* The degree may vary between zero and infinity. Thus, if all the inputs in a production function are increased by a constant (λ), the degree of the function (n) will be measured by the magnitude of the change in the value of the function. If the change in output is equi-proportional with λ, the production function is linearly homogeneous of degree one. In this situation, the firm is operating under constant returns to scale.

If the production function is homogeneous of degree 2 (non-linear-homogeneous), then following an increase in all inputs by a constant λ, the output will increase to a level equivalent to λ^2. In such a situation (when the production function is of degree greater than one), the firm operates under increasing returns to scale.

If the production function is homogeneous of degree less than one (non-linear homogeneous) then a firm operates under diminishing returns to scale, that is, output increases less than proportionately with a given increase in the level of all inputs.

Nature of Production Function

The nature of a production function may take the following forms:

(1) Homogeneous Production Function

(2) Non-Homogeneous Production Function

(3) Linear-Homogeneous Production Function

(4) Linear-Non-Homogeneous Production Function

(5) Non-Linear-Homogeneous Production Function

(6) Non-Linear-Non-Homogeneous Production Function

In the case of homogeneous production function, all inputs are changed in the same proportion or in other words, factor proportions are held constant over time. It refers to the situation of returns to scale.

In the case of non-homogeneous production function, only one input changes and others are kept constant. Therefore, it refers to the situation of laws of returns.

In the case of non-linear-homogeneous production, the firm operates under constant returns to scale.

In the case of non-linear non-homogeneous production function, the firm operates under law of constant returns.

In the case of non-linear-homogeneous production function, the firm operates under either increasing returns to scale or diminishing returns to scale.

In the case of non-linear non-homogeneous production functions, the firm operates under either increasing returns or diminishing returns.

Types of Production Functions

In economic theory, we normally discuss two types of input-output relations or production functions:

(1) Firstly, we study the production function when the quantities of some inputs are held constant and the quantities of one input (or quantities of few inputs) are varied. This kind of input-output relation forms the subject matter of the law of variable proportions.

(2) Secondly, we study the input-output relation by varying all inputs. This forms the subject matter of the laws of returns to scale.

A number of economists studied actual production functions and have used statistical methods to find out relations between changes in physical inputs and physical outputs. A most popular and empirical production function is the Cobb-Douglas production function. Originally, the Cobb-Douglas production function was applied not only to the production process of an individual firm but to the whole of the manufacturing production. In Cobb-Douglas production function, there are two inputs, labour and capital. In its general exponential form it is stated as:

$$Q = \alpha\ [K^{\beta}\ L^{1-\beta}]$$

where Q stands for the quantity of output, L and K stand for labour and capital inputs respectively and a and 13 are the positive parameters. In logarithmic form it can be written as:

$$\log Q = \log \alpha + \beta \log K + (1 - \beta) \log L.$$

This function is known as log linear production function.

3. The Laws of Production

The laws of production explain the characteristics of the production function. The laws of production are necessarily the generalisations which contain no precise quantitative results, and in fact their usefulness in economic theory turns on their applicability to all important forms of productive activity. The quantitative relationships between the factors of production and the output are, therefore, expressed in ordinal terms, such as, increasing or greater than, rather than cardinal terms, such as an increase of 15 per cent or so.

The productive factors land, labour, capital and the entrepreneur, combine to form units of production. It is important to look at the question of the proportions in which they are combined, or should be combined, to perform different tasks. These proportions vary widely from industry to industry. The production of commodity, such as, wheat requires a combination of a large amount of land with relatively small amounts of labour and capital, whereas the production of steel requires very large amount of capital, but small amounts of land and labour.

Normally, the laws of production are divided into two parts: The first branch known as the *law of variable proportions*[3], is concerned with the behaviour of the total product (*TP*) when only one productive factor input (say labour, *L*) is varied in quantity. The second branch, known as the *law of returns to scale of plant,* is concerned with the behaviour of the total product when all the productive factor-inputs are varied in the same quantity. These two branches of the laws of production will be discussed in the following section.

3. The law of variable proportion is also known as the law of proportionality, the law of diminishing returns, the law of non-proportional outputs, etc.

4. The Law of Variable Proportions or The Law of Diminishing Returns

This law is usually associated with the early 19th century economist, David Ricardo. Ricardo developed the relationship with land treated as the fixed input. Later economists demonstrated that the law holds whether the fixed input is land, labour, capital or organisation. Towards the end of the 19th century, Alfred Marshall indicated that "an increase in the capital and labour applied in the cultivation of (fixed) land causes in *general* a less than proportionate increase in the amount of produce raised, unless it happens to coincide with an improvement in the art of agriculture".[4]

Marshall stated that a tendency to diminishing returns holds due to the following conditions:

(*a*) that labour and capital are used in a fixed proportion and for higher levels of output, incremental units of both the inputs are to be used;

(*b*) that land is fully utilised; and

(*c*) that methods of production (i.e. the state of arts in agriculture) do not change.

In simple words, the law of diminishing returns defines a relationship between inputs (resources) and outputs (goods and services), *with a given level of technology*. It states that, as an increasing number of units of one factor-input are applied to a fixed number of units of other factor-inputs, output first increases at an increasing rate, then at a diminishing rate, and eventually decreases absolutely. That point in the application of the variable input beyond which output increases at a diminishing rate is known as the point of diminishing returns.

The assumption of a fixed technology is an essential part of the law of diminishing returns. The law does not deny that progress in the technical arts may delay indefinitely the tendency to diminishing returns. However, at a given moment of time, the production plan of the firm must be constructed with the use of specific techniques of production. Once the plan is in operation, it cannot be revoked overnight; the plant, building and machines cannot be revised every day. Thus the importance of the diminishing returns cannot be destroyed by the assumption of a fixed technology. If we consider a situation where the law does not apply, we find no economic problem in the world. The world's food problem can be solved by increasing the "doses" of labour and capital to a few plots of ground. Similarly, the total supply of any commodity can be increased by simply adding larger and larger quantities of labour and capital to one plant.

4. Alfred Marshall, *Principles of Economics* (8th ed.) Book IV, Chapters 1 and 3.

Illustration of the Law

Let us assume that we have a fixed area of land on which we are to grow a given crop, say, wheat. We shall also assume that the amount of capital equipment which is to be used is also fixed in supply. We can now vary the number of workers (L) who are put to work on this land (with the fixed supply of capital). The results which might be obtained from such an experiment are set out in Table 17.2. If we put 3 men then the total product from the land would be 270 units. If instead we put 4 men, the total product would be 300 units, and so on. The basic data in the first two columns are the production function. The third and fourth columns are derived from the first two. Column 3 shows the average product per worker employed and is obtained from the formula,

$$\frac{\text{Total Product}}{\text{Number of Men Employd}} = \text{Average Product} \text{ or } \frac{TP}{L} = AP$$

Table 17.2: Diminishing Returns Illustrated

(*in physical units*)

Number of Men (1)	*Total Product* (2)	*Average Product* (3)	*Marginal Product* (4)
1	100	100	100
2	220	110	120
3	270	90	50
4	300	75	30
5	320	64	20
6	330	55	10
7	330	47	0
8	320	40	–10

Column 4 shows the increase in the total product (*i.e.* the marginal product) which can be obtained from the employment of one more man. The addition of the sixth man adds ten units to the total product, while the employment of a fifth man adds twenty units to the total product. As farm (land) hands, the men are assumed to have equal efficiencies, so that there is nothing peculiar about the sixth man that causes his marginal product to be less than that of the fifth. The marginal product of any quantity of the variable input depends on the state of technology and on the amounts and quantities of the fixed inputs.

Table 17.2 also illustrates that both the average and the marginal products increase at first, and then decline. The marginal product declines faster than the average. When 6 men are employed, total product is maximum. No more is produced with 7 men; *i.e.* the marginal product of the 7 men is zero ($MP_L = 0$) and the marginal product of 8 men is minus 10 units (*i.e.* $MP_L < 0$).

The point of diminishing marginal product should not be confused with the point of diminishing total product. Total product will increase so long as marginal product is positive. But, the maximisation of total product would not be the optimum point of the product. In other words, as a matter of fact, we shall find that the optimum rate of use of the variable factor usually lies beyond the point of diminishing (marginal) returns but short of the point of diminishing total product.

The above idea can be more clearly illustrated with the help of a diagram as in Fig. 17.1.

Figure 17.1 shows the relationship between the product (output) of the firm and the number of units of labour (the variable input) employed

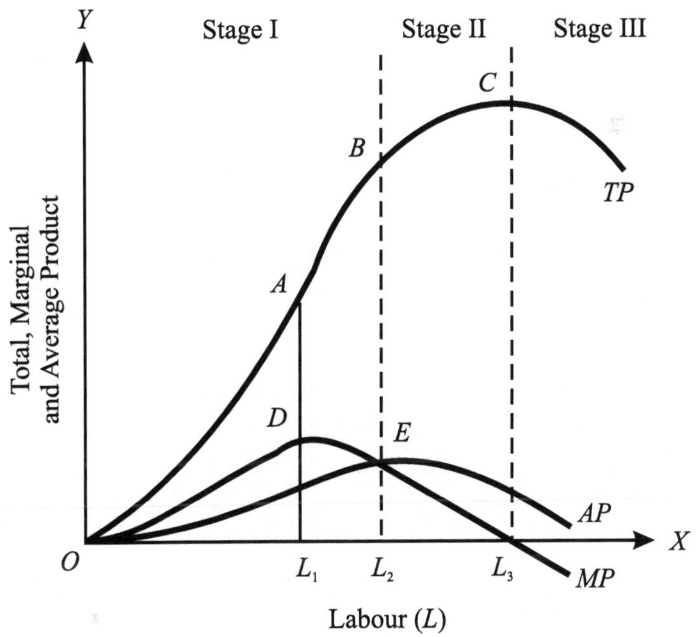

Fig. 17.1

by the firm. The units of labour are assumed to be of equal quality and to be used in conjunction with a fixed plant, i.e. in conjunction with a given-size "bundle" of land, capital and entrepreneurship. Inspection of the graph shows that the total output of the firm (*TP*) increases as the amount of labour hired increases, until the addition of a marginal labour causes total output to decrease. The total output curve is continuous because it is assumed that the units of the variable input can be made as small as desired. As the Figure suggests, the total product will usually first increase at an increasing rate, then at a decreasing rate until it reaches an absolute maximum and finally decreases to zero. The average product curve represents the total product of any given number of units of labour divided by the number; the marginal product curve represents the rate of increase of total product (*i.e.* the slope of the *TP-curve*). Thus, both of these curves may be derived geometrically from the total product curve. With these concepts in mind, it is possible to distinguish three stages of the law of proportion-ality. The summary has been given in Table 17.3.

Three Stages of Production

When one input is variable and others are held constant, the relations between the input and the product are conventionally divided into three "Stages". These three stages have been marked on Fig. 17.1 and described in Table 17.3.

Table 17.3: Properties of Total Product, Marginal Product and Average Product Curves and the Three Stages of Production

Total Product	*Marginal Product*	*Average Product*
Stage I		
first increases at increasing rate	increases	increases
then increases at diminishing rate	reaches a maximum, and begins to diminish	continues to increase and becomes maximum
Stage II		
continues to increase at diminishing rate and becomes maximum	continues to diminish and becomes equal to zero	becomes equal to MP and then begins to diminish
Stage III		
diminishes	becomes negative	continues to diminish but will always be greater than zero

Stage I. The first stage goes from the origin to the point where the average product curve reaches a maximum and where marginal and average products are equal. The marginal product first increases and then decreases in this region.

Stage II. The second stage begins from the point where the average product curve reaches a maximum and ends at the point where the marginal product becomes zero. The marginal product becomes zero when the total product reaches a maximum.

Stage III. The third stage begins from the point where the marginal product becomes zero, and ends at the point where the total product (and hence the average product) becomes zero. In other words, stage *III* of the variable input usage is that range over which marginal product is negative ($MP_L < 0$) or in which increasing use of labour yields smaller total product.

Clearly no firm would deliberately and voluntarily push its hiring of labour into stage *III*. Now the question is that where should the firm stop production? What number of men should it employ? No precise answers can be given to these questions on the basis of the present available information. For the precise answer we need to know the wages, which the firm would have to pay for each additional worker hired and the value of marginal product that the firm expects. Lacking this information, all that we can say is that the firm will try to balance extra revenues against extra cost in trying to determine the right size of employment. We can, of course, say that if the variable input is free, the entrepreneur will go to the end of the second stage. If, on the other hand, the fixed input is free, the entrepreneur will maximise the return per unit of variable input; that is, he will operate at the beginning of the second stage. The second stage where the marginal product is less than the average product but still positive, is the only economically significant region. Thus, to get the most out of the combination of all of the inputs used, the firm will normally be compelled to operate with a labour force and total output that places it somewhere in stage *II*.

In our above example, we have assumed labour as the variable input. But it does not mean that labour is always the variable input and that land, capital and entrepreneurship are always the fixed inputs. On the contrary, labour may be assumed as the fixed input, and land, capital or management or some combination of the three may be taken as the variable input. The law holds whatever the variable and whatever the fixed inputs. The law of diminishing returns applies when 'other things remain unchanged.' Improvements in techniques and equipment can offset the effects of the law.

6. The Laws of Returns to Scale

To get the maximum efficiency in production, we must ensure that the proportions in which the factors are combined are as near the optimum as possible. The most economic use of inputs means that we are getting the greatest possible output per unit of input. But there is a further law of production to be observed. This law is concerned, not with the proportions between the factors of production, but with the scale of production. The scale of production of the firm is determined by those factor inputs which it cannot change in the short period. The fixed factor inputs set the upper limit to the rate of output. In our above example, land was fixed and it was combined with the increasing units of the variable input, labour. The fixity of land determined the limits to the maximum output capacity of the firm. Within these limits the rate of output can be varied by changing the units of the variable input in the short run. But in the long period, the scale itself can be varied. Thus, in the long run, the previous assumption that some inputs are fixed amount can be avoided. The firm, therefore, can expand production by using more of all inputs-more labour, more capital and more land, etc.

In other words, the law of variable proportions explains the behaviour of output when changes are made in factor proportions, but the concept of returns to scale explains the behaviour of output when changes are made in the scale of production. To put it differently, in the case of law of variable proportions, some of the inputs are held constant while in the case of returns to scale all the inputs are changed in the same proportion. Here, we must also remember that factor-proportions do not change when the scale of production changes under the case of returns to scale.

Let us take a simple case when a firm is increasing all its inputs by 10 per cent at a time. As a result of this, the total product will increase. In the first stage, total product will increase by more than 10 per cent, and in the second stage by 10 per cent and in the third stage by less than 10 per cent. Now, if the increase in output is more than proportional to the increase in the quantities of the inputs, the returns to scale are said to be increasing. If instead, the increase in total output is proportional to the increase in the quantities of inputs, the returns to scale are said to be constant. And if the increase in total output is less than proportional, returns to scale are said to be decreasing.

Table 17.4 shows the manner in which total product might change as the scale of production increases. Up to the point where 40 men are employed on 50 units of land, output per man rises as the size of firm increases. The firm is experiencing increasing returns to scale. We use the words "to scale" to emphasise the fact that the proportions between the factor inputs are not being changed. The increasing returns arise from the growth in the size of the

Table 17.4: Situation of Returns to Scale

Units of Labour	*Units of Land*	*Total Product*	*Marginal Product*	*Average Product (Output per man)*
8	10	130	16.25	16.25
16	20	270	17.50	16.88
24	30	430	20.00	17.92
32	40	610	22.50	19.06
40	50	770	20.00	19.25
48	60	910	17.50	18.90
56	70	1,040	16.25	18.57
64	80	1,140	12.50	17.81
72	90	1,230	11.25	17.08

productive unit. In simple words, doubling the capacity of a firm might lead to more than double the previous output. In Table 17.4 as the size of the business unit increases from 8 men and 10 units of land to 16 men and 20 units of land (an increase of 100 per cent), total product changes from 130 units to 270 units (an increase of 108 per cent approx). As the firm increases in size, it is able to take advantage of certain economies of scale. But Table 17.4 also indicates the fact that as the size of the firm increases beyond the employment of 40 men and 50 units of land, the returns to scale are diminishing. This is because of the fact that beyond a certain size, the efficiency begins to diminish.

Now we shall discuss the causes of increasing returns to scale, constant returns to scale and diminishing returns to scale in the following sections.

Causes of Increasing Returns to Scale or the Economies of Scale

(1) *Economies of Increased Specialisation.* As the unit of production (firm) increases in size, it becomes possible to employ the principle of the division of labour to an increasing extent. The larger the firm, the greater are the opportunities for the specialisation of men and machines. According to Adam Smith, the cause of increasing returns to scale comes from higher degrees of specialisation. In a small industry, each labour has to perform a number of tasks and consequently, the efficiency of the work will be less. But when the industry increases its size, specialisation will take place. With more labour, the industry can subdivide tasks, with gains in the efficiency of labour. Similarly, with more machinery, the firm can buy special types and also assign special jobs even to standardised kinds of machinery. Thus, the economies of increased specialisation lead to increasing returns to scale.

(2) *Economies of Indivisibility of Plant.* A closely related cause of increasing returns to scale is indivisibility of the plant. In general, indivisibility means that equipment is available only in minimum sizes or in definite ranges of sizes.[5] As a firm's scale of operations increases, it can use the minimum sizes and then the larger sizes of more efficient equipment. But indivisibility is a matter of degree. Though there cannot be half a typewriter, a typewriter can be rented halftime. Similarly, there cannot be half an accountant, yet part-time accounting services can be employed. Indivisibility therefore, quickly exhausts itself as a cause of increasing returns to scale.

To put it differently, a large output of a standard product makes possible the continuous use of specialised machines. Some types of capital equipment can only be employed efficiently in units of a minimum size, and this minimum may well be too large for the small firm. There is a lower limit to the size of a blast furnace, a rolling mill, a car assembly line and a power press. This lower limit is often a technical limit; a smaller version of the equipment is

5. Donald S. Watson, *Price Theory and Its Uses* (1970), p. 166.

impracticable. More generally, the lower limit is an economic one, smaller versions of the equipment could be made but their usefulness would not justify their cost. Such indivisibility of plant means that small enterprises with small outputs cannot make use of large specialised plant and machinery. With a limited output it means that such plant would not be fully utilised, and would be standing idle for most of the time. The cost of using such equipment would be disproportionately high. Let us assume that a shoe-making machine available in the minimum size operates with of following cost structure.

Fixed costs	$2,000 per day
Variable costs	$10 per pair of shoes produced

(*i*) With a daily output of 1,000 pairs of shoes, the cost per pair attributed to this machine would be :

Fixed costs	$ 2,000
Variable costs	$10,000
Total costs	$12,000

Average cost per pair = 12,000/1,000 = $12

(*ii*) With a daily output of 100 pairs, the costs will be :

Fixed costs	$2,000
Variable costs	$1,000
Total costs.	$3,000

Average cost per pair = 3,000/100 = $30

This leads to the general conclusion that as the output is increased, the machinery comes to be utilised more intensively and consequently the cost of production per unit declines. This advantage of machinery and plant to produce large quantities at lower costs is referred to as *technical economies of production.*

(3) *Economies of Increased Dimensions.* We know that costs do not always increase proportionately with size. For example, a double-decker bus does not cost twice as much as a single-decker, nor does it use twice as much petrol. It only requires the same staff to operate it as does a single-decker. Similarly, if we double the dimensions of a ship we increase its capacity by eight times. A very large modern oil tanker of 80,000 tons is only twice the size of a 10,000 ton tanker in terms of its length, width and height. Also, if the diameter of a pipe is doubled, the flow through it is more than doubled. A wooden box that is a 3-foot cube can contain 27 times as much as a box that is a 1-foot cube, but only 9 times as much wood is needed for the larger box. Similarly, if the labour and materials in a motor car are doubled, its horsepower is more than doubled. All this states that as the size of a capital good increases, its total output capacity will increase at a rate greater than the costs involved in increasing its size.

This particular economy of scale accounts for the tendency of industries which use tanks, vats and furnaces, to operate larger and larger units.

(4) *Marketing Economies.* Larger firms can buy their (raw) materials and sell their products more cheaply than small firms. Normally, a larger firm is able to buy its requirements in large quantities. Bulk buying enables them to obtain preferential terms; it will normally obtain its goods at lower prices than the small firm, and will be able to dictate its requirements with regard to quality and delivery much more effectively. Large firms will be able to employ marketing experts, whereas in the small firm marketing will be a function of an employee who will require to perform a number of other tasks.

Further, the selling, advertising and packaging costs per unit will be very much lower for a large firm. This indicates that the larger is the size of the firm, lesser will be the (per unit) cost of production, i.e. more will be the returns.

(5) *Financial Economies.* The large firm has several financial advantages. This is fact that a large firm being well known will be able to borrow money more easily and more cheaply than the small firms. Its larger assets and greater selling potential provide the banks with greater security and make it possible for them to provide loans at lower rates of interest than would be charged to the smaller firms. Further, the large firms find it easy to raise funds through the sale of shares or bonds. This source of capital is only available to the large public company, and is only economic when large sums of money are required.

(6) *Risk-Bearing Economies.* Large firms are much better equipped to meet the risk of trading than are small firms. The larger the firm, the greater is the share of the total market under its control. A firm which has a large share of the total market is able to judge much accurately than the small firm the shifts which are taking place in the demand for the product and hence is able to adjust its production schedules accordingly. The small firms are not able to face such situation of risk.

The principle of averages operates to the benefit of the large firms. The large firms are able to reduce the risks of trading by means of a policy diversification. The large firms produce a variety of products. All their eggs are not in one basket. This variety of products means that a fall in the demand for anyone of them does not mean serious trouble for them; it may well be offset by a rise in the demand for one of the other products.

Causes of Constant Returns to Scale

The situation of increasing returns to scale cannot go on indefinitely. The firm then enters the phase of constant returns to scale. In other words, a stage comes when a given increase in all the inputs is followed by a proportionate increase in total output. In this situation *internal and external economies* are neutralised by *internal and external diseconomies.*

The situation of constant returns to scale can be brief, before decreasing returns to scale set in. When internal and external economies are more powerful than the internal and external diseconomies, the result is increasing returns to scale. When internal and external economies are exactly balanced with internal and external diseconomies, the result is constant returns to scale. And when the economies are less than the diseconomies, this will lead to diminishing returns to scale.

The concept of constant returns to scale occupies an important place in economics. It introduces a welcome simplification of theoretical analysis. Economists often use the language of mathematics in defining the constant returns to scale. A production function exhibiting constant returns to scale is said to be "linearly homogeneous" or "homogeneous of the first degree". The Cobb-Douglas production function, as we have already discussed in the previous chapter, is linearly homogeneous production function of degree one.

Causes of Decreasing Returns to Scale or the Diseconomies of Scale

When a firm continues to increase its size, even beyond the point of constant returns to scale, a stage will come when diminishing returns to scale set in. Increasing size brings many advantages, but it can bring disadvantages too. As a firm expands, it encounters growing diseconomies, which ultimately, more than cancel out the economies of large scale production and will cause average costs of production to start rising. Now the question is that why should costs begin to rise? What causes are at work to offset the economies of scale?

Most of the economists hold the view that the diseconomies or diminishing returns to scale occur primarily because of increasing marginal difficulties or the difficulties of co-ordination and control. As the firm continues to expand, the tasks of organisation and co-ordination become more and more difficult. Essentially, management consists of two basic activities, the taking of decisions and seeing that the decisions are carried. In the small firm, the entrepreneur can both decide and supervise. He is able to exercise all the functions of the management. He has to take all the key decisions and does not have to refer matters to anyone else. There is no 'communication problem.' But as the size of the firm grows, it is impossible for one man to carry out all the activities of management. The only solution is to subdivide the duties and responsibilities of control. It becomes necessary to create specialist departments, such as, production control, sales, purchasing, accounts and personnel departments. Now the lines of communication increase. A hierarchy of authority becomes established (managing director, director, head of the department, manager of section and foreman, etc.) and the decision making becomes all the more difficult. The managers, with whom the power to take decisions lies, are not very close to the actual level of production and must inevitably depend upon others for information. Thus, the reports move from the lowest level to the top and decisions are conveyed from the top to the levels below. This leads to unnecessary delays and untimely decisions. Efficiency suffers unavoidably. Hence, the economies of large scale production are swamped by the diseconomies of large scale management and that ultimately leads to decreasing returns to scale.

To put it differently, we may say that decreasing returns to scale will become operative when management becomes a problem. It is generally recognised that the problems of management are particularly serious in agriculture. Uncertainties over which man has hardly any control make it difficult for an agricultural undertaking being managed and run on a large scale. But in manufacturing industries scientific techniques of management can be more easily adopted. Many of the managerial problems are being solved these days with the help of electronic computers. Thus, the problems of management depend upon the nature of the industry. It becomes complicated as the size of the industry expands. But there is no such thing as the law of increasing, constant or decreasing returns to scale. The firms may remain in any of these situations.

Exercises

1. What is meant by a production function? What is the difference between short-run and a long-run production function?
2. Explain clearly the concept of production function.
3. Discuss the law of variable proportions and explain the conditions of its applicability.
4. "As we add more and more of a variable input to a fixed input, the amount of extra products will fall off Samuelson. Explain the conditions under which this law operates and discuss if it will also operate with several variable inputs.
5. Show in diagram the three stages of normal total product curve of a factor of production. How does the marginal product behave in each stage and why? Distinguish between increasing returns and increasing returns to scale.
6. Explain the various economies and diseconomies of scale.
7. State and explain the modern version of Law of Diminishing Returns and point out clearly the conditions under which it applies.
8. "As the proportion of one factor in combination of other factors is increased, after a point, the marginal and average product of the factor will diminish." Discuss the statement.
9. State and explain the law of returns to scale.

Multiple Choice Questions

10. (*i*) In general most of the production functions measure:
    (*a*) the productivity offactors of production
    (*b*) the relation between the factors of production
    (*c*) the economies of scale
    (*d*) the relation between changes in physical inputs and physical outputs [*Ans.* (*d*)]

(*ii*) Marginal product is
    (*a*) what is produced when all factors of production are employed at optimum efficiency
    (*b*) the extra output obtained from employing an additional unit of a factor
    (*c*) what is left to the entrepreneur after he has paid all his expenses
    (*d*) annual output of the most efficient firm in an industry [*Ans.* (*b*)]

(*iii*) Production is a function of
    (*a*) profits (*c*) price
    (*b*) factors (*d*) costs [*Ans.* (*b*)]

(*iv*) When average product is falling, it is
    (*a*) less than the marginal product
    (*b*) equal to the marginal product
    (*c*) greater than the marginal product
    (*d*) none of the above [*Ans.* (*c*)]

(*v*) When the marginal product is zero, total product is
    (*a*) zero (*c*) minimum
    (*b*) maximum (*d*) falling [*Ans.* (*b*)]

(*vi*) When the average product increases, the marginal product is
    (*a*) less than the average product
    (*c*) more than the average product
    (*b*) equal to the average product
    (*d*) none of the above [*Ans.* (*c*)]

(*vii*) If we have constant returns to scale and we increase the quantity of inputs by 10 per cent, output will
    (*a*) increase by 10 per cent
    (*b*) increase by less than 10 per cent
    (*c*) decrease by 10 per cent
    (*d*) decrease by less than 10 per cent [*Ans.* (*a*)]

(*viii*) The law of diminishing returns depends on the assumption that
    (*a*) land is a factor kept constant
    (*b*) the state of technical knowledge is unchanged
    (*c*) total output is constant
    (*d*) average output declines faster than marginal output. [*Ans.* (*b*)]

Chapter 18

Isoquant-Isocost Approach of Production Function

1. Introduction

This chapter presents a more general case of a production function with two variable inputs. It is assumed that the two inputs used for producing a good are labour and capital and that they are substituted for each other. The problem facing the firm is that using factor inputs, capital (*K*) and labour (*L*) in such production or in such a ratio that whatever the output produced, the cost outlay made for capital and labour will be as small as possible for that particular output. To put it differently, the firm should use the combination of capital and labour that will produce the greatest amount of product for a given outlay.

The production faced by the firm is very similar to the problem faced by the consumer in maximising satisfaction with a given income. Thus the technique that is being used here is very similar to that indifference curve used in consumption analysis.

2. Isoquants or Isoproduct Curves

A production function with two variable inputs can be represented by a family of isoquants. The word "isoquants" simply means equal quantities. They are also known as equal product curves or isoproduct curves. In other words, an isoquant is the firm's counterpart of the consumer's indifference curve. It is defined as the locus or path indicating different combinations of the two inputs, labour (*L*) and capital (*K*) which yield a specified level of output.

Let us take an example. Suppose that a firm can produce a given level of output of 10 units of a good by employing anyone of the alternative combinations of the two inputs, labour and capital as shown in Table 18.1.

Table 18.1: Isoquant Schedule

Combination	*Units of Labour*		*Units of Capital*	*Total Product (in units)*
I	1L	+	20K	100
II	2L	+	15K	100
III	3L	+	11K	100
IV	4L	+	8K	100

Table 18.1 indicates that an output of 100 units of a good can be produced either by one unit of labour and 10 units of capital or 2 units of labour and 15 units of capital or by any of the four combinations mentioned in the table. All combinations are equally likely because all of them produce the same level of output. Now, if we plot these combinations on a diagram and join. the points of various combinations of *L* and *K,* we can get a curve. This curve is known as an isoquant. In Fig. 18.1, we measure the units of labour along the horizontal axis and the units of capital along the vertical axis. The four combinations are shown as *a, b, c,* and *d.* After joining these points, we get the iso-product *Iq.* Here, we assume that technical production conditions are constant. Thus, an isoquant shows various combinations of the two inputs in the existing state of technology which produce the same level of output.

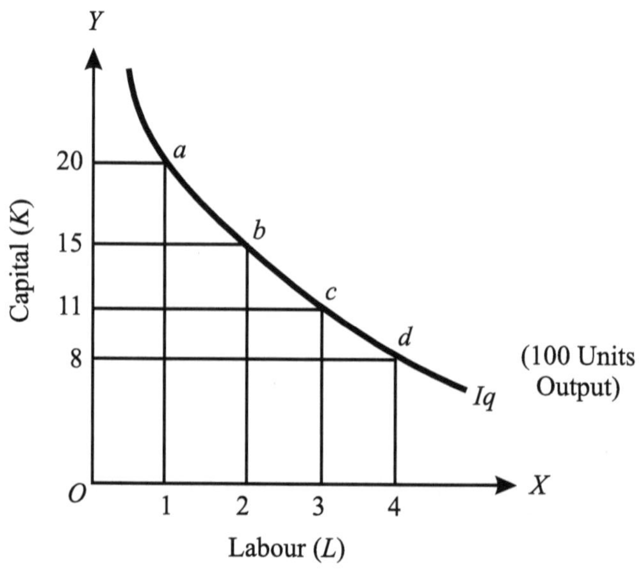

Fig. 18.1

Isoquants vs. Indifference Curves

The isoquant or the equal product curve *Iq* in Fig. 18.1 is similar to an indifference curve. It shows all those combinations of factor inputs which yield a given quantity of product, just as an indifference curve shows all those combinations of goods which provide a given level of satisfaction. Thus, the equal product curve is also known as the producer's indifference curve. However, there are some important differences between equal product and indifference curves, which we must note:

(1) An indifference curve indicates a level of satisfaction which cannot be measured in physical units. While an equal product curve measures output in physical units.

(2) We may very well say that a higher indifference curve will yield more satisfaction than a lower indifference curve, but we are unable to say that how much satisfaction is greater (lower) on a higher (lower) indifference curve. But in the case of equal product curves, it is easy to say by how much production is greater or less on one equal product curve than on another.

(3) Since satisfaction on indifference curves is not measured in physical units, we have to label them with such non-committal numbers as IC_1, IC_2, IC_3, etc. While we can label equal product curves in units of output.

Equal Product Map or Isoquant Map

Figure 18.2 shows a family of isoquants which is generally known as an isoquant 'map'. Each isoquant in this map indicates a different level of

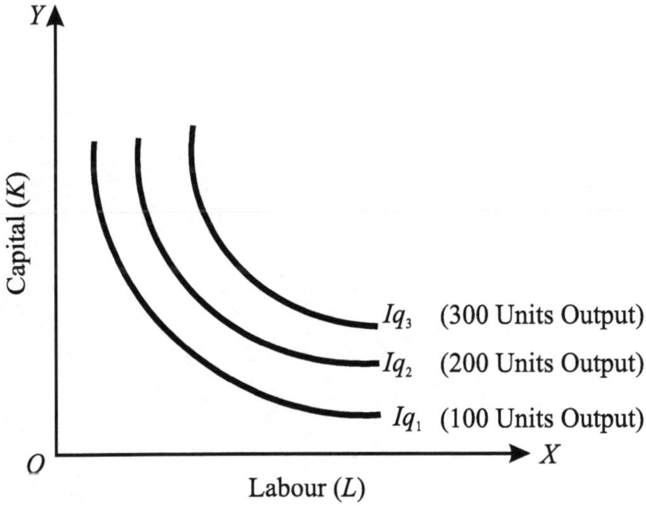

Fig. 18.2

output. The distance of an isoquant from the origin depicts the relative level of output. The farther the isoquant from the origin the greater will be the level of output along it. It may be noted, however, that the distance between two equal product curves does not measure the absolute difference in the volume of output. For example, the second isoquant (Iq_2) in Fig. 18.2 indicates that output is 200 units 100 units greater than on the first isoquant (Iq_1). Similarly, the third isoquant (Iq_3) represents an output 100 units greater than on the second isoquant 300 units instead of 200 units and so on.

The reason behind it is that as we go further from the origin more units of *L* and *K* (or at least more of one of them) are used; and therefore, the output on a higher isoquant will be greater than that on a lower isoquant.

Properties of Equal Product Curves

The following are the important properties or characteristics of isoquants:

(1) *The slope of an isoquant is negative.* Like indifference curves, the slope of isoquants is always negative. The reasons are the same. If the isoquant does not possess a negative slope, then the other probable shapes may be positively sloped, horizontal or vertical. If the isoquant slopes upward, it explains that a given level of output can be produced with less or more of both the factors of production. Under the assumption of constant technology and rationality in the behaviour of a producer such a situation seems to be highly implausible. Output cannot be the same when more or less of both the factor inputs are used. This situation has been shown in Fig. 18.3. The diagram shows that the amount of capital and labour used at point *A* is less than the amount of capital and labour used at point *B* and, therefore, the two points *A* and *B* will not yield the same level of output. In other words, the output at point *B* will be more than the output at point *A*. Thus the isoquant will never slope upward.

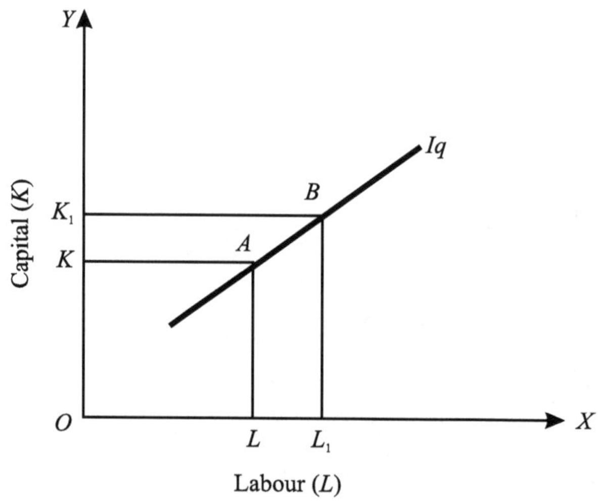

Fig. 18.3

Likewise, it can be demonstrated that a horizontal or a vertical isoquant is also inconceivable as it would indicate that output remains constant despite an increase (or decrease) in the application of one input. Fig. 18.4 indicates that if we go from point *A* to point *B* on the same isoquant then we are increasing the amount of labour while the amount of capital remains the same; the resulting output must increase. According to the definition of an isoquant they must produce the same level of output and, therefore, isoquants cannot be horizontal.

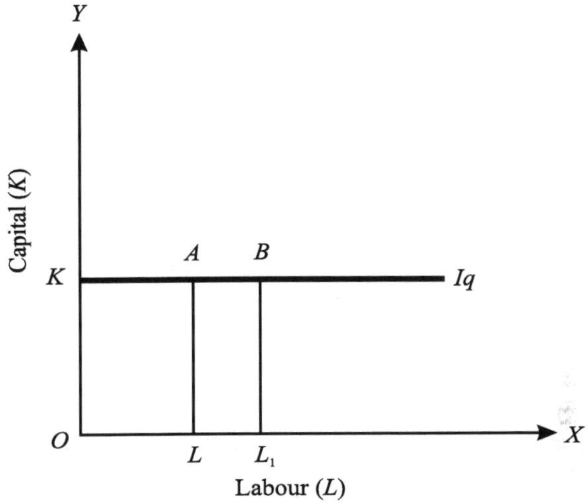

Fig. 18.4

In Fig. 18.5, we show a case when the isoquant is vertical. Here, the quantity of labour is fixed while the quantity of capital may change to any extent, but the output remains the same. This would not be the situation, because as we move from point *A* to point *B*, the quantity of capital input increases with the same quantity of labour and, therefore, output must increase.

Thus, isoquants cannot be vertical.

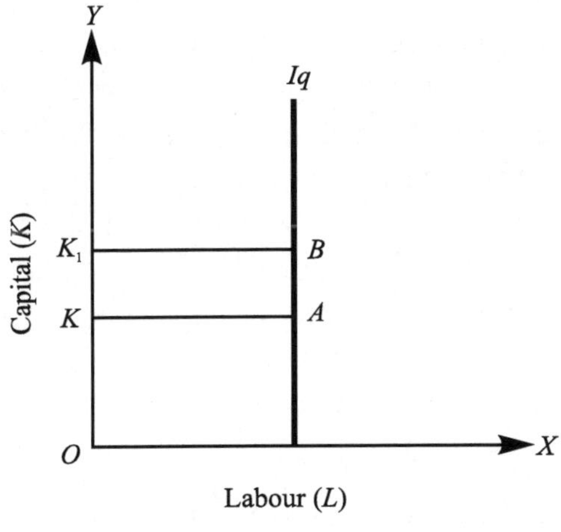

Fig. 18.5

Now, we have proved that the isoquant can neither slope upwards to the right nor it can be horizontal or vertical. It is, therefore, clear that they must slope downwards to the right. This is so because as the firm employs more units of labour, it has to give up some units of capital as the total outlay to be spent on two inputs is constant. A negatively sloping isoquant indicates all combinations of the two factors, labour and papital which will yield the same level of output. This has been shown in Fig. 18.6. At point A, the firm

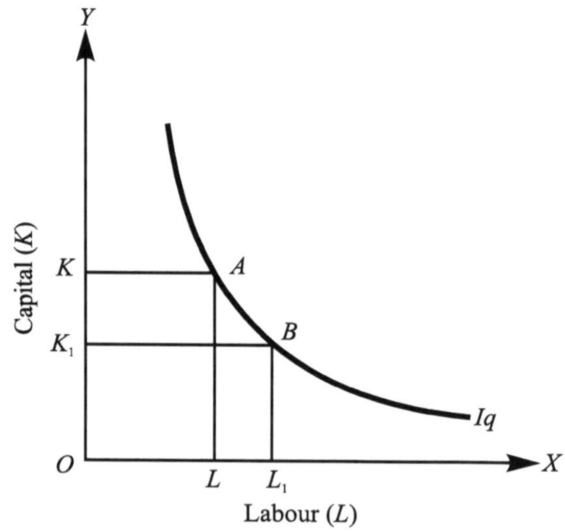

Fig. 18.6

employs OL units of labour and OK units of capital to produce a certain level of output which can also be produced by OK_1 units of capital and OL_1 units of labour at point B. This means that as we increase the units of labour, we decrease the employment of capital. At both the points the output remains the same.

The shape of the isoquants displays the substitutability of the two inputs. If the inputs are perfect substitutes, the isoquants would be straight lines. If they are good substitutes, the isoquants are slightly convex, as in Fig. 18.6. If the inputs are poor substitutes, the isoquants would be highly convex. If the inputs can be used only in a fixed ratio, then the isoquants are right angles.[1]

(2) *Isoquants need not be parallel to each other.* It so happens because the rate of substitution in different isoquant schedules need not be necessarily equal. Usually they are found different and, therefore, isoquants may not be

1. Sometimes equal product curves are drawn so as to be bent around like hairpins. Toward the Y-axis, such isoquants curl up and away from the axis; and at the other end, they curl up and away from the X-axis.

parallel as shown in Fig. 18.7. We may note that the isoquants Iq_1 and Iq_2 are parallel but the isoquants Iq_3 and Iq_4 are not parallel to each other.

(3) *Isoquants never cut each other.* Like indifference curves, isoquants can never cut each other. If they did, there would be a logical contradiction. This can be illustrated with the help of a diagram as in Fig. 18.8.

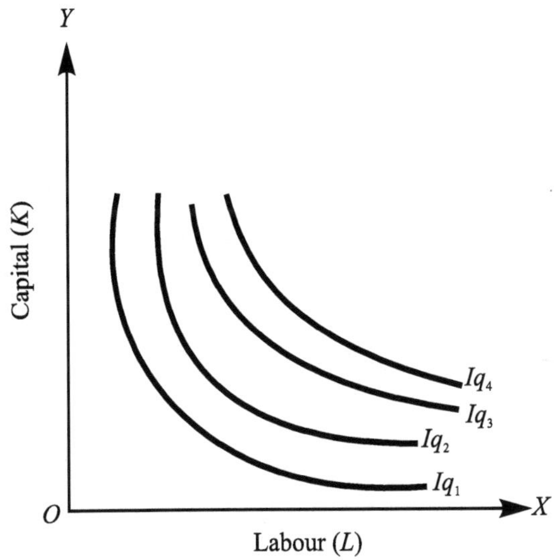

Fig. 18. 7

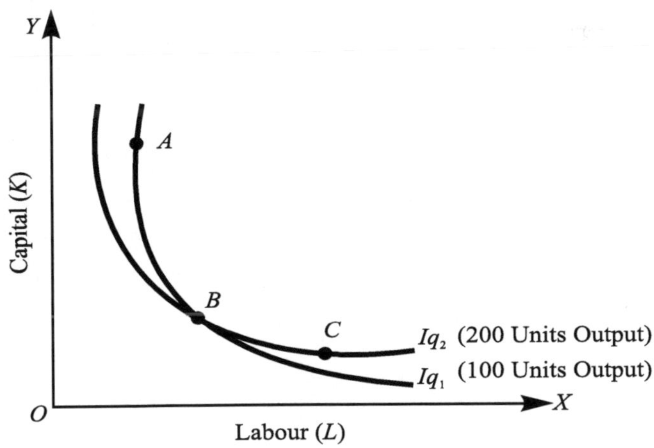

Fig. 18.8

Figure 18.8 indicates that isoquant Iq_1 cuts isoquant Iq_2 at point *B*. Now by definition we may write the following results:

On Iq_1 we have $A = B$

On Iq_2 we have $B = C$

Therefore, $A = C$

But A lies on a lower isoquant Iq_1 while C lies on a higher isoquant Iq_2. Thus, combination C must yield a greater level of output (200 units) than the combination A yields (100 units of output). Thus, by the definition of an isoquant A cannot be equal to C and, therefore, the two isoquants will never cut each other.

(4) *Isoquants are convex to the origin.* Like indifference curves, isoquants are convex to the origin. To prove this property we have to understand the concept of diminishing marginal rate of technical substitution (*MRTS*), because convexity of an isoquant implies that the *MRPT* diminishes along the isoquant. The marginal rate of technical substitution between L and K is defined as the quantity of K which can be given up in exchange for an additional unit of L. It can also be defined as the slope of an isoquant. Mathematically,

$$MRPT_{LK} = \frac{\Delta K}{\Delta L} = -\frac{dK}{dL} \qquad \ldots(1)$$

where ΔK is the change in capital and ΔL is the change in labour.

Equation (1) states that for an increase in the use of labour, fewer units of capital will be used. In other words, a declining *MRPT* refers to the falling marginal product of labour in relation to capital. To put it differently, as more units of labour are used, and as certain units of capital are given up, the marginal productivity of labour in relation to capital will decline.

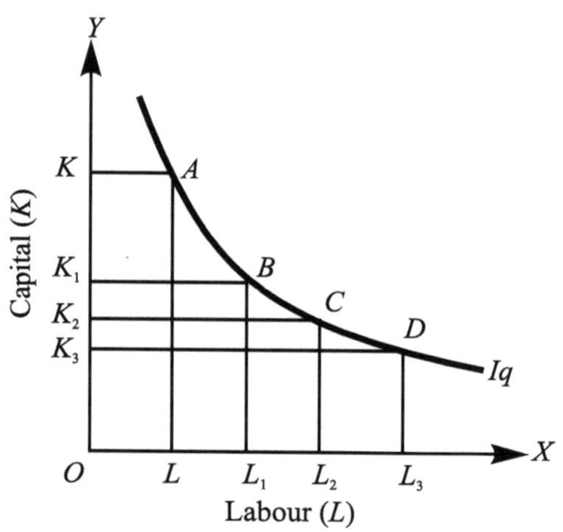

Fig. 18.9

This fact can also be illustrated in Fig. 18.9. As we move from point *A* to *B*, from *B* to *C* and from *C* to *D* along an isoquant, the marginal rate of technical substitution (*MRTS*) of capital for labour diminishes. Everytime we are increasing labour units by an equal amount (ΔL) but the corresponding decrease in the units of capital (ΔK) decreases.

Thus, it may be observed that due to falling *MRTS*, the isoquant is always convex to the origin.

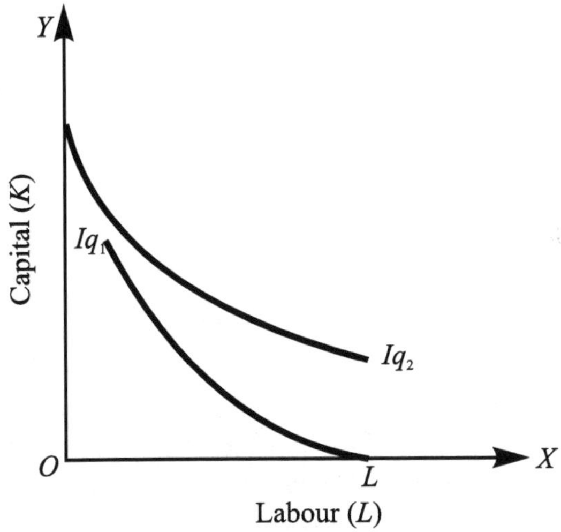

Fig. 18.10

(5) *No isoquant can touch either axis.* If an isoquant touches *X*-axis then it would mean that without using any capital the firm can produce output with the help of labour alone. But this is wrong because the firm can produce nothing with the *OL* units of labour alone. Similarly, without the use of labour the *OK* units of capital can produce nothing. Thus, the isoquants as shown in Fig. 18.10 will never exist in real life.

(6) *Each isoquant is oval-shaped.* (Construction of Ridge Lines and Economic Region of Production). It is elliptical which means that at some point it bends backward with positively sloped segments at both the ends. It indicates the fact that if the producer goes on employing more of capital or labour or both, a point will come when total product will decrease. Thus, the firm will continue production only to that part of isoquants which is convex to the origin and which lies between the ridge lines. The area between the ridge lines is known as the economic region of production.

This fact has been explained in Fig. 18.11.

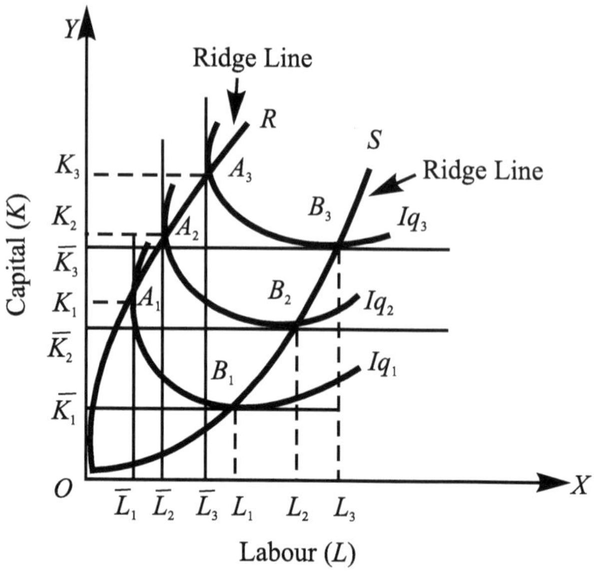

Fig. 18.11

Fig. 18.11 shows a family of three isoquants Iq_1, Iq_2 *and* Iq_3. All of them bend back upon themselves with positively sloped segments at both ends. Iq_1 assumes a positive slope at points A_1 and B_1. Similarly, Iq_2 assumes a positive slope at point A_2 and B_2 ; and Iq_3 assumes a positive slope at points A_3 and B_3 respectively. At point A_1, the firm is using OK_1 units of capital and at this level of output (Iq_1) the minimum amount of labour to be used is OL_1. Also, OK_1 will be the maximum amount of capital which a rational producer can use in order to produce a level of output represented by Iq_1. We may note that at point A_1, the slope of the isoquant (Iq_1) is infinite, or

$$\frac{\partial X}{\partial L} \Big/ \frac{\partial X}{\partial K} = \infty \text{ where } \partial X \text{ represents change in output } (X)$$

or $$\frac{\partial K}{\partial L} = \infty$$

This is infinite only when

$$\frac{\partial K}{\partial K} = 0$$

or $$MP_K = 0$$

It means that at point A_1, the marginal product of capital is zero. If more capital is used beyond OK_1, then the marginal product of capital will become negative, or

$$\frac{\partial X}{\partial K} < 0$$

Thus, the part of isoquant Iq_1 beyond point A_1 will not be economic for the firm. Similarly, for the output levels shown by Iq_2 and Iq_3, points A_2 and A_3 represent the intensive margins for capital input. Beyond these points, the use of capital will not be economic. Now, if we join these points A_1, A_2 and A_3, then the resulting curve is known as *Ridge Line.* It represents the boundary line for the economic region of production. In other words, beyond this ridge line *OR,* the marginal product of capital is negative and no rational firm would use capital input in this range, It may also be seen in the diagram 18.11, that beyond the ridge line *OR,* the isoquants bend back upon themselves and assume a positive slope.

Similarly, we may draw another ridge line *OS* which is the locus or path of all intensive margins for labour input. Beyond this ridge line *OS,* the marginal product of labour is negative and no rational firm would use labour input in this range. For example, the maximum amount of labour used to produce a level of output re-presented by Iq_1 is OL_1. At point B_1 the slope of the isoquants Iq_1 becomes zero, or

$$\frac{\partial X}{\partial L} \Big/ \frac{\partial X}{\partial K} = 0$$

which implies $$\frac{\partial X}{\partial L} = 0$$

or $$MP_L = 0$$

Now the use of labour beyond this point B_1 will not be economic in the sense that the marginal product of labour will become negative or

$$\frac{\partial X}{\partial L} < 0$$

Similarly, points B_2 and B_3 represent the intensive margins for labour input for producing the levels of output (x) represented by Iq_2 and Iq_3 respectively. Now if we join the points B_1, B_2 and B_3 then the resulting line as is another ridge line. It indicates all the points of intensive margins for labour. Beyond this ridge line *OS,* the isoquants bend back on themselves. In other words, beyond this line, the marginal productivity of labour becomes negative.

Thus, the area between the two ridge lines *OR* and *OS* represents the economic region of production. The area beyond these ridge lines is the area of uneconomic production.

3. The Principle of Diminishing Marginal Rate of Technical Substitution (Mrts)

As we have already explained that the downward slope of isoquants from left to right stems from the technical substitutability of factor inputs for one another, that is, upon the ability of one input to substitute for the other in the productive process. Generally, the combinations of factor inputs necessary to produce a given amount of product can be changed by substituting quantities of one input for another. Labour can be substituted for capital and vice versa. When factor inputs are technical substitutes, if less of one is used, more of the other must be used to compensate for its loss if total product is to remain constant. Now, the rate at which one factor input can be substituted for another keeping the total output constant is termed as the marginal rate of technical substitution or *MRTS.*

But we should remember the fact that while different factor inputs may be technical substitutes for each other, they are not perfect substitutes. Within limits they can be substituted for each other. For example, consider two factor inputs, labour and capital which are used to produce output *X*. Now the more labour and less capital used to produce the same output *X*, the more difficult it becomes to substitute additional units of labour for capital. Additional units of labour will just compensate for smaller amounts of capital. This is called the principle of diminishing marginal rate of technical substitution of labour for capital. In other words, the principle indicates the marginal significance of one factor input (*L*) in terms of another factor input (*K*). Table 18.2 illustrates this concept.

Table 18.2

Factor-Input Combinations	*Units of Labour*		*Units of Capital*		*Units of Output*	*MRTS of Labour for Capital*
A	1L	+	10K	=	100	–
B	9L	+	7K	=	100	1 : 3
C	3L	+	5K	=	100	1 : 2
D	4L	+	4K	=	100	1 : 1

In Table 18.2, we have indicated four situations *A, B, C,* and *D* which produce the same quantity of output, i.e. 100 units. They are all iso-product combinations of two factor inputs, labour and capital. In the initial situation, *A,* one unit of labour and ten units of capital are being used to produce 100 units of output. Now, if the output is to be kept constant while one unit of labour is added to the factor combination already being used, a certain quantity of capital must be dispensed with. Otherwise the total output would increase. Thus combination *B* indicates that 3 units of capital are to be given up for one additional unit of labour. In this situation, the marginal significance of labour in terms of capital or the marginal rate of technical substitution between labour and capital would be $1L = 3K$. If, further, one more unit of labour is used, then the producer cannot give up 3 units of capital to produce the same level of output, because the marginal significance of labour for capital has reduced. In other words, the more the units of labour are used, the lesser will be the marginal productivity of labour and the smaller the amount of capital used, the higher will be its marginal productivity. Thus, in the new situation of combination *C*, the producer gives up the use of only two units of capital for one unit of labour. It means that *MRTS* between labour and capital now is $1L = 2K$. Similarly, in the fourth situation of combination *D*, it becomes $1L = 1K$. It follows that the *MRTS* is diminishing.

The concept of *MRTS* can also be explained with the help of a diagram as in Fig. 18.12. Here, as the firm moves from point *A* to *D* along the isoquant *Iq,* the quantity of capital used decreases while the quantity of labour used increases. The increase in the quantity of labour is the same at each time but the corresponding decrease in the quantity of capital diminishes. For instance, if the firm moves from *A* to *B,* she employs one more unit of labour, but she has to reduce 3 units of capital. At point *C*, a further increase in the quantity of labour by one unit is accompanied by a reduction in the quantity of capital to the extent of two units. It is, thus, evident that every additional unit of labour is being substituted for a diminishing quantity of capital.

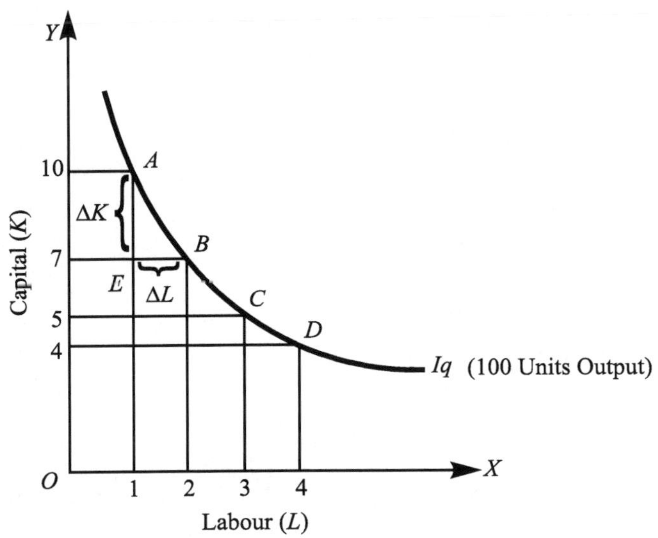

Fig. 18.12

To put it differently, the marginal rate of technical substitution (*MRTS*) of labour for capital is measured at any point on an isoquant by the slope of the isoquant at that point. It is the loss of certain units of capital which will just be compensated for by additional units of labour at that point. Thus

$$MRTS = \text{Slope of Isoquant}$$

$$= -\frac{\Delta K}{\Delta L}$$

In Fig. 18.12, the marginal rate of technical substitution at point *B* on isoquant *Iq* can be written as,

$$MRTS = -\frac{\Delta K}{\Delta L}$$

$$= \frac{AE}{EB}$$

Where *AE* are the units of capital that the firm gives up for *EB* units of labour.

The marginal rate of technical substitution of labour for capital can also be thought of as the ratio of marginal physical product of labour to the marginal physical product of capital. Thus

$$MRTS_{LK} = \frac{MPP_L}{MPP_K}$$

or $$MRTS_{LK} = \frac{\Delta K}{\Delta L} = \frac{MPP_L}{MPP_K}$$

or $$\Delta K \times MPP_K = \Delta K \times MPP_L$$

where $$\Delta K \times MPP_K = \text{Loss in output}$$

$$\Delta L \times MPP_L = \text{Gains in output}$$

$$\text{Since Loss in output} = \text{Gains in output}$$

$$\therefore \quad \frac{\Delta K}{\Delta C} = \frac{MPP_L}{MPP_K}$$

i.e. $$MRTS_{LK} = \frac{MPP_L}{MPP_L} \qquad \ldots(2)$$

---

2. The *MRTS* of labour for capital on any given isoquant is found by differentiating the isoquant equation as below:

$$X = f(L, K)$$

where X = Total output, L = Labour and K = Capital.
Since, total output on an isoquant remains the same, thus

$$dX = 0 = f_L\, dL + f_K dK$$

where d indicates the change and f_L and f_K are the partial derivatives of L and K respectively. From the above equation, we may write

$$\frac{dK}{dL} = \frac{f_L}{f_K} + MRTS_{LK}$$

The above relation can also be explained with the help of mathematics.[2]

We know that the law of diminishing marginal rate of technical substitution is based on the assumption that labour and capital can be substituted at a non-constant rate. The assumption is real.

Limitations of the Concept of Diminishing Marginal Rate of Technical Substitution

There are two important limitations (exceptions) to the principle of diminishing *MRTS*—(1) When the substitutability between labour and capital is not at all possible, and (2) When they are perfect substitute of each other.

(1) *Use of factor inputs in fixed proportions.* When the two factor inputs labour and capital are complements, then the *MRTS* between them will not diminish. Figure 18.13 indicates that labour and capital are used in fixed proportions. At point *A,* 5 units of capital and 1 unit of labour will be employed to produce 100 units of output. If the firm wants to double the output then she has to double the employment of both labour and capital. This means that at point *B,* the firm produces 200 units with the help of 10 units of capital

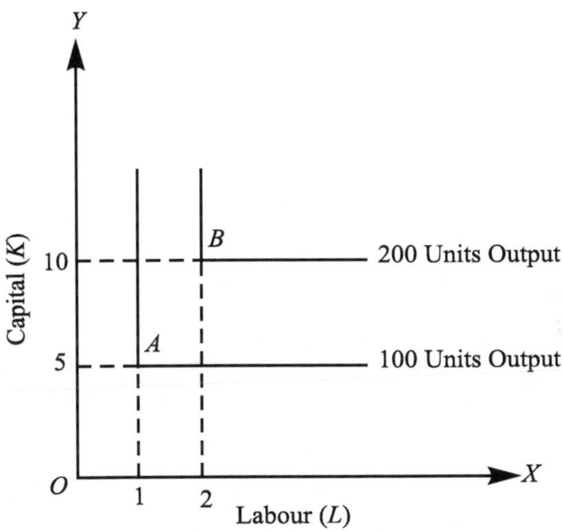

Fig. 18.13

$$\text{or} \qquad MRTS_{LK} = \frac{dC}{dL} = \frac{MPP_L}{MPP_K}$$

because the partial derivatives f_L and f_K represent the MPP_L and MPP_K respectively. If an isoquant is to be convex to the origin then

$$\frac{d\left(\frac{f_L}{f_K}\right)}{dL} < 0$$

and 2 units of labour. Here the isoquants will take the shape of the English letter '*L*' where a proportionate increase in both the inputs is required to make an increase in the total output. In such a case, the factor inputs are complementary and they cannot at all be substituted. The vertical portion of the isoquants indicates that the rate substitutability of labour for capital is zero, because the isoquants have no slope; while the horizontal part of the isoquants indicates an infinite marginal rate of technical substitutability.

(2) *Factor inputs are perfect substitutes.* Figure 18.14 indicates a situation when the two factor inputs labour and capital are perfect substitutes. The two isoquants Iq_1, and Iq_2 represent 100 units and 200

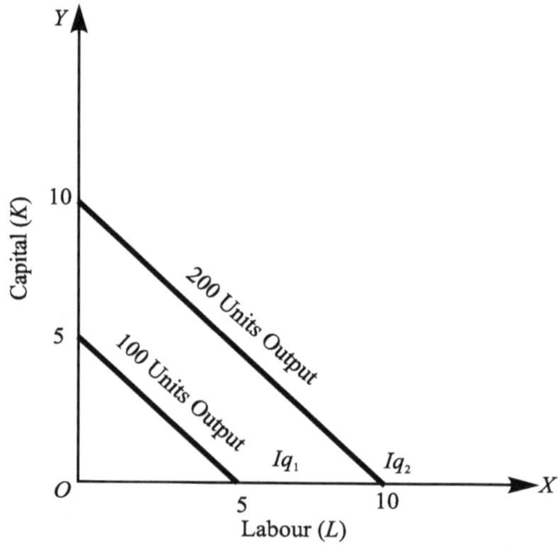

Fig. 18.14

units of out-put respectively. On Iq_1, 100 units of output can be produced either by 10 units of capital and zero unit of labour or by 10 units of labour and zero unit of capital. Similarly, Iq_2 indicates that 200 units of output can either be produced by 20 units of capital and zero unit of labour or by 20 units of labour and zero unit of capital. Thus, at all points of the isoquants the *MRTS* of labour for capital is constant (which is neither zero nor infinite). This situation is not a real situation because labour and capital are not the same factor inputs and thus, they cannot be perfect substitutes.

Optimum Combination of Inputs

The economic objective of the firm can be specified as the maximisation of output from the given cost outlay to be spent on labour and capital, or the minimisation of the cost of producing a given level of output. The graphical solution of this problem is very similar to the indifference curve solution to that of an individual consumer who maximises the satisfaction from his limited income. The theory of isoquants enables the producer to choose a input combination which produces maximum output at the minimum cost. This input combination is known as optimum input-combination.

A firm's equilibrium will be attained at a point where the isoquant touches the isocost line. We have already explained the isoquant map and now we need to explain the isocost line.

The isocost line is the counterpart of the budget line or price line. It shows all the combinations of the two inputs, labour and capital that the firm can purchase with a given total outlay and at given input prices. To make it more clear let us take an example. In Fig. 18.15, we assume that the price of capital is twice the price of labour.The price of capital is \$10 per unit and the price of labour is \$5 per unit. Now the line *MN* is an isocost line, representing a constant expenditure of \$1,000 on various combinations of the two inputs, labour and capital. In other words, the firm can purchase either 100 units of capital and zero unit of labour or 200 units of labour and zero unit of capital or any combination of the two inputs in between these extremes as shown by the *MN* isocost line. The isocost line will shift to the right if the firm's total outlay increases while the input prices remaining the same. Thus, the isocost lines of Fig. 18.15 refer to the costs of production inputs purchased on the market. So long as we assume that the market prices of factors (inputs) of production are unaffected by the amounts of the inputs that are purchased by the particular firm, the expenditure (outlay) incurred by the firm in

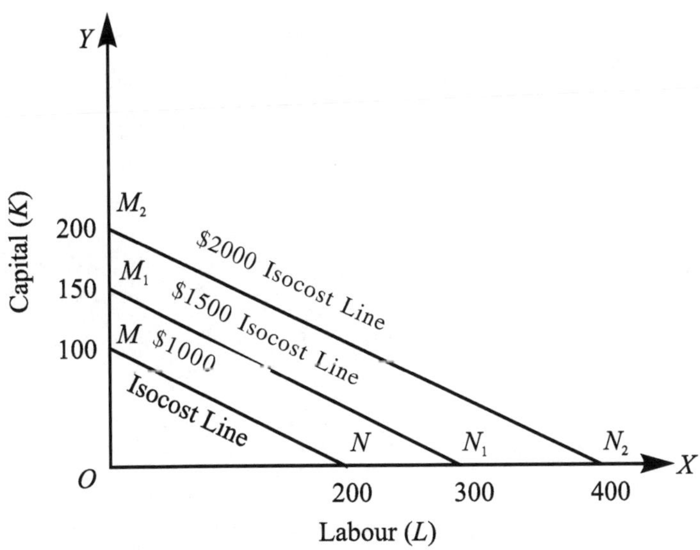

Fig. 18.15

purchasing different combinations of the two inputs can be represented graphically by a straight line (like *MN* in Fig. 18.15), the slope of the line being determined by the relative prices of the two factor-inputs.[3] The isocost line M_1N_1 in Fig. 18.15 represents a constant total outlay (expenditure) of \$1,500 on the combination of the two factor inputs, labour and capital, purchased on the market, and the isocost line M_2N_2 an expenditure of \$2,000. All the three isocost lines *MN*, M_1N_1 and M_2N_2 in Fig. 18.15 are parallel to each other which indicate the fact that prices of labour and capital remain the same despite a successive increase in the firm's total outlay to be spent on labour and capital.

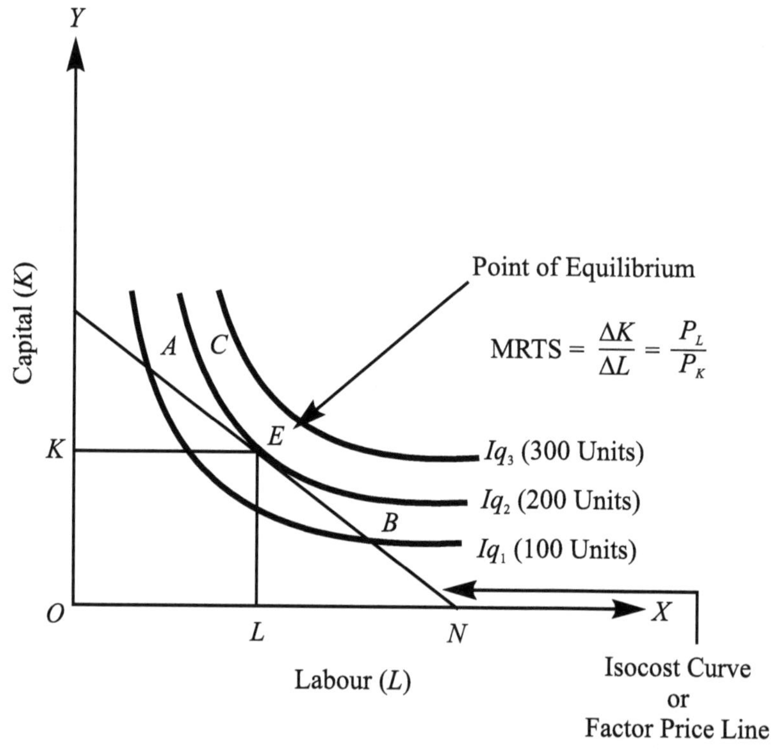

Fig. 18.16

3. The slope of the isocost curve is

$$\frac{C/P_K}{C/P_L} = \frac{C}{P_K} \cdot \frac{P_L}{C} = \frac{P_L}{P_K}$$

where P_L and P_K are the respective prices of labour and capital; and *C* is the firm's total outlay. The set of isocost curve confronting a firm using two factor inputs labour and capital can be represented by the equation

$$C = L \cdot P_L + K \cdot P_K$$

where *L* and *K* are quantities of labour and capital purchased by this firm.

Now we may solve the problem of the firm. The problem faced by the firm is that of getting on the highest possible isoquant that its given isocost curve will allow. To put it differently, it is that of getting the highest amount of output from the given cost outlay. This has been illustrated in Fig. 18.16.

Suppose the firm's isocost line is *MN*. The curves Iq_1, Iq_2 and Iq_3 are the lines of equal physical product or isoproduct lines (isoquants); Iq_2 referring to a greater quantity of output (200 units) than Iq_1 (100 units), and Iq_3 to a still greater quantity (300 units). In other words,

$$Iq_3 > Iq_2 > Iq_1$$

Since the isocost line *MN* reaches to its highest iso-product curve at point *E*, where it is tangential to the iso-product curve Iq_2, the position of *E* indicates the best combination of labour and capital. The firm will get maximum output (200 units) when it buys *OL* units of labour and *OK* units of capital.

Here, we should also note that the points *A* and *B* cannot be the equilibrium points although they satisfy the condition that the slope of isoquant equals the slope of isocost curve or factor price line and they also lie within the approach of the firm. But the fact is that at these points the firm remains at a lower isoquant Iq_1 which yields a lesser amount of product than that on Iq_2. Thus, the optimum factor combination will be attained at point *E*.

Also point *C* lies on Iq_2 and that yields the same units of output as point *E*, but to reach point *C* the firm has to incur more expenditure and that lies outside his constraint line *MN*. Thus, the only point which can be the equilibrium point is the point *E* where the isoquant Iq_2 touches the isocost curve *MN*.

The equilibrium position of the firm can also be explained in terms of the equality between *MRTS* and the factor price ratio. As we have already explained the slope of an isoquant indicates the marginal rate of technical substitution (*MRTS*) and the slope of the isocost line indicates the factor price ratio. The optimum input combination will be indicated by the point where the slopes of the two curves coincide with each other; or

$$MRTS = \frac{P_L}{P_K}$$

But, $MRTS$ = Slope of Isoquant $= \frac{\Delta K}{\Delta L} = \frac{MPP_L}{MPP_K}$

Thus $$\frac{P_L}{P_K} = \frac{MPP_L}{MPP_K} \qquad ...(3)$$

where MPP_L is the marginal physical product of labour and MPP_K is the marginal physical product of capital.[4]

Changes in Outlay and Expansion Path

Until now, while determining the equilibrium point, we have assumed firm's resources or total outlay to be constant. But if there is a change in its total outlay, the firm has to establish a new equilibrium point. The firm may produce a higher level of output if the total outlay has increased (assuming input prices to be constant). Since the marginal productivities of factor input are always not constant and not equal, change in outlay may reflect in varying degree of change in the use of different inputs.

The isocost line or the factor price lines will make a parallel shift following every change in the cost outlay, as the ratio of input prices has been assumed to be constant. As cost outlay increases, the firm would be able to purchase more of labour and more of capital. Figure 18.17 indicates a family of three isocost lines MN, M_1N_1 and M_2N_2. Now every increase in cost outlay will enable the firm to raise the level of employment of both the inputs and thus

---

4. This conclusion can also be derived with the help of some mathematics as below. To minimise the cost outlay,

$$C = P_L \cdot L + P_K \cdot K \quad \text{... } (i)$$

for a given level of output (i.e. constant)

$$X = f(L, K) \quad \text{...}(ii)$$

differentiate (*ii*) getting

$$\frac{dK}{dL} = -\frac{f_L}{f_K} \quad \text{...}(iii)$$

Then take the first partial derivative of C with respect to L and we get

$$\frac{\partial C}{\partial L} = P_L - P_K \frac{d_K}{d_L} \quad \text{...}(iv)$$

Substituting (*iii*) in (*iv*) and setting the derivative equal to zero, we get

$$\frac{\partial C}{\partial L} = P_L - P_K \frac{f_L}{f_K} = 0 \quad \text{...}(v)$$

or

$$\frac{P_L}{P_K} = \frac{f_L}{f_K} \quad \text{...}(vi)$$

This equation (*vi*) is the necessary condition for cost minimisation. This can also be put as

$$MRTS_{LK} = \frac{P_L}{P_K} \text{ or } \frac{MPP_L}{P_L} = \frac{MPP_K}{P_K} \quad \text{...}(vii)$$

The sufficient condition for cost minimisation is that at the point of tangency of the isoquant
and the isocost line, the isoquant must be convex to the origin, or

$$\frac{d^2K}{dL^2} > 0 \quad \text{...}(viii)$$

produce higher levels of output. The equilibrium points of input combinations will be E, E_1 and E_2. If we join these equilibrium points with the help of a curve, then this curve is known as the *expansion path* of a firm. Hence, an expansion path indicates different points of least cost combinations of labour and capital required to produce different levels of out-put. In other words, the expansion path curve (or scale line) shows the various *input-optima* as the firm expands the size of the output.

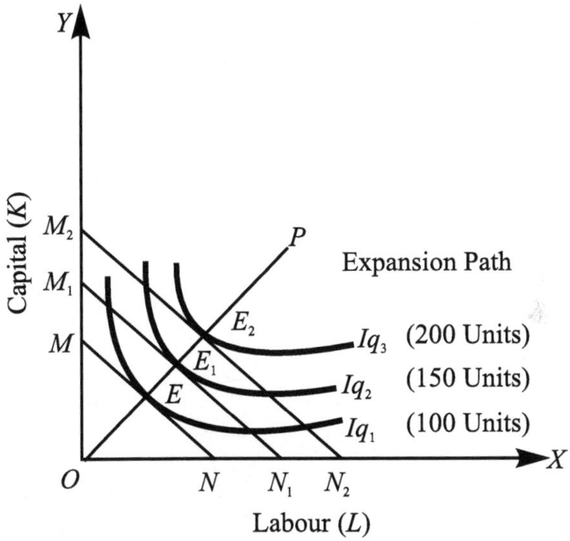

Fig. 18.17

The expansion path of a linear homogeneous production function (the constant-returns-to scale case) is always a straight line through the origin. This means that, given the prices of its inputs, the optimal proportion of the inputs of the firm will not change with the size of the firm's input budget[5] (cost outlay). This expansion path which is also known as an *isocline*[6] has been shown in Fig. 18.17. In such a particular case, the businessman does not have further input-proportion decision problems, as long as input prices do not change.

The expansion path of a general production function (where constant returns are absent) will not be a straight line; in that case an increase in the total outlay will be followed by varying proportions of capital and labour. It means that an increase in total cost outlay does not necessarily result in an equivalent increase in the use of both the inputs. In fact, the relative responsiveness of the use of an input will depend upon the value of *outlay elasticity* with respect to labour or capital as the case may be. The outlay

5. William J. Baumol, *Economic Theory and Operations Analysis* (Second Edition), p. 261.
6. According to Ferguson, an isocline is a locus of points along which the *MRTS* is constant. C.E. Furguson, *Micro Economic Theory* (1972), pp. 177-78.

elasticity will tell us the nature of the input. In the case of normal inputs, the outlay elasticity will be unity ($\eta = 1$). In the case of superior input, the outlay elasticity will be greater than one ($\eta > 1$). In case of inferior inputs, the outlay elasticity will be less than unity ($\eta < 1$).

An expansion path may also be termed as the *long-run expenditure curve* of a firm, as it relates various levels of output to different levels of total outlay. Also, from the firm's expansion path it is fairly easy to find the firm's total and average cost curves. As we know the *total cost curve* (*TC-curve*) is defined as a curve which shows how total cost outlays of a firm vary with firm's level of production. The average and marginal cost curves can easily be calculated by the total cost curve. In Fig. 18.17, isocost line *MN* represents a cost outlay *C* and its tangency point (equilibrium point) *E* tells us the maximum output obtainable, *i.e.* q_1 (100 units). This information is represented by point A_1 in Fig. 18.18. Similarly, point A_2 in Fig. 18.18 tells us that it will cost C_2 to produce output level q_2, and so on.

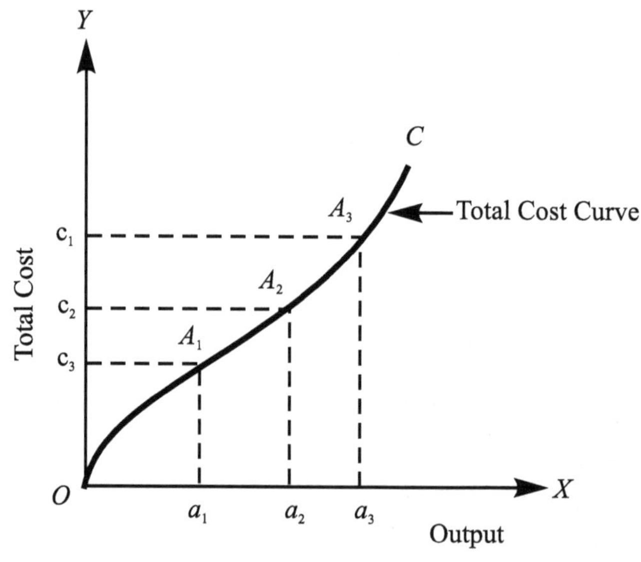

Fig. 18.18

The curve *OC* in Fig. 18.18 which is the locus of all points like A_1, A_2 and A_3 is the total cost curve of the firm.[7] Once the *TC* curve is obtained, we can also draw the firm's *AC* curve and *MC* curve from its *TC* curve.

---

7. Here we must remember that if all the information of points A_1, A_2 and A_3 of Fig. 18.18 has been taken from Fig. 18.17, then our resulting *TC*-curve will be a straight line like *OP* expansion path of Fig. 18.17. But here we have assumed that for all the time constant returns to scale (Linear Homogeneous Production Function) is not prevailing in the production process of the firm. Hence the *TC*-curve will be like that of Fig. 18.18. Likewise, the expansion path of Fig. 18.17 will turn to the shape of *TC-curve* in Fig. 18.18.

Changes in Input Prices

Figure 18.19 analyses the effect of a change in the relative prices of the two factors of production. The line *MN* in this figure is the original isocost curve. On this isocost curve, point *E* is the equilibrium point because the highest possible isoproduct curve Iq_1 touches this curve at this point *E*. It indicates that the firm purchases *OK* units of capital and *OL* units of labour. Now let us suppose that the prices of the two factor inputs labour and capital are reversed, so that the price of labour becomes the price of capital and price of capital

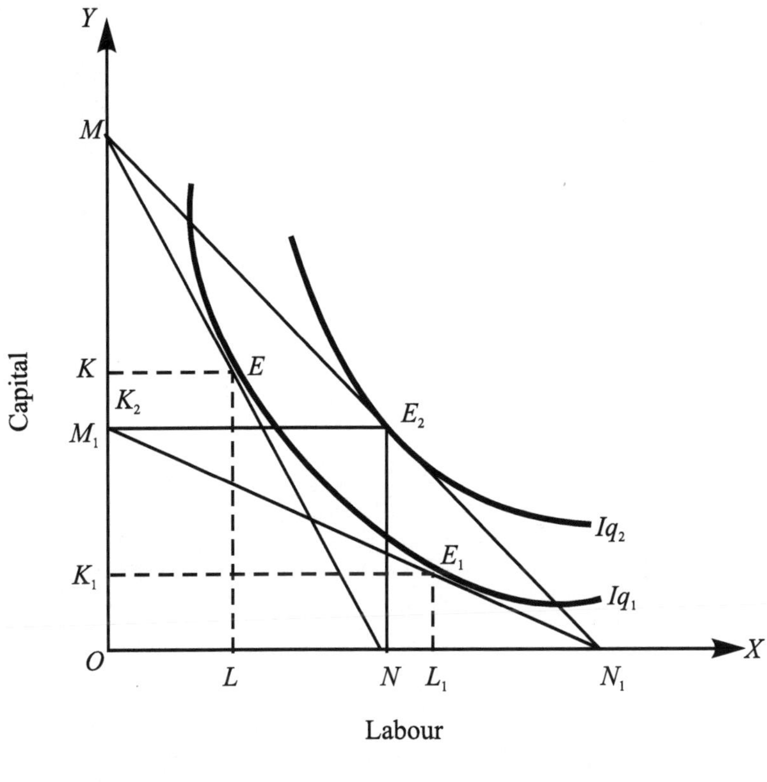

Fig. 18.19

becomes the price of labour. Now the new isocost line M_1N_1 represents the same cost outlay devoted to various combinations of the two inputs. Since in the figure the iso-product lines are symmetrical, the new isocost line M_1N_1 is tangential to the same isoproduct curve as the isocost curve *MN*, i.e. the isoquant Iq_1; but the point of tangency will be E_1 instead of *E*. With the new prices, the firm in equilibrium will purchase OK_1 amount of capital and OL_1 amount of labour. It means, as a change in the relative prices of factor inputs, the firm substitutes the cheaper factor input for the dearer, i.e. LL_1 of labour is substituted for KK_1 of capital.

It is quite possible that price of capital remaining the same while the price of labour declines. It means from the same cost outlay we may get more amount of labour (ON_1) or the same amount of capital (OM). The line MN_1 will be the new isocost line. This line is tangential to its highest isoproduct line at point E_2 on the curve Iq_2. Whereas on isocost line MN the optimum quantity of labour was OL and of capital was OK, the optimum quantities now (at MN_1 isocost curve) become OL_1 of labour and OK_1 of capital. An amount of LL_1 of labour is substituted for KK_1 amount of capital. Also, the new optimum position at point E_2, is on a higher iso-product line, Iq_2, so that total output is increased. Thus, here we find that a lower price for a factor of production gives the producer an advantage that he can get also from a greater cost outlay.

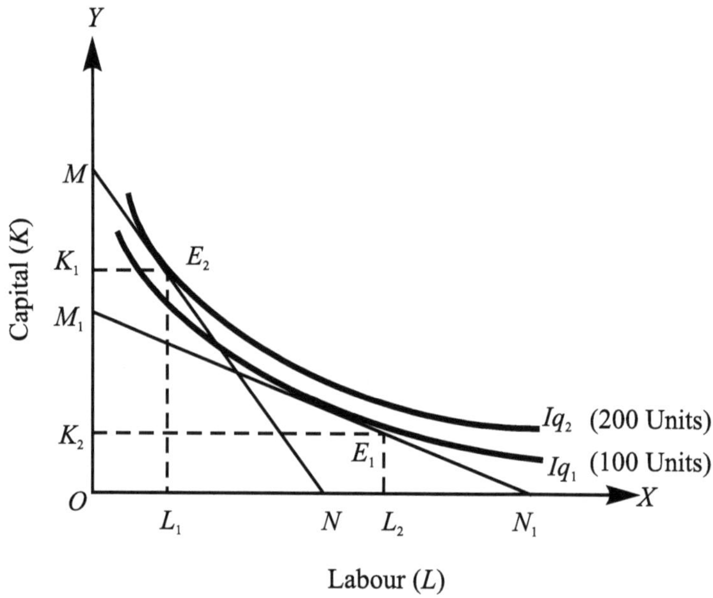

Fig. 18.20

In actual life, it is very unlikely that a set of isocost curves will be symmetrical, as in Figure 18.19. Figure 18.20 illustrates a situation in which the isoproduct curves are asymmetrical. The lines MN and M_1N_1 in this figure may be supposed to refer to a constant (or same) expenditure (outlay) on factors L and K. In spite of the same cost outlay, it will be noticed that MN and M_1N_1 are tangential to different isoproduct lines, MN to the higher iso-product line Iq_2 at E_2 and M_1N_1 to the lower iso-product line Iq_1 at E_1. The relative change in factor prices causes substitution of the factor input that has become cheaper for that which is relatively dearer; L_1L_2 of labour being substituted for K_1K_2 of capital. Also total production declines, the isoproduct line Iq_1 representing a smaller physical output (100 units) than the isoquant Iq_2 (200 units).

Output and Substitution Effect of a Fall in the Price of one Input (*Labour*). We know that a fall in the price of labour will lead to an increase in the quantity of labour used, assuming that it is a normal factor of production. As a fall in the price of labour while the price of capital remain the same, the resulting output will be greater than the previous level. Like a change in the price of a commodity, a change in the price of an input affects the demand for it via the substitution effect and the output (income) effect. Figure 18.21 illustrates the effect of a fall in the price of labour. In Fig. 18.21, the original isocost line or factor price line is *MN*. If the price of labour falls (while price of capital remains constant), then the factor price line MN_1 will indicate the new price ratio of capital and labour. The original equilibrium position is indicated by point E_1 on isoquant Iq_1 and OL_1 amount of labour is used by the firm. It is also evident that a fall in the price of labour enables the firm to move to a higher isoquant and the new equilibrium position is shown by point E_2 on the higher isoquant Iq_2. The new equilibrium point indicates that the firm uses OL_2 units of labour. A lower price of labour, therefore, has increased the use of labour from OL_1 to OL_2— i.e. an increase of L_1L_2, units of labour. This may be called *as the price effect* on the use of labour.

This price effect is partly due to the substitution effect the cheaper input, labour is substituted for relatively costlier input capital and partly due to output effect, i.e. a greater use of input as more output being used. Thus

Total Price Effect = Substitution Effect + Output Effect.

In Fig. 18.21, the change in labour input resulting exclusively from a given change in the ratio of input prices is shown by L_1L_3. Since labour is now relatively cheaper, the firm uses more labour by reducing the level of capital input nom OK_1 to OK_3 in order to produce the same level of output. This is the substitution effect. The factor price line M_1N_2 is parallel to the new isocost line MN_1 and thus reflects the (same) new input price ratio

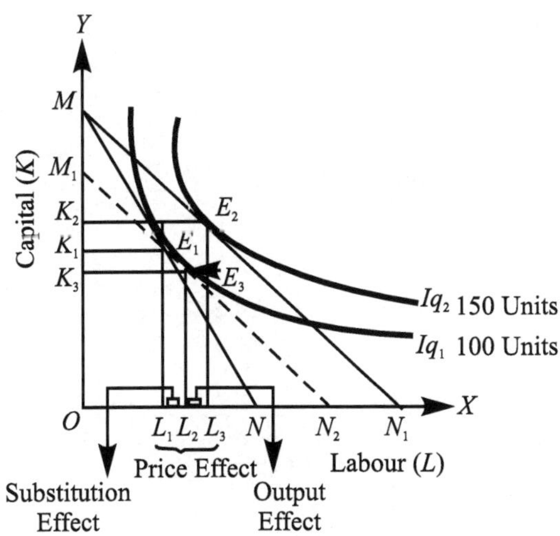

Fig. 18.21

$\left[\frac{OM}{ON_1} = \frac{OM_1}{ON_2}\right]$. However, the firm is capable of employing more units of capital and labour and thus produce a higher level of output (at point E_2). As a result, the firm further increases the use of labour by L_3L_2 and increases the amount of capital from OK_3 to OK_2, and produces a level of output represented by Iq_2 (150 units). This (L_3L_2) is the output effect of a fall in the price of labour.

To put it differently, as a fall in the price of labour, the firm increases its level of output from Iq_1 (100 units) to Iq_2 (150 units) by moving from equilibrium point E_1 to a new equilibrium point E_2. However, the movement from E_1 to E_3 is the substitution effect, and from E_3 to E_1 we have the output effect of a change in the ratio of input prices. In a summary form, we have

Total Price Effect = Substitution Effect + Output Effect

or $$L_1L_2 = L_1L_3 + L_3 L_2$$

In a similar way we may also demonstrate the price effect, substitution effect and output effect of a rise in the price of labour.

Optimum Combination of Outputs

In the above analysis we have discussed a case of two inputs and one output where the firm's problem was to get the optimum combination of factor inputs. This was achieved by the help of isoquant and isocost lines. Now, we shall discuss the problem that how a firm can maximise its revenue by producing an optimum combination of its outputs. Assume that the firm produces only two outputs *X* and *Y*. It is also assumed that the firm is working with fixed input quantity (fixed resources) within the framework of a given technology.

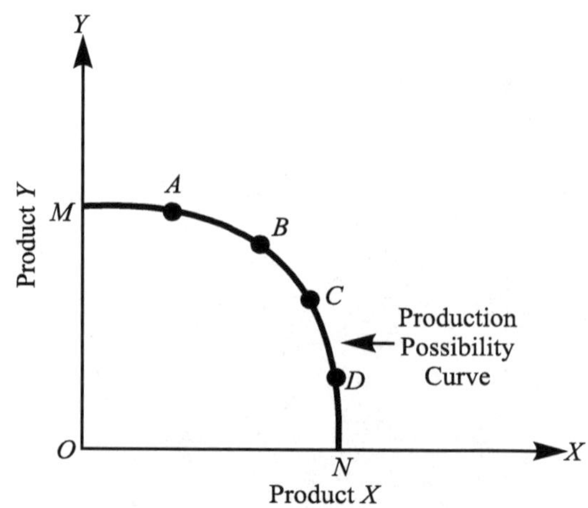

Fig. 18.22

The production possibility curve shows different points of combi-nations of outputs X and Y that the firm can produce with the fixed resources. This curve is also known as production transformation curve. In Fig. 18.22, the production possibility curve MN indicates that with the fixed resources, the firm can produce either OM quantity of product Y and zero quantity of product X, or ON quantity of product X and zero quantity of product Y, or any combination between these two extremes, such as A, B, C and D.

The production possibility curve is concave which indicates that for every additional unit of product X produced, the sacrifice of produce Y goes on increasing. This curve is also referred to as Product Transformations Curve, because when the firm moves from one point to another on the same curve, it transforms one product into another product through the transference of physical resources.

The slope of this curve is termed as marginal rate of product transformation (*MRPT*). *MRPT* is the rate at which one output is transformed into another output assuming the same production resources.

Mathematically, $$MRPT = \frac{-\Delta Y}{-\Delta Y} = \frac{-dY}{dX} \qquad \text{...(4)}$$

where ΔY is the change in output Y and ΔX is the change in output X.

The production possibility curve is concave to the origin point because of the law of increasing cost. To put it differently, the *MRPT* goes on increasing as the firm produces more of X and less of Y, and this is the increasing *MRPT* that is responsible for the concavity of the curve. The slope of this curve (*MRPT*) is always negative, because to increase the quantity of one output the firm has to sacrifice the production of other output; since the factor-inputs remain the same.

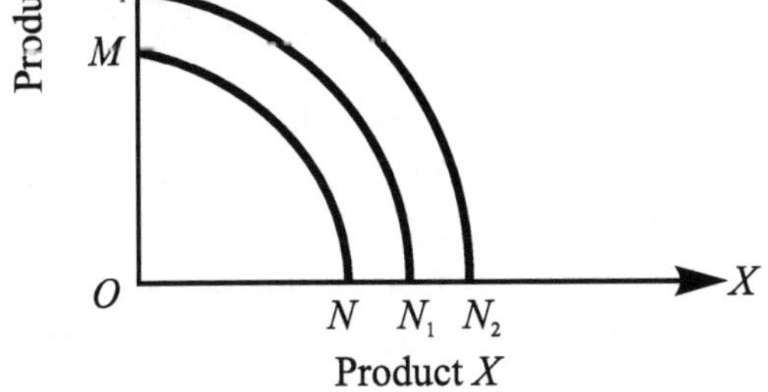

Fig. 18.23

We may also draw a map of production possibility curves according to the level of fixed resources. If the resources of the firm are increased, it is able to produce more of both the product. Figure 18.23 shows the three production possibility curves, *MN*, M_1N_1, and M_2N_2 which represent successive increments in productive resources of the firm.

Now, our problem is to find out the optimum combination of products from a number of available combinations such as *A, B, C, D* in Fig. 18.22. It requires a further explanation of the *Iso-revenue curves.* An iso-revenue curve can be defined as a straight line curve indicating different combinations of two outputs *X* and *Y* which yield the same amount of revenue to the firm. There may be a series of iso-revenue curves representing different levels of revenues. In Fig. 18.24, we have drawn three iso-revenue curves, *RS*, R_1S_1 and R_2 S_2 indicating different levels of revenues. The higher the iso-revenue curve, the more will be the revenue and vice versa. The iso-revenue curves are parallel to each other, indicating

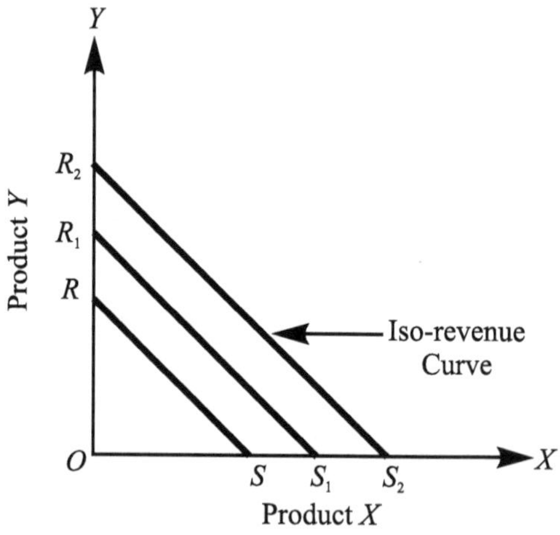

Fig. 18.24

that the prices of the two products *X* and *Y* are fixed. The slope of the iso-revenue curve indicates the price ratio. Thus

$$\frac{P_X}{P_Y} = \text{Slope of the iso-revenue curve} \qquad ...(5)$$

Now to get equilibrium point of the firm (where she will be able to get maximum revenue), we have to combine the two diagrams of the production possibility curve and the iso-revenue curves.

In Fig.18.25, point *E* is the equilibrium point, because it yields the highest possible maximum revenue represented by the iso-revenue curve R_1S_1. At this point *E*, the production possibility curve *MN* touches the iso-revenue line R_1S_1. At the other points on the *PP* curve, say *A* and *B*, the firm will not be able to get maximum revenue because they lie on a lower iso-revenue curve

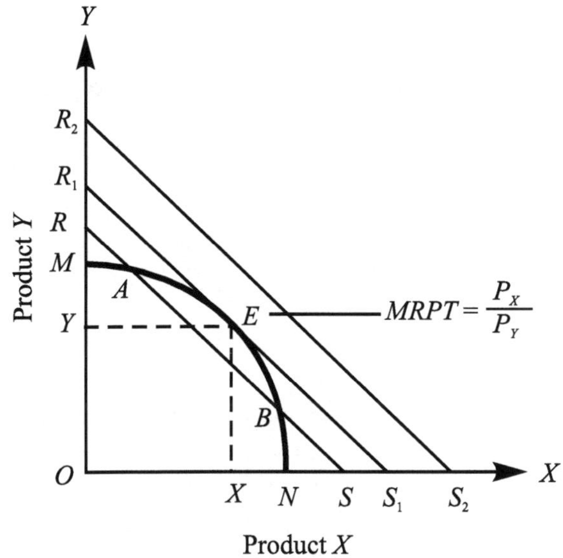

Fig. 18.25

RS. Thus, with the given resources, point *E* represents an optimum combination of two outputs *X* and *Y*. Here, the firm produces *OX* amount of *X* and *OY* amount of *Y*. Also, the optimum combination point indicates that the slope of the production possibility curve is equal to the slope of the iso-revenue line, or

$$MRPT = \frac{\Delta Y}{\Delta X} = \frac{P_X}{P_Y} \qquad \ldots(6)$$

Isoquants and Returns to Scale

Before we discuss the use of isoquants, we must understand that under the isoquants we can show the use of only two factors of production while in real situation, there are three or four factors of production. Thus, here we shall confine our discussion to two factors only which can easily be extended to situations with more than two factor inputs.

We are interested to explain the laws of production and we may look at the problem in two ways. In this section, we shall consider returns to two factors of production where both can vary returns with two variable factors. In the next section, we shall discuss returns to two factors where one can vary and the other is fixed, i.e. returns with one variable factor (or the law of variable proportions or the law of returns or the law of diminishing returns). Here, our main assumption is that there is perfect competition, i.e. all price lines are straight line curves.

From the isoquants map and the corresponding isocost lines (or factor price lines), we may derive the *scale line*. Here, we shall continue to assume that the firm wishes to produce each output as cheaply as possible. The amounts of factor inputs employed will depend on the relative prices of these factors as well as on the technical conditions shown in Fig. 18.26. In this diagram, we have shown the isoquants map consisting of three isoquants Iq_1 (100 units), Iq_2 (150 units) and Iq_3 (700 units) and the corresponding isocost lines MN, M_1N_1 and M_2N_2. In the existing situation the price of factor input labour divided by the price of factor input capital, i.e. the price ratio is equal to

$$\frac{OM}{ON} = \frac{OM_1}{ON_1} = \frac{OM_2}{ON_2}$$

Now, if the firm wishes to produce 100 units of output, it will be in equilibrium at the point E on the isoquant Iq_1 (100 units). At this point E, the isocost curve MN is tangential to the isoquant Iq_1 . Only at point E, the firm will be producing the 100 units of output as cheaply as possible. To reach any point other than E, on the equal product curve Iq_1 representing 100 units of output, the firm will have to spend more than ON in terms of labour or OM in terms of capital, for appropriate combinations of factors. Similarly, if the firm wishes to produce 150 units of output, it will be in equilibrium only at point E_1.ON_1 in terms of L (labour) or OM_1 in terms of K (capital), represents the lowest cost at which 150 units of output can be produced. Likewise, the firm shall be in equilibrium at the point E_2 if it wishes to produce 200 units of output. It will be noted that at all points such as E, E_1 and E_2, the marginal significance of labour input in terms of capital input is equal to the relative money prices of the two factors labour and capital, or

$$MRTS_{LK} = \frac{P_L}{P_K} \qquad \ldots(7)$$

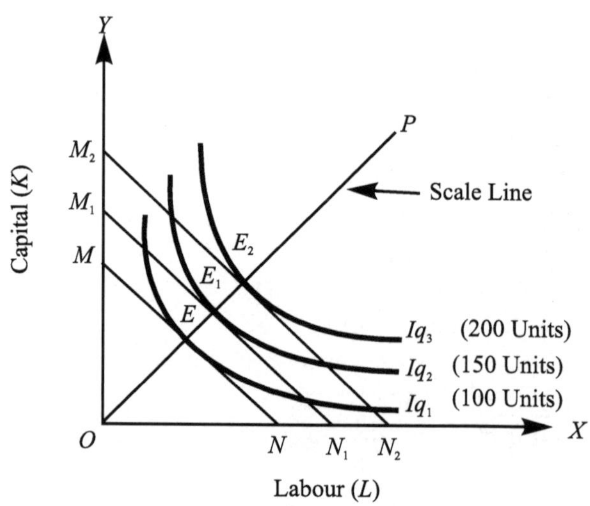

Fig. 18.26

The above condition is shown by the fact that each isoquant is tangential to the relevant price line. If we join the various points of equilibria, such as *E*, E_1 and E_2 we get a curve which is known as the *Scale Line.* In Fig. 18.26, *OP* represents the scale line. It is analogous to the income-consumption curve in the theory of indifference curve analysis. The scale line shows different amounts of the input produced at the minimum cost of production when the two factor inputs are variable and their relative prices (i.e. price ratio) are fixed. In other words, the scale line shows the way in which the firm adjusts the scale of its operation with given relative factor prices. It shows the cheapest way of producing each output in these circumstances (i.e. given the factor price ratio and the two factors are variable inputs). The scale line is also referred to as the expansion path of the firm. The shape of the scale line will depend both on the relative prices of the factors concerned (i.e. the factor price ratio) and on the shape of the isoquants. Now, having obtained the scale line corresponding to any particular factor price ratio, we can find out whether, as the factors are varied, total output to them increases at an increasing rate, or constant rate or diminishing rate.

(*i*) *Increasing Returns to Scale.* As the factors of production are increased or the scale of production is increased, the returns to outlay will be increasing in the beginning, because as output rises there are economies of scale to be repeated. It is likely, for instance, that where one of the factors is labour, the division of labour will increase output as the number of men employed rises. There are likely to be increasing returns to outlay in some parts of an equal product map, whether or not the scale lines are straight lines. This has been illustrated in Fig. 18.27.

In Fig. 18.27, *OP* is the scale line which is a straight line purely to simplify the construction of the diagram. It indicates how different quantities of output

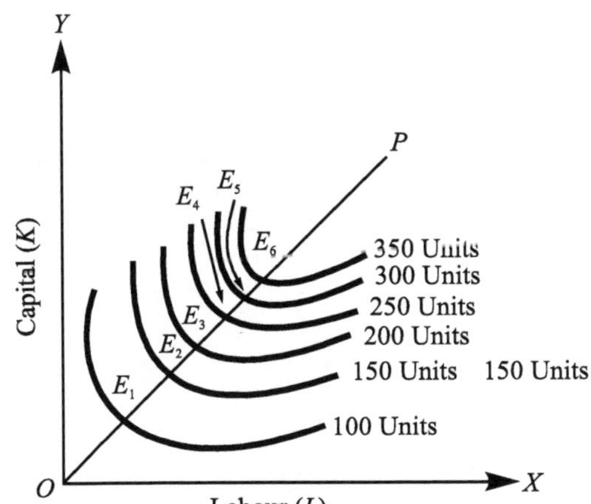

Fig. 18.27

could be produced at the minimum cost with the two factor inputs labour and capital. Along this scale line *OP,* as the output increases, the returns to outlay increase. The increasing returns to outlay are indicated by the gradual decrease in the distance between the isoquants.

For example,

$$E_1E_2 > E_2E_3 > E_3E_4 > E_4E_5 > E_5E_6$$

In other words, for a given increase in output from say 100 units to 150 units or from 150 units to 200 units, etc. cost outlay on capital and labour increases, but the increase in cost outlay is proportionately less than the increase in output. Therefore, Fig. 18.27 represents the situation of increasing returns to scale.

(ii) Constant Returns to Scale. It is possible sometime that returns to scale are constant. It implies that when the factors of production are changed in a certain proportion and the output also changes exactly in the same proportion, then the returns to scale are constant. This situation has been shown in Fig. 18.28.

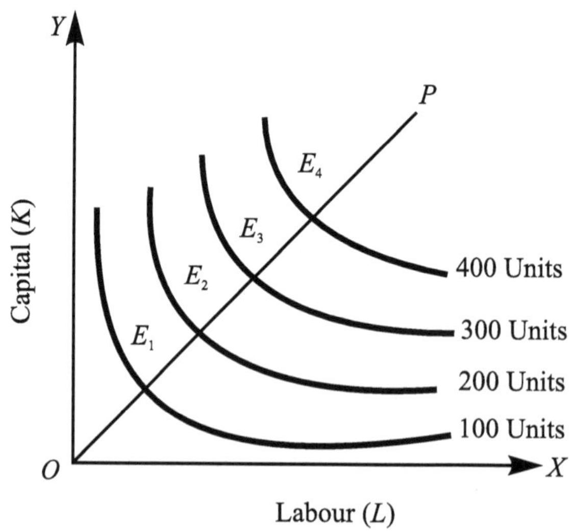

Fig. 18.28

In Figure 18.28, *OP* represents the scale line. It shows the different levels of output represented by various isoquants. The constant returns to outlay are indicated by the equal distances between the isoquants. In other words, if output is doubled from 100 units to 200 units then the quantity of factor inputs is to be doubled. This means,

$$OE_1 = E_1E_2 = E_2E_3 = E_3E_4$$

Thus, Fig. 18.28 illustrates the situation of constant returns to scale.

(*iii*) *Diminishing Returns to Scale.* We know that as the factors of production are increased, the returns to scale may be increasing in the first instance, but ultimately it will have to decrease. In the situation of diminishing returns to scale, the economies of scale which are responsible for increasing returns to scale will give place to diseconomies of scale. Diminishing returns to scale implies that for a given increase in output, a larger increase in quantities of factors of production is required. In other words, the proportionate increase in factor inputs will be more than the proportionate increase in output. This has been illustrated in Fig. 18.29.

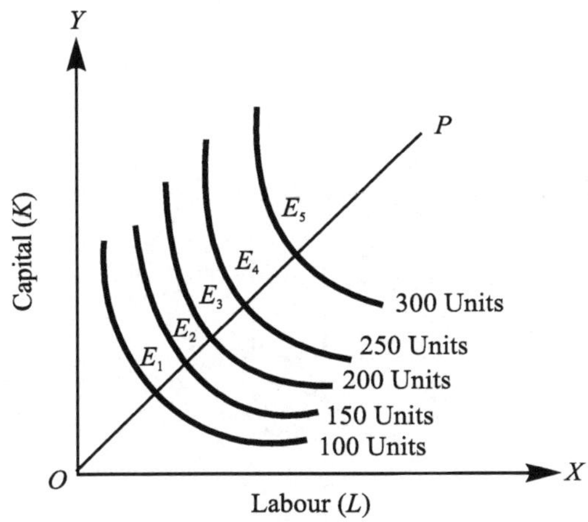

Fig. 18.29

In Fig. 18.29, *OP* is the scale line, which represents different levels of output indicated by various isoquants. The diagram indicates that for every additional increase of 50 units of output, the firm progressively increases its outlay on the two factors labour and capital, i.e. the distance between the isoquants increases as the firm produces higher levels of output. This means,

$$E_1E_2 < E_2E_3 < E_3E_4 > E_4E_5$$

Thus, Figure 18.29 shows the situation of diminishing returns to scale.

4. Isoquants and Laws of Returns or Returns to a Variable Input

In the above section, we have discussed the various situations of returns to scale when the two factor inputs labour and capital were variable. This kind of analysis is of limited use in economics because we do not find such situations of returns to scale in real world. In practice, at least one factor of production (say entrepreneurship) is usually fixed in amount. Thus, a more realistic analysis is of laws of returns. Here, we shall assume that one of the factors of production used by the firm is fixed while the other is variable. In Fig. 18.30, we assume that capital (*K*) is fixed and labour (*L*) is a variable input. *OM* amount of the fixed factor capital is used in conjunction with varying amounts of the variable input labour. The way in which returns to labour (*L*) change as the amounts of labour vary can be found by studying what happens along the horizontal line *MN* in Fig. 18.30.

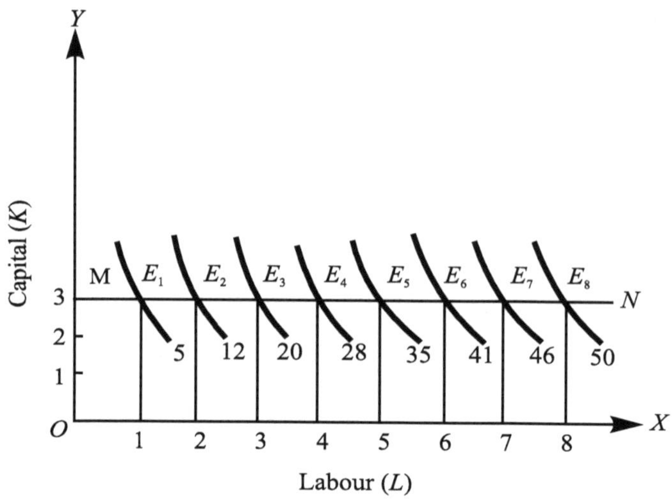

Fig. 18.30

At each point on the line *MN,* a fixed amount ($OM = 3$ units) of capital is being used in conjunction with a different amount of the variable input labour. We may show the physical returns to the variable factor in several ways. Just as we can represent costs and revenues by total, average and marginal cost curves, we can also represent the physical productivity of a variable factor of production (labour) by drawing total product curve, average product curve or marginal product curve. In the present section we shall draw the marginal physical productivity curve (or *MPP* curve) for labour.

It is assumed that the level of capital input is held constant at 3 units of capital and the firm adds one unit of labour input per unit of time. The isoquant map given in Fig. 18.30 presents a family of isoquants, each labelled with a numerical value signifying the level of output produced along it. Since the level of variable input (labour) increases by one unit each time, we can easily discover the marginal physical productivity of labour from the isoquant map. It (MPP_L) will be the difference between the numerical values between two isoquants. For instance, as employment increases from 1 unit of labour to 2 units of labour, total production rises from 5 units to 12 units. The marginal physical productivity of labour is therefore 7 units (12 units–5 units) of output. Similarly, the third unit of labour adds 8 units of output, the fourth unit of labour also adds 8 units of output and so on.

The derivation of marginal physical productivity curve of labour has been illustrated in Fig. 18.31. The upper part of Fig. 18.31 indicates that total output increases at an increasing rate until 3 units of labour are used. If the labour is employed beyond 4 units, output increases at a decreasing rate. For this reason, the marginal physical productivity curve of labour as shown in the lower part of Fig. 18.31 first shows a positive slope and then it falls downwards to the right. It is also possible to draw an average physical productivity curve, or (*APP* curve derived from the isoquants map by dividing total output at each level of employment by number of units of labour employed). This bears the

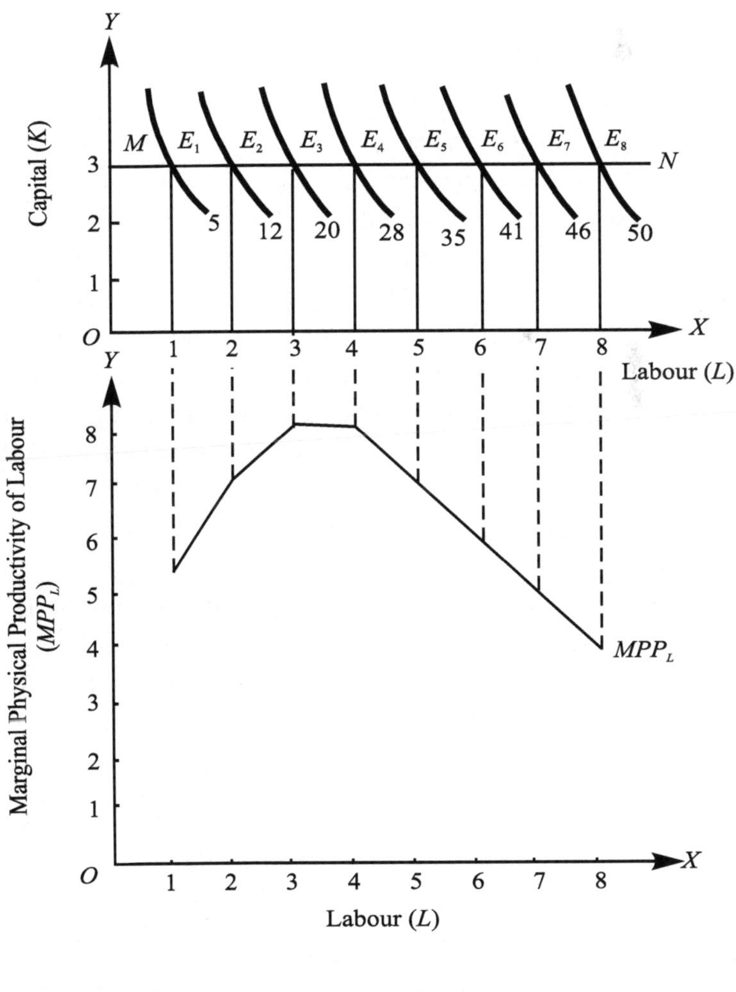

Fig. 18.31

usual average-marginal relationship to the marginal physical productivity curve and can, of course, be derived from the MPP_L curve itself. The total physical productivity curve of labour (TPP_L curve) can also be derived from the isoquant map or from the APP_L curve or MPP_L curve.

The phase of diminishing marginal physical productivity occupies an important place in economics. In the old time, it has usually been known as the *law of diminishing returns,* or more recently, the *law of variable proportions.* In this sense, the law of diminishing returns can be defined as "an increase in the amount of a variable factor added to a fixed factor causes, in the end, a less than proportionate increase in the amount of product, given technical condition."[8]

Thus, the law of diminishing returns in modern times is not defined in terms of diminishing marginal physical productivity, but it is couched in terms of proportionality.

5. The Cobb-douglas Production Function

The statistical investigations into the laws of production by C.W. Cobb and P.H. Douglas[9] are of great importance in the field of economics. Their production function is used as a fairly universal law of production. They have estimated it in numerous samples of manufacturing industries throughout the world. This exponential type of production function ($X = AL^{\alpha} K^{\beta}U$) has no more claim to general validity as a description of technology than other mathematical functions. Moreover, it possesses certain interesting properties which make it a very convenient choice of a researcher. Even before the research of C.W. Cobb and P.H. Douglas, the similar type of production function had been used by many economists. But, it was clearly developed and empirically verified by these two persons, Cobb and Douglas. It is why this function is almost always referred to as the *"Cobb-Douglas Production Function."*

The general form of the Cobb-Douglas production function is

$$X = AL^{\alpha} K^{\beta}U \qquad \text{...(8)}$$

where X = output, L = labour input, K = capital input, U = random disturbance term, A = a constant (may be treated as an efficiency parameter), and α and β = positive parameters

Also $L > 0$ and $K > 0$, $\alpha > 0$, $\beta > 0$.

8. Alfred Marshall, *op. cit.,* 150.
9. C.W. Cobb and P.H. Douglas, "A Theory of Production", *American Economic Review* (Supplement), 1928.

The sum of exponents ($\alpha + \beta$) represents the degree of homogeneity (or returns to scale) of this function which it assumes to be equal to one.

In this production function the output (X) is a function of two output L and K or symbolically,

$$X = f(L, K,) \text{ such that,}$$
$$f(\lambda L, \lambda K) = (\lambda L)^{\alpha} (\lambda K)^{\beta}$$
$$= \lambda^{\alpha+\beta} K^{\beta} L^{\alpha}$$
$$= \lambda^{\alpha+\beta} f(L, K)$$
$$= \lambda^{\alpha+\beta} X$$

Thus, if $\alpha+\beta = I$, the firm would be operating under the constant returns to scale

and the production function is homogeneous of degree one;
if $\alpha+\beta < 1$, it will have diminishing returns to scale;
if $\alpha+\beta > 1$, it will operate under increasing returns to scale.

Although the Cobb-Douglas production function in equation (8) *is non-linear, it can be transformed into a linear function* by converting all variables into logarithms. It is why this function is known as a log linear function. Thus, taking the log of equation (8) on both the sides, we have,

$$\log K = \log A + \alpha \log L + \beta \log K + \log U \qquad \ldots(9)$$

Properties of Cobb-Douglas Production Function

(1) *Constant Returns to scale prevails in the economy.* As we have seen that Cobb-Douglas production function assumes that ($\alpha+\beta$) = 1 which means constant returns to scale prevails in the economy. In other words, it proves the validity of *Euler's theorem.* Euler's theorem states that if factors of production are paid according to their marginal product then total product will just exhaust.

In other words, if factors are rewarded according to their marginal products, the combined share of the factors is equal to total output (X).

Since this condition is satisfied by production functions of degree one; the Cobb-Douglas production function which was used to attempt an empirical verification of the marginal productivity theory of distribution, statisfies Euler's theorem. We have,

$$\text{Log } X = \log A + \alpha \log L + \beta \log K + \log U$$

$$\therefore \qquad \frac{1}{X}\frac{\partial X}{\partial L} = \frac{\alpha}{L}$$

$$\text{or} \qquad \frac{\partial X}{\partial L} = \frac{\alpha}{L} X$$

or $$MP_L = \frac{\alpha}{L} \cdot X$$

∴ $$TP_L = MP_L \cdot L = \frac{\alpha}{L} \cdot X \cdot L = \alpha X$$

Similarly, $$\frac{1}{X}\frac{\partial X}{\partial K} = \frac{\beta}{X}$$

or $$\frac{\partial X}{\partial K} = \frac{\beta}{X} \cdot X$$

or $$MP_K = \frac{\beta}{X} \cdot X$$

∴ $$TP_K = MP_X K = \frac{\beta}{K} X \cdot K = \beta X$$

so that, $$TP_L + K = \alpha X + \beta X$$
$$= X(\alpha + \beta)$$

Now, if $(\alpha + \beta) = 1$ then $TP_L + K = X$ which proves the property.

Further, a production function should not specify, 'a priori', the degree of economies or diseconomies of scale. In mathematical terms if we deal with homogeneous functions and we will for the most part the function should be permitted to assume any degree of homogeneity that is dictated empirically. For non-constant returns to scale we have such important implications for the economies of growth and the study of market organisation, that it is wise to allow the empirical situation to stipulate the degree of scale.

In short, $(\alpha + \beta)$ is the degree of homogeneity of the Cobb-Douglas production function. Suppose that labour and capital have increased by 10 per cent then the Cobb-Douglas function becomes,

$$X = AL^{\alpha} K^{\beta} U$$

Now $$X = A\,(1.10L)^{\alpha}\,(1.10K)^{\beta} U$$
$$= A\,(1.10)^{\alpha+\beta} L^{\alpha} K^{\beta} U$$

Thus, output would increase by $(1.10^{\alpha+\beta})$ and if $(\alpha+\beta) < 1$, output would increase by less than 10 per cent, if $\alpha + \beta > 1$, output will increase by more than 10 per cent and if $\alpha + \beta = 1$, output will increase by exactly 10 per cent. In Cobb-Douglas production function, returns to scale are, therefore, characterised by the following:

$\alpha + \beta < 1$ → Diseconomies of scale,

$\alpha + \beta = 1$ → Constant returns to scale,

$\alpha + \beta > 1$ → Economies of scale.

Since the Cobb-Douglas production function can characterise any degree of returns to scale, it has been commonly used by many economists.

(2) *Elasticity of substitution* is *equal to one*. We may prove that the elasticity of substitution of the Cobb-Douglas production function (where constant returns to scale holds) is equal to unity everywhere and that it is the only function which satisfies this property. If the production function is linear and homogeneous, then the elasticity of substitution $\sigma = 1$ everywhere if and only if the function is

$$x = LA^{\alpha} B^{\beta} U \quad \text{where } \alpha + \beta = 1$$

or

$$\beta = 1 - \alpha$$

We know that elasticity of substitution can be defined as,

$$\sigma = \frac{\text{per cent change in factor quantity ratio}}{\text{per cent change in factor price ratio}}$$

Since the rate of technical substitution (RTS)

$$= \frac{\partial K}{\partial L} = \frac{MP_L}{MP_K} = \frac{P_L}{P_K} = R$$

then elasticity of substitution between two factors is defined by

$$\sigma = \frac{\partial \log\left(\frac{K}{L}\right)}{\partial \log R}$$

$$= \partial\left(\frac{K}{L}\right) \Big/ \frac{K}{L} \Big/ \frac{\partial R}{R}$$

where $\frac{K}{L}$ = factor quantity ratio and R = factor price ratio P_K/P_L.

Now we have

$$R = \frac{MP_L}{MP_K} = \frac{\partial X}{\partial L} \Big/ \frac{\partial X}{\partial K}$$

From our function we take the partial derivatives of X with respect to L and K respectively as;

$$X = AL^{\alpha} K^{\beta} U$$

$$\frac{\partial X}{\partial L} = \alpha AL^{\alpha-1} K^{\beta} U$$

also

$$\frac{\partial X}{\partial K} = \beta AL^{\alpha} K^{\beta-1} U$$

Now $$R = \frac{\partial X}{\partial L} \bigg/ \frac{\partial X}{\partial K}$$

$$= \frac{\alpha A L^{\alpha-1} K^{\beta} U}{\beta A L^{\alpha} K^{\beta-1} U}$$

$$= \frac{\alpha}{\beta}\left(\frac{K}{L}\right)$$

∴ $$R = \frac{\alpha}{\beta}\partial \cdot \left(\frac{K}{L}\right)$$

Hence, $$\frac{\partial R}{R} = \frac{\frac{\alpha}{\beta}\partial\left(\frac{K}{L}\right)}{\frac{\alpha}{\beta}\left(\frac{K}{L}\right)}$$

$$= \frac{\partial\left(\frac{K}{L}\right)}{\frac{K}{L}}$$

so that

$$\sigma = \frac{\partial\left(\frac{K}{L}\right)}{K/L} \bigg/ \frac{\partial\left(\frac{K}{L}\right)}{K/L}$$

$$= 1 \text{ Hence proved.}$$

The unitary elasticity of substitution is a famous property of the Cobb-Douglas production function, because it guarantees that relative income shares of capital and labour are constant for any changes in the relative supplies of capital and labour, and thus it provides a rationale for the 'relative' constant of factor shares observed in developed economies.

(3) *Expansion path generated by the Cobb-Douglas production function is linear and passes through the origin.* By the first order condition for the constraint optimisation, we have

$$\frac{f_L}{f_K} = \frac{P_L}{P_K}$$

where $\frac{f_L}{f_K}$ = ratio of their marginal productivities; $\frac{P_L}{P_K}$ = ratio of their prices

We have found from the function that,

$$\frac{f_L}{f_K} = \frac{\partial X}{\partial L} \Big/ \frac{\partial X}{\partial K} = \frac{\alpha}{\beta} \cdot \frac{K}{L}$$

or
$$\frac{f_L}{f_K} = \frac{P_L}{P_K} = \frac{\alpha}{\beta} \cdot \frac{K}{L}$$

or
$$\beta P_L \cdot L = \alpha P_K \cdot K$$

or
$$\beta P_L \cdot L - \alpha \cdot P'_K \cdot K = 0 \qquad \text{...(10)}$$

This equation (10) represents the expansion path implicit in the Cobb-Douglas production function $X = AL^{\alpha} K^{\beta} U$, which describes a straight line passing through the origin in the isoquant plane.

The equation (10) can be rewritten as

$$\frac{P_L \cdot L}{P_K \cdot K} = \frac{\alpha}{\beta} \qquad \text{...(11)}$$

The left hand side of equation (11) represents the share of income accruing to labour relative to that going to capital. Now that relative income shares are equal to $\frac{\alpha}{\beta}$, ($\frac{\alpha}{\beta}$= ratio of their elasticities of production or output) which is determined by the technology that governs the Cobb-Douglas production function. If α is high relative to β, then the labour share will be high relative to capital share of income. If technology is unchanging (or constant), it follows that a proportionate change in factor prices produces a compensating proportionate change in relative factor inputs and, therefore, relative share remains constant and equal to α/β.

Where upon it is evident that if $\sigma = 1$, the above expression of the Cobb-Douglas holds, but if $\sigma \neq 1$, a change in relative factor supplies alters relative income shares. Forgiven changes in relative factor supplies, the relative income share will rise or fall depending upon whether the elasticity of substitution exceeds or falls short of unity. In conclusion, we can say that, only for $\sigma = 1$, the relative income shares are constant for an unchanging technology and the Cobb-Douglas production function possesses this property.

(4) *α and β represents the labour share and capital share of the output respectively.* We have $X=AL^{\alpha}K^{\beta}U$

Taking the log on both the sides,

$$\log X = \log A + \alpha \log L + \beta \log K + \log U$$

$$\therefore \qquad \frac{\partial(\log X)}{\partial(\log L)} = \alpha$$

or $$\alpha = \frac{\partial X}{\partial L} \cdot \frac{L}{X}$$

or $$\alpha = MP_L \cdot \frac{L}{X} \qquad \text{...(12)}$$

where $$MP_L = \frac{\partial X}{\partial L}$$

In perfect competition we have,

$$VMP_L = P_L = P_X MP_L$$

where P_X = price of the output

or $$MP_L = \frac{P_L}{P_X}$$

Putting the value of MP_L in equation (12) we get,

$$\alpha = \frac{P_L}{P_X} \cdot \frac{L}{X} = \frac{\text{Wage Share}}{\text{Total Income}}$$

Similarly, $$\frac{\partial(\log X)}{\partial(\log K)} = \beta$$

or $$\beta = \frac{\alpha X}{\alpha K} \cdot \frac{K}{X}$$

$$= MPX \cdot \frac{K}{X} \qquad \text{...(13)}$$

In perfect competition, we have,

$$VMP_K = P_K = MP_K \cdot P_X$$

or $$MP_K = \frac{P_K}{P_X}$$

Putting the value of MP_K in equation (13) we get,

$$\beta = \frac{P_K}{P_X} \cdot \frac{K}{X} = \frac{\text{Rent Share}}{\text{Total Income}}$$

Hence, α = wage share of total income,
and β = rent share of total income,

Hence proved.

(5) α *and* β *are the elasticities of output with respect to labour and capital respectively.* In the case of Cobb-Douglas production function, α is defined as the partial elasticity of production (X) with respect to labour (L). It denotes the percentage change in labour input, *keeping capital input constant.* Similarly, β is defined as the partial elasticity of production (X) with respect to capital input (K), *keeping labour input constant.*

Since α and β represent individually the per cent change in output given per cent changes in labour and capital respectively, the two coefficients taken together measure the total per cent change in output for a given per cent change in labour and capital.

We noted, however, that the Cobb-Douglas production function took on a linear form when expressed in logarithmic instead of arithmetic units. We can, therefore, write,

$$\log X = \log A + \alpha \log L + \beta \log K + \log U$$

$$\frac{\partial(\log X)}{\partial(\log L)} = \alpha$$

or $$\alpha = \left(\frac{\text{change in logarithm of output}}{\text{change in logarithm of labour input}}\right) \text{(capital input constant)}$$

The change in the natural logarithm of some variable is the same thing as the percentage. We can, therefore, also write,

$$\alpha = \left[\frac{\text{per cent change in output}}{\text{per cent change in labour input}}\right] \text{(capital input constant)}$$

or $$\frac{\Delta X/X}{\Delta L/L} = \frac{\Delta X}{\Delta L} \cdot \frac{L}{X} = e_{XL} \text{ elasticity of output w.r.t. labour.}$$

or

Similarly, $$\frac{\partial \log X}{\partial \log K} = \beta$$

or $$\beta = \left[\frac{\text{per cent change in logarithm of output}}{\text{per cent change in logarithm of capital input}}\right] \text{(labour input constant)}$$

$$= \left[\frac{\text{per cent change in output}}{\text{per cent change in capital input}}\right] \text{(labour input constant)}$$

or $$\beta = \frac{\Delta X/X}{\Delta K/K} = \frac{\Delta X}{\Delta K} \cdot \frac{K}{X} = e_X \frac{\Delta X/X}{\Delta K/K} = \frac{\Delta X}{\Delta K} \cdot \frac{K}{X}$$

elasticity of output w.r.t. capital.

Hence proved.

(6) *If one of the inputs is zero, output will also be zero.* The Cobb-Douglas production function assumes constant returns to scale under which all the inputs are changed in equal proportions. If one of the inputs is zero, naturally other inputs are also held to be zero and the consequent output will also be zero.

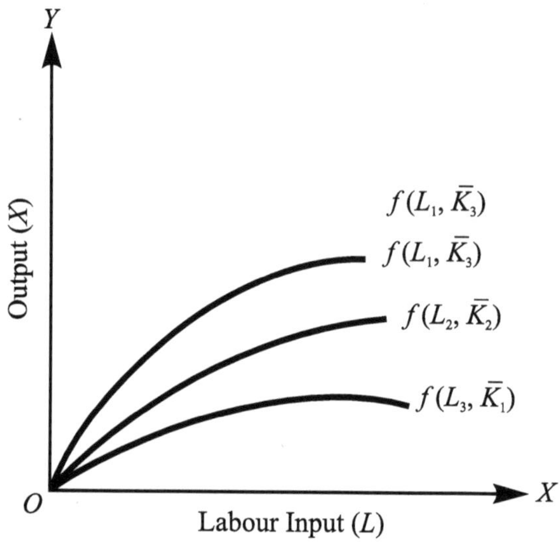

Fig. 18.32

Moreover, we have seen that the Cobb-Douglas function has constant elasticities of output variation with respect to labour or capital input. The relationship between output and input is non-linear (though we may convert it into a log-linear type of relationship). For constant levels of capital, the output-labour input relation is shown as the series of curved lines in the Figure 18.32.

If either input is zero ($L = 0$ or $K = 0$), output is zero ($X = 0$). Thus, both the inputs are necessary to the production process to take place. The curvature is such that marginal productivity falls as input grows. There is no asymptotic level of output (orceiling) beyond which production can not grow, but the rate of increase in output decreases as higher levels of input are employed in the production process.

Importance of Cobb-Douglas Production Function

As we have noticed earlier that Cobb-Douglas production function is most commonly used function in the field of economics. It graduates data on output and input well. Many economists used it independently under the name of "Cobb-Douglas Production Function." Hence there are a number of varieties of the Cobb-Douglas form which yield variable elasticities of production and substitution. We can quote three examples of this kind, as:

$$X = C^{1-\alpha} N^{\alpha} e^{\alpha N} \quad \rightarrow \text{Ferguson and Pfoubs}$$

$$X = AC^{\alpha} N^{\beta} e^{\gamma \log N \log e} \quad \rightarrow \text{Newmann and Read}$$

$$X = AC^{\alpha} N^{\beta} e^{\gamma C} e^{\alpha N} \quad \rightarrow \text{Heady and Dillon}$$

The Cobb-Douglas function is convenient in international or inter-industry comparisons. Since α and β are elasticity coefficients, they are pure number and easily be compared among different samples using varied units of measurement.

In a sense, one is able to capture the flavour of essential non-linearities of the production process and yet benefits from the simplifications of calculation from linear relationship by transforming to logarithms. The logarithmic function is linear in the parameters, which is an essential point to the statistician or to the economists.

Other functions may give a similar type of curvature and keep linearity in parameters. For example, we may write parabolic functions as,

$$X = \alpha_0 + \alpha_1 L + \alpha_2 K + \alpha_3 L^2 + \alpha_4 K^2 + \alpha_5 LK + U$$

However, this type of equation (parabolic) uses many more parameters than does the Cobb-Douglas yet the later (Cobb-Douglas) is economical in the use of degrees of freedom, or parameters and yet gives us non-linearity. The parameters of the Cobb-Douglas function, in addition to being elasticities, possess other attributes important in economic analyses. For example, the sum of the exponents ($\alpha + \beta$) shows the degree of "returns to scale" in production process.

Cobb-Douglas's research has been a test of the marginal productivity theory of wages (or theory of distribution) as well as descriptions of production technology.

Addressing the American Economic Association in 1947, Prof. Douglas summarised the results of his research on the measurement laws of production. Both time-series and cross-section studies were made by Douglas and others for the manufacturing industry of the USA, Canada, Australia, New Zealand and South Africa. In six cross section samples, Douglas found the average labour exponent (α) to be 0.63 and the average capital exponent (β) to be 0.34. In Australian studies, the average components in nine cross-section samples (1912-1937) are 0.60 for labour (α) and 0.37 for capital (β). In this way various comparisons were made between different states.

In this Cobb-Douglas type of production function the elasticity of substitution (σ) between labour (L) and capital (K) is compelled to take on a value of unity, whether or not the empirical situation so dictates. However, a less restricative and much more fruitful approach would be to allow the elasticity of substitution (σ) to vary in accordance with the empirical requirements under consideration.

Criticisms of Cobb-Douglas Production Function

Although Douglas has been a great pioneer and proponent of research into the laws of production, he has not overlooked the points at which his analysis is open to criticism. The main critics of the Cobb-Douglas function are K.J. Arrow, H.B. Chenery, B.S. Minhas and R.M. Solow. The critics have pointed out the following points of criticisms of the Cobb-Douglas production function.

(1) *The Cobb-Douglas function includes only two factor inputs*—capital and labour, but other factors are equally important in the production process. Moreover, the studies of the Cobb-Douglas function were often made for the manufacturing sector alone, raw materials do not conceal as intermediate goods produced and used within the same sector. Even for an economy as a whole, imported raw materials are significant factor inputs to be taken into account on the same footing as labour and capital inputs. In various countries of the world, we find open economies where raw material imports are of great significance in the production process.

(2) *The function assumes constant returns to scale can not be possible.* There are certain inputs of production which can not be increased in equal proportion, for example, entrepreneurship. Moreover, constant returns may take place only in the short-run. But in the long run we can not hope the same situation.

(3) As far as the measurement of labour-input is concerned we may count it in number or in man-hours, but it is very *difficult to measure capital input* due to its depreciation over time. Therefore, the whole problem of aggregation has been overlooked.

(4) Again, the *output measure is usually a form of aggregate value* added. This means that raw materials are not treated as a separate factor of production, but as an automatic subtraction from the total value of output. Raw materials, especially of the fuel variety, may not have the fixed relation to output (as is assumed under constant returns to scale) that is implied by the use of the value added concept.

(5) At different levels of productive operation there may be economies (increasing returns) or dis-economies (diminishing returns) in the use of materials (or factor inputs). It has been overlooked by the functions.

Here we may argue that the true underlying curve of production follows the usual S-shape as shown in Fig. 18.33.

Figure 18.33 shows that in an input-output relation there are phases of increasing, constant, and decreasing *marginal* returns. A sample of data usually approximates some portion of this curve and, therefore, form a limited number of observations, it is not possible to estimate the entire curve. It's quite possible that a sample heavily dominated by depression period may produce a portion of the curve showing increasing returns.

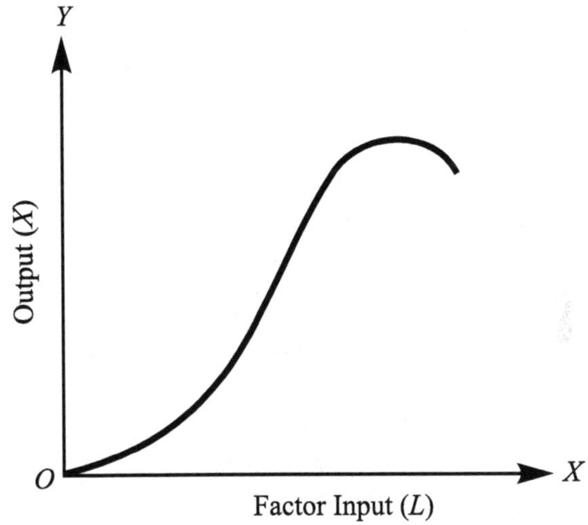

Fig. 18.33

Now if there are increasing returns to scale, we can not have factor shares equal to corresponding exponents (α and β) of the function because the sum of the exponents will exceed unity ($\alpha + \beta > 1$).

(6) *The function assumes that there is perfect competition* in the market and that is why the equalities between the shares and the exponents (α and β) exist. But if there is monopoly and monopolistic competition, the above relationship fails to hold in the economy.

(7) In Cobb-Douglas production function, *all labour units are considered as a homogeneous* input which is a great drawback of the function.

(8) We know that *Multicolinearity* is frequently encountered in economic time-series analysis. It is quite possible that there may be high inter-correlation between capital and labour in the estimation of a production function. Inter-correlation or multi co linearity is not necessarily a problem unless it is high relative to the over-all degree of multiple correlation among all variables simultaneously. In the case of Cobb-Douglas type of research, we have to face this problem of multi co linearity.

In spite of the above criticisms, the Cobb-Douglas production function is widely used in an economic research. It is mainly due to its unique properties that we have already discussed.

5. The Ces Production Function

A production function is presented here, which assumes that the basic measure of the degree of substitution is called but is not restricted 'a priori' to any value. It is called the Constant Elasticity of Substitution (*CES*) production. Clearly, the Cobb-Douglas and Leontief's production functions are special cases of the CES relation.

When the elasticity of substitution specified as constant, it only assumes that changes in relative factor inputs and prices do not alter the elasticity. The value of the elasticity is determined by the underlying technology; and changes in the underlying technology affect variations on the elasticity for every level of factor inputs and prices. Hence, the constancy of the elasticity refers to its invariance with respect to changes in relative factor supplies and not to transformations of the underlying technology.

The characteristics of an abstract technology are identified by the *CES* production function. That is to say that it permits us to measure changes in the efficiency of a technology, changes in the technologically determined returns to scale, changes in the capital intensity of a technology and changes in the substitution of labour for capital, etc.

The *CES* production function was derived independently by two different groups of economists: one consisting of K.J. Arrow, H.B. Chenery, B.S. Minhas and R.M. Solow; and the other group consists of Murray Brown and De Cani. The two derivations are dissimilar; also the latter permits any degree of returns to scale. Murray Brown and De Cani (1963) used the function in an ambitious attempt to separate the effect of output change; economies of scale, technical change and changes in the relative factor prices on labour demand; with U.S. economy data over the period 1890-1958.

Further, some of the recent studies used the constant elasticity of substitution (*CES*) function with a substitution elasticity below unity, is claimed to be more suitable for production function than the Cobb-Douglas form. Under the Cobb-Douglas production function, elasticity of substitution is equal to unity but in *CES* production function, as the name suggests, the elasticity of substitution is constant and not necessarily equal to unity. Four economists, Arrow, Chenery, Minhas and Solow have proposed this *CES* production function.

The equation of this function is,

$$X = \gamma[KC^{-\alpha} + (1-K)\,N^{-\alpha}]^{-\frac{\nu}{\alpha}}$$

$$(\gamma > 0; 0 < K < 1, \alpha > -1) \qquad \ldots(14)$$

where, X = output, C = capital input, N = labour input, γ = coefficient of technical efficiency or scale effect (or simply the efficiency parameter).

This parameter plays the same role in *CES* function as the coefficient A in the Cobb-Douglas function. It serves as an indicator of the general state of technology. Hence the greater the value of γ, the larger will be the output, regardless of inputs.

K = Capital intensity factor coefficient. It is also known as the distribution parameter and is similar to α in the Cobb-Douglas production function. This parameter shows the relative contribution of capital input (K) and labour input (L) to the total output (X).

$(1-K)$ = Labour intensity coefficient.

α = It is known as the substitution parameter and is closely related to the constant elasticity of substitution. The value of e^s (elasticity of substitution) depends on the value of this parameter.

ν = It represents the degree of homogeneity of the function or the degree of returns to scale.

Hence, this function consists of three variables (X, C and N) and four parameters (γ, K, α and ν). The variables are measured in index number terms with a common base period. And the four important parameters in the function represent the four different *characteristics of an abstract technology.* This is, in brief, the beauty of this particular production function over the Cobb-Douglas (or other types) production function.

Relation (14) can be written in anyone of the following forms:

$$(i)\quad X = \gamma\,[KC^{-\alpha} + (1-K)N^{-\alpha}]^{-\frac{v}{\alpha};\ \alpha=-\left[1-\frac{1}{\sigma}\right]}$$

$$(ii)\quad X = \gamma\,[KC^{\alpha'} + (1-K)N^{\alpha'}]^{-\frac{v}{\alpha'};\ \alpha'=\left[1-\frac{1}{\sigma}\right]}$$

$$(iii)\quad X = \gamma\left[\frac{N^{\alpha}C^{\alpha}}{KN^{\alpha} + (1-K)C^{\alpha}}\right]^{\frac{v}{\alpha}};\alpha = -\left[1-\frac{1}{\sigma}\right]$$

$$(iv)\quad X = \gamma\,[K_1C^{-\alpha}K_2N^{-\alpha}]^{-\frac{v}{\alpha'};\ \alpha=-\left[1-\frac{1}{\sigma}\right]}$$

where σ = elasticity of substitution

All the above four forms of the function will give us the same type of results.

Properties of CES Production Function

(1) *The value of the elasticity of substitution depends upon the value of* α. We define the elasticity of substitution as

$$\sigma = \frac{\partial\left(\log\dfrac{K}{L}\right)}{\partial \log R} = \frac{\partial\left(\dfrac{K}{L}\right)}{K/L} \Big/ \frac{\partial R}{R}$$

where $\frac{K}{L}$ = factor quantity ratio, R = factor price ratio

Now our function is,

$$X = \gamma[KC^{-\alpha} + (1 - K)N^{-\alpha}]^{-\frac{v}{\alpha}} \quad ...(15)$$

Taking the partial derivative of X w.r.t. N we get

$$\frac{\partial X}{\partial N} = \gamma\left(-\frac{v}{\alpha}\right)[KC^{-\alpha} + (1-K)N^{-\alpha}]^{-\frac{v}{\alpha}-1}\left[-\alpha N^{-\alpha-1}(1-K)\right]$$

$$= \gamma v[KC^{-\alpha} + (1-K)N^{-\alpha}]^{-\frac{v}{\alpha}-1}\left[N^{-\alpha-1}(1-K)\right] \quad ...(16)$$

Now we are again using equation (15) as

$$X = \gamma[KC^{-\alpha} + (1-K)N^{-\alpha}]^{-\frac{v}{\alpha}}$$

or $$\frac{X}{\gamma} = [KC^{-\alpha} + (1-K)N^{-\alpha}]^{-\frac{v}{\alpha}}$$

or $$\left[\frac{X}{\gamma}\right]^{-\frac{v}{\alpha}} = [KC^{-\alpha} + (1-K)N^{-\alpha}]$$

or $$\left[\frac{X}{\gamma}\right]^{-\frac{v}{\alpha}\left(-\frac{v}{\alpha}-1\right)} = [KC^{-\alpha} + (1-K)N^{-\alpha}]^{-\frac{v}{\alpha}-1}$$

or $$\left[\frac{X}{\gamma}\right]^{1+\frac{v}{v}} = [KC^{-\alpha} + (1-K)N^{-\alpha}]^{-\frac{v}{\alpha}-1} \quad ...(17)$$

Putting the value of (17) in equation (16) we get,

$$\frac{\partial X}{\partial N} = \gamma v\left[\frac{X}{\gamma}\right]^{1+\frac{\alpha}{v}} N^{-\alpha-1}(1-K) = \gamma^{-\frac{\alpha}{v}} vX^{1+\frac{\alpha}{v}} N^{-\alpha-1}(1-K) \quad ...(18)$$

Similarly we can find,

$$\frac{\partial X}{\partial C} = \gamma^{-\frac{\alpha}{v}} vX^{1+\frac{\alpha}{v}} C^{-\alpha-1}(K) \quad ...(19)$$

Now we can define the marginal rate of substitution as

$MRS = \frac{\partial X}{\partial C}\Big/\frac{\partial X}{\partial N} = \frac{\partial X}{\partial C} = R$ [because MRS is equal to the price ratio].

Putting the values from equations (18) and (19) we have,

$$\therefore \qquad R = \frac{\gamma^{-\frac{\alpha}{v}} vX^{1+\frac{\alpha}{v}} C^{-\alpha-1} K}{\gamma^{-\frac{\alpha}{v}} vX^{1+\frac{\alpha}{v}} N^{-\alpha-1}(1-K)}$$

$$= \frac{K}{1-K}\left(\frac{C}{N}\right)^{-\alpha-1} = \frac{K}{1-K}\left(\frac{N}{C}\right)^{1+\alpha}$$

Denoting $\frac{K}{1-K} = K'$ and $\frac{C}{N} =$ we get, $R = K' U^{1+\alpha}$

Taking the log on both the sides,

$$\log R = \log K' + (1+\alpha) \log U$$

$$\text{or} \qquad \frac{1}{R}\frac{\partial R}{\partial U} = (1+\alpha)\frac{1}{U} \quad \text{or} \quad \frac{\partial R}{R} = (1+\alpha)\frac{dU}{U}$$

$$\text{or} \qquad \frac{\partial U}{U} \Big/ \frac{\partial R}{\partial R} = \frac{1}{1+\alpha} \quad \text{or} \quad \sigma = \frac{1}{1+\alpha} \quad \text{where} \quad \alpha > 0$$

$$\text{also} \qquad \alpha = \left[\frac{1}{\sigma} - 1\right] = -\left[1 - \frac{1}{\sigma}\right] \qquad \text{...(20)}$$

If $\alpha = 0$ then $\sigma = 1$ and we shall get the situation of Cobb-Douglas production function. Hence the value of α depends upon the value of α. It assumes whatever the value of σ may be (depending upon α) but it is always constant.

(2) *The marginal products should be positive.* Our function is,

$$X = \gamma[KC^{-\alpha} + (1-K)N^{-\alpha}]^{-\frac{v}{\alpha}}$$

$$\text{or Now} \qquad MP_L = \frac{\partial X}{\partial N} = \gamma^{-\frac{\alpha}{v}} vX^{1+\frac{\alpha}{v}} N^{-\alpha-1}(1-K)$$

[Please see property No.1 for its calculation]

$$\text{or} \quad \frac{\partial X}{\partial N} = h_1 X^{+\frac{\alpha}{v}} N^{-\alpha-1} \quad \text{where} \quad h_1 = \gamma^{-\frac{\alpha}{v}} v(1-K) \qquad \text{...(21)}$$

If there are constant returns to scale then $v = 1$ (Here v refers to returns to scale or the degree of homogeneity of the function).

$$\text{If} \qquad v = 1 \text{ then, } \frac{\partial X}{\partial N} = h_1 X^{1+\alpha} N^{-\alpha-1}$$

$$= h_1\left(\frac{X}{N}\right)^{1+\alpha} = h_1\left(\frac{X}{N}\right)^{\frac{1}{\sigma}} \text{ where } \sigma = \frac{1}{1+\alpha} \quad ...(22)$$

[please see property No.1 for this]

Similarly, the Marginal Product of Capital is,

$$MP_K = \frac{\partial X}{\partial C} = \gamma^{-\frac{\alpha}{v}} vX^{1+\frac{\alpha}{v}} C^{-\alpha-1}K \quad \text{[See property No. 1]}$$

$$= h_2 X^{1+\frac{\alpha}{v}} C^{-\alpha-1} \quad \text{where} \quad h_2 = Kv\gamma^{-\frac{\alpha}{v}}$$

Again, if there are constant returns to scale, then $v = 1$ and

$$\frac{\partial X}{\partial C} = h_2 X^{1+\alpha} C^{-\alpha-1} \quad \text{or} \quad \frac{\partial X}{\partial C} = h_2\left(\frac{X}{C}\right)^{\frac{1}{\sigma}}$$

$$\text{where} \sigma = \frac{1}{1+\alpha} \quad \text{[See property No. 1]} \quad ...(23)$$

It is now obvious that the marginal products are positive.

(3) *The marginal product curves are sloping downward or*

$$\frac{\partial^2 X}{\partial N^2} < 0 \text{ and } \frac{\partial^2 X}{\partial C^2} < 0.$$

(4) *The marginal product of each factor will increase for increase in the other factor inputs.* To satisfy this property, the *RTS* (or *MRS*) of labour (*N*) for capital (*C*) can be derived in terms of *CES* production function by taking the ratio of MP_L and MP_K as :

$$\frac{\partial X}{\partial C} \Big/ \frac{\partial X}{\partial N} = R = K'U^{1+\alpha} \quad \text{where} \quad K' = \frac{K}{1-K} U = \frac{N}{C}$$

[See property No. 1]

$$1/\sigma$$

$$\text{or} \qquad R = K'\ U \qquad \text{where } \sigma = \frac{1}{1+\alpha} \quad ...(24)$$

This plays an important role in the following analysis. If the production process is highly *L*-intensive (small capital is used per unit of labour), MP_L is high compared to MP_K for each *N/C* ratio; thus a unit reduction in the labour rate has to be compensated for a larger increase in the rate of capital then if the process were to be less *L*-intensive. In this sense, *K* is a measure of capital intensity.

If σ is high, then capital is easily substitutable for labour and vice-versa. The expression for *R* tells us that if we reduce the rate of capital inputs by one unit, we have to increase the rate of labour input by more when factors are easily substitutable for each other then when they are ceteris paribus. Perhaps the easiest way to rationalise this is to recall that the more easily subsitutable are the factors for each other, the more similar they are from an economic point of view. If σ is low then the factors are dissimilar.

Advantages of CES Production Function over the Cobb-Douglas Production Function

(1) *CES* function represents a production function here all types of returns may be analysed. Since σ is not necessarily be equal to one ($\sigma \neq 1$), it represents a more general form of production techniques.

(2) As we have seen, the *CES* production function takes into consideration a number of important parameters. It, therefore, covers a wide range of variety, substitutability and efficiency.

(3) Estimation of this *CES* function is very easy. Of course, some transformation is needed, if we write output per unit of labour as a function of capital per unit of labour, that is,

$$\frac{X}{L} = f\left(\frac{K}{L}\right)$$

then this production function becomes very easy.

(4) It removes all the difficulties of Cobb-Douglas production function and is free from the unrealistic assumptions of the Cobb-Douglas production function.

Limitations of the CES Production Function

(1) The *CES* production function combines in one parameter two forces that affect it. In the first place, economies of scale can result from an expansion in the scale of operation for a given technology. Alternatively, given the scale of operation, a technological change can alter the rate of output. In empirical application both forces may affect the homogeneity parameter v, and it may not be possible to distinguish between them.

(2) Prof. H. Uzawa has attempted this function and concludes that it is difficult to generalise it to n-factors of production.

(3) A limitation of the *CES* production function is associated with its principal virtue the specification of elasticity of substitution which is invariant to changes in factor proportions. Recall that we have allowed the elasticity of substitution (σ) to changes in response to particular variations in the underlying technology not in response to changes in factor proportions. But this is an 'a priori specification'; we really do not know whether the elasticity of substitution (σ) should vary when factor proportions change. If the true structure

prescribes a variable elasticity due to changes in factor proportions and we claim that elasticity is changing for technology reasons then we are ascribing to technological change more than is due to it. Unless a completely general function is specified a polynomial of degree n i t seems this difficulty must be accepted. Since it is impossible with the available data and statistical techniques to obtain estimates of completely general production function and since they do not necessarily satisfy all neo-classical criteria (properties of *CES* function), we are forced for the immediate future to utilise the *CES* production function and live with the potential specification error.

(4) A fourth difficulty of this *CES* function is that *K*, the capital intensity parameter, is not dimensionless.

Besides these theoretical difficulties, there is an empirical problem; the *CES* production function is relatively difficult to fit to data.

Despite the above limitations, the *CES* production function is useful in its application to prove Euler's Theorem, to exhibit constant returns to scale to show that average and marginal product of capital (*K*) and labour (*L*) are homogeneous of degree zero, and to determine the elasticity of substitution.

6. Output Elasticity

If we deal with a production $X = f(L, K)$, then the output elasticity of input L is the ratio proportionate change in output (X) to the proportionate change in input (L), given the quantity of input K. Similarly, the output elasticity of input K is defined as the ratio of proportionate change in output (X) to proportionate change in input (K), given the quantity of input L. Mathematically,

$$E_{XL} = \frac{\Delta X/X}{\Delta L/L}$$

$$= \frac{\Delta X}{\Delta L} \cdot \frac{L}{X} \qquad \text{...(25)}$$

where ΔX = absolute in output X; ΔL= absolute change in input quantity L; X = initial

output; L = initial quantity of L

Similarly, output elasticity of input K can be written as,

$$E_{XK} = \frac{\Delta X/X}{\Delta K/K}$$

$$= \frac{\Delta X}{\Delta K} \cdot \frac{K}{X} \qquad \text{...(26)}$$

where ΔX = absolute change in output X; ΔK = absolute change in input K; X = initial output; K = initial quantity of input K.

Output elasticities can also be explained in terms of the ratios of the marginal and average productivities of the respective inputs. Hence, the output elasticity of input L is expressed as

$$E_{XL} = \frac{MP_L}{AP_L} \qquad \text{...(27)}$$

Similarly, output elasticity of input K is expressed as

$$E_{XK} = \frac{MP_K}{AP_K} \qquad \text{...(28)}$$

Now, if MP and AP are positive (i.e. $MP > 0$ and $AP > 0$), then the output elasticity is also positive.

The output elasticity of an input may be greater than, equal to or less than unity ($E_X > 1$ or $E_X = 1$ or $E_X < 1$) according as its MP is respectively greater than, equal to or less than its AP. The output elasticity can also be explained in terms of total productivity as the relations between MP, AP and TP are also known to us.

Further, the sum of output elasticities of input L and K would be equal to the degree of homogeneity. If the production function is homogeneous of degree one, then the sum of output elasticity of L and K also equals one.

7. Outlay Elasticity or Cost Elasticity

Total outlay is defined as the total cost which a firm is capable of incurring on labour and capital (if these are the only factor of production). If input prices (i.e. slope of the isocost lines) remain constant, an increase in the total outlay will enable the firm to increase the level of capital and labour, and thus to produce a higher level of output. However, increase in the total outlay does not necessarily result in an equivalent increase in the use of both the inputs. In fact the relative responsiveness of the usages of an input to a change in total outlay determines the nature of such an input. Such responsiveness is termed as the *outlay elasticity* or the *expenditure elasticity* Mathematically, it can be written as:

$$\eta_L = \frac{\Delta L/L}{\Delta C/C}$$

$$= \frac{\Delta L}{\Delta C} \cdot \frac{C}{L} \qquad \text{...(29)}$$

Similarly

$$\eta_K = \frac{\Delta K/K}{\Delta C/C}$$

$$= \frac{\Delta K}{\Delta C} \cdot \frac{C}{K} \qquad ...(30)$$

where η_2 and η_K represent the outlay elasticities with respect to labour (L) and capital (K) respectively.

In the above equations (29 and 30), $\frac{\Delta L}{\Delta C}$ shows the change in the level of labour input following a change in total outlay (C). Also $\frac{\Delta K}{\Delta C}$ represents the change in capital use in response to a change in total outlay (C).

Generally, an input level may be expected to change in the same proportion in which total outlay (C) changes. Such inputs are called *normal inputs.* On the other hand, a firm may increase the use of an input in a larger proportion than the (proportionate) increase in total outlay. Such inputs are known as *superior inputs.* Whereas in the case of normal inputs increase in total output is evenly distributed between both the labour and the capital, in case of superior inputs, a relatively larger share of overall increase in total outlay (assuming input prices unchanged) goes to one input (the superior one) and thus leaving the residual for the other input. Finally, there are *inferior inputs* whose use may actually decline despite an increase in total outlay.

Exercises

1. What is an isoquant? Explain its main properties.
2. What do you understand by Ridge Lines? How can you find out the economic region with the help of these ridge lines?
3. Explain the principle of diminishing marginal rate of technical substitution. What are its limitations?
4. Explain the producer's equilibrium position with the help of isoquants.
5. How does a firm succeed in securing the least-cost combination of the factors of production?
6. "Iso-product curves are the lines connecting all the points which yield the same product" Boulding. Discuss.
7. Explain the concept of 'returns to scale', with the help of isoquants.
8. Discuss the law of variable proportions with the help of isoproduct curves.
9. "The isoquant-isocost approach to production theory, like the traditional approach, explains the principles which underline costs, resource pricing and employment, resource allocation and product distribution." Explain the above statement with the help of diagrams.
10. Write brief notes on the following:
    (*i*) Production Possibility Curve,
    (*ii*) Expansion Path,
    (*iii*) Marginal Rate of Technical Substitution, and
    (*iv*) Marginal Rate of Product Transformation.
11. Explain output and substitution effects of a fall in the price of one input.
12. How does a firm get an optimum combination of two outputs? Illustrate your answer with the help of suitable diagrams.

13. Distinguish between returns to factor and return to scale. What will be the return to a factor if the returns to scale are increasing, constant and diminishing?
14. What is homogeneous production function? Discuss the properties of any such function.
15. Compare and contrast the Cobb-Douglas and *CES* production functions. Which of the two is conceptually superior and why?
16. Explain the following:
(*i*) Output Elasticity; (*ii*) Outlay Elasticity or Expenditure Elasticity; (*iii*) Factor Elasticity of Substitution.

Multiple Choice Questions

17. (*i*) Normally the isoquants slope
(*a*) upwards from left to right (*b*) upwards from right to left
(*c*) downwards from left to right (*d*) backwards from left to right [*Ans.* (*c*)]

(*ii*) An individual's production possibility boundary line
(*a*) contains all efficient combinations of productions
(*b*) forms boundary of the production possibility set
(*c*) indicates the marginal cost of an additional unit of either goods
(*d*) all of the above [*Ans.* (*d*)]

(*iii*) On a production-possibilities curve, the amount of *Y* foregone to produce another unit of *X* has been given a special name, what is it?
(*a*) substitute goods (*c*) opportunity cost
(*b*) production rate (*d*) price of production [*Ans.* (*c*)]

(*iv*) Imagine a firm employs the four factors of production namely *L, K, N* and *E*. The least cost combination of *L, K, N* and *E* will generally be the point at which
(*a*) $\frac{P_L}{P_K} = \frac{P_N}{P_E}$ (*c*) $P_L = P_K = P_N = P_E$
(*b*) $\frac{MP_L}{P_L} = \frac{MP_K}{P_K} = \frac{MP_N}{P_N} = \frac{MP_E}{P_E}$ (*d*) $MP_L = MP_K = MP_N = MP_E$ [*Ans.*(*b*)]

(*v*) Stage II of production function begins where the AP_L begins to decline
(*a*) always (*c*) sometimes
(*b*) never (*d*) often [*Ans.* (*a*)]

(*vi*) Within the relevant range, isoquants
(*a*) are negatively slopped (*c*) can not cross
(*b*) are convex to origin (*d*) all of the above [*Ans.* (*d*)]

(*vii*) If we plot capital on the vertical axis and labour on the horizontal axis, the slope of a straight line isocost curve drawn on such a graph is
(*a*) P_L/P_K (*c*) $-P_L/P_K$
(*b*) P_K/P_L (*d*) $-P_K/P_L$ [*Ans.* (*c*)]

(*viii*) At the point of producer's equilibrium
(*a*) the isoquant is tangent to the isocost curve
(*b*) $MRTS_{LK} = P_L/P_K$
(*c*) $MP_L/P_L = MP_K/P_K$
(*d*) all of the above [*Ans.* (*d*)]

(*ix*) The expansion path of production theory is analogous in consumption theory to the
(*a*) price consumption curve (*c*) income-consumption curve
(*b*) Engel curve (*d*) budget-constraint line [*Ans.* (*c*)]

(*x*) The elasticity of technical substitution is measured by
(*a*) the slope of the isoquant
(*c*) the ratio of factor inputs
(*b*) the change in the slope of the isoquant
(*d*) none of the above [*Ans.* (*d*)]

Chapter 19

Technical Progress and Production Function

1. Introduction

According to W.A. Lewis, "Economic growth or economic development depends both upon technological knowledge about things and living creatures, and also upon social knowledge about man and his relations with his fellowmen." One of the reasons of the economic backwardness of underdeveloped countries is low level of technological advancements. Economic development and technological advancements are positively correlated to one another. In the absence of technological advancement high rate of steady economic growth can not be ensured. A specific level of technological advancement is a necessary pre-requirement for rapid economic development and it is therefore this level of technology that acts as the index of economic development in the country.

The task of technological changes in underdeveloped countries is quite difficult because the social set-up is not conducive to technological improvements on any significant scale. It is fully accepted that in the absence of adequate technological changes, it will not be possible to accelerate rate of economic growth. Thus, efforts must be made to explore new technology in the underdeveloped economies from the industrially advanced economies.

2. Meaning of Technological Change

Generally speaking by the term 'technological change' we mean a change in the production function embodying all known techniques. It involves a change in the actual production function of a given enterprise. Such a change permits more product for the same resources or the same amount of product for less resources. This may be in the form of a new product yielding more utility rather than just

1. Charles Kindleberger, *Economic Development,* p. 95.

a larger amount of an old product.[1] In the context of economic development, technical change may be considered as any change in production methods used in an enterprise or industry and thus, it is synonymous with innovation. But a mere improvement in technical know-how cannot be called technical change. Some of the economists prefer a wider interpretation of the term technological change and they include within it the sociological changes that precede and make possible the technological change in a society. According to Frankel, "Technological change is not a mere improvement in the technical know-how. It means much more than this. It should be preceded by sociological change also, a willingness and desire on the part of the community to modify their social, political and administrative institutions so as to make them fit in with new techniques of production and the faster tempo of economic activity."[2] Thus, technological changes imply basic change in production function embodying all known techniques. It implies a change in actual production function of a given enterprise. This change may assume the form of a new product yielding more utility rather than just a larger amount of an old product.

Thus, in the context of economic development technological change may be conceived of as any change in production methods employed in an industry and is therefore synonym with innovation. A mere improvement in technical know-how can not be called technical change. Most economists include all the sociological changes that proceed and make the technological changes in the society possible.

3. Role of Technology in Economic Development

Level of technology is an important determinant of economic development in a country. It is only through higher technology that a rapid rate of economic growth can be attained. Technological change is the prime mover in the course of economic development. According to Prof. Schumpeter, innovation or technological progress is the only determinant of economic progress. If level of technology becomes constant, the process of growth will stop. It is technological progress that keeps the economy moving. Inventions and innovations have largely been responsible for rapid economic growth in developed countries.

The growth of real income in developed countries has taken place at rates that cannot be explained in terms of capital alone. A large part of this is due to increased productivity which has been the result of technological change.[3] Robert Solow estimated that 'technical change' accounted for about two-thirds of growth of the US economy, after allowing for growth in the labour force and capital stock. According to Dewhurst, "Technology, in fact,

2. Herbert S. Frankel, *Economic Impact of Underdeveloped Countries,* 1953, pp. 22-23.
3. Charles P. Kindleberger, *op. cit.,* p. 76.

can be thought of as the primary resource." Thus, technological change can contribute significantly in the economic development of underdeveloped countries. The impact of technological change on production function can be illustrated with the help of the diagram as in Fig. 19.1.

In Figure 19.1, we represent capital along the *Y*-axis and labour along the *X*-axis. In all the panels of Fig. 19.1, *Iq* is an isoquant of the production function before technological change, and Iq_1 represents the same quantities of output (100 units of *X*) after the innovation. In panel (*a*) innovation is neutral with respect to the two inputs of labour and capital. It means that no innovation takes place with respect to labour and capital. The new production function Iq_1 shows that the same output can be produced with less labour and less capital after technological advancement. In panel (*b*) the innovation is labour saving and Iq_1 shows that the same output can be produced with lesser inputs but the saving of labour is greater than that of capital. In panel (*c*) the innovation is capital saving and Iq_1 shows that the same output can be produced by less inputs after technological change but the saving of capital is greater than that of labour.

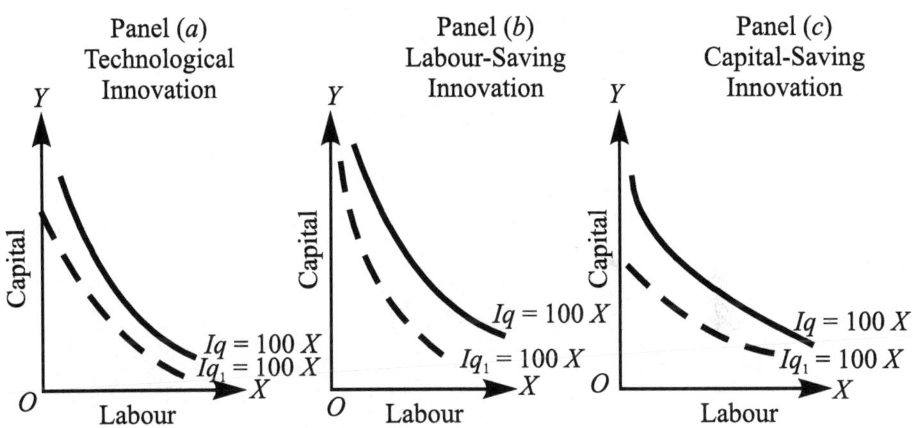

Fig. 19.1

Technological advance is even more important than capital formation. Capital formation alone can bring out economic development only to a limited extent and after sometime that progress stops if there is no technical change. Thus, in the process of economic development, technical advance is likely to outstrip thrift alone. It means that capital formation alone can ensure economic development to a limited extent thereafter it becomes to cessation. And later becomes dependent on the import of technology. A nation that spends more on science and technical research will tend to grow faster than another country accumulating more capital but spending less on technological development. This can be illustrated with the help of the diagram as in Fig.19.2.

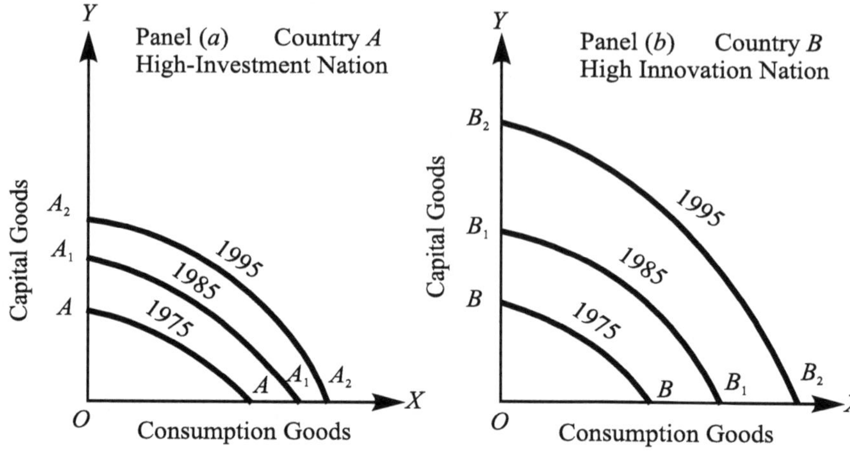

Fig. 19.2

In Figure 19.2 panel (*a*) country *A* is thrifty and advances by accumulating more capital goods. In Fig 19.2 panel (*b*) country *B* advances both with technical progress and capital accumulation. It is clear that the progress of country *B* from 1975 to 1985 is faster than that of country *A* which is due to high rate of technological development. From 1985 to 1995 it grows still faster, both methods, i.e. technical progress and capital formation.

The contention that technological progress is more important than capital formation can also be illustrated with the help of production function diagram as in Fig. 19.3.

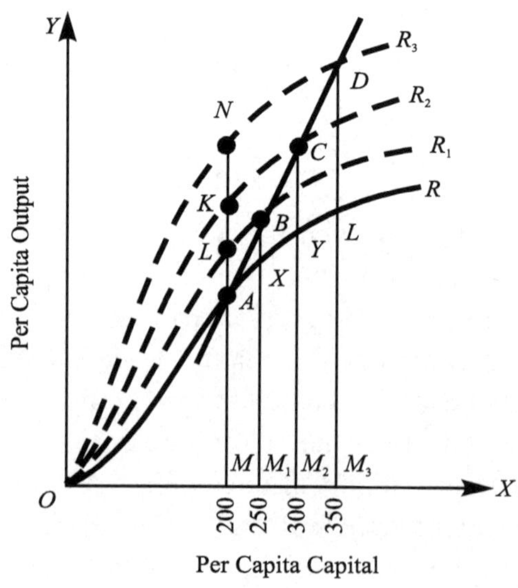

Fig. 19.3

In Figure 19.3, *OR* represents the production function which rises to OR_1, OR_2 and OR_3 with technological progress. On the production function *OR* if the amount of capital per worker is raised from \$200 to \$250 the output per worker is increased from *AM* to XM_1. When capital per unit of labour is \$350 the output per labour is ZM_3. The main characteristic of technical progress is that it makes possible a better utilisation of labour and other resources and hence the production function shifts upwards which means that more output per labourer can be obtained by the same amount of capital per worker. While the quantity of capital per labourer remains at \$200 the production per labourer goes on increasing from *AM* to *NM* due to the upward shifting of the production function. Similarly more can be produced at other levels of capital intensity. Technological progress results in shifting the production function upwards which enables more output per labourer with the same amount of capital per worker. Hence technological change can be an important source of economic development in a country.

4. Process of Technological Change

As we know, technological change consists in devising new goods and new ways of producing existing goods and services. The development of new technical knowledge can be defined as the growth of that new knowledge with the help of which goods can be produced at lesser cost; entirely new goods can be produced; new uses of goods can be discovered or new resources can be discovered. The process of growth of technical knowledge can be broken into following stages:

(*a*) Formulation of scientific principles.

(*b*) Application of these principles to given technical problems.

(*c*) Development of technical inventions to the point of commercial exploitation.

In the process of technological evolution the first stage is that of an advancement in scientific knowledge, the second is that of the application of this knowledge to some useful purpose and the third is that of the commercialisation of invention which may also be called innovation. Innovation has got special significance in the process of development of a country.

Innovation has to be clearly distinguished from invention. According to Prof. Schumpeter invention is the discovery of the new technique while innovation is the practical application of an invention in production for the market. It may also be called the commercialisation of an invention which springs from scientific advancement. While invention is a scientific fact, innovation is an economic fact. Invention is performed by inventors while innovation is the task of entrepreneurs. Innovation requires large capital investments at every stage, it needs not only a scientific attitude and bent on the part of the community but also an entrepreneurial skill of a high order with the ability to understand the possibilities of using scientific inventions for commercial purposes. The existence of expanding markets for the new product is also an important condition for the commercialisation of an invention.

5. Role of Entrepreneur

The entrepreneur or the innovator performs a very important function in bringing about technological development in the society. He has been the disseminator of technical knowledge. Unless new men come forward, interested in new goods and prepared to attempt new ways of doing and ready to assume the risks involved in the process of technological change, technological development will not be possible. If economic growth is to ensure from the application of technology, then some individual or group of individuals must act to put this new combination of resources in productive activity into effect. Some individual or group of individuals must make decisions required to replace old methods with new ones. This act has been called innovation and is an important entrepreneurial function.

Innovation is essential for rapid economic development. It has been a major factor in the economic growth of developed countries like USA, UK and Japan. It appears to be of growing importance in countries like India and China. Economic growth is bound to be slow unless there is an adequate supply of entrepreneurs looking out for new ideas and willing to take the risk of introducing them. "Entrepreneurs are stimulated to innovate by the desire for social success, by the hope of big profits or by the fear of great losses if they fail to innovate." Economic development is so intimately connected with the entrepreneurial function that they are sometimes defined as those who institute 'new combination.' The new combinations may involve new product, a new method of production, development of new market, the utilisation of new sources of productive factors or new forms of organisation.

In the past technological change took place without conscious change as the entrepreneurs found technological change profitable but now there is an awareness of the importance of technology and conscious efforts are being made by the governments to find the technological gap between countries. Under the capitalistic system the economic inducement to invention are a desire: (1) to share in widening markets, (2) to solve practical production problems, and (3) to take advantage of changes in relative prices. The inducement for the government to take initiative in this field seems to be the desire for military dominance as well as the social goal of increased productivity.

6. Types of Entrepreneurs

In order to understand the nature of entrepreneurial function that is necessary to stimulate the process of economic development and to increase the supply of suitable types of entrepreneurs, it is useful to classify the entrepreneurs on the basis of the functions performed by them. Danhof has classified entrepreneurs under the following heads:

(1) *Innovating Entrepreneurs.* This class includes those entrepreneurs who are always ready to put into practice the attractive possibilities at the first instance. They are aggressive in experimentation and the first to put new inventions into practice. They are actually the leaders of the process of technological change and hence their function is specially important in a developing society.

(2) *Imitative Entrepreneurs.* These entrepreneurs are always ready to adopt successful innovations initiated by the innovating entrepreneurs. This type of entrepreneurs are merely the followers of the successful entrepreneurs.

(3) *Fabian Entrepreneurs.* In this class are included those entrepreneurs who are very cautious in adopting new innovations. They adopt innovation only when it becomes clear to them that by not adopting them they will be losing their position in the enterprise.

(4) *Drone Entrepreneurs.* These entrepreneurs do not adopt new methods and inventions even when their income is reduced as compared to other producers.

For efficient technological advancement in a country innovating and imitating entrepreneurs are very necessary because it is they who initiate and carry forward the process of technical change. Thus, the major problem in the process of economic development is to increase the supply of innovating entrepreneurs and their followers.

7. Supply of Innovating Entrepreneurs

The rate of technological advance in a society depends upon the supply of innovating entrepreneurs. Entrepreneurship is a quality that is found in some members of the population which enable them to carry on the entrepreneurial activities. The supply of entrepreneurs is intimately connected to the motivations for innovations existing within the society. Few entrepreneurs will emerge if the motivation to induce output raising innovations is weak. The supply of entrepreneurs in a society can be increased by: (*a*) an expansion of the number of people possessing the entrepreneurial requisites, and (*b*) an increase in the capacities of the existing entrepreneurs.

The acquisition of requisite entrepreneurial skills by the people depends upon: (*i*) the innate ability, training and motivation of the people, and (*ii*) access to opportunities. The access to opportunities is an important determinant of the size of the entrepreneurial group. It depends upon the social and economic position of a person. Entrepreneurs generally come from upper class and hence their number will have a tendency to decline due to lower fertility of this group. The number of people having access to opportunity will increase only if there is economic and social mobility which depends upon the extent of economic expansion in the society.

The desire to acquire necessary entrepreneurial capacities and to engage in such activities depend upon the rewards for such activities. The greater the rewards for entrepreneurial activities the larger will be the number of people entering such activities. The rewards will depend upon the attitude of the community towards the entrepreneurial function. The desire to acquire entrepreneurial ability will also depend on the disappearance of alternative opportunities. The drying up of alternative economic and social opportunities in agriculture, civil service and non-entrepreneurial jobs will force the people to acquire abilities for the entrepreneurial job.

Another thing necessary for the growth of the entrepreneurial group is to increase the capacities of those who are already in the entrepreneurial group. It is a self-accelerating process-successful experience increases the capacities of the entrepreneurs. It brings in more capital for further investment and also increases one's ability to promote and organise new enterprises.

8. Technological Gap between the Rich and the Poor Countries

Underdeveloped countries can be termed as technologically backward countries. Their economies are low productivity economies as they have been operating on a lower level of technology. In these countries the techniques, particularly in agriculture, have stagnated for centuries. On the other hand, technology has grown very fast in advanced countries and the technological gap between the rich and the poor countries has been continuously widening. The rapid technological development in advanced countries has been due to the existence of inducements for invention and discovery and suitable socio-economic environment for undertaking the entrepreneurial function. In underdeveloped countries these conditions have largely been absent and the socio-cultural rigidities have prevented the people to assume the innovational role. Because of all these reasons these countries continue to be technologically backward. Speaking of the technological gap between countries, Dedijer points out that 95 per cent of the world's scientific research at the present time, is concentrated in approximately 30 of the advanced countries. The other 100 countries, encompassing two-thirds of the world's population, share the remaining 5 per cent between them. Bhabha also concludes that "what the developed countries have and the underdeveloped countries lack is modern science and an economy based on modern technology. The problem of developing the underdeveloped countries is, therefore, the problem of establishing modern science in them and transforming their economies to one based on modern science and technology."[4]

9. Problem of Technological Change in Underdeveloped Countries

Technological change is the foundation on which the process of economic development in underdeveloped countries must rest. With the vast store of technology that has been discovered and applied elsewhere, the need for technological change in developing countries has become most urgent. Positive motivations to induce innovations need to be increased and the resistance to the entrepreneurial function is to be minimised. There is hardly any hope of the modern technology automatically spreading to the broader fields of the economy of an underdeveloped country. Technological change in underdeveloped countries is a difficult process and requires special efforts on the part of the people and governments of these countries. According to a United Nations study: "Unless a special effort is made, the process of technological development in the underdeveloped countries will be relatively slow and the gap in technology will continue to grow wider as the cumulative scientific progress of the developed countries accelerates."[5]

The problem of technical change is not merely one of introducing new methods of production, and the instruments and tools or machines but it also involves a vast change in social beliefs and practices. Certain far reaching changes will have to be made to acquire technical changes. Knowledge has to grow; capital has to be created afresh on the basis of continuous experiment, and new hopes and beliefs have to be evolved to urge men and women to move forward.[6] The process of technical change becomes all the more difficult because we know very little of the processes involved in the change of the aptitudes of the people required for the purpose, of the time they may take, and the obstacles they encounter. Prof. Nurkse also speaks of the difficulty of adopting new methods of production. He observes that "it is much easier to

4. H.J. Bhabha, from a speech to the International Council of Scientific Union in Bombay, January 1966.
5. United Nations, *Measures for the Economic Development of Underdeveloped Countries,* 1951, p. 28.
6. Okun and Richardson, *Studies in Economic Development,* p. 412.

adopt superior consumption habits than improved production methods. Hence, fashions in consumption can spread more quickly than techniques of production."[7]

Inspite of various difficulties the process of technological change must be initiated in underdeveloped countries. For this, it is necessary at first to identify those branches of the economy which are in most urgent need of technological change. For this, combined efforts of a team of scientists, engineers and economists will be needed. The next step is to decide upon the most appropriate technologies for a particular situation in any country. Choice of appropriate technology is the most difficult job. The problem of definition and choice of 'appropriate technologies' is one of the most challenging in the entire field of economic development.[8] It is usually suggested that sufficient technologies exist in the world to meet all the needs of the developing countries for many years to come and that only a transfer of technology from the rich to the poor countries is required. It is also emphasised that if the appropriate technologies do not exist it is better that the research be done by the developed countries and the results be exported. These observations suggest that the problem of technological change in underdeveloped countries is merely a problem of transfer of modern technology from advanced countries to these countries. But it is difficult to agree with this contention and it has to be admitted that technological change is something more than a mere transfer of technology from the advanced to the backward countries. It also involves the evolution of suitable techniques in underdeveloped countries and the adaptation of imported technology to local conditions.

10. Choice of Technology

The choice of appropriate technology in underdeveloped countries is a difficult job. It is not possible to suggest a uniform pattern of technology for all the underdeveloped countries because they differ widely from each other in regard to factor endowments, level of income and capital formation, demographic patterns, institutional arrangements and stage of economic development. But it is possible to lay down certain considerations which must be kept in mind while making a choice of technology in a country. The following considerations are the most important ones in this respect.

(1) *Factor Endowment.* The prevailing factor endowment in a country will largely determine the type of technology that will be suitable for that country. If the country has abundance of labour and scarcity of capital then labour intensive techniques of production must be selected. On the other hand in labour scarce and capital abundant economies, labour saving and capital

---

7. Ragnar Nurlese, *Problems of Capital Formation in Underdeveloped Countries,* p. 62.
8. Gerald M. Meier, *Economic Development,* p. 323.

intensive techniques will be most appropriate. Thus, the type of factor endowment in a country is an important consideration in the choice of technology. As factor endowment cannot be altered in a short period, therefore, technology has to be adjusted to the prevailing factor endowment.

(2) *Technological Level Already Attained.* The prevailing level of technology forms the basis on which further technological change can take place. New technology has to be supported by the existing technology and hence only that type of technology should be adopted by a country which can be supported and nourished by the technology level already attained by the country. Abrupt changes in technology may not be in the interest of the economy.

(3) *Resources Available.* Technological development in a country is largely determined by the availability of resources for such development. The most important resource necessary for technological development is capital. In addition to that, skill, organisation and natural resources are also required. The availability of all these inputs largely determines the extent to which experimentation in new techniques and new forms of organisation can be undertaken. An over-ambitious programme of technological change will merely result in waste of productive resources of the country. Hence the technology to be adopted must be in accordance with the availability of necessary inputs.

(4) *Institutional Structure.* The institutional framework in a country also determines the type of technology that should be adopted by it. Economic, political and social institutions along with the aptitude of the people determine the technological level in a country. Spirit of indifference towards economic achievements cannot be very conducive for research and innovation and hence the level of technology will necessarily be low. The social system in a country may be rigid as not to permit any technological change. Under these circumstances social and institutional change must precede technological change.

11. Import of Technology and Underdeveloped Countries

It has widely been accepted that a mere transfer of modern technology from advanced to backward countries will not solve the problem of technological change in these countries. The type of technology developed in advanced countries cannot be very suitable and appropriate under the circumstances prevailing in underdeveloped countries. Hence the imported techniques have to be adapted to local conditions with suitable changes in them or appropriate techniques have to be developed by the underdeveloped countries. Most of the underdeveloped countries have got a vast reservoir of unemployed manpower and hence the labour saving and capital intensive techniques developed in the advanced countries do not suit to the underdeveloped countries.

Today underdeveloped countries have got the special advantage of importing already developed techniques from the advanced countries, but this has created several problems for them. The techniques they have to adopt have been evolved in advanced countries with a different economic. set-up and with a different factor supply situation. Hence, the modern technological knowledge gets super-imposed on a retrograde economic and social system. In view of the paucity of complementary factors like trained personnel, entrepreneurial ability and financial resources, adoption of modern technology in underdeveloped countries tends not only to be less productive and more expensive but it also causes a certain dislocation in the economy. The use of advanced technology requires highly trained manpower with scientific skill and understanding which is largely lacking in these countries. Hence, the underdeveloped countries cannot be much benefitted by the advanced technology of the West. There are "instances of production equipment which is well suited to the needs of industrialised countries but whose performance fails to measure upto expectations in the industrial environment of underdeveloped economies."[9]

The above analysis indicates the fact that the underdeveloped countries should not try to put themselves on the technological level of the industrially advanced countries. Present day western technology does not suit them. The technology which was suited to present day developed countries some years ago, say a century ago, would be suitable for underdeveloped countries of today. Perhaps techniques practised in a country which has not advanced to the level of highly industrialised countries of the West and where small scale production still continues to occupy a prominent place in the nation's economy, such as Japan, would be in a better position to meet the particular needs of pre-industrial economies.[10]

Imported technology is not only a misfit in the circumstances prevailing in the underdeveloped countries but it is also highly wasteful. The high initial investment required to introduce the highly sophisticated technique causes a severe strain on the financial resources of these countries. Moreover, most of the machinery has to be imported from advanced countries which drains away the precious and meagre foreign exchange resources of the developing countries. Another waste involved in the use of advanced technology is that the effective life of the imported expensive equipment in underdeveloped countries is likely to be much shorter due to the inexperience in handling the equipment, lack of technical skill and lack of proper maintenance.

Conclusively it can be stated that mere transfer of modern technology

---

9. UNO, *Industrial Enterprises in Underdeveloped Countries,* 1958, p. 177.
10. D.B. Singh, *Economic Development of Underdeveloped Countries,* p. 99.

from advanced to backward countries cannot solve the problem of their development. The problem is not that of transplanting technology available in industrially advanced countries. Imported technology has to be tested and adapted to the particular environment and needs of the underdeveloped countries. If appropriate technology is not available, it should be evolved by the scientists and technologists of the developing countries. Fresh researches are to be undertaken by these countries in fields in which developed countries are not interested. Besides, if at all, it is deemed imperative to import technology, it should be adapted to particular environments arid requirement of these countries.

Exercises

1. What do you mean by technological change? Explain neutral, capital-saving and labour-saving technical progress with the help of diagrams.
2. Explain the role of technology in the economic development of a country.
3. "Technological progress is more important than capital formation." Explain the statement with the help of a diagram.
4. Discuss the process of technological change.
5. "The entrepreneur peforms a very important function in bringing about technological development in the society." Explain the statement.
6. "Innovation is essential for rapid economic development." Explain.
7. Explain the technological gap between the rich and the poor countries. What is the problem of technological change in underdeveloped countries?
8. Explain the choice of technology for an underdeveloped economy. How far foreign technology is suitable for underdeveloped economies?

Multiple Choice Questions

9. (*i*) Economic development and technological advancements are
   (*a*) negatively correlated
   (*c*) uncorrelated
   (*b*) positively correlated
   (*d*) linearly correlated [*Ans.* (*b*)]

   (*ii*) Technological change means
   (*a*) more product for the same resources
   (*b*) the same amount of product with less resources
   (*c*) innovation
   (*d*) all of the above [*Ans.* (*d*)]

   (*iii*) According to Prof. Schumpeter which is not true?
   (*a*) invention is the discovery of the new technique
   (*b*) innovation is the practical application of an invention in production for the market
   (*c*) innovation is the commercialisation of an invention
   (*d*) innovation and invention both are one and the same thing [*Ans.* (*d*)]

   (*iv*) Technological efficiency
   (*a*) is the same thing as economic efficiency
   (*b*) is achieved when the output produced is maximum for the given level of inputs
   (*c*) is mainly an engineering or scientific problem
   (*d*) means that there is only one way to produce a given quantity of output
   [*Ans.* (*b*)]

PART FOUR

PRODUCT PRICING

Chapter 20

Nature of Costs and Elasticity of Costs

1. Introduction

Until now we were discussing the physical relationships between inputs and the output. These relationships have been summarised in the law of non-proportional outputs. Thus, the physical side of production can be translated into money costs of production by assigning prices to the resources (inputs) used. In this chapter we will look at production from the standpoint of a single business firm.

2. The Concept of Costs

Generally, the costs of production are assumed to be the money expenditure incurred by the business firm for the resources used to produce its product output. In other words, the ordinary accounting statements of costs cover only the money costs incurred in production, such as, the payments made for buying raw materials, rent for building, wage for labour, hiring of transportation and payments made for taxes, etc. Such accounting statements do not present a real picture of total costs of production. The firm's actual expenditures on resources constitute only a part of total cost. In economics the word 'cost' is given a special meaning, which is much broader than the sense in which a firm or the accounting authority uses it. Prof. Alfred Marshall made a distinction between the cost of production and the expenses (expenditures) of production by saying that "All the efforts and sacrifices made by the producer is the real costs of production while the money paid (to other factors of production) for these efforts is termed as the expenses of production."[1]

In general, what is called a cost is a payment made, or a sacrifice incurred, in order that a benefit may be secured. Regarded from the viewpoint of the

1. Alfred Marshall, *Principles of Economics* (Eighth Edition), pp. 282-83.

entire society, costs fall into two categories: (*i*) Factors of production are called into use, excluding any benefit which might arise from non-use. Thus, workers enjoy leisure when not working. (*ii*) Factors of production are withdrawan from productive uses, so that society loses their alternative products. Costs to individual producer or the business firm can be regarded in the same two ways. Either they can be looked upon as resources that are called into use, excluding benefits from non-use, or else they are assessed in terms of forgone alternative products.

In this context, we shall discuss the following two doctrines of economic costs: (1) The Opportunity Cost or Alternative Cost Doctrine; and (2) Explicit and Implicit Costs.

1. The Opportunity Cost or Alternative Cost Doctrine

Practically, every factor of production has many possible uses. Since it is scarce, it is impossible to employ it fully in all of them. To use it for anyone purpose means to forgo the opportunity of applying it to other purposes. Its use, therefore, costs whatever it might have been worth if it had been put to its possible alternative uses. An enterpriser in one industry must, then, pay for his factors of production as much as his competitors in other industries (or, for that matter, in his own industry) are willing to pay. The combined bidding of all the competitors for the limited supply of the factors of production thus establishes prices for them which, as we know, constitute the costs of production. This is known as the doctrine of opportunity cost. It may be stated as follows: the use of any factor in production involves a cost which is equal to the prices offered for that factor in its possible alternative uses.

Thus, economists define the cost of production of a particular product as the value of the forgone alternative products that resources used in its production could have produced. The costs of resources to a firm are their values in their best alternative uses. For example, a certain fixed amount of labour can be used in the production of either washing machines or refrigerators. Now the cost of the labour in the manufacture of washing machines is the value of refrigerators that the labour could have produced. Unless the manufacturer of washing machines pays that amount for the labour, it will go into or remain in refrigerator production. The principle of opportunity costs is very significant in the decision making of the productive firms.

In business management, frequently there are two or more opportunities for utilising factors of production, whether these are supplied by the enterpriser himself or procured from others. Choices are made whenever the enterpriser is confronted by alternative uses. At the time a worker is hired, the entrepreneur has a choice between hiring and not hiring. The opportunity cost of the labour at this time is the money outlay necessary to secure the worker's services. Once the labour has been hired, for the period of his contracted service the contracted wage no longer represents a practical alternative for the entrepreneur. The opportunities for utilizing the labour's services, now open to the entrepreneur, are the various employments which he has available for the labour, or the possibility of paying the worker to stand idle. The entrepreneur who aims at maximising his profit or minimising his loss will make his calculations on this basis. For instance, a building contractor may have an employee for whose services he has a year's contract, at a wage of $500 a month. During a slack season the contractor may have no employment for this labour. A local park service offers to pay the contractor $300 a month for the labour's service. Now $300 is a real alternative; but not the $500 since the employer's contract with the worker requires $500 to be paid regardless of how the labour is used. Thus, the doctrine of opportunity cost is very important in the decision making of the enterprisers.

The concept of opportunity cost can also be explained diagrammetically as in Fig. 20.1. In Figure 20.1, PP_1 is the production possibility curve which indicates the different combinations of labour and capital necessary to produce a given level of output. At point *R,* the producer employs *OL* units of labour and *OK* units of capital to produce a certain level of output. Now if he goes to point *S* then he employs more of labour and less of capital to produce the same level of output. Thus, at point *S*, he employs LL_1 more of labour and forgoes KK_1 units of capital. Thus, the opportunity cost of LL_1 quantity of labour is KK_1 quantity of capital.

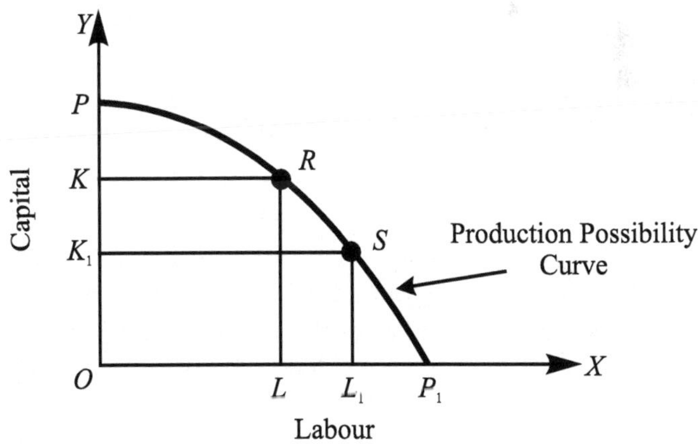

Fig. 20.1

Significance of Opportunity Cost Concept

The concept of opportunity cost is widely used in solving economic problems. Some of the points may be mentioned as follows:

(*i*) The concept of opportunity cost is applied in the determination of factor prices; i.e. rent, wages and interest, etc.

(*ii*) It is applied to explain the theory of comparative costs in the field of international trade.

(*iii*) It explains the consumer's surplus as well as the producer's surplus.

(*iv*) The Government makes use of it in the determination of various policies such as the policies related to expenditure and taxation, etc.

(*v*) It is also applied in the determination of consumer's equilibrium where the consumer wants to maximise his total utility function.

Limitations of Opportunity Cost Concept

The concept of opportunity cost has got the following limitations also:

(*i*) It can not be applied to those factors of production whose supply is fixed, i.e. in the case of specific factors of production which have no alternatives at their disposal and in such cases the opportunity cost becomes zero.

(*ii*) If the factors of production are immobile because of one reason or the other, then the concept of opportunity cost can not be applied. Sometimes the factors of production are prevented going abroad or entering into some field then this concept may not be applied, because their prices do not reflect the opportunity cost.

(*iii*) When the forgone alternative is not ascertainable then the concept of opportunity cost can not be applied.

(*iv*) This concept is based on the assumption of perfect competition which is not found in practical life.

2. Explicit and Implicit Costs

The modern economists divide the costs of production into two parts: (*i*) Explicit costs (overhead costs or money costs), and (*ii*) Implicit costs (or imputed costs). Explicit costs refer to the expenses incurred by a firm on buying the productive services owned by other factors of production. In other words, explicit costs are the contractual money payments that a firm makes to the factor owners. It hires workers and pays them wages. Similarly, the payments of interest for the capitalist, rent for the land owner, etc. are the contractual payments made by the firm. Besides, it spends money on raw materials, fuels, power, transportation and advertising. It also pays a number of taxes to the government. All these payments are termed as explicit costs of production. The ordinary accounting statements usually cover the *explicit or the money costs of production.* Alfred Marshall called them the expenses of production.

Implicit costs (or non-expenditure costs) on the other hand, do not involve any contractual payment made by the firm to any outsider; These may be the evaluation of the firm's own efforts and sacrifices incurred in production. More specifically, the *implicit costs* or the *imputed costs* refer to the reward which the firm would realise for self-owned, self-employed resources. According to Leftwich, the entrepreneur's salary as a cost can be easily explained. In accordance with the alternative cost doctrine the cost of single producer's services in producing his product is the forgone alternative product which would have been produced had he worked for someone else in a similar capacity. We consider as a part of the firm's costs, then, a salary for the entrepreneur equal to the value of his sevices in his best alternative employment. The other important implicit costs are depreciation of capital goods and a normal return on money capital invested by the firm. As far as the depreciation charges are concerned, some economists assume it as implicit costs because they are not contractual and accrue to the firm itself. But other economists, including Leftwich, consider the depreciation charges as explicit costs because according to them a cost accounting authority counts them as the firm's operating expenses. In fact, implicit costs include the normal return on his (entrepreneur's) investment, and the opportunity cost (alternative earnings) of his own labour.

Thus, for microeconomic analysis a more realistic approach of costs of production is to add both the explicit costs and the implicit or imputed costs of production. To make the approach still more realistic, the modern economists prefer to add 'normal profit' to the implicit and the explicit costs of production. According to Prof. Boulding, in economic analysis the concept of cost includes a normal profit because it is only after profit's inclusion in cost that an entrepreneur can show his incentive to combine different factors of production and offer certain quantity of the product for sale. Thus, total cost of production of a commodity is the sum total of (*i*) explicit costs, (*ii*) implicit costs, and (*iii*) normal profit.[2]

3. Vihaviour of Costs Over Time

As already mentioned, a cost function is defined as the relationship between costs and output. The production function of a firm and the prices it pays for its factor inputs determine the firm's cost function. As a production function may take different forms (with either one or some or all of the inputs variable), likewise a cost function may also take different forms. The two important cost functions are the short-run cost function and the long-run cost function.

Short-run is defined as that period of time in which some inputs are fixed in amount and the firm can expand or contract its output only by varying the amounts of other (variable) inputs. In the short-run, the firm attempts to minimise the cost of variable inputs. In other words, it tries to obtain the least cost combination of inputs. Output can range from zero, where the firm has to bear a maximum loss of the fixed inputs. Thus, in the short-run the firm's

2. K.F. Boulding, *Economic Analysis Vol. 1: Microeconomics,* p. 250.

decision making rests in the minimisation of the costs of variable inputs. In the long run, all inputs are variable in amount, a firm's output can range from zero to an infinitely large quantity. In other words, in the long-run the firm is capable of identifying the most efficient scales of its operation.

Now we shall explain the nature of short-run and long-run cost curves under the following section.

4. Short-run Cost Curves

Since in the short-run firm has fixed as well as variable inputs, short-run costs of the firm are also divided into fixed costs and variable costs.

Symbolically, $TC = TFC + TVC$

Total Fixed Costs (*TFC*) are, by definition, "fixed", that is whose total amount remains constant over a range of output. Having been incurred, it is sunk or remains unalterable with respect to a particular output range. In other words, total fixed costs exist no matter how much the firm produces. They consist of overhead expenses such as interest charges, depreciation of machinery and the plant, maintenance, and similar items.

Total Variable Costs (*TVC*) are those costs whose total amount changes with output. As the firm increases its level of production, it must purchase greater amounts of raw materials, hire more labour, use more fuel, etc. As output increases, these costs increase and vice versa. The variable costs will shrink to zero if operations are suspended, because then no materials need be purchased and none but the irreducible maximum of maintenance workers need be hired.

In fact, there is no sharp dividing line between fixed and variable costs. The one shades off into the other, so that the difference is one of degree, rather than of kind.For instance, interest on bonds will not change at all during the life of the bonds, but depreciation and executive staff are likely to vary a little as output is changed; fuel will vary considerably, but is hardly likely to increase or decrease as much as output; while raw materials and manual labour must change in very close correspondence with variations in the product. Here, then, are four different degrees of fixity and variability. In the long-run, all costs are variable, given time for old plant to wear out and new plant to be constructed, the size of the plant will be adjusted to the demand, involving greater or less costs for interest, taxes, etc. as the case may be. For the present, we are concerned with shorter periods, in which the plant is a fixed factor for the time being.

Thus, in the short-run, total cost is the sum of total fixed costs and total variable costs. These are indicated in Table 20.1 and in Fig. 20.2. It is important to note the trend of *TVC* (Total Variable Cost) curve in Fig. 20.2. The curve rises rapidly at first, then its slope becomes less and then rises rapidly again why is this? Since in the short-run period different quantities of variable factors are combined with a given scale of plant, law of variable proportions comes into play. As variable factor inputs are increased, physical marginal returns to the same increase in the first phase, are constant for a while and then begin

Table 20.1 *(in $s.)*

Quantity of X	*Total Fixed Cost (TFC)*	*Total Variable Cost (TVC)*	*Total Cost (TC = TFC +TVC)*
0	500	—	500
1	500	200	700
2	500	240	740
3	500	270	770
4	500	298	798
5	500	324	824
6	500	350	850
7	500	386	886
8	500	430	930
9	500	480	980
10	500	576	1,076
11	500	736	1,236
12	500	966	1,466

to decline. Consequently, as the total output increases from zero to upwards, the total variable inputs and hence costs increase at a falling rate to begin with, at a constant rate for a while and finally at an increasing rate. Thus, up to five units of output in Table 20.1, and Fig. 20.2, the successive increases in total variable cost (*TVC*) are smaller and smaller. For fifth and sixth units the successive increases in *TVC* are constant. Beyond six units of output the successive increases become larger and larger. It is because of this behaviour that in Fig. 20.2, the *TVC* curve is concave to the *X*-axis in the early stage and after a certain level of output it becomes convex to the *X*-axis. The *TC* (Total Cost) curve is nothing but the *TVC* curve and the *TFC* curve added vertically at each point. The vertical distance between *TC* and *TVC*, therefore, is constant throughout and is equal to *TFC*.[3]

3. The short-run total cost function can be defined in mathematical terms as below:

$$C = a + f(X)$$

where C = Total cost, a = Total fixed cost, $f(X)$ = Total variable cost.

Per Unit Cost Curves

Per unit cost curves are used fairly for the determination of output and price. The per unit cost curves are of following types:

(*i*) Average Fixed Cost (*AFC*) curve,

(*ii*) Average Variable Cost (*AVC*) curve,

(*iii*) Average Cost (*AC*) curve, and

(*iv*) Marginal Cost (*MC*) curve.

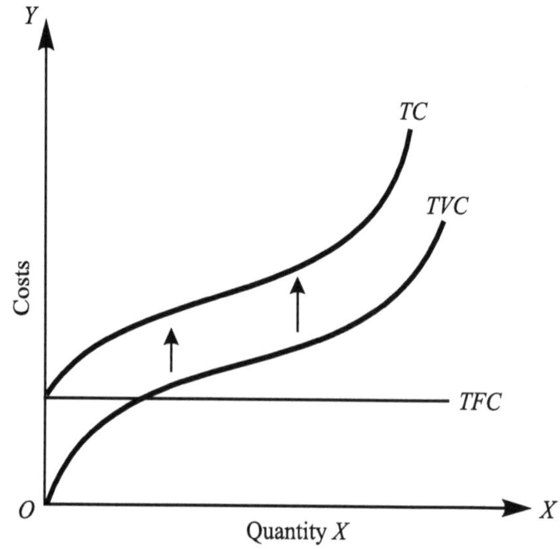

Fig. 20.2

(*i*) *Average Fixed Costs.* Average fixed costs are obtained by dividing total fixed costs by the level of output, or

$$AFC = \frac{TFC}{X}$$

In Table 20.2, the average fixed cost column is computed by dividing the total fixed cost column by the different quantities of *X*. As the rate of output increases, total fixed cost remaining the same, the average fixed cost will become smaller and smaller. The corresponding *AFC* curve, as shown in Fig. 20.3, is downward sloping to the right throughout its entire length.

As the quantity of *X* increases, it approaches but never reaches the quantity axis. Thus, a firm can reduce substantially its fixed costs per unit by producing larger quantities of output *X*. In other words, the *AFC* curve is a rectangular hyperbola asymptotic to the axis, i.e. the curve approaches the vertical and the horizontal at each end. For very small outputs, *AFC* per unit is high, and for larger outputs it is low. The *AFC* is a rectangular hyperbola because *AC* multiplied by output is always exactly the same amount.[4]

4. Donald S. Watson, *Price Theory and Its Uses,* Second Edition, p. 195.

Table 20.2

Quantity of X (*1*)	*TFC* (2)	*AFC* (3)	*TVC* (4)	*AVC* (5)	*TC* (6)	*AC* (7)	*MC* (8)
1	500	500	200	200	700	700	—
2	500	250	240	120	740	370	40
3	500	167	270	90	770	257	30
4	500	125	298	75	798	200	28
5	500	100	324	65	824	165	26
6	500	83	350	58	850	142	26
7	500	71	386	55	886	127	36
8	500	63	430	54	930	116	44
9	500	56	480	53	980	109	50
10	500	50	576	58	1,070	107	96
11	500	45	736	67	1,236	112	160
12	500	42	966	80	1,466	122	230

(ii) Average Variable Costs. Like average fixed costs, average variable costs arc obtained by dividing the total variable costs by the respective level of output *X*. Thus,

$$AVC = \frac{TVC}{X}$$

In the Table 20.2, we have computed the average cost column from the total variable cost column by using the above formula. Average variable costs behave in a different manner. Since in beginning total variable cost increases at a diminishing rate, average variable cost falls. Then, for some level of output, total variable cost increases at a constant rate, thus average variable cost becomes minimum at constant. Further, for higher levels of output, total variable cost increases at a increasing rate, and therefore, the average variable cost moves up for higher quantities of *X*. This has been clearly shown in Fig. 20.2. The *AVC* curve usually will have a *U* shape. It means that the *AVC* curve first falls, reaches a minimum and then begins to rise. In other words, it explains the three laws of production or cost.

(iii) Average Costs. Another cost which will be uscful to us is average cost or average total cost per unit of output. It is simply total cost divided by quantity (see Table 20.2). Thus,

$$AC = \frac{TC}{X} = \frac{TVC + TFC}{X} = \frac{TVC}{X} + \frac{TFC}{X}$$

where *AC* is average variable cost, *TC* is total cost, *TVC* is total variable cost, *TFC* is total fixed cost and *X* is the quantity of output. In Fig. 20.3 we have shown the *AC*-curve. It is the vertical summation of the *AFC* curve and the *AVC* curve. In Fig. 20.3, we note that it starts out at a very high point, then falls rapidly and finally rises again. Thus, the average cost curve, too, is usually thought to be a *U*-shaped curve. Its *U*-shape depends upon the efficiency with which both fixed and variable inputs are used. Given the scale of plant (quantity of fixed inputs), the greater the output of the firm, the greater the efficiency of the fixed inputs, i.e. the smaller the average fixed cost becomes. In other words, with increased production, fixed costs are spread over a larger number of units of *X; AFC* will fall and *AC* will fall with it. On the other hand, as production of *X* continues to increase, diminishing returns set in, inefficiencies occur and variable cost increases. It happens then, as in Fig, 20.3, that, as production increases, *AFC* move towards zero, but *AVC* rise and become a larger part of *AC* (since $AC = AFC + AVC$). This is illustrated as the *AC* and *AVC* curves come closer and closer together.

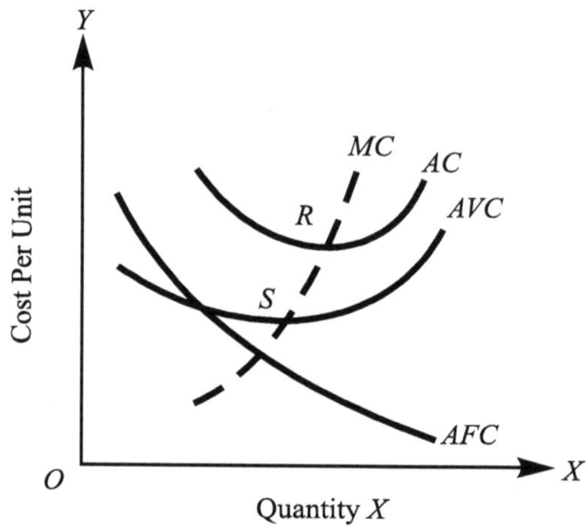

Fig. 20.3

With increasing quantity of *X*, fixed cost is spread over more units, and *AFC* has a declining influence in *AC*. At the same time however, *AVC* increases and causes *AC* to rise. The net effect of all this is that the *AC* curve is *U*-shaped. We must remember that the minimum point of the *AVC* curve must be to the right of the minimum point of the *AVC* curve. This is to say that the minimum point on the *AVC* curve lies at a lower output level than does the minimum point on the *AC* curve.[5]

---

5. We know that the short-run total cost function is

$$C = a + f(X)$$

Therefore, *AC*-function can be derived by dividing the total cost function by output as:

$$AC = \frac{C}{X} = \frac{a}{X} + \frac{f(X)}{X}$$

where $\frac{a}{X} = AFC$ and $\frac{f(X)}{X} = AVC$

(iv) Marginal Cost. Another cost in which the economists and businessmen are interested is the marginal cost (*MC*). It is defined as the extra cost of producing an additional unit. It can also be defined as the change in total cost resulting from a one unit change in output. Since a change in total cost is caused only by a change in total variable cost, marginal cost may also be defined as the increase in total variable cost resulting from a one-unit increase in output. Marginal cost depends in no way upon fixed cost. Marginal cost can either be computed from the total variable cost or from the total cost column (see Table 20.2). Thus, mathematically, where *n* stands for any volume of output.

$$\begin{aligned} MC_n &= TC_n - TC_{n-1} \\ &= [TVC_n + TFC] - [TVC_{n-1} + TFC] \\ &= TVC_n - TVC_{n-1} \end{aligned}$$

It, therefore, is clear that marginal cost is independent of the fixed cost. It makes no difference what the fixed cost is. The derivation marginal cost curve has been shown in Fig. 20.4.

The *MC* curve in Panel (*b*) of Fig. 20.4 has been drawn simply by taking the slopes of different tangents (first derivatives) on the *TC*-curve [Panel (*a*) of Fig. 20.4]. As output increases from OX_1 to OX_2, we move from point *E* to *G* along the *TC*-curve and total cost increases from OC_1 to OC_2. Therefore, at OX_2 level of output, the marginal cost will be C_1C_2.

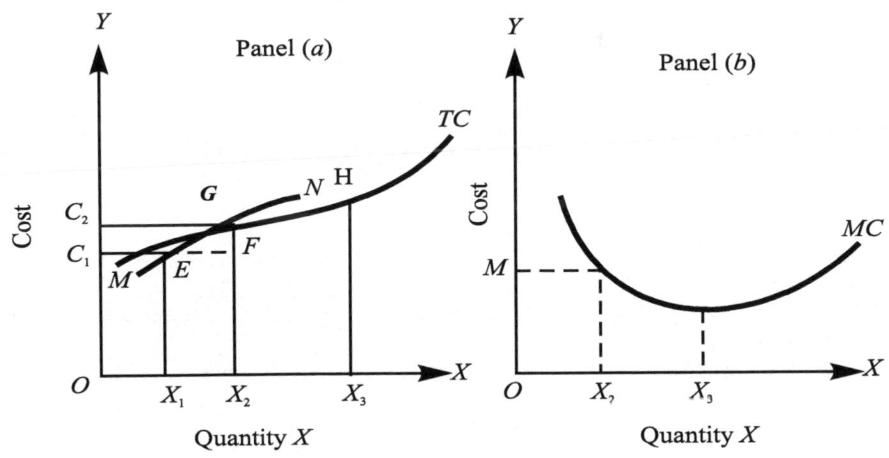

Fig. 20.4

The marginal cost of a unit of output at any level of output can be found in the same way. These information can be represented by the marginal cost curve as shown in Panel (*b*) of Fig. 20.4. Thus, at OX_2 level of output the marginal cost is *OM*, which is the same amount as C_1C_2.

The marginal cost curve usually is U-shaped and its shape comes from that of TC-curve. Upto OX_3 level of output, the TC-curve is concave to X-axis, which implies that each one unit increases in output upto that point (H) will increase total cost by a smaller amount than did the preceding one. Hence, marginal cost is decreasing as output is increased to OX_3 level. Point H on TC curve is the *point of inflection.* At output level OX_3, at which the point of inflection occurs, marginal cost takes on its minimum value. At outputs greater than OX_3, the total cost curve is convex to the horizontal axis which means that each one-unit increase in output increases total cost by more than the preceding one. Therefore, marginal cost will be increasing for outputs beyond OX_3. Thus, marginal cost first decreases and then increases as output increases.

Relationship of MC to AC and to AVC

In Fig. 20.2, it may be observed that the MC curve intersects the AVC and AC curves at their minimum points.[6] Also, when AVC and AC decline, MC is less than AVC and AC. When AVC and AC rise, MC is greater than AVC and AC. Furthermore, it may be observed in Fig. 20.3 that the MC curve intersects the AVC (at the latter's minimum level) at a smaller level of output than the level where it (the MC curve) intersects the AC curve. As already explained, this is due to the fact that AC comprises AFC and AVC.

---

6. Marginal cost is the derivative of total cost with respect to output:

$$C = a + f(X)$$

$$\therefore \quad MC = \frac{dC}{dX} = f'(X)$$

where C is total cost.

Also, the derivatives of TC and TVC are identical, because the fixed cost term disappears upon differentiation.

Now $MC = AC$, when AC is a minimum and for AC to be a minimum, its derivative is set equal to zero:

$$\frac{d\,(AC)}{dX} = \frac{d\left(\frac{C}{X}\right)}{dX} = 0$$

or
$$\frac{d\left(\frac{C}{X}\right)}{dX} = \frac{X\left(\frac{dC}{dX}\right) - C}{X^2} = 0$$

or
$$\frac{MC}{X} - \frac{C}{X^2} = 0 \text{ or } MC = \frac{C}{X} = AC$$

Similarly, we may also prove that $MC = AVC$, when AVC is minimum.

5. Long-run Cost Curves

In the above section, it has been assumed that each firm is working within the limits of an established plant whose capacity is fixed. Associated with this plant are certain fixed costs that remain the same regardless of the output produced. In the short-run nearly all firms find themselves in this kind of position. Over a longer period, a firm can change the size of its plant, and it will do so if its situation seems to require it. The existing plant can be allowed to wear out, and be abandoned; or perhaps it can be sold to another firm and converted to some other use. Thus, in the long-run the firm can build any desired scale of plant. All resources are variable and there will be no average fixed cost-curve. Thus, the firm would choose that size of operation (plant) at which it can maximise its profits, or where it can produce at the minimum cost.

When the firm plans to expand the scale of its operation, it may expect to have a different set of cost curves associated with each plant. In other words, we can think of the long-run as a series of alternative short-run situation into anyone of which the firm can move. Now we shall derive the long-run cost curves from the short-run cost curves.

Long-run Average Cost (LAC)

We may find that there is an optimum size of the firm which is more efficient than any other. A firm any smaller than the optimum will not be able to take full advantage of the economies of large-scale production, and it will not be able to get its costs down to as low a point as if it were larger. Beyond a certain point, however, there is no further advantage to be gained from increasing size (of the plant), and some diseconomies are even likely to result which interfere with efficiency, because as a firm gets larger, the difficulties of management become greater. Anyway, this characteristic of production

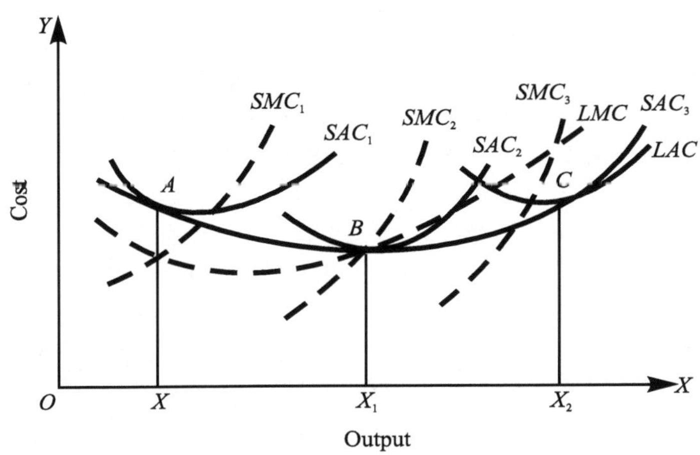

Fig. 20.5

costs to fall as we approach to the optimum size of firm, and to rise thereafter, is shown graphically in Fig. 20.5.

Here the curve *LAC* (long-run average costs) represents the lowest average costs that can be reached if a firm is required to produce most efficiently each of the various output levels measured on the horizontal axis. At output *OX*, the plant of most efficient size for that output can produce at minimum average cost of *XA*. A plant of the size most appropriate for output of OX_1 can produce more cheaply. Its minimum average cost would be X_1B. A firm, which produces still larger output as OX_2, will be less economical, and its per unit costs cannot be less than X_3C.

In formulating its policy, a firm will plan to build the plant most efficient for the volume of business it expects to do. The *LAC* curve indicates the best possibilities available for it. This is the reason why the *LAC* is sometimes known as a *planning curve*. Once the decision for the future has been made and the plant considered most appropriate has been constructed, it is not likely that it will always be possible to operate this plant at its most economical output. Changes in demand for the produce may force the firm to operate above or below its optimum size. The costs of production will, therefore, vary along the *SAC* curves. The reaction of *SAC* curves to the *LAC* curve is shown in Fig. 20.5. SAC_1 is the short-run average cost curve for the plant most appropriate to the output *OX;* and SAC_2 and SAC_3 are the corresponding short-run average cost curves for outputs OX_1 and OX_2. Now if a firm has a plant suited to the output *OX*, but is producing more or less (depending upon the demand for its product) than that in fact, its average costs will move to the left or right of *A* on SAC_1, and will deviate from *XA* accordingly. Thus, the level of output actually produced will depend upon the changes in demand for the product.

In Fig. 20.5, we have drawn *LAC* curve in such a way, that it is tangent to the *SAC* curves. Since the *LAC* curve so envelopes the *SAC* curves, it is also known as an *envelope curve*. Actually, there is a large number of short-run average cost curves tangent to the long-run average cost curve, but for the simplicity, we have shown only three *SAC* curves. It is interesting to note that SAC_2 curve is tangent to *LAC* curve at the former's lowest point. But we cannot generalise this statement with other *SAC* curves. Rather, it is the only one of the *SAC* curves of which this is true. The *LAC* curve does not touch the minimum points of any of the other curves. By definition, the *LAC* curve represents the lowest possible cost for each possible output. It means that, although the plant represented by SAC_1 is the most efficient plant that can be designed for output *OX*, that plant could operate even more efficiently at a somewhat greater output. It may be, for example, that this plant uses machinery that reduces its costs, but it cannot utilise this machine to its fullest capacity, i.e. the plant is underutilised. Yet it is the best plant possible for *OX* level of output. In contrast with this situation, the plant represented by SAC_3 is a bit over-utilised, yet even so, it constitutes the most efficient way of producing the output level OX_2. This proves the fact that *LAC* curve will not pass through the minimum point of all *SAC* curves, but it must be drawn as shown in Fig. 20.5.

The actual shape of the average cost curve in the long-run will depend on the assumptions we lay down. One assumption can be regarding the price of the factors of production. We can presume factor prices constant. Secondly, we have to lay down assumptions regarding the divisibility of factors. *If we assume that all the factors are infinitely divisible and no economies can be reaped from the division of labour, then the long-run average cost curve will be a horizontal straight line.* But in real life, it is difficult to find all the factors perfectly divisible. Usually we find that some factors are also indivisible even in the long-run. Management and entrepreneur are factors which are not perfectly divisible during the long period also. An entrepreneur will not be able to produce twice a given output as efficiently as he produces a given output. Therefore, it is rightly possible that a firm will produce more cheaply at some scales of output than at others, even in the long-run. This means that, in real life, the short-run average cost curves of a firm will have different minimum points.

Long-run Marginal Cost (LMC)

There is also long-run marginal cost curve shown in Fig. 20.5 the dashed line *LMC*. It indicates the extra costs entailed in enlarging production facilities so as to get greater quantities of output. It bears precisely the same relationship to the *LAC* curve that the *SMC* curve bears to its *SAC* curve.

The Optimum Scale of Plant

The optimum scale of plant means the most efficient scale plant that the firm can build. It is that plant where the short-run average cost curve forms the minimum point of the long-run average cost curve. In Fig. 20.4, this situation takes place at point *B* where SAC_2 curve is tangent to *LAC* curve at the minimum points of both. The optimum level of output is OX_1. Normally, firms will not operate at this level of output, but they will do so in the situation of perfect competition in the long-run. Economists believe that the tendency of competition is to force firms to that position; otherwise they could not remain in business. In the long-run, then, we must expect competition to bring the price down to X_1B. This idea will be more fully explained in the chapter that deals with pricing and output under perfect competition.

6. The Concept of Cost Elasticity

Elasticity of Total Cost

Cost elasticity measures the responsiveness of cost to changes in output. The total cost function can be written as:

$$C = f(x) \qquad \ldots(1)$$

where C = Total cost, and X= output

Now the elasticity of total cost can be defined as the ratio of the proportionate change in total cost to the proportional change in output. It may be written as:

$$\in = \frac{dC}{C} \bigg/ \frac{dX}{X}$$

$$= \frac{dC}{dX} \cdot \frac{X}{C} \qquad \ldots(2)$$

However, from the above description, we find $\frac{dC}{dX}$ to be marginal cost (MC) and $\frac{X}{C}$ to be the reciprocal of the average total cost (ATC or AC).

Thus,

$$\in = \frac{dC}{dX} \cdot \frac{X}{C}$$

$$= MC \cdot \frac{1}{AC}$$

$$= \frac{MC}{AC} \qquad \ldots(3)$$

Equation (3) states that cost elasticity ($\in$) is equal to the ratio of marginal cost to average cost. It follows the following conclusions:

(*i*) If $MC > AC$ then $\in > 1$
(*ii*) If $MC = AC$ then $\in = 1$
(*iii*) If $MC < AC$ then $\in < 1$

The above relations can also be explained diagrammatically in Fig. 20.6.

In Figure 20.6, at OX level of output $MC = AC$ and therefore $\in = 1$. It is the point L where the MC curve cuts the AC curve from below in the Figure. It is the case of constant returns.

When to the left of point L, $MC < AC$ and therefore $\in < 1$. It is the situation or the area where AC curve is falling and MC lies below AC curve. It is the case of increasing returns, or diminishing cost.

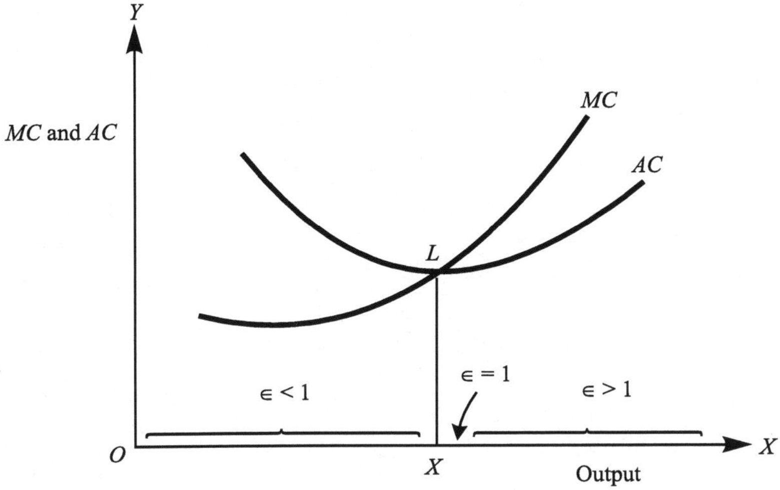

Fig. 20.6

When to the right of point *L*, *MC* >*AC*, and therefore ∈ >1. It is the situation or the area where *AC* curve is rising and *MC* curve lies above the *AC* curve. It is the final case of decreasing returns or increasing cost.

Since the *AC* and the *MC* are derived from the *TC* in relation to the output (*X*), the shapes of the *AC* curve and the *MC* curve can also be verified from the shape of the *TC* curve. It is shown in Fig. 20.7. Here *A* is the point on the *TC* curve at a given output *OX*, then the average cost is to be read off as the gradient of *OA* and marginal cost as the tangent at point *A*. Figure 20.7 shows

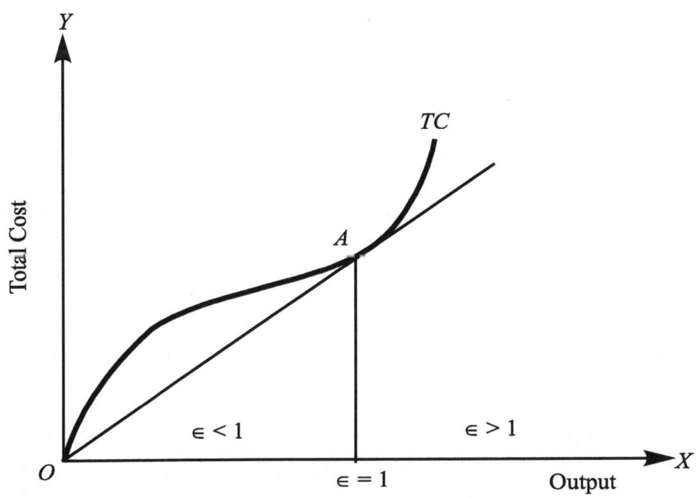

Fig. 20.7

that the elasticity of total cost increases continuously with increase in output from less than unity ($\in > 1$) to greater than unity ($\in > 1$) via unitary elasticity ($\in = 1$) at *OX* level of output.

In Fig. 20.7, we take a tangent point *A* where $\in = 1$ at output level *OX*. For output levels less than *OX*, the elasticity of total cost $\in < 1$ and for output levels higher than *OX*, the elasticity of total cost, $\in > 1$.

Elasticity of Average Cost

The elasticity of total cost is written as

$$\in = \frac{dC}{dX} \cdot \frac{X}{C}$$

Now, since average cost is $\frac{C}{X}$, therefore, we replace *C* by $\frac{C}{X}$, we may get the elasticity of average cost as under:

$$K \text{ (Average cost)} = \frac{d\left(\frac{C}{X}\right)}{dX} \cdot \frac{X}{\left(\frac{C}{X}\right)}$$

$$= \frac{X^2}{C} \cdot \frac{d}{dX}\left(\frac{C}{X}\right)$$

$$= \frac{X^2}{C}\left[X\frac{dC}{dX} - C\right]$$

$$= \frac{X^2}{C} \cdot \frac{1}{X^2}\left[X\frac{dC}{dX} - C\right]$$

$$= \frac{X}{C} \cdot \frac{dC}{dX} - 1$$

$$\therefore \qquad K = \in - 1 \quad \text{where } \in = \frac{dC}{dX} \cdot \frac{X}{C} \qquad ...(4)$$

If we know the value of $\in$ at different levels of output, we can conveniently verify the stage in which a firm is undertaking production. The following are the important conclusions:

(1) If $\in$ (i.e. the elasticity of total cost) is greater than, equal to or less than unity ($\in \gtreqless 1$), the elasticity of average cost is greater than, equal to or less than zero ($K \gtreqless 0$).

(2) The total cost elasticity exceeds the average cost elasticity by unity,

because by equation (4) we have

$$K = \in -1$$

$$\therefore \qquad \in = K + 1 \qquad \ldots(5)$$

Elasticity of Marginal Cost

The elasticity of total cost is written as

$$\in = \frac{dC}{dX} \cdot \frac{X}{C}$$

Now, since marginal cost is $\frac{dC}{dX}$, therefore, we replace C by $\frac{dC}{dX}$, we may get the elasticity of marginal cost as under:

$$\gamma \text{ (Marginal cost)} = \frac{d(dC/dX)}{dX} \cdot \frac{X}{(dC/dX)}$$

$$= \frac{d}{dX}(dC/dX) \cdot \frac{X}{(dC/dX)} \qquad \ldots(6)$$

Since

$$\in = \frac{dC}{dX} \cdot \frac{X}{C}$$

$$\therefore \qquad \in \cdot \frac{C}{X} = \frac{dC}{dX}$$

Substituting it into equation (6), we get

$$\gamma = \frac{d}{dX}\left(\frac{dC}{dX}\right) \frac{X}{\in\left(\frac{C}{X}\right)}$$

$$= \frac{d}{dX}\left(\frac{dC}{dX}\right) \frac{X^2}{\in C} \qquad \ldots(7)$$

Elasticity of Productivity

As we know that the output of a commodity is a function of various independent inputs. Assuming that all inputs are applied in the fixed proportions to produce output (X), then we may write the function as:

$$X = f(F) \qquad \ldots(8)$$

Now the elasticity of productivity is defined as the ratio of proportional change in output (X) to proportional change in inputs (F). It can be stated as:

$$\mu \text{ (productivity)} = \frac{dX}{X} \bigg/ \frac{dF}{F}$$

$$\frac{dX}{dF} \cdot \frac{F}{X} \qquad \text{...(9)}$$

Elasticity of productivity is applied in finding out the nature of production function in economic theory. The main conclusions are:

(1) If $\mu > 1$, it is the case of increasing returns because a small proportionate increase in input (say 5 per cent) leads to more than proportionate increase (more than 5 per cent) in output.

(2) If $\mu < 1$, it is the case of diminishing returns because a small proportionate increase in inputs (say 5 per cent) leads to a less than proportionate increase (less than 5 per cent) in output.

(3) If $\mu = 1$, it is the case of constant returns, because a certain proportionate increase in inputs (say 5 per cent) leads to the same proportionate increase (exactly 5 per cent) in output.

We have stated that the above concept of elasticity of productivity is based on the assumption of fixed proportions of inputs used in production of a commodity *X*, then total costs become proportional to inputs used. Thus μ (elasticity of productivity) is the inverse of $\in$ (elasticity of total costs). In other words

$$\mu = \frac{1}{\in} \qquad \text{...(10)}$$

Here inputs are used in fixed proportions only in the case μ and not for $\in$.

Exercises

1. Distinguish between fixed costs and variable costs as the terms are used by the economists.
2. Distinguish between the accounting costs and economic costs. Explain the importance of economic costs in economic analysis.
3. Distinguish between short-run cost curves and long-run cost curves. Why must the average cost curve be *U*-shaped? What does this shape precisely signify?
4. Define marginal cost. Indicate at what point the marginal cost curve cuts the average variable cost curve and the average cost curve and why it must cut them at these points.
5. Why is the long-run average cost curve known as a planning curve?
6. Define the terms "optimum size" and "normal capacity" and state which of the following costs will be at a minimum when a firm of optimum size is operating at normal capacity: *AC, AVC, AFC, MC.*
7. Discuss the nature of the short-run and long-run average cost curves. Why is the long run cost curve flatter than the short-run cost curve?
8. How do economies and diseconomies of scale affect the *LAC* curve?
9. Write notes on:

(*a*) Elasticity of Cost
(*b*) Elasticity of Productivity
(*c*) The Concept of Opportunity Cost
(*d*) Relation between *AC* and *MC*

Multiple Choice Questions

10. (*i*) Opportunity costs are also known as
(*a*) overhead costs (*c*) alternative costs
(*b*) money cost (*d*) social costs [*Ans.* (*c*)]

(*ii*) The opportunity cost of a factor of production is
(*a*) what it is earning in its present use
(*b*) what it can earn in the long period
(*c*) what it can earn in some other use
(*d*) what has to be paid to retain it in its present use [*Ans.* (*d*)]

(*iii*) All money costs can be regarded as
(*a*) implicit costs (*c*) opportunity costs
(*b*) explicit costs (*d*) social costs [*Ans.* (*b*)]

(*iv*) Implicit costs are the costs
(*a*) which are not incurred by the firm, and may accrue to the company
(*b*) of resources owned by the firm
(*c*) of resources supplied by the households
(*d*) all of the above [*Ans.* (*b*)]

(*v*) The fixed costs of a firm
(1) are fixed only in the short period
(2) when expressed as an average, do not change with output
(3) do not reflect diminishing marginal returns
(*a*) (1) and (2) only (*d*) (2) and (3) only
(*b*) (1) and (3) only (*e*) all of them
(*c*) (2) only [*Ans.* (*b*)]

(*vi*) Average fixed costs
(*a*) remain the same whatever the level of output
(*b*) increases as output increases
(*c*) diminishes as output increases
(*d*) show no pattern [*Ans.* (*c*)]

(*vii*) Fixed costs are known as
(*a*) special cost (*c*) prime cost
(*b*) direct cost (*d*) overhead cost [*Ans.* (*c*)]

(*viii*) In a short period, when production increases, the *AFC*
(*a*) increases (*c*) remain constant
(*b*) decreases (*d*) none of the above [*Ans.* (*b*)]

(*ix*) A firm's *TC* curve
(*a*) lies below its *TVC* curve
(*b*) rises more steeply than its *TVC* curve because *TC* includes fixed as well as variable costs
(*c*) is a horizontal curve
(*d*) is identical in shape to its *TVC* curve, but higher in position [*Ans.* (*d*)]

(*x*) All of the following curves are *U*-shaped except

(*a*) the *AVC* curve (*c*) the *AC* curve

(*b*) the *AFC* curve (*d*) the *MC* curve [*Ans.* (*b*)]

(*xi*) *MC* is given by

(*a*) the slope of the *TFC* curve

(*b*) the slope of the *TVC* curve but not by the slope of the *TC* curve

(*c*) the slope of the *TC* curve but not by the slope of the *TVC* curve

(*d*) either the slope of the *TVC* curve or the slope of the *TC* curve [*Ans.* (*d*)]

Chapter 21

Concept of Revenue

1. Introduction

In modern economics, the equilibrium of the firm is discussed in terms of cost and revenue. The profits of the firm are also calculated by the costs and the revenues of the firm. In the previous chapter we have explained the costs of production and now in the present chapter we shall describe the concept of revenue.

2. Total, Average and Marginal Revenue

The revenue of a firm consists of price times the number of units the firm can sell. Mathematically,

$$R = PX$$

where, R = Total revenue, P = Price, X = Quantity sold

Since the demand schedule of the firm tells us how much the firm can sell at each price, we can calculate the total revenue from it merely by multiplying price times quantity. In other words, the demand curve provides information to the firm about the total revenue it can get from its sales. In Table 21.1 we can see what total revenue would be at different price levels.

The information given in Table 21.1 can also be shown by a demand curve as in Fig. 21.1. We may see that the total revenue is maximum at price \$8 where 8 units of X are sold. If price increases from \$8, then total revenue will decline and if price decreases, total revenue will also decline. This fact can also be seen in Fig. 21.1. Since total revenue is PX, it can be represented by a rectangle underneath the demand curve. At price \$8, total revenue is shown by the area of shaded rectangle. At a price higher than \$8, total revenue will decrease, because the return per unit is higher but the gain in revenue due to higher price is not sufficient

Table 21.1

Quantity (Units) *X*	*Price or Average Revenue ($s.)* *P*	*Total Revenue ($s.)* *R = PX*	*Marginal Revenue ($s.)* *MR*
1	15	15	—
2	14	28	13
3	13	39	11
4	12	48	9
5	11	55	7
6	10	60	5
7	9	63	3
8	8	64	+1
9	7	63	−1
10	6	60	−3
11	5	55	−5
12	4	48	−7

to offset the loss in revenue due to reduced sales the demand at this level is elastic ($Ed > 1$), *i.e.* the percentage increase in price is less than percentage decrease in quantity sold. At a price lower than $8, more units will be sold but total revenue will decrease because demand is inelastic ($Ed < 1$, *i.e.* the percentage change in price is greater than percentage change in quantity). Thus any other rectangle under the demand curve of the firm will be of a smaller area than the one shown in Fig. 21.1. Thus, it is interesting to note that although the price $ 8 is not the highest price, yet the (total) revenue of

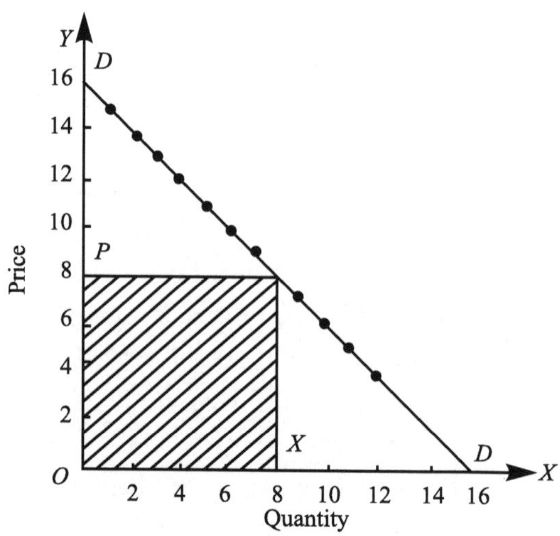

Fig. 21.1

the firm is maximum. But in the following chapters we shall note that the maximisation of revenue is not the objective of the firm it is maximisation of profit. Revenue does not give us the facts about profit. It requires a simultaneous information about the costs of the firm. We shall discuss this problem of equilibrium in the following chapters.

While discussing the revenue of the firm, we use three concepts: Total Revenue, Average Revenue and Marginal Revenue.

As we have already explained, total revenue is the total receipts of the firm through its sales, *i.e.* it is calculated by price per unit of the commodity multiplied by the total number of units sold.

Average revenue is the revenue per unit of the commodity sold. It is found by dividing total revenue by the number of units sold. Thus, average revenue means price. It is revenue for the seller and price for the consumer. Mathematically,

$$AR = \frac{TR}{X}$$

where, AR =Average revenue, TR = Total revenue, X= Number of units of the commodity sold.

Now, average revenue curve is the same thing as demand curve. As the consumer's demand curve is the graphic relation between price and quantity demanded, it also represents the average revenue or price at which the various quantities of a commodity are sold, since price offered by buyers is the revenue from the seller's point of view. Therefore, average revenue curve of the firm is really the same thing as demand curve of the consumers.

Marginal revenue (MR), on the other hand, is defined as the extra revenue secured from the scale of an additional unit of the commodity. It is then the revenue derived from the last unit sold. Since our demand curve (AR-curve) is downward sloping, the last unit can only be sold at a lower price. To calculate MR, we subtract total revenue of the sale of a unit or several units at some particular price from total revenue derived from the sale of the next. Algebraically, it is the addition to total revenue earned by selling units of the commodity instead of (n–1) units. Thus,

$$MRn = TRn - TRn - 1$$

where, MRn = Marginal Revenue of the nth unit, TRn = Total Revenue of n units, TRn –1= Total Revenue of n–1 units, n =Any given number of units sold.

In Table 21.1, we have calculated the MR column with the help of the above formula. For example, marginal revenue when two units are sold then would be \$13 (\$28 – \$15); when three units are sold, \$11 (\$39 – \$28) and so on. Here we should note that MR is not the same as price (or AR) because, in order to sell the third unit, it was necessary to reduce the price of the first two units to the selling price of the third, \$13. In other words, two units can be sold for \$14, but in order to sell three units, it is necessary to reduce the price to \$13. We suffer loss on all the units sold at the old price. Thus, the decrease in *MR* will be higher than the decrease in *AR*.

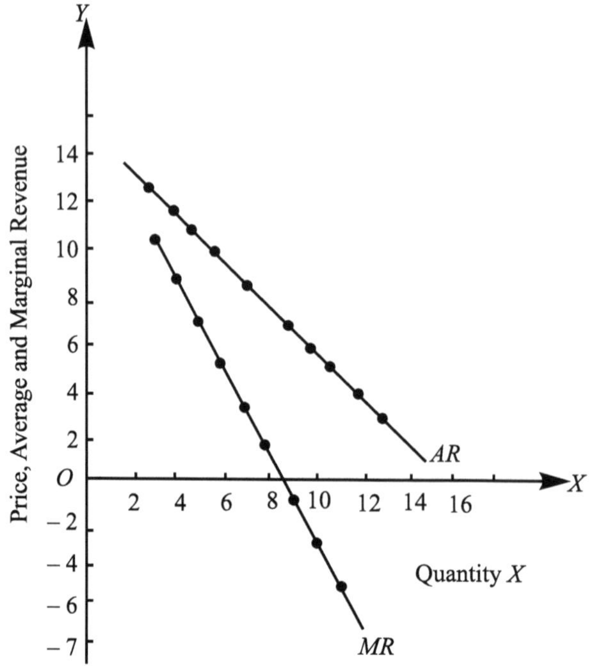

Fig. 21.2

Now, in Fig. 21.2, we draw the average revenue (demand) and marginal revenue curves on the basis of the data provided in Table 22.1, and see that *MR* will be less than *AR* (or price) at all levels. Notice that when nine units are sold, *MR* becomes negative: as price is lowered from \$8 to \$7. *TR* decreases from \$64 to \$63.

Generally speaking, marginal revenue is less than average revenue (or price) as indicated by the Fig. 21.2. But in perfect competition, when a firm has to sell any quantity at the ruling market price, marginal revenue is equal to average revenue, because there is no loss incurred on the previous units.

3. Revenue Curves for a Perfectly Competitive Firm

Perfect competition is the term applied to a situation in which the individual buyer or seller (firm) represents such a small share of the total business transacted in the market that he exerts no perceptible influence on the price of commodity in which he deals. Thus, in perfect competition an individual firm is a price taker, because the price is determined by the collective force of market demand and market supply which are not influenced by the individual. When price is the same for all units of a commodity, naturally average revenue (price) will be equal to marginal revenue (*AR* = *MR*).

Table 21.2: Demand and Revenue Schedule of a Competitive Firm

Quantity of X (in units)	*Price (P) or Average Revenue (AR)*	*Total Revenue (TR)*	*Marginal Revenue (MR)*
1	200	200	200
2	200	400	200
3	200	600	200
4	200	800	200
5	200	1,000	200

This can also be illustrated with the help of an imaginary revenue schedule as in Table 21.2. It indicates that price of $200 is given to the individual firm which is determined by the industry. As the firm sells more and more at the given price, its total revenue will increase but the rate of increase in total revenue is constant because *AR* = *MR*.

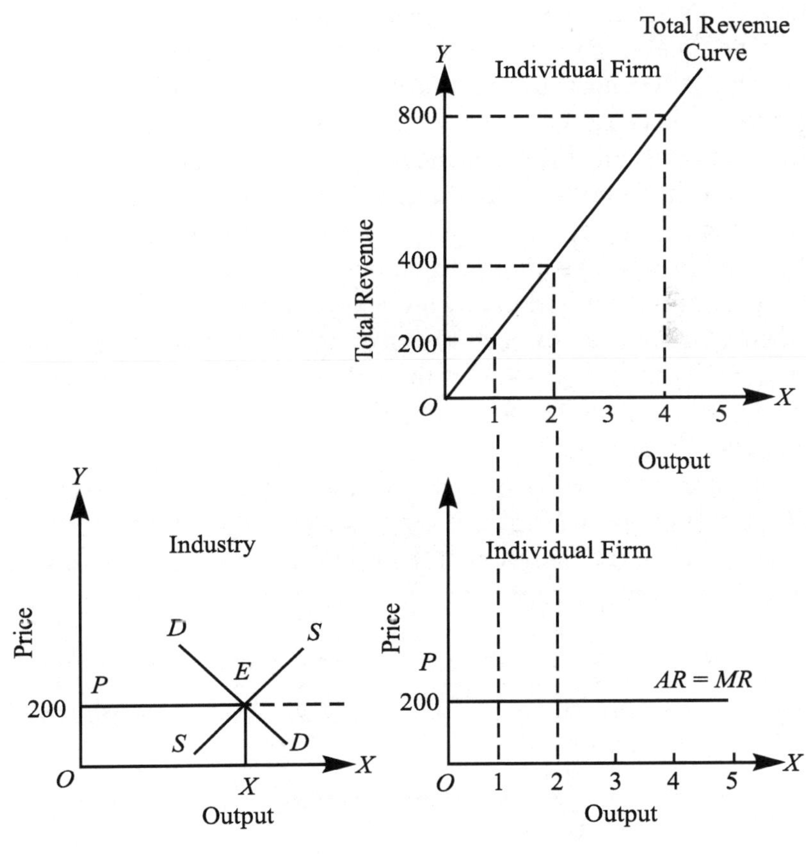

Fig. 21.3

The total revenue, marginal revenue and average revenue curves are also drawn in Fig. 21.3. It clearly shows that *OP* price is fixed by the industry and at this given price the firm can sell any quantity of the commodity. Its demand curve is horizontal and *AR* is equal to *MR*. The price of the commodity coincides with the sum received by the seller, per unit of sales, that is to say, with the seller's average revenue it stands at the same amount, regardless of the sales volume, its in this case it stands at $200 a unit. Marginal revenue is the additional sum that the firm receives from an additional unit of the commodity that it sells. It also coincides with the price, $200 in this example, since every additional unit sold brings this amount.

4. Revenue Curves for a Firm under Monopoly or Imperfect Competition

When a firm is working under conditions of monopoly or imperfect competition, its demand curve (or *AR*-curve) is less than perfectly elastic, the exact degree of elasticity being different in different market situations, depending upon the number of sellers and the nature of product. In other words, the demand (*AR*) curve has a negative slope and the *MR*-curve lies below it. This is because the monopolist seller ordinarily has to accept a lower price for his product, as he increases his sales. In the situation of monopoloy, he is the only seller, and he is faced by a situation that is generalised with respect to final goods by the law of demand: the market will absorb an additional quantity only at a lower price. Exceptionally, there may be situations where the market will absorb a larger quantity at the same or even a higher price, but they are uncommon and can be neglected here. If it is granted that the monopoly firm has to accept a lower price for her product, in order to sell a greater quantity, it is obvious that the *AR*-curve will be falling and the *MR* must always be less than *AR*, because a falling price must mean some loss on the sale of additional supply.

To make it more clear, let us construct an imaginary demand and revenue schedule for a monopoly firm. The first two columns of Table 21.3 give us the demand curve of the monopolist. It shows that price per unit and average revenue are one and the same. The quantity demanded will increase only

Table 21.3: Demand and Revenue Schedule of a Monopoly Firm

Quantity o/X (in units) (1)	*Price (P) or Average Revenue (AR)* (2)	*Total Revenue (TR)* (3)	*Marginal Revenue (MR)* (4)
1	100	100	100
2	90	180	80
3	80	240	60
4	70	280	40
5	60	300	20

when the price (*AR*) falls. Now to derive the column 4 of marginal revenue, we first calculate the total revenue column which is simply the product of price multiplied by the quantity sold. Now marginal revenue column can be derived from the total revenue column. As already explained, it (*MR*) is the net addition to the total revenue from the additional unit of commodity sold. Thus, in going from one to two units, the marginal revenue is $80 and this is found subtracting $100 from $180 and so on for the other unit.

These facts can also be explained in Fig. 21.4. It should be clear that the demand curve is sloping downward to show that more can be sold only at lower prices. The corresponding marginal revenue curve is below the *AR*-curve. From Table 21.3, it may be noted that when *AR* falls by $10, the *MR* falls by $20, i.e. the *MR* falls by double the rate of the fall in *AR*.[1]

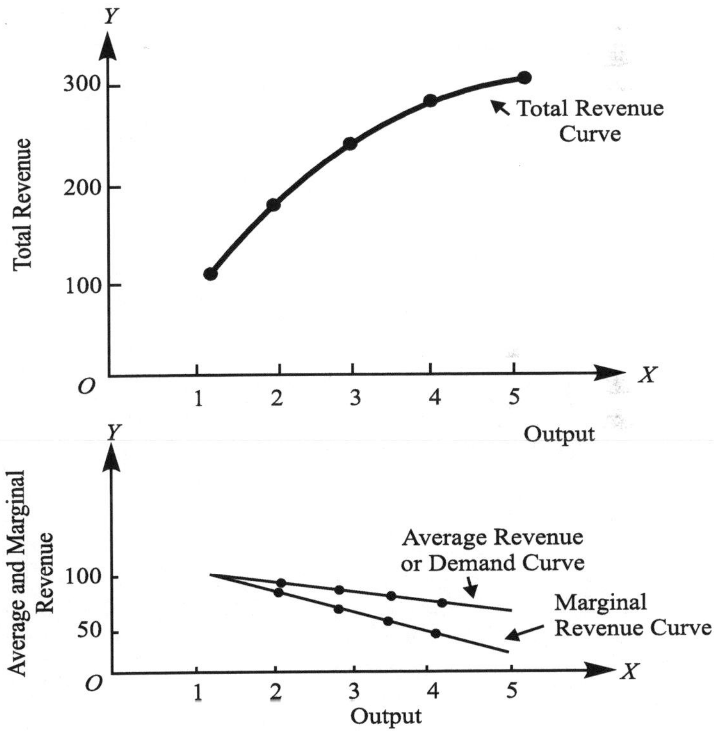

Fig. 21.4

1. This can be shown mathematically also that the rate of change to *MR* is twice the rate of change in *AR*.
   Let us assume, $AR = a - bX$ where a = constant
   $\therefore \quad TR = Xa - bX^2$ and b = slope of *AR* curve
   and $MR = \dfrac{d(TR)}{dX} = a - 2bX$ where $2b$ =slope of *MR*-curve which is twice that of AR-curve.

5. Relationship between Average and Marginal Revenue Curves[2]

In most of the following analysis of price theory, we shall be concerned only with average and marginal revenue curves, so that we can ignore total revenue curves. There are geometrical relationships between any average revenue curve and the corresponding marginal revenue curve. We have already explained some of the relationships between them. In this section, we shall discuss the main relationships between the average revenue curve and the marginal revenue curve with the help of Fig. 21.5.

So long as the average revenue curve is falling, marginal revenue must be less than average revenue. The marginal revenue curve itself may be rising, falling or horizontal according to the market situations or circumstances, but normally it falls downward. If we consider straight *AR* and *MR* curves as shown in Fig. 21.5, marginal revenue curve falls twice as much as the fall of average revenue curve. In other words, in such a situation, the marginal revenue curve will cut any line perpendicular to the *Y*-axis half-way to the average revenue curve. In Fig. 21.5, *AB* = *BC*. Now to prove this, let us consider the following steps:

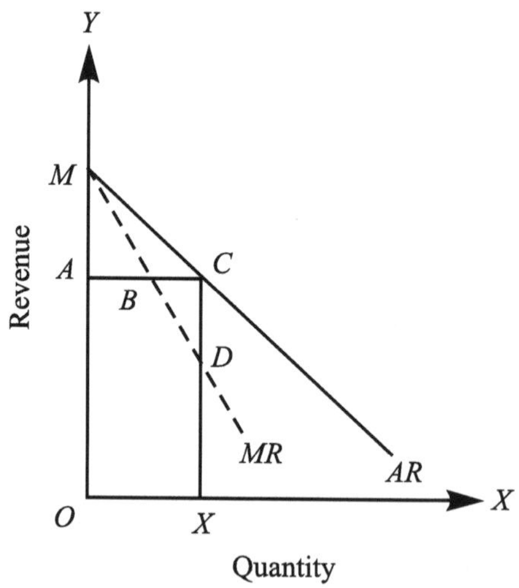

Fig. 21.5

$$\text{Area } ACXO = \text{Area } MDXO$$

where, $ACXO$ = Area of total revenue under demand curve at point *C*; and $MDXO$ = Area of total revenue under marginal revenue curve.

Also $$ACXO = ABDXO + \Delta BCD$$

---

2. Alfred, W. Stonier and Douglas, C. Hague, *A Textbook of Economic Theory,* Fourth Ed., pp.110-115. Also see the chapter on "Elasticity of Demand" of this book.

$$\text{and} \qquad MDXO = ABDXO + \Delta AMB$$

$$\therefore \qquad ABDXO + \Delta BCD = ABDXO + \Delta AMB$$

$$\text{or} \qquad \Delta BCD = \Delta AMB$$

Since ΔBCD and ΔAMB are congruent triangles, thus

$$AB = BC$$

Hence, it is proved that marginal revenue will cut any line perpendicular to the Y-axis half-way to the average revenue curve. But this happens only in the situation when the average and marginal revenue curves are straight lines.

When the average revenue curve is *concave upwards* or convex downward, as in Fig. 21.6 (*a*), the marginal revenue curve cuts any perpendicular less than half-way from the Y-axis to the average revenue curve. If the average revenue curve is concave downwards or convex upward as shown in Fig. 21.6 (*b*), the marginal revenue curve cuts any perpendicular more than half-way from the Y-axis to the average revenue curve.

Thus, in Fig. 21.6 (*a*), $AB < BC$ and
in Fig. 21.6 (*b*), $AB < BC$

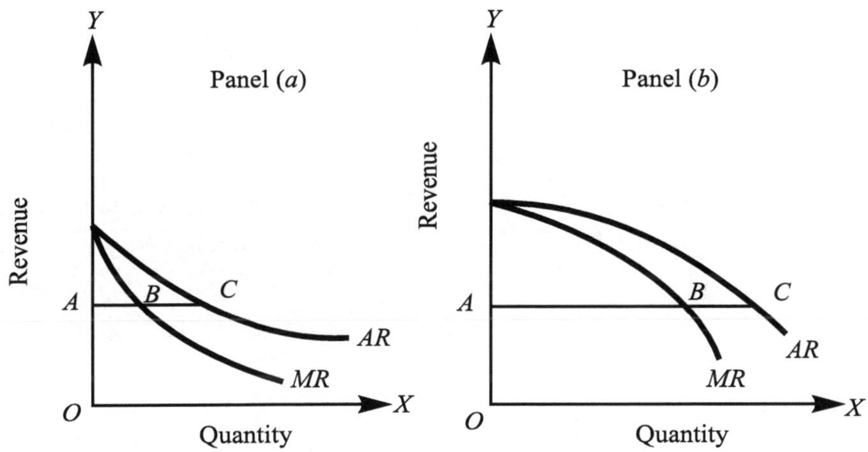

Fig. 21.6

So far we have discussed the relationship between the average and marginal revenue along a perpendicular to the Y-axis. Now, we shall discuss the relationships between average revenue and marginal revenue curves along a perpendicular to X-axis. In other words, we shall explain the relationship between marginal and average revenue at any level of output (which is measured along the X-axis). This type of relationship will assume a greater importance in economic analysis. This can be done in terms of elasticity of demand. Because, it is clear that the average revenue curve of a firm is really the same thing at the demand curve of consumers for the firm's product.

6. Average Revenue, Marginal Revenue and Elasticity of Demand

As we have already explained, the demand curve for the firm's product is the same thing as the average revenue curve of the firm. Thus, we shall measure the elasticity of demand on a firm's average revenue curve and then explain the relationship between *AR, MR,* and the elasticity of demand. It is also true that all average revenue curves (or for that matter demand curves) will not be straight lines. We, therefore, measure elasticity of demand on the average revenue curve which is really a curve.

In Fig. 21.7, the elasticity of demand at point *A* on the *AR* curve is equal to *NA/AM.* This can be proved in the following manner. As we know that elasticity of demand can be defined as:

$$Ed = \frac{\text{Percentage change in the quantity demanded for } X}{\text{Percentage change in the price of } X}$$

or

$$Ed = \frac{\frac{\Delta X}{X} \times 100}{\frac{\Delta P_X}{P_X} \times 100}$$

or

$$Ed = \frac{\Delta X}{\Delta P_X} \times \frac{P_X}{X}$$

where, Ed = Elasticity of demand; ΔX = Change in quantity demanded for X; ΔP_X = Change in the price of X; X = Original amount demanded for X; and P_X = Original price of X.

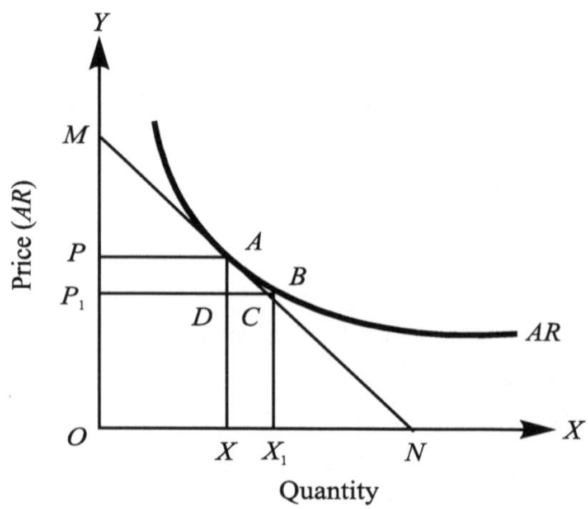

Fig. 21.7

Now, to measure elasticity at a particular point *A* on *AR* curve, it is necessary to draw a tangent (*MN*) to the curve at point *R*. The slope of the line *MN* is the same throughout its length. Thus, instead of measuring the elasticity of demand between points *A* and *B* on *AR* curve, we measure it between *A* and *C*. Since it is a case of point elasticity of demand, we assume that point *C* is very near to point *B*. Also, the slope of points *A* and *C* is the same and thus as a limiting case the distance *AC* is very small. If we supplement the required information from Fig. 21.7 to the above formula of elasticity of demanded, we get

$$Ed = \frac{XX_1}{PP_1} \cdot \frac{OP}{OX}$$

$$= \frac{DC}{AD} \cdot \frac{OP}{OX}$$

where $XX_1 = DC$; and $PP_1 = AD$

But since by a mathematical theorem, triangles *ADC* and *AXN* are similar, we can write $\frac{DC}{AD}$ as $\frac{AX}{XN}$. Thus

$$Ed = \frac{AX}{XN} \cdot \frac{OP}{OX}$$

$$= \frac{AX}{OP} \cdot \frac{OP}{OX} \quad \text{where } XN = OP$$

$$= \frac{AX}{OX}$$

But, since triangles *XNA* and *PAM* are similar, $\frac{AX}{OX} = \frac{NA}{AM}$. Thus, point elasticity of demand at point *A* is

$$Ed = \frac{AX}{OX} \cdot \frac{NA}{AM}.$$

It means, numerical point-elasticity of demand is given by dividing the length of the portion of the tangent above point *A* (*AM*) into the portion below point *A* (*AN*). With this measure of point elasticity of demand we can study the relationships between average and marginal revenue curves along any perpendicular on the *X*-axis.

For instance, in Fig. 21.8, the elasticity of demand at point *A* on *AR* curve is *AN/AM*. The two triangles *PMA* and *XAN* have equal angles. Therefore, *AN/AM* can be alternatively written as *AX/MP*. Now, we draw a, line from *M* which cuts the perpendicular *PA* at *C* and then passes through point *B*. This straight line MS is marginal to the tangent MN because it cuts the perpendicular PA at its mid-point, C.

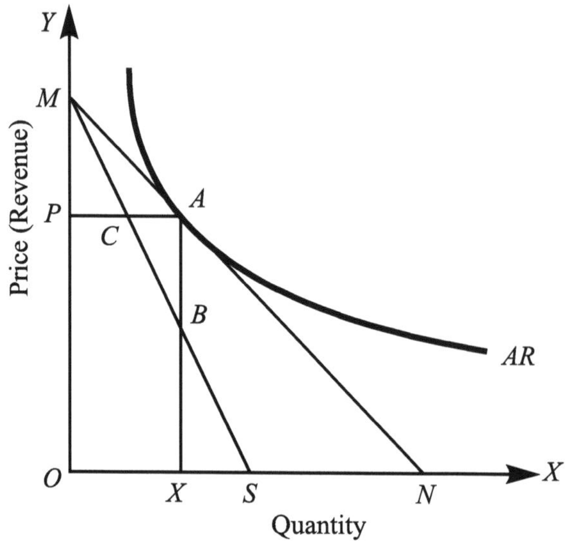

Fig. 21.8

Therefore, $PC = CA$

Also, angle PAM = angle ACB (being vertically opposite)

and, angle MPC = angle CAB (being right angles)

$\therefore$ $\Delta\ PMC = \Delta\ BCA$ (10 all respects)

In other words, the triangles PMC and BCA are the congruent triangles.

Thus,

$$MP = BA$$

Now, instead of explaining elasticity point A as $\frac{AN}{AM} = \frac{AX}{MP}$, we can write it as:

$$Ed = \frac{AX}{AB}$$

or
$$Ed = \frac{AX}{AX - BX}$$

where Ed = Elasticity of demand at the output OX

AX = Average Revenue

and, BX = Marginal Revenue

Thus, the above formula of elasticity of demand can be written as:

$$Ed = \frac{\text{Average Revenue}}{\text{Average Revenue} - \text{Marginal Revenue}}$$

$$= \frac{A}{A - M}$$

$$Ed\,(A - M) = A$$

$$EdA - EdM = A$$

$$M = \frac{EdA - A}{Ed}$$

or $$M = A\left(1 - \frac{1}{Ed}\right)$$

where, M = Marginal revenue, A = Average revenue, and Ed = Value of elasticity of demand.

Now, on the basis of above formula, we can find out the relationship between MR and AR at various point of elasticities of demand.

If $Ed = 1$, then $MR = 0$

If $Ed = 2$, then MR equals half the AR

If $Ed > 1$, then $MR > 0$

If $Ed < 1$, then MR is negative

These situations can also be illustrated with the help of a diagram as in Fig. 21.9.

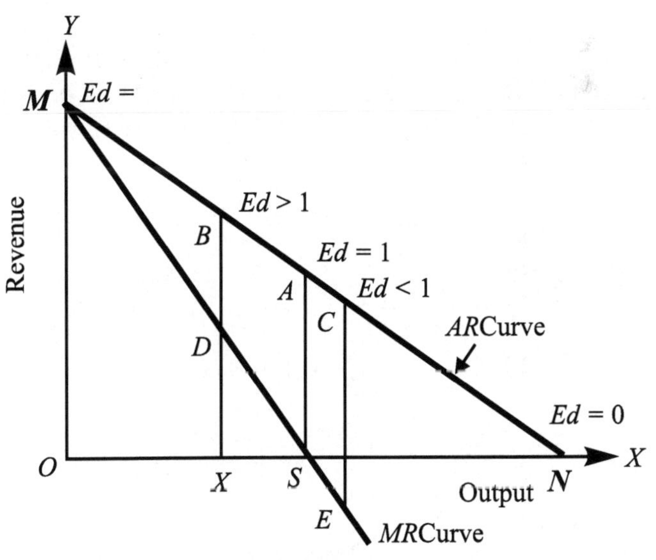

Fig. 21.9

Figure 21.9 indicates that at point A,

$Ed = \frac{AN}{AM}$ and since $AN = AM$, therefore, Ed=1. At this level of output *OS*, marginal revenue is zero. If elasticity of demand is greater than unity, marginal revenue will always be positive. In Fig. 21.9, this will be the case at any point between the range *A* and *M*. If elasticity of demand is less than one, then marginal revenue is negative. In Fig. 21.9, this will happen at any point between *A* and *N*.

7. Other Special Cases of Revenue Curves

Mrs. Joan Robinson[3] has mentioned many special cases of average and marginal revenue curves. Here we shall mention only the two types of special cases of average and marginal revenue curves.

(1) As we have already mentioned, if the elasticity of demand is unity throughout the length of *AR* curve, marginal revenue will be zero throughout. Thus, the resulting marginal revenue curve will coincide with the horizontal *X*-axis. This case has been shown in Fig. 21.10.

In Fig. 21.10, the demand curve of the firm's product or the *AR* curve is a rectangular hyperbola, having unitary elasticity throughout its length, or Ed =1.

If Ed=1 and putting this value in the formula $M = A\left(1 - \frac{1}{Ed}\right)$, we get the value of marginal revenue as:

$$M = A\left(1 - \frac{1}{1}\right)$$
$$= 0$$

Therefore, when the elasticity of demand at all points on the AR-curve (or demand curve) is equal to one, the marginal revenue will be zero throughout its length and in Fig. 21.10, the *MR* curve is nothing but the *X*-axis.

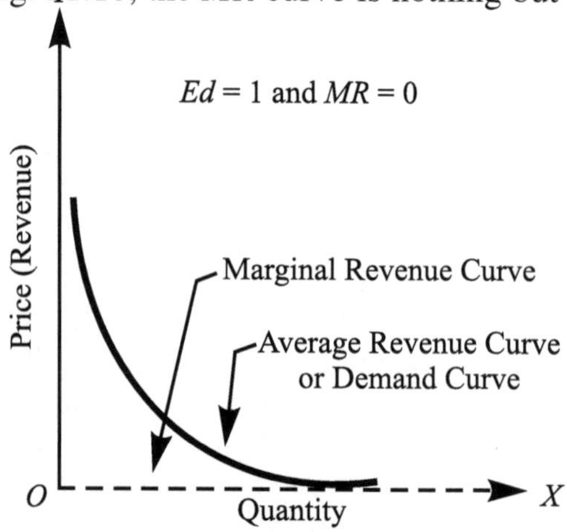

Fig. 21.10

3. Joan Robinson, *The Economics of Imperfect Competition,* Chapter 2.

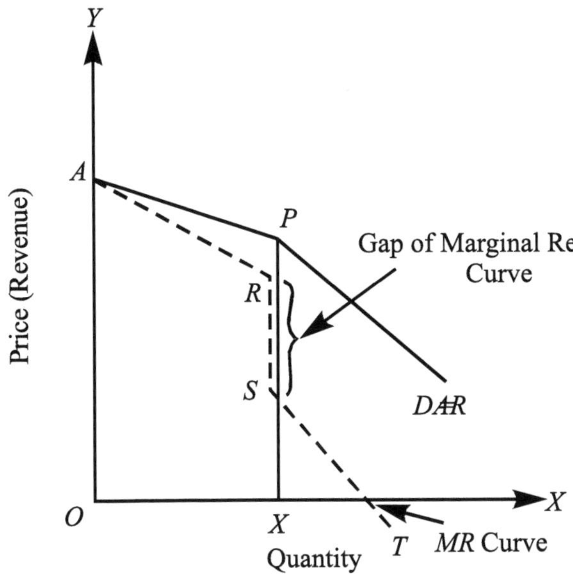

Fig. 21.10

(2) *In oligopoly situation,* a firm has to face a kinked demand curve or average revenue curve. It is shown in Fig. 21.11. Here, there is a kink at point *P.* This indicates that more or less the price is fixed for an oligopoly firm. The firm does not normally like to change the price, because it expects its competitors to follow price decreases but not increases. Thus, if the firm in question increases its price above existing level (i.e. *XP* in Fig. 21.11), its sales will decline rapidly because other firms in the market do not increase their prices. Similarly, if the firm reduces its price below the existing price, *XP,* then the other firms reduce their prices to a greater extent. This will again reduce the sales of the firm in question. It is in the interest of the firm to accept the existing price level.

Now, when there is kink in the average revenue curve, the marginal revenue is discontinuous at the point of the kink, as shown in Fig. 21.11. The discontinuous portion or gap in the marginal revenue curve can easily be drawn in a graph. In Fig. 21.11, it is clear that there are two parts of the demand curve, *AP* and *PD;* and therefore, the marginal revenue curves for these two parts of the *AR*-curve will be different. First draw the *MR*-curve corresponding to the demand curve *AP.* This *MR* curve is *AR* in Fig. 21.11. Then draw the *MR*-curve for the second part of the demand curve *PD.* This

MR-curve is *ST*. Thus, *RS* represents the discontinuous portion of the marginal revenue curve in Fig. 21.11.

Exercises

1. Explain the relationship between average revenue, marginal revenue and total revenue curves.
2. Show that an individual firm in perfect competition faces a perfectly elastic demand curve.
3. Explain the relationship between average revenue, marginal revenue and elasticity of demand.
4. Write a short note on the kinky demand curve of an oligopoly firm.
5. Prove that: Elasticity of Demand $= \dfrac{\text{Average Revenue}}{\text{Average Revenue} - \text{Marginal Revenue}}$
6. Explain the relationship between *AR* and *MR* curves of a firm under perfect competition and imperfect competition.

Multiple Choice Questions

7. (*i*) By Marginal Revenue (*MR*), we mean
   (*a*) the revenue of a firm earns when it has increased its output by one unit
   (*b*) the increase in costs a firm incurs when it increases its output by one unit
   (*c*) the change in revenue a firm earns when it increases its output by one unit
   (*d*) the change in fixed revenue but not the variable revenue due to a one unit change in sales [*Ans.* (*c*)]

   (*ii*) When $MR = 0$, elasticity of demand will be equal to
   (*a*) zero (*c*) infinity
   (*b*) unity (*d*) none of the above [*Ans.* (*b*)]

   (*iii*) When $MR > 0$ elasticity of demand will be
   (*a*) greater than unity (*c*) less than unity
   (*b*) equal to unity (*d*) equal to zero [*Ans.* (*a*)]

   (*iv*) When $Ed =$, we get
   (*a*) $MR = AR$ (*c*) $AR = MR = TR$
   (*b*) $MR = TR$ (*d*) $MR = MC$ [*Ans.* (*a*)]

   (*v*) When marginal revenue is zero
   (*a*) $TR = 0$ (*c*) *AR* is positive
   (*b*) $AR = 0$ (*d*) none of the above [*Ans.* (*c*)]

Chapter 22

Law of Supply and Elasticity of Supply

1. Introduction

The theory of supply is as much necessary as the theory of demand for the analysis of prices. In everyday use people often do not distinguish between the supply of a product and its quantity produced. However, the economists make a distinction between the two terms and they are not to be used interchangeably. Supply refers to the quantity to a good that is offered for sale in the market per period of time. Thus, the supply of a commodity is different from its stock of a point of time. The stock of a commodity refers to its total available quantity while the supply relates to only that quantity which is brought to the market for sale. It is noteworthy that the supply of a commodity differs at different prices. Hence, supply can be considered meaningfully only when it is seen in relation to some price. The concept of supply thus explained above suffers from the defect that it fails to relate supply to price. Keeping this fact in view that a more scientific definition must overcome the limitation we may define supply of a commodity as the quantity that will be available for sale in the market at a certain price per period of time. This definition of supply clearly suggests that it would be wrong to consider total stock of a commodity to be as supply. Indian mines are full of iron ore, but till such time iron ore is not extracted from the mines and is not offered for sale at a price. We cannot include it in the country's supply of iron ore. In the words of Meyers, "We may define supply as a schedule of the amount of good that would be offered for sale at all possible prices of anyone instant of time or during anyone period of time, for example a day or a week and so on in which the conditions of supply remain constant."

2. The Law of Supply

Supply of a commodity refers to the various quantities of it which a seller is willing and able to sell at a given price, in a given market and in a given period of time, other things remaining the same. It is the amount that is actually offered for sale at a given price, in a given market and in given period of time. Other things remaining the same, at any point of time a change in the price of a commodity itself results in a change in its supply. As a matter of fact there is a direct relationship between the price of a commodity and its supply. This implies that a rise in the price will induce producers to supply a larger quantity of the product while a fall in the price will result in its diminished supply. The behaviour of supply in response to changes in the price of the commodity is known as the law of supply. We may state *that ceteris paribus,* the quantity produced and offered for sale in a market varies directly with the changes in the price.

3. Factors Determining Supply

The important factors which determine the supply of a commodity are as follows:

(1) the price of the commodity in question;
(2) the prices of related commodities;
(3) the prices of the factors of production;
(4) the state of technology; and
(5) the goals of producers.

(1) *Price of the Commodity.* The supply of a commodity, depends upon the price of that commodity. Other things being equal, sellers of a commodity are normally willing to sell more of it if its price is high than if it is low.

(2) *Prices of Related Goods.* The supply of a commodity depends upon the prices of all other commodities. Generally a rise in the prices of other commodities will make production of the commodity whose price does not rise relatively less attractive than it was before. We thus expect, other things remaining the same, that the supply of the commodity will fall as the price of other commodities increase.

(3) *Prices of Factors of Production.* The supply of a commodity depends upon the prices of factors of production. An increase in the price of one agent of production may lead to a larger increase in the costs of making those commodities that use a great deal of that agent of production and only a small rise in the costs of producing those commodities that use a small amount of that factor of production. Thus a change in the price of one agent of production may cause changes in the relative profitability of different producers and this may cause producers to shift from one line of production to another and to cause changes in the supplies of different commodities.

(4) *State of Technology.* The supply of a commodity depends upon the state of technology. The tremendous results which have occurred in production, in national income, in per capita income and in the standard of living of the people and so on is very largely due to the improved methods of production. At

any time, what is produced and how it is produced depend upon what is known. Overtime, knowledge changes and so do the supplies of individual commodities.

(5) *Goals of Producers.* The supply of commodity depends upon the goals of the firms. If producers of some commodity want to sell as much as possible even if it costs them some profits to do so, more will be sold of that commodity than if they wanted to make maximum profits. If producers are not prepared to take risks, we would expect smaller production of any commodity the production of which was risky.

4. Supply Function

The supply of a commodity is a function of the price of that commodity, the prices of all other commodities, the prices of the factors of production, technology and the goals of the producers. The statement may be expressed in symbols by writing down what is called a supply function, as follows:

$$Sx = f(Px, Py, R, T, G)$$

where Sx is the quantity of commodity X supplied;

Px is the price of commodity X;

Py is the price of all other related commodities;

R is the price of factors of production;

T is the state of technology; and

G is the goals of the producers.

This is a very complicated functional relationship and we shall not succeed in developing a simple law of supply if we consider what happens to supply of a commodity when these things, i.e. prices of all other related commodities, prices of factors of production, changes in technology and the tastes of the producers all change at once. For a simple theory of price we want to know how the quantity supplied of a commodity varies with its own price. There is a functional relationship between price and amount supplied of a commodity. The functional relationship can alternatively be written as:

$$Sx = f(Px).$$

where Sx is the amount of commodity X supplied

Px is the price of the commodity X.

5. Supply Schedule and Supply Curve

Supply Schedule. A supply schedule is a relation between prices and quantities for a given commodity in a given market and in a given period of time. The quantity supplied of a commodity varies directly with the price. When the price falls supply will contract and when the price rises supply will extend. To illustrate the relation between the amount of a commodity supplied and its price, we shall take imaginary data for the prices and quantities of wheat.

Table 22.1: Supply Schedule

Price of Wheat ($s.)	*Quantity Supplied (kgs.)*
10	500
9	400
8	400
7	300
6	150
5	50

It is clear from the schedule in Table 22.1 that if the price of wheat increases, sellers will supply more wheat, on the contrary, if the price of wheat falls sellers will offer lower quantity of wheat for sale.

The Supply Curve. We can plot the data from the schedule on a graph with price on the vertical axis and quantity supplied on the horizontal axis. In the Fig. 22.1 we have shown such a graph. It gives the supply curve *SS*. It indicates the relation between the price and the quantity of that commodity.

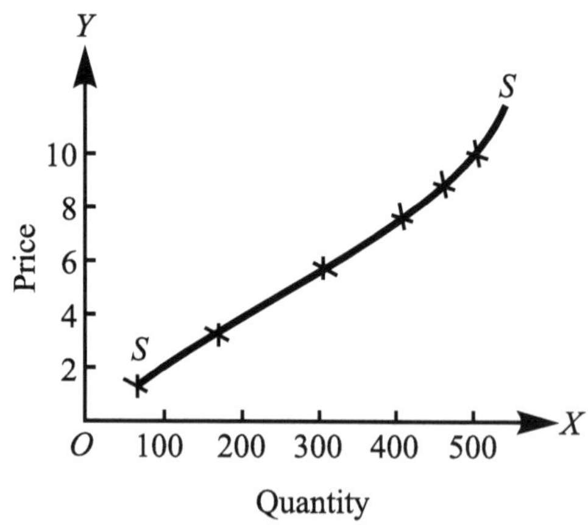

Fig. 22.1

6. Change in Supply and Change in Quantity Supplied

Under change in supply, we talk about increase in supply and decrease in supply while under change in quantity supplied we talk about extension of supply and contraction of supply. All these terms are explained as follows:

Increase in Supply. When more units of a commodity are supplied at the same price or the same units are supplied a lower price, it is an increase in supply with an increase in the supply of a commodity, the supply curve will get shifted to the right. This is shown in Fig. 22.2 when an increase in supply of a commodity occurs, supply curve also shifts from *SS* to *S′ S′*. It can be seen from Fig. 22.2 that at the same price *OP* now OX_1 units (instead of *OX*) of the commodity are supplied, i.e., an increase in supply or the same units *OX* are now supplied at a lower price OP_1.

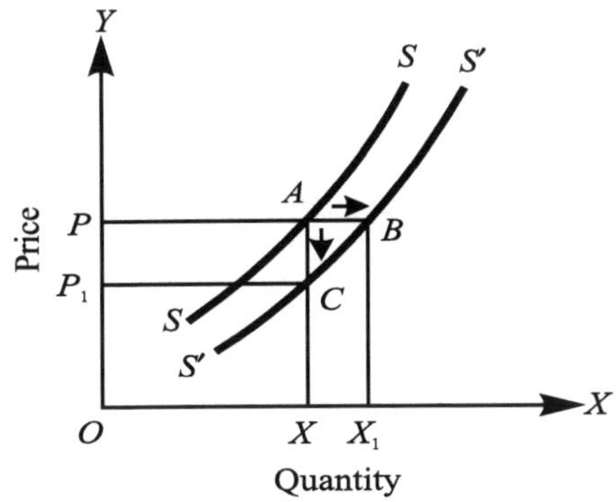

Fig. 22.2

Decrease in Supply. Decrease in supply means the same units of a commodity will be supplied at a higher price or at the same price less units of a commodity will be offered for sale. With a decrease in supply of a commodity the supply curve will get shifted to the left. This is shown in Fig. 22.3. When there is a decrease in the supply of a commodity, the supply curve shifts to *S′ S′*. At price *OP, OX* units of the commodity are offered for sale. When there is a decrease in supply of a commodity the same amount of the commodity (*OX*) is offered for sale at a higher price OP_1 or at the same price (*OP*) less quantity, i.e. OX_1 units are supplied.

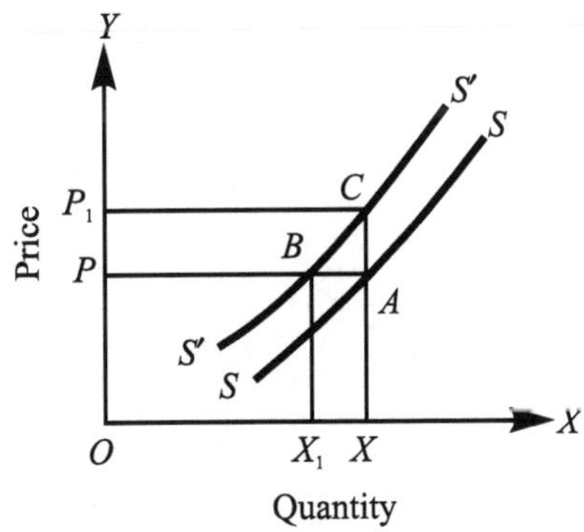

Fig. 22.3

Extension of Supply. When more units of a commodity are supplied at a higher price it is called the extension of supply. The extension of supply is shown in Fig. 22.4. Here at *OP* price *OX* units of commodity are supplied by the sellers. At price OP_1, the firm supplies OX_1 units of the commodity. At a still higher price OP_2, OX_2 units of commodity are supplied. Higher the price the larger will be the quantity supplied of a commodity.

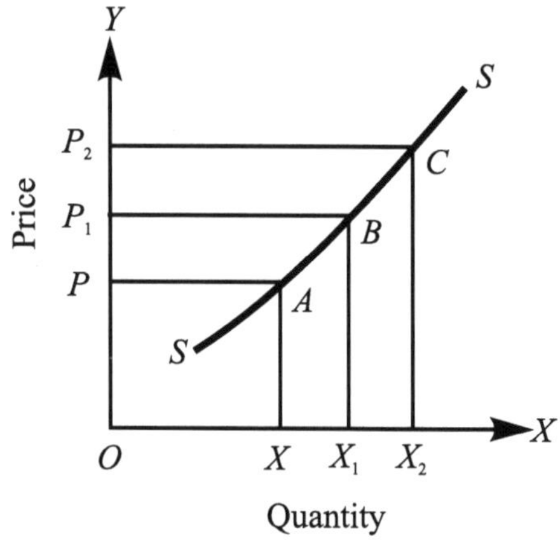

Fig. 22.4

Contraction of Supply. Contraction of supply means lower the price, smaller will be the quantity supplied of a commodity. The contraction of supply is shown in Fig. 22.5. At the price *OP* the firm supplies *OX* units of the commodity. At a lower price OP_1, the units of the commodity supplied will be reduced from *OX* to OX_1. At a still lower price OP_2, the units of commodity supplied will come down to OX_2. A movement along a supply curve indicates that a different quantity is being supplied because the price has changed.

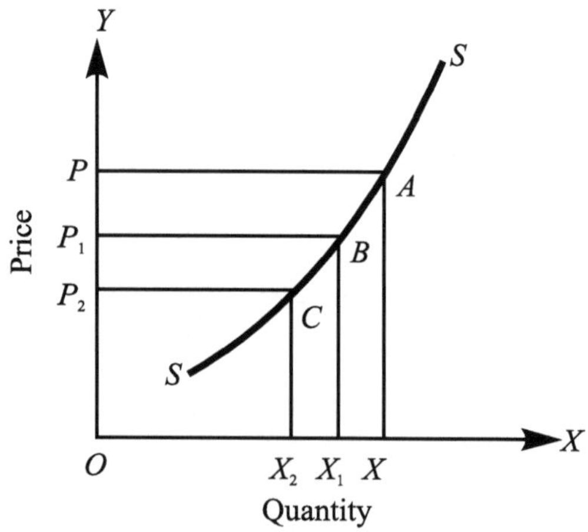

Fig. 22.5

7. Elasticity of Supply

The relationship between the proportionate (percentage) change in the quantity supplied and the proportionate (percentage) change in price is known as the

Elasticity of Supply. The formula for the elasticity of supply is similar to that for the elasticity of demand.

$$\text{Elasticity of supply} = \frac{\text{Per cent change in quantity supplied}}{\text{Per cent change in price}}$$

or
$$Es = \frac{\Delta X}{\Delta P} \cdot \frac{P}{X}$$

where
X = Original quantity supplied
P = Original price
ΔP = Absolute change in price
ΔX = Absolute change in quantity supplied

If this ratio $Es > 1$, supply is said to be elastic.

If this ratio $Es < 1$, supply is said to be inelastic.

If this ratio $Es = 1$, supply is said to have unit elasticity.

When the supply curve is perpendicular to the quantity axis, the elasticity of supply is zero ($Es = 0$).

When the supply curve is perpendicular to the price axis, the elasticity of supply is infinite ($Es = \infty$).

In fact, the steepness of supply curves varies with the commodity; certain supply curves tend to be elastic, others inelastic, and so on. This follows from the fact that an increase or decrease in price may bring about very little or a great change in the quantity producers are willing to supply. We see then that, when the percentage change in quantity is greater than the percentage change in price, supply is elastic [see panel (*a*) of Fig. 22.6], and when the proportionate change in quantity is less than the proportionate change in price, supply is inelastic [see panel (*b*) of Fig. 22.6]. In panel (*c*) of Fig. 22.6 we have the interesting case of supply having an elasticity of unity the proportionate changes in price and quantity being equal. Panel (*d*) of Fig. 22.6 illustrates a situation of a completely inelastic supply curve the vertical line *SS*. This is obviously the most extreme case of an inelastic supply in which a change in price results in absolutely no change in the production of the commodity, and its quantity is fixed. If we were to use our formula for determining elasticity, we would see that elasticity in this case is zero. Zero (which would be the percentage change in quantity divided by any number (the percentage change in price) is zero. The supply curve *SS* in panel (*e*) of Fig. 22.6 illustrates the other extreme case of perfectly elastic or infinitely elastic supply. In this case a small change in price results in an infinite increase in quantity. In instances such as this, or when the supply moves in the direction of horizontal line, we say that the elasticity of supply is infinite, or moves towards infinity.

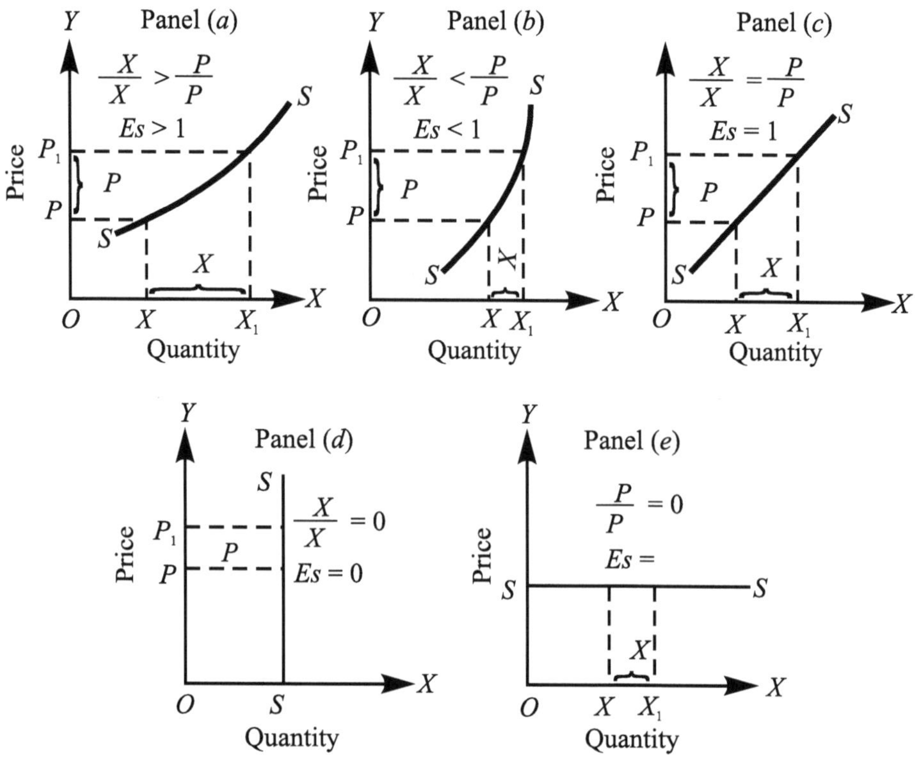

Fig. 22.6

The degree to which supply is elastic depends upon the flexibility of the productive resources. If production, with existing capacity, can be expanded easily and quickly in response to changes in demand, then supply will be elastic. An increase in the demand for many manufactured products could be met by employing more men, bringing into use stand-by equipment, and by working overtime. This would no doubt be true in the case of products such as footwear, hosiery and razor blades.

On the other hand, the supply of agricultural products must be fairly inelastic, because the quantity supplied in anyone year is governed by acreage planted in the sowing season. Some natural raw materials and some foodstuffs have supply curves which are extremely inelastic; rubber trees take five to seven years to reach maturity, and a significant increase in the size of dairy and beef herds would take several years. Hence, the element of time exercises an important influence on elasticity of supply. The longer the period of time, the more elastic is the supply likely to be.

8. Measurement of Elasticity of Supply

Elasticity of supply can be measured with the help of Fig. 22.7. The supply curve is *SS'* and *NM* is tangent to the supply curve between *R* and R_1 (*R* and

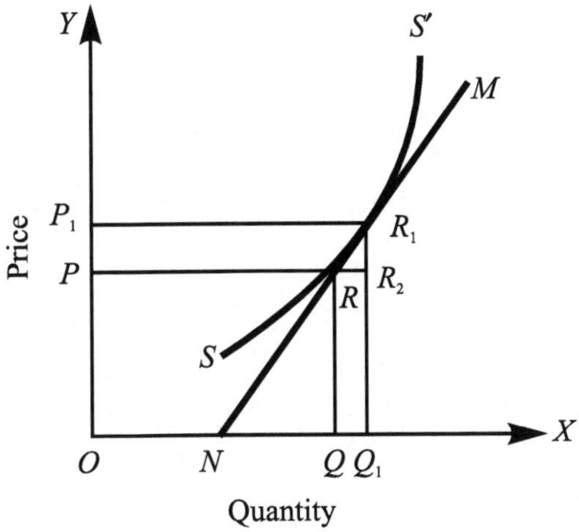

Fig. 22.7

R_1 should be close to each other). The rise in price is PP_1 or $R_2 R_1$; the increase in the quantity supplied is QQ_1 or RR_2.

Now the elasticity of supply formula is:

$$Es = \frac{\text{Percentage change in supply}}{\text{Percentage change in price}}$$

This formula of elasticity of supply is the same as elasticity of demand. It can be formulated as follows:

$$Es = \frac{\dfrac{\text{Change in supply}}{\text{Original supply}} \times 100}{\dfrac{\text{Change in price}}{\text{Original price}} \times 100}$$

$$= \frac{\text{Original supply}}{\text{Original supply}} \times \frac{\text{Original price}}{\text{Change in price}}$$

(Reorganising the above equation we get)

$$= \frac{\text{Change in supply}}{\text{Change in supply}} \times \frac{\text{Original price}}{\text{Original supply}}$$

Substituting the required information from the Fig. 22.7, we get

$$Es = \frac{RR_2}{R_1R_2} \times \frac{RQ}{OQ}$$

ΔRR_1R_2 and ΔNRQ are similar, therefore, the ratio of their sides is equal. This implies that

$$\frac{NQ}{RQ}\frac{RR_2}{R_1R_2} = \frac{NQ}{RQ}$$

$\therefore \qquad Es = \frac{NQ}{RQ} \times \frac{RQ}{OQ}$ [RQ may be cancelled from both sides]

$\therefore \qquad Es = \frac{NQ}{OQ}.$

This is how we measure elasticity of supply with the help of a diagram. It may be observed that in Fig. 22.7 NQ is less than OQ and therefore, elasticity of supply in this case will be less than one. On the other hand, if N coincides with the origin of the axis, NQ and OQ will be equal, consequently elasticity of supply will be equal to 1 or unity. If, finally, N happens to be beyond O, the elasticity of supply will be more than unity.

9. Elasticity of Price Expectation

A new concept of elasticity, known as elasticity of price expectation, was developed by the English economist J.R. Hicks in 1939. The demand for a commodity is influenced not only by the current price, but also by price expectations, i.e. the expected future price. The extent to which demand is affected by price expectations depends in good part upon the elasticity of price expectations. People's price expectations are influenced by several things, such as, political changes, current and recent economic developments, general opinion and the past experiences about the changes in prices. The elasticity of price expectation can be defined as the ratio of the relative change in expected future prices to the relative change in current prices.
Symbolically,

$$Ep = \frac{\text{Relative (percentage) change in expected future prices}}{\text{Relative (percentage) change in current prices}}$$

$$= \frac{\Delta Pf}{Pf} \Big/ \frac{\Delta Pc}{Pc}$$

where Ep = Elasticity of price expectation
Pf = Original future expected price
ΔPf = Change in future expected price
Pc = Original current price
ΔPc = Change in current price

Let us suppose that a consumer (or a businessman) sees that the current price of a commodity has increased by 20 per cent. Now, the consumer or the businessman expects a similar change in his original estimate of a future price of that commodity and raises the estimate of a future price by 40 per cent; so that, he has an elasticity of price expectations of 2.

Table 22.2 shows the possible ranges of elasticities of price expectations of consumers in a market.

If the elasticity of price expectation is elastic, increase in the current price of a product will cause its demand curve to shift to the right. In such a case the demand for the commodity will increase, because people want to buy more now to avoid the even higher prices they expect to prevail in the future.

Table: 22.2: Various Elasticities of Price Expectations
(Expectations of people toward an increase in current price)

Elasticity of price expectation	*Value of the coefficient (Ep)*	*People's expectation*
High Elasticity	$Ep > 1$	People expect that future prices will increase by a larger percentage than current prices.
Unit Elasticity	$Ep = 1$	People expect that future prices will increase by the same percentage as current prices.
Low Elasticity	$0 < Ep < 1$	People expect that future prices will increase by a smaller percentage than current prices.
Zero Elasticity	$Ep = 0$	People expect that an increase in current prices will have no effect on future prices.
Negative Elasticity	$Ep < 0$	People expect that an increase (or decrease) in current prices will be followed by a decrease (or an increase) in future prices.

If, on the other hand, the elasticity of price expectation is inelastic or negatively elastic, an increase in the current price of the product will cause its demand to shift to the left. In such a case, the demand for the commodity will decrease, because people will wait for the price to come down in the future.

If the elasticity of price expectation is unity, a change in current price of the commodity will make no effect on the current demand.

The concept of elasticity of expectations is of paramount importance in the speculative activities of the businessmen.

10. Supply Curve under Perfect Competition

The basis of the demand curve lies in the marginal utility of a commodity, while the basis of the supply curve lies in the costs of production. In considering how much of a commodity a firm is willing to supply, it is evident that its cost of production will be the major determinant.[1] We have already discussed the various types of costs in an earlier chapter; the most important types to be studied in relation to supply, are marginal cost and average cost.[2] As we know, marginal cost represents the cost of producing one more the addition to total cost resulting from the expansion of supply of output by one unit. The firm will continue to expand her output as long as the receipts from the sales of extra units exceed the cost of producing them. Here we assume that the firm always attempts to get maximum profits (or maximum loss). Maximum profits will be attained at that level of output where marginal cost is equal to marginal revenue ($MC = MR$).[3] As we know, marginal revenue represents the change in total revenue which results from the sales of one more unit. If price does not change as the number of units sold increases, then marginal revenue must be equal to the price ($MR = P$).

---

1. If the costs of production are raised, the supply curve will be pushed upwards; if costs of production are reduced, the supply curve will be pushed down. Thus, the cost is the vital determinant of supply. Yet, the supply will also depend upon its price and the technological progress.
2. In the short-run the firm will consider the average variable cost and not the average cost as the determinant of supply. In the long-run, average variable and average cost are one and the same thing.
3. We can also show this situation mathematically as

$$\pi = TR - TC$$

where π is total profit, TR is total revenue and TC is total cost. For profit (π) maximisation:

$$\frac{d\pi}{dX} = \frac{d(TR)}{dX} - \frac{d(TC)}{dX} = 0$$

$$\therefore \quad \frac{d(TR)}{dX} = \frac{d(TC)}{dX}$$

or

$$MR = MC$$

11. The Short-run Supply Curve of the Firm

As we have already explained, a firm is unable to change the sale of plant in the short period. Thus, there are some fixed factors of production in the short-run and firm can increase production only by increasing the quantities of variable inputs. The marginal and average cost of the individual firm are assumed to behave in the manner as shown in Fig. 22.8.

Figure 22.8 presents the firm's *MC* and *AVC* curves and the three exogeneously determined price levels.[4] *OP*, OP_1 and OP_2 are given prices and *OX*, OX_1 and OX_2 are the respective quantities of output where Price = Marginal Cost. Since we are assuming that the price remains constant over the range of output, price will be equal to marginal revenue ($P = MR$); each additional unit sold will add to the total revenue a sum of money which is equal to its price. Therefore, the equilibrium condition of the competitive firm can be written as:

$$\text{Price} = \text{Marginal Revenue} = \text{Marginal Cost}$$

Now our question is, what will be the level of supply? At a price of OP_2, the firm is willing to supply OX_2 quantity of output. At any level of output smaller than OX_2 the firm's profits (or losses) will not be maximized (minimised) because additions tocosts will be smaller than additions to revenue (or $MC < MR$), and the firm will gain by expanding her output to the extent of OX_2. Also, at higher levels of output than OX_2, the additions to costs will be greater than additions to revenue (or $MC > MR$), and it would pay the firm to reduce her output. Thus, at OP_2 price, the firm will maximise her profits (or minimise her losses) only at OX_2 level of output (where at point *C*, its $MC = MR$).

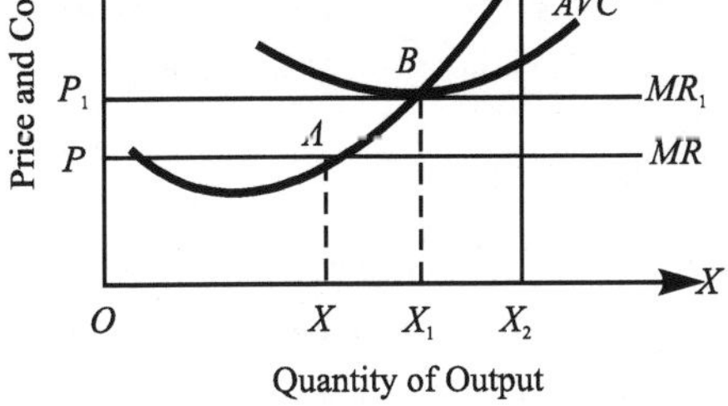

Fig. 22.8

4. Since it is the situation of perfect competition, the price of the commodity will be determined by the industry and not by the individual firm. The firm is a price-taker. Therefore, it (price) will be an exogeneous variable for the firm.

Further, at price OP_1, the firm will produce OX_1 quantity of output because at point B, $P = MR = MC$. In this particular case, price is also equal to average variable cost. It means that the revenue (price) only just covers the variable costs and there is a loss of fixed costs. But the loss of fixed costs is to be incurred even if the firm produces nothing. Thus at price OP_1, the firm is willing to supply only OX_1 quantity of out put.

But at any price below OP_1, the firm will produce nothing. In Fig. 22.8 at OP price, firm's (first order) profit maximising condition is satisfied at OX level of output. The equilibrium point is A where $P = MR = MC$. But at this level of output (OX), however, price is below average variable cost (or $P < AVC$). In such a situation production could only be carried on at a loss of available costs and no rational firm would like to bear it. Thus, at price OP, the firm would not produce at all. The minimum price acceptable by the firm is OP_1, and the corresponding (minimum) level of output would be OX_1.

Now we are able to answer the question, what quantities would a firm like to supply at any given price? The answer lies in the marginal cost curve, but only that part of marginal cost curve may be regarded as the supply which lies above the average variable cost curve. If we choose any price above OP_1, then the quantity supplied at the chosen price is determined by the intersection of the price line ($P = MR$) and the marginal cost curve.

Therefore, there is a "relevant range" of MC curve over which it assumes the form of a firm's short-run supply curve. In Fig. 22.8, this range is shown beyond the point B at which the AVC is minimum and is equal to the MC.

12. The Short-run Supply Curve of the Industry

The total (market) supply curve or the industry supply curve for the product can be obtained by adding the supply curve of the individual firms. Figure 22.9 illustrates the construction of the industry supply curve from the firms' marginal cost (supply) curves. For simplicity, let us assume that there are only two firms in the industry. In Fig. 22.9. Panels, (*a*) and (*b*) present the marginal cost curves of two firms in their relevant ranges where they face the situations as

$$P > \text{min. } AVC$$

because only then there can be assumed a positive supply.

Panel (*c*) in Fig. 22.9 shows the industry (market) supply curve *SS* which has been derived by taking the horizontal summation of the individual supply (*MC*) curves of the firms. The market supply curve is positively sloped which implies that each firm supplies a larger quantity of output at successively higher prices. In Fig. 22.9, it is clear that at price of $2, firm *I* will produce nothing because this price is below the minimum of its *AVC*, while firm *II* will produce 7 units of output; thus the total supply of the industry will be equal to 7 units. At price of \$4, firm *I* produces 5 units of output and firm *II* produces 15 units of output; thus the total supply of the industry at price of \$4 is equal to 20 units (5 units + 15 units). When price is \$6, firm *I* is willing to supply 8 units and firm *II* is willing to supply 20 units; thus the total supply of the industry becomes 28 units (8 units + 20 units) at price of \$6. Hence, the industry supply curve of the output is the horizontal summation of the individual firm's supply (marginal cost) curves.

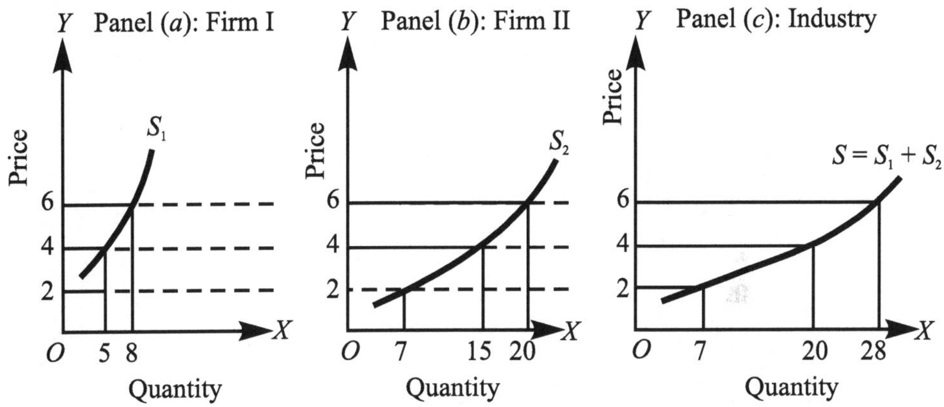

Fig. 22.9

13. The Long-run Supply Curve of the Firm and the Industry

Like the short-run supply curves of the firm and the industry, we may also derive the long-run supply curves of the firm and the industry. As we know, in the long-run, there are no fixed costs, thus the average variable cost curve of the short-run now becomes the average cost of the long-run. In the long-run, the minimum price acceptable by the firm for her product must be equal to the minimum of its average cost. Therefore, in the long-run, the supply of the firm will be determined by the equality of marginal revenue (price) and marginal cost ($MR = MC$), subject to the condition that the long-run price of the product must cover the average cost of production. The reason is that, in the long-run, no firm would like to bear the loss, how little it may be. In a situation when price is just equal to the average cost, i.e. there is no profit, no loss to the firm it would like to produce that level of ouput at which its $MR = MC$. Because, although the firm is not getting any abnormal profit, yet she is gaining normal profits which the economist includes in his average cost of production. Normal profit is defined as that level of profit which makes it just worthwhile for the firm to stay in its present line of business. Since this minimum level of profit is needed to keep the firm in production, it is legitimate to regard these profits as a cost of production.

At that level of output where price is below average cost, productions could only be carried on at a loss and we must assume that the firm would not, in the long-run, produce at this price. Although, in such a situation, our rule of profit maximisation ($MR = MC$) may be satisfied, yet, in such a case "maximum profits" must be read as "minimum losses". Hence, the minimum condition necessary for a firm to produce in the long-run is that the price must be equal to the average cost of production. If this condition is satisfied, then the firm will determine its exact supply of the product at a point where its marginal revenue (price) is equal to its marginal cost. The part of marginal cost curve of the firm which is above the minimum point of average cost curve is the supply curve of the firm in long-run. This has been illustrated in Fig. 22.10. Here, the part of *LMC* curve which is above point *A* is the supply curve of the firm. If the price is OP_2, the firm is willing to supply OX_2 units of output; because this is the level of output at which she gets maximum profit.

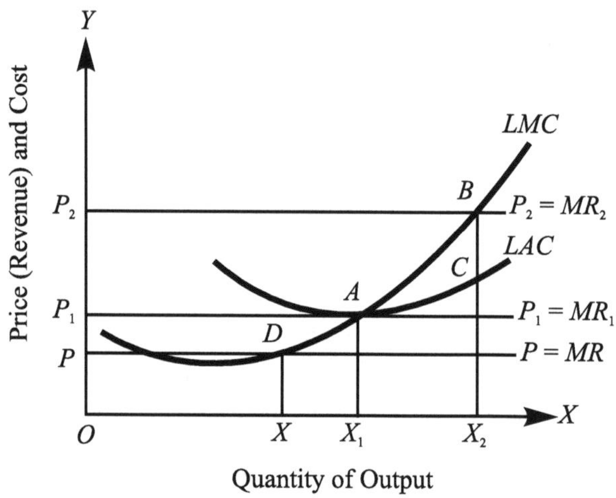

Fig. 22.10

At OX_2 level of output, the firm's per unit profit is equal to *BC*. If the firm produces a smaller amount than OX_2, its profit per unit will be reduced and if it produces more than OX_2 level of output, the addition to total cost (i.e. *MC*) is higher than the price (i.e. *MR*). Thus, at OP_2 long-run price the firm's long-run supply will be OX_2. The minimum price acceptable by the firm is equal to QP_1 at which the firm would like to produce OX_1 quantity of output. This price is just equal to its minimum long-run average cost. If price is below this level, then she will produce no output. For instance, at *OP* price, although firm's profit and output determination rule ($MC = MR$) is fulfilled at point *D*, where she requires to produce *OX* quantity of output. But this situation does not satisfy the other minimum long-run condition, that is, the price must be equal to the average cost. Hence, at *OP* price, the firm would like to no output and will change the line of business.

Now, the long-run supply curve of the industry can be obtained by the horizontal summation of the long-run supply (*MC*) curves of all the individual firms, the diagram will be the same as in Fig. 22.9. The shape of industry supply curve will depend upon the shape of marginal cost curves of the individual firms. Normally, the supply curve of the industry slopes upwards from left to right, indicating that more is supplied at higher price.

Changes in Supply. Changes in supply are made by changes in the scale of plant or the introduction of new techniques and methods of production. In each case the changes will mean that the costs of production have altered. An increase in scale or an improvement in the methods of production will mean a lowering of costs and new cost curves become applicable. Figure 22.11 shows the effects of a firm expanding and modernising its production processes. The original average and marginal cost curves are represented by *AC* and *MC*. An increase in the scale of plant and new techniques of productions result in greater efficiency and a lowering of its cost curves. Their new average and marginal cost curves are represented by AC_1 and MC_1 respectively. The supply curves of the firm are shown by heavier-lined sections of the marginal cost curves. Here, we may note that the increased efficiency of the firm shifts its supply curve to the right downward.

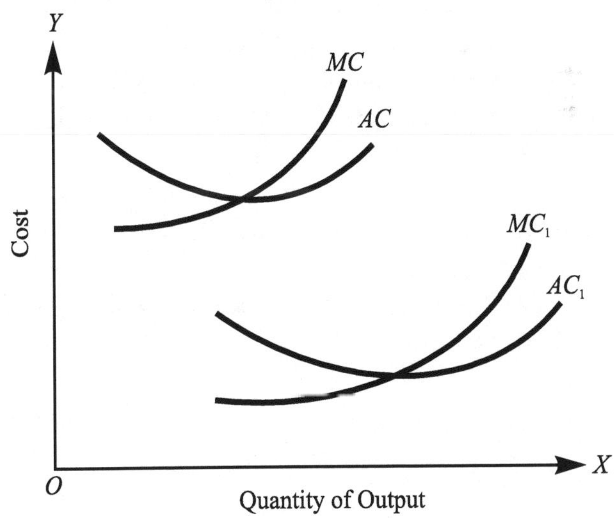

Fig. 22.11

14. Laws of Returns and the Long-run Supply Curve of an Industry

The Laws of Returns have an important bearing on the shape of the long period supply curve of an industry under perfect competition. The long period supply curve of the perfectly competitive industry will have different shapes depending upon the fact whether the industry is subject to constant returns, diminishing returns or increasing returns. The long period industry supply curve will be horizontal, if the industry in question is subject to the Constant Returns. It will slope upwards to the right if the industry is subject to Diminishing Returns. It will slope upwards to the left if the industry is subject to the Increasing Returns.

Industry Supply Curve under Constant Returns or Constant Costs

The cost of an industry subject to constant returns remain unchanged if the output of the industry is expanded through the application of additional doses of inputs. As the industry expands, the external economies resulting from it get cancelled with the external diseconomies flowing from it. The result is that the production costs remain constant. No doubt, the new firms will enter into industry in the long period but their costs will remain constant owing to the operation of the Law of Constant Returns.

This has been shown in Fig. 22.12 where the firm has achieved its equilibrium at the point *E*. At this point the *LMC* and *LAC* curves of the firm intersect each other. The firm is in equilibrium at the point *E* producing *OX* output at *OP* price. In the long period, the firm, expands its output but the costs remain constant. So the firm achieves its new equilibrium at the same point *E* without any rise in the average and the marginal costs of production. This applies to the new firms also which enter into the industry. Their costs do behave in the same manner as the cost of the firm in question. The result is that the long-run supply curve of the industry assumes a horizontal shape as shown in Fig. 22.12. It may be noted that for the purpose of this discussion, we assume all the firms to be indentical.

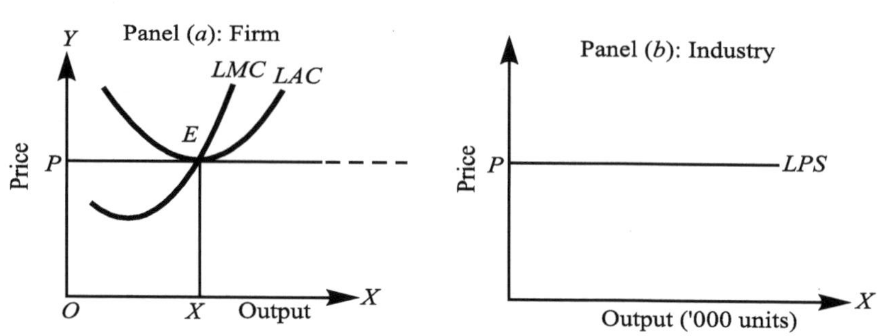

Fig. 22.12

Industry Supply Curve under Diminishing Returns or Increasing Costs

The costs of an industry subject to Diminishing Returns go on increasing if the output of the industry is expanded through the application of additional doses of inputs. As the industry expands, the external diseconomies resulting from it outweigh the economies flowing from it. The result is that the cost of production per unit goes on increasing with the expansion of output of the industry. In the long period, the new firms enter into the industry, there is increased pressure on the existing factors of production which now become scarce as a result of an increase in their demand. So the production costs start rising up with every expansion of the industry. This has been shown in Fig. 22.13. The firm is in initial equilibrium at the point *E* where the *LMC* and *LAC* curves intersect each other.

At this point, the price = *MC* = *AC*. The firm is in equilibrium producing *OX* output at *OP* price. With the expansion of industry production, the factors get scarced and the costs start mounting up. The firm now achieves equilibrium at the point E_1 where its LAC_1 and LMC_1 curves intersect each other. The firm, no doubt produces less output OX_1, but this output is achieved with higher costs. Since the number affirms is increasing and even if the individual firm's output is less but the output of the industry increases. As Fig. 22.13 shows, the firm achieves its new equilibrium at a higher costs and at higher prices. Since the production costs of all the firms register an increase, the industry will be able to supply increased quantities of the product only at a higher price. At the old *OP* price; the industry was supplying *OR* quantity of the commodity. At the new price OP_1 which is higher than the original price *OP;* the industry supply has increased to OR_1. This shows that the industry supply increases with every increase in the price of the commodity. It is for this reason that the *LPS* curve of the industry slopes upwards to the right.

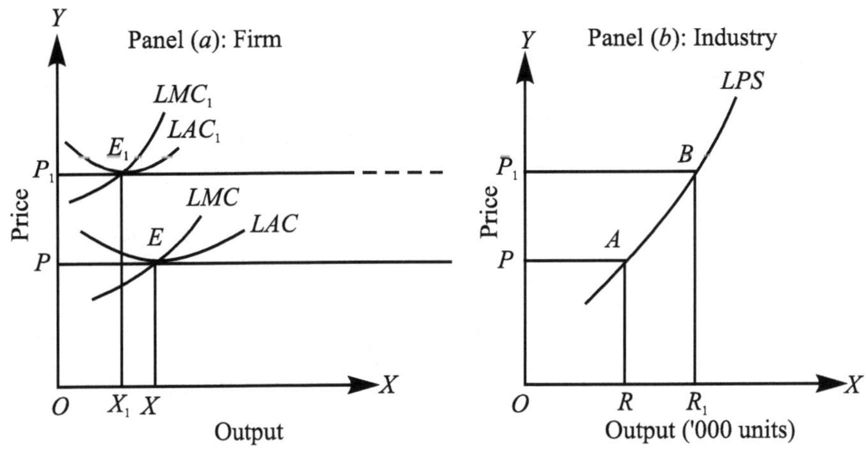

Fig. 22.13

Industry Supply Curve under Increasing Returns or Diminishing Costs

The costs of an industry subject to increasing returns go on diminishing as the output of the industry is expanded through the application of additional doses of inputs. As the industry expands the external economies resulting from it outweigh the external diseconomies flowing from it. The result is that the cost of production per unit goes on diminishing with every expansion of the output. In the long period, as the firm expands and the new firms enter into the industry, the production costs start declining with every expansion of the industry. This has been shown in Fig. 22.14. The firm is in initial equilibrium at the point E when the price $= MC = AC$. The firm is in equilibrium at the point E producing OX output at OP price. Then the firm in question starts expanding in production. It achieves the new equilibrium at the point E_1 where the LAC_1 and LMC_1 curves intersect each other. At this point, the firm produces the increased output OX, at the lower price OP_1, The Fig. 22.14 clearly shows the firm has achieved its new equilibrium at a lower cost and also at a lower price on account of the operation of the law of increasing returns or diminishing costs. The new firms which enter into the industry in the long period will also achieve equilibrium at lower costs and also at lower prices. Since the production cost of all the firms register a decline, the industry will be able to supply increased quantities of the product at lower prices. At this old OP price, the industry was supplying OR quantity of the commodity, At the new price OP_1 which is lower than the original price OP, the industry supplies increased output namely OR_1. This shows that the additional supplies from the industry are forthcoming at lower prices. It is for this reason that the LPS curve of the industry slopes downwards to the right.

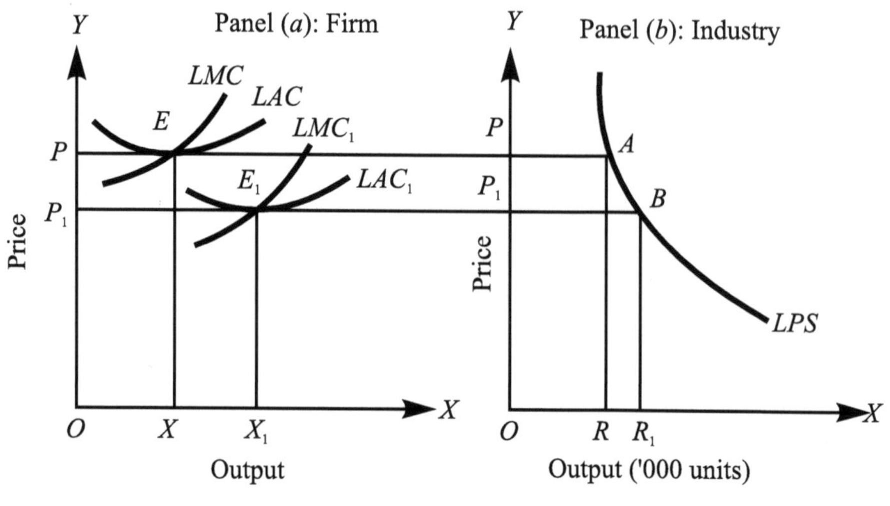

Fig. 22.14

15. Supply Curve under Monopoly or Imperfect Competition

We do not have a unique supply curve under imperfect competition or monopoly. It is because of the fact that price is simultaneously determined along with the quantity of the commodity produced unlike perfect competition, the price is not given to a firm under monopoly or monopolistic competition. Here the firm is a price-maker for her product. Thus, the firm fixes a price where it gets maximum profit. The supply of the commodity is determined by the market demand for its product. It is therefore impossible to talk of a supply curve under monopoly or monopolistic competition. The output supplied by the producer under such monopolistic situation will depend upon the market demand conditions for his product and no unique supply curve (as well as the supply schedule) can be drawn.

Exercises

1. Derive the short-run supply curve of a firm under perfect competition. How would you obtain the industry supply schedule?
2. Derive the long-run supply curve of the firm and the industry under perfect competition.
3. Explain the conditions under which the supply curve slopes downward.
4. Discuss why does the supply curve of the firm and the industry slope upward to the right in the short-run?
5. Explain the fact that the shape of the long-run supply curve depends on the laws of production.
6. "There is no unique supply curve under monopoly." Explain the statement.
7. State the law of supply and explain the elasticity of supply. How will you measure the elasticity of supply?
8. Distinguish between change in supply and change in quantity supplied.
9. Write a note on elasticity of price expectation.

Multiple Choice Questions

10. (*i*) Other things being equal, a rise in supply can be caused by
    (*a*) a rise in the price of the commodity
    (*b*) a rise in the income of the consumer
    (*c*) an increase in the income of the seller
    (*d*) all of the above [*Ans.* (*a*)]

    (*ii*) Given the supply of a commodity in the market period, the price of the commodity is determined by
    (*a*) the market demand curve alone
    (*b*) the market supply curve alone
    (*c*) the market demand curve and the market supply curve
    (*d*) none of the above [*Ans.* (*a*)]

(*iii*) At the shut-down point

(*a*) $TR = TVC$

(*b*) $P=AVC$

(*c*) the total losses of the firm equal *TFC*

(*d*) all of the above [*Ans.* (*b*)]

(*iv*) The short-run supply curve of the perfectly competitive firm is given by

(*a*) the rising portion of its *MC* curve over and above the shut-down point

(*b*) the rising portion of its *MC* curve over and above the break-even-point

(*c*) the rising portion of its *MC* curve over and above the *AC* curve

(*d*) the rising portion of its *MC* curve [*Ans.* (*a*)]

(*v*) An increase in output in a perfectly competitive constant cost industry which is in long-run equilibrium will come

(*a*) entirely from new firm

(*b*) entirely from existing firm

(*c*) either (*a*) or (*b*)

(*d*) partly from new firm and partly from existing firm [*Ans.* (*a*)]

Chapter 23

Equilibrium of the Firm and the Industry

1. Introduction

As we have already explained, equilibrium indicates a situation in which there is a complete adjustment of the various forces operating there and there is no inducement to change. It is an ideal stage. In Part Two of this book, we have analysed the behaviour of a consumer. A consumer is said to be in equilibrium when he is deriving maximum satisfaction. In Part Three of this book, we have analysed the behaviour of a rational producer (firm). He tries to minimise the cost of producing a given level of output or maximise his revenue (output) for given level of resource use. Thus, in the case of a producer, equilibrium is attained when he gets maximum output with the least cost-combination of different inputs.

In the present chapter, we shall discuss the equilibrium of the firm and the industry. A firm is said to be in equilibrium when it has no incentive either to expand or to contract its output. A firm would not like to change its level of output only when it is earning maximum profits. Hence, the firm attempts to maximise its profits, or to minimise its losses. Maximisation of profits or minimisation of losses (in case losses are met with) is a condition of a firm's equilibrium.s Similarly, an industry is said to be in equilibrium when the market demand and the market supply are perfectly equal and changes in demand and supply are absent.

2. Equilibrium of the Firm under Perfect Competition

The equilibrium of the firm can be discussed in terms of marginal cost and marginal revenue as well as in terms of total cost and total revenue. Many firms, nowadays, use a device known as a *break-even chart* for determining what output of their product would be most profitable in the market situation that confronts them. This kind of chart is based on a comparison of total costs for different outputs with the total receipts that it is anticipated can be derived from sales. It means that every firm intends to obtain the greatest return on its investment, or to maximise the difference between total revenue (receipts) and total cost. Suppose, a perfect competitive firm has to face with the costs and revenues as given in Table 23.1. Price for the firm has been assumed to remain constant. The fixed costs are assumed to be \$40. The sum of the fixed and variable costs for different outputs amounts to the figures shown in column 4. The total costs are plotted in the wavelike curve of Fig. 23.1. Table 23.1 also states that the price, \$20 per unit is fixed for the firm's output. The total revenue (receipts) from sales for various quantities sold will then be as shown in column 7 of the table. The figures of total revenue are also plotted on the diagram which gives us the diagonal straight line marked "Total Revenue Curve." The profit or loss resulting from sales for each unit is shown in the last column of the Table 23.1.

Table 23.1: Revenue, Cost and Profit for a Hypothetical Firm under Perfect Competition

Quantity of Output	*Total Fixed Cost*	*Total Variable Cost*	*Total Cost*	*Marginal Cost*	*Price*	*Total Revenue*	*Marginal Revenue*	*Profit or Loss*
1	*2*	*3*	*4*	*5*	*6*	*7*	*8*	*9*
0	40	—	40	—	—	—	—	–40
1	40	13	53	—	20	20	20	–33
2	40	24	64	11	20	40	20	–24
3	40	33	73	9	20	60	20	–13
4	40	40	80	7	20	80	20	0
5	40	48	88	8	20	100	20	+12
6	40	57	97	9	20	120	20	+20
7	40	77	117	20	20	140	20	+23
8	40	100	140	23	20	160	20	+20
9	40	140	180	40	20	180	20	0
10	40	183	223	43	20	200	20	–23

It can be observed from Table 23.1 and from Fig. 23.1 that the entrepreneur maximises his profit where the difference between total cost and total revenue is maximum. In equilibrium, he will produce seven units of output for maximisation of profit. We notice that for small outputs, the total costs exceed the total receipts obtained. This is because the fixed costs are not distributed over a large enough number of units to bring the cost per unit down below the selling price. But if more is produced, the losses shrink until a break-even point is reached (at 4 units of output), where the total revenue is just equal to total cost (\$80). This is shown in Fig. 23.1 at point *A* where the total cost curve cuts the total revenue curve. From point *A*, the total revenue exceeds the total costs, and results in a profit to the firm. The profits become larger with greater output, but after some point they will decline again as the maximum capacity of the plant is approached. Costs then creep up on the selling price until profits reduce to zero. In Fig. 23.1, point *B* shows that at nine units of output, profit becomes zero. Beyond this point *B*, losses would again be incurred. Thus, firm will always produce a level of output which is above the break-even point. It will try to increase its sales to that point where it gets maximum profit (7 units in our example).

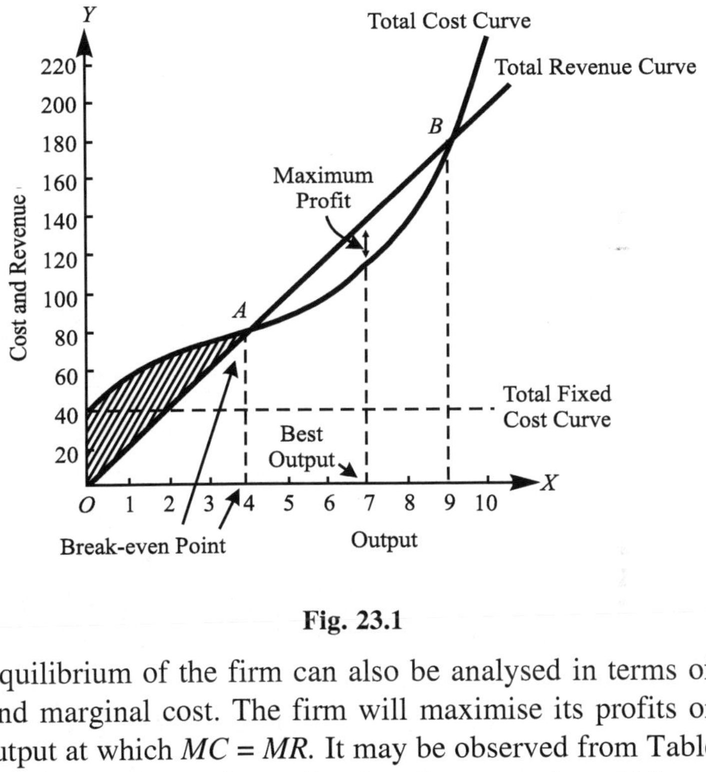

Fig. 23.1

The equilibrium of the firm can also be analysed in terms of marginal revenue and marginal cost. The firm will maximise its profits only at that level of output at which *MC* = *MR*. It may be observed from Table 23.1 that the firm maximises her profits at 7 units of output where *MC* = *MR* = $20. Beyond 7 units of output, marginal cost exceeds marginal revenue and, therefore, on each additional unit produced beyond this level, the firm incurs a loss. This means a reduction in total profits. This situation has been illustrated in Fig. 23.2. Panel (*a*) of Fig. 23.2 shows that profit is the vertical difference between *TR* curve and the *TC* curve. It indicates that profit is maximum when the firm produces 7 units of output. This is confirmed by Panel (*b*) of Fig. 23.1 in which the *MC* curve cuts the *MR* curve exactly at this level of output (7 units). The *MR* curve is horizontal to *X*-axis and is similar to the *AR* curve. The reason is that the price of the output is fixed for all units sold by the firm. If the firm produces more than 7 units of output, then the marginal cost will be greater

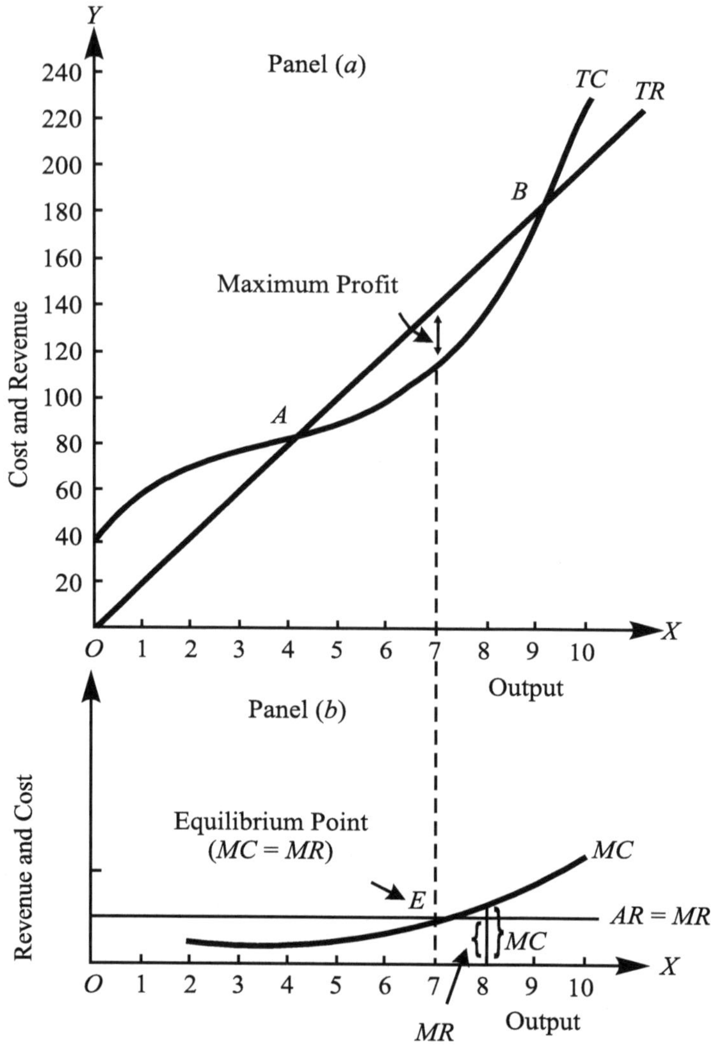

Fig. 23.2

than marginal revenue and the firm has to incur a loss. Thus, the best output is the one indicated by the equality of marginal revenue and marginal cost. If the firm produces this output, it is in equilibrium since there is no tendency for it to produce more or less than this output.[1]

1. This can also be stated mathematically as

$$\pi = R\,(q) - C(q)$$

where π indicates total profit of the firm and R and C are the respective total revenue and total cost of the firm. Both R and C are the functions of output (q). Now, for maximisation of π, the first derivative must be equal to zero. Thus,

$$\frac{d\pi}{dq} = R'\,(q) - C\;\;(q) = 0 \text{ or } MR = MC$$

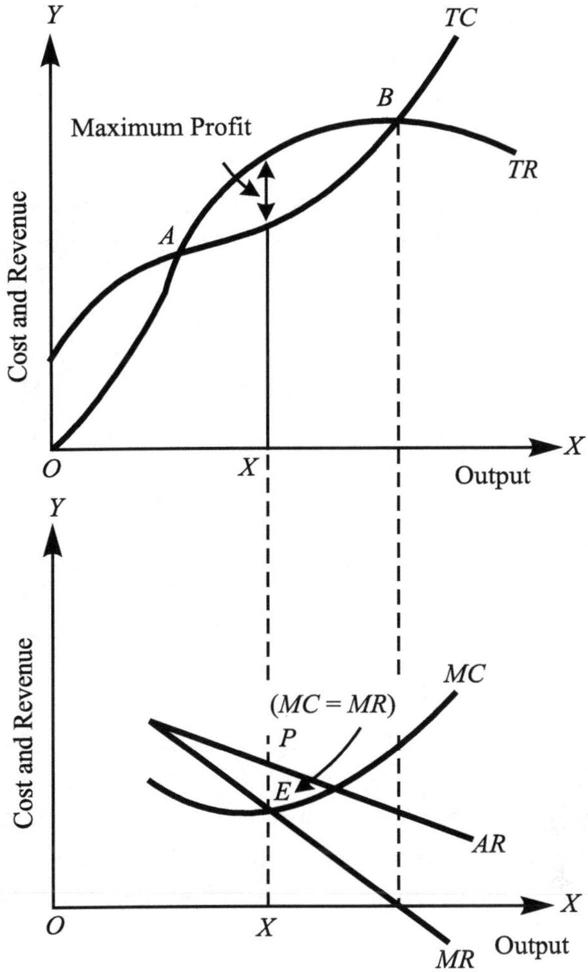

Fig. 23.3

3. Equilibrium of the Firm under Monopoly

The monopoly firm also tries to maximise her profits, and profits will be maximum at that level of output where the difference between total revenue and total cost is maximum or where the marginal cost is equal to marginal revenue.

This is the first order necessary condition of profit maximisation and the second order sufficient condition for profit maximisation requires:

$$\frac{d^2\pi}{dq^2} = R''(q) - C''(q) < 0 \text{ or } R''(q) < C''(q)$$

where $R''(q)$ is the change in marginal revenue and $C''(q)$ is the change in marginal cost.

Under perfect competition we assume that price is given to the firm and thus its *AR*-curve will be horizontal to *X*-axis. The *MR*-curve of the firm under perfect competition. is the same as the *AR*-curve. Since under perfect competition, the price remains constant regardless of the level of output or sales, the total revenue would be a straight line. But under monopoly, the firm has to face a negatively sloping demand curve (or *AR* curve) and the marginal revenue curve. The reason is that if at all she wants to sell more output, she has to reduce the price of her output. The consequent *TR*-curve for monopoly firm will not be a straight line but it will be as shown in Fig. 23.3. Now, for profit maximisation the same rules will be applied as we have discussed under the perfect competitive firm. Figure 23.3 indicates that profits will be maximum at that level of output at which the vertical difference between the *TR*-curve and the *TC*-curve is maximum. It is also observed that exactly at this level of output *MC*-curve cuts the *MR*-curve. Point *E* is the equilibrium point where the firm produces *OX* level of output and attains maximum profit. The second order condition is also satisfied, as if the firm produces beyond *OX* output, its *MR* will be less than its *MC*. Thus, the monopoly will always try to produce *OX* level of output. At this equilibrium level of output, the equilibrium price will be equal to *PX* (it is also the average revenue of the firm).

4. Equilibrium of the Industry

Under perfect competition, an industry consists of a number of firms producing identical or homogeneous output. The industry is said to be in equilibrium when the industry's demand and the industry's supply of the product are equal. In other words, the equilibrium price is given by the intersection of the demand and supply curves of the industry as shown in Fig. 23.4.

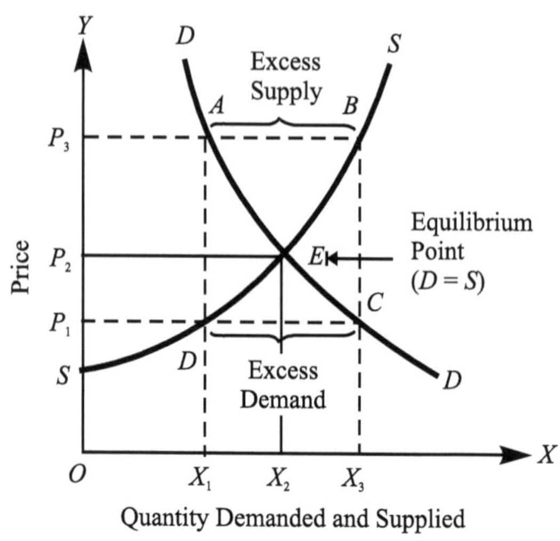

Fig. 23.4

In Fig. 23.4, the equilibrium price is OP_2, for only at this price are the quantities demanded and supplied equal. At prices higher than the market price (for example, OP_3), the quantity supplied (OX_3) exceeds the quantity demanded (OX_1), and this excess supply (*AB*) will mean that firms will be obliged to lower prices in order to dispose of their output; a situation sometimes referred to as a *buyers'market.* At lower prices (for example, OP_1), the quantity demanded will exceed the quantity supplied and competition between buyers will force up the price giving rise to conditions known as a *sellers' market.* Only at a price of *OP* are there no forces at work which are tending to change the price. Thus, in Fig. 23.4, OP_2 is the equilibrium price and OX_2 is the equilibrium quantity demanded and supplied.

5. Resource Allocation under Perfect Competition

There are two ways to deal with the problem of resource allocation under perfect competition:

(1) Resource Allocation under Partial Equilibrium

(2) Resource Allocation under General Equilibrium

(1) *Resource Allocation under Partial Equilibrium.* Under perfect competition in the long-run every firm builds the least cost plant and operates it at its optimal level of output, i.e. the per unit cost becomes minimum. Since each firm operates the plant at full capacity, so that the resources of the economy are allocated in the most efficient way within and between industries. This tendency will lead to full employment of resources within the economy. All the firms get normal profit and that leads to the following equilibrium condition to hold in the economy:

$$LMC = MR = P = AR = LAC \quad ...(1)$$

Under the above condition (1), the aggregate consumer satisfaction is also maximum as the goods are distributed among them according to their demands at the minimum per unit cost because price equals the marginal cost of the product. Given the above conditions under equation (1), we may explain below the optimal allocation of resources. In perfect competition, firms are simply price-takers and quantity-adjusters. Every firm has to accept the price determined by the industry demand and supply. In panel (*a*) of Fig. 23.5, price *OP* is fixed by the industry. It is given to every firm. Thus the demand curve for the firm's output is perfectly elastic where $AR = MR = P$. In panel (*b*) of Fig. 23.5, firm's profit maximisation output is *OX* where firm's $LMC = MR$ and also $MR = AR = P$.

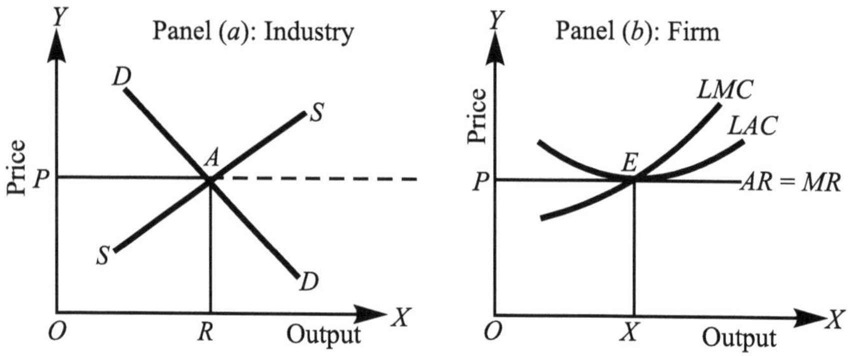

Fig. 23.5

(2) *Resource Allocation under General Equilibrium.* Here we assume that the economy produces only two goods *X* and *Y*, and allocates them optimally at the point where the community indifference curve is tangent to the production possibility curve or product transformation curve. Here it is assumed that there is perfect competition where the prices are given to all individual units both in the product market as well as in the factor market. Tastes and technology remain unchanged, i.e. we deal with only one production possibility curve only. The resources of the economy are fully employed. Under these assumptions, the optimal allocation of resources is shown in Fig. 23.6.

In Fig. 23.6, IC_1 IC_2 and IC_3 are the community indifference curves showing various possible combinations of goods *X* and *Y* available to the society for consumption. The slope of indifference curve is the marginal rate of substitution (*MRS*) between *X* and *Y*. Curve PP_1 is the production possibility

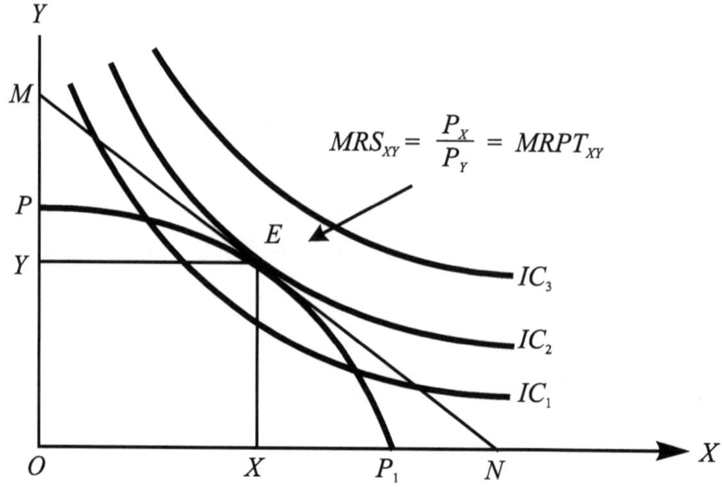

Fig. 23.6

curve which shows the various possible output combinations that the economy may produce under the given resources and technology. The slope of the PP_1 curve is the marginal rate of product transformation (*MRPT*) between *X* and *Y*. The *MRPT* measures the ratio of marginal social cost (*MSC*) of *X* to that of *Y*. In Fig. 23.6, *MN* is the price line or the constraint line whose slope shows the price ratio *Px/Py*. Now the society attains the optimal allocation of resources at point *E* where the slope of price line equals the slope PP_1-curve and the slope of the community indifference curve. It is the point where the product transformation curve touches the highest possible community indifference curve IC_2. At this point the society produces and consumes exactly. *OX* quantity of *X* and *OY* quantity of *Y*. Here, there is neither the situations over production nor the situation of under production but it is the situation of optimal production. From demand side, equilibrium is established at point *E* where the price line *MN* is tangent to the indifference curve IC_2. Thus at point *E*,

$$MRSxy = \frac{Px}{Py} \qquad \ldots(2)$$

From the supply side, the competitive equilibrium requires that the slope of the price line *MN* must be equal to the slope of PP_1-curve. Thus at point *E*,

$$\frac{Px}{Py} = MRPTxy \qquad \ldots(3)$$

Since $$MRPTxy = \frac{MCx}{MCy} = \frac{MSCx}{MSCy}$$

∴ from equation (2) and (3), we have

$$MRSxy = \frac{Px}{Py} = MRPTxy \qquad \ldots(4)$$

It follows that the resources are optimally allocated under perfect competition.

Exercises

1. Explain with the help of a diagram the firm's equilibrium under perfect competition.
2. Explain with the help of a diagram the equilibrium of the firm under monopoly.
3. How does the competitive industry attain its equilibrium position? Illustrate the answer with the help of a diagram.
4. Explain the equilibrium of a firm under monopoly.
5. State and show in diagrams the conditions of equilibrium of the firm and industry under perfect competition.
6. Explain how resources are optimally allocated under perfect competition.
7. "No firm can be in equilibrium unless its marginal revenue and marginal cost are equal." Comment on this statement.

Multiple Choice Questions

8. (*i*) When the perfectly competitive firm and industry are both in long-run equilibrium
   (*a*) $P = MR = SMC = LMC$
   (*b*) $P = MR = SAC = LAC$
   (*c*) $P = MR =$ lowest on the *LAC* curve
   (*d*) all of the above [*Ans.* (*d*)]

   (*ii*) When the perfectly competitive firm but not the industry is in long-run equilibrium
   (*a*) $P = MR = SMC = SAC$
   (*b*) $P = MR = LMC = LAC$
   (*c*) $P = MR = SMC = LMC \neq SAC = LAC$
   (*d*) $P = MR = SMC = LMC \neq SAC =$ lowest point on the *LAC* curve [*Ans.* (*c*)]

   (*iii*) Under perfect competition the economy attains general equilibrium when the resources are allocated in such a manner that
   (*a*) $MRSxy = \dfrac{Px}{Py}$
   (*b*) $MRPTxy = \dfrac{Px}{Py}$
   (*c*) $MRPTxy = \dfrac{MCx}{MCy} = \dfrac{MSCx}{MSCy}$
   (*d*) $MRSxy = \dfrac{Px}{Py} = MRPTxy$ [*Ans.* (*d*)]

Chapter 24

Pricing and Output under Perfect Competition

1. Introduction

We have so for been discussing the basic tools of analysis which we shall now use in the process of price and output determination under various market situations, such as, perfect competition, monopoly and imperfect competition. The analysis which will be carried out in the following chapters of Part IV, we shall assume that there is perfect competition between consumers. What we shall study is the difference in the kind of competition between firms.

In the present chapter, we assume that monopolistic elements are absent and proceed to consider how a price is arrived at under conditions of perfect competition. We shall look first at the conditions necessary for the existence of perfect competition and then at the process of price and output determination in various time per ods.

2. Characteristics of Perfect Competition

An industry (market) is said to be operating under perfect competition when the following requirements are met:

(1) Large number of buyers and sellers.
(2) Homogeneity of the products.
(3) Free entry or exit.
(4) Perfect mobility of factors of production.
(5) Absence of transport cost.
(6) Perfect knowledge of the economy.

(1) *Large Number of Buyers and Sellers.* There must be many buyers and many sellers, so that the behaviour of any one seller, or anyone buyer will have no influence on the market price. Each buyer comprises such a small part of the total (market) demand for the product, and each seller such a

small part of the total (market) supply that any change in their plans will have no influence on the market price. In other words, the price of the product is determined by the collective forces of industry demand and industry supply. The individual firm and the buyer must take the price of the product as given. The firm is a 'price taker'. As we have already explained in the previous chapters that demand curve of the firm in perfect competition is perfectly elastic. Each firm has to adjust her output or sale according to the prevailing market price.

(2) *Homogeneity of the Products.* In perfectly competitive industry, the product of anyone firm is identical to the products of all other firms. This means, all the firms in an industry produce perfectly identical or homogeneous products. Not only this, but all units of the commodity must be homogeneous (i.e. one unit is exactly like another). If this is so, then buyers will be completely indifferent as to the firm (seller) they approach, and the sellers will be indifferent as to the buyer to whom they sell. It does not make any difference to a consumer whether he buys the product from firm *A* or firm *B* or any other in the industry because the shape, packing, colour, weight, and other attributes of one product are identical to the products offered by other firms. As a consequence, a single price will rule over the entire industry. Since all the products are perfect substitutes, the elasticity of demand for the product will be perfectly elastic and the numerical value of the elasticity coefficient will be infinity. This will lead to the conclusion that the average revenue and marginal revenue of the perfect competitive firm will be the same.

(3) *Free Entry or Exit.* The third important feature of perfect competition is that there should be complete freedom for the firms to enter into the industry or to leave the industry. New firms must be permitted to set themselves up in the industry if they find it often an attractive opportunity otherwise competition would be restricted and hence it would not be perfect competition. This is not always listed as a separate condition, because it is considered to be implicit in the second. That is, if producers (firms) in an industry are many and small, acting independently of each other, there is not likely to be any bar to the entry of new firms. If profits are incurred in the short-run, new firms can enter the industry and/or the existing firms can expand the scale of their plants. The entry of new firms will shift the industry supply curve to the right and will tend to reduce the equilibrium price. After sometime this will lead to zero profits.

Similarly, if the firms are incurring losses in the industry in the short-run, a few firms may exit from the industry. This will reduce the supply of the industry and will raise the equilibrium price to the level of the long-run average cost. Again, this' will mean that only normal profits (which are included in *LAC*) will be attained by the competitive firms and the industry in the long-run. Thus, in perfect competition, due to free entry or exit, each firm will be of optimum size in the long run.

(4) *Perfect Mobility of Factors of Production.* Another assumption of perfect competition is that there must be perfect mobility off actors of production. It means, the factors of production (such as labour and capital) are mobile, not only geographically, but also among different jobs. Workers will move from one employer to another and entrepreneurs from one industry to another and by doing so, they can increase their returns or satisfaction. Thus, perfect mobility also implies that each firm is optimising the use of each factor input. While each factor owner gets its opportunity cost in a competitive market, each firm minimises the cost incurred on a particular factor use.

(5) *Absence of Transport Cost.* In perfect competition priced is the same. It is possible only when we assume that transport cost does not exist in a perfect competitive market. This assumption (ignoring the cost of transportation) will lead to price-equalisation of product and factor inputs geographically and also among all the alternative uses.

(6) *Perfect Knowledge of the Economy.* In a perfectly competitive market, all the buyers and sellers must possess a perfect knowledge about the market activities. Every buyer or seller knows the price of the product. In the absence of perfect knowledge, it is possible that some buyers may buy the commodity at higher prices when the same product is available at a lower price. Thus, in the situation of the absence of perfect knowledge, there will be different prices for the same product. Also, due to the perfect knowledge of buyers, it would not pay a firm to reduce the price. Because the reduction in price will be known immediately and the buyers will buy at the lowest prices. This forces sel1ers charging higher prices to lower their prices immediately. Conversely, the firm will lose all its sales if it increases the price. At the same time, advertisement and publicity would prove futile in a competitive market as al1 the products are homogeneous. Thus, the fact is that only a single price will prevail in the market for any particular product (or factor-input).

Sometimes, economists distinguish 'pure competition' from 'perfect competition.' The difference between them is one of degree. For pure competition, the first five assumptions mentioned above are normally considered necessary. For competition to be perfect, the additional requirement-is that all economic units (consumers, producers, and resource owners) must possess complete knowledge of the economy. In perfect competition, at all times, there must be one single ruling price for a particular product in the entire market. Given the price of the product, the individual firms take decisions independently. They have to decide, how much output should be produced at the given price. This is the reason that the examples of perfect competition are very rare.

When a situation of perfect competition exists, it means that one price, and only one price for the commodity will be established. Perfect knowledge ensures that buyers will not pay different prices. Perfect mobility ensures that consumers and factors of production will move to equalise any price differentials which may take place. Homogeneity of product ensures that preferences will not arise which might be converted into price differentials. Similarly, non-existence of transport cost ensures that price will be the same at all places it is sold. All of this means that an equilibrium price will be established which is due entirely to forces of supply and demand which cannot be influenced by individual buyers or sellers, and there will be no associations of buyers or sellers which might, by their actions, affect the market conditions. The only difference of degree between pure and perfect competition can be explained as: under conditions of perfect competition adjustments of the economy to disturbances in the conditions of demand and supply will be instantaneous; while under condition of pure competition, it will take longer for adjustment to occur because of incomplete knowledge on the part of buyers and sel1ers. We will, however, use the term perfect competition in our discussion of price and output determination.

3. Importance of Time Element in the Theory of Value (Marshall's Time Analysis of Value)

We know that price is determined by the forces of demand and supply, but the relative influence exerted by them on price varies with the period of time under consideration. Dr. Alfred Marshall was the first economist who recognised the influence of time on the determination of price. When demand for a commodity changes, its supply will also change. But changes in demand and supply are not instantaneous. For instance, an increase in demand will lead to an increase in supply, but the increase in supply will be made only after sometime. Thus, supply takes time to adjust itself to a change in demand. Further, the cost functions which are the basis of supply of a product also vary over time. In short period of time, the cost of production will be higher because there is not enough time to change the scale of plant. While in the long period, a firm is able to produce at a lower cost, because she can change the scale of plant to any extent she wishes. Hence, the element of time is very important in the determination of the price of a product. Marshall showed that there are four fundamental time periods in valuation: (*i*) The Market-Period or Very Short-Period, (*ii*) The Short Period, (*iii*) The Long-Period, and (*iv*) The Very Long-Period or the Secular Period. For the purposes of price determination, we shall consider only the first three types of time period. We shall include the secular period in the long period. Here it is important to note that Marshall did not classify the time periods in terms of calendar time but in terms of operational period (time) required for economic forces to work. Marshall divided the time periods on the basis of forces of supply and ignored the forces of demand. When the period is too short to change the supply of a product, it is referred to as market period or very short-period. When the supply of a product can be changed within the limits set by the given scale of plant, the period is said to be a short-period. When the supply takes a long time to adjust themselves to changes in demand, i.e. there can be any change in the supply of a product, the period is known as long-period.

We shall now discuss these time periods in the following section.

(1) *The Market Period or the Very Short-Period.* The market period or very short period is defined as the period in which the supply of a commodity is more or less fixed. For example, fish which has come to the market on a certain day and must be sold. Similarly, after the harvest is over, the amount of wheat coming to the market is absolutely fixed and it cannot be increased until the next harvest. Thus, the market period for wheat is approximately one year, while for vegetables it may be a week or a month or so. The market period for different commodities will be different. The main characteristic of this period is that supply of the product is absolutely fixed and, therefore, the supply curve of each firm will be a vertical line. The market supply curve is simply the horizontal summation of all individual firms supply curves. Thus, in such cases, price is determined primarily by demand. The equilibrium price is that price at which the entire supply is sold. If the demand is high, the price will be high; if the demand is low, the price will be low. The equilibrium price in the very short period is called the *market price.*

(2) *The Short-Period.* The short-period is defined as the period in which the firm is free to vary its output but does not have time to change its scale of plant. The number of firms in the industry will be fixed because new firms do not have sufficient time to enter into the industry, nor the existing firms will have time to leave the industry. Any changes in supply must come from the plant capacity of the existing firms. If the demand for a commodity increases, the individual firms will increase their output by intensive working of its existing capital equipment (plant or machine). Increase of supply with the existing equipment generally means increased marginal costs because ordinarily all firms operate their plants at the level where cost is minimum. The short-period supply curve of most commodities is, therefore, a line moving upwards. The point of equilibrium is the point at which the demand and supply curves intersect.

If, in the short-period, demand is low and the price is less than the average cost, firms will incur losses. But, by definition, the short-period is too short to change the scale of a plant, a producer (firm) will continue production even in the situation of loss. The reason is that if he stops production, the maximum loss will be equal to the fixed costs. For a time, therefore, the firms may carry on production if their variable costs are covered. In the long-run, however, the price must be high enough to cover both the variable costs and the fixed costs, otherwise production will be stopped. The equilibrium price in the short-period is called the *short-period normal price* which is determined by the intersection of the short-period normal supply and the short-period normal demand. The short-period normal demand will be nearly the same as market demand and the short-period normal supply curve will be less steep than the market supply curve.

(3) *The Long-Period.* The long-period is defined as the period long enough to enable the industry to adjust its supply of output completely to changes in demand. During this period of time, new firms may enter into the industry and the existing firms may leave the industry. Thus, the possibilities of output variation in a purely competitive industry are much greater in the long-period than in the short-period. In the long-period, the existing firms can vary output through increases or decreases in the utilisation of available plant-capacity as is the possibility in the short-period. But they can vary output more than this via changing their scales of plants to any extent. All the factors of production are the variable factors. There is no question of fixed cost. The minimum price of the product cannot be less than the average cost of production. Thus, there will be no loss to the firm. Also, during this period of time, complete adjustment of supply to demand is possible as all factors on which supply depends can be changed. The shape of the supply curve in the long period depends on the law of returns applicable to the production conditions of the commodity in question. It rises upwards under diminishing returns, slopes downwards under increasing returns and moves horizontally under constant returns. In all the situations, the point of equilibrium is the point at which the demand for the commodity and the supply of the commodity are equal. The equilibrium price in the long-period is called the *long-period normal price*. Market equilibrium price and output will oscillate round the long-period equilibrium price and output.

(4) *The Secular Period.* For the sake of completeness, Marshall also talked of a secular period or very long-period. The secular period will include all the changes in demand and supply which require a long-period of time, such as the changes in the size of population, supplies of raw materials, supply of capital, etc. These are the structural changes that we shall study in theories of growth. In other words, the very long-period is essentially a historical category.

4. Price Determination by the Industry under Perfect Competition

As we have already discussed that the price of a commodity will be determined at that point where industry demand for a product is equal to its supply. We have also seen in the previous chapters that market or industry demand is the sum total of all the quantities demanded by consumers at a given price and the market (industry) demand curve can be derived by the horizontal sum of all the individual demand curves. Similarly, the industry supply curve can be derived by aggregating the marginal cost functions of different firms in their relevant ranges. From the above discussion, it is also clear that time is an important factor to influence the industry price via supply variations. We shall now explain the equilibrium of the industry under three periods of time: the market period, the short-period, and the long-period.

Price Determination in the Market Period

In the market period the supply of the commodity is fixed and, therefore, price will depend upon the variation in demand. It does not mean that supply plays no role in the determination of price. The role of supply will depend upon the nature of the commodity. If a commodity is perishable, such as vegetables, fruits, fish, etc. such a commodity cannot stay fresh for some time and thus its entire supply must be sold at the same (market) time. The same is the case with the goods of purely seasonal interest like calendars and greeting cards. These goods deteriorate economically, but not physically; there will be no demand for them after a particular season is over. In all these cases, the supply curve of the commodity is a vertical line as shown in Fig. 24.1. Here, the costs of production do not come in the picture at all. The

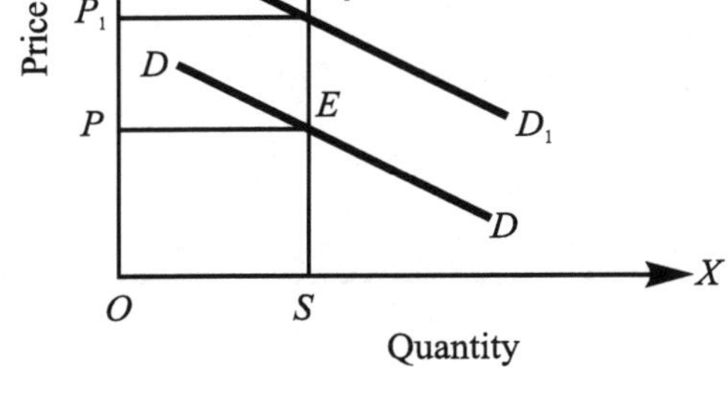

Fig. 24.1

vertical shape of the supply curve indicates that whatever the price is, the fixed supply is to be sold in the market. Now, the price will entirely be dependent upon the demand curve. Higher the demand, the more will be the price and the lower the demand, the lesser will be the price. In Fig. 24.1, if demand curve is *DD,* then the equilibrium price will be *OP.* If demand increases, and supply remains the same, price will increase. Let us assume that demand increases to D_1D_1, the price will become OP_1. Thus, in such a case, supply is fixed and demand exerts its full influence on the price of the product.

If, on the other hand, the commodity under consideration is a durable good, it can be stored. A firm selling such a commodity has a reservation price below which it will not like to sell it. The reservation price is influenced by the cost of production. In the market period, all costs are fixed costs and we know that fixed costs do not govern price. Thus, in the market period price will depend upon the variation in demand, but according to Marshall both demand and supply are equally needed for price determination. Now if demand for such (durable) goods is so low that the consumers offer a price less than the firm's reservation price, it will sell no output. This case has been illustrated in Fig. 24.2. The supply curve is *SS* which indicates that the firm will refuse to sell anything below the *OS* price. The quantity supplied increases up to the market price OP_1 but above this price, supply is the same (OX_1), however high the demand may be. The reason is that in the market period supply is fixed which cannot be adjusted to the variation (increase) in demand. Thus, even if a high price is offered by the buyers, the sellers are unable to supply accordingly. Thus, in Fig. 24.2, after point E_1, the supply takes the vertical shape. This type of behaviour takes place for durable and semi-durable goods.

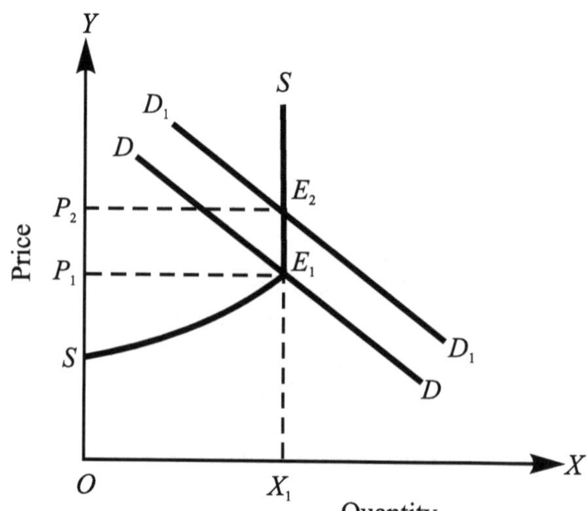

Fig. 24.2

Price Determination in the Short-Period

In the short period, the firm is able to vary its supply but does not have time to change its scale of plant. The number of firms in the industry will be fixed because new firms will not have time to enter into the industry and the existing firms have no time to leave the industry. Thus, the supply of the industry can be changed only within the limits set by the plant capacity of the existing firms. In other words, the supply curve will be upwards sloping and there will be no shift in the industry supply curve.

The short-period normal price is determined by the interaction of short-period supply and short-period demand curves. It has been illustrated in Fig. 24.3. *DD* is demand curve and *SS* is the supply curve. The equilibrium price is *OP* where the demand is equal to the supply of the product. Now, suppose that the demand increases from *DD* to D_1D_1, the supply curve remaining the same and the price will increase from *OP* to OP_1. At this OP_1 price, the quantity increases from *OX* to OX_1. This increase in quantity is made by an intensive use of the scale of plant. Similarly, if demand curve shifts from *DD* to D_2D_2, then the short-run equilibrium point will be E_2, where the quantity supplied is equal quantity demanded. It is reduced from *OX* to OX_2. This reduction in supply is made by a smaller use of the existing plant. It means, given the short-period supply curve (*SS*), a higher or lower price will be determined on the basis of the shift in demand. If demand increases, price will increase and if demand decreases, price will decrease.

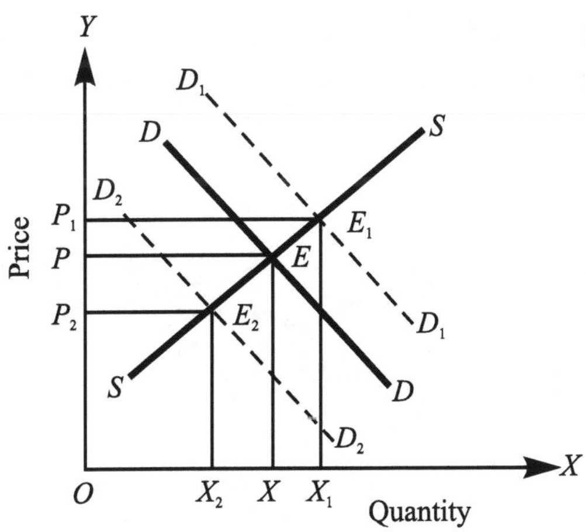

Fig.24.3

Relation between Market Period and Short-Period Price Determination

As we have explained, the equilibrium (market) price in the market period is determined at a point where the demand curve intersects the fixed (vertical) supply curve. While in the case of short-period, equilibrium price is determined at a point where the demand curve intersects the positively sloping supply curve. This means that in the short-period some adjustments in supply to demand are made by making a smaller or intensive use of the scale of plant. At any particular time, the market price may be more or less than the short-period equilibrium price, but all the time, it will tend to equate the latter.

Fig. 24.4 illustrates the relationship between the market period price and the short-period price. The supply curve in the market period is shown by a vertical straight line *MPS,* while the short-period supply curve is *SPS*. Suppose, *DD* is the initial demand curve. The initial equilibrium point is *'E,* where the demand curve cuts the market period supply curve *MPS.* The market period is *OP* and quantity sold by the firms taken together is *OX.* If it is also assumed to be a short-period, then the short-run supply curve *SPS* also cuts the demand curve *DD* at point *E* and, therefore, at price *OP,* the industry (all the firms together) offers *OX* units of quantity for sale in the market period also. This is why *DD, MPS* and *SPS* have a common point of intersection *E.* But it is clear that market period supply curve *MPS* is perfectly inelastic, showing that there is no possibility to change the level of output offered for sale. Shift in demand curve, therefore, makes no effect on quantity supplied. While in the case of short-period, the supply curve *SPS* is elastic, showing that there may be some adjustment in supply to demand for the commodity. For instance, if demand curve shifts from *DC* to D_1D_1; in the new demand conditions the new market equilibrium will be set at point *EM* where the market price increases from *OP* to OP_1 (subject to the condition that output remains the same). The short-period supply curve *SPS* shows that, in the short-period, the increased (variable) resources available allow supply to adapt itself in some degree to

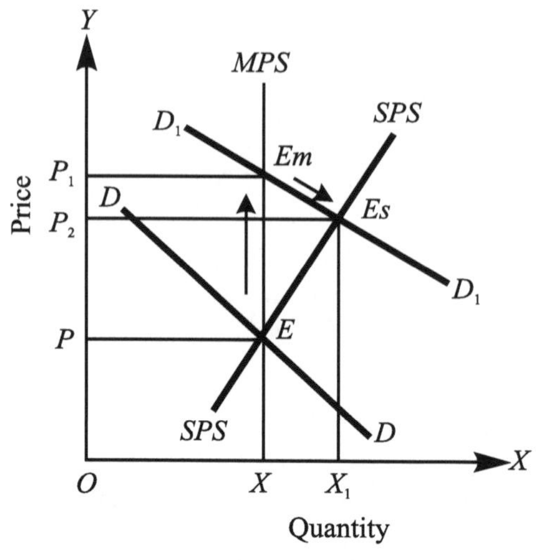

Fig. 24.4

the changed demand conditions. In other words, if this increase in demand promises to last for some time (short-period), the existing firms in the industry begin to use their existing plant and equipment more intensively. As a result a new short-run equilibrium is established at point *Es* where the short-period supply curve *SPS* intersects the demand curve D_1D_1. We may note here that the short-run normal price will be OP_2 and quantity will be OX_2. This new short-run equilibrium price OP_2 is higher than the initial market-period price *OP*, but not so high as the second market period price OP_1. The short-run supply has also increased from *OX* to OX_1. Thus, in the short-period more quantity is sold and price is not quite so high as in the market period (when the demand conditions are changed as shown by D_1D_1 curve in Fig. 24.4.

Price Determination in the Long-Period

In the long-period, the normal price of a commodity is determined by the long period demand and long-period supply of the industry. The long-period demand curve represents the various levels of collective demand of the buyers over a long-period of time. The long-period supply curve represents the various levels of collective supply of the firms which are placed on the market at different prices over a long period of time.

In the long-period the shift in demand will be met by greater output adjustments and smaller price adjustments than those that occurred in the short-period. There is ample time for the existing firms to leave the industry in the situation of loss and there is ample time for the new firms to enter into the industry in the situation of profit. As such, the supply of the commodity will be adjusted fully to the changed demand. Suppose that the demand for the commodity in question increases. This is assumed to be a once-for-all increase and no further change will take place during the process of adjustment. The new long-run price may be more than, equal to, or less than the initial price. It depends on whether the industry operates under increasing cost, constant cost or decreasing cost conditions. But it is sure that in the short run due to an increase in demand, the price will increase. Now to make a complete adjustment in supply to demand, the scale of plant will be varied and the resulting long-run normal price will depend upon the prevailing law of return in the industry. In the case of increasing cost (or decreasing returns), the new long-run equilibrium price will be higher than the old one. In the case of constant cost (or constant returns), (long-period) price, after a short-run increase will settle down at the old level. While in the case of decreasing cost (or increasing returns), new equilibrium long-period normal price after rising in the short-period will be actually lower than the initial price. Now, the determination of long-period normal price under the various cost conditions will be discussed in the following section.

Increasing Cost Industry

Here we assume that the industry is operating under increasing cost conditions. In this situation, the long-period supply curve of the industry rises upwards to the right as output increases. In other words, it has a positive slope. In Fig. 24.5, *LPS* is the long-run supply curve which slopes upward to the right. How can we get this supply curve? For this let us assume that the initial equilibrium point is *E* where the industry demand curve *DD* intersects the short-period supply curve *SPS* and the market supply curve *MP*. At this point the industry is supplying *OX* output at *OP* equilibrium price. Now suppose, demand curve shifts upward to D_1D_1. The short-run effect of this increase in demand is that the industry is able to supply only OX_1 output at OP_1 price. But in the long-run, the industry can fully adjust the supply to increase in demand. The existing firms can increase their plant capacities and the new firms can enter into the industry. Thus, the long-run increase in a supply will not be only OX_1, but it will be OX_2, because short-run supply curve also shifts to the right as SPS_1. The new equilibrium is established at point E_1 where price is OP_2 and output is OX_2. Now if we join points *E* and E_1, we get the long-period supply curve of the industry. The long-run equilibrium price (OP_2) is more than the initial price (*OP*). The extent to which the long-period price will differ from the original price will depend on the ease with which extra output can be produced in the long-run.

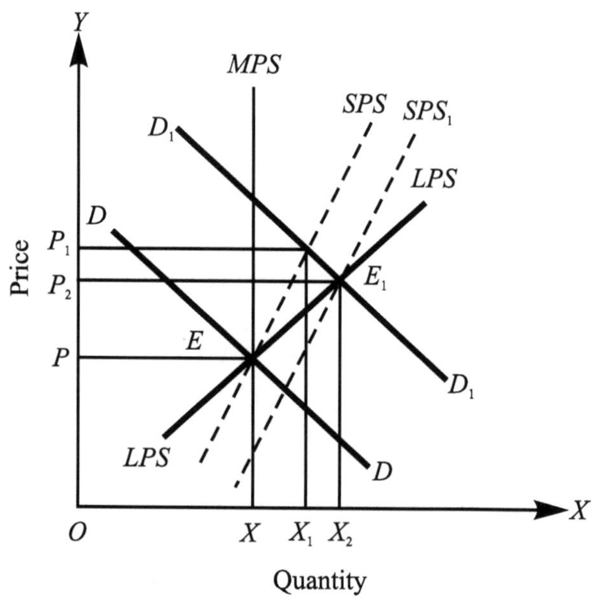

Fig. 24.5

Constant Cost Industry

Here we assume that the industry is operating under constant conditions. In this situation, the long-period supply of the industry is horizontal to X-axis as shown in Fig. 24.6 by the *LPS* straight line. Although the short-period price will increase as a result of increased demand, yet the price will fall again to the initial level in the long-run when the supply is fully adjusted to the changed demand conditions. For instance, let us assume that the initial equilibrium point is *E* in Fig. 24.6 where the equilibrium price is *OP* and quantity is *OX*. Now, if demand curve shifts from *DD* to D_1D_1, the short-run price will increase for *OP* to OP_1 and at this short-period price the industry is able to make OX_1 supply of the output. Since, in the long-period, there is enough time to increase the scale of plant, the short-period supply curve *SPS* shifts to the right as SPS_1. This leads to a new long-period equilibrium point E_1 where the long-period price is *OP* and long-period equilibrium quantity is OX_2. If we join the two points *E* and E_1, we get the long-period supply curve, *LPS* which is horizontal. This indicates that under conditions of constant cost, the long-period normal price is the same as the initial price while the output has increased.

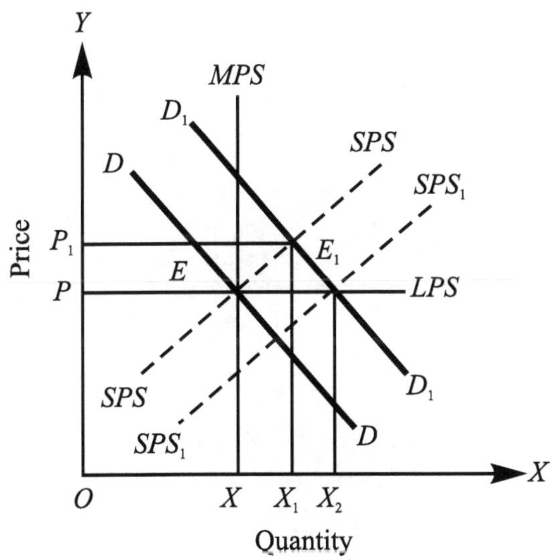

Fig. 24.6

Decreasing Cost Industry

Here we assume that the industry is operating under decreasing cost conditions. This situation is common. It is found only in the presence of external economies. As the industry expands in the long run, external economies take place. These external economies lead to the firms' cost curves shift downwards. In such a case the long-period supply curve of the industry slopes downwards. Although the short-period price will increase as a result of increased demand, yet the long-period price will be less than the initial price.

This case has been illustrated in Fig. 24.7. The initial equilibrium point is *E* where the price is *OP* and the output is *OX*. If demand increases from *DD* to D_1D_1, the short-period price will increase from *OP* to OP_1 and the short-period quantity increases from *OX* to OX_1. But in the long-period, the firms are able to increase their scales of plant. Thus, the short-period supply curve *SPS* shifts to SPS_1. New equilibrium will take place at point E_1 where the price is OP_2 and quantity demanded and supplied is OX_2. If we join the equilibrium points *E* and E_1, then the resulting curve is the long-period supply curve *LPS*. This curve *LPS* is falling. In Fig. 24.7, it is also clear that the long-period normal price OP_2 is less than the initial price *OP*. Also in the long-period the quantity demanded and supplied increases from *OX* to OX_2.

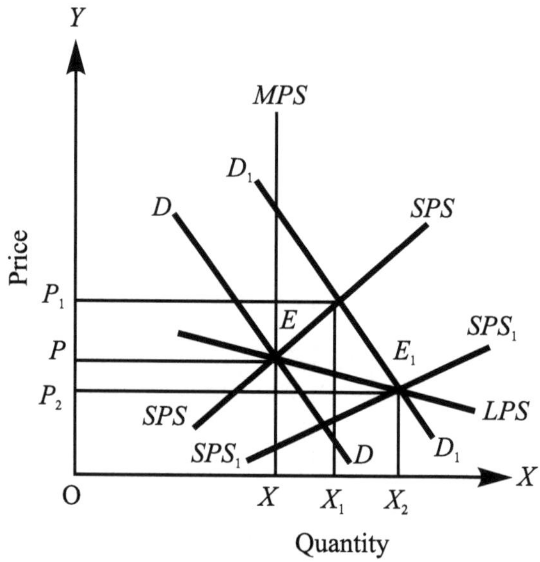

Fig. 24.7

Therefore, it is clear that the long-period normal price can be higher, lower or the same as the initial (original) market price, depending on supply (cost) conditions in the industry in question. It depends on whether or not there are internal and external economies or diseconomies of scale and how much they are. However, it is certain that the short-period normal price will invariably be higher than the long-period normal price.

5. Output Determination by the Firm under Perfect Competition

Under conditions of perfect competition, the individual firm supplies but a tiny fraction of the total supply. It is powerless to exert any influence on the price of the commodity. The price of the product is determined by the industry. A firm, in perfect competition has to accept the price given by the industry. In other words, the industry is a price-maker, while the firm is a price-taker. Thus, the only decision the firm has to take is how much to be produced at the given price? In the present section we shall show how the price affects the behaviour of the competitive firms. The demand curve for the products of such a firm must be a horizontal line, or more precisely, the demand curve is perfectly elastic. No matter how many units the firm sells, it cannot change the price. It can sell its entire output at the ruling market price. If it tries to sell at any higher price, there will be no demand for its products, and there is no incentive to sell at any lower price. This is true that firms will attempt to maximise profits at the point where marginal revenue (*MR*) equals marginal cost (*MC*), no matter what the degree of competition in the market.[1] Also, for profit maximisation, it is necessary that before the point where $MR = MC$, the marginal cost must be less than the marginal revenue and after the equilibrium point the marginal cost must be greater than the marginal revenue. This means that the *MC* curve must cut the *MR* curve from below and after the equilibrium point, it (*MC*) must lie above the *MR* curve. In perfect competition, the firm's *MR* curve is the same as its *AR* curve and the *MR* curve is horizontal to *X*-axis. Thus, the firm will be in equilibrium when the following condition is satisfied:

$$MC = MR = AR \text{ (price)}$$

By taking the help of the above fundamental rule, the firm will determine its equilibrium level of output. We shall discuss the firm's equilibrium under the three market periods: the market period, the short-period and the long-period.

Equilibrium of the Firm in the Market Period

In the market period, time is too short to change the supply of the product both for the firm and the industry. The price of the product is determined by the industry and at that price the firm sells its entire output. In Fig. 24.8 we

1. Mathematically, we may write

$$\pi = R - C$$

where π is profit, R is total revenue and C is total cost of the firm. The firm will maximise its total profit (π) when the first derivative of π with respect to output (X) is zero. Thus,

$$\frac{d\pi}{dX} = \frac{dR}{dX} - \frac{dC}{dX} = 0, \text{ or } \frac{dR}{dX} = \frac{dC}{dX} \text{ or } MR = MC$$

where $\frac{dR}{dX}$ is marginal revenue and $\frac{dC}{dX}$ is marginal cost.

have illustrated this case. In the industry, the supply curve is a straight vertical line and, therefore, demand plays a dominant role in determining the equilibrium price. The industry demand curve *DD* cuts the industry supply *MS* at point *E* and, therefore, the equilibrium price is *OP.* This price is given to the firm. At this given price *OP,* the firm can sell any level of output. In other words, the firm's demand curve is a horizontal line. Since, it is a case of market period, the firm will sell its entire output (inventory) at this given price.

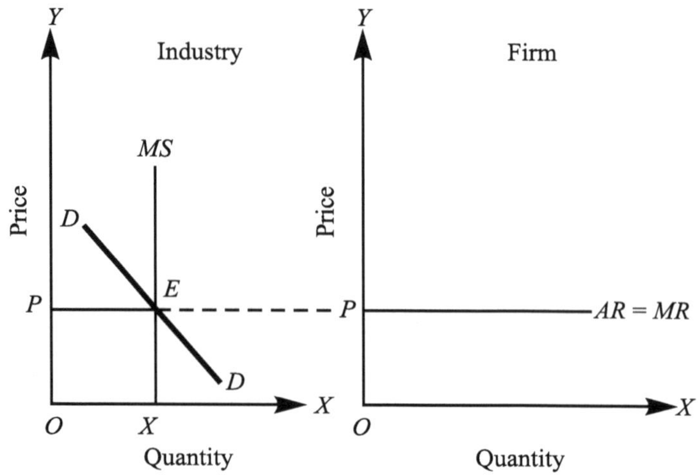

Fig. 24.8

Here, we may very well introduce the concept of reservation price which the firm assumes in the case of a durable product. For such a product, the firm will sell its output if reservation price[2] is less than or equal to the market price (*OP*) given to it. If the market price is lower than the reservation price, the firm will not sell its output.

Equilibrium of the Firm in the Short-Period

We have already explained how price is determined by the industry in the short-period. The price so determined by the short-period industry demand and industry supply is given to the individual firm. Now the firm adjusts its output accordingly. In other words, the firm has to decide whether to produce or not to produce. Also, if she is to produce, then how much should it produce? For this the firm has to see its costs of production. It is also clear to us that the purpose of the firm, in short-period, is either to maximise its profits or to maximise its losses. Its objective will be attained if it produces that level of output at which

2. The *reservation price* of the firm refers to the price below which the firm will not sell its output. This reservation price will depend upon many factors, such as the nature of the commodity, future expectations about the product price, the cost of storage, and the cost of production, etc.

its marginal revenue is equal to its marginal cost. In other words, the firm will be in short-run equilibrium when it holds the condition $MR = MC$. Now we shall discuss the two situations of the firm in the following manner.

Profit Maximisation. Figure 24.9 shows that the equilibrium price OP is determined by the industry at point E where the industry demand is equal to industry supply. The price so determined by the industry is passed on to the firm. This is shown by the horizontal demand curve of the firm. This line is also known as the price line. Since competition is perfect, the average revenue (demand) curve of the firm is also the marginal revenue curve of the firm. The firm's short-period average cost curve and short-period marginal cost curve are shown by SAC and SMC respectively in Fig. 24.9. The profits of the firm are maximum at the output at which marginal cost equals marginal revenue, that is, at output OX where $SMC = MR$. At any output less than OX, marginal revenue exceeds marginal cost, which would mean that if the firm produces more, its profits will increase. Also, at any output more than OX, marginal revenue becomes less than marginal cost, which would mean a loss if the firm exceeds output level OX. Thus, OX is the output of maximum profits. Total abnormal profits of the firm are equal to the shaded area. At the equilibrium point E, price is equal to EX, while average cost per unit equals AX. Abnormal profit per unit must be equal to EA (CP) and total abnormal profits will be equal to $PEAC$. Here we may note that at output OX, profit per unit is not maximised (for instance, the last unit of the output sold adds zero profit to the total profit), nor the firm is concerned with this. This objective of the firm is to maximise total profits and not the rate at which they are increasing.

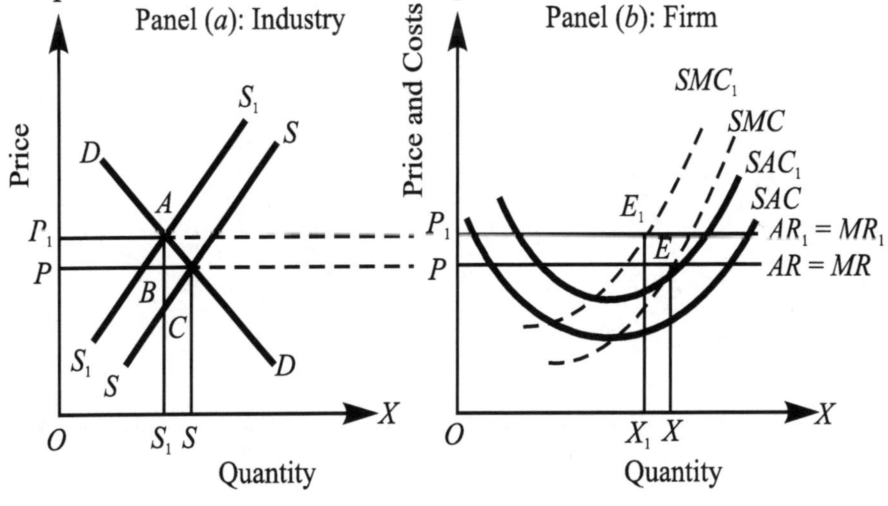

Fig. 24.9

Loss Minimisation. As has been explained, the determination of price is not a jurisdiction of an individual firm it can only determine its own output level on the basis of given price. If this price is too low and does not cover the average cost, the firm would be incurring losses. If on the other hand, the price is higher than the average cost, the firm would make abnormal profits. We have explained above the situation of profit maximisation and now we shall discuss the situation of loss minimisation. Although, the situation of short-run losses (or profits) would be wiped out in the long-run as in the long-run (industry) demand and supply both adjust themselves in such a fashion as to yield only the normal profits to the firm.

In Fig. 24.10 the firm's *AC* curve is above the price line (given by the industry). Its *MN* curve cuts the *MR* curve at point *E* and, therefore, point *E* is the equilibrium point where *MA* = *MC*. With the help of this point, the firm determines its equilibrium level of output *OX*. At this level of output the cost per unit is *OC*, while the price is *OP*. Therefore, the loss per unit will be equal to *PC*. The total loss of the firm is shown by the shaded area (*CAEP*). If the output level is less than or greater than *OX*, the firm's total loss would be more than at the level of optimisation. The maximum loss that a firm can bear would be equal to its fixed cost which is the difference between *AC* and *AVC*. At *OX* level of output, the firm's average variable cost is *XB*. The firm's average receipt (*AR*) is *XA*. The excess of *AR* (or price) over *AVC* is equal to *AB*. In other words, *AB* is the fixed cost per unit. Now at *OX* level of output, the firm is minimising its loss to *AE* per unit, because the maximum loss per unit that it could bear is *AB*. Hence, if the firm produces *OX* level of output, it covers *BE* part of its per unit fixed costs. If the price is less than the firm's average variable cost, *XB* (= *OV*) losses will be minimised by stopping production altogether, i.e. leaving losses equal to the total fixed costs.

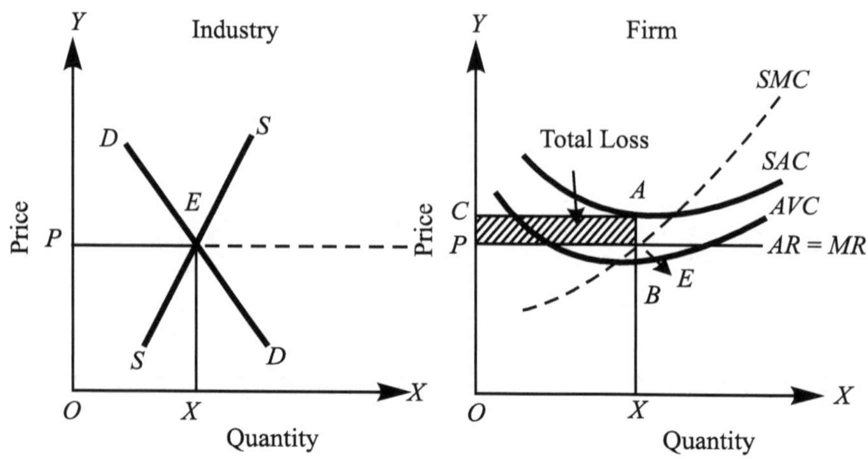

Fig. 24.10

Effect of a Tax on the Short-Run Equilibrium

A tax on commodity generally changes the optimum level of the individual firm. When a tax, such as sales tax, is imposed on a commodity, it has the same economic effect as an increase in the costs of production. Due to the imposition of sales tax, the marginal cost function will shift upward and as a consequence, the whole industry supply curve moves upwards and to the left. The cost of bringing the commodity to the market is now increased by the amount of tax being levied. Thus, the equilibrium price will be higher than before.

In Panel (*a*) of Fig. 24.11, the original industry supply curve is *SS* which shifts to S_1S_1 due to the imposition of tax. The distance between the two supply curves will depend upon the amount of tax levied on the commodity. As a consequence, price has risen from *OP* to OP_1 and the quantity supplied by the industry has fallen from *OS* to OS_1. It is also clear that the price has not increased by the full extent of the tax. The tax is equal to the amount *AC*, but the price has risen by the amount *AB* (= the increase in price, PP_1) and the producers or the firms are obliged to bear the amount *BC*.

Although the new price of the commodity is OP_1 (= AS_1), the industry (firm) only receives CS_1 while the government takes *AC* in taxation. In other words, the burden of tax on the industry depends upon the nature of the demand and supply curves.

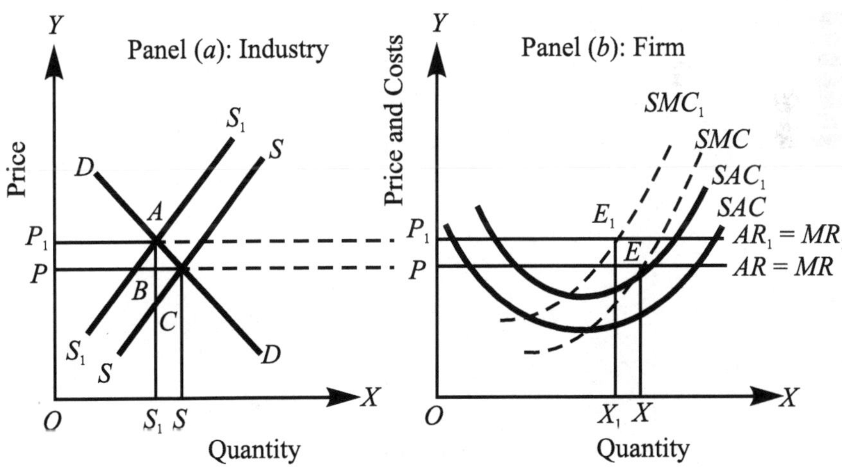

Fig. 24.11

In Panel (*b*) of Fig. 24.11, the effect of tax on the individual firm has been shown. Due to the composition of tax, its cost curves shift upwards as shown by SAC_1 and SMC_1. At *OP* price, the firm's equilibrium level of output is *OX;* while at the new increased price, its equilibrium level of output is OX_1. It shows that taxation on commodity reduces the optimum level of firm's output from *OX* to OX_1.

Equilibrium of the Firm in the Long-Period

We have seen that in the short-run a firm can adjust its output within the limits set by the fixed factors of production. But in the long-run, the firm can adjust its output to any extent because it can vary all factors of production. Thus, it is certain that the firm will not incur losses in the long-run. Also in the long-run, the tree entry of the new firms into the industry will wipe out the short-run abnormal profits of the firm. Hence in the long-run, the firm will be of optimum size where there is no (abnormal) profit-no loss. The firm gets only the normal profits which are included in the long-run average cost. In other words, under perfect competition the individual firm is in equilibrium, earning normal profits when

$$AR = MR = LAC = LMC$$

This point of equilibrium will be established at which the firm's horizontal *MR*-curve touches its *LAC* curve at the latter's minimum point. It is at this point also that *LMC* = *LAC*. This position has been illustrated in Fig. 24.12. The long-run equilibrium of the firm requires that short-run equilibrium exists at the same time. But the converse is not true. This means that short-run equilibrium of the firm can exist even though there is long-run disequilibrium of the firm. In Fig. 24.12, it is clear that to produce *OX* quantity of output at the minimum unit cost, the firm builds a plant associated with the short-run average cost curve, *SAC* whose minimum point is the same as that of the long-run average cost, *LAC*. Also *SMC* must intersect *SAC* at latter's minimum point. Thus, when a firm is in long-run equilibrium, the following condition will exist:

$$P = MR = LMC = LAC = SAC = SMC$$

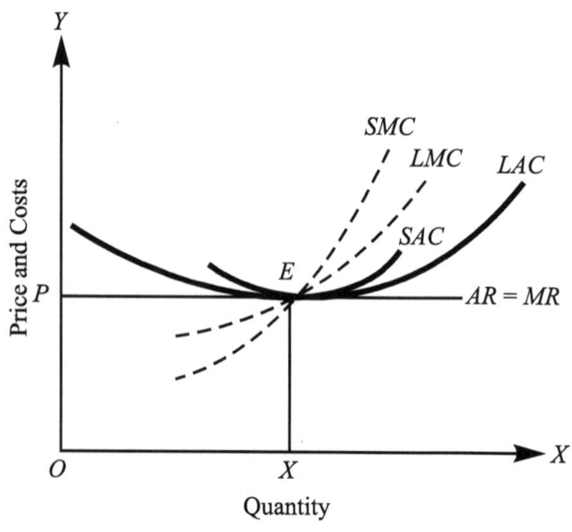

Fig. 24.12

The above long-run condition is applicable to all the firms in the industry. In other words, in the long-run, price must be equal to the minimum average cost of each firm. This is the situation, when no new firm will like to enter the industry and no old firm would like to leave the industry. The number of firms in the industry is fixed.

So far we have introduced the concept of long-period equilibrium of the firm in a perfect competitive industry. But it does not describe a complete analysis of the long-period adjustments within the industry that occur as a result of some disturbing force. Usually, cost changes as well as price changes will takes place as new firms, attracted by profits, enter the industry. The nature of the cost adjustments, if any, will depend upon whether the industry (or the firm) is operating under increasing costs, constant costs, or decreasing costs.

Increasing Costs. We have already explained the equilibrium of the industry under the increasing costs condition. Here we shall explain the long-run equilibrium diagrams for the industry and for a representative firm of the industry. The case of increasing costs has been shown in Fig. 24.13. Initially, the industry demand curve is *DD* and the industry supply curve is *SS*. The original price is *OP* where *DD* cuts *SS* at point *E*. This price is initially given to the firm. Now suppose, that at this price *OP*, the firm's short-run average cost, *SAC* and long-run average cost, *LAC* touch at point *A*. Since at point

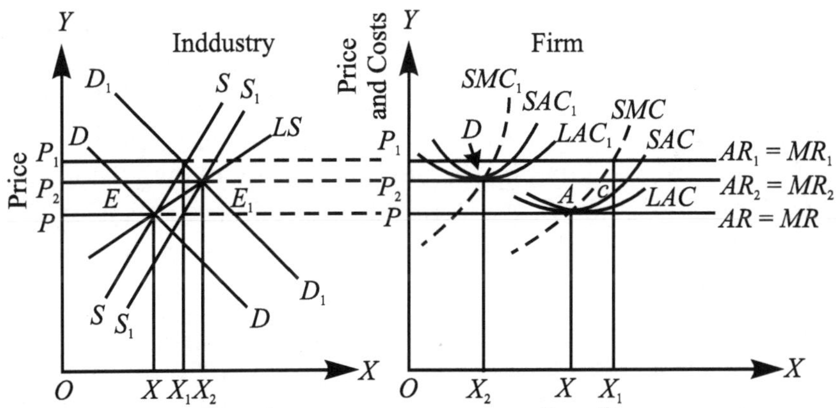

Fig. 24.13

A the *SAC* is minimum, therefore the *SMC* curve will cut the *SAC* at point *A*. Point *A* is the initial equilibrium point of the firm where $P = SMC = SAC = LAC$. The long-run marginal cost curve is omitted, because it is not essential for the present analysis and unnecessarily complicates the diagram.[3] Thus, initially, firm's

3. Here it is obvious that, when *LAC* is minimum at point *A*, it will also be equal to *L MC*. In other words, at point *A*, we shall have the condition.

$$P = MR = SMC = SAC = LMC = LAC.$$

equilibrium output is OX while industry output is OX which is the summation of individual firm's outputs at price OP. Here, the firm is using the optimum scale of plant at the optimum rate of output because there is no profit no loss.

Now, suppose, industry demand increases to D_1D_1 but at the same time supply cannot be adjusted according to demand. This means that such a shift in demand will raise the price to OP_1 in the short-run. Since in the short-run, the firm is not able to increase the size of the plant, it can make an intensive use of it by producing OX_1 output at price OP_1. This is the output (OX_1) at which SMC equals the new marginal revenue (MR_1). This allows the firm to make short-run profits equal to BC per unit. Thus, the short-run effects of the increase in demand are: (*i*) price has increased, (*ii*) output has increased to the extent that the existing plant-capacity is worked with greater intensity, and (*iii*) profits are attained by the existing firms.

But in the long-run, these short-run advantages of the firm will disappear. The existence of profits in the industry will attract new firms to enter into the industry in the long-run. As new firms enter the industry, the short-period supply curve (SS) of the industry will shift to the right as S_1S_1, The increase in supply will reduce the price from OP_1 to OP_2. At this price the firm will reduce output from OX_1 to OX_2. This is because the prices of factors of production, which were fixed in the short-run, have risen more than those of the other inputs. In other words, all inputs have become variable inputs and in order to economise inputs which are relatively more expensive, the firm builds a smaller plant.[4] In such a case, the total output of old firms will actually be less than that of initial situation. But since the total industry output has increased to OX_2, the increase in output by the new firms is more than the decrease in output by the old (existing) firms. Here, the conclusion is that in the long-run, the firm again establishes its equilibrium where there is no profit no loss to the firm. The firm as well as the industry is of optimum size.

The long-run industry supply curve is LS in Fig. 24.13. It joins all the points of long-run equilibrium for the industry such as, E and E_1. It demonstrates the fact that under increasing cost conditions, increased demand can be satisfied by the industry only at a higher supply price.

Constant Costs. In the case of constant costs, the firms in the industry can expand their scale of operations without causing any increase in factor

4. If all factor prices rise in the same proportion, the firm's cost curves would shift straight up and equilibrium output of the individual firm would be the same as before (in the initial situation). In such a case the entire increase in the industry output would be the result of the new firms. If, on the other hand, factor prices (which were fixed previously) rise less than the prices of other inputs, it would be cheaper to operate on a higher scale plant. In such a case, the increase in the industry output is partly due to the increase in the size of plants of the old firms and partly due to the output of new firms.

prices. In other words, the entire industry (all firms) was only a small part of the total supplies of various factors of production of the economy, so that its expansion or contraction will not affect the factor prices. As a result, the individual firm's cost curves will not be disturbed at all. The procedure of determining price and output is the same as that under increasing costs. This has been illustrated in Fig. 24.14. The initial equilibrium was at the price *OP* and each firm in the industry was producing *OX* quantity of the product. Now, suppose demand for the product increases and as a result, there is a shift in the industry demand curve from *DD* to D_1D_1. Since in the short-period, industry supply curve can not be shifted accordingly, thus price rises to OP_1. At price OP_1, each firm produces OX_1 quantity of the product. The existing firms are enjoying abnormal profits at this increased price. Now, in the long-run new firms are attracted by this profit and they enter into the industry. This leads the industry supply curve to shift to the right. Entry of new firms, and the corresponding shift in the industry supply curve will continue until the original price *OP* is restored, at which the individual firm produces *OX* quantity of the product and earns only the normal profit. We must remember that the cost curves of the industry will not shift in the changed conditions because the entry of new firms does not cause any increase in factor prices.[5] Also, the existing firms produce the same initial level of output.

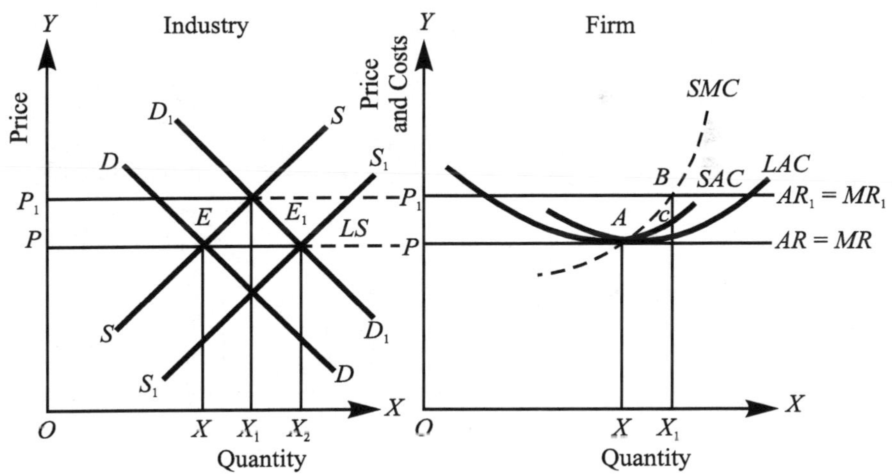

Fig 24.14

5. In a constant cost industry, the entry of new firms does not increase market demand resources sufficiently to cause their prices to increase. Of the total supply of resources necessary for the production of the commodity, this industry takes a small enough part so that no influence is exerted on their prices by the new firms coming in. This means that the cost curves will remain the same.

Thus, the increase in industry output (from OX to OX_1) will absolutely be the result of the output of new firms. This is the reason that the shift in industry supply curve is equivalent to the shift in demand curve. As a result, the long-run supply curve of the industry is LS and it is horizontal at the level of minimum long-period average costs. In such a situation the optimum size of the firm remains the same.

Decreasing Costs. In the case of decreasing costs, the firms in the industry meet the increased demand for the product at a lower price than the initial price. This case is not, in general, found in real life. It is possible only when the firms are unable to obtain external economies, such as cheap transportation, cheap power, technical information, etc. These external economies will lead to reduce the costs of production as they produce more. This has been illustrated in Fig. 24.15. The process of adjustment is the same as we have discussed under increasing or constant costs. The initial price is OP where the industry equilibrium output is OX and firm's output is OX. At this level of output the firm is getting no profit no loss. If industry demand curve shifts from DD to D_1D_1, the short-period price increases from OP to OP_1. At this price OP_1, the firm is getting abnormal profit to the extent of BC per unit at OX_1 level of output. In the long-run, new firms will enter into the industry

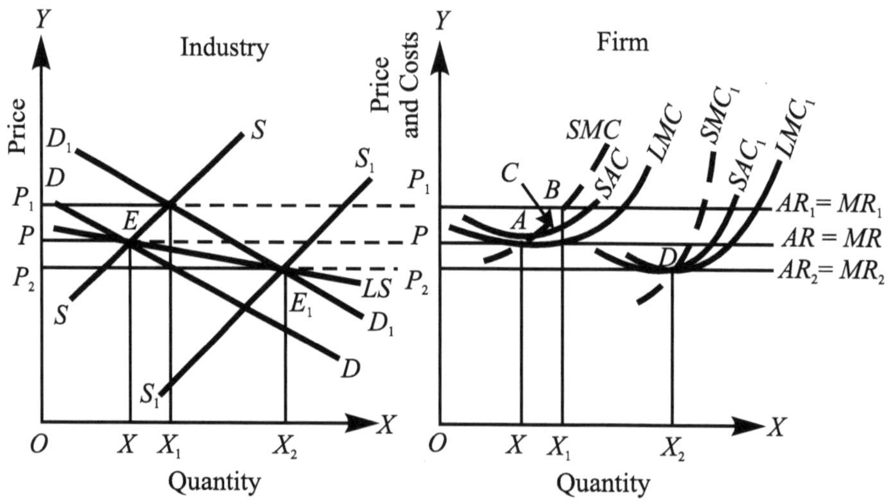

Fig. 24.15

and in the situation of decreasing costs, it will result input prices to decrease. The supply curve of the industry shifts from SS to S_1S_1. The increase (shift) in supply is more than the increase (shift) in demand. Consequently, the long-run supply price falls to OP_2.

On the other hand, as new firms enter into the industry, external economies take place and it will cause resource prices to fall. Consequently, the cost curves of the firm shift downwards. Both price' of the product and costs of production are decreasing. Thus the profits, attained by the firm in the short-run, disappear. At price OP_2: the firm produces OX_2 quantity of output, at which $P = MR = SMC = LMC = SAC = LAC$. The new industry output is OX_2 and the long-run supply curve of the industry is LS which is downward-sloping to the right. According to Ferguson, the decreasing supply curve is inconsistent with the assumptions of perfect competition. It is possible only in the situation of monopoly.

Exercises

1. Explain the effect of a shift in demand curve on the industry equilibrium in the short run under perfect competition.
2. Show the effect of a change in price on the short-run equilibrium of the individual firm under perfect competition.
3. Explain and illustrate diagrammatically the short-run and long-run equilibrium of the firm and the industry under the conditions of perfect competition.
4. What are the main characteristics of perfect competition? Distinguish between pure competition and perfect competition.
5. Explain the importance of time element in the theory of value.
6. Illustrate diagrammatically the long-run equilibrium of the firm and the industry under perfect competition assuming that increasing costs prevail in the industry.
7. Explain the market period equilibrium of the industry under perfect competition.
8. How is price of a commodity determined under perfect competition?
9. Discuss the conditions of short-run and long-run equilibrium of the industry under perfect competition.
10. Do you think that under perfect competition, in the short-run a firm may continue its production even in the situation of loss?
11. Write short notes on the following:
    (*i*) Effect of a tax on the short-run equilibrium under perfect competition.
    (*ii*) Long-run equilibrium of a perfect competitive firm and industry under increasing; constant and diminishing cost conditions.
12. Explain with the help of a diagram how price is determined in a perfectly competitive market.
13. Explain Marshall's three-period analysis on pricing of products in a competitive market. Illustrate with the help of diagrams.
14. Discuss the importance of time element in the theory of value.

Multiple Choice Questions

15. (*i*) Under perfect competition, the demand curve for an individual firm is
    (*a*) perfectly elastic
    (*b*) more elastic
    (*c*) less elastic
    (*d*) perfectly inelastic [*Ans.* (*a*)]

    (*ii*) The best level of output for a perfectly competitive firm is given by the point where
    (*a*) $MR = AC$
    (*b*) $MR = MC$
    (*c*) MR exceeds MC by the greatest amount

(*d*) $MR=MC$ and MC is rising [*Ans.* (*a*)]

(*iii*) At the best short-period level of output, the firm will be
(*a*) maximising total profits
(*b*) minimising total losses
(*c*) either maximising total profits or minimising total losses
(*d*) maximising profits per unit [*Ans.* (*c*)]

(*iv*) If price exceeds AVC but is smaller than AC at the best level of output, the firm is
(*a*) making a profit
(*b*) incurring a loss but should continue to produce in the short-run
(*c*) incurring a loss and should stop production immediately
(*d*) breaking even [*Ans.* (*b*)]

(*v*) Which of the following is the main characteristic of perfect competition market?
(*a*) Homogeneity of the product
(*b*) Free entry and free exit of the firm into the industry
(*c*) Perfect knowledge of the economy
(*d*) all of the above [*Ans.* (*d*)]

(*vi*) In the very short period, the supply curve of the industry is
(*a*) perfectly elastic (*c*) more elastic
(*b*) perfectly inelastic (*d*) less elastic [*Ans.* (*b*)]

(*vii*) In the very short period, under perfect competition the prices of vanish able items are determined by
(*a*) demand only
(*b*) supply only
(*c*) demand and supply
(*d*) partially demand and partially supply of the commodity [*Ans.* (*a*)]

(*viii*) In the short-period a firm will continue output if the following condition is satisfied
(*a*) $MC = MR = AC$ (*c*) Price $< AVC$
(*b*) Price $> AVC$ (d) Price $= MC = MR$ [*Ans.* (*b*)]

Chapter 25

Interdependent Prices[1]

1. Introduction

In the preceding chapters of pricing and output, we confined ourselves to the partial equilibrium analysis. The price of a single commodity was assumed to be determined by its demand and supply. When the price of a commodity is said to be determined by the conditions of demand and supply pertaining to it, it may seem as though this price is an isolated phenomenon, standing more or less apart from the prices of other goods; but this is an erroneous impression. We must always bear in mind that the prices of various commodities are rarely determined in isolation. They are, in fact, a system in which each is related to all the rest in greater or lesser degree. In other words, the price of a commodity is not the result of isolated factors of demand and supply for it alone, but of a multitude of interrelated factors in which the prices of many other goods are involved. Therefore, the entire price system comes under the analysis of general equilibrium.

Each price is related to every other price, for the simple reason that the money incomes (or purchasing powers) of consumers are limited, as are also the means (factors) of production. In simple words, the interdependence of all prices goes back to the fundamental fact of scarcity, which underlines all things economic. If a person spends a portion of his income for commodity *X*, he is unable to spend it for commodity *Y;* for the simple reason that he cannot eat his bread and have the money too. Every consumer has to decide how to spend his limited income or which commodities are to be purchased and how much of them is to be purchased. These decisions will affect the price of all the commodities the consumers buy. If the consumers decide that they need more amusement, and they spend more on theatres or on travel than they previously did, they must reduce their purchases of other

1. This analysis is also known as the Pricing of Related Goods.

commodities. By doing so, they add to the demand for theatres and such other commodities and thus tend to raise their prices. While on the other hand, the consumers reduce the demand for those goods which come under the second group, such as, clothing, furniture, etc. and therefore, tend to depress their prices. It means that a change in the consumption pattern may shift the direction of demand so as to affect strongly the prices of various goods produced in the economy.

Similarly, the principle of opportunity costs on the supply side will reinforce these observations. According to this principle of opportunity costs, any factor of production can be used in one industry only on the condition that firms in that industry will pay a price for it equal to what it would be worth in other industries. This establishes a price connection between all commodities in so far as they draw on the same basic resources of land, labour and capital.

Hence we find that the prices are not isolated, but are interrelated in an elaborate, coherent whole. This complex of prices is known as the price system. In the following section we shall examine some specific types of relations that are specially close, i.e. relations between the prices of related goods.

2. Substitutes and Complements

The two important types of related commodities are substitutes and complements. Some goods are fairly good substitutes for each other. The examples of such goods are cane sugar and beet sugar, aluminium and magnesium, television and movies, tea and coffee, etc. The degree of substitutability varies from the cases in which one commodity is an almost perfect substitute for another, to cases of only poor substitutability. Beet sugar is an almost perfect substitute for cane sugar, but vegetables are very poor substitutes for meat. Similarly, tea and coffee are assumed to be very close substitutes but bread and fruits are not close substitutes to each other. Thus, where the possibilities for substitution are good, changes in the price of one commodity will result in similar changes in the price of its substitute. For example, if the price of sugar increases, people will switch to the cheaper gur, then the increased demand for gur will cause its price to increase alongwith that of sugar, although not necessarily to the same degree. On the other hand, if sugar become cheaper, people will buy more sugar and less gur, resulting in the price of gur to go down and the fall in the price of gur is not necessarily the same.

The other type of goods are complements rather than substitutes. Complement goods are those goods which are jointly used. The examples of such complements are: ink and paper, tennis rackets and tennis balls, automobile and gasoline, window frames and window glass, etc. Here again, changes in the demand for, or price of, one of the complementary commodities will cause responsive changes in the demand for, or price of the other; but in this case the change will be in the opposite direction. For example, if tennis rackets become expensive (or the price of tennis rackets increases), people would play less tennis and this would lead to a reduction in the demand for tennis balls and finally resulting in the prices of both the complementary goods (here tennis rackets and tennis balls) to go down.

The extent of the changes in the demand and price of the related commodities can be measured by the cross-elasticity of demand. In simple words, cross-elasticity of demand states the extent to which the demand for one commodity responds to changes in the price of the other commodity. Mathematically, the formula of cross-elasticity can be written as below:

Cross-elasticity of demand between *X* and *Y* commodities =

$$\frac{\text{Percentage change in the quantity of } Y \text{ bought}}{\text{Percentage change in the price of } X}$$

When commodities *X* and *Y* are good substitutes for each other, the cross-elasticity will be positive and the magnitude will be high. If the substitutes are perfect, or nearly so, the value of cross-elasticity will approach infinity.

When commodities *X* and *Y* are complementary, the cross-elasticity will be negative. And the absolute magnitude of this elasticity coefficient will indicate the degree of complementarity between the two commodities.

The degree of substitutability is very important for the distinction between perfect competition, imperfect competition, product differentiation and pure monopoly. Where the products of different firms are perfect substitutes for each other, we have only one homogeneous commodity, then it will be a situation of pure competition. Where the products of different firms are fairly good but not perfect substitutes, i.e. the products are slightly different; then it will be a situation of product differentiation or monopolistic competition. Where the products of different firms are very poor substitutes, then each firm will act as pure monopoly.

But, for the present discussion of interdependent prices or mutually related prices, we assume that perfect competition prevails in commodity markets. There are four different ways in which the problem of interdependent prices may arise:

(*i*) Pricing under Joint Demand,

(*ii*) Pricing under Composite Demand,

(*iii*) Pricing under Joint Supply, and

(*iv*) Pricing under Composite Supply.

Now we shall discuss these different ways one by one in the following manner.

3. Pricing under Joint Demand

Joint demand exists when two goods are closely complementary. Two goods will be complementary in the sense that the use of one implies the use of the other. For instance, the demand for petrol is associated with the demand for motor cars, the demand for tennis balls is linked to the demand for tennis rackets, etc. An increase (or decrease) in the demand for one of these goods will be accompanied by an increase (or decrease) in the demand for the other. An increase in the demand for tea might well cause an increase in the price of sugar.

Joint demand is often associated with derived demand. This occurs in the building of a house, where there is a derived, joint demand for lumber, stone, plaster, cement, and other materials. In the production of most commodities, we find a similar situation. However, joint demand should not be confused with derived demand. Derived demand arises from the fact that goods at more or less remote stages of production are needed for the final use. It (derived demand) refers to the successive stages of production. Where joint demand refers to the situation in which a number of articles (goods) may be demanded simultaneously at anyone stage or by the consumer himself for the final use. This distinction between derived demand and joint demand rests in the difference between succession and simultaneity.

Thus, the case of joint demand may arise in both for factors of production and for the goods of final use. The valuation of complementary goods (goods demanded jointly) is complicated by the fact that the demand schedules of such goods are interrelated. The demand for motor cars will be seriously affected if petrol becomes scarce. We can draw a separate demand curve for motor cars only on the assumption that there would be no change in the supply conditions of petrol (or of any other product required for using a motor car). It is to be noted that Marshall's statement of the Law of Demand (and his concept of the Demand Curve) assumes "other things remaining the same." Therefore, the problem of pricing under joint demand is a complex one. It can be discussed under the following two situations (*i*) Situation of Varied Proportions; and (*ii*) Situation of Fixed Proportions.

In the situation of varied proportion, the purchaser of several commodities (or factor inputs) that are to be used jointly, can vary the proportions in which they are to be combined. In such a situation, it is possible to estimate the importance of each commodity, independently of the others. The method of *marginal analysis* is used to find out the importance of each commodity or factor input as the case may be. For example, a farmer wants to grow wheat. For this he demands several inputs together such as seeds, fertilisers, water, etc. Although, these factor inputs are used jointly, yet it is possible for the farmer to change the proportion in which they can be used to produce a given quantity of wheat. By doing so he is able to find out the individual demand schedules for these inputs. Suppose, he wants to find out the worth, or importance of fertilisers in the production of wheat. He will try a number of combinations of seeds, fertilisers, water, etc. by varying the proportion of fertilisers and keeping the quantities of other inputs constant. The different contributions of factor inputs applied to the production of wheat will result in different levels of output. In this way he can determine what the fertilisers are worth to him. Thus, it is possible to construct a separate demand schedule (or demand curve) for fertiliser, in spite of the fact that it is used in combination with other inputs. In such circumstances, we really have a case of simple derived demand and not a true case of joint demand at all. It is, therefore, possible to treat it as a problem of isolated price, by comparing separate demand and cost schedules, as we have used in the previous chapters on pricing and output under various market situations.[2]

The real problem of pricing under joint demand arises when the proportions in which complementary goods are employed are fixed by technical considerations which permit no variation. In such a situation it is impossible to separate the demand for one of the goods from that of the other. For example, in the making of eyeglasses, there is a joint demand for lenses and frames in a fixed proportion. Similarly, in the product of a number of other commodities, the factors of production are jointly demanded in the fixed proportion. The problem of price determination in such a case of fixed proportion can be solved by means of demand and supply curves not greatly different from those we have already discussed. Here, we have to set a single demand curve for eyeglasses (final output) against the two different supply (cost) curves for frames (the first factor input) and lenses (the second factor input) in such a way as to find the separate equilibrium prices for frames (first factor input) and lenses (second factor input). This case is illustrated in Panel (*a*) and (*b*) of Fig. 25.1. Here, we assume the situation of perfect competition. In Panel (*a*) of Fig. 25.1, S_fS_f curve represents the marginal costs of producing the frames. In Panel (*b*) of Fig. 25.1, S_LS_L represents the marginal costs of producing the lenses. Since two lenses (glasses) are used with each frame, the unit quantities shown on the horizontal axis indicate pairs of lenses and the prices shown on the vertical axis indicate the prices per pair of lenses.

2. The price is determined by applying the rule, $MC = MR$. Since marginal cost (MC) is given and marginal revenue (MR) is calculated by the above method of marginal analysis it becomes very simple to determine the price.

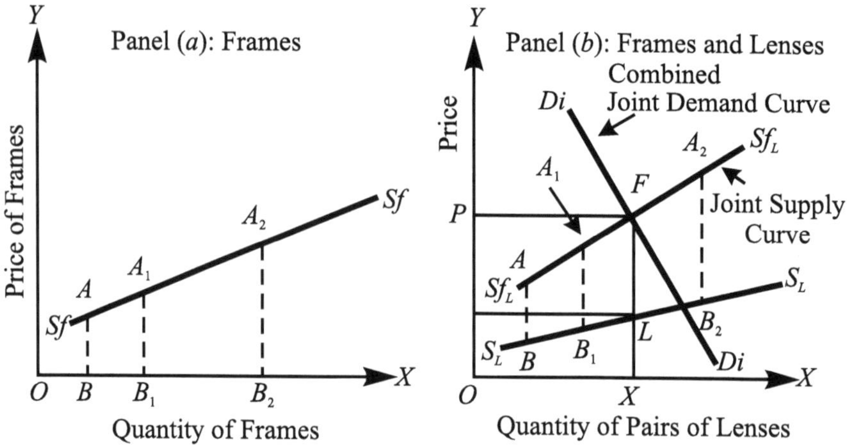

Fig. 25.1

Now, we combine the curves, $S_f S_f$ and $S_L S_L$ in order to obtain the combined cost of two factor inputs (frame and lenses) in the finished product (eyeglasses or finished glasses). We do this by superimposing the curve $S_f S_f$ upon the curve $S_L S_L$ in Panel (*b*) of Fig. 25.1. Thus, $S_{fL} S_{fL}$ curve is drawn by adding vertically the $S_f S_f$ curve of Panel (*a*) into the $S_L S_L$ curve of Panel (*b*). Therefore, the distances *AB*, A_1B_1 and A_2B_2 in Panel (*b*) will be exactly the same as the corresponding distances in Panel (*a*). Therefore, $S_{fL} S_{fL}$ is the combined cost (supply) curve for the two constituents (factor input) of the finished glasses (eyeglasses). Now let us assume that $D_j D_j$ is the joint demand curve for the two products in the finished glasses. It (D_j D_j) intersects the supply (cost) curve ($S_{fL} S_{fL}$) at point *E*. Therefore, at price *OP*, demand and supply are in equilibrium. In other words, the equilibrium price for eyeglasses is *OP*. At this level, the price for lenses (first factor input) should be equal to *XL* and the price for frames (second factor input) should be equal to *LF*. Hence, under joint demand, we may determine the separate equilibrium prices for the complementary products.

In the above analysis, we have discussed the price determination under joint demand, i.e. the determination of the prices of two complementary goods. Now we shall try to examine the relationship between the prices of two jointly demanded commodities. As we have already mentioned, changes in the price of one of the complementary commodities will cause an opposite change in the price of the other commodity.

This is illustrated with the help of Panel (*a*) and Panel (*b*) of Fig. 25.2. Panel (*a*) and Panel (*b*) of Fig. 25.2, explain the positions of demand, supply and price of the two complementary commodities, bread and butter respectively. Suppose, the price of bread increases (from *OP* to OP_1) due to some restrictions (tax) imposed by the government. Thus, the supply curve of bread has moved up (from SS to S_1S_1) by the extent of the tax (AB). Now at the higher price (OP_1), the demand for bread falls (from OX to OX_1). Now since the demand for bread has been reduced, there will be a similar reduction in the demand for butter. In other words, the demand curve for butter in Panel (*b*) shifts from DD to D_1D_1. As a result of this, the price of butter goes down from OR to OR_1. Here, we may see that the increase in the price of bread is more than the increase in the price of butter. The reverse will happen, if the price of bread falls instead of rising.

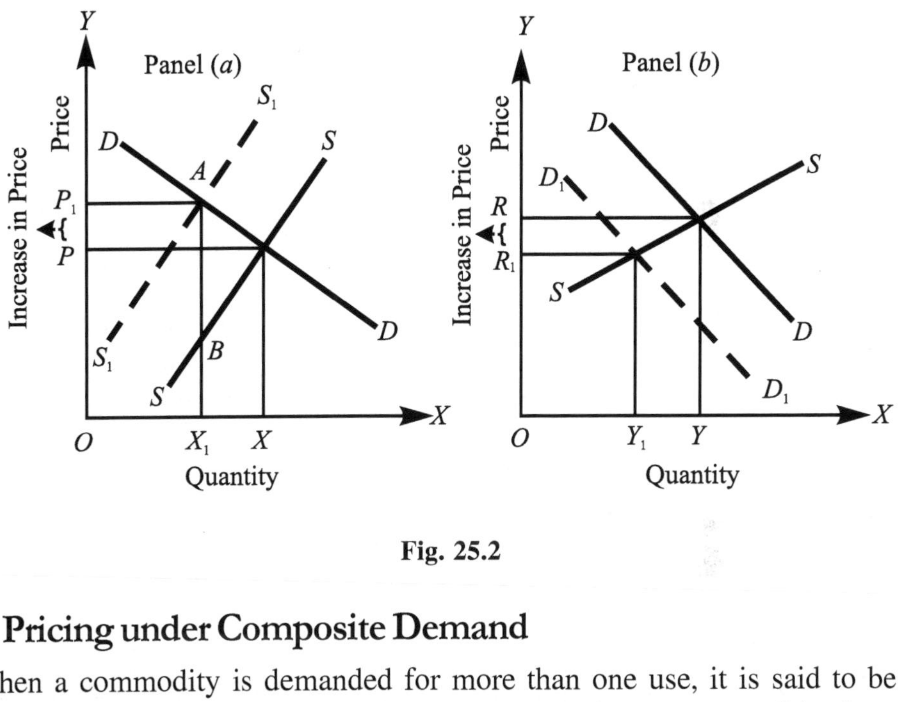

Fig. 25.2

4. Pricing under Composite Demand

When a commodity is demanded for more than one use, it is said to be in composite demand. The demand for such goods is the aggregate of the demand of the various users. For example, wool will be demanded by the textile industry, carpet manufacturers, blanket manufacturers, hosiery manufacturers, and many others. An increase in the demand for anyone use, say clothing, will raise the price of wool and affect the prices of all other commodities made from wool. Another good illustration of a commodity for which the demand is a composite of many separate demands would be electricity. It is demanded for light, heat and also for various production purposes. The same is true for the factors of production skilled and unskilled labour, land, and capital.

The determination of price of a commodity having composite demand is not a complex task. Like other commodities, the price of such a commodity is also determined by its demand and supply curves.

Where the demand for a good is composite, its total demand schedule (or demand curve) will be the sum of the demand schedules (curves) for it in all the different uses to which it is put. For example, at each price on demand schedule for wool, a certain quantity of it will be bought by the textile industry, a certain additional quantity will be bought by carpet manufacturers, a certain additional quantity will be demanded by blanket producers and hosiery manufacturers and so on. The sum of these quantities constitutes the total effective demand at each price. This will give us a demand curve of the usual type, i.e. it will be a negatively sloping curve. The supply (or cost) curve for wool is given. Now it will become a simple price problem. The equilibrium price will be attained at that point where the total effective demand, so computed, equals the total effective supply. Under perfect competition, in the long-run, the equilibrium price will tend to equal the optimum cost of production.

In the case of composite demand, because the total demand for the commodity is made up of many separate demands, a change in anyone of the component demand schedules will have only a slight (negligible) effect on the price. For instance, an increase in the demand for socks or mufflers will have very little effect upon the price of wool, because only an infinitesimally small portion of the total demand for wool is derived from that for socks or mufflers. On the other hand, a change in the conditions of supply (cost) for a commodity whose demand is composite may affect greatly the prices of all the products in which it is used.

5. Pricing under Joint Supply or Joint Costs

An interesting relationship, and one which gives rise to a number of economic problems, is that of joint supply. Joint supply exists when two or more products are automatically produced together. In such a case, joint costs arise; the cost of producing one of the commodities cannot be clearly separated from the cost of producing the other. In mining ore, the production of both silver and copper results in a joint cost. The production of coal gas entails the production of coke. The production of petrol leads to the production of benzene and fuel oil. Similarly, from the ginning of cotton there results, not only the cotton-fibre, but also the seed, from which a valuable oil can be extracted. Also in a meat-packing industry, hams, bacon, hides, blood, bone, hair, glue, fats, gut, and other useful raw materials are produced more or less together. All cases of so-called by-products fall in the same category. In these cases of joint supply, we have just the opposite of joint demand. Instead of several articles derived from separate sources being combined in use, and therefore, demanded jointly, we have several articles which are separately demanded but which are combined in production and, therefore, supplied jointly. Thus, *joint supply can be defined as that relation where two or more products are obtained at the same time, in a single production process.* It is also called joint costs, because, where two or more commodities are produced together, their costs of production cannot be entirely separated. We cannot produce beef unless we also produce hides. Similarly, when copper and silver are found in the same ore, how can one say what part of the cost of mining the ore is the cost of producing copper and what part of the cost of producing silver?

Therefore, in the case of joint products, the problem is, how to find the marginal cost of each of the products. If the marginal cost is found, we can apply the theory of value and say that the price of each of the joint products will tend to equal its marginal cost (assuming perfect competition in the market). For pricing under joint supply, we divide joint products into two categories:

(*i*) Joint products whose relative proportions can be varied, and

(*ii*) Joint products whose relative proportions are fixed.

In the case of the first type of joint products, it is possible to calculate the marginal cost of each of the products with the help of marginal analysis. Suppose, for example, 10 units of gas and 8 units of coke can be obtained by incurring a cost of \$200. Also, suppose that with a new production process it is possible to get 11 units of gas and 1 unit of, coke with a cost outlay of \$220. Then the marginal cost of gas is \$20 per unit. With variable proportions, the conditions of equilibrium are:

(*a*) in the situation of long-run perfect competition, $MC = P = MR$.

(*b*) in the situation of imperfect competition, $MC = MR$.

The real problem of pricing arises when the relative proportion of joint products is fixed. For example, the proportion between cotton-fibre and cotton-seeds is more or less fixed. To get more fibre, we have to increase the quantity of cotton. The problem here is to find out the separate marginal costs of the two products, i.e. their prices can be determined separately. The solution to this problem is the same as is worked out under the joint demand (Fig 25.1). Now, Panel (*a*) and Panel (*b*) of Fig. 25.3 illustrate this case. In Panel (*a*) of Fig. 25.3, d_fd_f *curve* shows the separate demand curve for cotton-fibres while in Panel (*b*) of Fig. 25.3, d_sd_s shows the separate demand curve for cotton-seeds. The combined demand curve for the fibres and seeds can be shown by superimposing d_fd_f and d_sd_s curves, using the latter (i.e. d_sd_s curve) as its base line. Therefore, in Panel (*b*) of Fig. 25.3. $D_{fs}D_{fs}$ indicates the combined demand curve for the two joint products (fibres and seeds). The construction of this curve ($D_{fs}D_{fs}$) is such that any distance between it and d_sd_s, such as A_1B_1, A_2B_2, or A_3B_3, exactly equal to the corresponding distances between d_fd_f and the horizontal axis in Panel (*a*) of Fig 25.3. In Panel (*b*) of Fig. 25.3, C_jC_j represents the marginal cost of producing the two commodities (cotton-fibres and seeds) jointly. We must remember that each unit space along the horizontal axis of Panel (*b*) indicates the combined unit of the two products

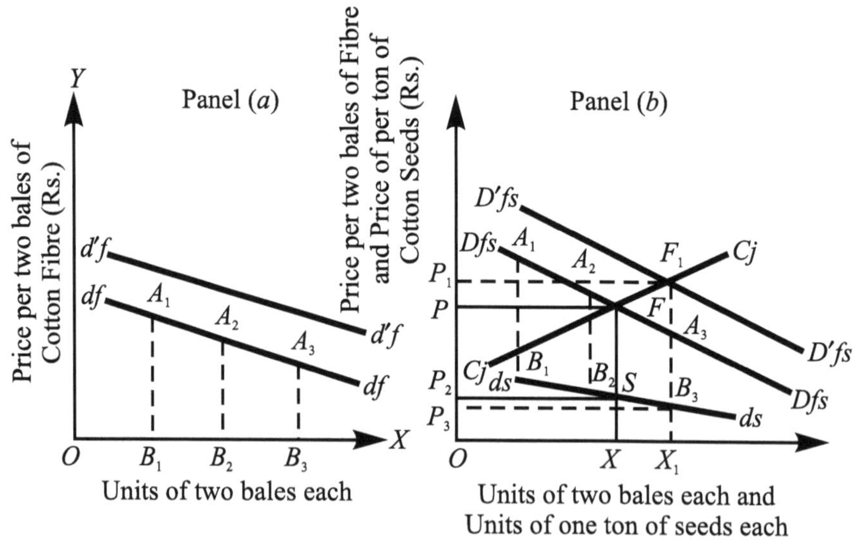

Fig. 25.3

(i.e. each unit may indicate, say, two bales of cotton and one ton of seeds). Similarly, along the vertical axis of Panel (*b*) we measure prices per two bales in the case of cotton-fibre and per ton in the case of cotton-seeds. Now equilibrium is reached at that point where the combined or effective demand curve $D_{fs}D_{fs}$ intersects the combined or effective supply (cost) curve C_jC_j. This point is *F* in Panel (*b*) of Fig. 25.3, where the equilibrium quantity of cotton-fibres and cottonseeds is equal to *OX*. The equilibrium price of the seeds will, therefore, be $SX(= OP_3)$ per ton, and the price of the cotton-fibres will be SF $(= P_3P)$ per two bales. Here, we observe that the costs are divided between the two products in proportion to their marginal demand prices.

Further, since the joint costs are apportioned between the two joint products according to the relative demand for them, the product, for which the demand is greater, will bear the larger part of the costs and consequently, it will be sold at a higher price than the price at which the other product would be sold. In the above diagram, the demand price of cotton-fibre is higher than that of cotton-seeds; therefore, cotton-fibre will be sold at a higher price than cotton-seeds. In Fig. 25.3, it is clear that the demand curve d_fd_f for cotton-fibre [see Panel (*a*)] is higher than the demand curve d_sd_s for cotton-seeds [see Panel (*b*)]. Consequently, the price *FS* of cotton-fibre is higher than the price *SX* of cotton-seeds.

Now, in case the demand schedule for anyone of the two (or more) joint products increases, its price will rise, and the price(s) of the other commodity(s) produced jointly with it may be expected to fall. For example, suppose, the demand schedule or demand curve for cotton-fibres in Panel (*a*) of Fig. 25.3 increases from $d_f d_f$ to $d'_f d'_f$; assuming the demand schedule (curve) for cotton-seeds remaining the same. Superimposing the new curve on $d_s d_s$, as before, we get the new combined demand curve $D'_{fs}D'_{fs}$ in Panel (*b*) of Fig. 25.3. This new combined demand curve D'_{fs} D'_{fs} intersects the cost (supply) curve C_jC_j at point F_1. Thus, point F_1 becomes the new equilibrium point. At this point, the output of both cotton-seeds and cotton-fibres increases from OX to OX_1. The increased demand for cotton-fibre has resulted in an increased supply of cotton-fibre. The price of cotton-fibre has increased from FS to F_1S_1 on account of rise in its demand. But the price of cotton-seeds has fallen from SX to S_1X_1, because its output has automatically increased with the increase in the production of cotton-fibre, though there is no increase in the demand for cottonseeds. The increased supply of cotton-seeds can be disposed of only by reducing its price. Cotton-fibre now bears a larger portion of the joint costs, cotton-seeds a smaller portion, than was formerly the case. Similarly, a decrease in the demand schedule of cotton-fibre will make the opposite effects.

6. Pricing under Composite Supply

Composite supply refers to that case where two or more goods are perfect substitutes. This case is the opposite of composite demand. In composite demand, we have one product used for two or more purposes. In composite supply, we have two or more goods used for one purpose. In other words, different commodities satisfying the same want are said to be in composite supply. Composite supply commodities are substitutes of one another e.g. tea and coffee, roadways and railways transport, butter and margarine, beet-sugar and cane-sugar, etc.[3]

Perfect cases of composite supply are rare, for it is not often that one commodity is a perfect substitute for another. Usually, there are slight differences which make one of them better adapted to certain uses than its competitor. In some cases, however, the differences are negligible; for instance, beet-sugar and cane sugar are so close that an average consumer cannot find the difference between them.

The prices of substitutes (composite supply goods) move in the same direction. If the price of tea falls, some people will use tea for coffee. The demand for coffee will fall and its price will fall. Goods which are substitutable for one another are also called *competing goods*.

3. The factors of production may also constitute a case of composite supply. For example, labour and capital, so far as the one can be substituted for the other, may be said to constitute a case of composite supply.

The price of commodities that are in composite supply will be determined by the cost of producing them and by their marginal utilities or marginal net products. In case the products (or factor inputs) are nearly perfect substitutes (such as beet-sugar and cane-sugar), they can be combined into one supply schedule, showing several quantities of each of the two substitutes that will be offered at each of a series of corresponding prices. That is, at one particular price, a certain quantity of beet-sugar and a certain quantity of cane-sugar will be produced; the sum of these constitutes the effective (combined) supply at that price, and so on for every possible price. Thus, we are able to draw the combined supply schedule of the close substitutes. The separate demand schedules for each are already known to us. Thus, the pricing problem of composite supply becomes very simple. Production of the two substitute commodities will be carried to the point where their marginal costs are the same, and the price (same for both) will be fixed at that level where the marginal demand-price equals its marginal cost.[4]

In conclusion, we can say that the problem of interdependent prices discussed above under the four main headings is of paramount importance. It touches almost every branch of production. The demand and supply of most of the commodities and resources are closely interconnected with each other. And the value of a thing may depend on the remote influences affecting the value of a thing. The price of petrol, for example, depends on the fare tables of the tramway company. For if the tram fare is reduced, more people would ride in them in preference to buses. The buses would be making smaller journeys in that case, and the demand for petrol would fall. Hence the prices of most commodities are interconnected with each other.

Exercises

1. Explain the problem of interdependent prices. How are the prices of commodities determined when they are produced jointly under perfect competition?
2. Write short notes on the following:
   (*i*) Joint Demand
   (*ii*) Composite Demand
   (*iii*) Joint Supply
   (*iv*) Composite Supply
3. Explain the pricing problem under joint demand and under joint supply (or joint costs).
4. Distinguish between, substitutes and complements. How can you measure the degree of substitutability and complementarity?

---

4. This case of composite supply has not been represented with the help of a diagram, but if so desired, it can easily be shown diagrammatically. Any change in the price of one of the substitute commodities will result in a similar change in the price of the other.

Multiple Choice Questions

5. (*i*) Which of the following pairs of commodities is an example of substitutes
   (*a*) Coffee and milk
   (*b*) Diamond and cow
   (*c*) Pen and ink
   (*d*) Mustard oil and coconut oil [*Ans.* (*d*)]

   (*ii*) For most consumers apples and oranges are substitute goods. Therefore, we would expect a rise in the price of apples to lead to
   (*a*) a fall in the price of oranges
   (*b*) an upward change in the demand curve of oranges
   (*c*) a leftward shift in the supply curve of apples
   (*d*) a rightward shift in the supply curve of oranges [*Ans.* (*b*)]

   (*iii*) A fall in the relative price for fruit would
   (*a*) lead to a fall in the demand for fruits
   (*b*) have no effect on the demand for potatoes
   (*c*) increase the quantity of sweets demanded
   (*d*) none of the above is correct [*Ans.* (*b*)]

   (*iv*) If two goods are complements, this means that arise in the price of one commodity will induce
   (*a*) an upward shift in demand for the other commodity
   (*b*) a rise in the price of the other commodity
   (*c*) a downward shift in demand for the other commodity
   (*d*) no shift in demand for the other commodity [*Ans.* (*c*)]

Chapter 26

Pricing and Output under Monopoly

1. Introduction

The classical economists, such as Adam Smith, David Ricardo and John Stuart Mill analysed the working of a competitive system. Later economists of the 19th century developed the "ideal" system of perfect competition from the earlier views. Since the time of Adam Smith, many economists showed their interest more in the theoretical perfection than in the actual developments of the capitalist system. They tried to show how an economic system based on the model of perfect competition would always mean: (*i*) production at the minimum possible cost, and (*ii*) consumer satisfaction at its maximum. But in the real world we hardly come across such a system of perfect competition. The exception to perfect competition which got serious attention during the 19th century was the concept of monopoly. This is, in fact, the antithesis of perfect competition.

Monopoly exists only when the entire supply of a given product is in the control of one seller, or of a group of sellers acting in close agreement. In other words, monopoly may be defined as that market form in which a single firm controls the whole supply of a single commodity which has no close substitutes. Thus, by definition, monopoly firm and industry refer to one and the same thing; a single firm constitutes the industry. It follows that the definition remains valid so long as no other firm is able to, or is allowed to, enter into the industry. Thus, the cases of monopoly in this sense of a single firm are rare as those of perfect competition. We may find certain examples of public utilities, such as water supply, gas, electricity, telephone, railways, etc. which are in the hands of (state) monopolies.

The term "monopoly" has been used by various economists in different ways. Some economists call it "pure" monopoly which implies that there is one and only one producer of the particular product in the market. According to John D. Summer, pure monopoly implies a perfectly inelastic demand in contrast to the perfectly elastic demand of perfect competitive firm. Piero Sraffa uses the word "absolute" monopoly which implies one firm controlling the supply of all goods in existence.

In technical language, we may define monopoly as a single firm/industry where the cross-elasticity of demand between the product of the monopolist and the product of the closest rival must be very low (near to zero), i.e. the product of a rival cannot take the place of the monopolised product.

2. Sources and Types of Monopoly

There are different types of monopolies as described below:

(1) *Natural Monopoly.* If the supply of a commodity is localised in a single place, then the monopoly is known as natural monopoly. For example, Bangladesh possesses the monopoly of raw jute and India possesses the monopoly of manganese.

(2) *Legal Monopoly.* When a firm is given the legal right to produce a unique commodity, it is known as legal monopoly. For example, the right of note issue has been given by law to the National Reserve Bank only in most countries, thus it is legal monopoly.

(3) *Public Monopoly.* When a monopoly is created for the interest of the public, it is known as, public monopoly. For example, the various public utility services, such as water supply, electricity, telephones, railways, etc. are the public monopolies. They provide their services to the public at reasonable prices. Some economists prefer to call them welfare monopolies.

(4) *Private Monopoly.* It is owned and operated by the private individuals or organisations for the purpose of getting maximum profits. Profit maximisation is the primary objective of private monopoly. Such monopoly is established by liquidating the competitors. This may also be classified into simple and discriminating monopoly. A simple private monopoly charges a single price for his product from all the consumers. While, on the other hand, a discriminating monopoly charges more than one price for the same product from different consumers.

3. Emergence and Assumptions of Monopoly

A monopolist has no control over the demand for the product, but he can control the supply of the product. A monopolist has the power to determine either: (*a*) the price of the product, or (*b*) the quantity to be sold in the market. He cannot determine both because he cannot control the demand. Thus, the main assumption of the monopoly firm is that its demand curve slopes downward; to sell more he must cut his price. Also when the demand curve (*AR*-curve) slopes downwards from left to right, marginal revenue in no longer equal to price. It will lie below *AR*-curve. While in the case of perfect competition, demand curve of the firm is a horizontal line. Thus, when the monopolist decides on the price at which he is prepared to sell, then the demand curve will determine the quantity sold at this price. This is determined to market a given quantity per month, then the demand curve will decide the price at which this quantity can be disposed of. If the monopolist produces a large quantity, the price will be low and profits would be low. If he produces a comparatively small quantity, the price will be high but the sales will be low and total profits will be low. The monopolist will, therefore, not follow either of these policies. He will fix his output in such a way as to secure the maximum possible net revenue or net profits.

The monopolist's power to influence price depends upon two factors:

(1) The availability of close substitutes, and

(2) The power to restrict the entry of new firms.

If a number of close substitutes are available in the market, then the monopolist will not be able to change his prices upwards to any significant extent, and his monopoly power will not be very high. In such a situation (when close substitutes are available), an increase in the price of the product will lead to heavy losses.

Again, if in some way, the entry of new firms is restricted, then the monopoly firm will continue to enjoy its privileged position even in the long-run. We have seen in chapter 24, that due to "free entry" in perfect competition, an individual firm enjoys only normal profits (which are included in long-run average costs) in the long-run. The monopolist can, on the other hand, protect his abnormal profits, even in the long-run, by preventing the entry of prospective competitors in the market. Thus, monopoly power can be defined as the ability to earn long-run abnormal profits without attracting competition.

Thus, the more effective the restrictions on the emergence of new competitors, and the fewer the close substitutes for his (monopolist's) product, the greater will be the power of the monopolist to charge higher prices. According to Prof. Robinson, "a monopoly firm can exist only so long as it is able to bar the entry of its potential competitors or rivals." Therefore, the essence of monopoly is the ability to 'restrict entry'. The following are the important measures which are used to debar the potential competitors from that particular industry by the monopoly firm.

(1) *Control over the Raw Materials.* We know that geographical distribution of natural and mineral resources is very uneven, and the known deposits of some minerals are concentrated into very small regions. In such a situation, there is a great incentive for producers to form a monopoly, in order to control the market, by manipulating the supply. When the monopoly firm can own all the deposits of some minerals, and if there are no other

deposits, it has to face no direct competitors. Thus, monopoly may emerge due to one single firm's control of raw materials, specially those the supply of which depends on nature.

(2) *Technical Barriers.* In modern capitalist states, there are a number of industries which are now dominated by a few giant firms. This is essentially true of the science-based industries where firms have been able to get very great technical economies of scale. For instance, tyre manufacturing, oil processing, chemicals and the motor-car industry may be cited as typical examples of the (monopoly) firms which are getting large technical economies of scale. They are operating on a large scale and making use of expensive capital goods. In such cases, the entry of new firms is almost impossible. The small new firms cannot compete with the existing large firms because the former will have a greater average cost of production. Firms already operating are in a protected position and this is always an inducement to form a monopoly.

According to Prof. Pigou, large-scale production possesses a number of advantages that it may be impossible for a new firm producing on a small scale to enter into the industry. The important advantages of a large firm are marketing research, availability of new processes of production, etc. These economies of scale reduce the per unit cost of production and thereby increase the monopoly power of the firm. Thus, monopoly may also be an outcome of the economies of large-scale production, especially the technical economies of scale.

(3) *Legal Barriers.* This is the most important factor to restrict the new entry into the industry. Here the law confers the monopoly right and prevents the entry of the potential competitors. In other words, monopoly may emerge as a result of some statutory regulations of the government. The government may issue licences to only some firm who can sell particular products. The rivals of these monopoly firms cannot enter into the market. For instance, in India a marketing society may be given an exclusive right to sell fertilisers in a group of villages or a 'fair price shop (*FPS*)' is given the exclusive right to sell some essential products within its jurisdiction. Such monopolies are made due to specific policies of the state.

The granting of patent rights in a further example of competition being limited by law. The firm holding the patent rights is protected from the threat of competition from new firms (or existing) making identical products, at least for the period of time for which the patent has been given to the firm by the government.

More recently, we have the example of the nationalised industries where the controlling boards have complete control over the supply of the goods and services produced by these industries.

(4) *Transport Costs and Tariffs;* Transport costs and tariffs are also the important factors which determine the monopoly power of a firm. Although

two (or more) firms may be operating at similar costs, it is possible for one (or more of the firms) to enjoy local monopoly (monopolies). For example, firm *A* will be able to sell more cheaply, in its own locality, than firm *B*, if firm *B* is producing in a location which is far from the local market of firm *A*. Therefore, firm A is able to raise its price in its local market by the amount of the transport costs which firm *B* has to incur if at all it wants to sell in firm *A's* local market.

Similarly, import tariffs are imposed to protect the domestic firm against the competition of foreign firms. The domestic firm can raise .the price by the extent of any differential between its own costs of production and the artificially high price (due to the imposition of import tariffs) of the foreign good.

The above are some of the important ways by which a firm occupies monopoly power in the market. But we must remember that the above measures are more or less temporary in nature. They cannot be made permanent. It is only in the case of social monopoly or public utility, that we may find a tendency to continue as monopoly. This is also socially desirable.

4. Price and Output Determination under Monopoly

As we have explained in the previous chapter that under perfect competition, the price of a product is determined by the interaction of market demand and market (industry) supply. Under monopoly conditions, too, there is bound to be interaction between the forces of demand and supply. But there is a difference between the two market situations. Under perfect competition the supply can completely be adjusted to demand in the long-run while under monopoly the supply is not free (because the entry of new firm is blocked) to adjust itself to demand. It is under the control of the monopolist. A monopolist is the sole producer of his product which has no close substitutes. He can easily influence the price by changing his supply. In fact, he sets the price. While in the case of perfect competition, an individual has nothing to do with the price. He is simply a price-taker.

Again, the demand curve for the product of the monopoly firm is the same as the demand curve of the industry. It is negatively sloped. This demand curve (or *AR*-curve) will show that it can sell more only by cutting down its price. As we have already explained in the earlier chapter, the corresponding marginal revenue curve of the monopoly firm will lie below the average revenue curve. If average revenue curve or the demand curve is a straight line negatively sloping curve, the *MR* curve will also be a straight line and its slope will be double that of the demand curve. This has further been illustrated in Fig. 26.1. In the case of perfect competition, the demand curve of the industry is slopping downward but the demand curve of the firm is a horizontal straight line. This would mean that *AR* and *MR* will be the same for a competitive firm.

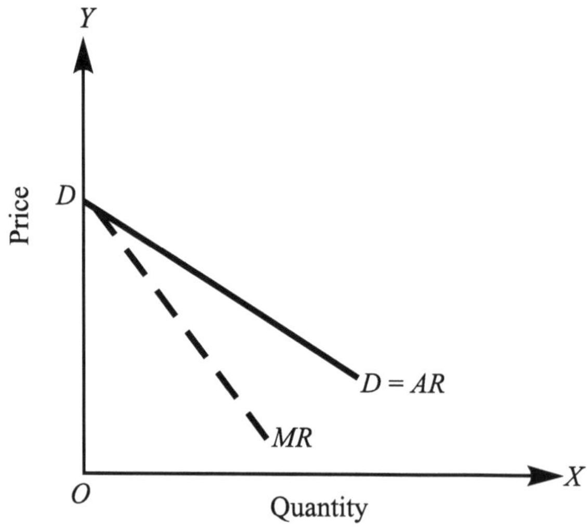

Fig. 26.1

The cost curves of a monopoly firm are generally the same as that of a perfectly competitive firm. The only difference, that we can say, is that a firm under perfect competition can purchase any quantity of resources (factors of production) at constant prices while a monopoly firm has to pay higher prices as it expands its output and needs more quantity of resources. As a result, the *MC*-curve of a monopoly firm will have an additional reason for rising at an increasing rate with the additional increase in the output.

Now, the aim of the monopolist is to make maximum profit. Hence he fixes the price of his commodity in such a way that he might earn maximum profit. According to Dr. Alfred Marshall, "The *prima facie* interest of the owner of a monopoly is clearly to adjust the supply to the demand...in such a way as to afford him the greatest possible net revenue."

In the case of perfect competition, the long-run equilibrium price will be equal to the (average) cost of production. Price cannot rise above the cost, for owing to the competition of several new firms anxious to secure extra profit, the supply of that product will increase, and the price will fall. Due to similar reason, the price cannot fall below the (average) cost of production. But in the case of monopoly, the cost of production sets only the *minimum limit* below which price would not fall. The price of the product may rise above cost and it will be the efforts of the monopoly firm to raise it as far as possible, so that it will be able to attain maximum monopoly profit. Cost of production, therefore, affects price under monopoly in a different way.

Under the given conditions of demand and supply (cost), the monopoly firm will always try to fix such a price of the product that gives him the maximum net revenue or profits. We also know that neither very high price nor a very low price will bring him the largest profit. If he keeps the price high, his sales will be less; and if he keeps the price low, he would be able to increase his sales. Which particular price will yield maximum profit, cannot be predicted. It depends upon the nature of the commodity. Thus, he must pay attention to both the demand schedule and the supply schedule of the commodity. If the demand for a commodity is highly elastic (such as comforts and luxuries), the monopolist can earn maximum profit by keeping the price at a low level. Because, in such cases, a low price will result in large sales and a smaller profit per unit but a large sale will then perhaps give them more (net) revenue than a larger profit per unit with reduced sales. Thus, for highly elastic goods, he will fix his price at a low level. If, however, the demand is inelastic (i.e. the article is of daily use), a lower price would not stimulate sales very much, but a higher price will make greater profits. Similarly, if the supply is restricted, the price would rise very high. In such a case, a larger profit per unit on a small sale will yield maximum profit to the monopolist. He will, then fix the price at a high level.

To determine a long-run price, the monopolist should also study the conditions of supply (cost). If the production of the commodity is subject to the law of constant returns, his cost per unit would remain the same, whatever the volume of the output. In such a situation, he will, fix the price according to the nature of the demand for the product and will allow the volume of output change with demand. If the production of the commodity is subject to the law of increasing returns (or the law of diminishing cost), i.e. every increase in output will lead to a decrease in costs per unit. In such a situation, the monopolist will put a larger output in the market. He will specially be induced to do so, if the demand for the commodity is elastic. Here he adopts the principle of smaller profit per unit on a larger output. If, on the other hand, the production of the commodity is subject to the law of diminishing returns (or the law of increasing cost), it will be in his interest to reduce output and thereby to reduce cost per unit. In such a situation he will fix a higher price. But if the demand for the commodity is highly elastic (i.e. a slight fall in price will lead to a larger increase in quantity demanded), it will be in his interest to reduce the price. The reason is that even though the cost per unit increases as output increases, yet the increase in cost per unit is less than the increase in profit per unit.

The above explanation clears that neither a high price nor a low price would serve the objective of the monopolist. For this he should carefully study the conditions of demand and supply (cost) of the commodity and fix his price at a level that will bring him the maximum profits possible. He will go on producing so long as additional units add more to revenue than to cost. He will stop at that point beyond which additional units of production add more to cost than to revenue.

In other words, the monopolist will be in equilibrium position at that level of output at which marginal revenue equals marginal cost. Mathematically, for profit maximisation, the monopolist requires[1]

$$\pi = R - C$$

$$\frac{d\pi}{dX} = \frac{dR}{dX} - \frac{dC}{dX} = 0$$

or $$\frac{dR}{dX} = \frac{dC}{dX}$$

or $$MR = MC$$

Where π = Total Profits

R = Total Revenue

C = Total Cost

X = Output

The monopolist will continue expanding output so long as marginal revenue exceeds marginal cost. He will do so because profits will go on increasing as long as marginal revenue exceeds marginal cost. At the point, where marginal revenue is equal to marginal cost, the profits will be maximised. If the production is carried beyond this point, profits will begin to decrease.

Now we shall discuss the price-output equilibrium of the monopolist in different time periods.

Price and Output Equilibrium of Monopoly in the Market Period

The total costs of the monopoly firm are fixed in the market period as those of a perfect competitive firm. Thus, by definition, these fixed costs do not affect the pricing policy of the monopolist during the market period. In chapter 24, we defined the market period as that period in which the supply of a

---

1. For profit maximisation, $\frac{d\pi}{dX} = 0$ is the first order necessary condition and for the second order sufficient condition to be satisfied, it requires that

$$\frac{d^2\pi}{dX^2} < 0$$

or $$\frac{d^2R}{dX^2} - \frac{d^2C}{dX^2} < 0 \text{ or } \frac{d^2R}{dX^2} < \frac{d^2C}{dX^2}$$

This means that change in *MR* must be less than change in *MC*.

product is absolutely fixed and shows no response to any price change. Therefore, in the market period, the monopolist possesses a certain quantity of a given commodity which he must dispose of. The price that he can charge for it entirely depends on the demand conditions. Costs do not come in the picture and this is a time of production without costs.

Let the monopolist have a fixed stock of the product shown by *OX* in Fig. 26.2 Panel (*b*). In Fig. 26.2 Panel (*b*), the demand curve facing the monopolist is linear and is represented by *AD* (which is the same as the *AR-curve* of the monopolist). The corresponding marginal revenue curve is represented by *MR*. Now, if the monopolist wants to sell its entire output *OX,* he has to keep his price at *OP.* But if he does so, marginal revenue (*MR*) will be negative and his total revenue (*TR*) will be less than the maximum level shown by point *E.* Now, in the market period, however, the monopolist would like to maximise his total

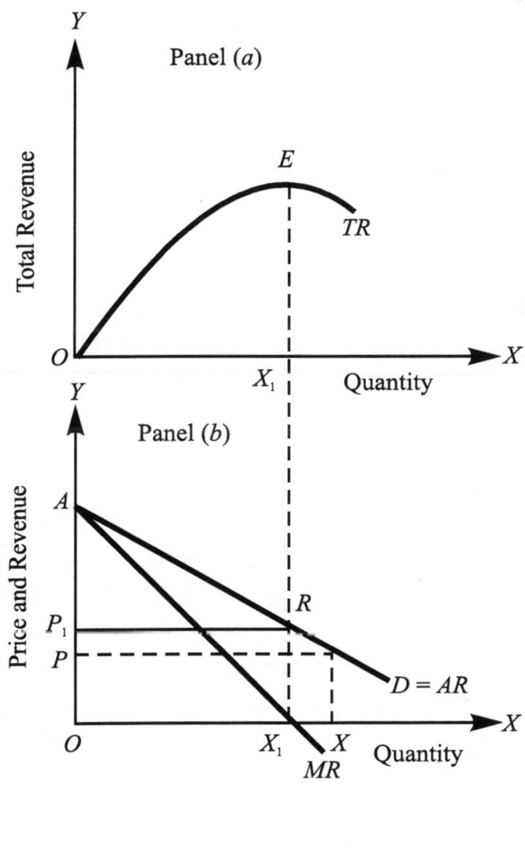

Fig. 26.2

revenue[2] as the costs of producing the present level of output OX have already been incurred by him. Moreover, instead of getting a negative return from the last unit (i.e. negative marginal revenue), he would always like not to sell it. Thus, the best thing for him is to sell only OX_1 quantity of output at price OP_1. At OX_1 level of output, he will maximise his total revenue where $MR = O$. When he sells OX_1 quantity out of the OX quantity, he remains with X_1X quantity in inventory. Even if the product is perishable, he would like to destroy it rather than to place it on the market. Because, placing it on the market reduces his total revenue. If, on the other hand, the product is not perishable, the monopolist will keep it with him for the next period. Also if the firm sells less than OX_1 quantity of output, his total revenue will not be maximum and he has to destroy a larger amount of the product (than X_1X). Thus, only at OX_1 level of output, the monopolist will maximise his receipts. Since he has no costs to consider, it will also maximise his profits. At point R, the average revenue curve (demand curve) will have an elasticity equal to one and the monopolist's total receipts (PR) will be at a maximum. Marginal revenue will be zero, as it always is when elasticity of demand is equal to unity. It will equal marginal cost, because marginal cost cannot be negative and the least it may be zero. This analysis also clears that a monopolist's equilibrium position will always be where the elasticity of demand for his product is greater than (or equal to in a special case of market period) one.

Price and Output Equilibrium of Monopoly in the Short-Period

As we know, in the short-period the scale of plant is fixed and the firm is unable to change it. Thus, like a purely competitive firm, the monopolist operates with a given plant during the short-period. If the monopolist desires to produce more, he can make an intensive use of the available plant. In other words, the monopolist will increase the supply of the product by increasing the variable factors (the fixed factors being fixed). Similarly, if the monopolist desires to reduce the supply, he can make a less intensive use of the fixed factors (such as machinery or plant, etc.) by decreasing the amount of variable factor inputs. The main thing is that the monopolist would like to maximise his profits (or to minimise his losses if at all he has to incur). For this, the equilibrium condition is the same as we have explained under perfect

2. Although we have said in the previous chapters that the objective of the monopolist is the maximisation of his profits (or minimisation of losses if it incurs in the short-period), yet in a very short period, he will be interested in the maximisation of revenue because costs do not enter into his price-decision.

competition. The monopolist will produce that level of output at which his marginal revenue is equal to his marginal cost.

Since the monopolist has to incur fixed costs in the short-run, the minimum price acceptable by him must be equal to his average variable cost. Thus, the monopoly price may be greater than, equal to, or less than the average costs in the short-run. It will depend upon the conditions of demand. If price is greater than average cost, the monopolist will earn abnormal profits. If price is equal to the average cost the monopolist will earn only the normal profits which are included in his average cost. If price is less than the average cost, the monopolist will incur losses. Anyway, the maximum loss that the monopolist would accept will be equal to his fixed costs. If the monopolist is to incur losses greater than the fixed costs, it will stop production. But in the short-period, he will continue production even in the situation of loss, if he is able to minimise the loss of his fixed costs. The minimisation of loss will be made at that level of output at which $MR = MC$. These three possible situations in the short-run are explained in the following section.

Profit Maximisation in the Short-Period. Profits of a monopolist are maximised at the output at which his short-period marginal cost (*SMC*) equals his marginal revenue (*MR*). This case has been illustrated in Fig. 26.3. Here, the monopolist's *SMC* curve cuts the *MR* curve at point *E* where the monopolist produces *OX* quantity of output. At *OX* level of output, the monopolist can charge *OP* price per unit because price is determined by the demand curve or the *AR-curve*. At *OX* level of output, the average cost is *OC*. Thus, the monopolist's per unit abnormal profit is equal to *CP* which is the difference between the price (*OP*) and the corresponding average cost of production (*OC*). The shaded area, *CPAB* in Fig. 26.3 represents the total monopoly

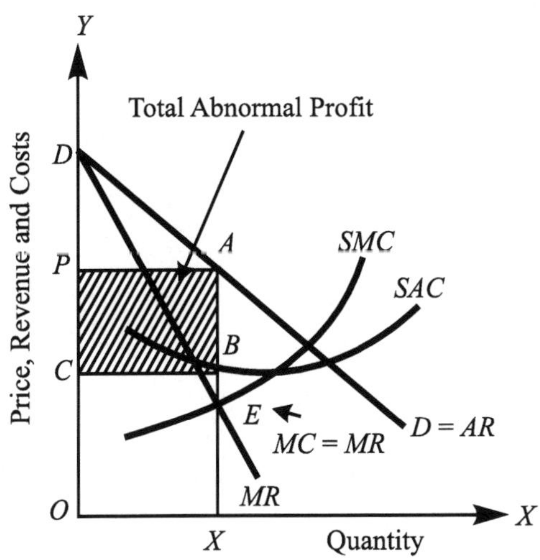

Fig. 26.3

profit. The total profits of the monopolist will be maximum only at *OX* level of output. At output smaller than *OX, MR* is greater than *SMC;* thus larger outputs upto *OX* add more to total receipts than to total costs and increase profits. At output beyond OX_1, *MR* is less than *SMC;* hence larger outputs beyond *OX* add more to total costs than to total receipts and cause profits to decrease. To sum up, the monopolist attains maximum profit at *OX* level of output where *SMC* = *MR* and at this level of output the second order condition of profit maximisation is also satisfied.[3]

Loss Minimisation in the Short Period. Generally, we find a misconception that a monopolist always makes profits. Whether the monopolist gets profits or not, depends upon the conditions of demand costs. It is not necessary that the monopolist should always operate at a (abnormal) profit. It is possible that his entire short-run average cost curve lies above the demand curve or *AR-curve.* In such a case, he has to incur losses. Sometimes, in the short-period, it is in his interest to operate even in the situation of loss, if the price of his product is high enough to cover his average variable cost. The situation of loss has been illustrated in Fig. 26.4. Here the monopolist's costs are so high and his market is so small that at no output will price (*AR*) cover average costs. In other words, his *SAC* curve lies above the *AR-curve.* Now his losses

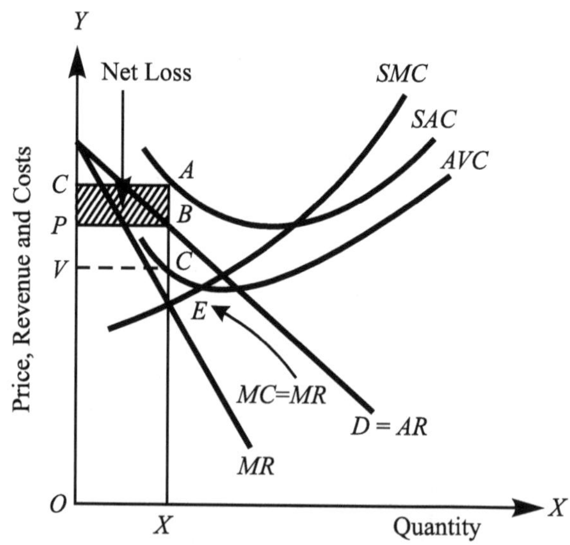

Fig. 26.4

3. The second order condition for profit maximisation is

$$\frac{d^2\pi}{dX} < 0$$

or change in *MR* must be less than change in *MC.*

are maximised at output *OX,* at which *SMC* equals *MR.* At this level of output, price is *OP* while cost per unit is *OC*. Thus, the monopolist has to incur losses to the extent of *CP* per unit. But the maximum loss that he is ready to bear in the short-run at *OX* level of output is *VC* per unit (which is equal to the fixed cost per unit). Since the average variable cost at *OX* output is *OV,* it is less than the price *OP;* thus a part of the maximum loss is covered by price. The total loss to be incurred by monopolist is shown in Fig. 26.4 by the shaded area *PCAB.* This is the minimum loss that the monopolist would incur in the short-period. If the level of output is less than *OX* or greater than *OX,* the total amount of loss would be greater than area *PCAB.*

Normal Profits in the Short-Period. In the short-period, it is possible that the monopolist neither makes abnormal profits nor incurs losses, but earns only normal profits. This happens only when the average cost curve of the monopolist is tangent to his average revenue curve and at the same time his marginal revenue curve cuts his marginal cost curve. In such a situation the monopolist must be producing at less than optimum size. This case has been illustrated in Fig. 26.5.

In Fig. 26.5, the monopolist is in equilibrium at *OX* level of output because at this level of output his marginal cost curve (*SMC*) cuts the marginal revenue curve (*MR*) at point *E* from below. Also, at the same level of output (*OX*), the monopolist's *AC* curve touches his *AR-curve* at point *A*. Thus, *OP* (= *XA*) is the monopoly price which is also equal to the cost per unit. Thus, the monopolist earns only normal profits his average revenue (price) being equal to his average cost; and the normal profit is included in the average cost of production.

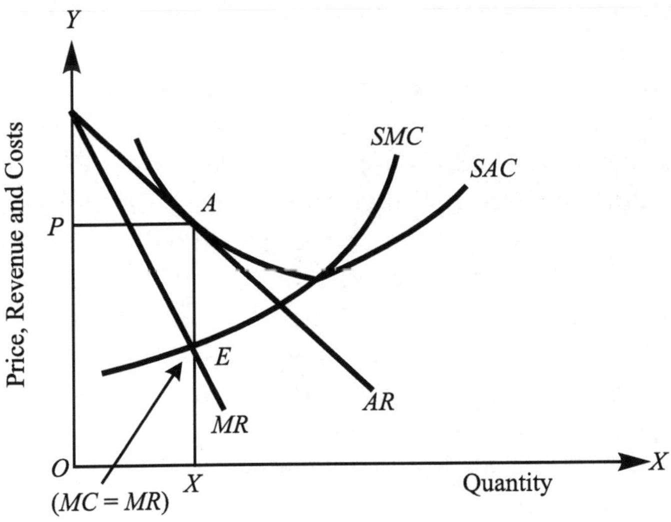

Fig. 26.5

From the above analysis of the short-period price and output equilibrium, it may be contended that profit maximisation or loss minimisation or the attainment of normal profit will be accomplished only at that level of output at which the marginal cost equals the marginal revenue.

Price and Output Equilibrium of Monopoly in the Long Period

Under perfect competition in the long period a firm gets only normal profits because of the free entry or exit of the firm into the industry. But under monopoly, entry of the new firms is not possible and therefore, the monopolist can easily protect his short-period abnormal profits in the long-run. The magnitude of the long-run profits will depend upon the cost conditions under which he has to operate production and the demand curve he has to face in the long-run. His long-period profits may be higher than or less than that of the short-period profits. But this is true that the monopolist, like a perfect competitive firm, will not accept any loss in the long period. The minimum price acceptable by the monopolist for his product must equal the long-run average cost. Under perfect competition we have seen that in the long-run every firm would be of optimum size where its long-period average cost (*LAC*) is minimum. But in the case of monopoly, the equilibrium level of output (where *LMC*=*MR*) mayor may not have the lowest long-run average cost. The monopolist will build the optimum plant only if his *MR* cuts his *LAC* at its lowest point. If *MR* passes through *LAC* before its (*LAC*) minimum point, the monopolist will build a smaller than optimum plant and operate it at a less than optimum rate. On the other hand, if *MR* cuts *LAC* beyond its (*LAC*) minimum point, the monopolist will build a plant greater than the optimum plant and operate it at a more than optimum rate.

Now we can say that since entry into the industry (market) is blocked, the monopolist adjusts his long-run output by means of scale of plant adjustments and there are three possibilities to exist: (*i*) the relation between his *MR* (or demand, *AR*) and his long-run average costs (*LAC*) may be such that he will build a less than optimum scale of plant, (*ii*) the relation between *MR* (or demand, *AR*) and *LAC* is such that he will build an optimum scale of plant, and (*iii*) the relation between *MR* (or demand, *AR*) is such that he will build a greater than optimum scale of plant. These three possible situations may be described in the following manner.

Less than Optimum Scale of Plant and the Law of Increasing Returns or Decreasing Costs. Here we assume that the monopolist has to operate under the conditions of diminishing costs which mean that as he produces more, his per unit cost of production decreases. But his market is so small that his marginal revenue curve cuts his long-run marginal cost curve to the left of *LAC's* minimum point. Thus, he is to produce only that level of output where

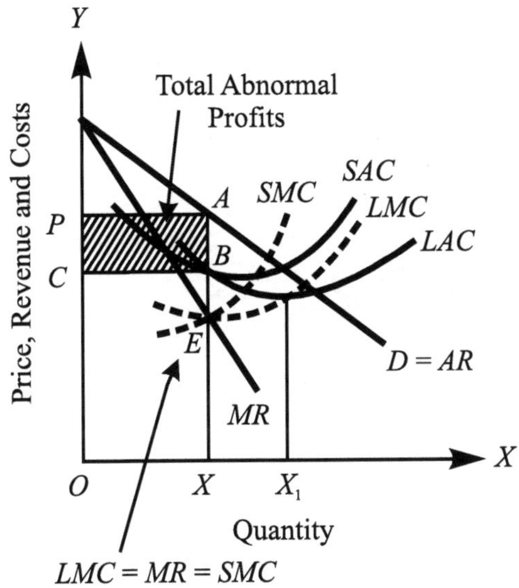

Fig. 26.6

his *MR* = *LMC*. Only at this level of output he maximises his profits. In other words, larger output cannot be produced if the demand is low. This case has been illustrated in Fig. 26.6.

The long-run equilibrium point is *E* where *LMC* = *MR*. Here, the output will be *OX* and price will be *Op*. The monopolist should build the scale of plant that will produce output *OX* at the least possible average cost. The monopolist's *SAC* (short-run average cost) curve should be tangent to *LAC* curve at output *OX*. If *SAC* is tangent to *LAC* at output level *OX, SMC* is necessarily equal to *LMC* at that output. This indicates that the long-run equilibrium of the monopolist is also the short-run equilibrium of the monopolist; because *SMC* = *LMC* = *MR*. At *OX* level of output the monopolist obtains maximum profits shown by the area *PABC*. This level of output is less than optimum level of output. The optimum level of output is that where the *LAC* is the minimum. In Fig. 26.6, the optimum level of output will be OX_1 but the monopolist will not produce more than *OX* quantity (and $OX < OX_1$), because he has no inducement to expand the existing plant size beyond *OX* as he is already getting maximum profits.

Optimum Scale of Plant and the Law of Constant Returns or Constant Costs. Here we assume that the monopolist has to operate under the conditions of constant returns or constant costs. In such a case the monopolist will build the optimum scale of plant only if his *MR* cuts *LMC* at the minimum point of *LAC*. This is shown in Fig. 26.7. Here point *E* is the equilibrium point at which *MR* = *LMC* = *LAC* = *SMC* = *SAC*. The optimum level of equilibrium output is *OX*. The monopolist is in both short-period and long-period

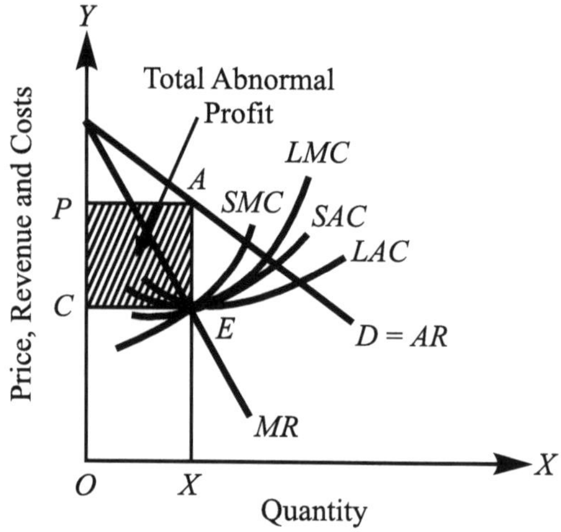

Fig. 26.7

equilibrium. His price of the product at *OX* level of output is *OP* and cost per unit is *OC*. Thus, the maximum abnormal profit per unit is *CP*. The shaded area *PAEC* represents his total minimum profits.

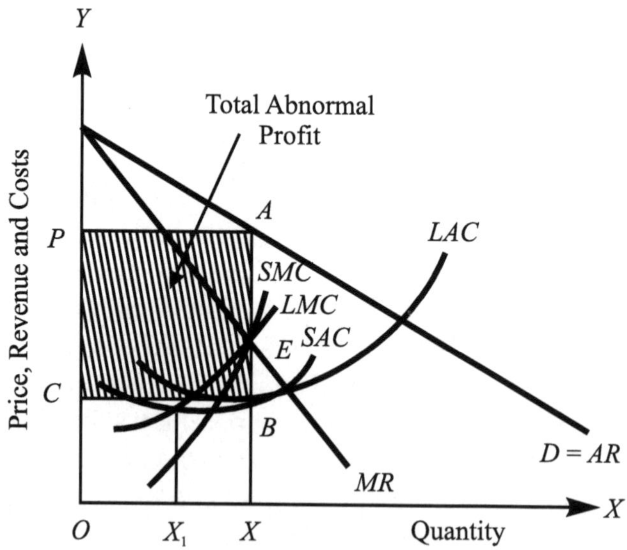

Fig. 26.8

Greater than Optimum Scale of Plant and the Law of Diminishing Returns or Increasing Costs. Here we assume that the monopolist has to operate under the conditions of increasing costs which means that as he produces more, his costs per unit of production will increase. In such a case the monopolist will try to reduce output and increase price. But his market is large enough for his marginal revenue to cut his *LAC* curve to the right of its (*LAC*) minimum point. In other words, the *MR* curve cuts the *LMC* curve beyond the minimum point of the *LAC* curve. This case has been illustrated in Fig. 26.8. Here the equilibrium point is *E* where *MR* = *LMC* = *SMC*. Thus, the profit maximising output level will be *OX*. The proper scale of plant to be used is *SAC* which is tangent to *LAC* at output level *OX*. In this situation, the monopolist builds a greater than optimum scale of plant and produces *OX* quantity of output which is more than the optimum level of output (as shown by OX_1 quantity of output in Fig. 26.8). At *OX* level of output, price is *OP*, cost per unit is *OC* and profit per unit is *CP*. The total maximum profits are shown by the shaded area *PABC*. In such a situation, his scale of plant is so large that diseconomies of scale occur (because per unit cost is more than the minimum of *LAC*), but a reduction of output would mean lower profits. Thus, he has no incentive to contract the plant size, as this would reduce his profits. Only at *OX* level of output, he is able to attain maximum profits.

5. Monopoly *vs.* Perfect Competition (Welfare Effects of Monopoly)

It can easily be demonstrated that a perfect competitive market is superior to monopoly as the latter has some adverse effects on the welfare of consumers.

We know that in a perfect competitive market price and output are determined at the point where the industry-supply curve (or the aggregate marginal cost curve) intersects the industry-demand curve. Now, we will see that a profit maximising monopoly will sell a smaller quantity of output at a higher price than a competitive industry faced with the same demand and cost situation. Fig. 26.9 compares the competitive and monopoly situations. We may assume here, that the monopolist has the same number of plants as the competitive industry, that costs are identical for both and that the industry absorbs only a small fraction of each input.

Fig. 26.9 indicates that *Ec* is the equilibrium point of the competitive industry where the industry demand and the industry supply of the product are equal. At this equilibrium point E_c, the industry price would be OP_c and output would be OX_c. In Fig. 26.9, point E_m is the equilibrium point of the monopolist where *MR* = *MC*. Therefore, the monopolist will produce OX_m quantity of output and will charge OP_m price. Now, we may conclude that under monopoly the consumers will enjoy OX_m quantity at OP_m price while under perfect competition, they will enjoy OX_c quantity at OP_c price. The output available in perfect competition is more than the output available in monopoly. Also the price charged by the monopolist will be higher than the price charged by the firms in perfect competition. In other words, introduction of monopoly in place of perfect competition will mean a loss of consumer's surplus to the consumers.

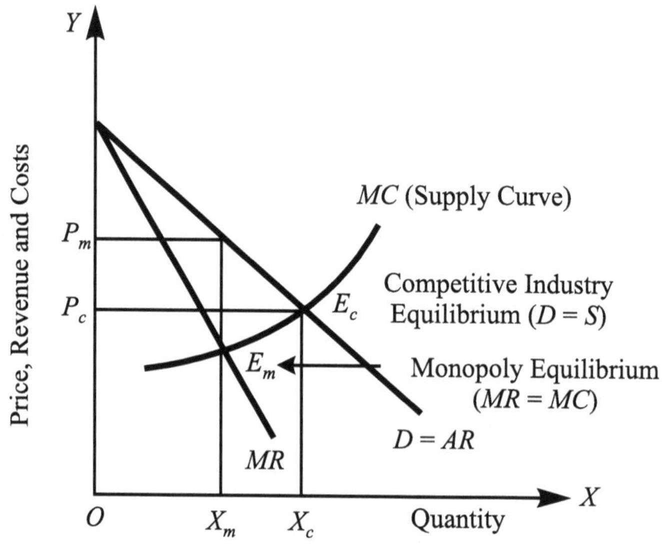

Fig. 26.9

6. Control and Regulation of Monopoly (Monopoly Pricing with Threat of Entry)

In this section we shall discuss some of the econonmic measures that can be used to prevent the monopolist from using his monopoly power to the full extent. The two important methods generally used by the state to control the operation of a monopoly firm are the following:

(1) Direct Regulation of Monopoly Price, and

(2) Regulation through Taxation.

Regulation of Monopoly Price

This method is generally used in the case of natural monopolies. Natural monopolies are very necessary to be controlled. If they are put in the hands of private entrepreneurs, and are free to work, it would lead to the exploitation of the people. Thus, the government should regulate them. This can be done either to control prices or to control output or control both price and output. The government appoints Price Tribunals or State Regulatory Commissions to govern the rates or prices charged by the public utility monopolies, such as gas and electric power companies, railways, etc. These commissions have to face a number of economic problems. The main economic problem involved is the determination of the price that will induce the monopolist to produce the greatest amount of the commodity consistent with his costs and with consumer demand. In other words, the price should be such that the monopolist should produce greater quantity of output to maximise his profits and at that price the consumers should also be ready to purchase greater amounts of the output. If price is fixed at a very low level, the market demand for the product will increase tremendously but at that price the monopolist will produce a smaller level of output which satisfies the rule $MC = MR$ (price). This will lead to black-marketing where the monopolist may charge a very high price for his product. Thus, a very small price would give rise to excess demand and unless price regulation is coupled with rationing, it would result in black-marketing by the monopolist. Therefore, the price commission must take care to fix a fair price for the product. This case has been illustrated in Fig. 26.10. In the absence of any restriction by the state authority, the monopolist maximises profits at that level of output where marginal cost equals marginal revenue. In such a free situation, the price he wants to charge is *OP* and the output he wants to produce is *OX*. At *OX* level of output his maximum profit per unit is *CP* (which is the difference between the price, *OP* and the cost per unit, *OC*).

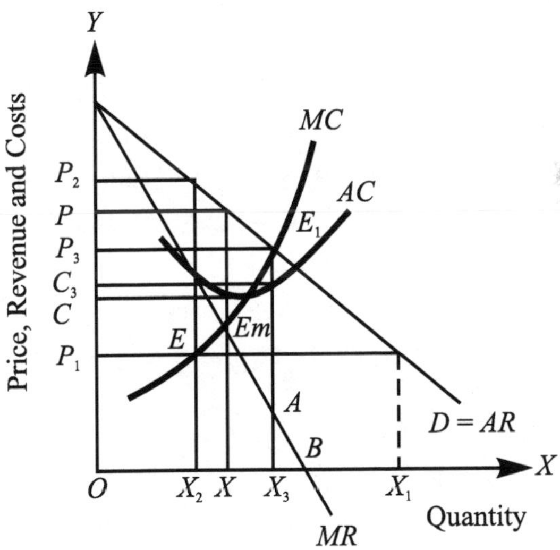

Fig. 26.10.

Now first suppose that the government authority (or the price tribunal) fixes a very lower price of the product as OP_1. It may be seen that at this price consumers demand OX_1 quantity of the product; but the monopolist produces OX_2 quantity of the product, because only at OX_2 output he is able to maximise his profits (whereas at point *E*, his *MC* equals the given price or marginal revenue). It is obvious that at OP_1 price, there will be an excess demand to the extent of X_2X_1. Now, at OX_1 level of output, the black-marketing price would be very high, OP_2. Thus, such a lower price will result in black-marketing by the monopolist.

Now, suppose that instead of fixing a very low price (OP_1), the regulatory commission fixes a maximum price OP_3 at which the monopolist's marginal cost curve cuts the demand curve at point E_1. In such a situation, the demand curve faced by the monopolist becomes P_2E_1D. It indicates that upto OX_3 level of output, the monopolist can charge OP_3 price but if at all he desires to sell more than OX_3 quantity of the output, he has to reduce the price below OP_3. Now the new demand curve P_3E_1D faced by the monopolist also changes his marginal revenue curve. Upto OX_3 the demand curve is perfectly inelastic as the demand curve faced by a perfect competitive firm and therefore marginal revenue will equal OP_3. Beyond output OX_3, the market demand curve and the original marginal revenue curve become relevant. At OP_3 price fixed by the commission, the monopolist's marginal revenue curve takes the shape as P_3E_1AB.

In this controlled situation, the monopolist will maximise his profits by producing OX_3 quantity of the output, because only at this level of output his marginal cost equals marginal revenue (price) at point E_1. At OX_3 output, his maximum profit per unit is C_3P_2. Thus, at OP_3 price, the monopolist acts as a perfect competitive firm beacause only in a perfectly competitive market $MR = P$ to an individual firm. Here, the price regulatory commission succeeds not only in lowering the monopoly price, but also in forcing the monopolist to sell larger quantity at this price as compared to the pre-control situation. This is all possible only when the commission is able to make the necessary calculations regarding the costs and price structure of the monopoly.

Regulation through Taxation

The second important method of regulation is taxation. Here we shall consider two types of taxes which the government can impose on the monopolist: (*i*) A Specific Tax which is a tax per unit on the monopolist's output, and (*ii*) A Lump-sum Tax which is a fixed amount of tax levied without regard to the monopolist's output level. The specific tax may be treated as a fixed cost. Now we shall explain the effects of these taxes on the monopolist's equilibrium with the help of diagrams in the following manner.

A Specific Tax. In Fig. 26.11, the original average cost and marginal cost curves of the monopolist are *AC* and *MC* respectively. His original equilibrium position is established at point E where $MC = MR$. The original price and output are OP and OX respectively. The original maximum profit per unit is CP (which is the difference between the price and the cost per unit). Now, suppose that a specific tax is levied on his output. This will lead to an increase in both the AC and MC of the monopolist. Thus, the imposition of a specific tax shifts the AC and MC curves upwards as AC_1 and MC_1 respectively. The MC curve also shifts upwards because this tax is a variable cost. The new marginal cost curve (MC_1) intersects the MR at point E_1 which lies to the left of the previous equilibrium point E. As a result, the profit maximising level of output is reduced from OX to OX_1, whereas the monopoly price rises from

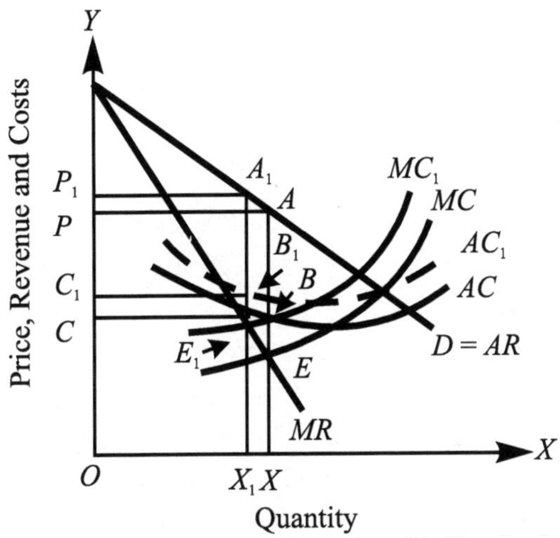

Fig. 26.11

OP to OP_1. The per unit cost at output OX increases from OC to OC_1. This reduces the monopolist's profits per unit from CP to C_1P_1; because the rise in price is less than the rise in costs. The monopolist's total profits fall from $PABC$ to $P_1A_1B_1C_1$.

However, the proportion of such a tax borne by the monopolist out of his profits will depend largely on the elasticity of demand for his product. Here we can say that the higher the elasticity of demand, the larger will be the proportion of the tax borne by the monopolist and vice versa.

A Lump-sum Tax. In Fig 26.12, we show the effects of a lump-sum tax on the monopolist. The original profit maximising output and price are OX and OP respectively. Originally, the monopolist earns CP profit per unit. Now,

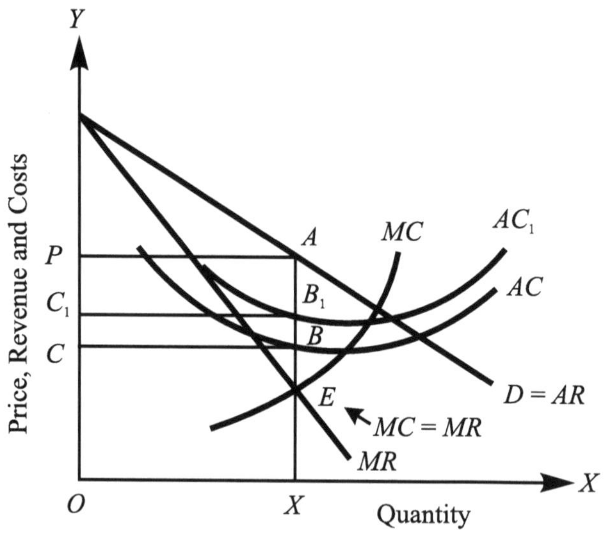

Fig. 26.12

suppose that a lump sum tax is levied on the monopolist. It is a fixed cost to the monopolist. Thus, it only shifts the average cost curve AC to AC_1, and makes no effect on the original marginal cost curve MC. Consequently, the profit maximising price and output remain at the original level as OP and OX respectively. The entire amount of the tax is paid by the monopolist from his profits. Thus, his profits fall from PC per unit to PC_1. In other words, the total profits fall from $PABC$ to PAB_1C_1. From consumers' point of view this method is the best method. Through this method all of the monopolist's profits may be taxed away with no effect on output and price.

7. Multiple Plant Monopoly in the Short-run

So far we have analysed the equilibrium of a monopoly firm which owns and produces with only one plant. But in the short-run, the monopoly firm can operate any number of plants of the same size or of different sizes. But in the long-run it operates only those plants which together bring him larger profits. In order to produce the profit maximisation output, the monopoly firm will operate each plant in such a manner that the MC in each plant is equal to the MR from selling the combind output. Now, let us suppose that the monopoly firm has two separate plants, both producing identical products. Since the two plants are not equally efficient and, therefore, the monopolist would have two cost functions representing the two plants. However, we assume that the monopolist fixes the same price as both plants produce homogeneous product. The profit of the monopolist is the difference between his total revenue and his total cost of production for both the plants. Thus, the equation of total profit can be written as:

$$\pi = R\,(q_1 + q_2) - C_1\,(q_1) - C_2\,(q_2) \qquad \text{... (1)}$$

where q_1 and q_2 are the quantities produced in the two plants, $R(q_1 + q_2)$ is his total revenue function, C_1 (q_1) and $C_2(q_2)$ are his cost functions for two separate plants. For profit maximisation, we set the partial derivatives of the monopolist's profit function equal to zero:

$$\frac{\partial \pi}{\partial q_1} = R'\,(q_1 + q_2) - C'_1\,(q_1) = 0 \qquad \text{...(2)}$$

and

$$\frac{\partial \pi}{\partial q_2} = R'\,(q_1 + q_2) - C'_2(q_2) = 0 \qquad \text{...(3)}$$

Since $R'(q_1+q_2)$ represents his overall *MR,* where as C'_1 (q_1) and C'_2 (q_2) depict the marginal cost associated with the two plants, from equation (2) and (3) we may state that a monopolist will obtain maximum profit when marginal revenue (*MR*) is equal to marginal cost of each plant and thus the marginal costs of both the plants are also equal. In other words, the first order condition for profit maximisation by a multi-plant monopolist requires that

$$MR = MC_1 = MC_2 = \ldots\ldots = MCn \qquad \text{...(4)}$$

8. Resource Allocation under Monopoly

The comparison between a perfectly competitive firm and a monopoly firm may clearly point out that monopoly leads to mal allocation of sources. For this one has to compare price, output and profits under both the situations. Under perfect competition in the long-run every firm satisfies the condition: Price = *AR* = *MR* = *LMC* = *LAC* at its minimum. This means that under perfect competition every firm gets only the normal profit which is included in the cost. Here the firms are of the optimum size and producing to their full capacity. But under monopoly, in the long-run, we have $p > LMC = MR$. Also the minimum point of the *LAC* curve is to the right of the equilibrium point ($LMC = MR$). It indicates the fact that the monopoly firm is of less than optimum size and does not produce to its full capacity and earns abnormal profit. Since, the monopoly firm has excess capacity, there is under allocation of resources to the monopoly firm and a misallocation of resources in the economy. It is also cleared in Fig. 26.9 (monopoly *vs.* perfect competition), that the monopoly price is higher than the competitive price and monopoly output is less than competitive output. Thus, the consumers are worse off under monopoly because they are supposed to pay more and get a smaller output than that under perfect competition. This is a net loss to consumers' welfare in the society.

Having examined the effects of monopoly on welfare of consumers and resource owners one would naturally be tempted to infer that monopoly is an evil and that every effort to introduce competition in a monopoly situation would increase social welfare. Yet there might be situations in which introduction of competition may do more harm than good. Particular situation may be explained when due to large plant capacity, the cost of production can be covered only if output is undertaken at a relatively sufficient scale. Thus, in Fig. 26.13, if there is only one firm in the market, it would produce OX_m output at OP_m price where his *MR* (i.e. D_1 and *MC* are equal at point E_m. It however another firm is allowed in the market (i.e. competition is being created in the market), then the demand curve now becomes *D* (instead of *D*) and the corresponding marginal revenue curve becomes *MR*. Each firm now produces *OX* quantity at *OP* price. In this new situation, price has fallen to consumers from OP_m to *OP,* but each firm produces at a very small scale and incurs a loss of *PCTS*. Thus, in such a situation where market is

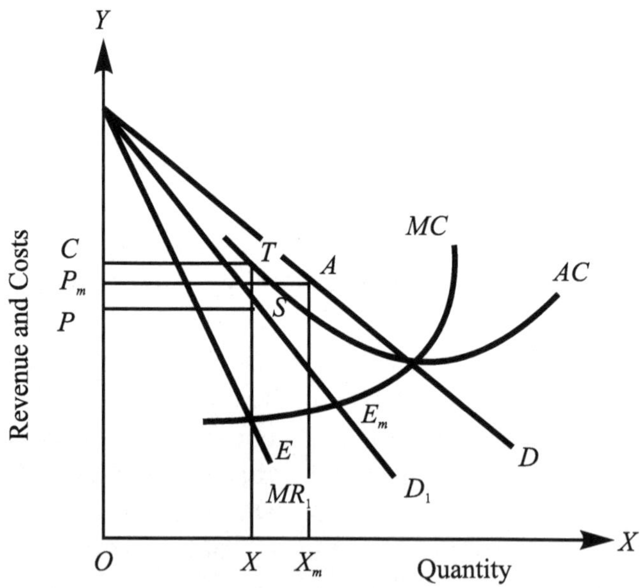

Fig. 26.13

small, an entry of second firm would imply unused capacity as well as net loss for both the firms in the market and this situation becomes more worse as more and more firms enter into the market. Hence monopoly may be desired instead of competition.

Further, monopoly may also be desired in the areas of public utility such as supply of water, electricity or the distribution of scarce goods through fair price shops.

Exercises

1. Describe the main assumptions of monopoly. How does monopoly emerge in real world?
2. How is price determined under monopoly?
3. Explain and illustrate diagrammatically the price and output determination of monopoly in the market period.
4. "The prima facie interest of the owner of a monopoly is clearly to adjust the supply to the demand, not in such a way that the price at which he can sell his commodity shall just cover its expenses of production, but in such a way as to afford him the greatest possible net revenue." Marshall. Discuss the above statement.
5. How does a monopolist determine the price and output of his product in the short-run? Would the monopolist like to continue his production in the situation of loss in the short-run?
6. Explain the price and output equilibrium of monopoly in the long-run.
7. Discuss in brief the welfare effects of monopoly.
8. How does the state control the operations of a monopoly firm?
9. How does a monopolist fix price of his product ? Is it inevitable that the monopoly price is higher than the competitive price?
10. How far is it possible for the state to induce the monopolist through price regulation, to furnish the greater amount of product consistent with his costs and consumer demand?
11. How are resources allocated under monopoly?
12. Explain the emergence and assumptions of monopoly.

Multiple Choice Questions

13. (*i*) Monopoly means
    (*a*) a single producer of a particular product in the world
    (*b*) a single producer of a particular product in India
    (*c*) a single producer of a particular product in a particular town or city
    (*d*) a single producer of a particular product in a single market [*Ans.* (*d*)]

    (*ii*) The demand for the product of a monopoly firm is
    (*a*) inelastic
    (*b*) elastic
    (*c*) unitary elastic
    (*d*) impossible to know without knowledge of the market demand elasticity for the product [*Ans.* (*d*)]

    (*iii*) If $P = \$10$ at the point on the demand curve where $ed = 0.5$, MR is
    (*a*) \$5 (*c*) \$1
    (*b*) \$ 0 (*d*) \$10 [*Ans.* (*d*)]

    (*iv*) The best level of output for the pure monopolist occurs at the point where
    (*a*) *TC* is minimum (*c*) *TR* and *TC* curves are parallel
    (*b*) $TR = TC$ (*d*) *TR is maximum* [*Ans.* (*c*)]

(*v*) At the best level of output for the pure monopolist

(*a*) $MR = SMC$ (*b*) $p = SMC$

(*c*) P = lowest SAC (*d*) P is highest [*Ans.* (*a*)]

(*vi*) In the short-period, the monopolist

(*a*) breaks even (*c*) makes a profit

(*b*) incurs a loss (*d*) any of the above [*Ans.* (*d*)]

(*vii*) Which form of monopoly regulation is most advantageous for the consumer?

(*a*) price control (*c*) per unit tax

(*b*) lump-sum tax (*d*) all of the above [*Ans.* (*a*)]

Chapter 27

Monopoly Price Discrimination

1. Introduction

Price discrimination means charging different prices from different buyers of the same product of service. This cannot be done under perfect competition where the individual firm is unable to influence the market-supply of the product. This can be done only under monopoly or it has some monopoly power. A monopolist need not always charge a single price to all his consumers. Since he is the only producer in the market, he has a control over the supply of the product. He can charge different prices to different consumers or in the different markets. In the preceding chapter it was contended that a monopolist may not derive any benefit from a price rise, as every increase in price is likely to induce consumers to buy smaller quantity of the product. He may, however, increase his profits by adopting price discrimination. *Discriminating Monopoly* or *Price Discrimination* occurs when a monopolist charges different prices for different units of a product, even though these units are identical in their physical characteristics. In general, price discrimination means that a firm charges two or more prices for the same thing at the same time.

2. Forms of Price Discrimination

Price discrimination may take place in many forms. We shall discuss only the important forms of price discrimination which are practised to increase the profits of the monopolist.

(1) *Personal Discrimination.* Personal discrimination occurs when different prices are charged to the different consumers in accordance with the intensity of either desire or according to their incomes. The monopolist can charge higher prices from the persons who are more eager to buy or whose ability to pay is more. A higher price is generally charged from the rich than

the poor. This type of discrimination is not always possible, for it may arouse violent resentment among the consumers. It is usually possible only in a disguised manner and will not be made openly. For example, the new book of a famous author may first be issued as a *de luxe* edition with a very high price, i.e. only the rich people buy it. Then a cheap-price edition may be issued for the low income groups. The price charged for a *de luxe* edition is significantly higher than the cost of producing it; and the price charged for a cheap-price edition is slightly higher than the cost of its production. Such type of discrimination may lead to maximum profits of the monopoly firm. This type of price discrimination is applied to railway passengers, and cinema tickets. People travelling in upper classes always pay more than the cost of providing the extra conveniences. Similarly, people purchasing balcony tickets or going to box always pay more than the cost of providing the extra comforts.

(2) *Local Discrimination.* In this situation different prices are charged from different localities. The monopolist charges a lower price at one place and a higher price at other places. 'Dumping' is the best example of local discrimination. In the case of dumping, the monopolist sells his output at a lower price in a foreign market and at a higher price in the domestic market.

(3) *Trade Discrimination.* It is also known as use discrimination. In this situation, the monopolist charges different prices for different uses. In other words, trade discrimination takes place when the monopolist charges a lower price to one trade than to another. For example, electric current may be sold at low price to industrial concerns, at a higher price for the purpose of domestic cooking, and at a still higher price for domestic lighting.

3. Conditions for Price Discrimination

In this section, we shall discuss the essential conditions for price discrimination. We have seen that it is impossible under perfect competition. In perfect competition, the firm is simply a price-taker and not a price-maker. The price is determined by the market (industry) demand and supply. The perfect competitive firm can never charge a higher price from any of her consumers simply because the consumers can easily shift to other firms who are selling the same product at a lower price. Nor the firm would like to charge a lower price from some of the consumers as she can sell her entire product at the market price. Thus, the demand curve of the perfect competitive firm is perfectly elastic and her *AR* equals *MR*. It follows that, price discrimination is not possible in perfect competition. It can be possible only when the firm possesses some degree of monopoly power.

But even in the case of monopoly, it does not always mean that the monopolist must practise discrimination. Ordinarily, no monopolist will adopt the policy of price discrimination unless it is profitable for him to do so. Price discrimination is profitable only if the following conditions are satisfied.[1]

1. *Two or More Separate Markets.* There must be two (or more than two) separate markets; otherwise, his product will be purchased in the market with the lower price and resold in the market with the higher price. This will iron out the price differential that the monopolist attempts to establish. Thus, the different markets must be such that no buyer of one market may enter the other market and vice versa.

2. *Differences in Elasticity of Demand.* The elasticities of demand in each market must be different. It means that if one market is less elastic, then the other should be more elastic. This condition is vital. If the demand elasticities in the different markets are equal, there will be no scope for price discrimination. If, on the other hand, elasticities are different, the monopolist will gain by selling his product at different prices in different markets.

Hence, the pre-requisites of price discrimination are the (two) separate markets and the differences of elasticity of demand between the markets. An old example is the monopoly that charges a high price of its product in the domestic market and a low price in foreign market. The two markets are kept separate by tariff wall; domestic buyers cannot buy goods at lower foreign price by importing them. The price is lower in the foreign market, because demand for the product is highly elastic (the product has to face competition from similar products); while price is higher in domestic market, because the monopolist is the only producer of it and the demand is inelastic. At the same time it is not necessary that the markets should be separated geographically. There are many other ways by which the markets can be separated. For instance, the markets of box seats, balcony seats and the first class seats in theatres are segregated by tickets, and ushers. Similarly, electric power companies use metres and other devices to separate the markets for electrical energy for lighting, cooking and other commercial and industrial uses. But price discrimination will take place only when the above two conditions separate markets and the different elasticity of demand in the market are satisfied.

4. Dcgrccs of Price Discrimination

Here, the question is how far a monopolist goes in charging different prices for his product? The extent to which price discrimination is possible will depend on the circumstances. Prof. A.C. Pigou, the English economist, created the idea of degrees of price discrimination and imperfect discrimination. Pigou speaks of the following three degrees of price discrimination.

---

1. Joan Robinson. *Economics of Imperfect Competition* (1993), Ch. 15 and 16; and George G. Stiglar, *The Theory of Price*. The Macmillan Company, New York, pp. 223-25.

Discrimination of the First Degree or Perfect Discrimination

In discrimination of the first degree, the monopolist knows the maximum amount of money each consumer will pay for any quantity. He will set the prices accordingly and take from each consumer the entire amount of his consumer's surplus. In other words, in the first degree of price discrimination, the price charged by the monopolist will be different for every individual unit of a homogeneous commodity. The monopolist tries to charge the highest price from each consumer that he will be ready to pay for each unit rather than go without it. Mrs. Robinson calls this situation as 'perfectly discriminating monopoly', because it is perfect only from the point of view of the monopolist.

Such discrimination is possible only if the consumers buy one unit each from the monopolist. The monopolist will charge different prices from different consumers, depending upon their willingness to buy it. If all of his consumers have different tastes, the monopolist has a different price for each one. In such a case, his minimum price will be determined by his costs. In a situation when the consumer buys more than one unit of the monopolist's product, then he will do so only at lower prices. The monopolist will now adjust his sales accordingly.

For example, in Fig. 27.1 the monopolist will sell one unit at OP_1 price, a second unit at OP_2 price, a third unit at OP_3 price and so on. Now assuming that the marginal unity of money is constant to the consumer; OP_1, OP_2, OP_3 can also be assumed as the prices which the consumer will pay for OX_1, OX_2 and OX_3 quantity of the product. Therefore, the demand curve DD will become the marginal revenue curve. If the monopolist sells OX_3 units of his total revenue will not be equal to the rectangle OP_3 CX_3 but will be equal to the

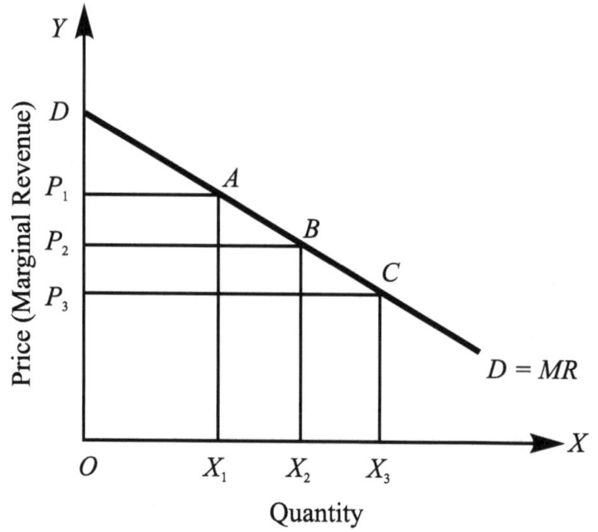

Fig. 27.1

total area under the (marginal revenue) curve, i.e. ODP_3X_3. Thus, assuming the marginal utility is equal to price, the area under the demand curve represents the total utility to the consumers. This indicates that under the first degree *of* price discrimination,

$$TV = TR$$

Where TV = Total Utility (in terms of money or price)

TR = Total Revenue

It also means that under the above situation, the monopolist takes away the entire utility obtained by the consumers in terms of the different prices charged by him and leaves no consumer's surplus with the consumers.

Price discrimination of the first degree is the limiting or extreme case. It can occur only rarely where a monopolist has only a few buyers of his product and where he is clever enough to judge the maximum prices that the consumers are willing to pay for his product. Thus, its technical feasibility would be limited because the monopolist usually does not possess a perfect knowledge of the demand of the consumers. It would be most unusual to find a single consumer being offered a number of units of an identical good, each at different prices. Discrimination between buyers is more usual than the discrimination between the units of a homogeneous product.

Discrimination of the Second Degree

In discrimination of the second degree, the monopolist is able to get a part of consumer's surplus but not the entire consumer's surplus of the consumers. In other words, the monopolist charges different prices from different consumers and different prices for different units of the same product, but not the maximum possible prices that the consumers could pay for it. He will be able to charge a lesser price than the maximum imaginary price of the consumers; leaving a certain amount of consumer's surplus with the consumers. The monopolist will sell the consumer several units at one price and another several units at a lower price, etc. Mrs. Joan Robinson meant it 'imperfect discriminating monopoly. This has been illustrated in Fig. 27.2.

In Fig. 27.2, DD is the demand curve of the consumers for the monopolist's product. It indicates that the monopolist charges a high price for a low level of output and for additional levels of output he charges lower prices. For instance, OX_1 output is sold at price OP_1, X_1X_2 (additional units) output is sold at OP_2 price and further X_2X_3 output is sold at OP_3 price. The demand curve shows that the consumers will consume these various output levels at the said prices. Now the total revenue of the monopolist will be equal to the total area under the demand curve upto point C and nor it will be equal to the rectangle OP_2CX_3 if the monopolist sells OX_2 quantity of output. But in this situation, the total revenue of the monopolist will be equal to the area

OP_1AX_1

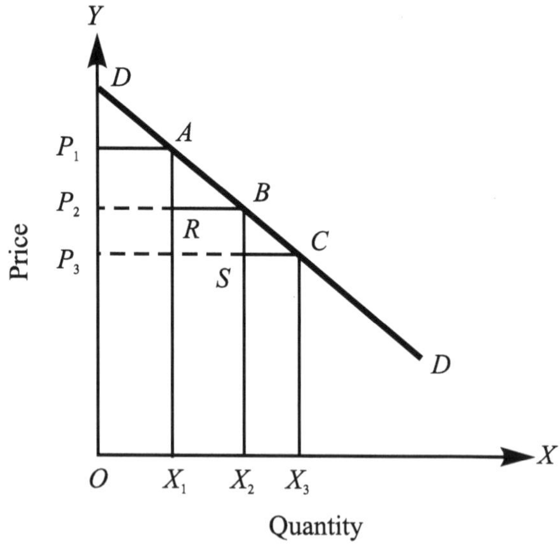

Fig. 27.2

$+ X_1RBX_2 + X_2SCX_3$. If the monopolist charges a single price OP_2 for his entire output sold, OC; his total revenue will be equal to the area OP_3CX_3 which would be smaller than the revenue derived under the second degree of price discrimination. Thus, with the three prices, the total revenue is the sum of the three rectangles. The monopolist in this way snatches a part of the consumer's surplus. The part which the monopolist leaves with the consumers is equal to the sum of the areas of the three little triangles as $\Delta DP_1A + \Delta ARB + \Delta BSC$.

This type of second degree price discrimination is normally practised in such markets where there are a number of buyers of the product. Since tastes and incomes of the consumers differ, the monopolist is able to seize some part of their consumer's surplus depending upon their (different groups of consumers) desire to buy the commodity.

Discrimination of the Third Degree

In discrimination of the third degree, the monopolist divides his consumers into two or more classes or groups or markets and charges different prices from different markets. This type of discrimination is most common in practice. The simplest form of this kind of price discrimination is that when the monopolist sells his output, already produced, in two separate markets. Since he has some given amount to sell, his costs of production can be ignored. When he sells his output only in the two markets, he adjusts the amount in each market such that the marginal revenue derived from the first market becomes equal to the marginal revenue derived from the second market.

Though the marginal revenues are equal in the two markets, prices are unequal due to different elasticities of demand in the two markets. Thus, discrimination of the third degree will occur only if the markets are separate and their respective elasticities of demand are different. In the following section we shall discuss the determination of price and output under the third degree of price discrimination which is the most common form of price discrimination.

5. Distribution of Given Output under Discriminating Monopoly

Let us assume that the monopolist has a given output already produced and merely wants to distribute it in the most profitable way between the two markets. As we have already mentioned, for price discrimination it is necessary that elasticities of demand must be different in the two distinct markets. Let us suppose that market *I* is less elastic and market *II* is more elastic. The respective marginal revenues of these markets *I* and *II* will also be different. Now, in order to maximise profits (revenues because costs are ignored here), the monopolist should distribute his given output among the markets in such a way that marginal revenue in each market is equal to the marginal revenue in the other market. If marginal revenue of market *I* is greater than that of

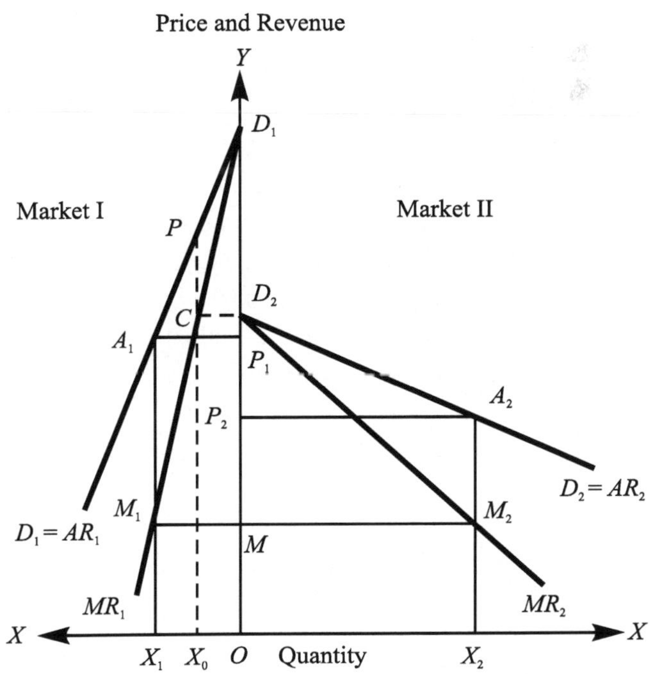

Fig. 27.3

market *II*, he will sell the additional unit of sales in market *I*. This type of substitution will go on until the marginal revenues in each market are made equal. Once marginal revenue in the two markets is equal, he will stop switching sales from one market to the other. He will gain nothing in switching a marginal unit of output and will actually lose if he continues the process because marginal revenue in the market with low elasticity of demand will eventually become less than marginal revenue in the other. Thus, the equality between marginal revenues will bring him (monopolist) the greatest total receipts from a given output. We can illustrate this case with the help of a diagram. In Fig. 27.3, AR_1 and AR_2 are the average revenue or demand curves of the two markets *I* and *II* respectively. Their corresponding marginal revenue curves are MR_1 and MR_2. Now, if the given amount of output is below OX_0, the monopolist should sell the entire amount in market *I* because upto this level of output the marginal revenue of the *I* market is higher than the marginal revenue of the *II* market. If his total output is equal to X_1X_2 $(= OX_1 + OX_2)$, he should sell OX_1 output in market *I* and OX_2 output in market *II*, so that marginal revenue in market *I* equals marginal revenue in market *II*. The level of marginal revenue in both the markets will be equal to OM $(=X_1M_1 = X_2M_2)$; or

$$MR_1 = MR_2$$

where MR_1 = Marginal Revenue of Market *I*

MR_2 = Marginal Revenue of Market *II*

This is the fundamental rule of output distribution when the costs are ignored. At this point the monopolist will be in equilibrium and his total revenue from the given output will be maximum. With this distribution of output, the price in market I will be OP_1 and the price in market *II* will be OP_2. It clears that the price in market *I* is higher than the price in market *II*. Also, output is more in market *II* than in market *I*. In other words, we can say that in equilibrium marginal revenue in the markets will be the same but prices will be different. Price will be higher in the market with the less elastic demand curve and vice versa. This can also be proved by the following mathematical formula:

$$MR = P\left(1 - \frac{1}{e}\right)$$

where MR = Marginal revenue

P = Price

e = Elasticity of demand

Since in equilibrium,

$$MR_1 = MR_2$$

where $$MR_1 = P_1\left(1-\frac{1}{e_1}\right)$$

$$MR_2 = P_2\left(1-\frac{1}{e_2}\right)$$

It follows that

$$P_1\left(1-\frac{1}{e_1}\right) = P_2\left(1-\frac{1}{e_2}\right)$$

Therefore, the price in market *I*, i.e. P_1 differs from the price in market *II*, i.e. P_2, when elasticities in the two markets are unequal. If elasticities were equal, prices in the two markets *I* and *II* would be the same and there would be no price discrimination.

Let us assume, $e_1 = 2$ and $e_2 = 4$. Putting these values in the above relation, we get

$$P_1\left(1-\frac{1}{2}\right) = P_2\left(1-\frac{1}{4}\right)$$

or $$\frac{1}{2}P_1 = \frac{3}{4}P_2$$

or $$P_1 = \frac{3}{2}P_2$$

Thus, $P_1 > P_2$ if $e_1 < e_2$. Similarly, if $e_1 = e_2$, then $P_1 = P_2$. Therefore, price discrimination is possible only when elasticities in the two markets are different.

6. Determination of Price and Output under (Third Degree) Discriminating Monopoly

The problem of the monopolist is to maximise his total profits. For this he must take account of his costs and revenues. He will maximise his profits when the marginal revenues in each of the two markets are equal and at the same time they are also equal to the marginal costs of the monopolist's entire output.

Suppose, in Fig. 27.4, the monopolist has two markets *I* and *II*. The average revenue curves or demand curves in the two markets are AR_1 and AR_2 respectively. The corresponding marginal revenue curves in the two markets are MR_1 and MR_2 respectively. These markets have different elasticities of demand at each price. Now the monopolist has to determine his entire output regardless of how it is distributed. For this he has to follow the profit maximising rule $MR = MC$. The total (combined) marginal revenue curve (ΣMR) and the marginal cost curve (MC) for the monopolist's whole output are shown in Panel (*c*) of Fig. 27.4. The marginal revenue for the entire output (ΣMR) is the horizontal summation of the two separate marginal revenues MR_1 and MR_2 of the individual markets. Now the monopolist will establish his equilibrium point at E where $MC = \Sigma MR$. His equilibrium level of output is OX. Now the problem before the monopolist is how to distribute the output OX between the two markets *I* and *II*. For this he will follow the rule $MR_1 = MR_2 = MC = \Sigma MR$. Following this principle[2], the discriminating monopolist will sell OX_1 output in market *I* and OX_2 output in market *II*. With this distribution of total output, marginal revenue in market *I* (OM_1) is equal to marginal revenue in market *II* (OM_2). The equilibrium points of market *I* and *II* are E_1 and E_2 respectively. The prices charged by the monopolist from market *I* and *II* are OP_1 and OP_2 respectively. The total maximum profit of the monopolist is equal to the shaded area *DRES* shown in Panel (*c*) of Fig. 27.4.

2. In the case of price discrimination, the monopolist's profit is the difference between his revenues on both the markets and his total costs:

$$\pi = R_1(q_1) + R_2(q_2) - C(q_1 + q_2)$$

where π is the total profit, $R_1(q_1)$ is the total revenue of market *I*, $R_2 < (q_2)$ is the total revenue of market *II* and $C(q_1 + q_2)$ is the total cost of the monopolist's output. Also, q_1 and q_2 are the quantities of output sold in market *I* and market *II* respectively. For profit maximisation, the partial derivatives are set equal to zero:

$$\frac{\partial \pi}{\partial q_1} = R_1'(q_1) - C(q_1 + q_2) = 0 \quad ...(i)$$

$$\frac{\partial \pi}{\partial q_2} = R_2'(q_2) - C'(q_1 + q_2) = 0 \quad ^{a}\ (ii)$$

From (*i*) and (*ii*) we have.

$$R_1'(q_1) = R_2'(q_2) = C(q_1 + q_2)$$

or $$MR_1 = MR_2 = MC$$

because $R_1'(q_1)$, $R_2'(q_2)$ and $C'(q_1 + q_2)$ are MR_1, MR_2 and MC respectively. Hence for profit maximisation the above condition must be satisfied where the two marginal revenues are equal to each other and to the marginal cost of the entire output.

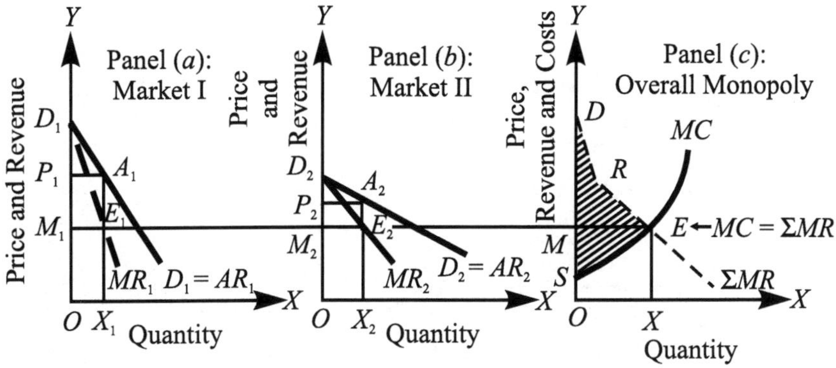

Fig. 27.4

This same solution can also be shown by combining the above three panels of Fig. 27.4 in a single diagram as in Fig. 27.5. The marginal and average cost curves of the monopolist are represented by *MC* and *AC* respectively. The combined marginal revenue curve $\sum MR$ is derived by taking the horizontal summation of the marginal revenue curves of the two markets. Market *I* starts from point D_1 while market *II* starts from point D_2. Thus, up to point *A*, the marginal revenue curve of market *I* will be relevant and thereafter we add the marginal revenue of market *II* to market *I* and get the total marginal revenue curve $\sum MR$ of the monopolist. The equilibrium level of output of the monopolist is *OX* which if distributed properly (by following the rule $MR_1 = MR_2 = \sum MR = MC$) in the two markets, then the profits in Market *I* will be equal to the area $CP_1\ TS$ and profit in market *II* will be equal to the area CP_2NR. Total profit of the monopolist will be equal to the profits of market *I* plus the profits of market *II*.

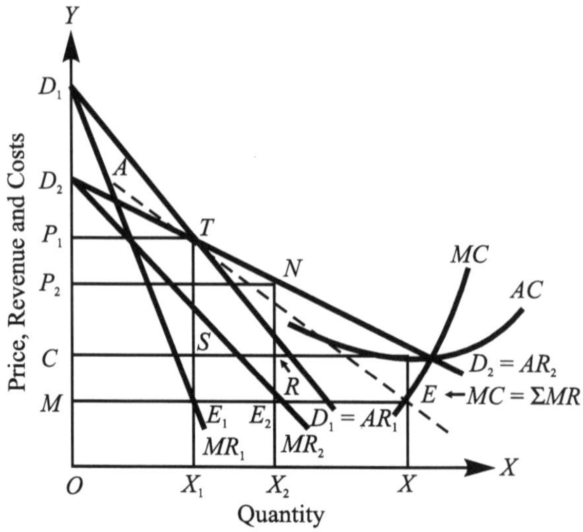

Fig. 27.5

7. Dumping: A Special Case of Price Discrimination

Dumping means charging a higher price in the domestic market and a lower price in the foreign market for the same product. Under the above forms of price discriminations both the markets were assumed to be imperfect; but under dumping, we assume that perfect competition exists in the foreign market while the monopolist enjoys monopoly power in the home (domestic) market. In other words, in the foreign market, the elasticity of demand for his product is infinite while in the home market, elasticity of demand for his product is very low. Thus, the monopolist has to face a horizontal straight line demand curve or average revenue for the foreign market. In the home market, the average revenue curve or the demand curve slopes downwards and the marginal revenue curve for the home market will be below it.

In Fig. 27.6, AR_d and MR_d are the average and marginal revenue curves for the domestic market which are one and the same. AR_f and MR_f are the average and marginal revenue curves for the foreign market. *MC* represents the marginal cost curve of the monopolist's total output. Now the problem of the monopolist is how much quantity of the output is to be produced? For this, he has to find out the equilibrium point where his marginal cost equals the combined marginal revenue. The combined marginal revenue curve is *AMNR*. On this curve, marginal revenue in the foreign market is added horizontally to the marginal revenue in the domestic market. The intersection of the monopolist's marginal cost curve with the combined marginal revenue at point *N* gives a total output of *OX* as that which maximises profits. The total output must now be distributed between the two markets the foreign market and the domestic market. Following the fundamental rule of distribution ($MR_1 = MR_2 = MC$), the monopolist sells OX output in the domestic market at a price of OP_d and a marginal revenue of MX_d. This leaves X_dX ($= OX - OX_d$) to be sold in the foreign market at a price of OP_f and with a marginal revenue NX ($= OP_f$).

It is clear from Fig. 27.6, that the marginal revenue of domestic market, MX_d, is the same as the marginal revenue of the foreign market NX; but price in the domestic market (OP_d) is higher than the price in the foreign market (OP_f). The monopolist's total profits are shown by the shaded area $AMNS$.

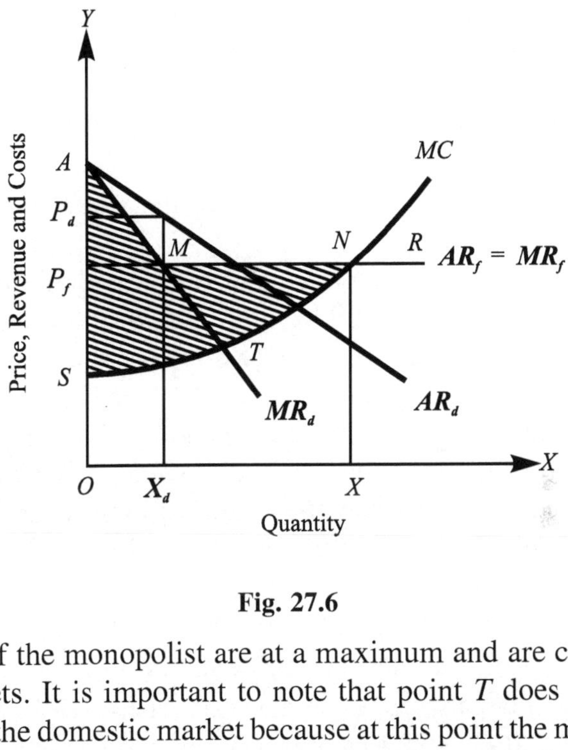

Fig. 27.6

These profits of the monopolist are at a maximum and are contributed to by both the markets. It is important to note that point T does not indicate the equilibrium of the domestic market because at this point the marginal revenue of the domestic market is less than the marginal revenue of the foreign market. Moreover, point T does not lie on the combined marginal revenue curve of the monopolist. Thus, point T will not be the relevant point for the output determination by the monopolist. For this, he has to follow the fundamental principle, $MC = MR_1 = MR_2 = \Sigma MR$.

8. Justification of Price Discrimination

In modern times, the theory of price discrimination has a number of applications of varied kinds. But in the ideal economy of the welfare theorists, there would be no price discrimination. The welfare theorists assume perfect competition throughout their economic analysis under which price discrimination is impossible any way. The natural monopolies in the ideal economy would set their prices equal to their marginal costs. Price differences between products would exactly equal differences in marginal costs, which is another way of expressing the absence of price discrimination. It means that the consumers pay the same prices at the same time for the same products is one of the marginal conditions for maximum economic welfare.

But it does not mean that for all the time price discrimination is not desirable. In the context of a partial welfare analysis, price-discrimination may assume a great importance. Partial welfare means the economic welfare flowing from one commodity or industry, considered by itself, and without regard to or for possible cross effects with other commodities or industries. Sometimes, the demand-cost relations of a monopolist are such that without discrimination he would not like to produce any quantity of the output. Also where the government regulates prices of the products, it may allow or even encourage price discrimination if it increases the welfare of the consumers and to the society as a whole.

There are many services, such as, rail transportation, or services of the doctors, etc. which cannot be provided profitably unless price discrimination is allowed to take place, because a single price for such services will mean low incomes to the entrepreneurs.

Another reason to justify price discrimination by the government is that it will reduce the inequalities of personal real incomes. Normally, the reduced price or low price is meant for the poor class while the higher price is meant for the rich class. Here the equity criterion pushes aside the efficiency criterion. Tenants in public-housing projects, who must have incomes below specified levels pay rents that are in general fairly below the full costs.

Now, we can say that whether price-discrimination is economically justified or not will depend upon the question whether it is advantageous or disadvantageous to the welfare of the society. Anyway, the classification of buyers or of markets for charging different prices must satisfy legal tests of 'reasonableness'. Price differences must also be 'reasonable', which usually means that they must conform to demonstrable differences in costs as measured by accounting standards. In fact, differences in elasticities of demand are hardly ever put on an equal footing with differences in costs. The recognition given to elasticities of demand is oblique or implicit. A monopoly regulated by the government may be allowed to charge a lower price for its product where it has to face tough competition as we have seen under dumping. Sometimes, the discriminating monopolist resorts to price discrimination with the selfish motive of destroying his rivals and keeping his own monopoly power in the bargain. He adopts this policy both in the domestic market as well as the foreign market. Thus, if price discrimination leads to larger outputs of the society, it must be justified because larger output implies greater economic welfare. If, on the other hand, it leads to smaller output than that of simple monopoly, it must not be justified.

Exercises

1. What do you understand by price discrimination? Explain the conditions for price discrimination.
2. How far a monopolist goes in charging different prices for his product?
3. "A discriminating monopolist adjusts his sales in such a way that the marginal revenue obtained from selling an additional unit in anyone market is the same for all the markets" Explain die statement.
4. Explain discriminatory pricing under monopoly. Is price discrimination economically justifiable?
5. (*a*) What conditions must be present for 'price discrimination' to be possible under monopoly? Under what circumstances might price discrimination be possible, but not profitable?
   (*b*) How far is it possible for the state to induce the monopolist, through price regulation, to furnish the greatest amount of product consistent with his costs and consumer demand?
6. State the conditions under which monopolistic price discrimination is possible. How will a discriminating monopolist determine his output and the output to be sold in each market? Will the price be higher in the more elastic market?
7. "The main aim of the monopolist is to sell in such a manner that he may get maximum monopoly profit." Discuss.
8. Explain price and output determination under discriminating monopoly.
9. What do you understand by dumping? How are price and output determined under dumping?

Multiple Choice Questions

10. (*i*) Pursuing a policy of price discrimination will increase the profits of a monopolist who sells in two sub-markets
    (*a*) only if he sells more than one product
    (*b*) if the price elasticity of demand for his output differs in two markets
    (*c*) if buyers in either sub-market can easily resell his output to buyers in the other sub-market
    (*d*) only during the short-run when capital stock is fixed [*Ans*. (*b*)]

    (*ii*) Price discrimination will always lead to
    (*a*) increase in output (*c*) no change in output.
    (*b*) decrease in output (*d*) none [*Ans*. (*c*)]

    (*iii*) Discriminating monopoly is possible if two markets have
    (*a*) rising cost curves
    (*b*) rising and declining cost curves
    (*c*) different elasticities of demand

Chapter 28

Monopsony and Bilateral Monopoly

1. Introduction

Monopsony refers to a market situation when there is a single buyer of a commodity or service. According to Professor Liebhafsky, "Monopsony can be formally defined as a case of a single buyer who is not in competition with any other buyers for the output which he seeks to purchase, and as a situation in which entry to the market by other buyers is impossible." Such a situation may arise when the consumers of a certain commodity are organised or when a certain individual happens to have a taste for some commodity which no one else requires! It may also happen when a single big factory in an isolated locality is the sole buyer of some commodity from different firms.

A bilateral monopoly on the other hand is a market situation in which a single seller faces a single buyer. As we have studied earlier, a monopolist is the single seller of a product (or a factor) in the market. When he faces a single buyer, or the monopsonist, this situation is termed as a bilateral monopoly. Since both the firms are capable of exercising their respective strength, there will be bargaining and the stronger of the two will have a better bargain by having the more favourable terms than the other fellow.

2. Pricing and Output under Monopsony

The process of monopsony price determination is very similar to that under monopoly. The monopsonist aims at the maximisation of his surplus while the monopolist tries to maximise his profit. For profit maximisation, the monopolist applies the condition $MC = MR$. The monopsonist tries to make his purchases in such a way that $MC = MU$. It is only at this point that the monopsonist gets maximum consumer's surplus.

Fig. 28.1 explains the process of price determination by a monopsonist. The *AC*-curve of the monopsonist is the supply curve of the industry or of the market. It is from the industry that he buys the product. In Fig. 28.1, *AC* and *MC* curves are the average and marginal cost curves respectively. *MU* is the marginal utility curve of the monopsonist. The equilibrium point is *E* where the *MC* curve cuts the *MU* curve. Thus, the monopsonist purchases *OX* quantity at *EX* price, which is the supply price for that output. The surplus obtained by the monopsonist is the area *CPER*. This is the difference between what he is prepared to pay (*ODEX*) and what he actually pays (*OCRX*).

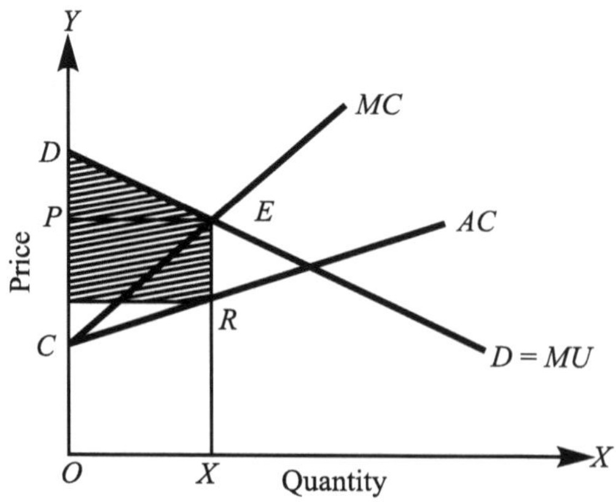

Fig. 28.1

3. Comparison between Monopsony and Perfect Competition

(1) *Constant Cost Case.* In Fig. 28.2, the supply price is constant, and therefore the *AC* and *MC* curves wil1 coincide. Here *E* is the equilibrium point where *OX* quantity of the output is purchased at *EX* (= *OP*) price. The *OX* quantity bought at *EX* price under monopsony is the same as under perfect competition because *MC* curve will cut the horizontal *AR* = *MR* curve from below under perfect competition at the equilibrium point *E*.

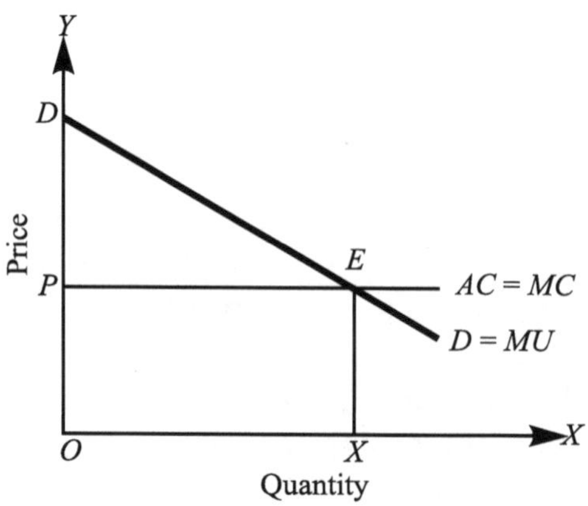

Fig. 28.2

(2) *Increasing Cost Case.* Quantity Under increasing cost situation, *AC*

and *MC* curves are rising, the monopsonist will pay less price than that under perfect competition, and he will buy a little more than half the competitive amount. This case is presented in Fig. 28.3. Here monopsonist equilibrium

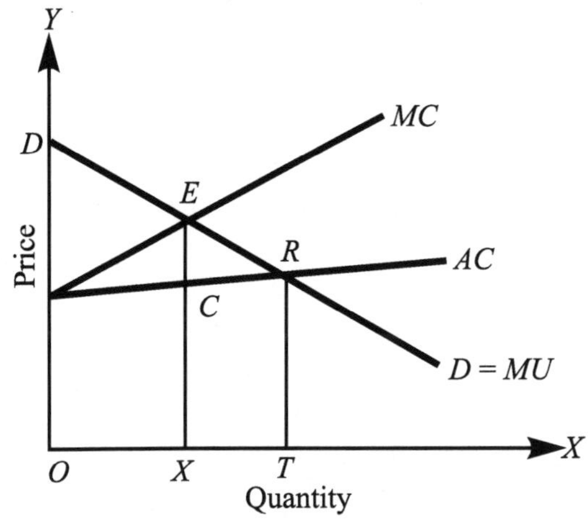

Fig. 28.3

point is *E* while the perfect competitive buyer's equilibrium point will be *R*. Thus, the monopsonist's price is *CX* which is less than the competitive price *RT.* Also, the quantity purchased by the monopsonist is *OX* which is less than competitive quantity *OT.*

(3) *Diminishing Cost Case.* It is shown in Fig. 28.4. Here *AC* and *MC* curves slope downwards. In such a situation the monopsonist buys more than

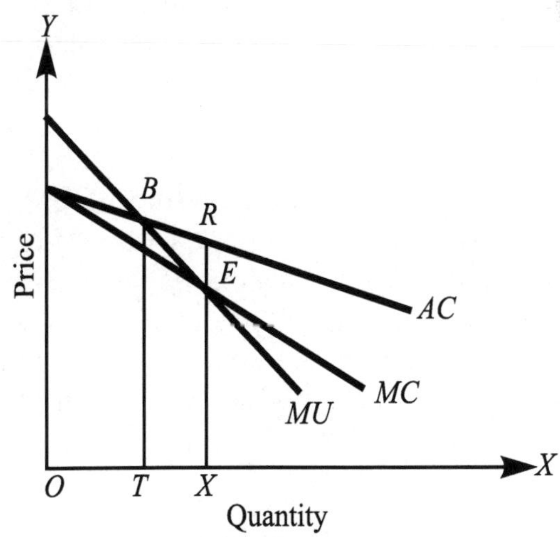

Fig. 28.4

that under perfect competition. Here monopsonist's equilibrium point is *E* where he buys *OX* quantity at *RX* price. Under perfect competition, the equilibrium point is B where the price is BT and quantity is OT. Hence it is clear that $OX > OT$ and price $BT > RX$.

4. Pricing and Output under Bilateral Monopoly

In Fig. 28.5, the monopsonist consumer's demand for the product is shown by DD or AR; the corresponding marginal revenue is shown as MR. The monopolist's marginal cost of production is shown by MC. If the monopolist

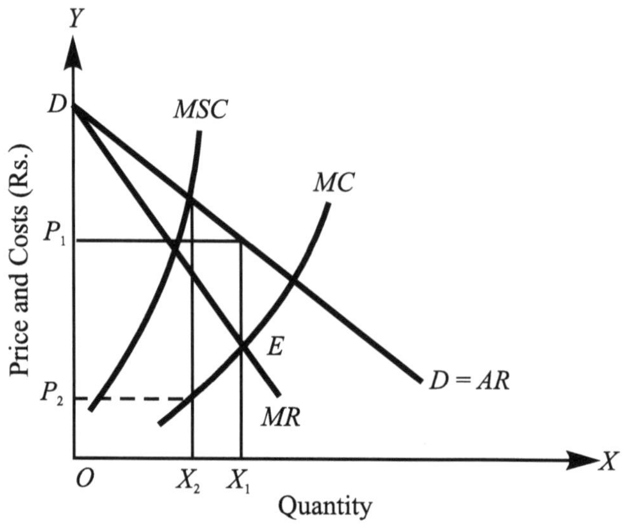

Fig. 28.5

alone were to exercise his monopoly power, he would maximise his profits by producing OX_1 where $MC = MR$. On the other hand, if the monopsonist alone were to set price, subject to the cost conditions of the supplier, then he would regard MC as the seller's supply curve. Thus, MC represents the schedule of the average supply price of the product. The corresponding marginal supply cost (MSC) curve would, therefore, be MSC. The monopsonist would prefer to buy that quantity at which the seller's MSC would be equal to the price he is willing to pay, but assuming that he can exercise his monopolistic power, he would offer only OP_2 dollars per unit for OX_2 units. At what price the two "giants" agree to trade the particular product will depend on their relative strength. This price will, however, lie between OP_1 and OP_2 which are the highest and lowest price levels acceptable to the monopsonist buyer and the monopolist seller respectively.

Exercises

1. What do you understand by the term monopsony? How is monopsony price determined?
2. Distinguish between monopsony pricing and perfect competitive pricing under different cost conditions.

3. Explain pricing under bilateral monopoly.

Multiple Choice Questions

4. (*i*) When there is a single buyer of a commodity in the market, it is known as
   (*a*) monopoly
   (*b*) monopsony
   (*c*) bilateral monopoly
   (*d*) none of the above [*Ans.* (*b*)]

   (*ii*) Bilateral monopoly refers to a market situation in which
   (*a*) a single producer (monopolist) of a product faces a single buyer (monopsonist) of that product
   (*b*) there is only one seller in the market
   (*c*) there are two sellers in the market
   (*d*) there are two buyers in the market
   [*Ans.* (*a*)]

Chapter 29

Monopolistic Competition

1. Introduction

In the preceding chapters we have examined the polar extremes of perfect competition and monopoly. In real life, competition is rarely perfect. In the majority of cases, there is neither a single individual who controls the total supply, nor are there many sellers so that their individual shares are negligible in relation to the total supply of the market. Thus, the real situation is of imperfect competition where there is neither perfect competition nor absolute monopoly. This market situation is also known as monopolistic competition.

The classical economists and the neo-classical economists (of the late 19th century, such as, Marshall and Pigou) assumed competition and monopoly as mutually exclusive and always emphasised the competitive market situation as it would always increase material welfare. Imperfect competition as a market situation was given no importance. It was only after 1926, that the modern economists felt that absolute monopoly and perfect competition were unrealistic market situations. The Cambridge economists, Piero Sraffa, H. Hotelling and Zeuthen, etc. were of the opinion that the models of perfect competition and monopoly do not depict the real market situations. Further in 1933, the simultaneous publication of *The Economics of Imperfect Competition* by Mrs. Joan Robinson of England and *The Theory of Monopolistic Competition* by Prof. E.H. Chamberlin of America, revolt against the traditional theories related to perfect competition and monopoly. According to Mrs. Joan Robinson, even in the presence of a large number of firms producing a particular product, a buyer may prefer to buy from a seller of his choice and may also be willing to pay a relatively higher price. It means price will not be the same in the market and it will never be a situation of perfect competition. Mrs. Robinson calls it the situation of imperfect competition.

On the other hand, Prof. Chamberlin introduces competitive forces in a monopoly market. He does not assume the presence of a large number of firms producing identical products but concentrates on the individual firm whose product is a close substitute of the other firms' products. According to him, in real world we do not find an absolute monopoly. Product differentiation exists in the market and that limits the monopoly power of the firm. Thus, due to the availability of substitutes, a firm enjoys "limited monopoly". Prof. Chamberlin calls it the situation of monopolistic competition.

Thus, the terms imperfect competition or monopolistic competition[1] are used to describe the market situations found in modem capitalist states, the basic features being a large number of firms selling differentiated products. Sometimes the term monopolistic competition is also referred to as *Group Equilibrium.*

2. Main Features of Monopolistic Competition

According to Prof. Chamberlin, the main features or characteristics of monopolistic competition are the following:

(1) *Relatively Small Number of Firms.* Under perfect competition, we assume that there are a number of firms which produce identical products. It means no individual firm can influence the market price which is determined by the industry demand and industry supply. In monopolistic competition, the number of firms is less than that under perfect competition. Due to this reason that a firm enjoys some monopoly power. Since the firms under monopolistic competition sell differentiated products, they are able to charge different prices for their products.

(2) *Product Differentiation.* Product differentiation is the main feature of monopolistic competition. According to Prof. Chamberlin monopolistic competition is a market situation in which there are many firms of a particular product, but the product of each firm is in some way differentiated from the product of every other firm in the market. Product differentiation may take the form of brand names, trade-marks, etc. This means that the product of a firm may find close substitutes and its crosselasticity of demand is very high.

This is the reason that Chamberlin's analysis of monopolistic competition deals largely with the individual firm and does not refer directly to the industry. The commodities produced by any industry are not homogeneous; the technique of branding differentiates the product of anyone firm from the products of other firms in the same industry. Thus, each firm has an independent demand schedule, but at the same time, each demand schedule reflects the

1. Imperfect competition is a much wider and more comprehensive term than monopolistic competition. In fact monopolistic competition is only one of the many sub-categories of imperfect competition. In the present chapter we shall discuss the theory of monopolistic competition which was developed by Prof. E.H. Chamberlin.

competitive nature of the market. According to Prof. Chamberlin, the concept of industry equilibrium has no relevance in the context of product differentiation. Although we can talk about the equilibrium of the group of firms producing similar products, yet it is difficult to make an effective combination of all firms producing similar products into a product group, as the degree of product substitutability is not well defined. For this reason the case of monopolistic competition differs from that of monopoly only in the degree of competition that is present. No monopolist is entirely free from competition. If a monopolist charges an exorbitant price for his product, there are usually other products of close substitutes, that can be used in its place. These possibilities of substitution give some elasticity to the demand curve, and this limits the price. If the substitutes are not close, the demand may be rather inelastic and the monopoly power will be great, but if good substitutes are available, the demand will be more elastic and the monopoly power will be less. This last is usually the case with product differentiation or monopolistic competition.

(3) *Freedom of Entry of New Firms.* Under monopolistic competition, the individual firm has a monopoly of its own product, but it faces keen competition from firms making very similar products, and it does not have the power to restrict the entry of new firms.

(4) *Competitive Advertisement.* Product differentiation is also emphasised by the practice of competitive advertising. In fact, the practice of competitive advertising is the more striking feature of monopolistic competition. Advertising is employed to heighten, in the mind of the consumer, the differences between Brand *A* and Brand *B*. It is important to realise that we are concerned with the differentiation of goods in the economic sense and not in the technical sense. Two branded products may be almost identical in their technical features or chemical composition, but if advertising and other selling practices have created different images in the consumer's mind, then these products are different from our point of view, because the consumers will be prepared to pay different prices for them. Thus, advertisement or sales promotion technique is the important feature of monopolistic competition.

(5) *More Elastic Demand.* The shape of the demand curve faced by the firm under monopolistic competition comes from product differentiation. In the absence of product differentiation, the demand curve of the firm will be perfectly elastic like the demand curve of a perfectly competitive firm. But due to a differentiated product, the individual firm possesses some monopoly power and therefore its demand curve will be more elastic. In other words, under monopolistic competition, each producer is a monopolist and the demand curve for his product will slope downwards, but the availability of close

substitutes will mean that the demand curve for his product will be more elastic. Thus, diagrammatically, the demand curve of a firm under monopolistic competition will be less steep as compared to that of monopoly firm. This means that a small decrease in the price of the product will lead to a large increase in the demand for her product assuming the prices of other firms remain the same.

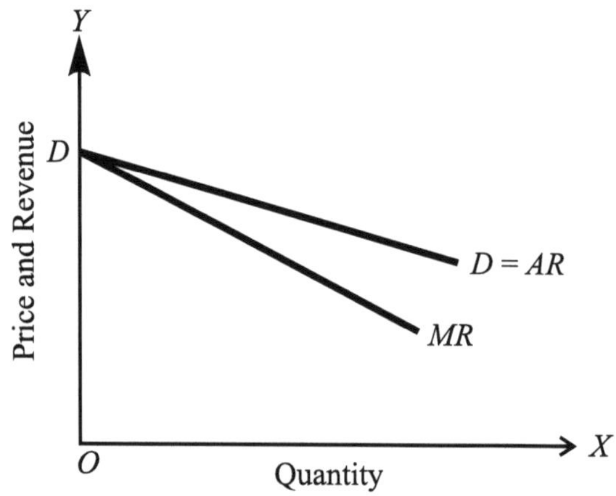

Fig. 29.1

It has been illustrated in Fig. 29.1. *DD* is the demand curve or average revenue curve of the firm under monopolistic competition. It is more elastic and not perfectly elastic. The corresponding marginal revenue curve lies below the demand curve. These curves are drawn on the assumption that the prices of other firms remain the same in response to the changes by a particular firm.[2] The slope of these curves will depend upon two factors: (*i*) the importance of the individual firm in the market, and (*ii*) the extent of product differentiation or product homogeneity. Product differentiation leads some consumers to prefer the products of particular sellers over those of other sellers. Consequently, the demand curve faced by an individual firm has some downward slope to it and enables the firm to exercise a small degree of control over her price. Ordinarily, the demand curve faced by the firm will be very elastic within its relevant range of prices because of the numerous good substitutes available for its product.

Here, the firm may expect a substantial expansion in sales by contemplating a price-cut. This also implies that the demand for the firm's product is highly elastic. Therefore, each firm seeks to maximise her profits only by varying the price of her product.

2. This is an important assumption, especially when price changes are of the nature of price cutting.

3. Monopoly Index

We have seen that in monopolistic competition, a firm has monopoly as well as competition. The more close substitutes of its product are, the less will be the monopoly power of the firm and vice versa. The output of the firm under monopolistic competition must be smaller, and its unit cost and price higher than it would be under pure competition. Here the question is that how can we measure this monopoly power of a firm? The following formula (which is known as a monopoly index) may be used to calculate the monopoly power of a firm.

$$M = P\left(1 - \frac{1}{|e|}\right)$$

where M = Marginal revenue, P = Price, $| e |$ = Elasticity of demand

Given the value of the coefficient e (elasticity of demand), one can find out the relation between price and marginal revenue.

In perfect competition, elasticity of demand of a firm is infinite ($e = \infty$), then price will be equal to the marginal revenue ($P = M$).

In monopoly, the demand curve is more inelastic, so that the coefficient 'e' has a smaller value, say $e = 2$.

then, $$M = P\left(1 - \frac{1}{2}\right)$$

or $$M = \frac{1}{2}P$$

or $$P = 2M$$

which means price will be twice the MR or price is 100 per cent higher than marginal revenue.

In monopolistic competition, the demand curve of the firm is more elastic, i.e. the coefficient 'e' has a larger value, say $e = 20$,

then $$M = P\left(1 - \frac{1}{20}\right)$$

$$= \frac{19}{20}P$$

or $$20M = 19P$$

This means that price is nearly 5 per cent more than the marginal revenue. In other words, the firm has a monopoly power to increase price by 5 per cent more than the price in perfect competition (where $P = MR$).

Hence, above formula explains the monopoly power of a firm.

4. Price and Output Determination under Monopolistic Competition

As we have already explained, under monopolistic competition due to product differentiation, it is rather impossible to present the analysis of the industry in graphic terms. In the case of perfect competition, where the product differentiation, is absent, we can draw industry demand and industry supply curves to determine the equilibrium price and output of the industry. But under monopolistic competition, construction of industry (market) curves is a rather unsatisfactory practice. Unless the differentiated products are converted in terms of a common denominator, it will be difficult to measure the quantity of the industry along the horizontal axis. Further, no single price prevails for differentiated products of the industry and that creates another difficulty of presenting the industry analysis in graphic terms. Therefore, under monopolistic competition, we shall confine our diagrammatic analysis to the individual firm. The market as a whole is there, but we shall discuss it only in terms of theoretical analysis.

Here our main assumption is that each firm in this market situation operates with an impression that its action would go unnoticed by its rivals in the market. The firm will attempt to maximise her profits only by varying the price of her product. Prof. Chamberlin also assumes that demand and cost functions are uniform throughout the product group. The equilibrium of the firm under monopolistic competition involves the usual conditions as discussed under other market situations. Now we shall discuss the equilibrium position of the firm and the group under the following section.

Short-Period Equilibrium of the Firm under Monopolistic Competition

Short-period equilibrium of a monopolistically competitive firm is very similar to that of a monopolist. Here the firm produces a differentiated product and attains some degree of monopoly power. In short-period, the firm does not have time to change its scale of plant and no new firms will enter the industry. Now, in order to maximise its profits, the monopolistically competitive firm will produce that level of output at which its marginal cost equals marginal revenue. This case has been illustrated in Fig. 29.2. The firm's demand curve is represented by *AR*, which is negatively sloped. The corresponding marginal revenue (*MR*) curve lies below it. The firm's short-run average cost and marginal cost curves are *SAC* and *SMC* respectively. The *SMC*-curve cuts the *MR*-curve at point *E*. Thus, the equilibrium level of output is *OX*, price is *OP* and cost per unit is OC. At *OX* level of output, the firm enjoys *PC* abnormal profit per unit. The total maximum profit of the firm is represented by the shaded area *CPAB*.

The short-period equilibrium does not mean that all the firms charge the same price. In fact the firms charge different prices for their differentiated products. Each firm seeks its own profit maximising position.

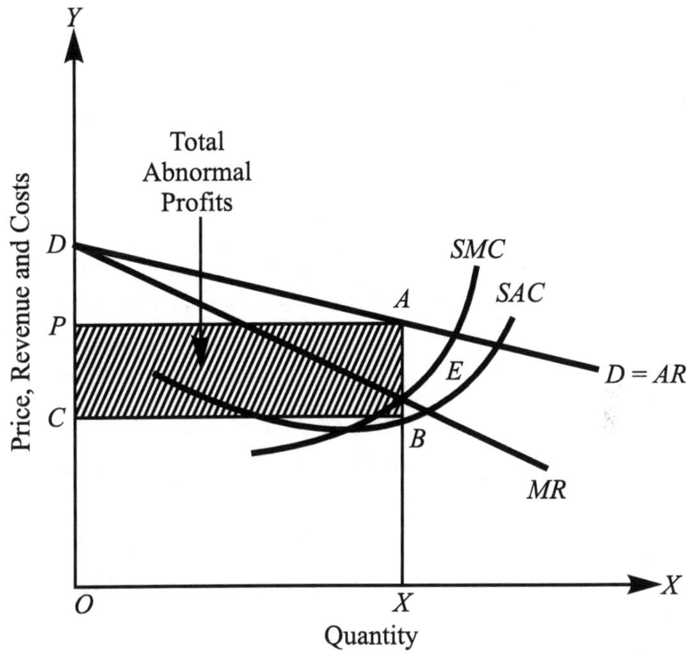

Fig. 29.2

Figure 29.2 indicates the equilibrium of a representative firm under monopolistic competition. The other firms also attempt to maximise their individual profits in the same manner. We must, however, remember that it is not necessary that under monopolistic competition all the firms will attain abnormal profits in the short-period. It is possible that some firms may take abnormal profits while at the same time others may incur losses or make normal profits only. Like other market situations, the firm under monopolistic competition has to incur certain fixed costs in the short-run which are not related to the volume of output. Thus, the minimum price acceptable by the firm in the short-run will be equal to its average variable cost. When the price of a firm's product is equal to its *AVC,* the firm's maximum loss will be equal to its entire fixed costs. If price is higher than the *AVC,* but less than the *AC,* the firm's short-run objective will be the minimisation of its loss. Thus, the two other possible situations of the short-period equilibrium (i.e. the situation of normal profits and the situation of losses) are shown in Fig. 29.3.

Panel (*a*) of Fig. 29.3 illustrates the situation when the firm gets only the normal profits which are included in the costs. The equilibrium level of output is *OX*. At *OX* output the price is *OP* which is also equal to its cost per unit.

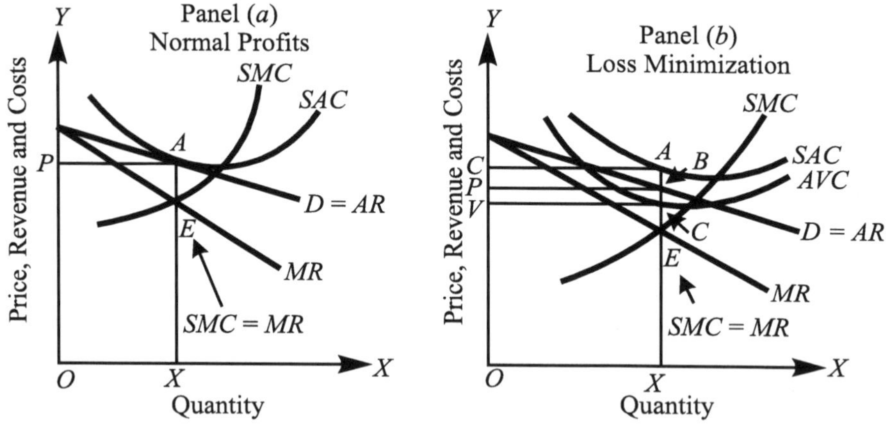

Fig. 29.3

Thus, the firm's abnormal profit is zero. In Panel (*b*) of Fig. 29.3, we have shown a case when the firm is minimising its losses. The equilibrium level of output is *OX* where the firm could bear *VC* amount of loss per unit (equal to fixed cost per unit). But since at *OX* output, price is *OP* and cost per unit is *OC*, the firm has to incur only *PC* amount of loss per unit (*PC* < *VC*). Therefore, the firm is minimising its losses by producing *OX* quantity of Output in short-run equilibrium.

Long-Period Equilibrium of the Firm under Monopolistic Competition

In the long-period, all factors of production used by the firm are variable and therefore, the firm can change its scale of plant to any extent. The firm will always try to build the scale of plant which makes the per unit cost minimum. As we have mentioned, the monopolistic competitive firm in the long-period can increase its sales by introducing a policy of price-cut for his own product. Here the firm assumes that its actions (i.e. price-cuts) will not be reacted by its rivals in the market. Thus, it will be able to get the full benefits of its economies of scale. For sometime the entry of the new firms will be blocked, but when the firms enjoy high level of short-run profits, it will induce the entry of new firms into the industry. Thus, the long-period equilibrium of the firm under monopolistic competition can be discussed in two ways: (*i*) when entry of new firms is blocked, and (*ii*) when entry of new firms is free.

Long-Period Equilibrium of the Firms when Entry of New Firms is Blocked. Under monopolistic competition, the case of blocked entry into an industry will not be the usual case. But for sometime it may happen. In such a situation, the industry has an optimal number of firms; each would attempt to adjust its scale of plant to the size required for long-period profit maximisation. The firm under monopolistic competition adopts the policy of

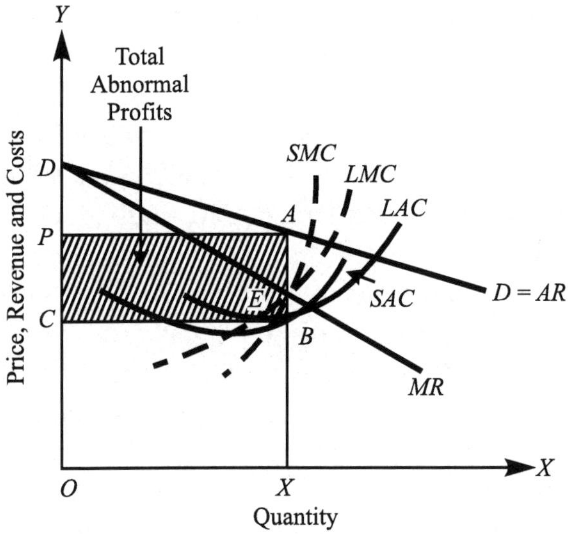

Fig. 29.4

price-cut to increase its sales. Thus, it will go on reducing its price until it produces that level of output at which its cost per unit becomes minimum possible and the profit maximising conditions are satisfied. This case has been depicted in Fig. 29.4. The demand curve faced by the firm is *DD* and the marginal revenue curve is *MR*. The respective long-period average cost curve and marginal cost curve are *LAC* and *LMC*. Profits will be maximised at output *OX,* at which long-period marginal cost equals marginal revenue at point *E*. The equilibrium price is *OP.* Now to produce output *OX,* at the least possible cost per unit, the firm should build the scale of plant which has its short-period average cost curve tangent to the long-period, cost curve at that output. In Fig. 29.4, *SAC* is tangent to *LAC* at output *OX* and at the same time *SMC* = *LMC* = *MR*. Thus, cost per unit is *OC* at output *OX*. The firm gets the maximum abnormal profits *CP* per unit. The total profits are shown by the shaded area *CPAB*.

Now, the firm has no incentive to cut its price below *OP* and to increase its sales beyond *OX* because the cost of producing an additional unit of output will be more than the revenue it gets from it (i.e. *MC* > *MR*) and, therefore, its profits would decline. Nor the firm would like to produce less than *OX* quantity of output, because in that case (when *MR* > *LMC*) it would not be able to maximise its profits. Therefore, in the long-period when the entry of new firms into the industry is blocked, the firm will produce that level of output at which two conditions are satisfied: (*i*) *SMC* = *LMC* = *MR,* and (*ii*) *SAC* = *LAC*.

Long-Period Equilibrium of the Firm when Entry of New Firm is Open. When the existing firms in the monopolistic competition are earning abnormal profits, there will be a tendency in the long-period for new firms to enter the industry. As new firms enter, they encroach upon the markets of existing firms, causing the demand curve and the marginal revenue curve faced by each firm to shift downward. In other words, the entry of new firms into the industry creates larger output without any' significant increase in the total sales of all the firms. The increase in supply (and in the number of suppliers) pushes the whole cluster of price ranges for individual firms downward. Thus, the firms will reduce their prices to check the decline in their individual sales as a result of the wholesale entry of new firms into the market.

On the other hand, the entry of new firms into the industry will also affect the costs of production for the existing firms. If the industry (i.e. all the existing firms) is operating under increasing cost conditions, the entry of new firms would cause factor-prices to rise which would shift the cost curves of existing firms upward. If it is operating under constant costs, the entry of new firms would have no effects upon factor-prices and upon the cost curves of individual firms. In an unusual case of decreasing costs, the entry of new firms would cause resource prices to decrease and cost-curves of the firms to shift downward. Here, we shall illustrate the case of increasing costs only.

Thus, the effects of the entry of new firms into the industry will be : *(i)* to shift the demand curves faced by the individual firms downward, and *(ii)* to shift the cost curves of the existing firms upward. These two simultaneous effects will cause profits of the existing firm to decrease. But the new firms will continue to enter so long as profit possibilities remain. Thus, in the long-run when entry is open, abnormal profits will be squeezed and the firms will get only the normal profits.[3] This means, in the long-run, price or average revenue is just equal to average cost. The same argument can be given when there are losses in the short-run and the exit of firms will lead to eliminate the losses in the long-period. Therefore, the basic difference between monopoly and monopolistic competition is that in the long-period profits are possible in monopoly simply because new firms are not allowed to enter the industry while such profits are impossible in monopolistic competition, simply because new firms are allowed to enter the industry.

This situation has been illustrated in Fig. 29.5. The relevant demand (or average revenue) and marginal revenue curves are *AR* and *MR*. respectively; and the long-period average cost and marginal cost curves are *LAC* and *LMC*

3. Thus, the large-period equilibrium of the firm under monopolistic competition, when the entry is open, is very much similar to that of a perfect competitive firm.

respectively.[4] Since we want to show the final long-run position of the adjustments in the scale of plant, the tangency between the firm's *LAC* and *AR* curves is the fundamental condition. Now the firm will get normal profits only at the situation where *LAC* = *AR* at that point at which *LMC* = *MR*. Thus the firm's equilibrium output is *OX* at which *SMC* = *LMC* = *MR* and *LAC* = *AR*. Any deviation from *OX* level of output with scale of plant *SAC* will cause losses to be incurred. The industry as a whole will be in equilibrium since the firms are operating at no profit-no loss. In such a situation the number of firms in the industry is fixed because there is no incentive for the firms to enter into or exit from the industry. This is usual position that occurs in the long-period.

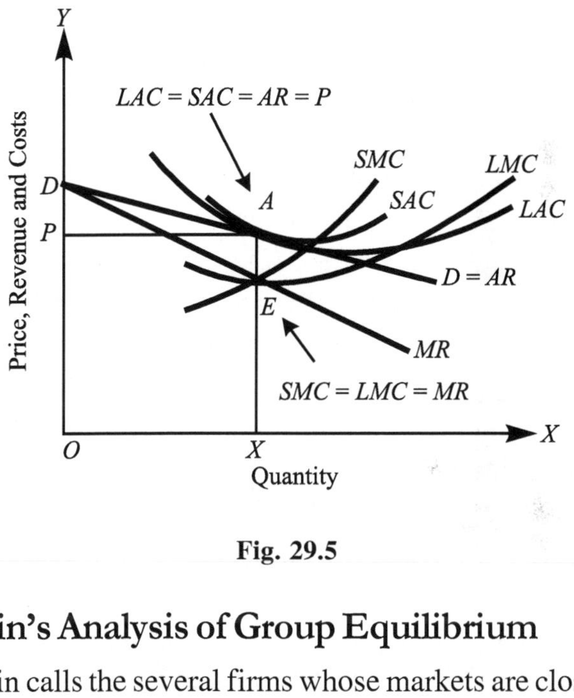

Fig. 29.5

5. Chamberlin's Analysis of Group Equilibrium

Prof. Chamberlin calls the several firms whose markets are closely interwoven as "group." An industry can consist of two or more groups of closely competing firms. Since the firms in a particular group produce goods which possess a greater degree of homogeneity and, therefore, within any group, close competition exists. But competition between the groups is not keen. The Chamberlin's group is vague because it is very difficult to draw sharp lines between groups. Moreover, the firms in a group are producing

4. The demand and marginal revenue curves are shifted downward as compared to the initial situation which has been discussed in Fig. 29.4. Similarly, the *LAC* and *LMC* curves are shifted upward as compared to the initial position of Fig. 29.4. This is all due to the present assumption that entry of new firms into the industry is open.

differentiated products and they will have their different revenue and cost curves. The prices charged by the firms in a group are also different. All this enables us to draw a group revenue curve or a group cost curve under monopolistic competition. While under perfect competition, it is possible to draw the supply curve of the industry and the revenue and cost curves of the individual firms.

Chamberlin tries to overcome these difficulties by making simple assumption with the basic objective of ignoring the diverse conditions surrounding each firm. His assumptions are:

(*i*) All the firms in the group are producing more or less identical product.

(*ii*) All firms have equal share of the market which means that all of them have similar demand curves (similar in elasticity and position).

(*iii*) All firms have equal efficiency in production, and therefore, have similar cost curves.

(*iv*) The number of firms in the group is so large that each firm regards itself independent, i.e. one firm's action regarding price and output will have a negligible effect upon the numerous competitors.

The first three assumptions are known as the "uniformity assumptions" and the last one is known as the "symmetry assumption". Given these assumptions, it is possible to explain group equilibrium in the long-run. Existence of super normal (or abnormal) profits in the short-run and the anticipation of the same in the long-run will attract new firms to enter the industry or induce the existing firms to expand. On the other hand, existence of losses in the short-run and the anticipation of the same in the long-run will induce existing firms to leave the industry.

If the new firms are set up or existing firms expand there will be a tendency for prices to decline and equal the average cost. New firms in the industry will mean large production but will not mean a significant increase in the total sales. The existing market wilI now have to be shared between a large number of sellers. In the long-run there comes a situation when every firm will tend to be a no profit-no loss firm and will reap only normal profit.

Thus, under monopolistic competition, the behaviour of a group must be reflected in the behaviour of one firm. For this, Prof. Chamberlin calls his heroic assumption, namely, that each firm has identical demand and cost curves. If the demand curves are the same, it would mean that the firms in a group have equal shares of the market (of the commodity). If there are 100 firms in a group, then each firm has one per cent of total sales of the group.

Now keeping this assumption in mind, we can illustrate both the individual equilibrium and the group equilibrium with the help of a diagram.

Suppose, in Fig. 29.6, each firm's demand curve is d_1d_2 and the long-run average cost curve is *LAC*. Initially, in the short-period, each firm can make large abnormal profits. In Fig. 29.6, we have not drawn the marginal cost curve and marginal revenue curve and, therefore, we have not shown the

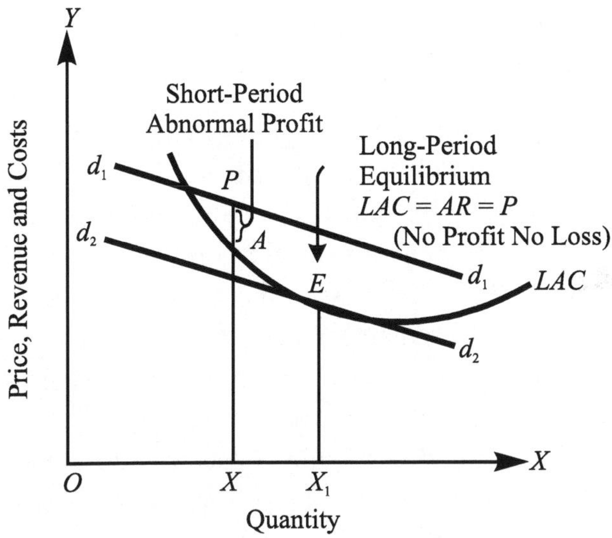

Fig. 29.6

short-period abnormal profits of each firm. It can be easily visualised in the imagination. Since all firms are assumed to be identical and, therefore, the total abnormal profits of the whole group will be high enough. The distance between the demand curve and the average cost curve will show the profits of each firm at some level of output (determined by the rule $MC = MR$). But we are in the long-period in which new firms can enter and put new products on this market. As a result of the entrance of new firms in the group, the demand curve (d_1d_1) of each firm shifts to the left as d_2d_2. The reason is that the new products reduce the sales of the existing firms. Now the firms are forced to reduce their prices in order to check the constant decline in their sales. The process of price-cutting will go on so long as profits of the group (or each firm) are present. The process stops when the demand curve, d_2d_2 slides far enough left to become tangent to the long-period average cost curve *LAC*. Here we must remember that due to the assumption of constant costs,

LAC will remain the same. Now the tangency point *E* will become the long-period equilibrium point of the group. This implies that price (*AR*) equals average cost and there is no profit-no loss in the group. With tangency, the firm can neither raise nor lower its price without suffering losses. This is the point where the number of firms in the group is fixed, that is, no firm has the incentive to enter the group or to exit from the group. Hence the group is in equilibrium.

6. Selling Costs and Their Implications on Equilibrium under Monopolistic Competition

Unlike a perfect competitive firm or a monopoly, a monopolistically competitive firm has to incur certain costs on advertisement or publicity. In perfect competition, all products in the industry are homogeneous and, therefore, the price is the same. In monopoly, no substitution is generally possible for the monopolist's product. For this reason, the firm in perfect competition or monopoly need not advertise the attributes or special features of its product. But in the case of monopolistic competition, each firm sells a differentiated product and for this reason, advertisement or selling costs would be crucial. According to Prof. Chamberlin, "Selling costs are those costs which are to be incurred in order to alter the position or shape of the demand curve for a product." Therefore, the expenditures on advertising do increase the demand for a product, all other things price, quality, incomes of the consumers, etc. being equal.

According to Prof. Baumol, the decision as to how far to carry advertising cost will depend upon the firm's objective whether it wants to maximise its sales or to maximise its profits. He says that total revenue increases with increasing advertising expenditures, but it will not always be the case. After a point diminishing returns will take place. Thus, the level of advertising outlay at which the differences between total revenue and total costs is maximum must be incurred for profit maximisation.

Prof. Buchanan, on the other hand, is of the opinion that advertising cost is a fixed cost and, therefore, it has no relationship with the volume of output. The average selling cost or advertising cost will decline as output increases. According to him, net returns to advertising expenditures depict the difference between the increased total revenue emanating from selling costs and the increased total costs (costs of production plus costs of advertising).

The task now is to set up a relationship between the advertising expenditures of a firm and the unit sales of its product. The relationship can

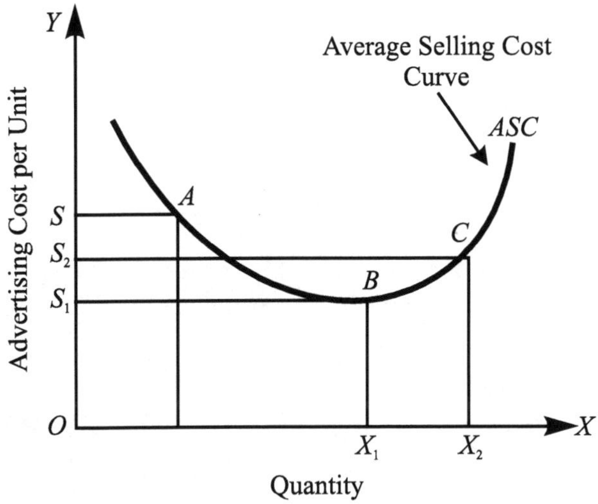

Fig. 29.7

be shown by the selling cost curve. This is another contribution of Chamberlin to economic theory. Figure 29.7 presents the average selling cost curve, *ASC*. This is a *U*-shaped cost curve. It shows that as output increases, selling costs per unit will decrease, but after a certain point an increase in output will lead to an increase in selling costs per unit of output. At *OX* level of output, the advertising cost per unit is *OS*. The minimum advertising cost is OS_1, when the firm sells OX_1 quantity of output. If the firm wants to sell more than OX_1 quantity of its product, then the per unit cost of advertising will increase. For instance, at OX_2 units of sales, the per unit cost of advertising is OS_2. Thus, the curve *ASC* first declines, because of initial economies of scale in advertising; advertising expenses that are too small are said to be wasteful. After reaching a minimum level, the curve rises indicating the diseconomies of scale in advertising. In all likelihood, the curve *ASC* finally becomes vertical when the sales have reached the "saturation point". The vertical part of the curve will indicate that any further increase in advertisement expenditure will make no increase in the sales of the firm. Selling costs or advertising expenditures may be very high or very low. No generalisation is possible. The shape and position of the selling cost curve will depend upon a number of factors, such as, the price of the product, availability of substitutes and the degree of substitution, the quality of the product and the qualities of its substitutes, the incomes of the consumers and their tastes, etc. A change in any of these factors will vary the shape and the position of the curve.

Now the question is how much should a firm spend on advertising? The profit-maximising firm spends an amount on advertisement such that the combined marginal cost of production and of advertising is equal to the price (or average revenue) the firm gets for its product. The last unit sold is just

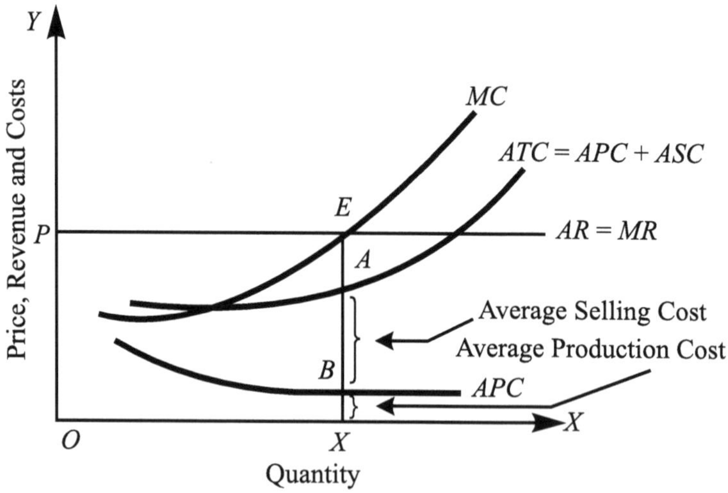

Fig. 29.8

worth the cost of producing and selling it. Figure 29.8 explains this situation. The price of the product is *OP*. The horizontal line from *P* can be viewed as if it were a marginal revenue curve because by advertising, the firm can sell more without having to lower its price. In Fig. 29.8, the average production cost is *APC*. The average total cost is the summation of the average production cost and average selling cost which is shown by *APC* + *ASC*. The *MC* curve gives the marginal cost associated with the average total cost. The equilibrium or optimum level of output sold is *OX*, because at this level of output *MC* = *D* = *MR*. At *OX* output, the firm's advertising expenditure, *AB*, per unit is optimum because here profits are maximised. Any level advertising expenditure than this will reduce the profits of the firm.

7. Waste of Monopolistic Competition (Problem of Resource Allocation under Monopolistic Competition)

As we know, under perfect competition and monopoly, there is no need of advertisement by the individual firms and as such there will be no waste in the economy. Under monopolistic competition, the firm in the market has to incur a lot of expenditure to increase its sales. This expenditure is a waste of the economy because it adds nothing to the total output of the economy. When there are profits in the industry, this waste further increases. New firms enter into the industry and increase the supply of the industry. Since the total demand of the industry more or less remains the same, the surplus production becomes a waste of the economy. Again, the waste will be more when the consumer's preferences are changed.

Prof. Rothschild has pointed out five kinds of wastes of monopolistic competition. These are: (1) Unemployment, (2) Excess Capacity, (3) Cross Transport, (4) Failure to Specialise, and (5) Competitive Advertising.

1. *Unemployment.* There are certain types of unemployment which will be found under all conditions. In imperfect competitive situation, the problem of un employment is aggravated by various reasons. For one thing, part of the productive capacity may remain unused. Cyclical unemployment may be intensified through price maintenance in place of production maintenance. Finally, monopolistic factors may increase the share of profits in national income which will reduce property to consume without creating a comparable increase in the desire to invest.

2. *Excess Capacity.* Under monopolistic competition, firms will not produce optimum output at the lowest average cost point. Since competition is not perfect, the demand curve for a firm is not perfectly elastic and, therefore, is not equal to the lowest average cost point. This is the well known fact of excess capacity or unused capacity with its corollary of non-minimum production costs and price above marginal cost. Excess capacity is regarded as a waste of monopolistic competition.

3. *Cross Transport.* The waste of cross transport arises when under monopolistic and oligopoly situations, markets are not clearly divided between different producers in different regions. Cloth produced in Kanpur may be sold in Delhi, and cloth produced in Delhi may be sold in Kanpur. The cost of cloth to the consumer is necessarily increased to include transport charges. If the market for cloth is conveniently divided so that the southern market is served by Louisiana mills and Michigan market and northern regions are served by Michigan mills, transport costs can be reduced. The wasteful use of transport facilities is the direct result of product differentiation and as such is similar in nature to the problem of excess capacity.

4. *Failure to Specialise.* Another disadvantage of monopolistic competition is the sufficient specialisation. The cost advantages arising out of specialisation cannot be escaped under monopolistic competition because the sales of the firm cannot be expanded without reducing the prices. To some extent, the failure to specialise and the costly maintenance of several lines of production is also owing to a desire to reduce the risks which are involved in too great a dependence on the demand for one a few products. In such a case, this waste is due to the uncertainty of competition.

5. *Advertising.* The waste of advertising is the outcome of the absence of perfect competitive conditions. Marshall in his book, *Industry and Trade* distinguished between constructive and comparative advertisements. Constructive advertisement is to spread information of a product and this is

compatible with pure competition where knowledge of the product is not perfect. It may be remembered that perfect competitive system with perfect knowledge is an impossibility and therefore, this type of advertisement cannot be regarded as a waste. But the bulk of the advertisement is of the combative type, connected with the boosting up of differentiated products. Such advertisement is clearly wasteful for it leads to unnecessary competition among rivals and high cost to the consumers. Some may argue that advertisements increase consumer's satisfactions by adding to the prestige, the glamour and the desirability of the advertised goods to the buyers. But against this argument, Rothschild states that the dissatisfaction created by advertisements in people who cannot buy the advertised goods may amount to much more this is psychological waste arising out of advertising.

Thus, imperfect or monopolistic competition involves many inherent defects or wastes. These defects are mainly due to the preferences of consumers for different varieties; or there are imaginary differences which have been increased by competitive advertisement. It is the interest of the community, if there is a reduction in the number of varieties of a product, reduction in the number of firms, elimination of cross transport and advertisement expenditures.

Figure 29.9 illustrates the waste of the economy under monopolistic competition. Here the demand for the firm's product is d_1d_1. Assume that the consumers have perfect information about the product, i.e. about the quality and about the prices and qualities of all other available substitutes. The long-period equilibrium of the firm will be established at point E where the

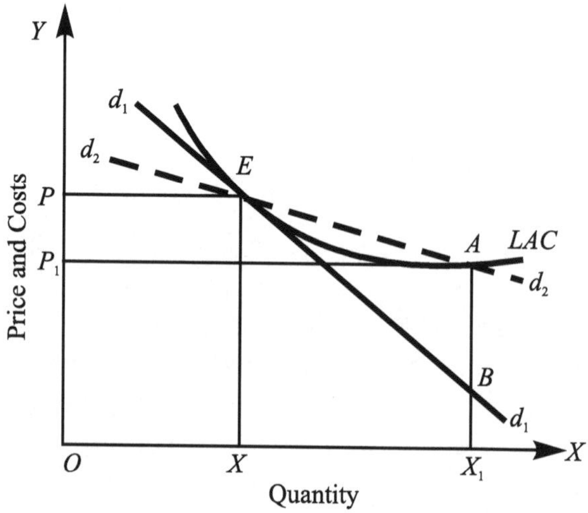

Fig. 29.9

long-period average cost curve touches the demand curve d_1d_1. At this tangency point it is implied that $MR = MC$ (which are not shown in the diagram). At this equilibrium point *E*, the consumers buy *OX* quantity at *OP* price. The most efficient output level to be produced by the firm is OX_1 where the average total cost of production is minimum, i.e. AX_1 per unit. At OX_1 output, the minimum long-period price acceptable by the firm must be equal to the average cost. This means that the firm will produce the most efficient level of output OX_1 only if the price is OP_1. But the consumers' demand curve for the product (d_1d_1) shows that they are unwilling to pay X_1B price for OX_1 quantity. They are ready to pay only BX_1 price for OX_1 quantity. At this low price the firm will not like to produce any amount of the product because it has to incur a great loss. The consumers would prefer to pay a higher price for a smaller quantity. If their demand curve were d_2d_2, which it is not, the consumers would be indifferent between the two choices; that is, they would be ready to purchase *OX* quantity at *OP* price or OX_1 quantity at OP_1 price. Since the actual demand curve faced by the firm is not d_2d_2 but d_1d_1, the firm will never produce the most efficient output OX_1 but accept to produce *OX* output where he gets only the long-period normal profits. Therefore, it is the net loss of efficiency of the firm as well as of the economy. It is also known as the excess capacity of the firm under monopolistic competition. It is the excess of what a firm can produce with its given plant size over what it actually produces in order to maximise its profit.

In perfect competition, all the firms in the industry produce at optimum level, i.e. at that level where the long-period average cost is minimum. But it is possible only when the demand curve for the product is horizontal. When the demand curve is negatively sloped, as in the case of monopolistic competition and monopoly, demand curve cannot be tangent to *LAC* curve, and the profit maximising level of output is, therefore, less than optimum in the long-run.

This situation of excess capacity or unused capacity leads to unemployment in the economy. Further, the over-abundant multiplication of small firms, each producing a differentiated product, leads to a faulty distribution of factors of production. Monopoly or oligopoly (where the industry consists of a few firms) may probably lead to a better resource-use than monopolistic competition.

In spite of the above wastes or disadvantages of monopolistic competition, it possesses some ethical values also. It provides consumers a wide range of types, styles and brands of particular products. It provides the opportunity to choose a product which the consumer likes most. According to Prof. Chamberlin, although a firm fails to produce the "sort of ideal" level of output, firms may tacitly agree to avoid any type of price competition. Moreover, the theory of monopolistic competition presents the actual situation of the market. The economists and the policy makers should try to remove the shortcomings of this realistic situation.

Exercises

1. Define monopolistic competition. Why does it tend to be a multi-price market form? Examine the performance of a monopolistically competitive industry from the point of view of economic efficiency.
2. What are the main characteristics of monopolistic competition. Explain the equilibrium of the firm in the short and long-run under monopolistic competition.
3. Explain the differences between perfect competition, monopolistic competition and monopoly. Show with the help of a diagram, how price is determined under monopolistic competition.
4. Explain the concept of group equilibrium under monopolistic competition.
5. What are the selling costs? Explain the equilibrium of monopolistic competitive firm under selling costs.
6. State and show in diagrams the conditions of equilibrium of the firm and the industry under perfect competition and monopolistic competition (with open entry). Bring out the main differences between these two equilibrium positions.
7. What do you understand by product variation? How does a firm reach equilibrium with product variation?
8. Is it true that under monopolistic competition firms possess much "excess capacity" and yet remain "undersized"?

Multiple Choice Questions

9. (*i*) A monopolistically competitive market is distinguished from a perfectly competitive market by the fact that
   (*a*) it contains few buyers
   (*b*) it contains few sellers
   (*c*) it deals in a differentiated products
   (*d*) all of the above [*Ans.* (*c*)]

   (*ii*) Under imperfect competition degree of monopoly power depends upon difference between
   (*a*) *MR* and *MC* (*c*) *AC* and *MC*
   (*b*) *MR* and *AC* (*d*) none of the above [*Ans.* (*d*)]

   (*iii*) When entry into the industry is open (the usual case) and the industry is in long-run equilibrium, the monopolistic competition will produce at the lowest point on its *LAC* curve
   (*a*) always (*b*) never
   (*c*) sometimes (*d*) can not say [*Ans.* (*b*)]

Chapter 30

Oligopoly

1. Introduction

The term "Oligopoly" is developed from two Greek words, "Oligoi" meaning a few and "pollein" meaning to sell. Oligopoly refers to that market situation in which there are a few enough sellers of a particular product (or differentiated products) for the activities of one to be of importance to the others. Oligopoly differs from monopoly where there is only one seller, and from perfect and monopolistic competition where there are many sellers. In oligopoly, a single seller occupies a position of sufficient importance in the commodity market for changes in his market activities to have repercussions on the others. Other sellers react to the market activities of the one and their reactions in turns have repercussions on him. The individual seller is aware of this and in changing his price, output, sales promotional activity or quality of his product, he must take into account the reactions of others. Hence, the oligopoly situation has one important feature which distinguishes it from other forms of market situations. This is the interdependence in the decision making of the various firms, an interdependence which is recognised by all of them. Every seller in such a situation knows that at least some of his rivals' decisions depend on his own behaviour, and he must take this fact into account in his own decision making.

The reason is that changes in the output and price of one firm will affect the amounts which other firms can sell and the prices which they can charge. Hence other firms will react in one way or another to price output changes on the part of one. Individual firms are, therefore, not independent as they are under perfect competition or under monopoly.

This feature has made the formulation of a systematic analysis of oligopoly very difficult. The analysis of pricing and output under oligopoly lacks the neatness and precision of the theory of perfect competition and the theory of monopoly. This is partly because of oligopolistic uncertainty (in many cases an oligopolistic cannot be sure what his rivals' reaction will be to various kinds of activities on his part) and partly because oligopoly covers such a wide range of cases, each with its own unique characteristics. This is why we cannot find a general theory of oligopoly. As a result, the literature of oligopoly is full of different models.

Before we define different models of oligopoly, let us clear one more point. An oligopoly situation invites collusion among the firms in an industry because of three reasons: (*i*) by reducing the degree of competition the collusion may enable the firms to act monopolistically and thereby increase their profits; (*ii*) a collusion may reduce oligopolistic uncertainty; and (*iii*) a collusion may restrict the new firms from entering into the industry. Once a collusion is made, only a high profit incentive may initiate a firm to leave the collusion and to act independently.

2. Collusion and Blocked Entry

The kind of pricing that is likely to develop in the conditions of oligopoly depends mainly on the degree of collusion among the several firms and the extent to which free entry is possible into the industry concerned. Collusion is more likely to prevail if the number of firms is few than if there are many, and it is most effective if it can be put in the form of a formal agreement. However, where (as in the case of United States) the antitrust laws make any combination or agreement in restraint of trade illegal, formal agreements may be replaced by some kind of tacit understanding. A spirit of 'live and let live' among the rival firms may come to prevail, because each knows that he has most to gain by refraining from active competition, especially price-cutting. Each is conscious of the price policies pursued by the others, and fears retaliation on their part if he becomes too aggressive. Or, tacit understanding can be fostered by occasional informal meetings, trade conferences, and like. But collusion of this kind is naturally precarious, and this gives an element of instability to oligopoly pricing. The greater the number of firms in the industry, the more likely is the competition to prevail; because it is difficult to make the contacts for concerted policy among a great many concerns (firms), and where each one is small in relation to the total output of the industry, a firm is less conscious of the effects of its policies on the market (industry) as a whole.

Furthermore, collusion requires some kind of a pooling arrangement for giving each party a satisfactory share of the market. This must take into consideration the capacity of each plant, its costs, geographical location, the quality and variety of its products, etc. All this is more difficult to work out if there are many firms. Even where cartels[1] are legal (as in Europe), these

1. A cartel is a combination of firms in an industry where competition is restrained by an agreement among them concerning prices, the share of the market to be allotted to each, the interchange of patent rights, or the other matters of similar kind.

factors have made them rather easily broken up. The presence of numerous firms, however, need not be an insuperable bar to collusion if, one of them is so much larger than the rest that it can assume a position of price leadership.[2]

How effectively oligopolies can exploit their position will depend also on the difficulty or ease with which new firms can come into the industry or market. If entry is easy, high prices will soon attract competitors, and they will force the price down. This may deter the present oligopolists from pursuing too greedy a policy, and induce them to keep their prices moderate. But, if entry into the industry or market is difficult, the position of the oligopolists is more secure, and hence they are likely to set their prices higher. Entry may be difficult if the industry is a manufacturing one in which the economies of large scale production are great. Here large firms already established may be able to produce so much more cheaply than new firms, that no newcomer can hope to compete successfully. Again, when the oligopoly industry is based on some natural resources found in only a few areas, other new firms cannot enter the industry. Further, patents are often a means of blocking entry into an industry. These are the basis of oligopolistic situations in the manufacture of electric pumps, cameras, radios, pastes and many other products.

Thus, the effectiveness of oligopoly depends upon the degree of collusion among the firms and the power to restrict new firms to enter into the industry.

3. Classification of Oligopoly

Oligopoly situation can be classified on different bases:

(1) *Basis of Product Differentiation.* On the basis of product differentiation, oligopoly may be classified as Pure or Perfect Oligopoly and Imperfect or Differentiated Oligopoly. In the case of pure oligopoly, the product of different firms in the industry is identical or homogeneous while in the case of differentiated oligopoly, the products of different firms are not identical but rather differentiated products. Thus, differentiated oligopoly will exist where the competing firms produce products which are close substitutes but not perfect substitutes.

The distinction between pure oligopoly and differentiated oligopoly does not play a significant role in the analysis. In real situation, firms in most oligopolistic industries produce differentiated products. But theoretically we may determine price and output in both kinds of oligopoly.

(2) *Basis of Entry of Firms.* On the basis of the possibility of entry of new firms into the industry, oligopoly may be classified as Open Oligopoly

2. In the case of price leadership, the leader sets a price high enough to assure a reasonable profit for all, and the small firms (or followers) accept the price without attempting to alter it.

and Closed Oligopoly. An open oligopoly provides full freedom to new firms to enter into the industry. In the situation of open oligopoly there is no restriction of any kind for the desiring firms to enter into the market. A closed oligopoly, on the other hand, refers to that market situation where only the few firms control the entire market and new firms are not allowed to enter the industry.

(3) *Basis of Price Leadership.* On the basis of presence or absence of price leadership, oligopoly may be classified as Partial Oligopoly and Full Oligopoly. Partial oligopoly refers to that market situation where the industry is dominated by one large firm (known as the leader) and the other firms (known as the followers) of the industry follow the price policy determined by their leader. Full oligopoly, on the other hand, refers to that market situation where there is no leader and no followers.

(4) *Basis of Agreement.* On the basis of agreement, oligopoly is classified as Collusive Oligopoly and Non-collusive Oligopoly. A collusive oligopoly refers to that market situation where the firms of the industry follow a common policy of pricing. In other words, they combine together to avoid competition among themselves regarding the price and output of the industry. A non-collusive oligopoly refers to that market situation where there is no agreement among the firms regarding the price and output of the entire market. In other words, the firms under non-collusive oligopoly act independently.

4. Characteristics of Oligopoly

In order to distinguish oligopoly from other market situations, such as, perfect competition, monopoly and monopolistic competition, etc. it is necessary to understand the characteristics or assumptions or features of oligopoly situation. The main characteristics of oligopoly are the following:

(1) *Very Few Sellers of the Product.* The important feature of oligopoly situation is that the number of sellers dealing in a homogeneous or differentiated product is very small. It means that the pricing and output policy of an individual seller in the market can influence the industry price and output. Each firm controls a large share of the markets and therefore, it is able to make a noticeable effect on the market activities by changing his output.

(2) *Interdependence.* Under perfect competition, no individual can influence the market demand, supply and price. The firms are simply price-takers in perfect competition and they take their output decisions independently. No firm is worried about the actions or reactions of the other firms in the perfect competitive industry. Similar is the case under monopoly. The monopoly firm takes its decision independently. Although, the monopolist has to see the market elasticity of demand for his product while determining the price of the product,

yet he does not bother about the pricing decisions of other firms.

It is only under oligopoly, that a firm has to take into consideration the actions and reactions of other firms while determining its price and the level of output. As we have already mentioned, there are only a few firms in oligopoly market, each producing a homogeneous or a slightly differentiated product (close substitute). Since a firm controls a large share of the market, it is able to make a significant influence on the price and output of the oligopoly market. Thus, the firms in oligopoly are independent and each has to take into account the actions and reactions of the others. The cross-elasticity of demand for their products is very high because of the availability of close substitutes. This is the reason that no firm would normally like to change its existing price. Only in some abnormal cases they may dare to take independent decisions.

(3) *Presence of Monopoly Power.* As we have said that the number of firms in oligopoly market is very small and, therefore, collusion among them is possible. Under collusion, the firms act as monopoly and they may charge higher prices for their products. Also, different firms sell differentiated products and to that extent each may charge a high price. The element of monopoly becomes still more conspicuous when the consumers become habitual of consuming particular products.

(4) *Existence of Price Rigidity.* In oligopoly situation, each firm has to stick to its price. If any firm tries to reduce its price, the rival firms will retaliate by a higher reduction in their prices. This will lead to a situation of price war which benefits none. On the other hand, if any firm increase, its price with a view to increase its profits, the other rival firms will not follow the same. Hence, no firm would like to reduce the price or to increase the price. The price rigidity will take place.

(5) *Excessive Expenditure on Advertisement.* As we have seen that the firms under oligopoly produce close substitutes and they are interdependent. Each firm has to stick to its prevailing, price. Now the only way to increase the sales is the advertisement and the improvement (or variation) in the design and quality of the product. Each firm spends a lot on advertisement. It plays an important role in determining the demand function of the firm's product.

Thus, thc primary purpose of advertising is to shift to the right the demand curve faced by the firm, and also to make it less elastic. This will enable the firm to sell a larger volume of output at the same price or probably at higher price without the risk of price-war. Each firm tries to encroach upon the markets of others through advertising instead of through price-cutting.

Under oligopoly, the products of various firms can be differentiated effectively only by advertising. Each firm tries to attract consumers to its particular brand name by advertising; although basically the product of each firm may be the same as that of other firms in the industry. Variations in quality and design of particular products are usually used along with advertising to differentiate the product of one firm from another.

The object of quality variation is the same as that of advertising. The primary object is to shift the demand curve to the right and to make it less elastic. In addition to it, quality variation may also be used to extend the market vertically different qualities to appeal to different classes of the consumers. In both, advertising and quality variation, retaliation by the rivals will take place. Individual firms may succeed in increasing their market shares temporarily, but if a permanent increase is to be obtained, such firms must be able to keep ahead of their rival firms.

5. Cost Curves and Demand (Revenue) Curves of the Oligopolistic Firm

Here we assume that the oligopolistic firm buys its resources from a perfect competitive factor market and, therefore, its cost curves are like those of the purely competitive firm or those of the pure monopolist.

It is the demand side that distinguishes oligopoly from other market situations. Mutual interdependence of firms creates an atmosphere of uncertainty for all the firms under oligopoly market. It is very difficult for a firm to visualise its price-output policy with any degree of certainty. What one firm is able to do in attempting to make its profits as large as possible is conditioned by the ways in which other firms react to the market activities of the one. The extent of oligopolistic uncertainty is highly variable from case to case. As such, the demand or average revenue curve of the oligopolistic firm cannot be definite or determinate, because the firm in question cannot correctly estimate the reactions of its rivals to its price-output policy.

We have, therefore, two observations to make regarding the shape of the demand curve of an oligopoly firm: (*i*) The demand curve can be definite, certain and determinate only if the reactions of the rivals are predictable or known, and (*ii*) The oligopolistic firm has only a series of conjectures regarding the probable reactions of its rivals.

The 'kinked' demand curve does provide a simple way of conceiving an average revenue curve for the oligopolistic firm which helps us to understand oligopoly pricing problems. It explains the oligopolistic price regidity. The case of kinked demand curve occurs only if certain assumptions are fulfilled. Figure 30.1 assumes that there is a small group of firms, each producing the same product. It also assumes that a price *OP* has been accepted by all the firms in the industry. At this price *OP*, our particular firm sells *OX* quantity of its product; other firms may sell more or less than *OX*, depending on the relative popularity of their particular products and the extent to which they

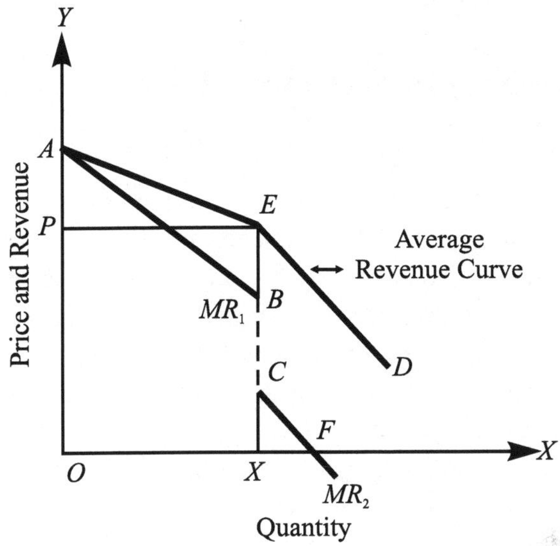

Fig. 30.1

are being advertised. In Fig. 30.1, the demand curve *AED* (which is also the average revenue curve of the firm) has a kink at point *E*. It divides the demand curve into two parts *AE* and *ED* respectively. *AE* part of the demand curve is more elastic while *ED* part of the demand curve is less elastic. The reason of the kink at point *E* is as follows. We assume that if this particular firm raises its price, none of its rivals follow, because they feel that a higher price would lead to lower sales. Since price-increase is not followed by the rivals, a small increase in the price of this particular firm's product will lead to a very large fall in its sales; demand is very elastic if one firm alone increases its price. On the other hand, if this particular firm cuts its price, its rivals will react and cut their prices to exactly the same extent. Although a general price-cut will be unprofitable to all, yet it takes place to maintain the old market share of each firm. Consequently, the kinked point *E,* the average revenue curve slopes downwards very steeply. Since all firms are assumed to be charging the same price, anyone of them gains extra sales only to the extent that the sales of the whole oligopoly group can be expanded through the general price-cut. Therefore, the demand curve of the oligopoly firm can be drawn only under certain assumptions such that a single price or a cluster of prices has been established in the industry and a price-increase by one firm is not followed by its rivals while a price-decrease by one firm is followed by its rivals. In Fig. 30.1 the demand curve faced by the firm for price increases is *AE* and at each possible price it will have a considerably greater elasticity than the market demand curve. Also, for price decreases, the demand curve faced by the firm is *ED* and it will have about the same elasticity at different prices as the market demand curve.

The kinked demand curve *AED* has important implications for the marginal revenue curve of the oligopolistic firm. The marginal revenue curve is discontinuous at *OX* output, that is, it has a gap which is shown by the dashed line *BC* in Fig. 30.1. It (gap) comes from the abrupt change from the more elastic to the less elastic parts of the demand curve.

We can draw such a marginal revenue curve by assuming two separate demand curves and their respective marginal revenue curves. In Fig. 30.2, this case has been illustrated. The *AE* portion of the demand curve and its dashed extension gives one demand curve while the *ED* portion and the demand curve and its dashed extension upto the price axis gives another demand curve. Now we draw the appropriate marginal revenue curve MR_1 and MR_2 for the respective smooth demand curves AR_1 and AR_2. Since the dashed parts of the distinct demand curves do not exist, their respective portions of the marginal revenue curves will become irrelevant for our purposes. In other words, *AB* portion of *MR.* and *CF* portion of MR_2 will be relevant for

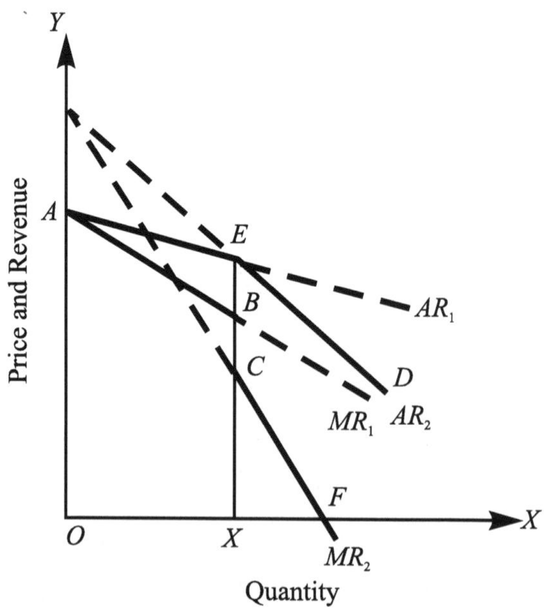

Fig. 30.2

the given portions of the firm's demand curve. The same conclusion can be drawn in terms of elasticity of demand. If the demand curve were a continuous curve, elasticity would be changing continuously as we move from higher to lower prices. Since $MR = (1\text{-}l/e)$, the marginal revenue curve would also be continuous as we move down the demand curve. However, at point E the demand curve breaks. Elasticity at an output infinitesimally below OX is substantially greater than elasticity at an output infinitesimally above OX. Thus, marginal revenue must drop sharply at output OX. Hence, it is proved that in the case of a kinked demand curve or average revenue curve, the marginal revenue curve will have a gap in it at the kinked point of the demand curve.

6. Price and Output Determination under Oligopoly

As we have mentioned above, the interdependence of the demand curves of the firms in oligopoly poses serious difficulties in establishing a theory of the determination of prices and outputs. No firm, under such conditions, is sure of the price and output combination which would maximise its profits or revenues (sales). According to William J. Baumol there are three possible approaches to the oligopoly problem.[3] A firm may adopt anyone of the following alternative approaches:

(1) *Ignoring Interdependence.* The very simple approach is to ignore the interdependence and take independent decision. The firm may follow its own independent line of action, on the assumption that its competitors will also do in their own interests. In such a situation the entire theory becomes the simple theory of monopoly where firm attempts to maximise its profits in the conventional manner, i.e. it produces that level of output at which its $MR = Me$.

(2) *Estimating the Competitors' Countermoves.* The second approach is that the oligopoly firm attempts to estimate or anticipate the nature of competitive reactions on the basis of past experience. For example, the firm estimates that his competitors will follow (or react) its price changes within a few days, so that, the firm will adopt such a strategy which is optimal in terms of this assumption.

(3) *Preparing against Optimal Moves by the Competitors.* Unlike the second approach, the firm in this case does not guess at its competitors' reactions, but it calculates the optimal moves of its opposition (his competitors' best possible strategies) and prepares its own defences and counter-moves accordingly. Therefore, the approach is associated with the theory of games.

Now we shall discuss the determination of price and output under oligopoly situation in the following manner Equilibrium under Independent Action, and Equilibrium under Collusion.

3. William J. Baumol, *Economic Theory and Operations Analysis,* Third Edition, pp. 353-54.

7. Equilibrium under Independent Action (The Sweezy Model of Kinked Demand Curve)

Cases of independent action are just what the name implies. Here we assume a single firm, operating without overt collusion, but aware of the fact that what it does will be closely watched by the other oligopolists in the industry, and will very likely be met by some competitive retaliation on their part. Thus, independent action often touches off price wars when the reactions of rivals to actions of one are retaliatory in nature.

Under independent action an oligopoly firm faces a kinked demand curve. Therefore, the solution of oligopoly problem under independent action is also known as the Kinked Demand Curve Solution. The kinked demand curve was first used by Prof. Paul M. Sweezy to explain price rigidity under oligopoly. The kinked demand curve represents the behaviour of an oligopoly firm which has no incentive either to increase or to decrease its price. Each firm in the oligopoly industry has learned by experience what the reactions of rivals will be to actions on her part and may voluntarily avoid any activity that will lead to the situation of price war. It is also possible that each firm is reasonably well satisfied with present prices, outputs and profits and is content to let things continue as they are, rather than chance starting a chain reaction. Hence, firms usually do not change their price-quantity combinations in response to small shifts in their cost curves.

The most significant aspect of Sweezy Solution is the existence of a 'kink' in the demand curve of an oligopoly firm. At this kink, the firms sticks to its price. It does not raise it for the fear of being disobeyed by its rivals. On the other hand, it does not cut its price as all the rivals will follow. Therefore, there is a rigidity in price at the kink point of the demand curve, and under normal conditions, the firm will not move in either direction from this point. Sweezy argued that at this kinked point we have finite discontinuity in the *MR-curve* of the firm. It is because of the fact that price is rigidly fixed at this point.

This case has been illustrated in Fig. 30.3. The price prevailing for the moment is assumed to be *OP*, and sales for this oligopoly firm are *OX*. This price may be the aftermath of prior competition, in which the firms have come to a common price.

Now if the firm raises its price and its competitors do not, many of its customers will shift their patronage to others, so that its sales will decline sharply. This gives the demand curve for this firm a nearly horizontal slope (such as *AE* portion of demand curve) for prices higher than *OP*. If the product of this firm is identical with that of its rivals, the curve will actually be horizontal, and it will make no sales at all at higher prices; but if it has a differential advantage (however slight) in the eyes of at least some of its consumers, the curve will be as shown (highly elastic demand curve). Under these circumstances, so long as the prevailing price is yielding a reasonable profit, there is little or nothing to be gained by raising it.

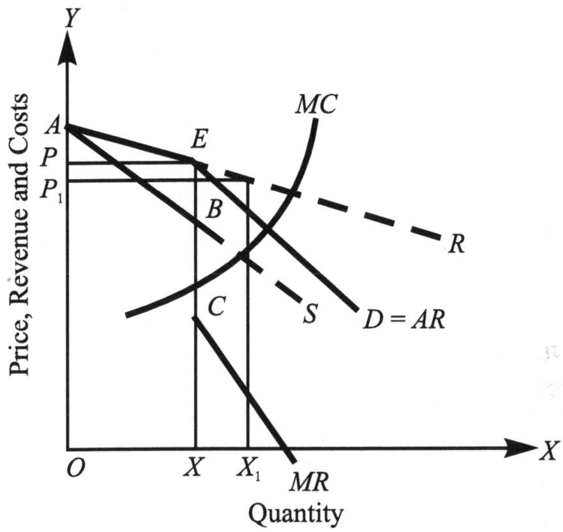

Fig. 30.3

Now suppose this oligopoly firm reduces its price with a view that it will be able to increase its sales at the expense of its competitors. If this firm could be sure that its rivals would not follow the price cut, it could assume that its demand curve would continue along the slope *AE* to *R*, and the marginal revenue curve would extend on from *AB* and *S*. With marginal costs or *MC*, the most profitable output would then be OX_1 where its marginal cost (*MC*) is equal to its marginal revenue (*MR*). The firm could reach this optimum output (OX_1) and maximise its profits by cutting the price to OP_1. But in fact, if this firm cuts its price from *OP* to OP_1, it is probable that its rivals would cut their prices too, and some of them might cut below OP_1. This would cause some consumers to shift to the other firms, so that the demand curve would dip downward at *E* to *D*, instead of going out along *ER*. Thus, the demand curve of the firm under individual action will be a kinked demand curve and the resulting marginal revenue curve will have a gap at the kink point.

This type of situation tends to give oligopoly prices a sort of rigidity or stability. It means that each oligopolist in the market hesitates to disturb the existing price even if his cost curves shift upward or downward. But the price-rigidity takes place only within the limits determined by the gap of marginal revenue curve. That is, the firm would not like to change the price so long as the cost curves shift between the discontinuous part of the marginal revenue curve. In a situation when the cost curves shift beyond this limit, the firm has the incentive to change the price accordingly. But it happens only when all the firms of the oligopoly industry realise the same situation. For instance, if costs have been rising and profits declining for all the firms, a boost in the price may be indicated, yet each one fears to quote a higher price. Now if one has the courage to do so, all the rest will follow suit, and each will occupy the same relative position with respect to the others as before. On the other hand, if costs are falling and profits are so high that there is the danger of entering new firms into the industry, a price-cut by one firm may merely be the signal for others to cut their prices to the same level. A new position of stability will then be reached without a price war, with the relative positions of the oligopoly firms remaining the same.

8. Equilibrium under Collusion

Most of the modern economists are of the opinion that independent price determination cannot exist for long in oligopoly. It leads to a sense of antagonism, uncertainty and insecurity and to overcome them there is a tendency among oligopolists to act collectively by tacit collusion. In addition, the firms can gain the economies of production. All the firms in oligopoly tend to enlarge their size and lower their costs of production per unit and capture as large a share of the market as possible.

Literally, collusion means the "act of playing together". In common parlance, collusion is used with the idea of deceit or fraud or trickery. But in economics, collusion means the act of agreeing on a common live-and-let-live policy by legally independent and potentially competitive firms or organised groups of resource owners or a combination of firms and resource owners. The collusion may be legal or illegal, depending upon the laws of the country concerned. In this section we shall deal with the collusion among the oligopolistic firms. We can distinguish among cases of perfect collusion and cases of imperfect collusion.

Perfect Collusion in Oligopoly

Cases of perfect collusion consist primarily of cartel arrangements. A cartel is an explicit agreement, usually formal, among independent firms on prices, output, and often on other matters such as division of sales territories. In other words, a cartel is a formal organisation of the firms within a given industry. Cartels are often short-lived. Firms do have the desire for large joint profits; this desire gives the impulse to form cartels. Firms are likely, however, to quarrel over the division of joint profits; this propensity is the leading cause of the break-up of cartel arrangements. Here we shall discuss oligopoly pricing under two types of cartel arrangements: (1) Pricing under the centralised cartel, and (2) Pricing under the market-sharing cartel.

In the centralised cartel, we shall assume that decision making with regard to pricing, output, sales and distribution of profits is possessed by the central association. The market sharing cartel, on the other hand, is a somewhat lower form of organisation. Here, we assume that firms forming the cartel agree on market shares with or without an understanding regarding prices. Under the market-sharing cartel, member firms perform their own marketing activities, but they are careful to observe the cartel agreement made by them.

(1) *Pricing under the Centralised Cartel* (*Joint Profit Maximisation Perfect Cartel*). A centralised cartel or a perfect cartel is an agreement among the firms in an industry that results in the maximisation of the joint profits of the member firms.[4] Thus, the cartel can act as a single monopolist. It is assumed that the constituent firms of the cartel produce a homogeneous product. The market demand for the product now becomes the cartel's demand. It is assumed that the board of control, established by the cartel, has full knowledge of the demand for the product of the industry at each possible price. Therefore, the board of control can calculate marginal revenue for the industry. The board of control also knows the marginal costs of all of the firms and can easily find out the marginal cost of each volume of output of the industry.[5]

For simplicity we assume that the demand curve or average revenue curve of the cartel is linear and, consequently, the marginal revenue curve

---

4. Mathematically, let us assume that there are only two firms in the cartel. Thus, we have

$R = R\ (q_1 + q_2)$ = total revenue of the cartel

where q_1 and q_2 are the outputs of firm *I* and firm *II* respectively. Also,

$C_1 = C_1\ (q_1)$ = total cost for firm *I*

$C_2 = C_2\ (q_2)$ = total cost for firm *II*

Then, the total profits of the cartel would be

$$\pi = R - (C_1 + C_2)$$
$$= R\ (q_1 + q_2) - C_1\ (q_1) - C_2\ (q_2)$$

To maximise joint profits, we require:

$$\frac{\partial \pi}{\partial q_1} = 0 = R'(q_1 + q_2) - C'_1\ (q_1)$$

and $$\frac{\partial \pi}{\partial q_2} = 0 = R'(q_1 + q_2) - C'_2\ (q_2)$$

or $R'(q_1 + q_2) = C'_1\ (q_1) = C'_2\ (q_2)$

where $R'\ (q_1 + q_2)$ is the marginal revenue (*MR*), $C'\ (q_1)$ is the marginal cost of firm *I's* output and $C'_2\ (q_2)$ is the marginal cost of firm *II's* output. Therefore, in equilibrium, we have

$$MR = MC_1 = MC_2.$$

5. The marginal cost (*MC*) curve of the industry or the market can be calculated by adding horizontally, the *MC*-curves of the individual firms of the industry.

will also be linear. This case has been illustrated in Fig. 30.4. Here it is assumed that we have five firms *A, B,* C, *D* and *E;* each with differing capacities and somewhat different cost schedules. The curve *MC* represents the sum of the marginal costs for all these firms combined, that is,

$$\Sigma MC = MC_a + MC_b + MC_c + MC_d + MC_e.$$

The demand curve for the product of the industry is shown by *DD* and *MR* is the marginal revenue curve derived from it. As in pure monopoly, the most profitable output is where the *MC* curve cuts the *MR* curve. Hence, the

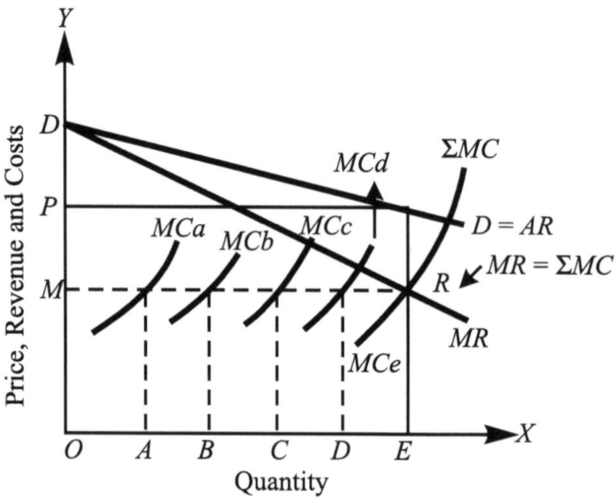

Fig. 30.4

equilibrium point is *R.* where *MC* = *MR.* The optimum output level of the cartel is *OE* and the equilibrium price is *OP.* At this price *OP,* the output shares of firms *A, B,* C, *D* and *E* are *OA, AB, BC, CD* and *DE* respectively. This is really a case of pure monopoly, and, therefore, it permits of a determinate solution.

Allocation of output will be done on the basis of efficiency of firms. If there are a number of firms, the inefficient firms may be asked to close down either temporarily or permanently. In a few extreme cases, member firms of a cartel may agree to share the market equally. It is possible only if the firms have identical cost curves. But this is not true in practice.

Now profits can be calculated on a firm-by-firm basis and then summed for the industry. It is also true that the larger the number of firms forming the cartel, the harder it will be to hold the cartel together, particularly if the individual firms' shares of the industry profits are small. There exists a strong incentive for individual firms to leave the cartel and operate independently.

(2) *Pricing under the Market-Sharing Cartel.* In this case the firms of the industry produce a homogeneous product and agree upon the share of the

market that each is to receive at each possible price. Homogeneity of the product will establish the rule of a single price in the product market. In other words, each firm is to limit its sales to the given districts, states or regions. One common price will prevail in the entire market. Such a system can, however, function only when the cost functions of different firms are the same.

To simplify the cost of market-sharing cartel, let us assume that there are only two firms in the industry. The two firms have identical cost functions and agree to share the market half and half. If the context of the above

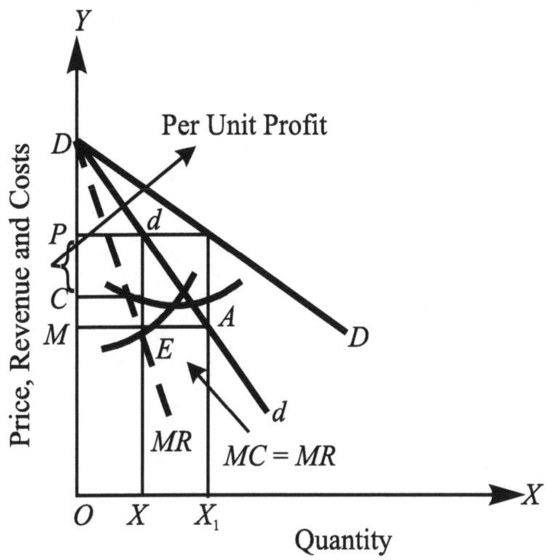

Fig. 30.5

assumptions, the two firms will charge similar prices for their products and will sell equal shares of the sales of the market.

In Fig. 30.5, *DD* is the demand curve of the industry and for each firm the relevant demand curve is *dd.* Since cost functions of the two firms are identical, *AC* and *MC* may be assumed as the respective average cost and marginal cost curves of the two firms. The marginal revenue curve faced by each firm is *MR* (because it is common to both). The profit-maximising output for each firm will be *OX* at which *MC* is equal to *MR.* Each firm will charge *OP* price and will sell *OX* output. If firm *I* sells *OX* output, the other firm will sell XX_1 output (= $OX_1 - QX$). The total output of the industry at price *OP* is equal to *OX.* The output of each firm will be the same (i.e. $OX = XX_1$) only if the individual firm's demand curve *dd* lies halfway between the market demand curve and the vertical axis. In this situation, per unit profit of each firm will be equal to *CP.*

In the above case we have assumed that the firms in the industry agree to share the market half and half; but it is possible that they may agree on different market shares. It will depend upon their individual capacities. High-capacity firms may receive larger market shares than low capacity firms.

Even in this situation the process of equilibrium will be the same. The total marginal cost curve can be obtained by the horizontal summation of the individual firm's marginal cost curves. Applying the rule of profit maximisation ($MR = \sum MC$), we may find out the industry output and the common price to be charged by the firms in the industry. Now the output distribution will be made according to the agreement between the firms of the industry.

Market-Sharing case is possible only when the cost functions of the member firms are identical. In fact, costs of production for the individual firms are likely to differ rather than being identical. Thus, the differences in costs and the degree of independent action will make pricing and output problems much more uncertain than they have been discussed in the above oligopoly model. In case, it exists, it has a very short life.

Imperfect Collusion in Oligopoly

As we have mentioned above, the cases of perfect collusion (centralised cartel and Market-Sharing cartel) do not exist in real world. The case of a perfect collusion stands as a polar extreme where the maximisation of joint profits is emphasised. But mutual distrust among member firms and their unwillingness to give up all of their sovereignty make it most unlikely that cases of perfect collusion could long endure. The better and more lasting cases than that of perfect collusion are the cases of imperfect collusion. In fact, collusion is always imperfect. The cases of imperfect collusion also try to raise prices and profits, but they never assume the position of monopoly. We may find a number of cases of imperfect collusion, but in the present section, we shall discuss the important case of price leadership. Price leadership is said to exist when the price at which most or all of the firms in the industry offer to sell is determined by the leader (one of the firms of the industry). This method was devised by the German economist, Prof, Heinrichvon Stackelberg. This device is also known as Leadership Solution or Followership Solution.

In the words of Prof. Arthur Bums, "If changes are usually or always inaugurated by the same firm and usually or always followed with similar price changes by other sellers, price competition may be said to involve price leadership." In real world, there are many types of price leadership. But among them, the two important types of price leadership are the following (1) Price Leadership by a Low-Cost Firm, and (2) Price Leadership by a Dominant Firm.

(1) *Pricing under Price Leadership by a Low-Cost Firm.* Here we take a simple case of two firms industry. Suppose, the first firm is a high-cost firm while the second firm is a low-cost firm. In Fig. 30.6, the average cost and

marginal cost curves of the high-cost firm are AC_1 and MC_1 respectively, while those of the low-cost firm are AC_2 and MC_2 respectively. The industry demand curve is *DD,* and each firm has an equal share of the market. Therefore, *dd* is the demand curve for each firm. The corresponding marginal revenue curve for each firm is *MR*. Now given the demand curves and cost curves, each firm will like to fix that level of output and price at which it will get the maximum profits. Thus, the first firm will like to produce OX_1 output and charge OP_1 price, while the second firm would like to produce OX_2 output and charge OP_2 price.

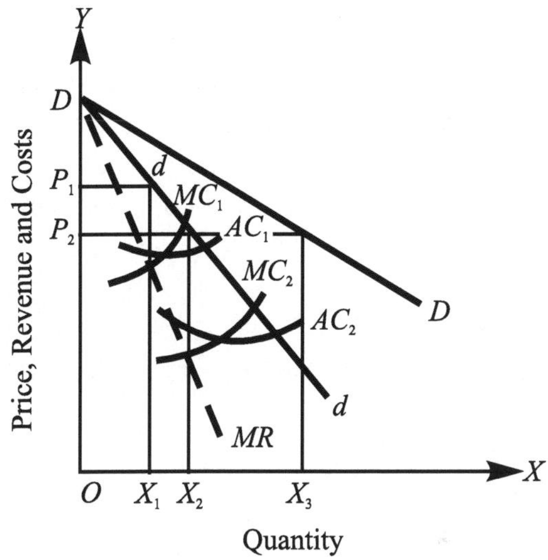

Fig. 30.6

Now, if we assume that the two firms are producing a homogeneous product, then the only price possible in the market is OP_2. Since the low-cost firm can afford to sell at a lower price than can the high-cost firm, the latter will have no alternative than to sell at the price (OP_2) fixed by the low-cost firm. Therefore, in such a situation, the low-cost firm (second firm) becomes the price leader and the high-cost firm (or firms) will become the follower. If, in this situation, the high-cost firm does not want to become follower, then the low-cost firm can drive out the high-cost firm from the market by fixing a price lower than the average cost of the (first) high-cost firm. In such a situation the entire output (OX_3) will be sold at OP_2 price.

(2) *Pricing under Price Leadership by a Dominant Firm.* Generally, in an oligopolistic industry, one or more large firms are found, together with a number of small firms. In the present analysis, we assume that the industry comprises a large dominant firm and a number of small firms. A dominant

firm, if it so desires, can drive out all its rivals by a price war. Now, to avoid large-scale price cutting, tacit collusion may occur in the form of price leadership by the dominant firm. In this situation the dominant firm fixes the price for the industry and allows the small firms to sell all they desire to sell at that price. Thus, the small firms of the industry are simply the price-takers. The residual of the industry demand at this price (set by the dominant firm) will be supplied by the dominant firm. This type of price-leadership is also called as partial monopoly. The partial monopoly is more than just a price leader, because he yields more or less monopoly power.

Under this situation, each small firm of the industry behaves like a perfect competitive firm. The price of the product is set by the dominant firm and this price is given to all the small firms. In other words, the demand curve for the small firm is perfectly elastic or it is horizontal to *X*-axis. The marginal revenue curve of the small firm coincides with the demand curve; therefore, $AR = MR$. Now to maximise profits the small firm produces that level of output at which its marginal cost is equal to its marginal revenue. The combined supply curve for all the small firms can be obtained by summing horizontally the individual marginal cost curves of all the small firms. This combined supply curve shows how much all firms together will supply at each possible price. In Fig. 30.7, this combined supply curve of the small firms is indicated by ΣMC.

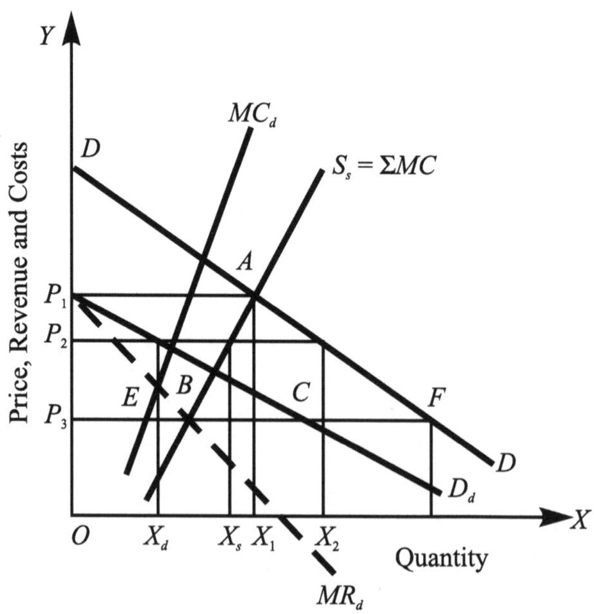

Fig. 30.7

In Fig. 30.7, the industry demand curve is *DD* which shows different combinations of price and output that the consumers would like to purchase. The ΣMC curve shows how much the small firms combined will sell at each possible price. The horizontal differences between the two curves—DD and ΣMC at all possible prices show how much the dominant firm can sell at those prices. Thus, the demand curve faced by the dominant firm is P_1D_d; which is obtained by subtracting horizontally the ΣMC curve from the DD curve.

To show in detail how the demand curve of the dominant firm is obtained, the following analysis is relevant. As we have mentioned, the dominant firm sets the price for the industry and allows the small firms to sell whatever they want to sell. The residual of the market demand will be filled up by the dominant firm. Now, suppose the dominant firm sets the price at OP_1 where the total market demand for the product is OX_1. At this price OP_1, the entire market demand will be met by the small firms as their supply curve ΣMC cuts the market demand curve DD at point A. At this price, there will be zero demand for the dominant firm's product. If the dominant firm reduces price from OP_1 to say OP_2; then the market demand increases from OX_1 to OX_2. Now, at this new lower price OP_2, the small firms would like to supply only OX_S quantity and the rest OX_d (i.e. $OX_2 - OX_S = X_SX_2$ or which is equal to OX_d) will be met by the dominant firm. Now suppose, the dominant firm sets the price at OP_3, then the market demand will be P_3F. From this the small firms will sell only P_3B amount of the product and rest BF (which is equal to P_3C) will be met by the dominant firm. In this way we get the demand curve of the dominant firm (P_1D_d) from the market demand curve (DD) and the aggregate supply curve of the small firms (ΣMC).

Now, once the demand curve of the dominant firm is obtained, it is very easy to draw the marginal revenue curve of it. In Fig. 30.7 MR_d is the marginal revenue curve of the dominant firm corresponding to its derived demand curve P_1D_d. The marginal cost curve of the dominant firm is MC_d. In this situation, the dominant firm will fix that price at which its profits become maximum. For profit maximisation, the dominant firm takes the help of the fundamental rule, $MC = MR$. Thus, profits are maximum for the dominant firm at an output level of OX_d at which MC_d is equal to MR_d. The equilibrium price fixed by the dominant firm is OP_2. Each small firm maximises profits by producing the output at which its marginal cost is equal to its marginal revenue, and here marginal revenue for each small firm is equal to the price OP_2. Total output for the small firms combined is OX_S, where $\Sigma MC = MR$ (Price). Thus, the profit maximising quantity and price for the dominant firm would be OX_d and OP_2 respectively. At this price, total market demand is OX_2, out of which small firms supply OX_S quantity and the *rest* X_SX_2 ($= OX_d$) is supplied by the dominant firm.

9. Welfare Effects of Oligopoly (Resource Allocation under Oligopoly)

We can draw certain conclusions regarding the welfare effects of oligopoly market situation as compared with other market situations in the following manner.

Competition versus Collusion

It appears likely that some output restriction and increase in prices will occur in oligopolistic market as compared with purely competitive markets. Generally, this final result of a collusive agreement is that all the firms in the agreement end up operating so far short of their normal capacities; and with such high cost per unit (average cost) that all profits disappear. This outcome, in a sense, resembles that reached through pure competition in the long-run where the long-run abnormal profits become zero. The social results, however, are very much less satisfactory under oligopolistic situations. In perfect competition, in the long-run, all the firms of the industry are operating at normal (optimum) capacity and selling relatively large quantities at prices just covering the minimum average total costs. On the other hand, in collusion (oligopoly situation), a larger number of firms would be operating at below capacity and providing consumers with smaller quantities at a higher price. Thus, the excess capacity and the excess management tied up in these operations of oligopoly represent a waste of valuable resources. Moreover, the reduced employment increases job applications in other and more competitive industries and drives wages there to lower levels than would otherwise prevail. Therefore, collusive practice reduces the national income and increases the inequalities in its distribution.

Panel (*a*) and Panel (*b*) of Fig. 30.8 illustrate the difference in the end results (long-run outcomes) of these two no-profit situations one under pure competition and the other under oligopoly or collusive agreement. Panel (*a*) of Fig. 30.8 states that under perfect competition, consumers would get a larger quantity of the product at price *OP* from all the firms in the industry operating at their most efficient scales, and each firm supplies *OX* units of the product. Whereas Panel (*b*) of Fig. 30.8 states that under the collusive agreement consumers get a smaller quantity at the higher price *OP,* a larger number of firms, each producing *OX'* units of the product and operating at high cost and inefficient plant (*SAC'*) at point *A'*. Therefore, an oligopolistic firm will produce less than a perfect competitive firm and would charge higher price than the latter. This would be so because an oligopoly firm has to face a negatively sloped demand curve.

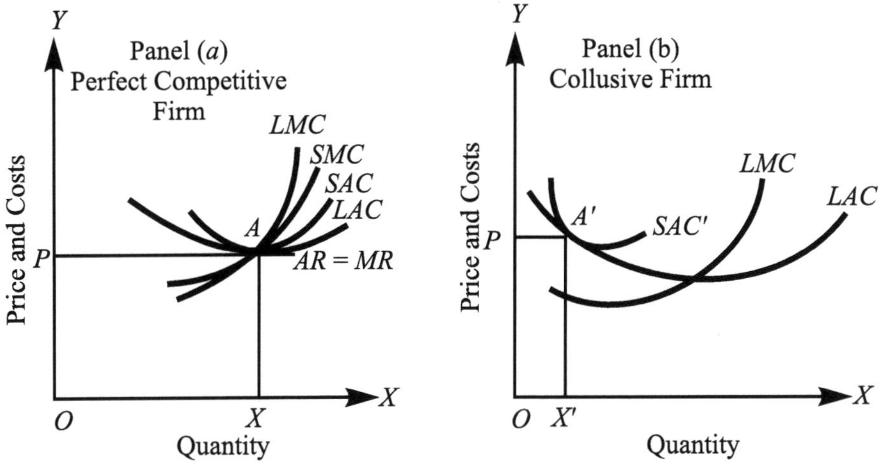

Fig. 30.8

Monopoly versus Collusion

We know that both the monopoly firm and the collusive firm have to face a negatively sloped demand curve, yet the monopoly solution may be preferable from the social point of view. The monopolist would control productive capacity and see to it that this capacity was effectively utilised. The wastes involved in indefinitely tying up excess capacity and excess management (which is always a scarce and very valuable resource in any society) would be avoided. To the extent that the competition of substitutes did not protect the consumer, government regulation or government ownership would be necessary. Either of these solutions would be preferable to overt government encouragement of collusion.

Moreover, under oligopoly, the non-price competition through advertising and introduction of variations in quality and design involve some cost which has to be borne by the consumers of the society. Although advertising enables the consumers to make a choice between a wide range of commodities available in the market, yet too much expenditure on non-price competition may not be socially desirable. This non-price competition involves a heavy social cost.

Collusion and Factoral Rewards

Monopolistic practices under oligopoly tend to depress the rewards going to resource owners. If the resource owners have zero reservation prices for their services, i.e. if they accept any reward offered, rather than allow their resources to go idle, the economy will operate at the full employment level and the factorprices (wages, interest, rent, etc.) going to factor-owners will be determined by their ,marginal productivity in the competitive sector of the economy. Firms operating in the non-competitive sector (oligopoly firms) will be obliged to pay only enough to secure from the competitive sector the resources required for their operations, and the scale of their operations will be determined by the considerations discussed in the preceding section. The firms operating in the competitive sector (perfect competitive firms) will operate at zero profits and the owners of the resources will receive in wages, interests, and rents the equivalent of the value output from this sector of the economy. There will be persistent profits in the non-competitive sector, yet these profits will not, in and of themselves, induce expansion. They will go to the owners of the equity capital and, if expected to persist, they will become capitalised by the process of capital formation. Thus, how adversely the long-run interests of the society are affected by monopolistic practices of oligopoly will depend upon the relative size of the non-competitive sector, the spending and investing habits of the profit earners and the capital requirement of the society. For instance, on balance the US economy has gained from the monopolistic practices of the 19th century.

Moreover, oligopoly provides consumers with a broader range of products among which they can make the choice than does either pure competition or pure monopoly. It also possesses the advantage of promoting research and development in the society, because it gives emphasis on variations of quality and design of the products. It is indication of dynamism in the society.

Exercises

1. Define oligopoly and show how price is determined under it: (*i*) with product differentiation, and (*ii*) without product differentiation.
2. Why there is a kink in the demand curve of an oligopoly firm? How do you draw the marginal revenue curve of the oligopoly firm?
3. What are the main characteristics of oligopoly? Is it correct to say that pricing under oligopoly is indeterminate?
4. Define collusion. Describe the conditions on the side of supply and of demand that favour collusive practices. Show why collusion tends to break down unless it is legalised and enforced by government.
5. Explain the kinky demand curve solution under independent action.
6. What are the main types of collusion? Explain briefly the pricing problem of oligopoly under the centralised cartel and under market sharing cartel.
7. What do you understand by price-leadership? Explain the pricing process under price leadership by a low-cost firm and by a dominant firm.
8. Write a short note on the welfare effects of oligopoly.
9. Does the kinky demand curve solution offer a satisfactory explanation of price-output decision under oligopoly?

Multiple Choice Questions

10. (*i*) Oligopoly describes
    (*a*) a kind of monopolistic competition in which each seller is aware of the influence of his actions on the other sellers
    (*b*) an industry engaging in more competition than a monopoly but less than perfect competition
    (*c*) an industry with more than one firm
    (*d*) none of the above [*Ans.* (*a*)]

    (*ii*) An oligopolistic firm
    (*a*) is a price-taker
    (*b*) sells a product for which there are no good substitutes
    (*c*) does not influence the actions of the other firms
    (*d*) none of the above [*Ans.* (*d*)]

    (*iii*) Which of the following most closely approximates our definition of oligopoly
    (*a*) the cigarette industry
    (*b*) the barber shops in a city
    (*c*) the gasoline stations in a city
    (*d*) wheat farmers in the midwest [*Ans.* (*a*)]

Chapter 31

Duopoly

1. Introduction

Duopoly refers to that market situation in which there are two sellers of the product. There is no basic difference between the theory of duopoly and the theory of oligopoly. In fact, duopoly is a limiting form of oligopoly. According to Cohen and Cyret, "When there are exactly two sellers in the market, this is a special case of oligopoly called duopoly." Like oligopoly, duopoly can be with or without product differentiation.

As there are only two duopolists in the market, each is fully aware of this fact that whatever he does will affect his rival's price-output policies, in the same way as he would react according to what his rival does. In this case, each duopolist tries to make a correct estimate (guess) of his rival's motives and actions. It is possible that the two duopolists may agree to form a tacit cartel after experiencing that competition between them is harmful to both. It is also possible that they may agree to charge a single price and free otherwise, i.e. competition is restricted to advertisement only. Anyway, it is very difficult to generalise as to which situation the duopolists would like to adopt. The older classical models of duopoly assume that the firms are of equal size and sell homogeneous product. It is also assumed that the costs of each firm are the same, or at any rate not very different. The unit costs of the firms are constant over any range of output that would come into question. Further, the total demand in the market they share is linear. Both the producers behave in the same way and want to maximise their individual profits.

In the context of the above assumptions of older classical models, we shall discuss the Cournot Solution, the Edgeworth Solution, the Bertrand Model, the Stakleberg Model, the Hotelling Model and the Chamberlin Solution of duopoly problem in the following section. The Cournot solution does not assume the interdependence of the firms in the industry. According to him, the firms do not conspire; they do not agree even tacitly. Each one sees what the other is doing, assumes he will continue to do the same thing, and then acts accordingly. According to them, the duopolists adjust their outputs, not their prices. The Chamberlin Solution, on the other hand, assumes the presence of interdependence between the firms in the industry. Prof. Edgeworth is of the opinion that each seller assumes the price of his rival constant.

All those models are classical models of duopoly because they are based on classical assumptions and do not deal with the current economic problems.

2. The Cournot Model

Augustin Cournot, a 19th-century French economist, was the first person who introduced the theory of duopoly in 1838. He was of the opinion that there is some independence in the decision-making of the competing firms (duopolists). The main assumption of his model is that each seller assumes the supply of his rival constant. Cournot takes the example of two mineral springs situated side by side and owned by two persons (duopolists) *A* and *B*. The persons have to incur no costs of producing water and each expects that his rival will never change the level of his output. This case has been illustrated in Fig. 31.1.

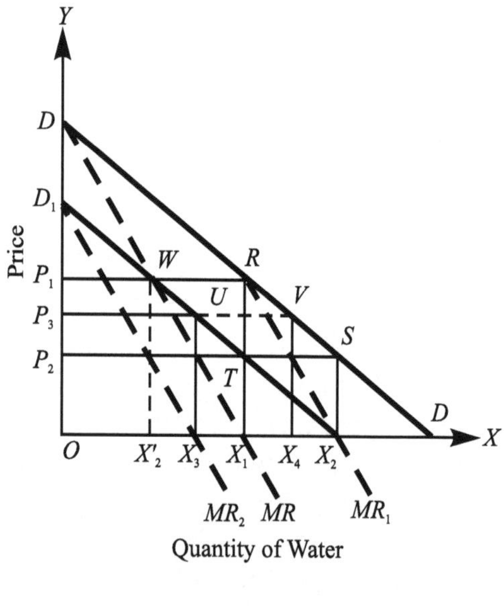

Fig. 31.1

In Fig. 31.1, *DD* is the market demand curve for water and the corresponding marginal revenue curve is *MR*. Suppose, initially firm *A* exists in the market. According to Cournot, for profit maximisation, *A* will sell OX_1 quantity of water as at this level $MR = MC = 0$. If *A* produces more than OX_1 quantity, then his marginal revenue becomes negative. Therefore, he would like to produce only OX_1 quantity and charge a price OP_1 for this quantity. His total profits will be equal to area OP_1AX_1.

Now suppose, firm *B* enters into the market with the assumption that *A* will not change his level of output, i.e. he (*A*) will continue to sell OX_1 quantity. If it is so, then *B* has to consider the segment *RD* (the remaining portion of the market demand curve *DD*) as his individual demand for water. Now the corresponding marginal revenue curve for *B* becomes MR_1. Given this demand curve and marginal revenue curve for *B,* he would like to sell X_1X_2 quantity of water as at this level his $MR = MC = 0$. For this output level, *B* charges a price OP_2 $(= X_1T)$ and expects to get a profit equivalent to the area X_1TSX_2.

Now, since the product is homogeneous and therefore, *A* has to accept the price OP_2 fixed by *B.* This will reduce A's profits from OP_1RX_1 to OP_2TX_1. Further, *A* assumes that *B* will always produce and sell X_1X_2 quantity of water (which is equal to X_2D). It means, still X_2 demand for water remains unsatisfied because

$$X_2D = OD - OX_1 + X_1X_2$$

where OD = total market demand for water

OX_1 = quantity sold by *A*

X_1X_2 = quantity sold by *B*

In other words, *A* thinks that only a quarter of the total demand for water is sold by *B* and therefore, assumes that his market demand will not be equal to OX_1 but now he is able to sell OX_2 quantity of water. In other words, *A* may visualise his new demand and marginal revenue curves to be as D_1X_2 and MR_2 respectively. These curves are linear straight lines and are parallel to the original demand and marginal revenue curves. Now assuming these new demand and marginal revenue curves, *A* would like to sell OX_3 quantity at OP_3 price; because at OX_3 output his $MR = MC = 0$. At OX_3 output, *A's* profits will be equal to the area OP_3UX_3. Here we notice in Fig. 31.1 that OX_3 output is just half the distance OX_2.

Now, *B* will observe that the market situation has changed and in this new situation the demand for his output left is X_3D $(= OD - OX_3)$. Thus, he again assumes his straight line demand and marginal revenue curves and would like to produce half of the X_3D quantity as he follows the profit maximising rule $(MR = MC = 0)$.[1]

In this way, every time each duopolist in the market will adjust his price and output assuming other's output to be constant. Changes in price and quantity sold by *A* and *B* will occur until the two have sold out equal quantities. In Fig. 31.1, the final quantity sold by *A* will be OX_3 and by *B* will be X_3X_4 and the market price would be fixed at OP_3. The equilibrium total profits of *A* and *B* will be equal to the area, $OP_3\ UX_3$ and the area X_3UVX_4 $(= OP_3UX_3)$ respectively.

1. Actually, we have not drawn these new demand and marginal revenue curves for *B*, but it is always implied, due to the linear nature of the curves.

The above Cournot model can also be extended even to more than two firms. As more and more firms enter into the oligopoly industry, the equilibrium output and price of the industry will lead to perfectly competitive output *OD* and zero price.

The Cournot Model in Terms of Reaction Curves

Some economists have used the reaction curves to explain Cournot's duopoly model. The reaction curves may be output reaction curves or price reaction curves depending upon whether it is the output or the price which is the adjustment variable. Since in Cournot model, it is the output which is subject to the adjusting variation, output reaction curves are relevant. It should be carefully notified that these reaction curves do not indicate the reactions which a seller expects will be forthcoming from his rivals but to the sellers' own reactions to the moves of his rival. In Fig. 31.2, output reaction curves of producers *A* and *B* are drawn as *MN* and *ST* respectively. *A's* output reaction curve *MN* explains how *A* will react to any change in output of *B,* that is, *A's* output reaction curve shows how much output *A* will determine to produce for each output level of producer *B*. In other words, it indicates, the most profitable output for *A* for each given output level of *B*. Similarly, *B's* output reaction curve *ST* explains how much output *B* will determine to produce for each output level of producer *A*. For example, if *B* produces output OB_1, *A's* output reaction curve *MN* shows that *A* will produce output OA_2 in response

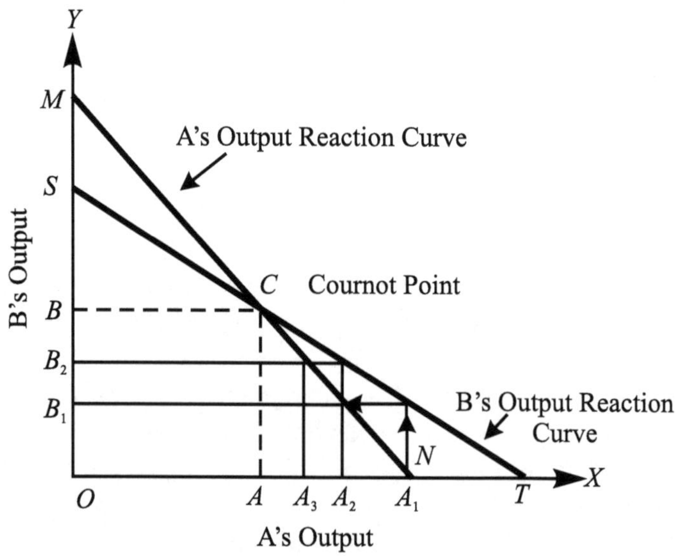

Fig. 31.2

to *B's* output OB_1. Likewise, for all other output levels the reaction can be explained. On the other hand if *A* produces OA_2, *B's* output reaction curve shows that *B* will produce OB_2 and so forth for all other levels of output. This reaction in the output of one to the other's output will continue till both reach the Cournot point C where both *A* and *B* produce the same output. *A's* output *OA* equals *B's* output *OB*. The same conclusion follows if we move from lower right to upper left. Thus, the reaction curve analysis also provides us with a unique and stable equilibrium in terms of the Cournot model.

It will be noted from Fig. 31.2 that output reaction curves have been drawn to be straight lines. This is due to the assumption that the marginal costs of production of both *A* and *B* are constant (at zero). It should be noted that output *ON* is the monopoly output since producer *A* will produce *ON* if producer *B's* output is zero. In other words, producer *A* will produce and sell *ON* if he were the monopolist. On the other hand output is the output which *B* must produce in order to force the producer *A* to produce zero output. Given the marginal costs as zero, producer *A* will be forced to produce zero output when the price has fallen to zero, and therefore production is no longer profitable. Output *OM* will be produced under conditions of pure competition since at output *OM* the price will be zero and therefore equal to marginal cost which is assumed to be zero in the present case. Thus, while *ON* is the monopoly output, *OM* is the purely competitive output. We assume the two producers *A* and *B* to be completely identical, therefore, OS will be equal to *ON,* and *OT* will be equal to *OM.*

Output reaction curves, as explained above, can be used to explain Cournot's duopoly solution. Each producer, as before, assumes that his rival will continue producing the same amount of output regardless of what he might himself decide to produce. To begin with, suppose producer *A* goes into trade first and is, therefore, initially a monopolist. Thus, *A* produces output *ON.* Suppose now *B* also enters into trade. *B* will assume that he will keep his output constant to *ON. B's* output reaction curve *ST* reveals that for output *ON* of *A,* he will produce OB_1. But when *A* sees that *B* is producing OB_1, he will reconsider his previous decision. Assuming that *B* will produce OB_1, *A* will produce OA_2 in reaction to OB_1. Now when *B* observes that *A* is producing OA_2, then he will react and will produce OB_2 in reaction to OA_2 of producer *A.* But when *A* observes that *B* is producing OB_2, he will again react and produce OA_3. This process of adjustments and readjustments will continue until the point is reached where the two reaction curves intersect each other at point C when both *A* and *B* are producing *OA* and *OB* output respectively. Here the duopolists attain stable equilibrium when they will not make any readjustment. This will be the most profitable output for both of them.

3. The Bertrand Model

In 1883, Joseph Bertrand, a French mathematician, criticised Cournot's duopoly solution on its assumption that the supply of the rival duopolist is constant. Instead, he presented his own model based on the assumption that each producer believes the price of his rival would remain constant and keeping all other assumptions of the Cournot model the same. It means that under Bertrand model, the producers first set the price of the product and then produce the output which is dependent at that price and not output (as is the case under Cournot model).

Let there be two producers *A* and *B*. Suppose that *A* goes into business first. Now since *A* is the only producer in the market at present, he sets the price at monopoly level, which is the most profitable for him. Then *B* enters the market on the assumption that *A* will continue to charge his monopoly price and sell the same quantity of output. *B*, therefore, reduces the price of his product. Consequently *B* takes away some of the customers of *A*. Now *A* thinks that *B* will continue to charge this price and therefore he reduces his price to a lower level than *B*, thereby taking away some of *B*'s customers. In this way, they will indulge in price war till both reach the perfectly competitive level of output and price in the long-run. Once the price reaches the competitive level, neither of the two duopolists *A* and *B* would like to lower or raise the price further. If any of the duopolist reduces his price below the competitive level, he would be incurring losses. On the other hand if one of them increases the price above the competitive level, then he is likely to lose his entire sales to his rival on the presumption that the latter would continue to charge the competitive prices. Hence, here the stable equilibrium is reached at the competitive price where the total output is equally divided between the two duopolists.

The above analysis of Bertrand model can also be explained with the help of Fig. 31.3. In Fig. 31.3, *OY* is the price axis of both *A* and *B*. *YA* and *YB* are their demand curves respectively. The maximum quantity of output that *A* can produce is *OA* and that *B* can produce is *OB*. Thus, the total competitive output is $OA + OB$. If they happen to share the market jointly, they sell ^ $(OA + OB) = OA_1 + OB_1$ at the price *OP*.

Let us suppose that there is no collusion between *A* and *B*. Also suppose that *A* is already selling OA_1 output at *OP* price. Now *B* assumes that *A* will not change his price, so he fixes a lower price OP_1 where he is able to sell OB_2 quantity. Now *A* finds his sales being reduced (because of B's action), he reduces his price to OP_2 (lower than *B*'s price OP_1) and sells OA_2 output by attracting some of *B*'s customers. Now it is *B*'s turn to react and he fixes a still lower price OP_3 and sells a larger quantity OB_3. This type of price

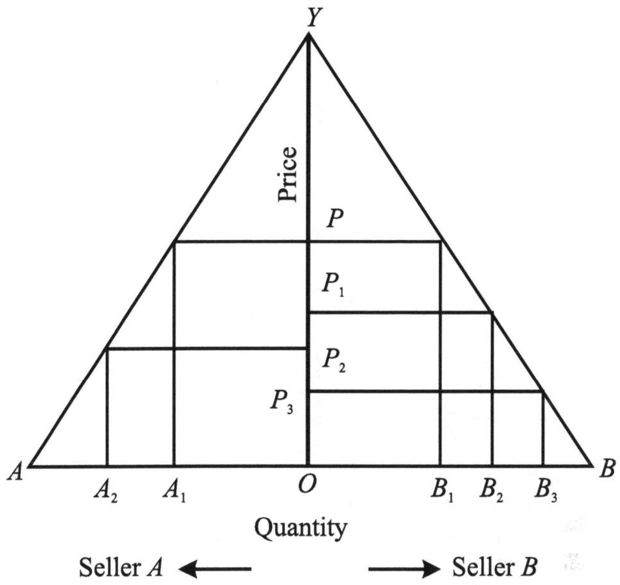

Fig. 31.3

war (action and reaction) will continue on the part of both *A* and *B* till both sell their entire output *OA* and *OB* at the zero competitive price. This is stable equilibrium in Bertrand model.

It is clear from the above analysis of the Cournot and Bertrand models of duopoly that the fundamental assumption about the behaviour of the duopolists in the two models is the same. The assumption of zero cost of production is unrealistic because no firm will be prepared to sell its product at zero competitive price. They are also closed models which do not allow entry of firms. Further the assumption that each duopolist can act without any price-reaction from the other is unrealistic. Further these models are static models which do not explain the time period involved in the action and reaction process of price moves by the duopolists.

4. The Edgeworth's Model

In 1897, Prof. F.Y. Edgeworth developed another classical model of duopoly. This model is based on the same classical assumptions as were taken by Cournot's model, except one that it assumes that each seller takes the price of his rival as constant, instead of assuming the supply of his rival to be constant. Prof. Edgeworth has presented his solution of duopoly problem with the help of Fig. 31.4. Here, it is assumed that there are only two firms in the industry (*A* and *B*) selling homogeneous product and incurring zero marginal cost

($MC = 0$). It is assumed that the market is shared equally by both the duopolists. In Fig. 31.4, DD_A is the demand curve for A and DD_B is the demand curve for

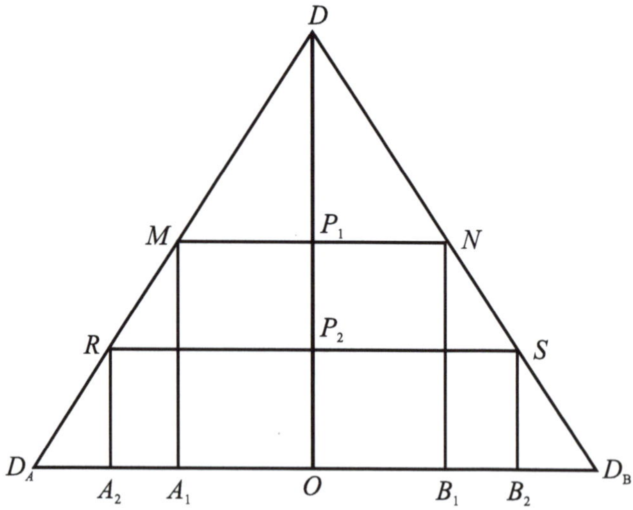

Fig. 31.4

B. OA_1 ($=A_1D_A$) and OB_1 ($=B_1D_B$) are the maximum probable outputs (where $OA_2 = OB_2$) at which the marginal revenue (MR) = marginal cost (MC) = 0. If both the duopolists have got some sort of tacit agreement then they will sell OA_1 and OB_1 quantities respectively at OP_1 price. In other words, under collusion, they will act as a monopoly.

But suppose there is no collusion of any type between the two firms in the industry and also assume that initially firm A exists in the market. Being a single seller in the market, A's behaviour is very similar to that of a monopolist. In equilibrium, A would like to sell OA_1 quantity at OP_1 price and his total profit at this level will be equal to the area A_1MP_1O.

Now, B enters into the market and sets a lower price than OP_1 with the assumption that A will keep his price constant at OP_1. By doing this he (B) will be able to increase his sales sufficiently. But, on the other hand, when A observes this new situation, he fixes a price lower than B's price assuming that B will keep his price constant. A will now sell more than before and will be able to catch a large part of B's market. This will be followed by reappraisal of the market situation by B and he will again fix a price lower than the new price set by A, assuming that A will keep his price constant.

In this way, a situation of price-war will take place in the market. The price-war will continue until the price comes to be OP_2. At this price both the firms will sell OA_2 and OB_2 quantities of their products respectively. In other words, the firms will reach their maximum capacity. But according to Edgeworth, OP_2 price will not be understood as the equilibrium price, because at this price OP_2, the firms' total sales will be equal to A_2B_2 and still D_AA_2 and D_BB_2 consumers will not be satisfied by the firms. Thus, these consumers would be ready to purchase the quantity at any price below *OD*. Therefore, let us assume that *A* begins to raise his price with the assumption that *B* has already placed his entire capacity on the market and he will keep his price constant. But, on the other hand, at the same time *B* has a similar strategy to increase the price and get advantage of the remaining market. It means that the market price starts rising until it again reaches OP_1. This is the maximum limit of price-increase. After this, the only possibility remains is to start reducing the same and the same process of price-war starts which we have already discussed. Thus, price-war is the main feature of duopoly situation. According to Edgeworth, price will always oscillate between OP_1 and OP_2. In other words, price is indeterminate in Edgeworth's Model of Duopoly.

The Edgeworth model is, however, an improvement upon the Cournot model in that price rather than output is used as the decision variable, though it leads to indeterminacy.

5. The Stackleberg Model

A German economist, Heinrich von Stackleberg provided an interesting solution to the duopoly problem. It is based on the assumption that each seller recognises the interdependence of other's actions. Each duopolist either regards himself a leader or a follower. Each duopolist determines the maximum profits he can get both by being a leader and a follower. He will then choose to play whatever role brings him greater profits.

Let us assume that *A* and *B* are the two sellers and that each desires to play the role of a leader, leaving the other fellow to act as a follower. *A*'s maximum profit from followership is determined by substituting *B's* optimum leadership output level in *A*'s reaction function. Each seller can determine his maximum profit from leadership on the assumption that his rival obeys his reaction function and acts as a follower. To put it differently, each duopolist determines his maximum profits levels from both leadership and followership and desires to play the role which yields the *larger maximum.* Four outcomes are possible: (1) *A* desires to be a leader and *B* a follower, (2) *B* desires to be a leader and *A* a follower, (3) both desire to be leaders, and (4) both desire to be followers. Outcome (1) results in consistent behaviour and therefore a determinate solution. *A* assumes that *B* will act as a follower, and he does, *B* assumes that *A* will act as a leader, and he does. Likewise outcome (2) also results in a determinate solution. But if outcomes (3) and (4) are obtained, the expectations of *A* and *B* are not realised, as under (3) each assumes that the other will act as a follower which he does not, while under (4) each assumes that the other will act as a leader which he does not. In the latter case neither of the reaction functions is obeyed and we have a Stackleberg disequilibrium.

The above cases can be explained with the help of reaction curves as follows:

(1) *Seller A desires to be a leader, and B a follower.* It is presented in Fig. 31.5 where the "variable" is interpreted as price. In this case, each seller will raise his price, if the rival's price increases. If *A* acting as the leader raises his price from L_B upward, *B* follows him by raising his price from L_A upward, so that both finally reach the equilibrium point *E*. Thus, here the model is determinate.

(2) *If B desires to be a leader and A as a follower.* Here also the solution is determinate because both follow consistent behaviour patterns. In Fig. 31.5 when *B* as a leader raises his price from L_A upward, *A* follows him by raising his price from L_B upward, till both reach the equilibrium point *E*. Thus, the model is determinate.

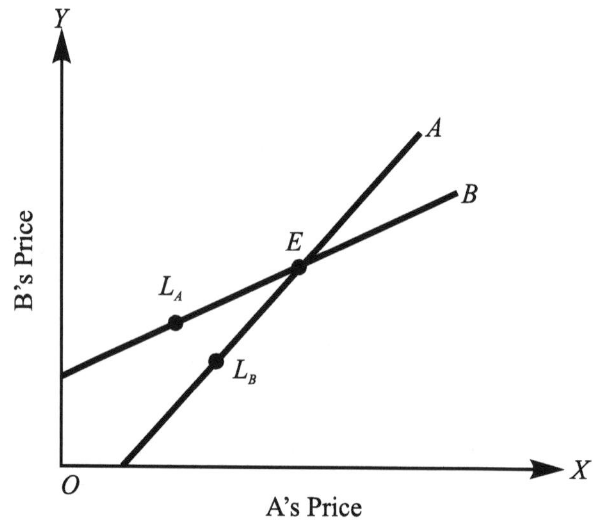

Fig. 31.5

(3) *If both A and B desire to be leaders.* Here each assumes that the behaviour of the other is governed by his reaction function but, in fact, neither follows the reaction function of the other. Thus, there is no equilibrium situation. This is known as the "Stackelberg disequilibrium." It is shown in Fig. 31.6 where the variable is interpreted as the quantity of output. Each seller suffers

from the rise in the output of his rival. The profit maximisation output of one seller falls when his rival's output increases. If *B* acts as the leader and increases his output from L_A onward, the reaction on *A* would be to reduce his output from L_B downward. But *A* does not follow *B* because he also considers himself a leader and so does not reduce his output from L_B downward. So there is no possibility of equilibrium at point *E*. This is the Stackelberg disequilibrium.

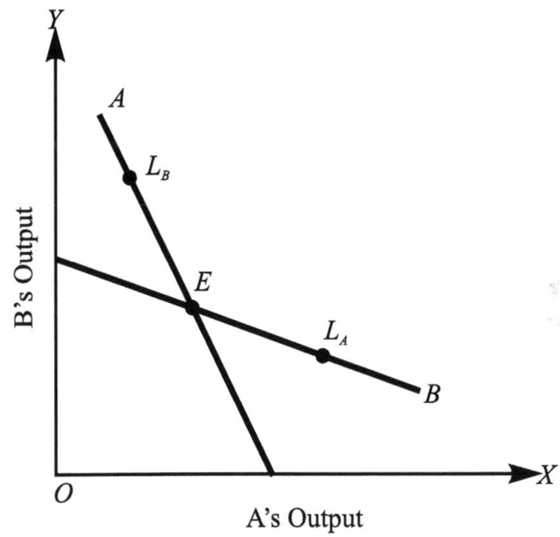

Fig. 31.6

(4) *If both A and B desire to be follower.* In Fig. 31.5 above seller *B* thinks that seller *A* has raised the price of his product, so *B* will follow him by raising the price of his product. Now it is *A's* turn to follow *B* in raising the price of his product. Then *B* will follow him and so on till both reach equilibrium point *E*. Thus, the followership solution is determinate.

6. The Hotelling Model

In 1929 Harold Hotelling presented an empirical analysis of the market behaviour and constructed a model which is generally known as the Hotelling's stable solution.

Once again, we find *A* and *B* as the two entrepreneurs who produce a homogeneous product at zero marginal cost. However, the two products appear differentiated to the consumers due to differences in the locations of the two sellers. In Hotelling's view, markets are commonly sub-divided into regions within each of which a seller enjoys a quasi-monopolistic position. As shown in Fig. 31.7, buyers are uniformly distributed along a line of length *L*, which may be the main street. *A* and *B* are initially located at points *A* and *B* in this market.

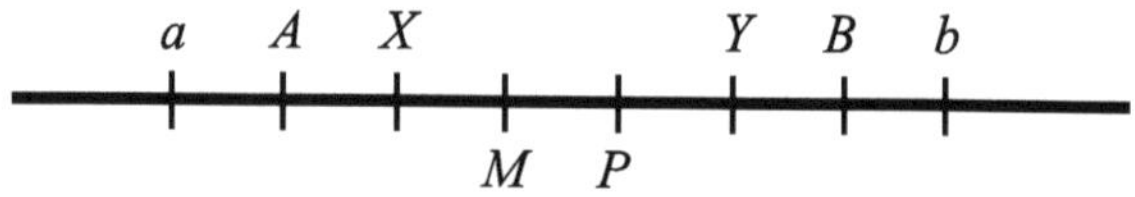

Market - *L*

Fig. 31.7

Every buyer must go to the vending point and transport his purchases home at a cost *C* per unit distance (say kilometre) carried. Thus, a buyer located *X* kilometers distance from *A* must pay a transportation cost of *ex* for each unit of product he buys.

Hotelling then assumes that there are *a* buyers situated to the left of *A* and *b* buyers situated to the right of *B*. Assuming that each buyer purchases only one unit of the product, *A* and *B* will have protected or sheltered markets in respect of *a* and *b* buyers located to their left and right respectively. The total sales of *A* and *B* will be $L=a+x+y+b$.

A and *B* both have some leeway in setting their price, although neither will set a price so high that buyer in his sheltered market find it less expensive to buy from his rival. Since the products differ only in transportation cost, delivered price must be equal. In other words, if price charged by *A* and *B* are assumed to be P_A and P_B, together with transportation costs we should have $P_A + cx = P_B + cy$. *A's* total profit will be $P_A\ (a + x)$ while *B*'s profit will be $P_B(b+y)$. In the initial stages P_A may be different from P_B, but eventually they are equalised.

Hotelling believes that in the long-run both *A* and *B* attempt to expand their respective "sheltered" markets. As a result, *A* starts moving to the right, *B* moves to his left and ultimately both are located at *M*, selling the product at the same price. The incentive which different sellers have to conglomerate in the central part of a city or in the down-town areas is but a reflection of the market behaviour of different sellers highlighted by Hotelling.

Hotelling provided a stable and determinate solution to the oligopoly problem and argued that in the long-run both *A* and *B* charge the same price and sell the same quantity.[2]

7. The Chamberlin's Model (Small Group Model)

Prof. Chamberlin's model of duopoly gives a result quite different from those of the older classical models the Cournot's model and the Edgeworth's model, etc. Although, the Chamberlin's model is based on the same assumptions of classical models, yet it recognises the mutual dependence between the price

2. See C.E. Ferguson, *Microeconomic Theory*, pp. 311-12 for a mathematical proof.

and output of the duopolists in the market. Here, the firms are assumed to have full and far-sighted recognition of their interdependence and its consequences. The Cournot model and the Edgeworth model assume the firms to be independent, i.e. do not give recognition to the interdependence between the firms. This is the main point of difference between the Chamberlin's model and the other classical models of duopoly.

Chamberlin's model can be understood by both (*i*) the output adjustment, and (*ii*) the price adjustment. First we discuss the output adjustment. For this we go back to Fig. 31.1 to understand the model. In Fig. 31.1 Cournot has represented his model assuming the non-existence of interdependence between *A* and *B*. With the same Fig. 31.1, we may understand the Chamberlin's model by adding the assumption that on *B*'s entry in the market *A* recognises their mutual interdependence.

In Fig. 31.1, we observe that initially *A* was selling OX_1 quantity of his product at OP_1 price. Being a single seller of the product, he behaved like a monopolist. Thus, *A*'s initial total profits were equal to the area OP_1RX_1.

Now, *B* enters the market and intends to sell X_1X_2 quantity at OP_2 price. Now the moment *B* enters the market, Prof. Chamberlin assumes that interdependence between *A* and *B* arises. Under this assumption of mutual interdependence, *A* will not expect drat *B* will keep his price and output constant but he (*A*) realises that *B* will always try to maximise his profits. Thus he (*A*) reduces his supply to X_1X_2 (= OX_2^1). Thus, the total supply of the industry will be $OX_2^1 + X_1X_2 = \hat{}$ (*OD*). In this way at OP_1 price the total supply OX_1 [= ^(*OD*)] is equally divided between *A* and *B* (i.e. $OX_1 = OX_2^1 + X_2^1X_1$), Here, *A* and *B* will also share the monopoly profits of the market (OP_1RX_1) equally. *A*'s $X_2^1WRX_1$ profits will be equal to the area $OP_1WX_2^1$; and *B*'s profits will be equal to the area (= $OP_1\ WX_2^1$). Thus, the total profits of the industry would be $OP_1RX_1 = OP_1WX_2^1 + X_2^1WRX_1$. Therefore, OP_1 will be a stable equilibrium price. No duopolist would like to vary output at this price. If one attempts to do so, it leads to a harmful situation to both of them.

Now, under the second method of price adjustment (instead of output adjustment as discussed above) also, we shall be getting the same result. Here we shall take help of Fig. 31.4 which represents the Chamberlin's model. Let us now assume that some price takes place between OP_1 and OP_2. If *A* increases his price to OP_1 for maximising his profits, then *B* will also do the same immediately. In this way *B* also increases his price to OP_1 for attaining maximum profits. Once OP_2 price is fixed, no duopolist would like to reduce it because each duopolist knows that by doing so he would be reducing his total profits. Thus, at OP_1 price, the equilibrium becomes stable and joint profits are at a maximum.

The equilibrium in Chamberlin's model is stable, stable as granite, because each firm is looking to its ultimate interest never gives a moment's thought to any other possible course of action. In this model there is no collusion in any meaningful sense. Each firm acts independently, while it recognised the mutual dependence of all the firms in the industry. This recognition of mutual dependence leads to a stable equilibrium or a sort of monopolistic equilibrium in duopoly (or oligopoly).

Exercises

1. Define duopoly. How is price determined under duopoly?
2. Show why price is indeterminate under duopoly conditions and point out how this difficulty can be overcome?
3. Write short notes on the following:
   (*i*) Cournot's Model of Duopoly Problem
   (*ii*) Edgeworth's Model of Duopoly Problem
   (*iii*) Chamberlin's Model of Duopoly Problem.
4. Explain the characteristic features of the Cournot model of duopoly.
5. Discuss the Stackleberg solution to the duopoly problem.
6. Explain the Bertrand solution of duopoly problem. How does it differ from the Cournot solution?
7. Discuss the Hotelling solution to the duopoly problem.

Multiple Choice Questions

8. (*i*) With reference to the Cournot model, determine which of the following statements is false?
   (*a*) The duopolists do not recognise their interdependence
   (*b*) Each duopolist assumes the other will keep its quantity constant
   (*c*) Each duopolist assumes the other will keep its price constant
   (*d*) The solution is stable [*Ans.* (*c*)]

   (*ii*) With reference to the Edgeworth model, determine which of the following statement is correct?
   (*a*) The duopolists recognise their interdependence
   (*b*) It explains price regidity
   (*c*) Each duopolist assumes the other keeps its price constant
   (*d*) Each duopolist assumes the other keeps its quantity constant [*Ans.* (*c*)]

   (*iii*) If there is a market structure in which there are only two buyers for a commodity, it is called
   (*a*) Duopoly (*b*) Duopsony
   (*c*) Discrimination market (*d*) None of the above [*Ans.* (*b*)]

Chapter 32

Limit Pricing Theories

1. Introduction

The limit price theory was first formulated by Joe S. Bain[1] in 1949 and then later refined in 1956. In his original article Joe S. Bain showed that the oligopoly firms with collusion may be threatened by potential entry of firms. Although the products may not have close substitutes, yet if a high price is fixed for the product, then there may be the fear of entry by the potential rival firms in the market. In such a situation, there is always a maximum price which is known as the limit price. It is the price which the existing firm may charge from the customers without attracting the entry of new firms in the market.

Sylos-Labini in his book *Oligopoly and Technical Program* (1957) extended the main model of limit pricing to entry-preventing price based on scale economies. Further Franco Modigliani in an article[2] in 1958 presented a generalised model based on the Sylos-Labini version by relaxing some of his restrictive assumptions. In 1968, Pashigian[3] introduced time-period analysis in the Sylos model while in 1970 Jagdish Bhagwati[4] extended the Modigliani model to a growing market in a dynamic setting. In the present chapter we shall deal with the theories of Bain and Sylos-Labini.

2. Bain's Limit Pricing Theory

According to Bain, limit price is the price which the established firms can charge without attracting the entry of new firms into the industry. This price may be lower than the profit maximising price in the short-run and will depend

1. J.S. Bain, "A Note on Pricing in Monopoly and Oligopoly". *A.E.R.*, March 1949.
2. Franco Modigliani, "New Development on the Oligopoly Front", *J.P.E.*,1958.
3. P. Pashigian, "Limit Pricing and the Market Share of the Leading Firms", *Journal of Indus/rial Economics,* 1968.
4. J.N. Bhagwati, "Oligopoly Theory, Entry Prevention and Growth", *O.E.P.*, 1970.

upon the relative costs of firms within and outside the group, and on demand conditions in the market. Bain assumes the limit price as the maximum price above the competitive price which is fixed by the existing firms in the industry.

The main assumptions of the Bain model are the following:

(1) There are long-run price and output adjustments.

(2) There are some established firms in the industry.

(3) The market demand curve for the commodity is not affected by price adjustments by the established firms or by the entry of new firms into the industry.

(4) The collusion among the firms is based upon the dominant leader firm.

(5) The other firms in the group follow unified price policy.

(6) The leader firm fixes the limit price below which entry will not take place.

The Bain Model

Bain explains the limit price model by defining the condition of entry. The condition of entry is the premium or percentage by which established firms can increase the price above the competitive price without attracting the entry of new firms into the group. Mathematically, the conditions of entry can be written as:

$$E = \frac{P_L - P_C}{P_C} \qquad ...(1)$$

or

$$P_L = P_C(1 + E) \qquad ...(2)$$

where

P_L = Limit price

P_C = Competitive price

E = Premium or percentage which the established firms may get.

Now if the established firms fix P_L above P_C, they can get more than normal profits because the competitive price $P_C = LAC$ which includes normal profit.

Thus, E is the margin or percentage or premium above P_C which the existing firms earn by fixing a higher (limit) price P_L. The Bain model states that the time period involved in the condition of entry of new firms is long enough which mostly depends upon the changing conditions of demand and input prices, etc. The longer the time period required by a new firm to establish itself, the lesser will be the degree of threat of its entry and the larger will be the gap between P_L and P_C. This gap between P_L and P_C is known as entry barrier or entry gap.

Entry Barriers and Determination of Limit Price

Here we may discuss the following two major sources of entry barriers:

(1) Product Differentiation, and

(2) Economies of Scale

(1) Product Differentiation. This case may be explained with the help of a diagram as in Fig. 32.1. Here we assume that *LAC* is the long-period average cost curve which is held constant and *OPC* is the competitive price. The demand curve of the group or in Bain' s analysis the most advantage firm is *DD*. OP_L is the limit price or the entry preventing price fixed by the group or the most advantage firm. Accordingly OX_L is the limit output. If the firm charges OP_L price, the demand of the potential entrant firm is D_ED_E which does not permit it to enter the oligopoly market (group) because the D_ED_E curve is tangential to the *LAC* at point *R*, leaving no level of output at which it exceeds the firm's average cost of production. If the established firms increase the price to OP_H which is the entry inducing price, its output will be reduced to OX_1. This attracts the potential entrant firm to enter the oligopoly market and its demand curve shifts to $D_{E1}D_{E1}$. The new firm can produce any quantity upto OX_E. The amount by which P_L exceeds P_C is the entry gap or the "height" of the entry barrier which is equal to *AB* (or P_CP_L) in Fig. 32.1.

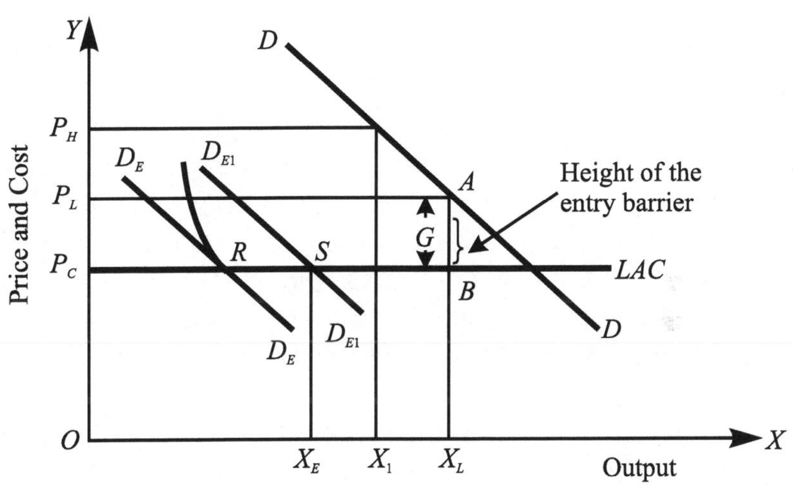

Fig. 32.1

(2) **Economies of Scale.** The economies of scale arise due to indivisibilities and the advantages of specialisation and division of labour in both production and management. The effects of economies of scale on the level of limit price depend upon (*a*) the expectation of potential entrant firm about the reactions of the existing firms after entry, and (*b*) the expectations of the existing firms about the behaviour of the entering firm. The following are the two possibilities:

(*i*) *Price Constant.* In this case the entrant firm expects the price to be the same at the post-entry level. In Fig. 32.2, *DD* is the market demand curve of the existing firms which produce *OX* output at their optimum scale plant and sell it at the competitive price OP_C. If the established firms charge the entry-preventing price (limit price) OP_L, the limit output is OX_L. At price OP_L, they

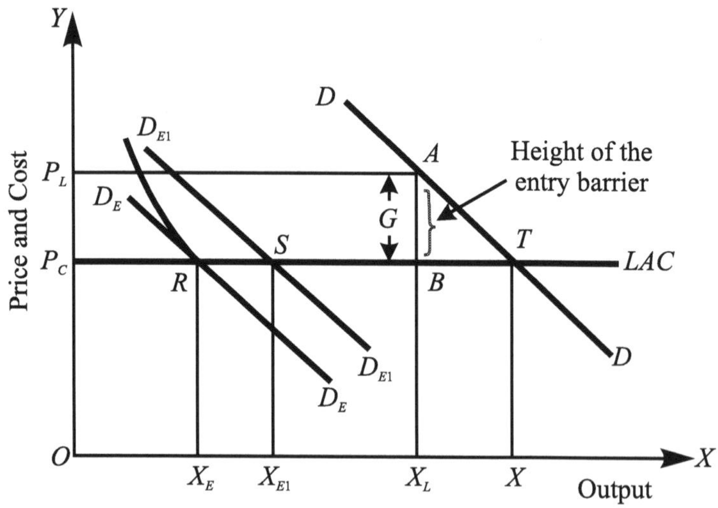

Fig. 32.2

will sell XX_L ($OX - OX_L = X_LX$) less output than their optimum scale plants. This price will prevent the potential entrant firm to enter the market when it is producing OX_E output at its minimum scale plant. The demand curve for the entrant firm is D_ED_E which is parallel to the market demand curve *DD*. This curve D_ED_E is tangential to the *LAC* curve at point *R* to that there is no level of output at which the price exceeds the firm's average cost. The gap between OP_L and OP_C is the scale barrier or the entry gap which prevents the firm to enter the market. If the entrant firm increases the scale plant the existing firms will accommodate it by allowing it to sell OX_{E1} quantity when its demand curve is $D_{E1}D_{E1}$. It means that the established firms will sell $OX_{E1} - OX = X_{E1}X$ output instead of pre-entry level of *OX* output at OP_C constant price, and the entrant firm will sell OX_{E1} output.

(*ii*) *Quantity Constant.* In this case the entrant firm expects the existing firms to keep their output constant at the pre-entry level. In Fig. 32.3 check the entry, the existing firms will produce the limit output OX_L and sell the same at limit price OP_L, given their optimum scale of plant. The potential entrant firm's minimum optimal scale plant produces OX_E output which just covers its *LAC*. Thus, the entry gap for the firm is *AB*. If the existing firms keep their output at OX_L level and allow the entrant firm to enter their market and sell its minimum output OX_E, the total output in the market will increase

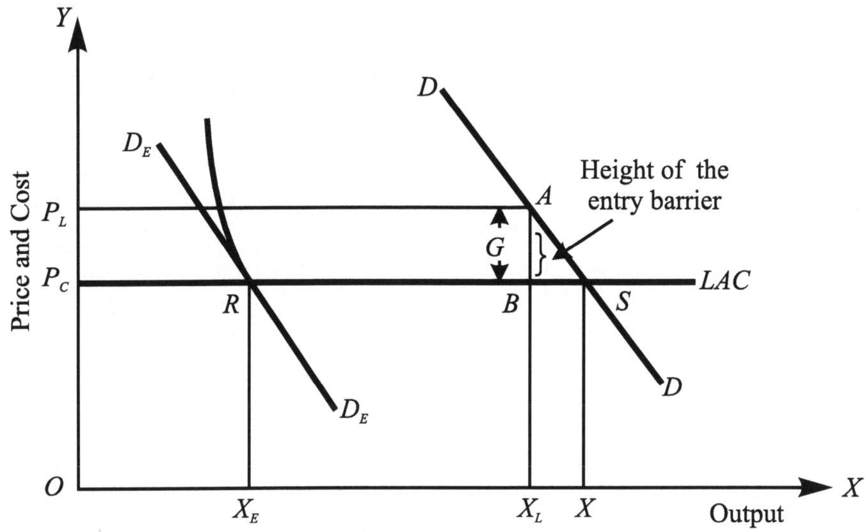

Fig. 32.3

by this quantity OX_E. Now it will be $OX = OX_E + OX_L$. As a result of this, the market price will fall just below the competitive price OP_C because the existing firms keep their output at the pre-entry level.

3. Sylos-Labini Model of Limit Pricing

In his book *Oligopoly and Technical Program* (1957), Sylos-Labini developed a long-run model of limit pricing in oligopoly market based on scale barriers to entry. Here the limit price or the entry preventing price is fixed by the largest firm in the oligopoly market. Since the cost structure of different firms will not be the same, the limit price would be greater than the *LAC* of the smallest firm in the market. The limit price covers not only the *LAC* but also the minimal normal rate of profit determined by the industry. This price must be acceptable by all the existing firms in the oligopoly group. Thus, the equilibrium price is

$$P_i = LAC_i (1 + r) \quad \ldots (3)$$

Where P_i = Equilibrium price for the *i*th plant

LAC_i = Long-run average cost of the *i*th plant

r = Minimum normal rate of return or profit which Sylos assumes as 5 per cent.

Now if the new firm has a scale plant of a size larger than the smallest firm in the group, it would bring down the price. This is because the Sylos-Labini model assumes that the established firms would continue to produce the same output. The additional output of the entrant firm would reduce the price and the minimum rate of profit in the industry. This case has been illustrated in Fig. 32.4. Here *DD* is the market demand curve and LAC_L, LAC_M and LAC_S are the long-run average cost curves of the large scale plant, medium scale plant and the small scale plant firms respectively. The largest firm fixes a price OP_S at the LAC_S of least efficient smallest firm. All other firms in the industry accept this price (OP_S) at the output level *OX* to prevent entry of new firms, the leader firm fixes the limit price OP_L and the limit output OX_L which is equal to $OX - OX_S$. This price OP_L is the equilibrium price because it

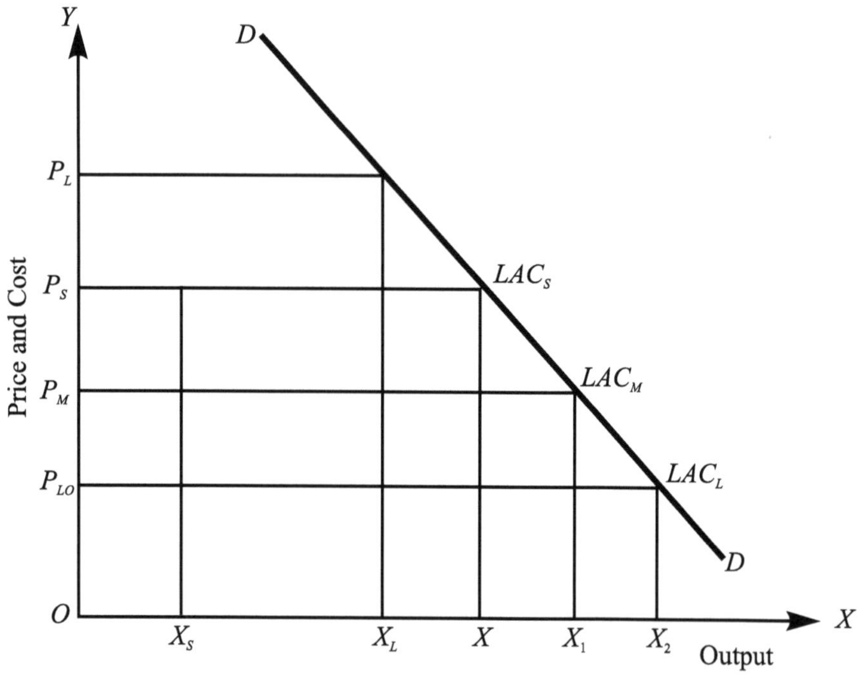

Fig. 32.4

prevents the new firm from entering the oligopoly group. In case a new firm enters the group, the total output of the group will rise to the level *OX* and it will reduce the price just below OP_S. At limit price OP_L, the limit output is OX_L. If a new firm enters the market with the scale plant of the size of the smallest firm, the total output of the industry will exceed OX_L which will bring down the price to a level just below the *LAC* of the entrant firm. The *LAC* of the new firm is, in fact, equal to the LAC_S of the smallest existing firm. This prevents the firm to enter the group because if it enters, its price will fall below its *LAC* and this will not be acceptable for it.

Thus, the equilibrium price will not be higher than the entry preventing price OP_L and lower than OP_S. This will not prevent entry.

Similarly, the equilibrium output can not be larger than the entry preventing output OX_L and any output smaller than this will not prevent entry. This is because of the assumption of the model that the existing firms will produce the same level of output even after the entry of new firms.

According to Sylos, there is no unique determinate solution but the "price tends to settle at a level immediately above the entry preventing price of the least efficient firms which it is to the advantage of the largest and the most efficient firms to let live".

Exercises

1. Explain clearly the Bain's limit pricing theory.
2. Explain the sources of entry barriers as described by Bain. How is limit price determined?
3. Examine the Sylos-Labini model of limit pricing.

Multiple Choice Questions

4. (*i*) Who was the first economist to formulate the limit price theory?
   (*a*) Joe S. Bain
   (*b*) W.J. Baumoi
   (*c*) John F. Due
   (*d*) None of the above [*Ans.* (*a*)]

   (*ii*) According to Sylos-Labini model, the equilibrium price is equal to
   (*a*) long-run average cost
   (*b*) normal profit
   (*c*) long-run average cost plus the normal rate of profit
   (*d*) marginal cost [*Ans.* (*c*)]

Chapter 33

Full-Cost Pricing Theory

1. Introduction

In the previous chapters we have explained those theories of price and output determination under oligopoly which are based on profit maximisation assumption. After the marginalist revolution, profit maximisation by the firm is generally explained by the marginal analysis, that is, by the use of marginal revenue and marginal cost concepts. An important alternative approach to profit maximisation and marginal analysis based upon it is the full-cost pricing theory which does not assume that rational firms seek to maximise profits. It may be pointed out in the beginning that full-cost theory has been given several names. Full-cost pricing theory is also known as *average-cost pricing* theory, since in this theory price of a product is fixed on the basis of average cost. It is also called *cost-plus pricing,* or *mark-up pricing* theory, since this theory visualises that in order to fix price businessmen add a mark-up to their average cost of production.

Two Oxford economists, Hall and Hitch, found empirically in 1939 that instead of equating marginal cost with marginal revenue, many firms engage in *full cost pricing.* To quote them, "The way in which businessmen decide what price to charge for their products and what output to produce, casts doubt on the general applicability of conventional analysis of price and output policy in terms of marginal cost and marginal revenue and suggest a mode of entrepreneurial behaviour which current economic doctrine tends to ignore." They suggest that after the sellers have worked out their total cost in respect of the level of output expected for the next period of time, they would add to this a *satisfactory* profit margin. The price would be equal to *full cost* including an acceptable profit margin. They contended that the firms' main preoccupation is price and not the output as implied by the traditional theory.

However, in order to arrive at such an acceptable profit margin the rival firms must have some sort of mutual understanding, tacit collusion, moral conviction of fairness, consideration for long run cost and demand. Generally oligopolistic firms keep their prices rigidly fixed. It was also discovered by Hall and Hitch that marginal costs and marginal revenue are very difficult to work out, hence firms emphasise on full-cost pricing.

Hall and Hitch's findings may be summarised as follows: Firstly, unlike the classical and neo-classical belief, the firms do not behave atomistically. The behaviour of interdependent oligopolistic firms, as Hall and Hitch put it, could not be dealt with within the framework of the traditional theory. They found that firms do not attempt to maximise their profit by applying the marginalistic rules, but normally attempt to ($MC = MR$) set their price on the *average-cost principle* or as they put it, on the lines of *full-cost* pricing. That is,

$$P = AVC + AFC + \text{Normal profit margin}$$

Hall and Hitch gave two reasons for the breakdown of marginalistic rules: (*a*) Firms do not know the tastes and preferences of consumers and so are not aware of their demand function, nor their marginal costs, hence the application of the marginalist rule ($MC = MR$) becomes impossible. (*b*) Firms believe that the full cost price is the "right" price as it covered normal profit over the cost of production when the plant was normally utilised. However, if a firm wanted to secure a big order, it may not insist on the average-cost pricing, or if it thought that such pricing may damage its goodwill or endanger its future position.

Finally, it was found by Hall and Hitch that prices of manufacturers were fairly sticky, despite changes in demand and costs. Traditional theory predicted a change in price and output in the event of changing costs and/or demand. In the real world, however, this was not observed. Referring to the apparatus of the kinked demand curve, they argued that normally businessmen set the price equivalent to average cost ($AVC + AFC$ + Profit margin) and the kink would occur at that price. It was reported by most firms that they did not have any collusive agreement with their rivals for raising the price, as they had a fear of potential entrants who may endanger the position of established firms. Likewise, firms did not think that collusive reduction in the price would be profitable to the 'group'. Furthermore, in the firms' view, frequent changes in price were disliked by their customers.

In 1948, R.A. Gordon also endorsed these views. He contended that the real industrial world is extremely complex and the determinants of demand and costs vary so frequently and so continuously that a firm can not extrapolate their past and have a realistic set of marginal cost and demand functions. In short, due to uncertainty prevailing in the modern industrial/business world, marginalist behaviour (i.e. maximisation profit by the rule $MC = MR$) has lost its relevance.

2. Full-cost Pricing and Kinked Demand Curve

Hall and Hitch combine full-cost pricing with kinked demand curve analysis. Current price is fixed on the basis of full-cost[1] (as defined above), and a kink in the demand curve is formed at this price. Full-cost pricing together with the kinked demand curve analysis is illustrated in Fig. 33.1. Here let us assume that the firm decides to produce *OX* output. This output is fixed on the basis of expected sales. At *OX* level of output the average cost is equal to *KX* which includes the direct cost and the normal profit. Thus, the firm will fix a price *OP* which is equal to its average cost.

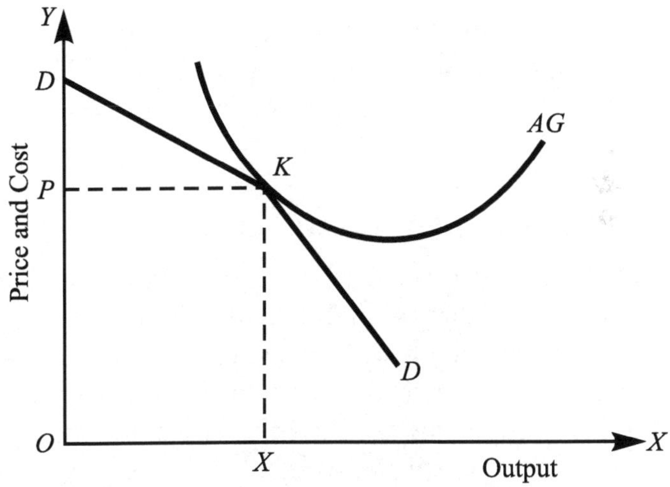

Fig. 33.1

Kinked demand curve analysis as used by Hall and Hitch along with his full-cost pricing theory provides an explanation for the stability or rigidity of prices under oligopoly in the short run. Increases or decreases in demand will usually shift the kink to the right or left but will leave the price unchanged. But Hall and Hitch have mentioned the following two exceptions to this general rule in which case price of the product changes:

(1) If the demand remains at a low level for some time, there is every likelihood that price will be reduced so as to maintain output. According to Hall and Hitch, the explanation for this reduction in price in the context of depressed demand is that one entrepreneur may become panicky and his irrational behaviour forces the others to cut prices.

---

1. As we mentioned in the previous chapter on oligopoly that Sweezy version of kinked demand curve theory of oligopoly cannot explain how the current price came to be what it is. This flaw is not present in Hall and Hitch's version of kinked demand curve analysis.

(2) If the *AC* curves of all firms shift by similar amounts on account of changes in factor prices or technology, then this is "likely to lead to a revaluation of the full cost" price. However, Hall and Hitch point out that "there will be no tendency for prices to fall or rise more than the wage and raw material costs".

It should be noted that, given that the average cost curve falls for quite a large range of output, the full-cost pricing suggests that price of the products will vary inversely with output; smaller levels of output will involve higher cost per unit and therefore higher prices will be fixed. But, according to Hall and Hitch, the oligopolists will not produce small outputs and therefore will not charge higher prices. This is because oligopolists (1) prefer price stability, (2) are prevented by the kink to raise price, and (3) they have propensity to produce larger levels of output or, in the words of Hall and Hitch, they desire to "keep plant running as full as possible, giving rise to a general feeling in favour of price concessions".

3. Full-cost Pricing and Andrews' Version

As we have noted that the kinky demand curve analysis has created some complications in the explanation of full-cost pricing, Prof. Andrews has developed a modified version of the full-cost pricing. His analysis is similar to that of Hall and Hitch, but there are some differences between the two. An important difference between the two lies in the use of the concept of *costing-margin* by Andrews. The costing-margin is conceived by Andrews as an addition to *constant* average direct cost and "will normally tend to cover the costs of the indirect factors of production and provide a normal level of net profit". Thus, like the analysis of Hall and Hitch, addition of costing margin to the average variable cost for fixation of price of the product goes against the price fixation on the basis of profit-maximisation principle of the traditional theory of value. Thus, the concept of costing margin of Andrews is similar to the mark-up of Hall and Hitch, but there is a difference in that whereas Hall and Hitch visualise a *constant or inflexible* mark-up or a margin for overhead cost and normal profit, Andrews discusses at length the circumstances in which there might be some *flexibility* in the costing margin in response to competitive and market forces. As shall be brought out later, on the introduction of flexibility in the costing margin brings Andrews' full-cost price theory closer to the price theory based on profit maximisation principle. Another difference between Andrews and Hall and Hitch's versions of full-cost pricing theory is that while the latter use kinked demand curve along with full cost pricing, the former does not make use of the kinked demand curve hypothesis in his full cost theory. Still another important difference between the two is that whereas Hall and Hitch consider that average cost varies with output and average cost curve is U-shaped, Andrews visualises that for a large relevant range of output, average direct (variable) cost remains constant.

The usual formula for costing-margin (or mark-up) is,

$$M = \frac{P - AVC}{AVC}$$

$$\therefore \quad P = AVC(1 + M)$$

where

$$M = \text{Mark-up}$$

$$P = \text{Price}$$

$$AVC = \text{Average Variable Cost}$$

Suppose that firm's AVC = \$1000, and the firm sets M = 0.20 (or 20 per cent). They would fix price P = \$1000 (1 + 0.20) = \$1200. Once this price is fixed by the firm, the costing-margin will remain constant, given its organisation, whatever the level of its output. But it will change with any general permanent changes in the prices of the indirect factors of production.

The theory of full-cost pricing as put forward by Andrews is illustrated in Fig. 33.2. In Figure 33.2 AC represents the average direct cost (*i.e.* average variable cost). It will be seen that average direct cost curve AC is saucer-shaped, that is, it first falls, then remains constant for quite a large increase in output and then eventually rises. Corresponding to this, MC is the marginal cost curve; MC curve falls in the beginning and lies below AC, then it coincides with AC curve and eventually MC lies above AC. In order to proceed to fix the price, besides average direct cost, a business firm has to calculate the total indirect costs (*i.e.* fixed costs) and also the amount of profits it wishes to earn. The total indirect costs plus the amount of profits planned will yield a *fixed sum of money* which will remain constant for fixation of price in the short-run. The 'costing-margin', according to Andrews, is obtained from this fixed sum of money by dividing it by "some chosen output".

This chosen output used for the purpose of estimating costing margin can be determined in several ways. Firstly, it may be fixed on the basis of *capacity output* with the given plant when by the capacity output is meant the maximum output that can be produced with the given plant. Output can be fixed by a business firm as some percentage of this capacity output. Secondly, the chosen output can be fixed on the basis of *sales of product made in the preceding production period,* or average of sales achieved over a number of previous production periods. Thirdly, the output may be determined on the basis of *expected sales in a future period* for which output is being produced.

If a new firm has to set the price of its product, or if the firm has introduced a new product for which it has to set the price, then the above mentioned second way of choosing the output for estimating the costing-margin is ruled out and in these circumstances only the first and third methods become relevant.

In fact, when the firm is a new one or where an existing firm is introducing a new product, then the first and third methods of choosing output amount to the same thing. This is because the designed capacity of the plant will be determined by the expected sales of the product in the future periods.

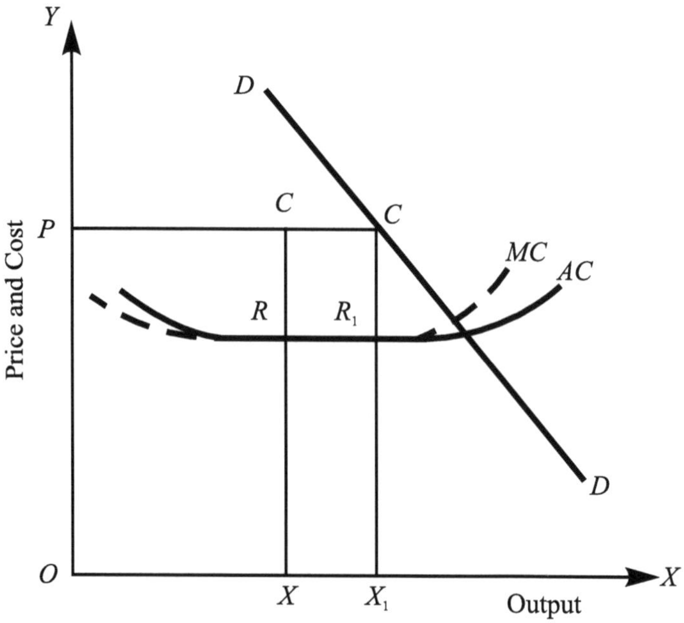

Fig. 33.2

In Figure. 33.2, let us assume that the firm has chosen output *OX* for estimating costing margin and for fixing price of the product. Further, suppose that if the given fixed sum of money, representing the total overhead (indirect) costs and the normal level of profits is divided by the chosen output *OX* it yields *RC* amount which will be the costing margin to be added to the average direct cost for determining the price of the product. It will be seen in Fig. 33.2 that at *OX* level of output, average direct cost is *RX*. If we add costing margin *CR* to *RX*, we get full-cost equal to *CX*. Thus, the price *OP* will be fixed equal to full-cost *CX*. It should be noted that *price OP fixed on the basis of full cost CX will remain unchanged* whatever the amount *demanded and the actual output produced in the given period.* Now, if the demand for the product is given by the curve *DD*, then it will be seen from the figure that at *OP* price,

2. It should be noted that output *OX* must lie within the maximum capacity output of the film if the given demand is to be fully met. However, if *OX* exceeds the maximum capacity and the film has accumulated stock of the product from the previous periods, then it can draw upon the stocks to meet the demand.

OX quantity of the product will be demanded and therefore produced.[2] Now, even if the *demand for the product increases or decreases, the price will remain unaltered at OP, provided the amount demanded lies within the range of constant average direct cost, that is, within its horizontal straight line portion;* and further provided that costing margin remains unaltered. Thus, we see that according to Andrews' version of full-cost theory also, price will change as a result of the changes in direct and indirect costs of production and not as a result of alteration in demand. Thus, according to full-cost theory "The price will not be altered in response to changes in demand, but only in response to changes in the prices of the direct and indirect factors."

Limitations of Full-Cost Pricing Theory

The theory of full-cost pricing is adopted on the assumption that a firm does not have the information required about demand conditions, nature and degree of competition, technology used, etc. Further, modern business conditions are extremely uncertain. Besides, a firm may be producing or selling a number of varieties of goods and to calculate prices on the basis of profit maximisation may be almost impossible. The cost-plus method is convenient since the firms have only to add some standard mark-up to their cost. Over a period of time, through trial and error, they can find out the proper mark-up. It is argued that this is what happens in practice. It is difficult to assess whether fixing price on the basis of a particular mark-up and changing the mark-up according to changing market conditions will result in actually maximising profit. This will, in fact, depend upon the ability of the management of a firm.

Another weakness of the full-cost pricing theory is its assertion that firms do not maximise their profits. In the opinion of most economists, profit maximisation is always the major and often the only objective of firms, though there can be other supplementary aims also, such as security. Besides, empirical studies of firms by Hall and Hitch and many others do not really invalidate profit maximisation assumption because businessmen and industrialists do often contradict themselves when they have to explain their views on profits, pricing, etc. Many of them speak about their social responsibilities and hide their real motive of profit maximisation.

Although full-cost pricing theory was formulated as an alternative to marginal principle, there is no contradiction between the two approaches; in fact, the marginal principle is consistent with the full-cost pricing theory. It is pointed out that even under the full-cost pricing theory, firms attempt to calculate the mark-up on the basis of profit maxim is at ion assumption, i.e. the mark-up is the maximum percentage which a firm thinks it can charge under the given circumstances. Besides, firms do change the mark-up according to changes in the demand and cost conditions and this implies that they are following profit maximisation approach while fixing prices and output on the basis of full cost.

Further it is difficult to fix a satisfactory profit margin in full-cost pricing, yet it would be possible for firms to get some idea of profit margin over a period of time. The normal or conventional profit margin will enable a firm to find out the prices it should charge. In general, therefore, the full cost pricing will roughly give us the same conclusion as the marginal cost analysis.

The full-cost pricing is also criticised on the ground that there is no clear motivation in choosing a price on the basis of full cost or fixing a particular mark-up. Under the marginal analysis the basic motive of every firm is to maximise its profits. Such a motivation is absent in the full-cost pricing theory. Naturally, it is difficult to predict how a firm fixes a particular mark-up or how a firm changes its price when demand and cost conditions change. But this criticism is not well founded since under the full-cost principle, firms do have some motivation or objective, *i.e.* they aim at a *reasonable or satisfactory* level of profit. But this concept of *reasonable* or *satisfactory* level of profit is much less precise than the concept of *maximisation of profit*. Moreover, the motive of reasonable and satisfactory level of profit comes under suspicion when firms raise their mark-up during business booms. If a firm is satisfied with a reasonable level of profit, why should it raise its mark-up during a business boom when making more profit is relatively easy?[3] The full-cost pricing principle has obviously no answer to such a question.

The theory of full-cost pricing attempts to explain price determination on the basis of full-costs of every firm. But a real problem arises when the industry is composed of a number of firms of different sizes and efficiencies producing a similar product. In fixing prices, each firm will have to consider, not only its cost of production but also the cost of production of others. In practice, it may not be possible to find out the cost of other firms. But there will always be some one firm whose price (based on its average cost) will serve as the standard price for the other firms. Such a firm will be the price leader and all other firms will become price-followers. Full-cost pricing without reference to price leadership does not, therefore, explain price determination in modern business realistically.

---

3. Sometimes a firm may not raise its price to the maximum level possible even when the demand for its product exceeds its supply and, thus, there is scope for raising price. This may be because the firm does not want to give the impression that it is exploiting the consumers. Or the boom conditions may be short lived and, therefore, price may have to be lowered later. In general, goodwill of consumers and profit maximisation in the long-run may induce firms to forgo short-run profit maximisation.

Merits of Cost-Plus Pricing

Despite these limitations, full-cost pricing principle attempts to explain the practice of price determination by manufacturing firms on the basis of their cost production. It offers a realistic explanation to the common business practice of maintaining prices for a long-period despite changes in demand. It is safer to set price on the basis of cost which is more stable. Besides, under conditions of competition, when prices are more or less the same, fixing price on the basis of full-cost and maintaining it will avoid price-wars and assure price stability.

Joel Dean argues that full-cost pricing is quite safe in pricing a new product. If the prevailing price in the market is such that it will not cover the estimated cost of the new product, the firm can as well not produce and market the product and thus avoid the loss.

4. Rate of Return Pricing

A refined version of cost-plus pricing has been developed in terms of Rate of Return Pricing. This system too makes use of the two concepts of full-costs and mark-up.

Under this system of pricing, the management is assumed to have a clear and definite rate of return on its investment. That is,

$$\text{Rate of Return} = \frac{\text{Earnings}}{\text{Capital invested}}$$

This rate of return on investment becomes the basis for the mark-up.

The management of the firm makes an estimate of the *normal rate of production,* by taking a period of years, viz. the normal output is the average of good and bad years. Then, the management makes an estimate of the total cost of production of this normal output; this is the *Standard Cost* of production. The next stage is for the management to calculate the ratio of invested capital to the year's standard cost. This gives us the capital turnover.

$$\text{Capital turnover} = \frac{\text{Investment}}{\text{Standard costs}}$$

Finally, the management calculates the mark-up, by multiplying the capital turnover by the expected rate of return on investment. For example,

Mark-up = Capital turnover   Rate of Return on Investment

$$= \frac{\text{Investment}}{\text{Standard Cost}} \times \frac{\text{Earnings}}{\text{Investment}}$$

$$= \frac{\text{Earnings}}{\text{Standard Cost}}$$

The mark-up is thus carefully planned and calculated, as different from the arbitrary percentage used in the cost-plus pricing.

The mark-up is then added to standard cost to determine the price:

Price = Standard Cost + Mark-up.

The management will regard this price as the base price applicable over a period of time. However, when cost of production changes as a result of changes in the prices of raw materials or due to changes in the levels of wages, the management can change the price suitably. Besides, the base price can be modified suitably according to changes in demand and competitive conditions in the market.

Evaluation of Rate of Return Pricing

As we mentioned at the outset, rate of return pricing is a refined version of full-cost or cost-plus pricing. It is refined-and, therefore, superior to cost-plus pricing in two ways:

(*a*) The analysis is based on standard cost which is computed on the basis of normal output; and

(*b*) The profit mark-up is based on planned rate of return on investment and not on any arbitrary figure.

All the merits and limitations of the cost-plus method of pricing apply to Rate of Return Pricing method also.

5. Target Pricing

Another version of full-cost pricing is known as target pricing. A firm might set before itself the target of getting a rate of return for its investment and fix its price to achieve that rate of return. In fact, a firm may have three alternative targets while fixing or changing the pricing of its product, viz.

(*a*) maintain a given rate of return on investment,

(*b*) maintain a given mark-up over costs,

(*c*) maintain a given rate of profit from total sales.

The target rate of return will be different in all the three cases. Let us illustrate target pricing with the help of a numerical example. The following information is available for a firm about its costs, sales, etc.:

1. Total investment in buildings, plant, etc.: $ 400,000
2. Total variable cost on materials, labour, etc.: $ 390,000
3. Total fixed cost on administration and overheads: $ 150,000
4. Total sales at $12 per unit: 50,000 units

Now, the total revenue is $6,00,000 (i.e. price = $12) and total cost is

$5,40,000; net profit is $ 60,000. If the variable cost of production increases by 10 per cent, how will the firm adjust its price?

Constant Rate of Return on Investment

Suppose that the firm wants to maintain a constant rate of return on investment. In that case:

$$\text{Return on investment} = \frac{60{,}000}{400{,}000} \quad 100 = 15 \text{ per cent}$$

If the firm sets the target of 15 per cent return on the net investment of $400,000, it has to maintain its net profit at the level of $60,000. Now 10 per cent increase in variable costs will mean total variable cost rising to $429,000 ($390,000 + 39,000).

Total variable cost	$ 429,000
Total fixed cost	$ 150,000
Total cost	$ 579,000
Net profit (constant)	$ 60,000
Total revenue targeted	$ 639,000
Total output	50,000 units

∴ Price to be fixed is $12.78 per unit.

Thus, a 10 per cent increase in the variable cost of production will necessitate a rise in price by 78 paise if the firm has to maintain a constant rate of return on investment.

Constant Mark-up over Costs

Suppose that, on the other hand, the firm aims at a given mark-up over costs. The present position is:

$$\text{Percentage mark-up over costs} = \frac{60{,}000}{540{,}000} \quad 100$$

$$= \frac{100}{9} = 11.1 \text{ per cent}$$

If the firm decides to maintain the mark-up of 11.1 per cent over total costs in the faqe of 10 per cent rise in the variable cost of production, the position would be:

Total cost = $ 579,000
Mark-up over cost = 11.1 per cent
Total revenue = 579,000 11.1 per cent

$$= 579,000 \quad \frac{100}{9}$$

$$= \$643,332$$

Number of units produced = 50,000

∴ Price per unit = $12.87

It is clear that the firm has to raise the price of its product by 87 paise if it aims at constant mark-up over cost.

Constant Rate of Profit from Total Sales

Suppose that the firm aims at a constant rate of profit from total sales. The position before the increase in cost of production is:

$$\text{Percentage profit on sale} = \frac{\$\ 60,000}{\$\ 600,000} \quad 100 = 10 \text{ per cent}$$

The firm aims at maintaining 10 per cent profit on sales, despite the 10 per cent increase in total variable cost of production. In such a case let us assume that the total revenue is X and 10 per cent of X would be $X/10$. The equation to solve is

$$X - \frac{X}{10} = \$\ 579,000$$

(multiplying all variables by 10)

$$10X - X = \$\ 579,0000$$

$$9X = \$\ 579,0000$$

$$X = \$\ 643,332$$

That is, the total revenue is $643,332. Number of units produced is 50,000 units. Hence price per unit is $ 12.87.

It is thus clear that a firm can decide about the change in the price of its product provided it has clear idea about target rate of return. But the basic weakness of this approach to pricing is that it tends to ignore demand and fails to consider competition adequately.

6. Other Methods of Pricing

Marginal Cost Pricing

Marginal Cost Pricing is said to be better than full-cost pricing. Under full-cost pricing, price is based on total costs comprising fixed and variable costs. Under marginal cost pricing, fixed costs are ignored and pricing is determined on the basis of marginal cost which refers to the cost of producing additional units. The price fixed must cover the marginal cost and total cost which will have to be covered in the long run. Price based on marginal cost will be much more aggressive than the one based on total cost. Besides, where a firm has large unused capacity, it should explore the possibility of producing and selling more it should cover the cost of producing the additional units (marginal cost). The real difficulty is that the management may not always be aware of the concept of marginal cost.

Going Rate Pricing

Under this system, a firm fixes its price according to the general pricing structure in the industry or according to the price set by the price leader. In a sense, each firm has "monopoly" power over its produce and it can, if it chooses, fix a monopoly price and face all the consequences of monopoly. In practice, however, it prefers the easier and more practical method of *choosing price going in the market.* It will change its price only when other firms do the same. Such a price policy is useful and safe to a firm under certain circumstances. For instance, the firm may not have an accurate idea of its costs or it may like to play safe and not provoke the larger firm to go for cut-throat competition. Besides, it is difficult for each firm to calculate the full implication of change in costs and prices and it is much better to follow the same pattern of pricing adopted by others. Even a large firm may be satisfied with going-rate pricing list a change in price by it unnecessarily disturbs the whole market. No firm would like to "spoil" the common market by reducing the price.

Customary Pricing

There are certain goods whose prices tend to be fixed more or less in the minds of consumers these are known as the "Charm" prices. A good example is the price of most soft drinks called by various names of cola. Most or all the soft drinks sell at the price at the same price; customers are accustomed to this price. Change in costs of production if the change is moderate will not affect the price, as the firms will not and cannot change price. Accordingly, a rise in cost of production may probably lead to reduction in quality of the product but not to a rise in price. Likewise, a fall in cost of production may not be accompanied by a decline in price. Pricing-in this case may be known as *customary pricing*.

Exercises

1. What do you understand by the term full-cost pricing? How is price determined under the principle of full-cost?
2. Explain the full-cost pricing theory: Mention its merits and demerits.
3. What do you mean by cost-plus pricing? Outline the pricing procedure by this method and evaluate its effectiveness.
4. Outline the pricing procedure by "rate of return pricing" method and bring out its merits and demerits.
5. Explain full-cost pricing and Andrews' version diagrammatically.
6. Write notes on the following:
   (*a*) Target Pricing (*b*) Marginal Cost Pricing
   (*c*) Customary Pricing (*d*) Going Rate Pricing

Multiple Choice Questions

7. (*i*) What is full-cost?
   (*a*) Average Direct Costs
   (*b*) Average Overhead Costs
   (*c*) Normal Margin for Profit
   (*d*) All above taken together [*Ans.* (*d*)]

   (*ii*) According to Hall and Hitch, business firms under oligopoly and monopolistic competition do not determine price and output by comparing *MC* and *MR* but fix prices on the basis of
   (*a*) full average cost of production
   (*b*) full fixed cost of production
   (*c*) satisfactory margin of profit
   (*d*) none of the above [*Ans.* (*a*)]

   (*iii*) Under oligopoly, the price of the product is fixed at the point
   (*a*) of kink in the demand curve (*b*) where $MC = MR$
   (*c*) where $AC = MC$ (*d*) where $AC = MR$ [*Ans.* (*a*)]

Chapter 34

Managerial and Behavioural Theories of the Firm

1. Introduction

As in actual practice, particularly in case of large corporations, there is a split between ownership by stockholders and control by managers, the profit-maximising approach (representing the interests of owners only) seems to be a partial approach. On the other hand, the managerial approach has been analysed and developed by, among others, W.J. Baumol, Oliver E. Williamson and R.L. Marris.

According to W.J. Baumol, managers get salaries plus allowances and, therefore, they are interested in their salary, power and prestige, which vary with the size of the firm; they would thus like to maximise sales rather than net profits. "The typical oligopolist's objective," he observes, "can usefully be characterised approximately as sales maximisation subject to minimum profit constraint."

According to Marris also, the manager of a modern firm tries to maximise the rate of growth of his firm.

It was however left to Williamson to develop a full-fledged managerial theory of the firm. He agrees with Baumol that the personal goals of managers include salary, status, power, prestige, seniority, professional excellence, social service, etc. He has himself proposed an economic model of the firm in which the managers (the decision-makers) of the firm seek to maximise *their utility* (subject to owners' minimum profit constraint), which depends on: (1) their salaries and other emoluments, (2) the size and quality of the staff reporting to them, (3) the magnitude of the discretionary investment expenditure by them, and (4) the type and amount of perquisites and prestigious facilities (the "management slack", e.g. lavishly furnished office, luxurious company cars, large expense accounts, lodging and boarding in big hotels when away on business, etc.) that they receive from the firm over and above the amount required for the firm's operations.

Again there are many ramifications of this theory. A standard approach by Kalman J. Cohen and Richard M. Cyert is as follows: "In particular, as one looks closely at the behaviour of actual firms, the justification for the assumption of profit maximisation seems to weaken. When one adds uncertainty to the firm's decision-making process, even defining the meaning of profit maximisation becomes difficult to do in an empirically meaningful way. The behavioural theory of the firm takes the position that arguments over motivation are somewhat fruitless. The critical issue is not whether one assumes profit maximising instead of satisfactory behaviour. Instead it is fruitful to develop an understanding of the process of decision-making within the firm." But there must be some objective or goal behind this internal decision-making process. According to this theory there are *multiple goals,* not just one goal. Profit-maximisation and sales-maximisation are the personal goals of the owners and managers respectively. Richard M. Cyert and James C. March have suggested, in addition, four possible *functional* goals of the firm: production goal, inventory goal, sales goal, and market-share goal. Within a firm there are different groups of people with different interests, and though they have to cooperate with each other, their group-interests may be mutually conflicting.

The *behaviour* of a firm depends upon its *form* (single entrepreneurial enterprise, partnership, joint-stock company, cooperative enterprise, government enterprise, etc.) and the *structure of market* (perfect competition, monopoly, monopolistic competition, oligopoly, bilateral monopoly, etc.) the firm operates in. The behaviour of a multinational corporation may be further different. The labour unions and the government also do exercise their influence on the behaviour of the firm. Nevertheless, if we *assume* that the *basic objective function* of the firm is to *maximise long-run net profits subject to a number of constraints* (financial, technical, organisational, institutional, managerial, etc.) *we will not be far away from the truth.* Both the owners and managers of the firm are interested in the growth of the firm, larger sales and capturing of new markets, prestige of the firm, its liquidity and security and do have in their mind the interests of workers, consumers and the government. The production goal, inventory goal, market-share goal, etc. are *subsidiary* to this basic long-term objective function which is more amenable to equilibrium analysis and objective quantification.

The second important element in the economic theory of the firm is the production transformation process or processes which enable it to convert some finite number of inputs into a finite number of different outputs. However, in the neo-classical marginal analysis the multiproduct, multifactor firm is assumed to function under the following production conditions:

(1) The firm possesses a production process capable of transforming a maximum of m variable factors of production into p product. There are, however, no limitations on the availability of the factors.

(2) The production function is continuous (with nonzero first- and second-order partial derivatives) and relates the set of independent factor variables to the set of independent product variables.

(3) The exact nature of the production function is predetermined by a set of technical decisions made by the firm's engineers and technicians.

(4) The firm's (well-behaved) production function is characterised by a decreasing marginal rate of technical substitution between any two factors; a decreasing marginal product for all factor-product combinations; and an increasing marginal rate of product transformation between any two products.

(5) All the firm's factors and products are perfectly divisible.

(6) The parameters which determine the firm's production function will not change over the time period considered.

(7) The parameters of the production function are not permitted to be random variables.

The firm is assumed to have access to three different types of information: (1) product-demand information; (2) factor-supply information; and (3) product-technology information.

We have already discussed the problems associated with product-demand information. The firm knows, either the prices of its products (and these prices are assumed to be constant, e.g. under perfect competition) or it knows its total revenue function (say, under imperfect competition).

Similarly, the firm is assumed to know and use the up-to-date state of technology, and has advance knowledge of factor-prices and factor-supply functions.

The firm needs more information under monopolistic and oligopolistic competition, e.g. regarding salesmanship and advertisements, reaction curves of competitors, etc.

On the basis of a given set of goals and given product-demand, factor-supply, and production-technology information, the firm makes two different types of decisions input decisions and output decisions.

The firm has also to take investment decisions, i.e. purchase and use of durable factors of production, such as equipment, plant, machinery, etc.

Now we shall consider some of the behavioural and managerial theories of the firm such as the Simom's Satisficing Theory, the Behavioural Theory of Cyert and March, Williamson's Managerial Decision Theory, Marris's Growth Maximisation Theory, and Baumol's Sales Maximisation Theory.

2. Simon's Satisficing Theory

Nobel Laureate, Herbert Simon was the first economist to formulate the behavioural theory of the firm. He says that the main objective of the firm is not maximising profits but satisficing profits. According to him, "We must expect the firm's goals to be not maximising profits but attaining a certain level of rate of profit, holding a certain share of the market or certain level of sales." Since the firm has to run under uncertainty, it can not be sure whether profits are being maximised or not. Here Simon makes a comparison between the behaviour of an organisation and the behaviour of an individual person.

A firm, like an individual, has its aspiration level in keeping with its needs. Its aspiration level depends on its different goals such as production, price, sales, profits, etc. and on its past experience. The aspiration level draws the boundary between satisfactory and unsatisfactory outcomes. Here the firm may face the three possible alternative situations: (*a*) the actual achievement may be less than the aspiration level, (*b*) the actual achievement may be more than the aspiration level, and (*c*) the actual achievement may be equal to the aspiration level. The first alternative may be due to much fluctuations in economic activity or because of qualitative deterioration in the performance level of the firm. The firm is satisfied with the second alternative which is due to its commendable performance. The firm is also satisfied with the third alternative. Hence the firm is not satisfied with the first situation when its actual achievement lags behind the aspiration level. It may be that the firm has fixed its aspiration level very high. It will therefore revise it downwards and start a search activity to fulfil its various goals. The advantage of search activity must be balanced against its cost.

Criticisms

The Simon's satisficing theory has been badly criticised. The main weakness of the theory is that Simon has not specified the 'target' level of profits which a firm aspires to reach. Further, Simon does not clarify a satisfactory level of performance based on a certain level or rate of profit. This is in no way better than the profit maximisation model. The profit maximisation model indicates an optimum level of profits, but in the Simon model there are many 'satisfactory levels' depending upon the groups that operate in the firm. It is very complicated to choose a single rate of profit which may satisfy all in the group.

3. Behavioural Theory of Cyert and March

Cyert and March[1] have also formulated a behavioural theory of the firm. According to this theory, the modern business firm is a complex organisation in which the decision-making process is related to different goals of the firm. The goals are fulfilled by the managers, workers, shareholders, suppliers, customers and so on. Cyert and March theory explains the following five types of goals of the firm:

1. *Productoin Goal.* This goal is related to output decisions. It depends upon stable employment, case of scheduling, development of acceptable cost performance and growth. Hence the goal represents in greater part the demand for those coalition members who are associated with production.

2. *Inventory Goal.* It represents the demand of coalition members who are associated with inventory such as salesmen and customers. It is related to decisions in output and sales areas.

3. *Sales Goal.* It aims at fulfilling the demand of coalition members associated with sales.

4. *Market-Share Goal.* It is an alternative to the sales goal. It is associated with the demand of sales management. Thus, the market-share goal is related to sales decisions.

5. *Profit Goal.* It is related to pricing and resource allocation decisions.

According to the Cyert and March theory, all the goals are to be satisfied because they are relevant to prices, output and sales strategy decisions of the firm. If any of them is not satisfied, i.e. the individual related to that activity is not satisfied then a search will be conducted to meet that goal. The search will be based on the rules of thumb which are also based on the past experience of the firm and the people within the firm.

The decision-making process in the Cyert-March theory rests with the top management and the lower levels of administration. The top management fixes the goals of the firm and allocates the given resources to the various departments based on their share of the total budget of the firm. The share of the budget depends on the bargaining power and the skill of each manager. The bargaining power will depend upon the past performance of each department. In this process of allocation, the top management retains some funds to be allocated at its discretion at any time to any department of the firm.

Once the budget share is fixed to each department, each manager of the department has considerable discretion in spending the funds at his disposal. Decisions taken by managers are implemented by the lower level staff based on their experiences.

---

1. R.M. Cyert and J.C. March, A *Behavioural Theory of the Firm,* 1963.

The Cyert and March theory has been criticised by Koutsoyiannis and Hawkins. According to them, it, in fact, is not a theory. It only deals with particular cases where as a theory is expected to be a general approximation of the behaviour of firm. It does not explain the interdependence and interaction offirms. It does not take into account the conditions of entry or the effects on the behaviour of existing firms of a threat of potential entry by new firms.

4. Williamson's Managerial Discretion Model

Williamson has formulated a managerial-utility-maximisation model as against profit maximisation model. It assumes that the shareholders and the managers of a firm are two separate groups. The shareholders want to maximise the returns on their investments, i.e. maximisation of profits. The managers are meant to have considerations other than profit maximisation in their utility functions. Thus, sthe managers are interested not only in their own emoluments but also in the size of their staff and expenditure on them.

Hence Williamson's theory is related to the maximisation of the manager's utility which is a function of expenditure on the staff and emoluments and discretionary funds.

Mathematically,

$$U = f(S, M, D) \qquad \ldots(1)$$

where

U = Utility Function

S = Staff Expenditure

M = Management Stock

D = Discretionary Investments

Also, $S \geq 0, M \geq 0, \text{ and } D \geq 0$

The model assumes that the law of diminishing marginal utility applies so that when additions are made to S, *M* and *D*, they would yield diminishing marginal utility to the manager.

Further Williamson assumes price (*P*) as a function of output (*X*), expenditure on staff (S) and the state of environmental (*E*), thus the demand function can be written as,

$$P = f(X, S, E) \qquad \ldots(2)$$

Also $$\frac{\partial P}{\partial X} < 0, \; \frac{\partial P}{\partial S} < 0 \text{ and } \frac{\partial P}{\partial E} > 0$$

The above relationships indicate that the demand for *X* is negatively related to 0, but is positively related to *S* and *E*. When the demand increases, the output and expenditure on staff will also increase which will lead to increase the costs of the firm and consequently the price will rise, and vice versa.

Now in order to develop a model, Williamson takes about four different types of profits: actual, reported, minimum required, and discretionary profits.

The equation of actual profits can be written as:

$$\pi_A = R - C - S \qquad \ldots(3)$$

where R = Revenue

C = Total Production Costs

S = Staff Expenditure

Now if the amount of managerial stock or emoluments (M) is deducted from the actual profits, we may get the reported profits:

$$\pi_R = \pi_A - M \qquad \ldots(4)$$

$$= R - C - S - M$$

Here, reported profits are taxable profits which are meant to pay taxes and dividends. The minimum required profits π_o, are the lowest level of profits after paying taxes which the shareholders must get in order to hold shares of the firm. Since discretionary profits (π_d) are what remains with the managers after paying taxes and dividend to sharehoders, therefore,

$$\pi_d = \pi_R - \pi_o - T \qquad \ldots(5)$$

where T = Taxes

To maximise managerial utility, the last unit of money (or dollar) spent on S, M, and D must yield the same marginal utility, so that the equilibrium condition is:

$MU_S = MU_M = MU_D\,(1 - t)$ where t is the tax on profits. ...(6)

5. Growth Maximisation Model of Marris

Robin Marris[2] has developed a dynamic balanced growth maximising model of the firm. According to him, "Modern big firms are managed by the managers and shareholders are the owners who decide about the management of the firms." The managers of the firm aim at maximisation of the growth rate of the firm and the shareholders aim at the maximisation of their dividends and share prices. To maintain a link between the growth rate and share prices, Marris has developed a balanced growth model. Here the managers fix such a growth rate at which the firm's sales, profits, assets, etc. grow. If the manager fixes a higher growth rate, he will have to incur more expenditure on advertisement and on R&D in order to create a larger demand for its products. He will, therefore, retain a larger proportion of the total profits of the firm and the share of the profits to be distributed among the shareholders in terms of dividends will fall. Consequently the share prices will also fall in the market.

Since the managers are more concerned about their job security and growth

2. Robin Marris, *The Economic Theory of Managerial Capitalism* (1964).

of the firm, they will fix that growth rate which maximises the market value of Shares, give satisfactory dividends to shareholders, and avoid the takeover of the firm. At the same time, the owners (i.e. shareholders of the firm) also desire balanced growth of the firm because it ensures fair return on their investment. Thus, both the managers as well as the shareholders have to achieve the same objective.

Marris's growth model has been criticised by Koutsoyiannis and Hawkins. They say that the theory assumes a given price structure for the firms and, therefore, does not explain how prices of the products are determined in the market. The theory has also ignored the problem of oligopolistic interdependence of firms in non-collusive market. According to Koutsoyiannis, "Marris's model is applicable basically to those firms which produce consumers' goods. The model is not appropriate for analysing the behaviour of manufacturing business or traders."

6. Baumol's Sales Maximisation Model

William J. Baumol[3] has presented a managerial theory of the firm based on the sales maximisation. According to this principle, the objective of a business firm is *sales maximisation* rather than *profit-maximisation.* (Let it be remembered that in terms of the traditional marginalist principle the objective of a firm is to maximise its profit or the firm is looked upon as the maximiser of profits.) But, according to this new principle, the ultimate objective of a firm is *not* to maximise its profit, but to maximise its sales. According to Baumol, every modern business firm wishes to maximise its sales revenue (i.e. price multiplied by quantity) rather than its profit. In other words, it desires to capture as large a portion of the market as possible, though in doing so it may not succeed in earning the maximum profit for itself. Why? The reason is to be found in changes that have taken place in the constitution and structure of the modern business corporation in recent years. As is well known, ownership and control do not vest in the same hands in a modern business firm. The ownership lies in the hands of shareholders while the actual control and management vest in the hands of professional managers. The shareholders are, undoubtedly, interested in maximum profits, but the professional managers are not. The latter are more interested in maximising the sales revenue rather than in maximising the profits. The reason is that the remuneration of the professional managers is very often related to the sales revenue rather than to the profits of the firm. Further, maximisation of sales revenue also adds to the prestige, reputation and standing of the firm in question. Hence, profit-

3. W.J. Baumol, *Business Behaviour, Value and Growth* (1959).

maximisation is no longer the sole or even the major objective of a modern business firm. This, however, does not imply that Baumol has ignored completely the profit-motive or profit-considerations in the pricing policy of a business firm. According to him, the firm should fix a price which not only covers the cost of production, but also yields adequate profit for the shareholders. After all, the satisfaction of the shareholders is of primary concern for the professional managers. If the sales maximising output does not bring adequate profit to the shareholders, the firm will have to select another level of output which will yield sufficient profit, even though it may not maximise the sales of the firm. In Baumol's words, "The typical oligopolist's objective can usually be characterised approximately as sales maximisation subject to profit constraint."

Baumol's sales maximisation principle can be illustrated with the aid of Fig. 34.1.

In Fig. 34.1, we have compared two equilibria of the firm; the first equilibrium is the equilibrium of the firm when its objective is sales or revenue maximisation while the second equilibrium represents the equilibrium of the

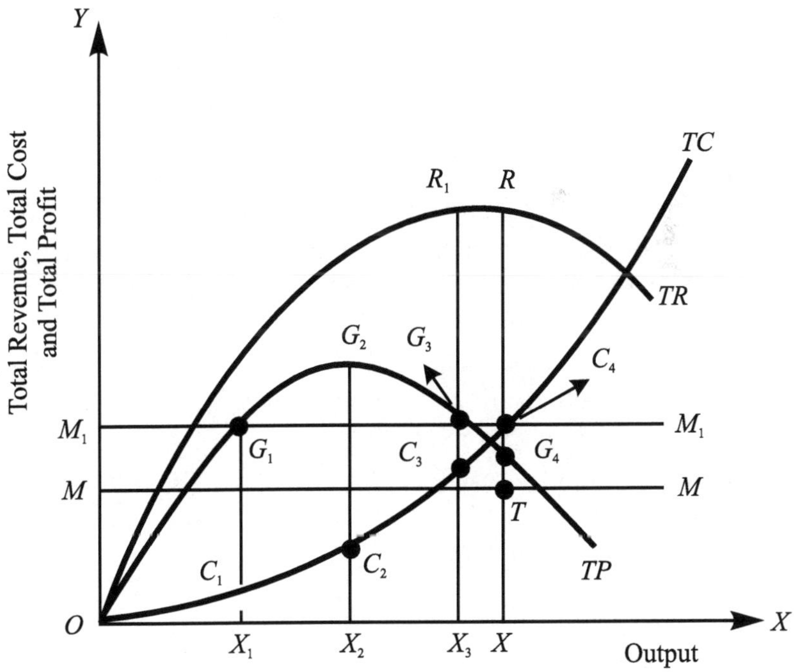

Fig. 34.1

firm when the objective is profit-maximisation. We have shown three curves in Fig. 34.1—*TR* (Total Revenue), *TC* (Total Cost) and *TP* (Total Profit) curves. The *TP* curve represents the difference between *TR* and *TC*. The *TP* curve reaches its peak at G_2 and G_2X_2 is the highest or maximum profit. OX_2 is the profit-maximising output in the diagram. If the objective of the firm is to maximise its profit, then it shall produce OX_2 output. Likewise, the *TR* curve reaches its peak at *R*, and *RX* is the maximum sales revenue of the firm. *OX* is the sales revenue maximising output. If sales maximisation is the objective of the firm, it will produce *OX* output. [It should be observed that the sales-maximisation output (*OX*) is larger than the profit maximising output (OX_2).] Now let us suppose that the sales maximisation objective of the firm is subject to the *minimum profit constraint*. In other words, the firm is required to earn a minimum amount of profit to satisfy the shareholders. Suppose, the minimum profit constraint is represented in the diagram by the line *MM*. Now the minimum profit constraint *OM* (or *TX*) is smaller than the actual profit (G_4X) being earned by the firm when it produces the sales-maximising output of *OX*. So the firm in question will go ahead by producing the sales-maximising output of *OX* as shown in the diagram. Now suppose that the minimum profit constraint is *OX* instead of being *OM*. The line M_1M_1 indicates the newly-risen minimum profit constraint. The sales-maximising output OM_1 now does not yield the minimum profit represented by the line M_1M_1. The firm will now give up its sales-maximising objective and retreat backwards to produce OX_3 output. This output does not bring maximum sales revenue to the firm, but it does assure the minimum profit of OM_1 (or, G_3X_3) to the shareholders. In other words, the firm waters down the sales maximisation objective to assure minimum profit to its shareholders. It may be pointed out that the minimum profit constraint line M_1M_1 intersects the Total Profit curve (*TP*) at the point G_1 as well. This implies that the firm can, if it likes, produce OX_1 output also. But, in actual practice, the firm will not opt for this output because at this output the total sales revenue is much less that what it is at the output OX_2. The firm will, thus, go in for OX_2 output because it assures larger sales revenue to it. Thus, the output is much larger under the sales maximisation objective (with minimum profit constraint) than under the objective of profit maximisation.

The main advantage of Baumol' s sales maximisation hypothesis lies in the fact that it provides still another motive to the modern business firm for its operations, namely, the motive of sales maximisation in addition to the motive of maximum profit. Baumol's hypothesis also furnishes a more realistic explanation of the behaviour of an oligopolistic firm. The oligopolistic firm, as is well known, is influenced more by the sales-maximisation motive than by the consideration of profit-maximisation. Baumol's hypothesis also explains, why an oligopoly firm resorts to non-price competition (i.e. advertising, publicity, product differentiation, quality improvement, etc.) in relation to the other oligopolistic firms. In other words, the oligopoly firm in question does not adopt price-cutting as a method to compete with other firms in the market.

The reason is obvious. The effect of price-cutting by the firm on its sales-revenue is uncertain. Price-cutting by the firm will be followed by price-cutting by other firms as well. The result is that there shall be little or no improvement in the sales-revenue of the firm in question. Price-cutting may not, thus, bring about any increase in the sales revenue of the firm concerned. But expenditure on advertisement, publicity, product differentiation, etc., is bound to increase the sales of the firm. It is on account of this that an oligopoly firm keeps the price of its product fixed but competes with its rivals through increased expenditure on advertisement, etc.

The main drawback of Baumol's hypothesis is that it has not been able to divest itself completely of the profit-motive. Though Baumol emphasises sales-maximisation as the objective of the firm, yet he does not rule out the profit-motive altogether. He stresses the importance of earning adequate profit by the firm to satisfy the shareholder. He goes so far as to say that a firm should select that level of output which yields adequate profit to the shareholders, even though it may not lead to sales-maximisation. In other words, he is prepared to sacrifice the objective of sales-maximisation to ensure adequate profit to the shareholders of the firm.

Effect of Changes in Overhead Costs on Price and Output

Baumol's sales maximisation hypothesis also gives rise to an important conclusion with regard to the influence of changes in overhead or fixed costs on the price and output of a commodity produced by a firm. The traditional price theory (based on the assumption of maximisation of profit) held the position that a change in overhead or fixed costs did not influence the equilibrium output of the firm, because the equilibrium output was determined as per the marginalist principle by the equality of *MR* and *MC,* and the *MC,* in its turn, was not affected by changes in overhead costs. Hence, changes in overhead costs had no effect on the equilibrium level of output. Nor did changes in the overhead costs affect the price in the short period. Thus, the conclusion of the traditional price theory was that changes in overhead costs produced no effect on the output or price of the commodity in the short period. Baumol, however, challenged this assertion of the traditional price theory with his sales maximisation hypothesis, and pointed out that changes in fixed costs do affect prices and outputs of the firm even in the short period. Baumol's argument can be illustrated with the help of Fig. 34.2.

In Fig. 34.2, *TP* is the total profit curve in the initial situation. The minimum profit required to be earned by the firm is indicated by *OM* and *MM* line is the minimum profit constraint line for the firm. If the objective of the firm is profit-maximisation, then it shall produce *OX* output, because at this output *GX* profit is the maximum. But if the objective of the firm is sales maximisation subject to the minimum profit constraint, it shall produce OX_2

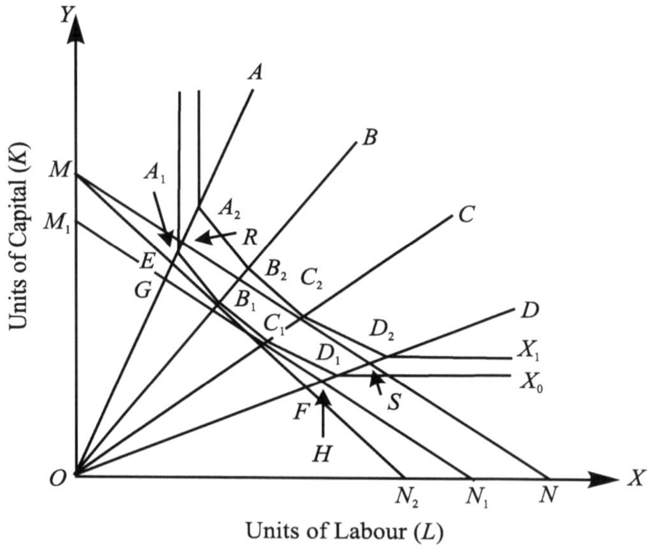

Fig. 34.2

output. Now let us suppose that the government levies a lump sum levy on the profit of the firm to the extent of TT_1. This means that the overhead or fixed cost of the firm will rise by this amount, or in other words, the profit of the firm will be reduced by this amount. The reduced profit of the firm is indicated in the diagram by the dotted curve TP_1. In other words, the total profit curve descends downwards on account of the increased fixed costs consequent upon the imposition of the levy. The new profit curve TP_1 (dotted curve) runs parallel to the original curve *TP*. Despite the increase in fixed costs, the profit-maximising output remains constant at the old *OX* level, confirming the conclusion of the traditional price theory, namely, that the changes in fixed costs do not change the output and price in the short period. But, as pointed out earlier, according to Baumol's sales maximisation hypothesis, changes in fixed costs do influence outputs and prices to the short period. Before the imposition of the governmental levy, the firm was producing an output of OX_2, and was earning a profit of R_2X_2 at this output. But after the imposition of the levy, the firm's profit at this level of output is reduced to FX_2. Now this FX_2 profit is less than the minimum profit constraint of *OM* (or, R_2X_2). Obviously, the firm shall not stick to this output of OX_2. It will reduce its output to OX_1, because this output enables it to earn the minimum profit of R_1X_1 indicated by the line *OM*. Due to the reduction in the output, the firm will also raise the price of the product. Thus, according to Baumol's hypothesis, the firm will change the output and price of the commodity even in the short period in response to changes in fixed costs.

Baumol has also applied his hypothesis to explain the incidence of corporation tax levied by the government on the profit of the firm. According to the traditional price theory (based upon the profit maximisation assumption), the entire money burden of the corporation tax will fall on the firm. The tax will, undoubtedly, increase the fixed costs (or, lower down the profit) of the firm as explained in the above diagram. But the firm shall not be able either to lower down its output or to raise the price to be charged from the consumers, meaning thereby that the entire burden will fall on the firm itself. But according to Baumol's hypothesis, the imposition of the corporation tax will reduce the total profit of the firm and compel it to cut down its output and raise the price of the product. Thus, a part of the money-burden of the corporation tax will be passed on to the shoulders of the customers, according to Baumol's sales maximisation hypothesis.

Exercises

1. Explain the behavioural theory of Cyert and March.
2. What are the important goals of a modern firm ? How do conflicts arise and resolved among them?
3. Explain the sales maximisation model of Baumol. What are its important assumptions and limitations?
4. Write notes on the following:
   (*i*) Simon's Satisficing Theory
   (*ii*) Williamson's Managerial Discretion Model
   (*iii*) Growth Maximisation Model of Marris.

Multiple Choice Questions

5. (*i*) The managerial approach has been analysed and developed by
   (*a*) W.J. Baumol (*b*) Oliver E. Williamson
   (*c*) R.L. Marris (*d*) All of the above [*Ans.* (*d*)]

   (*ii*) According to W.J. Baumol, the typical oligopolist's objective is
   (*a*) sales maximisation subject to minimum profit constraint
   (*b*) to attain maximum profit
   (*c*) to incur minimum cost
   (d) to get maximum output with minimum cost [*Ans.* (*a*)]

   (*iii*) Cyert and March theory of the firm explains the following goal of the firm
   (*a*) Production goal and market-share goal
   (*b*) Inventory goal and sales goal
   (*c*) Profit goal and production goal
   (*d*) All of the above [*Ans.* (*d*)]

   (*iv*) Williamson has formulated the following model
   (*a*) Managerial utility maximisation model
   (*b*) Sales maximisation model
   (*c*) Profit maximisation model
   (*d*) Cost minimisation model [*Ans.* (*a*)]

Chapter 35

Theory of Games and Price Determination

1. Introduction

The theory of games was developed by John Yon Neumann and Oskar Morgenstern in their famous work entitled *the Theory of Games and Economic Behaviour* in 1944. This theory determines the standards of rational behaviour in situations where the outcomes depend on the action of interdependent individuals. Actually the game theory is applicable to a diversity of problems, such as situations of duopoly, oligopoly, bilateral monopoly (where a market consists of a single seller and a single buyer) often fit into its category. We shall discuss the theory in relation to oligopoly (or duopoly) alone.

As we know, a player of the game has to select one among a variety of possible courses of action technically known as *strategies.* This applies to the duopolist as well. A duopolist's strategy consists of selecting a particular value for each of the variable under his control. For instance, there are three possible strategies open to the duopolist: (*i*) Changing the price; (*ii*) Changing advertisement expenditure; and (*iii*) Changing the quality of the product.

Now the duopolist may select any strategy best suited to its interests. Since there are three variables under his control, a strategy consists of selecting particular values for these three variables. Each duopolist (or the participant) is assumed to possess a finite number of strategies though the number may be very large. Before we analyse the solution, we should clear its *assumptions.* They are the following:

(*i*) The game theory assumes that while selecting its strategy, a duopolist will assume that his rivals will adopt a strategy which will be most unfavourable to its interests.

(*ii*) The game theory also assumes that a duopolist knows all the possible strategies open to it as well as those strategies available to his rivals.

The games are classified on the basis of two criteria: The number of participating firms or persons and the net outcome. The first criterion involves a counting of the number of persons with conflicting interests. There are *one-person, two-person, three-person,* and in the general case, *n-person games.*

The second criterion distinguishes between *zero-sum* and *non-zero-sum-games.* A zero-sum game is, one in which the algebraic sum of the outcomes, e.g. profits, for all the participating firms equals zero for every possible combination of strategies. If the net outcome of a game is different from zero for at least one strategy combination, it is classified as a non-zero-sum game.

A *one-person, zero-sum game* is not interesting because here a monopoly firm occupies the entire market and he gains nothing regardless of his strategy choice. A monopoly situation may be considered in a *one-person, non-zero-sum game.*

The *two-person, zero-sum game* is applied to a duopolistic market in which one duopolist's gains are always equal to the other's losses.

2. Two-person Constant-sum or Zero-sum Game

As we know the theory of games attempts to reach at a number of equilibrium solutions based on the rational behaviour of the market participants. The main idea behind the game theory is that each participant in a game is confronted with a solution whose outcome depends not only upon his own strategy but also upon the strategy of his opponent. *A strategy* is a particular application of the rules leading to specific result. *A move* is made by one player leading to a situation having alternatives. *A choice* is the actual alternative selected by the player. The various strategies adopted by each player in relation to the other is known as his pay-off. *The saddle point* in the game is the equilibrium point.

In a constant-sum or zero-sum game between two players the gains of one player are exactly equal to the losses of the other player. "There is for each player, a strategy which gives him the mathematical expectation of a gain not less than or of a loss not greater than, a certain particular value. It also shows that, if the players actually behave in this way, then those expected gains and losses are actually realised and the game has a determinate solution."

The game theory applied to oligopoly, gives good results only for the "two-person constant-sum game". In other words, the theory is applicable to a pair of duopolists who are competing for some given total profit. What is gained by one is lost by the other. In technical language, such a game is referred to as "strictly adversary game".

Assumptions

The two-person constant-sum game is based on the following assumptions:

(1) A duopolist market solution exists with duopolist *I* and *II,* each trying to maximise his profits.

(2) Each is engaged in constant-sum game so that what one duopolist gains, the other loses.

(3) One duopolist's interest is diametrically opposed to the others.

(4) Each duopolist is in a position to guess the strategy of the other as against his own strategy so as to construct the pay-off matrix of both.

(5) Each duopolist assumes that his opponent will always make a wise move and he would try to countermove that to protect himself from any possible loss.

Pay-off Matrix

The two-person, zero-sum game is also termed as *two-person, constant-sum game*. The present analysis is restricted to this situation only. Here, the theory is applicable to a pair of duopolists who are competing for some given total profit. What is gained by one is lost by the other. In other words, "the constant-sum game" implies that the profits to the two duopolists always add to a constant amount. For example, the profits to be shared by the two duopolists amount to Rs. 100. If duopolist *I* receives Rs. 60, the duopolist *II* will get Rs. 40. If, on the other hand, duopolist *I* gets Rs. 30, then the other duopolist will get Rs. 70. So that the aggregate profits will always be Rs. 100.

Now, the duopolists may have their different strategies to adopt so that each may be able to achieve its objective. In general, if duopolist *I* has *m* and duopolist *II* has *n* strategies, the possible outcomes of the game are given by the following *profit matrix*.

The profit matrix is also known as *pay-off matrix*.

$$\begin{bmatrix} X_{11} & X_{12} & \cdots & X_{1n} \\ X_{21} & X_{22} & \cdots & X_{2n} \\ \vdots & & & \\ X_{m1} & X_{m2} & \cdots & X_{mn} \end{bmatrix}_{m \times n}$$

where $Xij(i = 1,2, ...m \text{ and } j = 1, 2, ...n)$ is the profit of duopolist *I*, if duopolist *I* adopts i^{th} strategy and duopolist *II* adopts its jth strategy. Since the game is "zero-sum game", the corresponding profit earned by duopolist *II* will be $(-Xij)$.

For example, if duopolist *I* reduces his price by 10 per cent, then duopolist *II* may adopt three possible strategies: (*i*) he may reduce the price by 10 per cent or more than 10 per cent; (*ii*) he may increase his advertising expenditure; (*iii*) he may improve the quality of his product. As against a 10 per cent price reduction by duopolist *I*, his pay-offs (or profits) will be different for different counter strategies followed by duopolist *II*. Similarly, for a different strategy adopted by duopolist *I* to increase his sales, his pay-offs will be different, depending upon the counter strategy adopted by duopolist *II*.

For a specific example, consider the *I's* pay-off matrix presented in Table 35.1.

Table 35.1: Duopolist I's Pay-off matrix under Zero-Sum Game

	Duopolist II's Strategies					
	1	2	3	4		*Row Minima*
Doupolist *I*'s Strategies	1	16	80	40	10	10
	2	20	60	–20	–16	–20
Column Maxima		20	80	40	10	10 = 10

In Table 35.1, two strategies are open to duopolist *I*. As against these, duopolist *II* has four strategies to adopt. If duopolist *I* employs his first strategy and duopolist *II* employs his second strategy, then *I*'s profit will be 80 and *II*'s is –80 (because one's profit is other's loss in zero-sum game). If *I* adopts his second strategy arid as against it *II* adopts his third strategy, then *I*'s profit is –10, and *II's* profit will be 10.

But the duopolist's decision problem consists of choosing an optimal strategy. In Table 35.1, *I*'s pay-offs from his own strategies are given row-wise. Since *II* would like to minimise *I*'s gain (because *I*'s gain will be *II*'s loss), he will counter every move taken by *I* which minimises *I*'s gain. For example, when *I* selects his first strategy, *II* will select his fourth strategy and the outcome will be 10.

Similarly, if *I* selects his second strategy, then *II* will immediately adopt his third strategy and the outcome will be –20.

Hence *II* will always attempt to minimise *I*'s gain from his counter strategy. Thus, the minimum pay-offs (profits) to *I* doupolist from his two strategies are given under the column of *row minima.* Now it will be in the interest of *I* to choose that strategy which yields maximum of these minimum values. In other words, duopolist *I* will *maximise* and select his great strategy.

In Table 35.1, pay-offs to *I* from *II*'s strategies are given columnwise. If *II* selects his first strategy, *I* would immediately select his second strategy and the outcome will be 20. Here, given *II*'s strategy, as first *I* will maximise his pay-off (or profit) by choosing second strategy and the outcome will be 80. Thus, the maximum pay-offs which *I* will obtain, given *II*'s strategies, are given under the row of *column maxima.* Now it will be in the interest of *II* to choose that strategy which yields minimum of these maximum values (or pay-off) obtained by *I* from *II*'s strategies. In other words, duopolist *II* will *maximise* and select his fourth strategy.

Hence the optimum combination of strategies is 10 where *I* adopts exactly his first strategy and *II* adopts his fourth strategy. Here *I* obtains that much pay-off (profit) as *II* wants to him. Any combination of strategies other than this will not be optimum as one of two duopolists may not agree on it. Only at this optimal combination, the duopolists' decisions are consistent, and an equilibrium is established.

In general, for a zero-sum game, consistent decisions and attainment of equilibrium will require:

$$\max_{i}.\min_{j}., X_{ij} = \min_{j}.\max_{i}., X_{ij} = X_{14} = 10.$$

The Saddle Point

The saddle point is the equilibrium point. In the pay-off matrix of Table 35.1, duopolist *I*'s pay-off from its maximum strategy 4 exactly equal *II*'s pay-off from its minimax strategy 1 (10 = 10). When the minimax and the maximin in a pay-off matrix are equal, it is strictly determined game. Both the players (duopolists) are guaranteed a common amount of win (profit). They cannot win more because there is a saddle point in the pay-off matrix which occurs both in the 'Row Minima' and 'Column Maxima'. It is the equilibrium point 10, common to both *I* and *II* duopolists. Thus, a constant-sum two person game is strictly determined only if it has a saddle point arrived at with pure strategy.

Solution without Saddle Point

When there is no saddle point, then the solution is indeterminate for there is no equilibrium point in the 'Row Minima' and the 'Column Maxima'. In this case when duopolist *I* selects a strategy with a high pay-off, duopolist *II* selects some other strategy with a still higher pay-off. The pay-off matrix in Table 35.2 explains this case.

If duopolist *I* selects strategy 1 to have a pay-off of 14, there is nothing to prevent duopolist *II* from selecting strategy 3 for obtaining the pay-off 16. If duopolist *I* chooses strategy 3 for the pay-off 10, duopolist *II* might select

Table 35.2: Pay-off Matrix

Duopolist I's Strategy →	*Duopolist II's Strategy* ↓			*Row Minima*
	1	2	3	
1	10	14	8	8
2	4	6	10	4
3	20	12	16	12
Column Maxima	20	14	16	$12 \neq 14$

strategy 1 to get a profit of 20 and so on. In this pay-off matrix there is no equilibrium or saddle point. If any one of the two duopolists adopts his own strategy, it will be counteracted by the other's strategy. If duopolist *I* sticks to its maximum strategy 3, duopolist *II* will gain by choosing the non-minimax strategy 1. It will have a pay-off 20 against *I's* 12. The only solution to such a problem is to employ the maximin-minimax strategies. When duopolist *I* adopts the maximin strategy, it gains 12 while duopolist *II* gains 14 by adopting the mimax strategy. Each fears that the other might discover its choice of strategy and so wants to play it safe to be sure of a certain minimum of profit 2, the difference between 14 and 12 measures the extent of indeterminacy. This is because the maximin and the mimax are unequal $12 \neq 14$. Thus the solution is not stable. It means that where the pay-off matrix has no saddle point minimax always exceeds the maxi-min, as is clear in Table 35.2. The reason is obvious that player *I* in the game always chooses the maximum of the minimum rows, whereas player *II* always selects the minimum of the maximum columns.

Mixed Strategies

The duopoly problem without a saddle point can be solved by permitting each duopolist to choose mixed strategies. A mixed strategy refers to the introduction of an element of chance in choice making on a probabilistic basis. Thus, it is a probability distribution that assigns a definite probability to the choice of each pure strategy in such a manner that the sum of the probabilities in unity for each participant.

Under this technique a set of dice is given to each duopolist to throw and determine the strategy to be selected. Each duopolist has a pair of mixed strategies that leads to an equilibrium position. Each duopolist tries to adopt the most desirable expected value of the pay-off as against his rival; and is, therefore, in search of a set of probabilities for his mixed strategy so as to get the highest expected pay-off. This is termed as the *optional mixed strategy.* Suppose the game has a value denoted by *V*. Now the duopolist *I* tries till he gets the highest expected pay-off *V* by playing his mixed strategy, playing the same mixed strategy, duopolist *II* will try to keep *I*'s expected pay-off to the minimum of *V*.

In Table 35.3 we have shown a pay-off matrix where each duopolist has two strategies 1 and 2. It has no saddle point. Both the duopolists resort to the game of dice to reach at a solution. The rule is that if duopolist *I* throws the dice and the result is 1 or 2, he will select strategy 1 and if the outcome is 3, 4, 5, or 6, then he will select strategy 2. Applying this rule of the game, the probability of duopolist *I* selecting strategy 1 is 1/3 and of selecting strategy 2 is 2/3. Duopolist *II* will adopt the same strategies but with opposite probabilities in order to keep *I*'s expected pay-off to the minimum. The probability of duopolist *II* selecting strategy 1 is 2/3, and of selecting strategy 2 is 1/3. Thus, each must select both the probabilities. The expected values of the game V for duopolist *I* =1/3   2/3   6 + 1/3   1/3   4 + 2/3   2/3   2 + 2/3   1/3   6 = 36/9 = 4. Similarly, the expected value of the

game V for duopolist II = 2/3   1/3   6 + 2/3   2/3   2
+ 1/3   1/3   4 + 1/3   2/3   6 = 36/9 = 4.

Here each duopolist will attempt to maximise the "mathematical expectation of his profit", rather than the profit itself. The expected pay-off or the mathematical expectation of profit for each of the duopolist equals the value of the game (V= 4) when both choose their optimal probabilities. If duopolist *I* applies his optimal mixed strategy, his expected pay-off cannot

Table 35.3: Pay-off Matrix

Duopolist *I*'s Strategies	Duopolist *II*'s Strategies	↓	1	2
	II's Probabilities / *I*'s Probabilities		2/3	1/3
1	1/3		6	4
2	2/3		2	6

be less than *V*, whatever duopolist *II*'s choice of strategies may be. Similarly if duopolist *II* applies his optimal strategy, his expected loss cannot be greater than *V*, whatever duopolist *I*'s choice of strategies may be. Hence the solution becomes determinate when mixed strategies are applied.

3. Non-constant-sum Games

In real life most economic problems are of non-constant type where more than two persons are involved in the game. But such an analysis is highly complicated and is therefore not attempted here.

4. Limitations of Game Theory

Some economists have pointed out holes in the game theory in its application to the oligopoly problem. *Firstly,* the game theory is applicable to the duopolists. Complications ensue when it is sought to be applied to firms numbering more than two. *Secondly,* the theory is based upon the assumption that the duopolist always pursues a policy of "playing it safe". He suffers from the perpetual fear complex that his rival will play a strategy which will prove most unfavourable to his (duopolist's) interests. So he adopts a conservative and over-cautious policy. This behaviour is not supposed to be realistic. In the real world, the duopolist often undertakes risks to increase his profits. The "safety" assumption underlying this theory is, thus, far from being realistic. *Thirdly,* the oligopoly game is not a "constant-sum game", as assumed by the game theory. The duopolists do not fight to share profits of a *fixed* size. *Fourthly,* it is pointed out that the duopolists in the real world do *not* possess as complete a knowledge of the strategies open to them as well as to their rivals as assumed by the game theory. What to talk of the rival, a duopolist may not even be aware of all the strategies open to him. *Fifthly,* the game theory assumes that both the duopolists would adopt the most rational course of action open to them, i.e. both would play their maximin or minimax strategies. In case, one of the duopolists fails to adopt a rational course of action, the game theory would break down. It is on account of these inherent difficulties that the game theory has failed to offer a satisfactory explanation of oligopolistic behaviour. According to Prof. D. S. Watson, the contribution of the game theory to the advancement of knowledge about oligopolistic behaviour has been a vast disappointment.

Exercises

1. Show how the duopoly problem can be solved by assuming that the duopolists are engaged in a two-person zero-sum game.
2. What do you understand by a "mimax strategy"? Do you think it provides a meaningful explanation of firms behaviour than the traditional principle of profit maximisation?
3. Consider a two-person constant-sum game without a saddle point. Show in such a situation, with pure strategies a "mimax" always exceeds the "maximin". How would you solve such a game by a proper choice of mixed strategies?
4. Critically explain the theory of game as developed by John Von Neumann and Oskar Morgenstern.

Multiple Choice Questions

5. (*i*) Who developed the theory of game?
   (*a*) Neumann and Morgenstern (*b*) William J. Baumol
   (*c*) J. R. Hicks (*d*) Samuelson P.T. [*Ans.* (*a*)]

   (*ii*) What is a saddle point?
   (*a*) Balanced growth point (*b*) Imbalanced growth point
   (*c*) Equilibrium point (*d*) Unstable equilibrium point [*Ans.* (*c*)]

   (*iii*) In a constant-sum game, what is true?
   (*a*) what one player gains, the other loses
   (*b*) both players get equal gains
   (*c*) both players adopt the same strategy
   (*d*) mixed strategies are adopted by the players. [*Ans.* (*a*)]

   (*iv*) When the minimax and the maximin in a pay-off matrix are equal
   (*a*) it is a strictly determined game
   (*b*) it is a indeterminate solution
   (*c*) it can not be solved by a two-person constant-sum game
   (*d*) it can not be solved by a zero-sum game. [*Ans.* (*a*)]

Chapter 36

Input-Output Analysis

1. Introduction

The input-output technique was first introduced by the famous French economist Quesnay. He developed his *Tableau-Economique* which was later introduced in the form of 'input-output money flow system' by Harvard University's Wassily W. Leontief. Prof. Leontief popularised this technique in the field of Economics in 1951, for which he was honoured with the 1973 Nobel Prize.

Input-output analysis is the basic econometric reasearch under the theory of programming. The theory of programming is divided into two parts. The first part deals with the *internal consistency* of programmes, i.e. the co-ordination of various interdependent decisions which must be brought into agreement for the programme to be realised. The second part of the theory of programming deals with the question of *optimality of programmes,* i.e. there may be a number of internally consistent programmes and the task is to select the best (optimal) out of all the possible programmes. The present chapter is concerned mainly with the first part of the theory of programming.

The establishment of internal consistency of programmes constitutes a basic objective of socialistic planning. It is accomplished by means of so-called *balances of national economy.* According to Prof. D.M. Nachne, "Basically an input-output table is nothing but a particular kind of a macroeconomic balance sheet." The input-output is also called as the analysis of inter-industry or inter-sector flows or the analysis of inter-industry relations. According to Prof Lange, "The analysis of inter- industry relations, usually referred to as input-output analysis, serves the purpose of establishing the quantitative relations between various branches of production in the national economy. It studies the conditions of natural consistency of the output, of the various branches of the national economy which result from the fact that the output of one branch is the source of input in another branch."

2. Meaning of Input-output Analysis

Before we develop the technique of input-output analysis, it is necessary to understand the meaning of this term. The term, 'input' implies that object or material which is demanded by the entrepreneur or producer for purpose of production, where as the term 'output' is defined as the outcome of the productive effort. According to Prof. Hicks, input is that object which is purchased with a view to use it in an enterprise, whereas output is the thing made and sold by the entrepreneur. In this way, the input is received by the firm or entrepreneur whereas the output is produced by the entrepreneur. In other words, the input is a firm's expenditure and the output is its income. From this point of view, the money value of inputs is the firm's total cost while the money value of total output is the firm's total revenue.

On the basis of the concept of input-output analysis one finds inter-industry relations and interdependencies in the entire economy because the input of one industry is the output of another. This is the reason why input-output analysis is also named as inter-industry analysis. As Prof. W.J. Baumol states, "Input-output analysis is the name given to the attempt to take account of general equilibrium phenomena in the empirical analysis of production." Whatever is used up in the production of a commodity, is called input and whatever is produced, is called output. Therefore, the input-output analysis explains the interdependence of inputs and outputs.

3. Main Features of Input-output Analysis

According to Henderson and Quandt, "The input-output system is an empirically oriented multi-market analysis. Its assumptions represent a considerable simplification of the general multi-market equilibrium analysis (*Leon Walras's Model*). Utility functions are omitted, and consumer demands are stated on the basis of outside information without regard to the equilibrium of individual consumers. The industry, rather than the firm, is the unit of production. The production function for each industry is of the constant-coefficient type, and there are no optimisation problems in the productive share." In other words, there are three important points to be noticed in the problem of input-output analysis.

According to Prof. J.K. Mehta, "Input-output analysis plays an important part in preparing an economic policy for economic forecasting in developed countries and for economic planning (programming) in developing countries."

(1) We observe that the analysis deals almost with production. Demand theory plays no role in the input-output analysis. Here, the problem is necessarily technological. A producer is always curious to determine what can be produced and how much quantity of raw materials should be utilised in the production process.

(2) Again, the distinctive feature of input-output analysis is its devotion to empirical investigation. This feature distinguishes it from Walras analysis of general equilibrium. Input-output employs a model which is more narrow than the Walrasian general equilibrium theory, because it (input-output model) encloses fewer phenomena. It exclusively emphasises the production side of the economy and ignores, completely the demand side of the economy.

(3) The outputs found by this method need not satisfy market equilibrium conditions. Here, the general equilibrium phenomena are used just for the sake that input-output analysis seeks to take account of the interdependence of the various sectors of the economy. In other words, the input-output model is characterised by the, "general" without the equilibrium.

The interdependence arises because each industry employs the outputs of the other industries as its raw materials. Its output, in turn, is often used by other industries as an input. For example, steel is used by railway industry and petrol industry; similarly railways (as the means of transporting steel) and petrol (fuel) are used by steel industry. Hence, the basic problem is to find what can be left over for final consumption (consumer, military, etc.), and how much of each output will be used up in the prodution process (as inputs) to obtain these net outputs. Successful trials on such problems result in many applications. It can be used in producing requirements if usable demand estimates can somehow be obtained. It can be used for economic planning including problems of economic development in 'backward areas'. The most important use of input-output analysis is the formation of a national income accounting matrix.

Assumptions

The input-output analysis is based on the following important assumptions. They may be relaxed to some extent in practice.

(1) The economy is in perfect equilibrium.

(2) The whole economy is divided into a number of sectors and sub-sectors.

(3) It assumes that there are n-industries and n-commodities. *No two commodities are produced jointly.* Each industry produces only one homogeneous output.

(4) In any productive process, all inputs are employed in fixed proportions. The use of these inputs expands in proportion with the level of output. In other words, it assumes a linear homogeneous production function. This assumption is normally relaxed in practice.

(5) Production technology is assumed to be static, because input coefficients remain constant.

(6) Inputs and outputs are expressed in terms of money values.

(7) The total output of anyone industry is used as an input by some other industry, by the same industry or by the final demand sector.

(8) Production relations are assumed to be linear.

(9) There are no external economies and diseconomies of production.

4. Construction of Input-output Tables

An input-output table consists of several rows and columns. Every row explains the output distribution of a particular sector and every column explains the inputs of this particular sector of the economy. In this way, each sector of an economy consists of a row and a column. Let us take an example where the economy is divided into four sectors as: Agriculture, Industry, Power and Transport. We also assume that these sectors use each other's output as input but do not use their own outputs as inputs. A part of each output is used for export, capital formation and consumption. This part is put under the name of final demand. Again, the input which various sectors of the economy get from import) government and consumers in terms of labour (or in any form) is called *primary input.* The relevant information has been put in Table 36.1. This table is an example of input-output money flows (in $10M). Sum of final items (outputs) will give national income or product (*GNP*). Each sector's output is listed twice by row and by column. Each row shows what happens to its output. Each column shows its needed inputs.

The Table 36.1 clearly shows that Agricultural sector uses the outputs of industrial sector worth $360M, power worth $520M and transport worth $760M. Besides, it uses primary inputs (or the output, say labour of household sectors) worth $3,560M. In this way, the gross input of Agricultural sector comes to be of the cost $5,200M. Its gross output amounts to be of $5,200M, which it distributes to various sectors of the economy as, industry worth $400M, power worth $500M, transport worth $700M and the rest worth $3,600M goes to final demand sector of the economy. In a similar way, other sectors of the economy also get their inputs and distribute their outputs. In equilibrium (or the economy), it is necessary that input and output of each sector must be equal. In other words, under conditions of general equilibrium, each branch (sector) of the economy would produce just what was required of its products (or output) by all the other branches, so that there would be no needs unfulfilled and no products unsold anywhere in the economy.

Table 36.1: Input-Output Table

(*$ in 10m*)

	Sectors of the Economy	Purchasing Sectors (1) Input to Agriculture	(2) Input to Industry	(3) Input to Power	(4) Input to Transport	(5) Final Demand	Total Output or Total Revenue
Selling Sectors	1. Agriculture	—	40	50	70	360	520
	2. Industry	36	—	44	76	244	400
	3. Power	52	74	—	40	414	580
	4. Transport	76	66	66	—	472	680
	5. Primary Inputs Supplied by Household Sector	356	220	420	494	—	1490
	Total Input or Total Cost	520	400	580	680	1490	3670

Hence, on the basis of input-output table, a planner may easily know the consistent objectives of various sectors of the economy. If the optimal output level of a particular sector is known, then the optimal output levels of other sectors can easily be found because it is possible to calculate the technical coefficients of each sector with the help of this input-output matrix. Technical coefficient shows the per unit input requirement of a given level of output. For example, the total output of agricultural sector amounts to $520 M and for this output level, it requires input worth $360M from industrial sector. Therefore, the technical coefficient of agricultural sector to industrial sector will be 36/520 = 0.06. On the other hand, the technical coefficient of industrial sector to agricultural sector will be 40/400 = 0.1. Similarly, we may calculate the technical coefficient for each sector and may easily find out the optimal level of output of a particular sector which should be produced to maintain the equilibrium condition.

In other words, we may develop two types of equations from the input-output matrix (table)[1] : (*i*) with the help of columns, and (*ii*) with the help of rows. These equations are called *Balance Equations* or *Structural Equations.* The basis of these equations is the technical coefficients. For each sector, we may have three technical coefficients. But, in a situation when each sector

1. It is also referred to as the *Transaction Matrix.* The transaction matrix is an array of rows and columns. It clarifies the manner in which the total output of anyone industry is to be distributed as the inputs of other industries and the final demand sector.

also consumes its own output, then we may have four technical coefficients. Now, we shall convert Table 36.1 in the form of input-output coefficients as shown in Table 36.1.

Table 36.2: Input-Output Coefficients

	Sectors of the Economy	Purchasing Sectors				
		(1) Agriculture (X_1)	(2) Industry (X_2)	(3) Power (X_3)	(4) Transport (X_4)	(5) Final Demand (X_5)
Selling Sectors	1. Agriculture	(X_1) —	0.10	0.09	0.10	0.24
	2. Industry	(X_2) 0.06	—	0.08	0.11	0.16
	3. Power	(X_3) 0.10	0.19	—	0.06	0.28
	4. Transport	(X_4) 0.15	0.16	0.11	—	0.32
	5. Primary Inputs Supplied by Household Sector	(X_5) 0.69	0.55	0.72	0.73	—
	Gross Total	1.00	1.00	1.00	1.00	1.00

In the situation of general equilibrium we may develop the following five *Balance Equations* (in terms of column-input coefficients only) for the five sectors as:

$$X_1 = 0.06X_1 + 0.10X_1 + 0.15X_1 + 0.69X_1$$
$$X_2 = 0.10X_2 + 0.19X_2 + 0.16X_2 + 0.55X_2$$
$$X_3 = 0.09X_3 + 0.08X_3 + 0.11X_3 + 0.72X_3$$
$$X_4 = 0.10X_4 + 0.11X_4 + 0.06X_4 + 0.73X_4$$
$$X_5 = 0.24X_5 + 0.16X_5 + 0.28X_5 + 0.32\,X_5$$

Similarly, we may also obtain the following *five Balance Equations* in terms of rows of coefficients as:

$$X_1 = 0.10X_2 + 0.09X_3 + 0.10X_4 + 0.24X_5$$
$$X_2 = 0.06X_1 + 0.08X_3 + 0.11X_4 + 0.16X_5$$
$$X_3 = 0.10X_1 + 0.19X_2 + 0.06X_4 + 0.28X_5$$
$$X_4 = 0.15X_1 + 0.16X_2 + 0.11X_3 + 0.32X_5$$
$$X_5 = 0.69X_1 + 0.55X_2 + 0.72X_3 + 0.73X_4$$

In order to make use of the input-output table, it is necessary to transform the above table into a general example, and for this a transactions matrix is to be constructed. The transactions matrix clarifies the manner in which the total output of any one industry is to be distributed as the inputs of other industries and final demand sector. Now the transactions matrix for the economy has been shown in Table 36.3.

Table 36.3: Transactions Matrix

	Sectors	*Purchasing Sectors*				*Final Demand*	
		Agriculture	*Industry*	*Power*	*Transport*	*or Consumption Sector*	*Total Output*
		(1)	(2)	(3)	(4)	(5)	
Selling Sectors	1. Agriculture	X_{11}	X_{12}	X_{13}	X_{14}	α_1	X_1
	2. Industry	X_{21}	X_{22}	X_{23}	X_{24}	α_2	X_2
	3. Power	X_{31}	X_{32}	X_{33}	X_{34}	α_3	X_3
	4. Transport	X_{41}	X_{42}	X_{43}	X_{44}	α_4	X_4
	5. Household	X_{51}	X_{52}	X_{53}	X_{54}	0	X_5

In Table 36.3, we have zero figure in the fifth column and fifth row, which indicates the fact that household sector is simply a spending (consuming) sector that does not sell anything to itself. In other words, we can say that labour is not directly consumed. Table 36.3 can also be shown in the form of production function (by taking column-wise):

$$X_1 = f_1 (X_{11}, X_{21}, X_{31}, X_{41}, X_{51})$$
$$X_2 = f_2 (X_{12}, X_{22}, X_{32}, X_{42}, X_{52})$$
$$X_3 = f_3 (X_{13}, X_{23}, X_{33}, X_{43}, X_{53})$$
$$X_4 = f_4 (X_{14}, X_{24}, X_{14}, X_{44}, X_{54})$$

Similarly, the distribution of total output among various sectors can be written as (by adding row-wise):

$$X_1 = X_{11} + X_{12} + X_{13} + X_{14} + \alpha_1$$
$$X_2 = X_{21} + X_{22} + X_{23} + X_{24} + \alpha_2$$
$$X_3 = X_{31} + X_{32} + X_{33} + X_{34} + \alpha_3$$
$$X_4 = X_{41} + X_{42} + X_{43} + X_{44} + \alpha_4$$
$$X_5 = X_{51} + X_{52} + X_{53} + X_{54}$$

In order to explain the behaviour of the economy, Leontief has elaborated two kinds of relations, which he calls the *"fundamental relations of balance and structure"*. The first is called the balance equation, since it indicates the internal stability or equilibrium of each sector in the economy. The second is called the 'structural equation', since it shows the external equilibrium of each sector or inter-sector relationships. If it is assumed that the total production of industry i ($i = 1, 2, \ldots n$) is used by n industries, then the balance equation will take the form:

$$X_i = X_{i1} + X_{i2} + X_{i3} + \dots X_{in} = \alpha_i$$

where α_i the amount of X_i which is distributed to the household sector (consumers). Leontief has also accepted the assumption of constant coefficient, that is, the inputs of every industry X_{ij} make use of the constant ratio of production. In this case, 'technological or input coefficient' of the industry will be found as below:

Technological coefficient, or $a_{ij} = X_{ij}/X_j$ where X_{ij} indicates that part of output of ith industry which is consumed by j^{th} industry and X_j denotes the total output of jth industry. Therefore,

$$X_{ij} = a_{ij}X_j$$

This equation clarifies the quantity or proportion of the total output of one industry that is used in another industry. This equation is known as the structural equation. Since, it is assumed in the input-output analysis that the total output of one industry is consumed by other industries and final demand sector, it clarifies the structure and flow of the entire economy. Therefore, a combination of many structural equations suffices to clarify the existing technological situations of the economy. A table of various input-output coefficients is called the '*technological matrix*', which has already been discussed in Table 36.2.

5. Applications of Input-output Analysis in Planning

The basic concept of input-output analysis has been adopted by many socialist states as well as other states which have undertaken programmes of economic development. One of the most constructive ideas in the programmes of both the socialist countries and the communist countries is the proposal to integrate the whole economic process into a well co-ordinated, consciously unified system. They regard competitive industry as wastefully disorganised. therefore, they usually place the socialist industry under the central guidance of national planning body (as National Development and Reform Commission in China). It is the task of this body to survey the needs of the community, to set against those needs the supply of various productive resources available and then to direct the employment of those resources in the ways best calculated to maximise the social welfare. The various operations of industries, instead of being left to the individual judgement of the thousands of enterprisers, would be directed in accordance with an overall plan.

We may calculate, what part of the products of each branch of industry is absorbed by the other branches. By this process (of input-output matrix), it is possible for the statisticians to have a precise picture of the input-output relationship of the whole economic process. Collectivists believe that this would result in a much smoother flow of material through the various stages of manufactures and distribution to consumers without the numerous shortages and surpluses. The various branches of industry would be optimally fitted to each other and there would be no depression of serious unemployment.

Again, the input-output analysis, which shows the relationship between the various branches of production in an economy, comes handy to planners of the economy. An unplanned economy relies upon the process of the trial and error that goes on in the free markets of commerce to keep these inter-industry relations in balance with each other. A planned economy would try to eliminate the error in this process by working out the needed relationship in advance and then directing the industry accordingly. No doubt, the central planning body might use an immensely more accurate and improved form of input-output table to guide it.

Socialistic countries which have adopted planning on a massive scale to bring about a smooth growth in their economy, have made a good use of the input-output analysis in their economic plans. With the aid of statistics, collected from all parts of the country, the central planning body works out annual industrial budgets for the nation, appraising the needs and possibilities for various sectors of production and devising longer programmes, projecting for fixed periods the direction and growth of all economic activities.

The Leontief input-output tables may be used for purposes other than studying the inter-sector relations between various sectors of production. We may construct a table similar to the Leontief table, except that instead of sectors of production we may consider various administrative regions of the country or various countries. We then get a scheme facilitating the study of input-output flows between regions (of a country) or countries.

Again, input-output tables are also used for the study of railway freight traffic. The role of sectors of production in the railway traffic tables, which have been drawn up for years, now, are played by the various railway stations. "Inter-sector flows" have been replaced by the tonnage of freight sent from one station to other.

From the above discussion, it appears that the Leontief input-output tables may be interpreted in all sorts of manner and may be applied in different econometric studies concerning phenomena relating to inter-flows between sectors, regions and countries, etc.

6. Use of Input-output Analysis in Indian Five-year Plans

Input-output analysis has been fairly used in Indian Planning also. Although collectivism provides for a more suitable climate for direction and supervision of the economic activities of a nation than mixed economy which prevails in India, yet suitable modifications and improvisations in the input-output concept and practice should enable our country to achieve industrial and agricultural advancement through proper procedure of targeting and their implementation and by appropriate linking of relationship between various branches of a production in the economy.

The industrial policy laid down by the Government of India since independence has provided for fixation of priorities in the economy among various sectors and their division in various categories public sector, private sector and the mixed sector. The increasing role of the state in the country's economy, as evidenced by the expansion in the public sector plan outlays, is paving the way for developing the economy into a well-planned manner to achieve the objectives of various sectors.

Now we come to the question of adaptability of the input-output technique to India's economic planning, we have to find out a consistent flow-pattern yielding a desired set of the final products through material balancing. Suppose, our planners wish an increase in the net output of steel over a certain time period. By developing an input-output matrix, the planners can immediately see with the help of the input-output techniques how much coal, iron, transport, labour, etc. will be needed to produce goods which in turn can be used in steel production. The calculation will also show how much steel expansion will be needed to sustain the level of additional production of the various goods needed for steel making. The solution is rapid and exact. While, by a process of successive approximation it is possible to apply the Leontiefs solution, the fact that all the balances are duly balanced does not indicate that the solution has been reached. The system of material balances does not show the magnitude of technical coefficients, because the matching of inputs from one balance with the output from another presents great difficulties.

Recently P.P. Pillai has, for the first time, constructed an input-output structure of Kerala's industrial economy. He presents an inter-industry transaction table and a matrix of production coefficients for the organised industry sector in Kerala for the year 1964. For the purpose of analysing the structure of the economy, he identified the following twenty-four production sectors: (1) Plantation, (2) Food-grains, (3) Fishery, (4) Animal Husbandry, (5) Other Agriculture, (6) Food Industries, (7) Cashew-processing, (8) Oil Industry, (9) Textiles, (10) Coir Manufacturing, (11) Paper and Paper Products, (12) Wood and Cork Industry, (13) Chemicals, (14) Drugs and Pharmaceuticals, (15) Soaps and Glycerine, (16) Basic metal and metal products, (17) Machinery except electricals, (18) Transport Equipments, (19) Electric Light and Power, (20) Rubber and Rubber Products, (21) Electrical Equipments, (22) Miscellaneous Industries, (23) Transport, and (24) Construction.

The first five sectors constitute the Agriculture and Allied sectors in the state (Kerala) income accounting classification and sectors 6 to 22 constitute the Industrial sector. He says that compilation of this 24 24 input-output matrix requires a larger volume of data. Unfortunately, many of these data are not readily available, though not completely lacking. One searching for necessary data for this purpose gets perplexed and discouraged. That many essential and important data about the state's economy are lacking; will be realised only when one begins to do quantitative exercise of the kind we require. Although many state agencies are collecting these data but they don't serve the purpose. This lacuna in data is the major difficulty in the use of such an input-output analysis in our country. Only due to his reason, Mr. Pillai has limited his study on the Industrial sector of the state's economy. He has included 17 sectors (from 6 to 22 of the above-mentioned sectors which constitute the industrial sector of the economy).

He concludes that the economy of Kerala is essentially an open economy in the sense that it trades with the rest of India and with other countries. The transaction matrix shows that the main intersectoral forward linkage sectors in the industrial economy, in the sense of commodity disposal, are paper and paper products, wood and cork, chemicals, basic metal and metal products, and electric light and power. There are no sectors with important backward linkage in the sense that they depend for inputs on many of the other sectors. No sector receives inputs from more than seven sectors. Except the sectors chemicals, basic metal, machinery, transport equipment and electric light and power, all other sectors are dependent on agricultural crops. Cashew processing industry is the one most heavily dependent on agriculture. Other sectors which depend heavily on agriculture for their inputs are oil industry, food industries, textiles and coir manufacturing.

Again, the transaction table indicates that the production in the oil industry is far below the demand for it. It means, a large part of our demand for oil is fulfilled by its imports from abroad. Similar is the position in basic metal and metal product industries.

On all-India basis, some work on input-output tables was started by Indian Statistical Institute in 1950-51. Only a limited number of big sectors of the economy was studied, because sufficient data were not available. A 36 36 Transaction-Matrix was prepared in 1951-52 (the initial year of the First Five-Year Plan). A modification was made in the classification of the sectors included in the 36 36 old transaction-matrix. In 1952, Planning Commission started working on input-output analysis through the Central Statistical Organisation (C.S.O.) agency. In 1960-61, a matrix was prepared by the Long-run Planning Cell.

The production-targets in the draft outline of Fifth Five-Year Plan (1975-79) were determined on the basis of a detailed 66 66 matrix. Therefore, it divides the whole economy into 66 sectors for the purposes of fixing production targets. Also, a 4 4 matrix was used to estimate the economic sources of the plan. In the Seventh and Eighth Plan also, the Planning Commission made an extensive use of input-output analysis. Hence, input-output analysis occupies an important place in India's economic planning.

7. Limitations of Input-output Analysis

Despite its obvious advantages, the Leontiefs input-output system cannot be wholly accepted for purposes of planning. The input-output analysis developed by Wassily Leontief is based on the following two fundamental assumptions:

(1) Labour is the only scarce factor-input,

(2) The input-output coefficients are fixed.

Neither of these assumptions is valid or useful for short-term plans for which we are more interested. The important limitations of input-output analysis can be explained under the following points:

(1) In short-term plans, one of the fundamental problems is how to utilise the existing capacity. In making balancing adjustments planners must reckon with capacity limitations which limits the possibility of upward adjustments in balances.

(2) Capacity limitations can be taken into account in the course of balancing, since each balance is treated as a separate entity. In a Leontief system, where the solution is carried simultaneously for the whole economy, capacity limitation cannot be included so easily. Of course, it is possible to portion the transaction matrix and obtain solutions for sub-sectors, thus it makes sure that the capacity limitations are not violated by the system. The abandonment (complete self-surrender) of the overall approach equivalent to the abandonment of simplicity, and the superiority of the Leontief solution becomes more questionable.

(3) Further, the labour scarcity assumption of input-output analysis is quite inappropriate for a country like India which has a fast growing labour force and often underutilises its manpower. But, when labour shortages occur, they usually take the form of excess demand for a specific skill rather than an overall demand for manpower.

(4) The input-output analysis assumes input-output ratios to be constant. But in preparing material balances, planning technicians search for possibilities of increasing output without a proportional increase in all inputs. Thus, the approximation method allows balancing through coefficient modification and disproves the validity of the assumption of Leontief input-output analysis.

(5) Planning in socialist countries does not make any assumptions about the functional or proportional relationship between variables under the input-output system. The planners with material balancing can alter the factor proportion at every step (whenever changes in variables occur).

(6) Moreover, the physical measurement units of different commodities are different. It creates a great difficulty in the formation of input-output tables

and technical coefficients. We may normally include money prices into our system to get rid of this difficulty; but money prices are influenced by the index of general price level. The ratios which are calculated on the basis of money prices, will be proper in future dates (due to the prevailing degree of inflation). Hence, conclusions based on these fixed input-output coefficients will not tell us the true picture of the economy.

(7) The assumption of constant returns to scale will not hold for a long time. Hence, changes in technological factors and scale of plant have not been viewed in the Leontief's input-output analysis.

(8) Some factor inputs such as services, insurance, transportation, etc. are expressed only in monetary terms. It means, the balancing equations of input-output analysis in terms of physical units will not be able to predict the correct situation of the economy.

In spite of these difficulties and limitations in the use of Leontief input-output analysis for short-term planning, mathematical methods are gaining increasing importance. Mathematical Programming[2] is used to get the solution of the problems involving capacity limitations, while broad input-output calculations are made to ensure overall consistency of plans. As yet, these methods do not yield striking results because of inherent limitations in the data performance reports are inaccurate and they come in with a considerable time lag. Worst of all, the statement of policy goals cannot readily be quantified and the goals themselves are subject to modifi-cation in the course of the balancing process.

Exercises

1. What are the main features of input-output analysis? How do we construct the input-output tables?
2. Explain the various applications of input-output analysis in planning. What are its limitations?
3. Explain briefly the use of input-output analysis in Indian five-year plans.

Multiple Choice Questions

4. (*i*) Who invented the technique of input-output analysis?
   (*a*) Wassily W. Leontief (*b*) Watson Donald S.
   (*c*) P.T. Ellsworth (*d*) C.E. Ferguson [*Ans.* (*a*)]

   (*ii*) The input-output analysis is also known as
   (*a*) analysis of inter-industry demand
   (*b*) inter-sector flows
   (*c*) inter-industry relations
   (*d*) all of the above [*Ans.* (*d*)]

2. Linear programming as an advanced technique has been discussed in Chapter 37 of this book.

Chapter 37

Linear Programming

1. Introduction

The technique of linear programming was developed in 1947 by the American mathematician, George B. Dantzig, for the purpose of scheduling the complicated procurement activities of the U.S. Air Force. Actually, it was however, the Russian mathematician, L.V. Kantorovich, who first formulated the technique of linear programming. Several other economists have made important contributions to this technique. Notable among these are T.C. Koopmans, R. Dorfaman, and W.W. Cooper. But we must undoubtedly award the honour to mathematician George Dantzig, inventor of the first successful (and still one of the most efficient) general computational techniques, the *simplex method.* Since 1947, the technique of linear programming has made considerable advances both in theory as well as in its applications to practical problems in industry . The post-war development of computers has greatly contributed to the growth of linear programming as a device to solve the business problems of individual firms. Linear programming means the systematic planning or decision- making which is made by the firm in relation to production. In the absence of this technique, the mechanics of making all the calculations of all the possible combinations of the productive inputs would pose a difficulty, if not an impossible task of the firm. Under the technique of linear programming the variables are put into equations and the equations are generally solved through the use of high-speed computers.

2. Meaning of Linear Programming

According to Prof. Leftwich, "Linear programming is the simplest and most widely used of the mathematical programming techniques that have come into vogue since world war II... It is a technique for solving maximisation and minimisation problems confronting decision-making agencies subject to certain side conditions or constraints that limit what the agencies are able to do." This definition of linear programming states that linear programming is entirely a mathematical technique. Like the calculus of any branch of mathematics, it can only help us to find out the implications of the economic information which we are willing to assume. Thus, linear programming is a mathematical tool for the analysis of optimum decisions subject to constraints in the form of linear inequalities. Mathematically speaking, it applies to those problems which require the solution of maximisation or minimisation problems subject to a system of linear inequalities in terms of certain variables. In real sense, linear programming problems are concerned with the efficient (optimum) use or allocation of limited resources to fulfil desired objectives.

Now we shall discuss the assumptions of linear programming problems.

3. Characteristics or Assumptions of Linear Programming

(1) *The Constraints.* In linear programming problems, the firm[1] is assumed to face a number of limitations within which it has to operate. For example, there may be quantity limitations on particular kinds of inputs or facilities used by the firm. The firm is also assumed to have limited number of alternative production processes. Here a production process is defined in terms of a constant ratio of inputs. Therefore, production carried on with a given production process can be increased or decreased until input quantity limitations are reached. .

(2) *Constant Price.* In linear programming problems, it is also assumed that all input and output prices are constant. It means that linear programming techniques follow the purely competitive approach to prices. Perfect competition prevails in both the markets-the commodity market and the factor market. As a result, prices are exogenously given to the individual firm.

(3) *Linearity.* In linear programming problems, it is assumed that the firm's input-output, output-output and input-input relations are linear. This assumption implies that the input-output coefficients are fixed in respect of all the available inputs and the number of products to be produced. In other words, a firm purchasing an input at a constant price faces a linear *TC*-function for that input. Similarly, *TR*-function will also be linear when the product is sold at a constant price. Linearity of the input-output relations would also mean a constant *MRTS* and the resultant linear isoquant in respect of each item to be produced. Although, an isoquant is ordinarily a non-linear constant product curve for two resources, the linear-programming counterpart is a series of connected linear relations. Similarly, actual production functions may very well show non-linear relations between input and output. In linear programming problems they are assumed to be homogeneous of degree one.

---

1. For simplicity, we discuss the case of a firm, but linear programming techniques can be and are used by agencies other than firms, for example, military procurement units, or governments, etc.

4. Maximisation Problems

Here, we shall consider two maximisation problems:

(1) One Output-Two Inputs Case,

(2) Multiple Outputs-Multiple Inputs Case.

1. One Output-Two Inputs Case

It can be considered in two ways (*a*) Cost-outlay constraints, and (*b*) Input quantity constraints.

(*a*) *Cost Outlay Constraints.* Here we assume that a firm, producing one output *X* and using two inputs *L* and *K* seeks to maximise output subject to a given cost outlay. This problem is simple and similar to the previous theory of production. In our previous analysis we assumed the possibilities of continuous substitution between Land *K* but now we drop this assumption and instead suppose that there are only four processes (possible ratios of *K* to *L*) by which the firm can produce the product (*X*). By assumption, the firm faces constant input and output process.

Figure 37.1 illustrates that the four processes for the firm are the *A, B,* C, and *D.* They are linear production rays. On each process the ratio of inputs is constant. Say, process *A* requires 3 units of *K* and 1 unit of *L* to produce 20 units of *X.* Now if we want to double the output level, then 6 units of *K* and 2 units of *L* will be needed, i.e. the ratio remains the same (3 : 1). Similar will be the case for other production processes. The points on the various production rays showing any given level of output (*X*) can be joined by a series of straight lines and the resulting kinked curve is known as an isoquant. Also, the higher the output level, the farther from the origin the isoquant lies. The linear segment

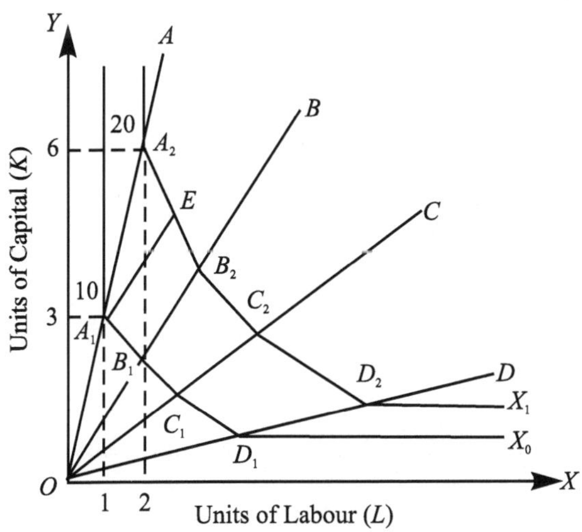

Fig. 37.1

of an isoquant between two production processes will always be parallel to the corresponding linear segment of any other isoquant.

Further, any point such as E on isoquant X_1 in Fig. 37.1 represents the simultaneous use by the firm of two processes to produce a given level of output (X_1). In this case the firm is using processes A and B. Now at point E, quantity OA_1 of X is produced by process A and the remaining quantity of X ($A_1E = B_1B_2$) is produced by process B.

Now the cost outlay constraints of a firm can be represented by an isocost curve. An isocost curve is also known as the budget line or the factor price line. In Fig. 37.2, the cost outlay of the firm has been represented by *MN* isocost curve which shows various points of the combinations of L and *K* available to the firm with the given cost outlay. Therefore, the isocost curve and production processes *OA* and *OD* tell the limits within which the firm is able to produce output. Any point on or within the triangles *ORS* is a possible combination of inputs *L* and *K* and lies on some isoquant of the firm. The area bounded by *ORS* is called *the area of feasible solutions* to the firm's problem. No production possibilities outside this area are open to the firm so far as input prices and cost outlay are constant.

From the feasible solutions to the firm's solution, *the optimal solution* must be found. The optimal solution will be one that maximises the firm's output subject to the cost outlay constraints. The optimal solution, here will occur at point C_2 at which the isocost curve touches the highest possible isoquant X_1, Therefore, to produce output level X_1, the firm will use process *C*. No other process than this *C*, will produce output level as high as X_1,

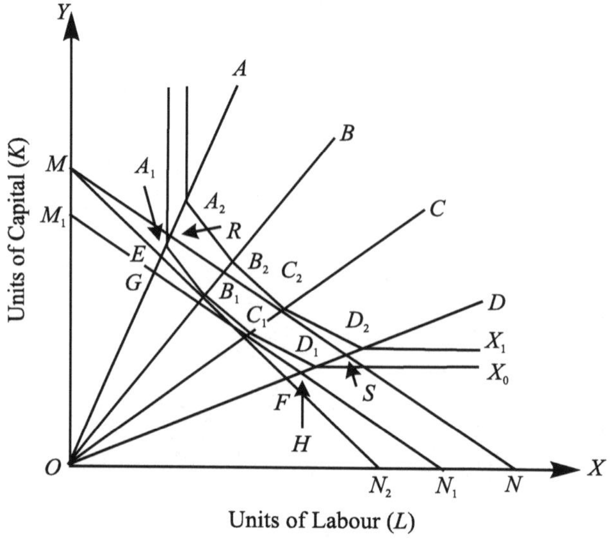

Fig. 37.2

Further, a change in the cost outlay with the prices of factor inputs remaining the same, will not affect the process used, but will certainly affect the level of output. If cost outlay is reduced, i.e. the isocost curve takes the shape M_1N_1 in Fig. 37.2. Now *the area of feasible solutions* is *OGH*. The firm maximises output at point C_1 by using the same process *C*. The maximum output is X_0.

Further, an increase in the prices of input (*L*) while price of *K* and cost outlay remaining the same, will shift the isocost position as MN_2 and the *area of feasible solutions* becomes *OEF*. Here, *the optimal solution* will be at point B_1 where the firm produces output X_0 by using production process *B*.

(*b*) *Input Quantity Constraints.* Here, first we assume that one of the inputs is limited and the other input is abundant. In Fig. 37.3 only K_0 of input *K* is available to the firm and input *L* is available in an unlimited quantity. In such a situation, *the area of feasible solutions* will be the triangle ORD_1. On this feasible solution, *the optimal solution* will be at point D_1 where the isoquant X_1 represents the highest output level available with quantity K_0 of *K*. Process *D* used at level OD_1 will maximise the firm's output.

On the other hand, if input *L* is limited to L_0 where input *K* is available in an unlimited quantity, the area of feasible solutions will be OA_3T and on which the optimal solution will be at *point* A_3. The relevant isoquant is X_3 and the maximum output level OA_3 will be produced by process *A*.

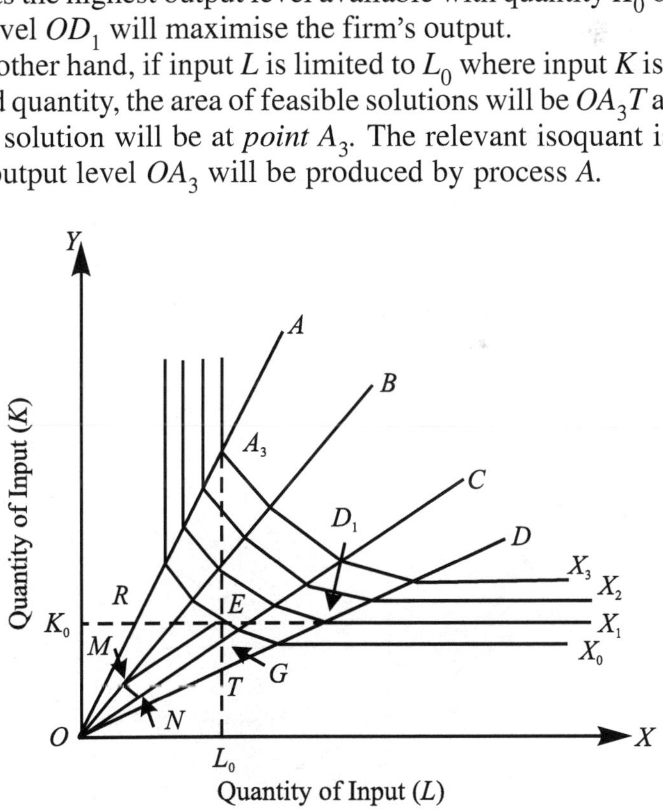

Fig. 37.3

Now, *if both the inputs are limited* in quantity as input *L* is limited to L_0 and input *K* is limited to K_0 in Fig. 37.3. Subject to these limitations, *the area of feasible solutions* is *ORET. The optimal solution* lies at point *E*. The maximum output of the firm X_0 which will be produced by process *B* and process C. Output *OM* will be produced by process *B* and the remaining output *ME* (= *NG*) will be produced by process C.

2. Multiple Outputs—Multiple Inputs Case (Maximising Revenue)

Here we assume that the firm is producing two different outputs, *X* and *Y*. Also, the firm possesses four kinds of facilities (or the constraints), each of which is fixed in capacity. These facilities are shown in Fig. 37.4 as *M, N, R,* and *S*. These facilities could be such things as the assembling, painting, packaging and transport departments of the firm. These departments have limited capacities. The firm's attempt to produce the maximum output is limited by these constraints.

Profit (or rent) derived per unit of *X* and per unit of *Y* will depend upon the prices received for each of the outputs and the average variable cost (*AVC*) of each. The *AVC* is constant because the fixed units of variable inputs are needed per unit of *X* and *Y* regardless of the amount of *X* and *Y*. Profit (or rent) per unit of the output is equal to the price of the product minus its *AVC*, and thus will be a constant amount. The profits per unit of *X* and *Y* may be denoted by π_X and π_Y respectively.

Now the *objective function* can be established as below which the firm wants to maximise within the given constraints.

$$\pi_X X + \pi_Y Y = \pi \qquad \ldots(1)$$

where

π = total profits (total rent)

$\pi_X X$ = profit (rent) of product *X*

$\pi_Y Y$ = profit (rent) of output *Y*

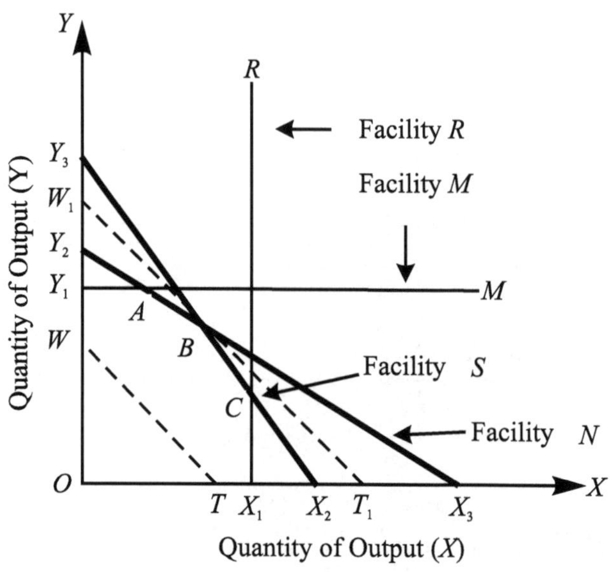

Fig. 37.4

The objective equation (1) is the equation for a family of isorent curves (for different values of π).

In Fig. 37.4, we illustrate how the firm will maximise its profits (π) from two outputs *X* and *Y*. The production of these commodities *X* and *Y* is subject to the constraints *M, N, R,* and S. Constraint *M* limits the production of *Y*; no more than OY_1 of *Y* can be produced. Constraint *R* limits the production of *X*; no more than OX_1 of *X* can be produced. The rectangle formed by the lines Y_1M and X_1R indicates the combined effects of the two constraints *M* and *R*. However, constraints *N* and *S* limit the production of both *X* and *Y*.

The shaded area in the Fig. 37.4 represents *the area of feasible solutions.* In other words, Y_1A, *AB, BC,* and CX_1 constitute the linear-segmented production possibility curve. Now, the point of *optimal solution* on this area of feasible solutions will depend upon the relevant isorent curve. In Fig. 37.4, *WT* is the isorent (or isorevenue) curve. Since, the optimal solution consists of the maximum revenue and, therefore, the isorevenue line W_1T_1 (which has the same slope as *WT*) hits the area of feasible solutions at point *B*. At this point *B*, the firm produces more of *Y* than of *X*. If there is some disturbance in the relative prices of *X* and *Y*, other things being the same, will also disturb the slope of isorevenue curve and thereby the point of optimal solution as well.

5. Mathematical Treatment of the Linear Programming Problem

A linear programming model may be used to find an optimum solution for one or more than one output. Let us assume that a firm is producing *n* number of outputs and each of them is produced by a linear production activity[2] using *m* inputs. We also assume that a particular output may be produced by more than one activity. Activities are linear in the sense that the quantity of the ith input required to support the jth activity or output (X_{ij}) is a linear function of the level of the jth activity,

$$X_{ij} = a_{ij}q_j \qquad \ldots(2)$$

$(i = 1, \ldots m), (j = 1, \ldots n)$

where a_i = a set of coefficients (combination of inputs) describes an activity to produce the output in question.

q_j = specified quantity of jth output.

a_{ij} = quantity of ith inputs required to produce one unit of q_j.

The jth activity is completely described by its coefficients for the *m* inputs: $(a_{1j}, a_{2j}, \ldots .a_{mj})$. Further, the concept of marginal productivity of an input is of no importance within the purview of linear programming, because it is not

2. In present context an activity can be regarded as a particular way of combining inputs for the production of an output.

possible to increase an activity level (or output level) by increasing the quantity of a single input. All inputs must be increased proportionately.

Now, to reach an optimum solution (maximisation of revenue or minimisation of cost) we require (*i*) the objective function, (*ii*) the constraints, (*iii*) input-output coefficients, and (*iv*) prices of inputs and outputs.

Here, for simplicity, we consider the problem of a firm where the firm wants to maximise its revenue subject to the given resource constraints. The firm's total revenue (R) is a linear function of its activity (output) levels.

The linear programming model is:

Maximise, $R = p_1q_1 + p_2q_2 + \ldots + P_nq_n$ ...(3)

Subject to the n activities

$$\left.\begin{array}{l} a_{11}q_1 + a_{12}q_2 + \ldots + a_{1n}q_n \le X_1 \\ a_{21}q_1 + a_{22}q_2 + \ldots + a_{2n}q_n \le x_2 \\ \} \\ a_{m1}q_1 + a_{m2}q_2 + \ldots + a_{mn}q_n \le x_m \end{array}\right\} \quad \ldots(4)$$

where $p_1, p_2, \ldots p_n$ are the fixed prices of n outputs

$$a_1, q_2, \ldots q_n; (q_j \ge 0) \quad \ldots(5)$$

a_{ij} ($i = 1, 2, \ldots m$) and $j = 1, 2, \ldots n$) are the input-output coefficients.

The constraints (4) are expressed as weak inequalities, because the firm is free to use less than its endowments.[3]

Linear Programming Solution: Revenue Maximisation

The firm's linear-programming problem is to maximise (3) subject to the constraints given by (4) and (5). The inequality shown in equation (4) states that the requirement of ith input in producing n number of outputs will be equal to or less than the available quality of ith input. Now to convert them into equalities we define m new variables $U_i(i = 1, \ldots m)$ which give the quantities of the m inputs not used for productive activities. The definition of these variables allows the transformation of (4) into the following set (6) of equalities.

$$\left.\begin{array}{l} a_{11}q_1 + a_{12}q_2 + \ldots + a_{1n}q_n + U_1 = X_1 \\ a_{21}q_1 + a_{22}q_2 + \ldots + a_{2n}q_n + U_2 = X_2 \\ \} \\ a_{m1}q_1 + a_{m2}q_2 + \ldots + a_{mn}q_n + U_m = X_m \end{array}\right\} \quad \ldots(6)$$

It must be noted that the coefficient of $U_i(i = 1, \ldots m)$ is + 1 for the relevant input and zero for all others.

3. This may be due to the point constraint limitations which a firm has to face. Moreover, inputs are used in fixed proportions.

For simplicity we take *a case of two outputs and two inputs.* First, we must see how an inequality is represented graphically. Consider the inequality $2X + Y = 5$. Here, if only Y is produced (*i.e.* $X = 0$), the maximum output of Y will be equal to 5 units (= OM in Fig. 37.5). Similarly, if only X is produced (i.e. $Y= 0$), then the maximum of X will be equal to $2X + 0 = 5$ or $X = 2.5$ units (= ON units in Fig. 37.5).

Now, if we join these two extreme points M and N, with the help of a straight line, then it will tell us the various possible combinations of X and Y to be produced under full capacity.

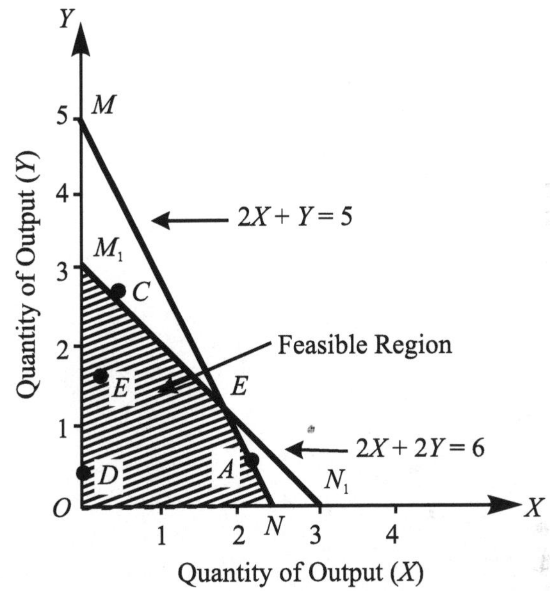

Fig. 37.5

In Fig. 37.5 any point such as A on the line MN which represents the equation $2X + Y = 5$ (and represents full use of capacity) clearly satisfies the inequality. But point such as B and C, or D which lies before the line MN also satisfies the inequality because it involves values of X and Y smaller than those which completely use up the capacity. Therefore, we observe that while a two-variable equation is represented by a line, a two-variable inequality is represented by a region.

We shall also see that the variables must also satisfy a second inequality, say $2X + 2Y \leq 6$ which is represented by a straight line M_1N_1 in Fig. 37.5. Now all the points which satisfy both inequalities must lie below both the lines MN and M_1N_1, i.e. below the area OM_1EN. It also satisfies $X \leq 0$ and $Y \leq 0$. This area is known as the *feasible region* to the linear programming problem.

Now we can represent the following problem diagrammatically in Fig. 37.6.

$$\text{Maximise } R = 8X + 7Y$$
$$\text{Subject to } X + 2Y \leq 10 \ (X \geq 0 \text{ and } Y \geq 0)$$
$$2X + Y \leq 12$$

where R = Total Revenue which is constant

X and Y are two outputs

From revenue function, it is clear that price of X is equal to 8 (or $P_X = 8$) and price Y is equal to 7 (or $P_Y = 7$) because $R = P_X.X + P_Y.Y$.

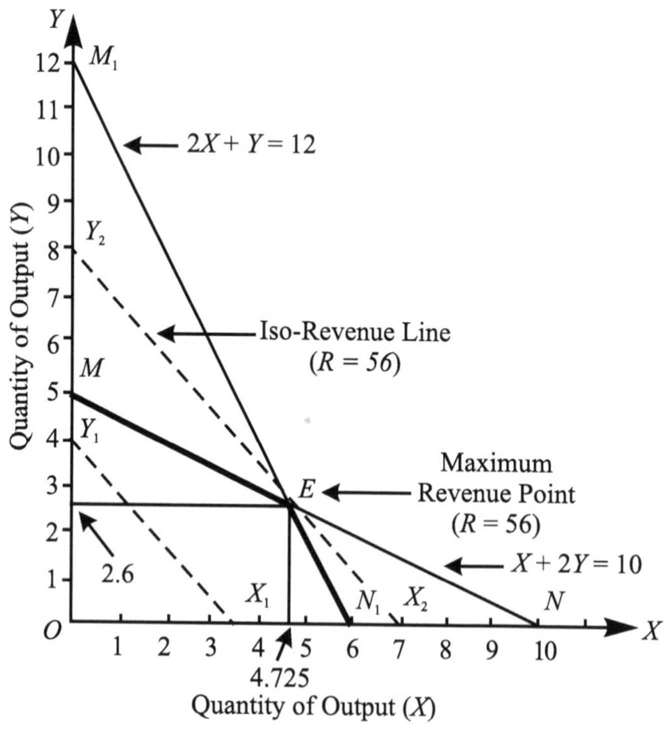

Fig. 37.6

Now, the constraints are represented by the lines $MN(X + 2Y = 10)$ and M_1N_1 $(2X + Y = 12)$ respectively. These two lines (or constraints) produce the area of feasible solutions which is $OMEN_1$ in Fig. 37.6. Now the solution to our above linear programming problem will lie either on or within the *feasible region* $OMEN_1$. For this we have to include our given objective function into our Fig. 37.6. It can be represented by the isorevenue curves. We convert our objective function in term of the isorevenue equation as,

$$Y = \frac{1}{7}R - \frac{8}{7}X$$

We may find a set of such equations (or lines) by assigning different values to R. Taking the partial derivative of Y w.r.t. X we get,

$$\frac{\partial Y}{\partial X} = \frac{8}{7}$$

or
$$-\frac{\partial Y}{\partial X} = \frac{8}{7}$$

Since in equilibrium, $MRTS = \frac{P_X}{P_Y}$

$$\therefore \qquad -\frac{\partial Y}{\partial X} = MRTS = \frac{P_X}{P_Y} = \frac{8}{7} = \text{slope of isorevenue curve.}$$

The isorevenue curve can be represented by Y_1X_1 line in Fig. 37.6. To get the optimal solution we go on increasing the value of R, i.e. shifting our isorevenue curve to the right (having the same slope because output prices are held constant) till we reach point E on our feasible region. At this point E we will obtain maximum possible revenue ($R = 56$). At this point, the firm produces 2.6 units of output Y and 4.725 units of output X. Therefore, the basic feasible solution or the optimal solution consists of,

$$R = 56$$
$$X = 4.725 \text{ units}$$
$$X = 2.6 \text{ units.}$$

Linear Programming Solution: Cost Minimisation

Cost minimisation is known as the dual problem of linear programming when the primal problem is of maxim is at ion. Here, under the linear inequalities[4] (constraints), we must consider the fact that the value of all inputs used (input prices) to produce one unit of X_1 must be at least equal to the price of output or average revenue. Likewise, the value of all inputs used in producing one unit of X_2 must be at least equal to its price (price of X_2).

Let us assume that the firm's objective function and constraints are given as follows:

Minimise, $C = 3X_1 + 5X_2$

Subject to $5X_1 + 2X_2 \geq 10$

$X_2 + X_2 \geq 4$

$X_1 + 3X_1 \geq 6$

4. The positive constraints are imposed in order to emphasise that the imputed values of "shadow-prices" of inputs cannot be negative.

where C = Total cost, X_1 and X_2 are the two inputs.

The above problem can be represented diagrammatically in Fig. 37.7. The three inequalities (constraints) have been represented by MN, M_1N_1, and M_2N_2 respectively. The lower boundary of the feasible region has been shown by $MABN_2$.

Now, from the objective function we get the isocost equation as,

$$C = 3X_1 + 5X_2$$

or $$X_2 = \frac{1}{5} - \frac{3}{5}\, 5\, X_1 \text{ (Isocost equation)}$$

$\therefore$ $$\frac{\partial X_2}{\partial X_1} = -\frac{3}{5}$$

or $$-\frac{\partial X_2}{\partial X_1} = \frac{PX_1}{PX_2} \text{ (In perfect competitive condition)}$$

where PX_1 =Price of input X_1, and PX_2 = Price of input X_2.

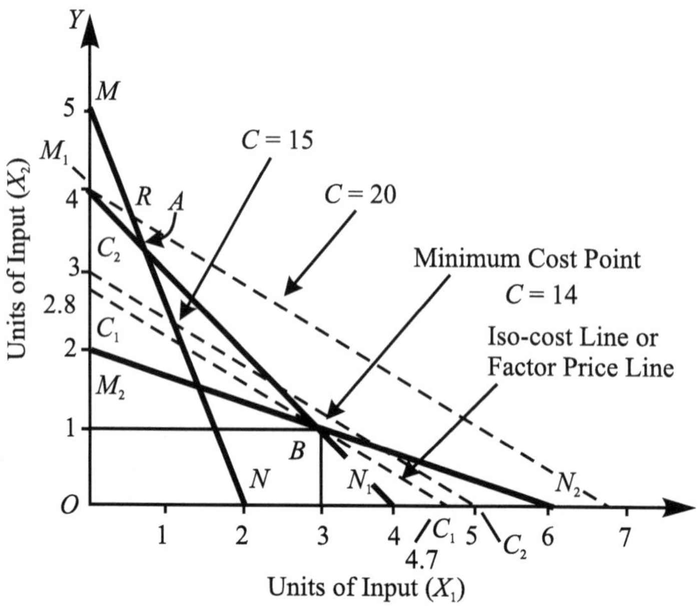

Fig. 37.7

If we give different values to C (input prices remaining the same), we may get a family of isocost curves and we will choose that which minimises the objective function. We draw the isocost equation in Fig. 37.7 as C_1C_1 which touches our feasible region $MABN_2$ at point B. Therefore, point B will be the minimum cost (C) point. No other point than B in our feasible region will be minimum cost point. For example, at point R, the firm has to incur $C = 20$. Therefore, the optimal solution will be at point B which will consist of,

$$C = 14$$
$$\text{Input } X_1 = 3 \text{ units}$$
$$\text{Input } X_2 = 1 \text{ unit}$$

6. Applications of Linear Programming in Indian Economy

We know that in a developing country like India, the factors of production such as skilled labour, capital and raw material, etc., are very scarce. The econometrician is, therefore, faced with the problem of scarce resource allocation to meet the competing demands and conflicting objectives. The traditional methods of hunch are losing their importance in the present time economy. Therefore, the Indian planners are constantly in search of objective and result-oriented techniques for decision making at all levels of planning. The decisions may be of two types: (*i*) Non-programmed decisions, and (*ii*) Programmed decisions.

Non-programmed decisions consist of capacity expansion, plan location, product line diversification, etc. These are one time decisions. On the other hand, programmed decisions consist of budgeting, replacement, purchasing, transportations, maintenance, etc. Those decisions are changing decisions over time and, therefore, repetitive in nature. They require the cooperation of different departments holding different responsibilities.

In modern times, a number of new methods, techniques and tools have been developed by world econometricians. All these findings come under the science known as operations research. Some of these operations research techniques have been successfully applied in Indian situations, such as, business forecasting, inventory models and linear programming, etc.

Linear programming approach enables the Indian entrepreneurs to arrange for that combination of inputs which optimises the cost of production or the production profit or any other given objective function. The *LP*-approach is also used to a class of problems where the limited resources are to be allocated in an optimum manner to the different competing facilities. There are not enough resources (or inputs) to perform all activities (or facilities) in an efficient manner.

Specifically, such problems are the following:

(*a*) How to minimise the use of scarce factor inputs, such as, imported raw materials, skilled labour, foreign capital, etc., in order to get maximum profit?

(*b*) What should be the best combination of products or product mix to be produced in order to reach the maximum profits.

(*c*) How many salesmen should a company have, such as, its cost is minimized?

(*d*) How to allocate the scarce resources of the country into different sectors of the economy?

The main applications of the linear programming are the following:

(1) We know that at the national level, well known *Mahalanobis Four Sector Model* was used to fix the objective of the *Second Five-Year Plan.* Therefore, in the formulation of the country's Five-Year Plans, the *linear programming approach* and *econometric-models* are being used in various areas, such as, foodgrain storage, transportation, multi-level planning (national, state and district levels) and urban system.

(2) Again, Indian Railways have applied linear programming in a number of areas. For instance, the location of Rajendra Bridge over the Ganges linking South Bihar with North Bihar at Mokama in preference to other sites has been done with the help of linear programming approach. For other decisions, such as routing, transportation of various goods, etc. LP-approach is being tried. In order to facilitate this, a senior officer in charge of application of operations research techniques is appointed at Rail Bhavan at New Delhi.

(3) Again, linear programming approach is being used in agriculture also. It has been tried on a limited scale for crop rotation mix of cash crops and food crops, and fertiliser mix.

(4) Again, the national airlines are also using linear programming in the selection of routes and allocation of aircrafts to various routes. This has been facilitated by the computer system located in the headquarters. The officials found it most suitable and appropriate tool in solving their problems. Their decisions are totally based on the results of these computers.

(5) Again, the commercial institutions as well as the individual traders are also using linear programming techniques for cost reduction and profit maximisation. The oil refineries are using *LP*-technique for blending decisions and for the improvement of finished products.

(6) Again, the paint industry decisions pertaining to the selection of the product mix and location of warehouse for distribution are taken with the help of *LP*-techniques. TELCO uses *LP*-approach for deciding what casting and forgings to make in their own shops and what should be bought from outside suppliers.

(7) Again, the steel-plants are using linear programming techniques for determining the combination of the final product such as billets, rounds, bars, plates and sheets.

(8) Again, the organisation like Hindustan Lever uses *LP*-approach for the distribution of consumers goods throughout the country. *LP*-approach is

also used for capital budgeting decisions like the selection of one project from a number of different projects.

Hence, the linear programming approach can be applied to a variety of decision-making problems in planning which seeks to optimise a goal (or objective) from the total system's point of view, such as, resource allocations, product-mix, transportation, aircrafts routing, etc.

7. Limitations of Linear Programming Approach

(1) Linear programming technique assumes linearity between input-output, or output-output or input-input relations. Since, most of such relations are non-linear, this approach can be used for a limited number of cases.

(2) Linear programming technique also assumes that inputs are used in different production lines (different facilities) which are additive. This means that the sum total of input-use is less than or equal to the available input quantity. The problems where additivity of different activities is not possible, it cannot be solved by this technique (*LP*) of operations research. For example, the machine time needed for producing X_1 and X_2 cannot be added because some time is required in converting the machine to its different uses.

(3) This approach is based on the assumption of constant returns in the economy which is not realistic.

(4) This approach again assumes input prices and output prices as parameters. In other words, there must be perfect competition in both the markets the product market and the factor market. In real world, the situation of perfect competition cannot be seen.

(5) Sometimes, the inequalities define the constraints of a *LP*-problem. For simplicity, we use stack variables to remove these inequalities of the constraints. But, in such cases, a firm has to move accordingly. In fact, the firm is helpless to accept these changes partly due to its (input) indivisibility and partly due to non-availability of scarce inputs. Therefore, we may of course, get optimal solution from *LP*-approach; however, it is not of much help to the firm in question.

Exercises

1. What do you understand by linear programming? Explain its important assumptions.
2. Explain the linear programming approach to the theory of production.
3. What are the chief applications of linear programming? Explain briefly the limitations of linear programming.
4. Solve the following linear programming problem by the diagrammatical method.

   Maximise $R = X + 4Y$

   Subject to $2X + 3Y \leq 4$

   $3X + Y \leq 3$

   $(X \leq 0 \text{ and } Y \geq 0)$

   Where R is total revenue and X and Y are the two respective outputs.

Multiple Choice Questions

5. (*i*) Linear Programming is a technique to solve the problem of
   (*a*) maximisation (*b*) minimisation
   (*c*) anyone of the above (*d*) none of the above [*Ans.* (*c*)]

   (*ii*) Linear Programming can be defined as a method to decide
   (*a*) the optimum combination of factors to produce a given output
   (*b*) the optimum combination of products to be produced by a given plant and equipment
   (*c*) between a variety of techniques to produce a commodity
   (*d*) anyone of the above [*Ans.* (*d*)]